THE THIRD REICH FROM ORIGINAL SOURCES

THE NUREMBERG TRIALS

THE COMPLETE PROCEEDINGS

Vol 2: The Indictment - The Four Charges

3rd-14th December 1945

Edited and introduced by Bob Carruthers

C⊕DA
BOOKS LTD

This edition published in Great Britain in 2011 by
Coda Books Ltd, The Barn, Cutlers Farm Business Centre, Edstone,
Wootton Wawen, Henley in Arden, Warwickshire, B95 6DJ
www.codahistory.com

A CIP catalogue record for this book is available from the British Library

ISBN 978 1 908538 78 9

Originally published as
"The Trial of German Major War Criminals
Proceedings of the International Military Tribunal Sitting at Nuremberg,
Germany"
under the authority of
H.M. Attorney-General by His Majesty's Stationery Office
London : 1946

CONTENTS

Introduction

The trial of the German major war criminals is better known to posterity as the Nuremberg Trials. This was a revolutionary new form of justice which was without parallel in the history of warfare.

In the wake of six years of savagery, inhumanity and turmoil it was sensed that a series of summary executions would not bring closure to the years of violence which had seen unheralded scenes of brutality as civilian populations were targeted for bombardment on a scale never before witnessed.

In 1945, faced with the stark evidence of the appalling crimes against humanity committed by the Nazi regime, there was an understandable clamour, particularly from the Soviet camp, for a series of quick summary executions to draw the line under the past and allow the world to get back to civilised behaviour. Given the scale of the crimes and the gruesome evidence emerging from Dachau, Auschwitz and Bergen-Belsen, it was certainly difficult to argue against making a rapid example of men like Hermann Göring, the father of the Gestapo.

Fortunately clearer heads prevailed and it was felt necessary to create some form of judicial process which would mark the transition back from barbarism to the rule of law. However there was then no such thing as an international court and there was no precedent for the legal trial of defeated belligerents. The plan for the "Trial of European War Criminals" was therefore drafted by Secretary of War Henry L. Stimson and the War Department. Following Roosevelt's death in April 1945, the new president, Harry S. Truman, gave strong approval for a judicial process. After a series of negotiations between Britain, the US, the Soviet Union and France, details of the trial were finally agreed. The trials were to commence on 20th November 1945, in the Bavarian city of Nuremberg.

At the meetings in Potsdam (1945), the three major wartime powers, the United Kingdom, the United States, and the Union of Soviet Socialist Republics finally agreed on the principles of punishment for those responsible for war crimes during World War II. France was also awarded a place on the tribunal.

The legal basis for the trial was established by the London Charter, issued on August 8th, 1945, which restricted the trial to "punishment of the major war criminals of the European Axis countries". Some 200 German war crimes defendants were ultimately tried at Nuremberg, and 1,600 others were tried under the traditional channels of military justice. The legal basis for the jurisdiction of the court was that defined by the Instrument of Surrender of Germany. Political authority for Germany had been transferred to the Allied Control Council which, having sovereign power over Germany, could choose to punish violations of international law and the laws of war. Because the court was limited to violations of the laws of war, it did not have jurisdiction over crimes that took place before the outbreak of war on September 3rd, 1939.

Leipzig, Munich and Luxembourg were briefly considered as the location for the trial. The Soviet Union had wanted the trials to take place in Berlin, as the capital city of the 'fascist conspirators', but Nuremberg was chosen as the site for the trials for two specific reasons: firstly because the Palace of Justice was spacious and largely undamaged (one of the few civic buildings that had remained largely intact through extensive Allied bombing), and secondly that a large prison was also part of the complex.

Nuremberg was also considered the ceremonial birthplace of the Nazi Party, and hosted annual rallies. It was thus considered a fitting place to mark the Party's symbolic demise.

As a compromise with the Soviet Union, it was agreed that while the location of the trial would be Nuremberg, Berlin would be the official home of the Tribunal authorities. It was also agreed that France would become the permanent seat of the IMT and that the first trial (several were planned) would take place in Nuremberg.

Each of the four countries provided one judge and an alternate, as well as a prosecutor.

- Major General Iona Nikitchenko (Soviet main)
- Lieutenant Colonel Alexander Volchkov (Soviet alternate)
- Colonel Sir Geoffrey Lawrence (British main and president)
- Sir Norman Birkett (British alternate)
- Francis Biddle (American main)
- John J. Parker (American alternate)
- Professor Henri Donnedieu de Vabres (French main)
- Robert Falco (French alternate)
- The chief prosecutors were as follows
- Attorney General Sir Hartley Shawcross (United Kingdom)
- Supreme Court Justice Robert H. Jackson (United States)
- Lieutenant-General Roman Andreyevich Rudenko (Soviet Union)
- François de Menthon (France)

Assisting Jackson was the lawyer Telford Taylor, Thomas J. Dodd and a young US Army interpreter named Richard Sonnenfeldt. Assisting Shawcross were Major Sir David Maxwell-Fyfe and Sir John Wheeler-Bennett. Mervyn Griffith-Jones, later to become famous as the chief prosecutor in the Lady Chatterley's Lover obscenity trial, was also on Shawcross's team. Shawcross also recruited a young barrister, Anthony Marreco, who was the son of a friend of his, to help the British team with the heavy workload. Assisting de Menthon was Auguste Champetier de Ribes.

The International Military Tribunal was opened on October 18th, 1945, in the Palace of Justice in Nuremberg. The first session was presided over by the Soviet judge, Nikitchenko. The prosecution entered indictments against 24 major war criminals and six criminal organizations – the leadership of the Nazi party, the Schutzstaffel (SS) and Sicherheitsdienst (SD), the Gestapo, the Sturmabteilung (SA) and the "General Staff and High Command," comprising several categories of senior military officers.

The indictments were for:

- Participation in a common plan or conspiracy for the accomplishment of a crime against peace
- Planning, initiating and waging wars of aggression and other crimes against peace
- War crimes
- Crimes against humanity

Under the circumstances the Proceedings of the International Military Tribunal just about passes muster as an exercise in establishing a platform from which to dispense a reasonably balanced form of justice. There was, of course, the questionable involvement of Stalin's legal team and it was ironic that his crimes against peace and humanity matched, if not surpassed those of Adolf Hitler. Ribbentrop and Molotov between them had secretly carved up Poland and in so doing had certainly been guilty of crimes against peace, planning war. Stalin had also waged an aggressive was against Finland and had annexed the Baltic States. Had Stalin been on trial his own actions would have condemned him to a guilty verdict on all four counts, but history is always written by the victors, and Stalin's crimes were airbrushed out of history in order that his team could sit in judgement as if nothing untoward had ever happened.

It has been asked many times were the trials fair. In strict legal terms they certainly were not. Declaring the instruments of the Nazi state to be illegal was illogical and unreasonable, but this was certainly no Stalinist show trial with a guilty verdict and a hangman's noose already awaiting the defendants. Under the circumstances the court was incredibly well balanced as was evidenced by the fact that three of the Defendants were acquitted and others received comparatively light sentences. Of the twenty-four accused only twelve received death sentences.

Ultimately the process had its flaws but it did provide a civilised alternative to Stalin's suggestion that 50,000 to 100,000 German officers should be executed without trial, and it was to serve as a forerunner for the International Court now located at the Hague.

This is the second volume in the complete proceedings of the Nuremberg trial of the German major war criminals before the International Military Tribunal sitting at Nuremberg, Germany.

Taken from the original court transcript this volume covers the proceedings from 3rd to 14th December 1945 and represents an essential primary source for scholars and general readers alike. The transcripts are complete and contain the whole of the proceedings as taken from the original court documents.

This volume contains the continuation of the Indictment brought against the Defendants, including further details of the four counts of waging aggressive war, crimes against peace, war crimes and crimes against humanity, as originally published under the authority of H.M. Attorney-General by His Majesty's Stationery Office London in 1946.

Bob Carruthers

Eleventh Day:
Monday, 3 December 1945

THE PRESIDENT: I call on the prosecutor for the United States.

SIDNEY S. ALDERMAN (Associate Trial Counsel for the United States): May it please the Tribunal, it occurs to me that perhaps the Tribunal might be interested in a very brief outline of what might be expected to occur within the next week or two weeks in this Trial.

I shall immediately proceed with the aggressive war case, to present the story of the rape of Czechoslovakia. I shall not perhaps be able to conclude that today.

Sir Hartley Shawcross, the British chief prosecutor, has asked that he be allowed to proceed tomorrow morning with his opening statement on Count Two and I shall be glad to yield for that purpose, with the understanding that we shall resume on Czechoslovakia after that.

Thereafter, the British prosecutor will proceed to present the aggressive warfare case as to Poland, which brought France and England into the war. Thereupon the British prosecutor will proceed with the expansion of aggressive war in Europe, the aggression against Norway and Denmark, against Holland, Belgium, and Luxembourg, against Yugoslavia and Greece. And in connection with those aggressions the British prosecutor will present to the Tribunal the various treaties involved and the various breaches of treaties involved in those aggressions.

That, as I understand it, will complete the British case under Count Two and will probably take the rest of this week.

Then it will be necessary for the American prosecuting staff to come back to Count One to cover certain portions which have not been covered, specifically, persecution of the Jews, concentration camps, spoliation in occupied territories, the High Command, and other alleged criminal organizations, particularly evidence dealing with individual responsibility of individual defendants.

Roughly, I would anticipate that that would carry through the following week-two weeks. However, that is a very rough estimate.

Thereupon, the French chief prosecutor will make his opening statement and will present the evidence as to Crimes against Humanity and War Crimes under Counts Three and Four as to Western Occupied countries.

Following that, the Russian chief prosecutor will make his opening statement and will present corresponding evidence regarding War Crimes and Crimes against Humanity in the Eastern countries.

That, in very rough outline, is what we have in mind to present.

I turn now to the third section in the detailed chronological presentation of the aggressive war case: Aggression against Czechoslovakia. The relevant portions of the Indictment are set forth in Subsection 3, under Section IV (F), appearing at Pages 7 and 8 of the printed English text of the Indictment.

This portion of the Indictment is divided into three parts:

(a) The 1936-38 phase of the plan; that is, the planning for the assault both on Austria and Czechoslovakia.

(b) The execution of the plan to invade Austria; November 1937 to March 1938.

(c) The execution of the plan to invade Czechoslovakia; April 1938 to March 1939.

On Thursday, last, I completed the presentation of the documents on the execution of the plan to invade Austria. Those documents are gathered together in a document book which was handed to the Tribunal at the beginning of the Austrian presentation.

The materials relating to the aggression against Czechoslovakia have been gathered in a separate document book, which I now submit to the Tribunal and which is marked "Document Book 0."

The Tribunal will recall that in the period 1933 to 1936 the defendants had initiated a program of rearmament, designed to give the Third Reich military strength and political bargaining power to be used against other nations. You will recall also that beginning in the year 1936 they had embarked on a preliminary program of expansion which, as it turned out, was to last until March 1939. This was intended to shorten their frontiers, to increase their industrial and food reserve, and to place them in a position, both industrially and strategically, from which they gourd launch a more ambitious and more devastating campaign of aggression.

At the moment-in the early spring of 1938-when the Nazi conspirators began to lay concrete plans for the conquest of Czechoslovakia, they had reached approximately the half-way point in this preliminary program.

The preceding autumn, at the conference in the Reich Chancellery on November 5, 1937, covered by the Hossbach minutes, Hitler had set forth the program which Germany was to follow. Those Hossbach minutes, you will recall, are contained in Document 386-PS as United States Exhibit Number 25, which I read to the Tribunal in my introductory statement a week ago today.

"The question for Germany," the Fuehrer had informed his military commanders at that meeting, "is where the greatest possible conquest can be made at the lowest cost."

At the top of his agenda stood two countries, Austria and Czechoslovakia.

On March 12, 1938 Austria was occupied by the German Army, and on the following day it was annexed to the Reich. The time had come for a redefinition of German intentions regarding Czechoslovakia. A little more than a month later two of the conspirators, Hitler and Keitel, met to discuss plans for the envelopment and conquest of the Czechoslovak State.

Among the selected handful of documents which I read to the Tribunal in my introduction a week ago to establish the corpus of the crime of aggressive war was the account of this meeting on 21 April 1938. This account is Item 2 in our Document Number 388-PS, as United States Exhibit Number 26.

The Tribunal will recall that Hitler and Keitel discussed the pretext which Germany might develop to serve as an excuse for a sudden and overwhelming attack. They considered the provocation of a period of diplomatic squabbling which, growing more serious, would lead to an excuse for war. In the alternative- and this alternative they found to be preferable-they planned to unleash a lightning attack as the result of an incident of their own creation.

Consideration, as we alleged in the Indictment and as the document proved, was given to the assassination of the German Minister at Prague to create the requisite incident.

The necessity of propaganda to guide the conduct of Germans in Czechoslovakia and to intimidate the Czechs was recognized. Problems of transport and tactics were discussed, with a view to overcoming all Czechoslovak resistance within 4 days, thus presenting the world with a *fait accompli* and forestalling outside interventions.

Thus, in mid-April 1938, the designs of the Nazi conspirators to conquer Czechoslovakia had already reached the stage of practical planning.

Now all of that occurred, if the Tribunal please, against a background of friendly diplomatic relations. This conspiracy must be viewed against that background. Although they had, in the fall of 1937, determined to destroy the Czechoslovak State, the leaders of the German Government were bound by a treaty of arbitration and assurances freely given, to observe the sovereignty of Czechoslovakia. By a formal treaty signed at Locarno on 16 October 1925 - Document TC-14, which will be introduced by the British prosecutor- Germany and Czechoslovakia agreed, with certain exceptions, to refer to an arbitral tribunal or to the Permanent Court of International Justice matters of dispute. I quote, they would so refer:

"All disputes of every kind between Germany and Czechoslovakia with regard to which the parties are in conflict as to their respective rights, and which it may not be possible to settle amicably by the normal methods of diplomacy."

And the preamble to this treaty stated:

"The President of the German Reich and the President of the Czechoslovak Republic equally resolved to maintain peace between Germany and Czechoslovakia by assuring the peaceful settlement of differences, which might arise between the two countries; declaring that respect for the rights established by treaty or resulting from the law of nations, is obligatory for international tribunals; agreeing to recognize that the rights of a state cannot be modified save with its consent, and considering that sincere observance of the methods of peaceful settlement of international disputes permits of resolving, without recourse to force, questions which may become the cause of divisions between states, have decided to embody in a treaty their common intention in this respect."

That ends the quotation.

Formal and categoric assurances of their good will towards Czechoslovakia were both coming from the Nazi conspirators as late as March 1938. On March 11 and 12, 1938, at the time of the annexation of Austria, Germany had a considerable interest in inducing Czechoslovakia not to mobilize. At this time the Defendant Goering assured Masaryk, the Czechoslovak Minister in Berlin, on behalf of the German Government that German-Czech relations were not adversely affected by the development in Austria and that Germany had no hostile intentions towards Czechoslovakia. As a token of his sincerity, Defendant Goering accompanied his assurance with the statement, "Ich gebe Ihnen mein Ehrenwort (I give you my word of honor)."

At the same time, the Defendant Von Neurath, who was handling German foreign affairs during Ribbentrop's stay in London, assured Masaryk, on behalf of Hitler and the German Government, that Germany still considered herself bound by the Arbitration Convention of 1925.

9

These assurances are contained in Document TC-27, another of the series of documents which will be presented to the Tribunal by the British prosecutor under Count Two of the Indictment.

Behind the screen of these assurances the Nazi conspirators proceeded with their military and political plans for aggression. Ever since the preceding fall it had been established that the immediate aim of German policy was the elimination both of Austria and of Czechoslovakia. In both countries the conspirators planned to undermine the will to resist by propaganda and by Fifth Column activities, while the actual military preparations were being developed.

The Austrian operation, which received priority for political and strategic reasons, was carried out in February and March 1938. Thenceforth the Wehrmacht planning was devoted to "Fall Grun" (Case Green), the designation given to the proposed operation against Czechoslovakia.

The military plans for Case Green had been drafted in outline from as early as June 1937. The OKW top-secret directive for the unified preparation of the Armed Forces for war-signed by Von Blomberg on June 24, 1937, and promulgated to the Army, Navy, and Luftwaffe for the year beginning July 1, 1937-included, as a probable war-like eventuality for which a concentrated plan was to be drafted, Case Green, "War on two fronts, with the main struggle in the southeast."

This document-our Number C-175, Exhibit USA-69-was introduced in evidence as part of the Austrian presentation and is an original carbon copy, signed in ink by Von Blomberg. The original section of this directive dealing with the probable war against Czechoslovakia-it was later revised-opens with this supposition. I read from the bottom of Page 3 of the English translation of this directive, following the heading II, and Subparagraph (1) headed "Suppositions":

> "The war in the East can begin with a surprise German operation against Czechoslovakia in order to parry the imminent attack of a superior enemy coalition. The necessary conditions to justify such an action politically, and in the eyes of international law must be created beforehand."

After detailing possible enemies and neutrals in the event of such action, the directive continues as follows:

> "(2) The task of the German Armed Forces" - and that much is underscored- "is to make their preparations in such a way that the bulk of all forces can break into Czechoslovakia quickly, by surprise, and with the greatest force, while in the West the minimum strength is provided as rear-cover for this attack.
>
> "The aim and object of this surprise attack by the German Armed Forces should be to eliminate from the very beginning and for the duration of the war, the threat by Czechoslovakia to the rear of the operations in the West, and to take from the Russian Air Force the most substantial portion of its operational base in Czechoslovakia. This must be done by the defeat of the enemy armed forces and the occupation of Bohemia and Moravia."

The introduction to this directive sets forth as one of its guiding principles the following statement- and I now read from Page 1 of the English translation, that is, the third paragraph following Figure 1:

"Nevertheless, the politically fluid world situation, which does not preclude surprising incidents, demands constant preparedness for war on the part of the German Armed Forces:" - and then- "(a) to counterattack at any time; (b) to make possible the military exploitation of politically favorable opportunities should they occur."

This directive ordered further work on the plan for "mobilization without public announcement." I quote:

" . . . in order to put the Armed Forces in a position to be able to begin a sudden war which will take the enemy by surprise, in regard to both strength and time of attack."

This is, of course, a directive for staff planning, but the nature of the planning and the very tangible and ominous developments which resulted from it, give it a significance that it would not have in another setting.

Planning along the lines of this directive was carried forward during the fall of 1937 and the winter of 1937-38. On the political level, this planning for the conquest of Czechoslovakia received the approval and support of Hitler in the conference with his military commanders on 5 November 1937, reported in the Hossbach minutes, to which I have frequently heretofore referred.

In early March 1938, before the march into Austria, we find the Defendants Ribbentrop and Keitel concerned over the extent of the information about war aims against Czechoslovakia to be furnished to Hungary. On 4 March 1938, Ribbentrop wrote to Keitel, enclosing for General Keitel's confidential cognizance the minutes of a conference with Sztojay, the local Hungarian Ambassador, who had suggested an interchange of views. This is Document 2786-PS, a photostat of the original captured letter, which I now offer in evidence as Exhibit USA-81. In his letter to Keitel, Ribbentrop said:

"I have many doubts about such negotiations. In case we should discuss with Hungary possible war aims against Czechoslovakia, the danger exists that other parties as well would be informed about this. I would greatly appreciate it if you ;would notify me briefly whether any commitments were made here in any respect. With best regards and Heil Hitler."

At the 21 April meeting between Hitler and Keitel, the account of which I read last week and alluded to earlier this morning (Document 388-PS, Item 2), specific plans for the attack on Czechoslovakia were discussed for the first time. This meeting was followed, in the late spring and summer of 1938, by a series of memoranda and telegrams advancing Case Green (Fall Grun). Those notes and communications were carefully filed at Hitler's headquarters by the very efficient Colonel Schmundt, the Fuehrer's military adjutant, and were captured by American troops in a cellar at Obersalzberg, near Berchtesgaden. This file, which is preserved intact, bears out Number 388-PS, and is United States Exhibit Number 26. We affectionately refer to it as "Big Schmundt" -a large file. The individual items in this file tell more graphically than any narrative the progress of the Nazi conspirators' planning to launch an unprovoked and brutal war against Czechoslovakia. From the start the Nazi leaders displayed a lively interest in intelligence data concerning Czechoslovakian armament and defense. With the leave of the Tribunal I shall refer to some of these items in the Big Schmundt file without reading them. The documents to which I refer are Item 4 of the Schmundt file, a telegram from Colonel Zeitzler, in General Jodl's office of the OKW, to Schmundt at Hitler's headquarters.

THE PRESIDENT: Are you proposing not to read them?

MR. ALDERMAN: I hadn't intended to read them in full, unless that may be necessary.

THE PRESIDENT: I am afraid we must adhere to our decision.

MR. ALDERMAN: If the Tribunal please, I should simply wish to refer to the title or heading of Item 12, which is headed, "Short Survey of Armament of the Czech Army," dated Berlin, 9 June 1938, and initialed "Z" for Zeitzler, and Item 13, "Questions of the Fuehrer," dated Berlin, 9 June 1938, and classified "Most Secret." I should like to read four of the questions which Hitler wanted authoritative information about, as shown by that document, and I read indicated questions on Pages 23, 24, 25, and 26 of Item 13 of Document 388-PS.

"Question 1: Hitler asked about armament of the Czech Army. I don't think it necessary to read the answers. They are detailed answers giving information in response to these questions posed by Hitler.

"Question 2: How many battalions, et cetera, are employed in the West for the construction of emplacements?

"Question 3: Are the fortifications of Czechoslovakia still occupied in unreduced strength?

"Question 4: Frontier protection in the West."

As I say, those questions were answered in detail by the OKW and initialed by Colonel Zeitzler of Jodl's staff.

As a precaution against French and British action during the attack on Czechoslovakia, it was necessary for the Nazi conspirators to rush the preparation of fortification measures along the western frontier in Germany. I refer you to Item 8, at Page 12 of the Big Schmundt file, a telegram presumably sent from Schmundt in Berchtesgaden to Berlin, and I quote from this telegram. It is, as I say, Item 8 of the Schmundt file, Page 12 of Document 388-PS: "Inform Colonel General Von Brauchitsch and General Keitel." And then, skipping a paragraph: "The Fuehrer repeatedly emphasized the necessity of pressing forward greatly the fortification work in the West."

In May, June, July, and August of 1938 conferences between Hitler and his political and military advisors resulted in the issuance of a series of constantly revised directives for the attack on Czechoslovakia. It was decided that preparations for X-Day, the day of the attack, should be completed no later than 1 October. I now invite the attention of the Tribunal to the more important of these conferences and directives.

On 28 May 1938 Hitler called a conference of his principal advisors. At this meeting he gave the necessary instructions to his fellow conspirators to prepare the attack on Czechoslovakia. This fact Hitler later publicly admitted. I now refer and invite the notice of the Tribunal to Document 2360-PS, a copy of the Volkischer Beobachter of 31 January 1939. In a speech before the Reichstag the preceding day, reported in this newspaper, reading now from Document 2360-PS, Hitler spoke as follows:

"On account of this intolerable provocation which had been aggravated by a truly infamous persecution and terrorization of our Germans there, I have determined to solve once and for all, and this time radically, the Sudeten-German question. On 28 May I ordered first: That preparation should be made for military action against this state by 2 October. I ordered second: The immense and accelerated expansion of our defensive front in the West."

Two days after this conference, on 30 May 1938, Hitler issued the revised military directive for Case Green. This directive is Item 11 in the Big Schmundt file, Document 388-PS. It is entitled, "Twofront War, with Main Effort in the Southeast," and this directive replaced the corresponding section, Part 2, Section II, of the previous quote, "Directive for Unified Preparation for War," which had been promulgated by Von Blomberg on 26 June 1937, which I have already introduced in evidence as our Document C-175, United States Exhibit Number 69. This revised directive represented a further development of the ideas for political and military action discussed by Hitler and Keitel in their conference on 21 April. It is an expansion of the rough draft submitted by the Defendant Keitel to Hitler on 20 May, which may be found as Item 5 in the Schmundt file. It was signed by Hitler. Only five copies were made. Three copies were forwarded with a covering letter from Defendant Keitel to General Von Brauchitsch for the Army, to Defendant Raeder for the Navy, and to Defendant Goering for the Luftwaffe. In his covering memorandum Keitel noted that its execution must be assured -I quote: "As from 1 October 1938 at the latest." I now read from this document, which is the basic directive under which the Wehrmacht carried out its planning for Case Green, a rather lengthy quotation from the first page of Item 11, Page 16 of the English version:

"1. Political prerequisites. It is my unalterable decision to smash Czechoslovakia by military action in the near future. It is the job of the political leaders to await or bring about the politically and militarily suitable moment.

"An inevitable development of conditions inside Czechoslovakia or other political events in Europe, creating a surprisingly favorable opportunity and one which may never come again, may cause me to take early action.

"The proper choice and determined and full utilization of a favorable moment is the surest guarantee of success. Accordingly the preparations are to be made at once.

"2. Political possibilities for the commencement of the action. The following are necessary prerequisites for the intended invasion:

a. Suitable obvious cause and with it,

b. Sufficient political justification,.

c. Action unexpected by the enemy, which will find him prepared in the least possible degree.

"From a military as well as a political standpoint the most favorable course is-a lightning-swift action as the result of an incident through which Germany is provoked in an unbearable way for which at least part of world opinion will grant the moral justification of military action.

"But even a period of tension, more or less preceding a war, must terminate in sudden action on our part, which must have the elements of surprise as regards time and extent, before the enemy is so advanced in military preparedness that he cannot be surpassed.

"3. Conclusions for the preparation of Fall Grun.

"a. For the 'armed war' it is essential that the surprise element, as the most important factor contributing to success, be made full use of by appropriate preparatory measures, already in peacetime and by an unexpectedly rapid course of the action. Thus it is essential to create a situation within the first 2 or 3 days which plainly demonstrates to hostile nations, eager to intervene, the hopelessness of the Czechoslovakian military situation and which, at the same time, will give nations with territorial claims on Czechoslovakia an incentive to intervene immediately against Czechoslovakia. In such a case, intervention by Poland and Hungary against Czechoslovakia may be expected, especially if France-due to the obvious pro-German attitude of Italy-fears, or at least hesitates, to unleash a European war by intervening against Germany. Attempts by Russia to give military support to Czechoslovakia mainly by the Air Force are to be expected. If concrete successes are not achieved by the land operations within the first few days, a European crisis will certainly result. This knowledge must give commanders of all ranks the impetus to decided and bold action.

"b. The Propaganda War must on the one hand intimidate Czechoslovakia by threats and wear down her power of resistance; on the other hand issue directions to national groups for support in the 'armed war' and influence the neutrals into our way of thinking. I reserve further directions and determination of the date.

"4. Tasks of the Armed Forces. Armed Forces preparations are to be made on the following basis:

"a. The mass of all forces must be employed against Czechoslovakia.

"b. For the West, a minimum of forces are to be provided as rear cover which may be required, the other frontiers in the East against Poland and Lithuania are merely to be protected, the southern frontiers to be watched.

"c. The sections of the Army which can be rapidly employed must force the frontier fortifications with speed and decision and must break into Czechoslovakia with the greatest daring in the certainty that the bulk of the mobile army will follow them with the utmost speed. Preparations for this are to be made and timed in such a way that the sections of the army which can be rapidly employed cross the frontier at the appointed time, at the same time as the penetration by the Air Force, before the enemy can become aware of our mobilization. For this, a timetable between Army and Air Force is to be worked out in conjunction with OKW and submitted to me for approval.

"5. Missions for the branches of the Armed Forces.

"a. Army. The basic principle of the surprise attack against Czechoslovakia must not be endangered nor the initiative of the Air Force be wasted by the inevitable time required for transporting the bulk of the field forces by rail. Therefore it is first of all essential to the Army that as many assault columns as possible be employed at the same time as the surprise attack by the Air Force. These assault columns-the composition of each, according to their tasks at that time must be formed with troops which can be employed rapidly owing to their proximity to the frontier or to motorization and to special measures of readiness. It must be the purpose of these thrusts to break into the Czechoslovakian fortification lines at numerous points and in a strategically favorable direction, to achieve a break-through, or to break them down from the rear. For the success of this operation, co-operation with the Sudeten-German frontier population, with deserters from the Czechoslovakian Army, with parachutists or airborne troops and with units of the sabotage service will be of importance. The bulk of the army has the task of frustrating the Czechoslovakian plan of defense, of preventing the Czechoslovakian army from escaping . . ."

THE PRESIDENT: Is it necessary to read all this detail?

MR. ALDERMAN: I was just worried about not getting it into the transcript.

THE PRESIDENT: It seems to me that this is all detail, that before you pass from the document you ought to read the document on Page 15, which introduces it and which gives the date of it.

MR. ALDERMAN: I think so. It is a letter dated:

"Berlin, 30 May 1938; copy of the fourth copy; Supreme Commander of the Armed Forces; most secret; access only through officer; written by an officer. Signed Keitel; distributed to C-in-C Army, C-in-C Navy, C-in-C Air Force.

"By order of the Supreme Commander of the Armed Forces, Part 2, Section II, of the directive on the unified preparations for war of the Armed Forces dated 24 June 1937, (Ob. d. W)" -with some symbols, including "Chefsache" (top secret) "(two-front war with main effort on the Southeast-strategic concentration Green) is to be replaced by the attached version. Its execution must be assured as from 1 October 1938 at the latest. Alterations in other parts of the directives must be expected during the next week.

"By order of Chief of the Supreme Command of the Armed Forces, signed, Keitel.

"Certified a true copy, Zeitzler, Oberstleutnant on the General Staff."

In line with the suggestion of the presiding Justice, I shall omit the detailed instructions which are set out for action by the Luftwaffe and by the Navy, and I turn next to the last paragraph of the directive, which will be found on Page 19 of the English version:

"In war economy it is essential that in the field of the armament industry a maximum deployment of forces is made possible through increased supplies. In the course of operations, it is of value to contribute to the reinforcement of the total war-economic strength-by rapidly reconnoitering and restarting important factories. For this reason the sparing of Czechoslovakian industrial and factory installations, insofar as military operations permit, can be of decisive importance to us."

In other words, the Nazi conspirators, 4 months before the date of their planned attack, were already looking forward to the contribution which the

Czech industrial plant would make to further Nazi war efforts and economy.

And the final paragraph of this directive, Paragraph 7, on Page 19:

"All preparations for sabotage and insurrection will be made by OKW. They will be made, in agreement with, and according to, the requirement of the branches of the Armed Forces, so that their effects accord with the operations of the Army and Air Force as to time and locality.

"Signed Adolf Hitler.

"Certified a true copy, Zeitzler, Oberstleutnant on the General Staff."

Three weeks later, on 18 June 1938, a draft for a new directive was prepared and initialed by the Defendant Keitel. This is Item 14 at Pages 27 to 32 of the Big Schmundt file. It did not supersede the 30 May directive. I shall read the third and fifth paragraphs on Page 28 of the English translation, and the last paragraph on Page 29:

"The immediate aim is a solution of the Czech problem by my own free decision; this stands in the foreground of my political intentions. I am determined as from 1 October 1938 to use to the full every favorable political opportunity to realize this aim."

Then skipping a paragraph:

"However, I will decide to take action against Czechoslovakia only if I am firmly convinced, as in the case of the occupation of the demilitarized zone and the entry into Austria, that France will not march and therefore England will not intervene."

And then skipping to the last paragraph on the 29th page:

"The directives necessary for the prosecution of the war itself will be issued by me from time to time."

"K" - initial of Keitel, and - "Z" -initial of Zeitzler.

The second and third parts of this directive contain general directions for the deployment of troops and for precautionary measures in view of the possibility that during the execution of the Fall Grun (or Case Green) France or England might declare war on Germany. Six pages of complicated schedules which follow this draft in the original have not been translated into English. These schedules, which constitute Item 15 in the Schmundt file, give a timetable of specific measures for the preparation of the Army, Navy, and Luftwaffe for the contemplated action.

Corroboration for the documents in the Schmundt file is found in General Jodl's diary, our Document Number 1780-PS and United States Exhibit Number 72, from which I quoted portions during the Austrian presentation. I now quote from three entries in this diary written in the spring of 1938. Although the first entry is not dated it appears to have been written several months after the annexation of Austria, and here I read under the heading on Page 3 of the English translation:

"Later undated entry:

"After annexation of Austria the Fuehrer mentions that there is no hurry to solve the Czech question, because Austria had to be digested first. Nevertheless, preparations for Case Green will have to be carried out energetically. They will have to be newly prepared on the basis of the changed strategic position because of the annexation of Austria. State of preparation, see Memorandum 1-A of 19 April, reported to the Fuehrer on 21 April.

"The intention of the Fuehrer not to touch the Czech problem as yet will be changed because of the Czech strategic troop concentration of 21 May, which occurs without any German threat and without the slightest cause for it. Because of Germany's self-restraint the consequences lead to a loss of prestige for the Fuehrer, which he is not willing to take once more. Therefore, the new order is issued for Green on 30 May."

And then the entry, 23 May:

"Major Schmundt reports ideas of the Fuehrer.... Further conferences, which gradually reveal the exact intentions of the Fuehrer, take place with the Chief of the Armed Forces High Command (OKW) on 28 May, 3 and 9 June, -see inclosures (War Diary)."

Then the entry of 30 May:

"The Fuehrer signs directive Green, where he states his final decision to destroy Czechoslovakia soon and thereby initiates military preparation all along the line. The previous intentions of the Army must be changed considerably in the direction of an immediate break-through into Czechoslovakia right on D-Day "-X-Tag-" combined with aerial penetration by the Air Force.

"Further details are derived from directive for strategic concentration of the Army. The whole contrast becomes acute once more between the Fuehrer's intuition that we must do it this year, and the opinion of the Army that we cannot do it as yet, as most certainly the Western Powers will interfere and we are not as yet equal to them."

During the spring and summer of 1938 the Luftwaffe was also engaged in planning in connection with the forthcoming Case Green and the further expansion of the Reich.

I now offer in evidence Document R-150, as United States Exhibit 82. This is a top-secret document dated 2 June 1938, issued by Air Group Command 3, and entitled "Plan Study 1938, Instruction for Deployment and Combat, 'Case Red.' "

"Case Red" is the code name for action against the Western Powers if need be. Twenty-eight copies of this document were made, of which this is number 16. This is another staff plan, this time for mobilization and employment of the Luftwaffe in the event of war with France. It is given significance by the considerable progress by this date of the planning for the attack on Czechoslovakia.

I quote from the second paragraph on Page 3 of the English translation, referring to the various possibilities under which war with France may occur. You will note that they are all predicated on the assumption of a German-Czech conflict.

"France will either (a) interfere in the struggle between the Reich and Czechoslovakia in the course of Case Green, or (b) start hostilities simultaneously with Czechoslovakia. (c) It is possible but not likely that France will begin the fight while Czechoslovakia still remains aloof."

And then, reading down lower on the page under the heading "Intention":

"Regardless of whether France enters the war as a result of Case Green or whether she makes the opening move of the war simultaneously with Czechoslovakia, in any case the mass of the

German offensive formations will, in conjunction with the Army, first deliver the decisive blow against Czechoslovakia."

By mid-summer direct and detailed planning for Case Green was being carried out by the Luftwaffe. In early August, at the direction of the Luftwaffe General Staff, the German Air Attache in Prague reconnoitered the Freudenthal area of Czechoslovakia south of Upper Silesia for suitable landing grounds.

I offer in evidence Document 1536-PS as Exhibit USA-83, a report of the Luftwaffe General Staff, Intelligence Division, dated 12 August 1938. This was a top-secret document for general officers only, of which only two copies were made.

Attached as an enclosure was the report of Major Moericke, the German Attache in Prague, dated 4 August 1938. I quote the first four paragraphs of the enclosure:

"I was ordered by the General Staff of the Air Force to reconnoiter the land in the region Freudenthal-Freihermersdorf . . ."

THE PRESIDENT: Page 3 of the document?

MR. ALDERMAN: Yes. ". . . for landing possibilities.

"For this purpose I obtained private lodgings in Freudenthal with the manufacturer Macholdt, through one of my trusted men in Prague.

"I had specifically ordered this man to give no details about me to Macholdt, particularly about my official position.

"I used my official car (Dienst Pkw) for the journey to Freudenthal taking precautions against being observed."

By 25 August the imminence of the attack on Czechoslovakia compelled the issuance by the Luftwaffe of a detailed intelligence memorandum, entitled "Extended Case Green"; in other words, an estimate of possible action by the Western Powers during the attack on Czechoslovakia.

I now offer this document in evidence, Number 375-PS as Exhibit USA-84. This is a top-secret memorandum of the Intelligence Section of the Luftwaffe, General Staff, dated Berlin, 25 August 1938. Based on the assumption that Great Britain and France would declare war on Germany during Case Green, this study contains an estimate of the strategy and air strength of the Western Powers as of 1 October 1938; the target date for Case Green. I quote the first two sentences of the document. That is under the heading "Initial Political Situation":

"The basic assumption is that France will declare war during the Case Green. It is presumed that France will decide upon war only if active military assistance by Great Britain is definitely assured."

Now, knowledge of the pending or impending action against Czechoslovakia was not confined to a close circle of high officials of the Reich and the Nazi Party. During the summer Germany's allies, Italy and Hungary, were apprised by one means or another of the plans of the Nazi conspirators. I offer in evidence Document 2800-PS as Exhibit USA-85. This is a captured document from the German Foreign Office files, a confidential memorandum of a conversation with the Italian Ambassador Attolico, in Berlin on 18 July 1938. At the bottom is a handwritten note headed "For the Reichsminister only", and the Reichsminister was the Defendant Ribbentrop. I now read this note. I read from the note the third and fourth paragraphs:

"Attolico added that we had made it unmistakably clear to the Italians what our intentions are regarding Czechoslovakia. He also knew the appointed time well enough so that he could take perhaps a 2 months' holiday now which he could not do later on.

"Giving an idea of the attitude of other governments, Attolico mentioned that the Romanian Government had refused to grant application for leave to its Berlin Minister."

THE PRESIDENT: Would this be a convenient time to break off for 10 minutes?

MR. ALDERMAN: Yes, Sir.

[A recess was taken.]

MR. ALDERMAN: May it please the Tribunal, a month later Mussolini sent a message to Berlin asking that he be told the date on which Case Green would take place. I offer in evidence Document Number 2791-PS as Exhibit USA-86, a German Foreign Office note on a conversation with Ambassador Attolico. This note is signed "R" for Ribbentrop and dated 23 August 1938. I now read two paragraphs from this memorandum:

"On the voyage of the Patria Ambassador Attolico explained to me that he had instructions to request the notification of a contemplated time for German action against Czechoslovakia from the German Government.

"In case the Czechs should again cause a provocation against Germany, Germany would march. This would be tomorrow, in 6 months, or perhaps in a year. However, I could promise him that the German Government, in case of an increasing gravity of the situation or as soon as the Fuehrer made his decision, would notify the Italian Chief of Government as rapidly as possible. In any case, the Italian Government will be the first one who will receive such a notification."

THE PRESIDENT: You did not tell us what the initial was, did you?

MR. ALDERMAN: The initial "R" for Ribbentrop, and the date 23 August 1938.

Four days later Attolico again asked to be notified of the date of the pending attack. I offer Document Number 2792-PS as Exhibit USA-87 -another German Foreign Office memorandum, and from that document I read three paragraphs under the heading "R. M. 251."

"Ambassador Attolico paid me a visit today at 12 o'clock to communicate the following:

"He had received another written instruction from Mussolini asking that Germany communicate in time the probable date of action against Czechoslovakia. Mussolini asked for such notification, as Mr. Attolico assured me, in order 'to be able to take in due time the necessary measures on the French frontier.' Berlin, 27 August 1938; 'R" -for Ribbentrop, and then:

"N. B. I replied to Ambassador Attolico, just as on his former demarche, that I could not impart any date to him; that, however, in any case Mussolini would be the first one to be informed of any decision. Berlin, 2 September 1938."

Hungary, which borders Czechoslovakia to the southeast, was from the first considered to be a possible participant in Case Green. You will recall that in early March 1938 Defendants Keitel and Ribbentrop had exchanged letters on the question of bringing Hungary into the Nazi plan. At that time the decision was in the negative, but by mid-August 1938 the Nazi conspirators were attempting to persuade Hungary to join in the attack.

From August 21 to 26 Admiral Horthy and some of his ministers visited Germany. Inevitably there were discussions of the Czechoslovak question. I now offer Document 2796-PS as Exhibit USA-88. This is a captured German Foreign Office account signed-by Von Weizsacker of the conversations between Hitler and Ribbentrop and a Hungarian Delegation consisting of Horthy, Imredy, and Kanya aboard the S. S. Patria on 23 August 1938. In this conference Ribbentrop inquired about the Hungarian attitude in the event of a German attack on Czechoslovakia and suggested that such an attack would prove to be a good opportunity for Hungary.

The Hungarians, with the exception of Horthy, who wished to put the Hungarian intention to participate on record, proved reluctant to commit themselves. Thereupon Hitler emphasized Ribbentrop's statement and said that whoever wanted to join the meal would have to participate in the cooking as well. I now quote from this document the first two paragraphs:

"While in the forenoon of the 23rd of August the Fuehrer and the Regent of Hungary were engaged in a political discussion, the Hungarian Ministers Imredy and Kanya were in conference with Von Ribbentrop. Von Weizsacker also attended the conference.

"Von Kanya introduced two subjects for discussion: Point 1, the negotiations between Hungary and the Little Entente; and 2, the Czechoslovakian problem."

Then I skip two paragraphs and read the fifth paragraph:

"Von Ribbentrop inquired what Hungary's attitude would be if the Fuehrer would carry out his decision to answer a new Czech provocation by force. The reply of the Hungarians presented two kinds of obstacles: The Yugoslavian neutrality must be assured if Hungary marches towards the north and perhaps the east; moreover, the Hungarian rearmament had only been started and one to two more years time for its development should be allowed.

"Von Ribbentrop then explained to the Hungarians that the Yugoslavs would not dare to march while they were between the pincers of the Axis Powers. Romania alone would therefore not move. England and France would also remain tranquil. England would not recklessly risk her empire. She knew our newly acquired power. In reference to time, however, for the above-mentioned situation, nothing definite could be predicted since it would depend on Czech provocation. Von Ribbentrop repeated that, ' Whoever desires revision must exploit the good opportunity and participate.'

"The Hungarian reply thus remained a conditional one. Upon the question of Von Ribbentrop as to what purpose the desired General Staff conferences were to have, not much more was brought forward than the Hungarian desire of a mutual inventory of military material and preparedness for the Czech conflict. The clear political basis for such a conflict-the time of a Hungarian intervention-was not obtained.

"In the meantime, more positive language was used by Von Horthy in his talk with the Fuehrer. He wished not to hide his doubts with regard to the English attitude, but he wished to put on record Hungary's intention to participate. The Hungarian Ministers were, and remained even later, more skeptical since they feel more strongly about the immediate danger for Hungary with its unprotected flanks.

"When Von Imredy had a discussion with the Fuehrer in the afternoon he was very relieved when the Fuehrer explained to him that in regard to the situation in question he demanded nothing of Hungary. He himself would not know the time. Whoever wanted to join the meal would have to participate in the cooking as well. Should Hungary wish conferences of the General Staffs he would have no objections."

I think perhaps that sentence, "Whoever wanted to join the meal would have to participate in the cooking as well," is perhaps as cynical a statement as any statesman has ever been guilty of.

By the third day of the conference the Germans were able to note that, in the event of a German-Czech conflict, Hungary would be sufficiently armed for participation on 1 October. I now offer in evidence Document Number 2797-PS as Exhibit USA-89, another captured German Foreign Office memorandum of a conversation between Ribbentrop and Kanya on 25 August 1938. You will note that the English mimeographed translation bears the date 29 August. That is incorrect; it should read 25 August. I read the last paragraph from that document, or the last two:

"Concerning Hungary's military preparedness in case of a German-Czech conflict Von Kanya mentioned several days ago that his country would need a period of one to two years in order to develop adequately the armed strength of Hungary.

"During today's conversation Von Kanya corrected this remark and said that Hungary's military situation was much better. His country would be ready, as far as armaments were concerned, to take part in the conflict by October 1 of this year." -Signed with an illegible signature which probably is that of Weizsacker.

The account of the German-Hungarian conference again finds its corroboration in General Jodl's diary, Document Number 1780-PS, from which I have already several times read. The entry in that diary for 21 to 26 August on Page 4 of the English version of the document reads as follows:

"Visit to Germany of the Hungarian Regent. Accompanied by the Prime Minister, the Minister of Foreign Affairs, and the War Minister Von Raatz.

"They arrived with the idea that in the course of a great war after a few years, and with the help of German troops, the old State of Hungary can be re-established. They leave with the understanding that we have neither demands from them nor claims against them, but that Germany will not stand for a second provocation by Czechoslovakia, even if it should be tomorrow. If they want to participate at that moment, it is up to them.

"Germany, however, will never play the role of arbitrator between them and Poland. The Hungarians agree; but they believe that when the issue arises a period of 48 hours would be indispensable to them to find out Yugoslavia's attitude."

The upshot of the talks with the Hungarians proved to be a staff conference on 6 September.

I quote again from Jodl's diary, the entry for 6 September, beginning at the end of that same page:

"Chief of General Staff, General of Artillery Halder, has a conference with the Hungarian Chief of General Staff Fischer. Before that he is briefed by me on the political attitude of the Fuehrer, especially his order not to give any hint on the exact moment. The same with OAI, General Von Stulpnagel."

It is somewhat interesting to find a high-ranking general giving a briefing on such political matters.

Then we come to final actual preparations for the attack. With a 1 October target date set for Case Green, there was a noticeable increase in the tempo of the military preparations in late August and September. Actual preparations for the attack on Czechoslovakia were well under way. The agenda of the Nazi conspirators was devoted to technical details, the timing of "X-days," questions of mobilization, questions of transport and supplies.

On 26 August the Defendant Jodl initialed a memorandum entitled, "Timing of the X-Order and the Question of Advance Measures." This is Item 17 at Pages 37 and 38 of the English translation of the Schmundt file on Case Green, our Number 388-PS.

I should like to invite the special attention of the Tribunal to this memorandum. It demonstrates beyond the slightest doubt the complicity of the OKW and of Defendant Keitel and Jodl in the shameful fabrication of an incident as an excuse for war. It reveals in bare outline the deceit, the barbarity, the completely criminal character of the attack that Germany was preparing to launch.

I ask leave to read this document in full:

"Chief Section L; for chiefs only; written by General Staff officer; top secret; note on progress of report; Berlin, 24 August 1938; access only through officer; 1 copy.

"Timing of the X-Order and the Question of Advance Measures.

"The Luftwaffe's endeavor to take the enemy air forces by surprise at their peacetime airports justifiably leads them to oppose measures taken in advance of the X-Order and to demand that the X-Order itself be given sufficiently late on X minus 1 to prevent the fact of Germany's mobilization becoming known to Czechoslovakia on that day.

"The Army's efforts are tending in the opposite direction. It intends to let OKW initiate all advance measures between X minus 3 and X minus 1 which will contribute to the smooth and rapid working of the mobilization. With this in mind OKH also demands that the X-Order be given to the Army not later than 1400 on X minus 1.

"To this the following must be said:

" 'Operation Green" '-or Aktion Grun-" will be set in motion by means of an 'incident' in Czechoslovakia which will give Germany provocation for military intervention. The fixing of the exact time for this incident is of the utmost importance." I call special attention to that sentence- "The fixing of the exact time for this incident ;s of the utmost importance.

"It must come at a time when the over-all meteorological conditions are favorable for our superior air forces to go into action and at an hour which will enable authentic news of it "-news of this prepared incident-" to reach us on the afternoon of X minus 1.

"It can then be spontaneously answered by the giving of the X-Order at 1400 on X minus 1.

"On X minus 2 the Navy, Army, and Air Force will merely receive an advance warning.

"If the Fuehrer intends to follow this plan of action, all further discussion is superfluous.

"For then no advance measures may be taken before X minus 1 for which there is not an innocent explanation as we shall otherwise appear to have manufactured the incident. Orders for absolutely essential advance measures must be given in good time and camouflaged with the help of numerous maneuvers and exercises.

"Also, the question raised by the Foreign Office as to whether all Germans should be called back in time from prospective enemy territories must in no way lead to the conspicuous departure from Czechoslovakia of any German subjects before the incident.

"Even a warning of diplomatic representatives in Prague is impossible before the first air attack, although the consequences could be very grave in the event of their becoming victims of such an attack (that is the death of representatives of friendly or confirmed neutral powers).

"If, for technical reasons, the evening hours should be considered desirable for the incident, then the following day cannot be X-Day, but it must be the day after that.

"In any case we must act on the principle that nothing must be done before the incident which might point to mobilization, and that the swiftest possible action must be taken after the incident (X-Fall).

"It is the purpose of these notes to point out what a great interest the Wehrmacht has in the incident and that it must be informed of the Fuehrer's intentions in good time-insofar as the Abwehr Section is not also charged with the organization of the incident.

"I request that the Fuehrer's decision be obtained on these points." - signed - "J" -(Jodl).

In handwriting, at the bottom of the page of that document, are the notes of the indefatigable Schmundt, Hitler's adjutant. These reveal that the memorandum was submitted to Hitler on August 30; that Hitler agreed to act along these lines, and that Jodl was so notified on 31 August. There follows Jodl's initials once more.

On 3 September Keitel and Von Brauchitsch met with Hitler at the Berghof. Again Schmundt kept notes of the conference. These will be found as Item 18 at Pages 39 and 40 of the Document Number 388-PS. I shall read the first three short paragraphs of these minutes:

"Colonel General Von Brauchitsch reports on the exact time of the transfer of the troops to 'exercise areas' for 'Grun'. Field units to be transferred on 28 September. From here will then be ready for action. When X-Day becomes known field units carry out exercises in opposite directions.

"Fuehrer has objection. Troops assemble field units a 2-day march away. Carry out camouflage exercises everywhere." -Then there is a question mark.- "OKH must know when X-Day is by 1200 noon, 27 September."

You will note that Von Brauchitsch reported that field troops would be transferred to the proper areas for Case Green on 28 September and would then be ready for action. You will also note that the OKH must know when X-Day is by 12 noon on 27 September.

During the remainder of the conference Hitler gave his views on the strategy the German armies should employ and the strength of the Czech defenses they would encounter. He spoke of the possibility, and I quote, "of drawing in the Henlein people." The situation in the West still troubled him. Schmundt further noted, and here I read the final sentence from Page 40 of the English transcript:

"The Fuehrer gives orders for the development of the Western fortifications: Improvement of advance positions around Aachen and Saarbrucken; construction of 300 to 400 battery positions (1600 artillery pieces). He emphasizes flanking action."

Five days later General Stulpnagel asked Defendant Jodl for written assurance that the OKH would be informed 5 days in advance about the impending action. In the evening Jodl conferred with Luftwaffe generals about the co-ordination of ground and air operations at the start of the attack. I now read the 8 September entry in General Jodl's diary, Page 5 of the English translation of Document 1780-PS.

"General Stulpnagel, OAI, asks for written assurance that the Army High Command will be informed 5 days in advance if the plan is to take place. I agree and add that the over-all meteorological situation can be estimated to some extent only for 2 days in advance and that therefore the plans may be changed up to this moment (X-Day minus 2) "-or as the German puts it- "X-2 Tag."

"General Stulpnagel mentions that for the first time he wonders whether the previous basis of the plan is not being abandoned. It presupposed that the Western Powers would not interfere decisively. It gradually seems as if the Fuehrer would stick to his decision, even though he may no longer be of this opinion. It must be added that Hungary is at least moody and that... Italy is reserved."

Now, this is Jodl talking:

"I must admit that I am worrying, too, when comparing the change of opinion about political and military potentialities, according to directives of 24 June '37, 5 November '37, 7 December '37, 30 May 1938, with the last statements. In spite of that, one must be aware of the fact that the other nations will do everything they can to apply pressure on us. We must pass this test of nerves, but because only very few people know the art of withstanding this pressure successfully, the only possible solution is to inform only a very small circle of officers of news that causes us anxiety, and not to have it circulate through anterooms as heretofore.

"1800 hours to 2100 hours: Conference with Chief of High Command of Armed Forces and Chief of General Staff of the Air Force. (Present were General Jeschonnek, Kammhuber, Sternburg, and myself) We agree about the promulgation of the X-Day order "-

X-Befehl-" (X-1, 4 o'clock) and preannouncement to the Air Force (X-Day minus 1"-X minus 1 day-" 7 o'clock). The 'Y' time has yet to be examined; some formations have an approach flight of one hour."

Late on the evening of the following day, 9 September, Hitter met with Defendant Keitel and Generals Von Brauchitsch and Halder at Nuremberg. Dr. Todt, the construction engineer, later joined this conference, which lasted from 10 in the evening until 3:30 the following morning. Schmundt's minutes on this conference are Item 19 in the large Schmundt file, on Pages 41 to 43 of Document 388-PS.

In this meeting General Halder reviewed the missions assigned to four of the German armies being committed to the attack, the 2d, the 10th, the 12th and the 14th German Armies. With his characteristic enthusiasm for military planning, Hitler then delivered a soliloquy on strategic considerations, which should be taken into account as the attack developed. I shall quote only four paragraphs, beginning with the summary of General Von Brauchitsch's remarks, on the bottom of Page 42:

"General Oberst Von Brauchitsch: 'Employment of motorized divisions was based on the difficult rail situation in Austria and the difficulties in getting other divs' "-that is for divisions" 'ready to march into the area at the right time. In the West vehicles will have to leave on the 20th of September, if X-Day remains as planned. Workers leave on the 23d, by relays. Specialist workers remain according to decision by Army Command II.'

"The Fuehrer: 'Does not see why workers have to return home as early as X-ll. Other workers and people are also on the way on mobilization day. Also the railroad cars will stand around unnecessarily later on.'

"General Keitel: 'Workers are not under the jurisdiction of district commands in the West. Trains must be assembled.'

"Von Brauchitsch: 235,000 men RAD (Labor Service) will be drafted, 96 construction battalions will be distributed (also in the East). 40,000 trained laborers stay in the West.' "

From this day forward the Nazi conspirators were occupied with the intricate planning which is required before such an attack. On 11 September Defendant Jodl conferred with a representative of the Propaganda Ministry about methods of refuting German violations of international law and of exploiting those of the Czechs. I read the 11 September entry in the Jodl diary at Page 5 of the English translation of 1780-PS:

"In the afternoon conference with Secretary of State Hahnke, for the Ministry of Public Enlightenment and Propaganda on imminent common tasks. These joint preparations for refutation"-Widerlegung-"of our own violations of international law, and the exploitation of its violations by the enemy, were considered particularly important."

This discussion developed into a detailed study compiled by Section L, that is, Jodl's section of the OKW.

I now offer in evidence Document C-2 as Exhibit USA-90, which is a carbon copy of the original, signed in pencil. Seven copies of this captured document, as it shows on its face, were prepared and distributed on 1 October 1938 to the OKH, the OKM, the Luftwaffe, and the Foreign Office.

In this study anticipated violations by Germany of international law in connection with the invasion of Czechoslovakia are listed and counterpropaganda suggested for the use of the propaganda agencies. It is a highly interesting top-secret document and with a glance at the original you can see the careful form in which the study of anticipated violations of international law and propagandistic refutations thereof were set out.

The document is prepared in tabular form, in which the anticipated instances of violation of international law are listed in the left hand column. In the second column are given specific examples of the incidents. In the third and fourth column the position to be taken toward these incidents, in violation of international law and in violation of the laws of warfare, is set forth.

The fifth column, which in this document unfortunately is blank, was reserved for the explanations to be offered by the Propaganda Minister. I first quote from the covering letter:

"Enclosed is a list drawn up by Section L of the OKW, of the violations of international law which may be expected on the part of fighting troops.

"Owing to the short time allowed for the compilation, Columns c-1 and c-2 had to be filled in directly therefore, for the time being.

"The branches of the Armed Forces are requested to send in an opinion so that a final version may be drawn up.

"The same is requested of the Foreign Office.

"The Chief of the Supreme Command of the Armed Forces. "By order" - signed - "Burckner."

I am sorry that I perhaps cannot take the time to read extensively from this document. I shall confine myself to reading the first 10 hypothetical incidents for which justification must be found from the second column, Column b of the table:

"First: In an air raid on Prague the British Embassy is destroyed."

"Second: Englishmen or Frenchmen are injured or killed."

"Third: The Hradschin is destroyed in an air raid on Prague."

"Fourth: On account of a report that the Czechs have used gas, the firing of gas projectiles is ordered.

"Fifth: Czech civilians, not recognizable as soldiers, are caught in the act of sabotage (destruction of an important bridge, destruction of foodstuffs and fodder) are discovered looting wounded or dead soldiers and thereupon shot.

"Sixth: Captured Czech soldiers or Czech civilians are detailed to do road work or to load munitions, and so forth.

"Seventh: For military reasons it is necessary to requisition billets, foodstuffs, and fodder from the Czech population. As a result, the latter suffer from want.

"Eighth: Czech population is, for military reasons, compulsorily evacuated to the rear area.

"Ninth: Churches are used for military accommodations.

"Tenth: In the course of their duty, German aircraft fly over Polish territory where they are involved in an air battle with Czech aircraft."

From Nuremberg on the 10th of September, Hitler issued an order bringing the Reichsarbeitsdienst (the German Labor Service) under the OKW. This top-secret order...

THE PRESIDENT: Are you passing from that document now?

MR. ALDERMAN: Yes.

THE PRESIDENT: Would you read the classification with reference to gas?

MR. ALDERMAN: Perhaps I should, Sir.

THE PRESIDENT: It is number 4.

MR. ALDERMAN: Incident number 4?

THE PRESIDENT: Yes.

MR. ALDERMAN: Well, number 4 was the supposed incident. "On account of a report that the Czechs have used gas, the firing of gas projectiles is ordered." Under the column, "Attitude of International Law Group":

> "According to the declaration agreed to in June 1925 by 40 states, including Czechoslovakia, the employment of poison gases, chemical warfare agents, and bacteriological substances is expressly forbidden. Quite a number of states made the reservation to this declaration on the prohibition of gas warfare."

Then, under the column headed "Justification by the Laws of War":

> "If the assertion, that the opponent-in this case the Czechs used a prohibited gas in warfare, is to be believed by the world, it must be possible to prove it. If that is possible, the firing of gas projectiles is justified, and it must be given out in public that it can be proved that the enemy was the first to violate the prohibition. It is therefore particularly important to furnish this proof. If the assertion is unfounded or only partially founded, the gas attack is to be represented only as the need for carrying out a justified reprisal, in the same way as the Italians did in the Abyssinian war. In this case, however, the justification for such harsh reprisals must also be proved."

From Nuremberg on the 10th of September, Hitler issued an order bringing the Reichsarbeitsdienst (the German Labor Service) under the OKW . . .

THE PRESIDENT: There is another short passage which seems to be material.

MR. ALDERMAN: I was very much tempted to read the whole document.

THE PRESIDENT: The justification of number 10.

MR. ALDERMAN: Number 10 was, "In course of their duty, German aircraft fly over Polish territory where they are involved in an air battle with Czech aircraft."

Under the heading, "Attitude of the International Law Group":

> "According to Article 1 of the Fifth Hague Convention of 18 October 1907, the territory of neutral powers is not to be violated. A deliberate violation by flying over this territory is a breach of international law if the neutral powers have declared an air barrier for combat aircraft. If German planes fly over Polish territory this constitutes a violation of international law, provided that this action is not expressly permitted."

Now, under the heading, "Justification by the Laws of War," is this:

> "An attempt at denials should first be made; if this is unsuccessful a request for pardon should be made (on the grounds of miscalculation of position) to the Polish Government and compensation for damage guaranteed."

I had referred to an order issued by Hitler on 10 September 1938 from

Nuremberg, bringing the German Labor Service under the OKW. This top-secret order, of which 25 copies were made, is Item 20 in the Schmundt file, Page 44. I will read that order:

"1. The whole RAD organization comes under the command of the Supreme Command of the Army effective 15 September.

"2. The Chief of OKW decides on the first commitments of this organization in conjunction with the Reich Labor Leader (Reichsarbeitsfuehrer) and on assignments from time to time to the Supreme Commands of the Navy, Army, and Air Force. Where questions arise with regard to competency he will make a final decision in accordance with my instructions.

"3. For the time being this order is to be made known only to the departments and personnel immediately concerned.

"Signed, Adolf Hitler."

Four days later, on 14 September, Defendant Keitel issued detailed instructions for the employment of specific RAD units. This order is Item 21 in the Schmundt file, at Page 45 in the English translation. I do not think I need read the order.

There is another order issued by the Defendant Jodl on 16 September, Item 24, at Page 48 in the Schmundt file. I think I need only read the heading or title of that:

"Subject: Employment of Reich Labor Service for maneuvers with Wehrmacht. Effective 15 September the following units will be trained militarily under direction of the Commander-in-Chief of the Army."

Two further entries in the Defendant Jodl's diary give further indications of the problems of the OKW in this period of mid-September, just 2 weeks before the anticipated X-Day.

I now read the answers for the 15th and 16th September, at Pages 5 and 6 of the English translation of the Jodl diary.

"15 September: In the morning, conference with Chief of Army High Command and Chief of General Staffs of Army and Air Force, the question was discussed as to what could be done if the Fuehrer insists on advancement of the date, due to the rapid development of the situation.

"16 September: General Keitel returns from the Berghof at 1700 hours. He graphically describes the results of the conference between Chamberlain and the Fuehrer. The next conference will take place on the 20th or 21st in Godesberg.

"With consent of the Fuehrer, the order is given in the evening by the Armed Forces High Command, to the Army High Command, and to the Ministry of Finance, to line up the v.G.a.D. along the Czech border." -That I understand to have reference to the reinforced border guard.

"In the same way, an order is issued to the railways to have empty rolling stock kept in readiness, clandestinely, for the strategic concentrations of the Army, so that it can be transported starting 28 September."

The order to the railroads to make rolling stock available, to which General Jodl referred, appears as Item 22, at Page 47 of the Schmundt file. In this order the Defendant Keitel told the railroads to be ready by 28 September but to continue work on the Western fortifications even after 20 September in the interest of camouflage. I quote the first four paragraphs of this order:

"The Reichsbahn (the railroads) must provide trains of empty trucks in great numbers by September 28 for the carrying out of mobilization exercises. This task now takes precedence over all others.

"Therefore the trainloads for the limes job" -I understand the "limes job" to have reference to defense fortification in the West- "will have to be cut down after September 17 and those goods loaded previous to this date unloaded by September 20.

"The Supreme Command of the Army (Fifth Division of the Army General Staff) must issue further orders after consultation with the authorities concerned.

"However, in accordance with the Fuehrer's directive, every effort should be made to continue to supply the materials in as large quantities as feasible, even after 20 September 1938, and this for reasons of camouflage as well as in order to continue the important work on the limes."

The penultimate stage of the aggression begins on 18 September. From that date until the 28th a series of orders was issued advancing preparations for the attack. These orders are included in the Schmundt file and I shall not take the time of the Tribunal by attempting to read all of it.

On the 18th the commitment scheduled for the five participating Armies, the 2d, 8th, 10th, 12th, and 14th, was set forth. That is Item 26 in the Schmundt file at Page 50 of the English translation. Hitler approved the secret mobilization of five divisions in the West to protect the German rear during Case Green, and I refer to Item 31 in the Schmundt file at Page 13-I beg your pardon, it is Page 55, I had a misprint. I might refer to that. It is a "most-secret" order, Berlin, 27 September 1938, 1920 hours; 45 copies of which this is the 16th:

"The Fuehrer has approved the mobilization without warning of the five regular West divisions (26th, 31st, 36th, 33d, and 35th). The Fuehrer and Supreme Commander of the Armed Forces has expressly reserved the right to issue the order for employment in the fortification zone and the evacuation of this zone by the workers of the Todt organization.

"It is left to the OKH to assemble as far as possible, first of all the sections ready to march and, subsequently, the remaining sections of the divisions in marshalling areas behind the Western fortifications." - signed - "Jodl."

THE PRESIDENT: I think this would be a good time to adjourn. We will meet again at 2 o'clock.

[A recess was taken until 1400 hours.]

MR. ALDERMAN: May it please the Tribunal, my attention has been called to the fact that I misread a signature on one of the documents to which I adverted this morning. It is Item 31 of the Schmundt minutes. I read the name "Jodl" as being the signature on that item. I should have read Keitel.

In the course of presenting details of the documents which are being offered in evidence, I think it would be well to pause for a moment, and recall the setting in which these facts took place. The world will never forget the Munich

Pact, and the international crisis which led to it. As this crisis was developing in August and September of 1938, and frantic efforts were being made by the statesmen of the world to preserve the peace of the world, little did they know of the evil plans and designs in the hearts and the minds of these conspirators.

What is being presented to the Tribunal today is the inside story, in their own words, underlying the Pact of Munich. We are now able to spread upon the pages of history the truth concerning the fraud and deceit practiced by the Nazi conspirators in achieving for their own ends, the Pact of Munich as a stepping stone towards further aggression. One cannot think back without living again through the dread of war, the fear of war, the fear of world disaster, which seized all peace-loving persons. The hope for peace which came with the Munich Pact was, we now see, a snare and a deceit-a trap, carefully set by the defendants on trial. The evil character of these men who were fabricating this scheme for aggression and war is demonstrated by their own documents.

Further discussions were held between the Army and the Luftwaffe about the time of day at which the attack should be launched. Conference notes initialed by the Defendant Jodl, dated 27 September, reveal the difference in views. These notes are Item 54, at Page 90 in the translation of Document 388-PS. I shall read these first three paragraphs as follows: The heading is:

"Most secret; for chiefs only; only through officers.

"Conference notes; Berlin, 27 September 1938; 4 copies, first copy. To be filed Grun.

"Co-ordinated Time of Attack by Army and Air Force on X-Day.

"As a matter of principle, every effort should be made for a co-ordinated attack by Army and Air Forces on 1. X-Day. "The Army wishes to attack at dawn, that is, about 0615. It also wishes to conduct some limited operations in the previous night, which however, would not alarm the entire Czech front.

"Air Force's time of attack depends on weather conditions. These could change the time of attack and also limit the area of operations. The weather of the last few days, for instance, would have delayed the start until between 0800 and 1100 due to low ceiling in Bavaria."

Then I'll skip to the last two paragraphs on Page 91: "Thus it is proposed:

"Attack by the Army-independent of the attack by the Air Force-at the time desired by the Army (0615), and permission for limited operations to take place before then; however, only to an extent that will not alarm the entire Czech front.

"The Luftwaffe will attack at a time most suitable to them."

The initial at the end of that order is "J" meaning, I think clearly, Jodl.

On the same date, 27 September, the Defendant Keitel sent a most-secret memorandum to the Defendant Hess, and the Reichsfuehrer SS, Himmler, for the guidance of Nazi Party officials. This memorandum is Item 32 in the Schmundt files at Page 56 of the English translation. I read the first four paragraphs of this message.

"As a result of the political situation the Fuehrer and Chancellor has ordered mobilization measures for the Armed Forces, without the political situation being aggravated by issuing the mobilization (X) order, or corresponding code words.

"Within the framework of these mobilization measures it is necessary for the Armed Forces authorities to issue demands to the various Party authorities and their organizations, which are connected with the previous issuing of the mobilization order, the advance measures or special code names.

"The special situation makes it necessary that these demands be met (even if the code word has not been previously issued) immediately and without being referred to higher authority.

"OKW requests that subordinate offices be given immediate instructions to this effect, so that the mobilization of the Armed Forces can be carried out according to plan."

Then I skip to the last paragraph:

"The Supreme Command of the Armed Forces further requests that all measures not provided for in the plans which are undertaken by Party organizations or Police units, as a result of the political situation, be reported in every case and in plenty of time to the Supreme Command of the Armed Forces. Only then can it be guaranteed that these measures can be carried out in practice.

"The Chief of the Supreme Command of the Armed Forces, Keitel."

Two additional entries from the Defendant Jodl's diary reveal the extent to which the Nazi conspirators carried out all of their preparations for an attack, even during the period of negotiations which culminated in the Munich Agreement. I quote the answers in the Jodl diary for 26 and 27 September, from Page 7 of the translation of Document 1780-PS. 26 September...

THE PRESIDENT: Have you got in mind the dates of the visits of Mr. Chamberlain to Germany, and of the actual agreement? Perhaps you can give it later on.

MR. ALDERMAN: I think it will be covered later, yes.

THE PRESIDENT: Very well.

MR. ALDERMAN: The agreement of the Munich Pact was the 29th of September, and this answer then was 3 days before the Pact, the 26th of September:

"Chief of the Armed Forces High Command, acting through the Army High Command, has stopped the intended approach march of the advance units to the Czech border, because it is not yet necessary and because the Fuehrer does not intend to march in before the 30th in any case. Order to approach towards the Czech frontier need be given on the 27th only.

"Fixed radio stations of Breslau, Dresden and Vienna are put at the disposal of the Reich Ministry for Popular Enlightenment and Propaganda for interference with possible Czech propaganda transmissions.

"Question by Ausland whether Czechs are to be allowed to leave and cross Germany. Decision from Chief of the Armed Forces High Command: 'Yes.'

"1515 hours: The Chief of the Armed Forces High Command informs General Stumpf about the result of the Godesberg conversations and about the Fuehrer's opinion. In no case will X-Day be before the 30th.

"It is important that we do not permit ourselves to be drawn into

31

military engagements because of false reports, before Prague replies.

"A question of Stumpf about Y-Hour results in the reply that on account of the weather situation, a simultaneous intervention of the Air Force and Army cannot be expected. The Army needs the dawn, the Air Force can only start later on account of frequent early fogs.

"The Fuehrer has to make a decision as to which of the Commanders-in-Chief is to have priority.

"The opinion of Stumpf is also that the attack of the Army has to proceed. The Fuehrer has not made any decision as yet about commitment against Prague.

"2000 hours: The Fuehrer addresses the people and the world in an important speech at the Sportpalast."

Then the entry on 27 September:

"1320 hours: The Fuehrer consents to the first wave of attack being advanced to a line from where they can arrive in the assembly area by 30 September."

The order referred to by General Jodl was also recorded by the faithful Schmundt, which appears as Item 33 at Page 57 of the file. I'll read it in its entirety. It is the order which brought the Nazi Army to a jumping-off point for the unprovoked and brutal aggression:

"28. 9. 38.; most secret; memorandum.

"At 1300 hours 27 September the Fuehrer and Supreme Commander of the Armed Forces ordered the movement of the assault units from their exercise areas to their jumping-off points.

"The assault units (about 21 reinforced regiments, or seven divisions) must be ready to begin the action against Grun on 30 September, the decision having been made 1 day previously by 1200 noon.

This order was conveyed to General Keitel at 1320 through Major Schmundt" -pencil note by Schmundt.

At this point, with the Nazi Army poised in a strategic position around the borders of Czechoslovakia, we shall turn back for a moment to examine another phase of the Czech aggression. The military preparations for action against Czechoslovakia had not been carried out in vacuo.

They had been preceded by a skillfully conceived campaign designed to promote civil disobedience in the Czechoslovak State. Using the techniques they had already developed in other uncontested ventures underhandedly, the Nazi conspirators over a period of years used money, propaganda, and force to undermine Czechoslovakia. In this program the Nazis focused their attention on the persons of German descent living in the Sudetenland, a mountainous area bounding Bohemia and Moravia on the northwest and south. I now invite the attention of the Tribunal to Document Number 998-PS and offer it in evidence as an exhibit.

This exhibit is entitled, "German Crimes Against Czechoslovakia and is the Czechoslovak Government's official report for the prosecution and trial of the German major war criminals. I believe that this report is clearly included within the provisions of Article 21 of the Charter, as a document of which the Court will take judicial notice. Article 21 provides:

"The Tribunal shall not require proof of facts of common knowledge but shall take judicial notice thereof. It shall also take judicial notice of official governmental documents and reports of the United Nations, including the accounts and documents of the committees set up in the various Allied countries for the investigation of war crimes and the records and findings of military or other tribunals of any of the United Nations."

Since, under that provision, the Court will take judicial notice of this governmental report by the Czech Government, I shall, with the leave of the Tribunal, merely summarize Pages 9 to 12 of this report to show the background of the subsequent Nazi intrigue within Czechoslovakia.

Nazi agitation in Czechoslovakia dated from the earliest days of the Nazi Party. In the years following the first World War, a German National Socialist Workers Party (DNSAP), which maintained close contact with Hitler's NSDAP, was activated in the Sudetenland. In 1932, ringleaders of the Sudeten Volkssport, an organization corresponding to the Nazi SA or Sturmabteilung, openly endorsed the 21 points of Hitler's program, the first of which demanded the union of all Germans in a greater Germany. Soon thereafter, they were charged with planning armed rebellion on behalf of a foreign power and were sentenced for conspiracy against the Czech Republic.

Late in 1933, the National Socialist Party of Czechoslovakia forestalled its dissolution by voluntary liquidation and several of its chiefs escaped across the border into Germany. For a year thereafter, Nazi activity in Czechoslovakia continued underground.

On 1 October 1934, with the approval and at the urging of the Nazi conspirators, an instructor of gymnastics, Konrad Henlein, established the German Home Front or Deutsche Heimatfront, which, the following spring became the Sudeten German Party (SDP). Profiting from the experiences of the Czech National Socialist Party, Henlein denied any connection with the German Nazis. He rejected pan-Germanism and professed his respect for individual liberties and his loyalty to honest democracy and to the Czech State. His party, nonetheless, was built on the basis of the Nazi Fuehrerprinzip, and he became its Fuehrer.

By 1937, when the powers of Hitler's Germany had become manifest, Henlein and his followers were striking a more aggressive note, demanding without definition, "complete Sudeten autonomy". The SDP laid proposals before the Czech Parliament which would in substance, have created a state within a state.

After the annexation of Austria by Germany in March 1938, the Henleinists, who were now openly organized after the Nazi model, intensified their activities. Undisguised anti-Semitic propaganda started in the Henlein press.

The campaign against Bolshevism was intensified. Terrorism in the Henlein-dominated communities increased. A storm-troop organization, patterned and trained on the principles of the Nazi SS was established, known as the FS, Freiwilliger Selbstschutz (or Voluntary Vigilantes).

On 24 April 1938, in a speech to the Party Congress in Karlovy Vary, Henlein came into the open with what he called his Karlsbad Program. In this speech, which echoed Hitler in tone and substance, Henlein asserted the right of the Sudeten Germans to profess German political philosophy which, it was clear, meant National Socialism.

As the summer of 1938 wore on, the Henleinists used every technique of the Nazi Fifth Column. As summarized in Pages 12 to 16 of the Czech

Government official report, these techniques included:

(a) Espionage. Military espionage was conducted by the SDP, the FS, and by other members of the German minority on behalf of Germany. Czech defenses were mapped and information on Czech troop movements was furnished to the German authorities.

(b) Nazification of German organizations in Czechoslovakia. The Henleinists systematically penetrated the whole life of the German population of Czechoslovakia. Associations and social cultural centers regularly underwent "Gleichschaltung", that is purification, by the SDP. Among the organizations conquered by the Henleinists were sports societies, rowing clubs, associations of ax-service men, and choral societies. The Henleinists were particularly interested in penetrating as many business institutions as possible and bringing over to their side the directors of banks, the owners or directors of factories, and the managers of commercial firms. In the case of Jewish ownership or direction, they attempted to secure the cooperation of the clerical and technical staffs of the institutions.

(c) German direction and leadership. The Henleinists maintained permanent contact with the Nazi officials designated to direct operations within Czechoslovakia. Meetings in Germany, at which Henleinists were exhorted and instructed in Fifth Column activity, were camouflaged by being held in conjunction with "Sanger Feste" (or choral festivals), gymnastic shows, and assemblies, and commercial gatherings such as the Leipzig Fair. Whenever the Nazi conspirators needed incidents for their war of nerves, it was the duty of the Henleinists to supply them.

(d) Propaganda. Disruptive and subversive propaganda was beamed at Czechoslovakia in German broadcasts and was echoed in the German press. Goebbels called Czechoslovakia a "nest of Bolshevism" and spread the false report of Russian troops and airplanes centered in Prague. Under direction from the Reich, the Henleinists maintained whispering propaganda in the Sudetenland which contributed to the mounting tension and to the creation of incidents. Illegal Nazi literature was smuggled from Germany and widely distributed in the border regions. The Henlein press, more or less openly, espoused Nazi ideology before the German population in the Sudetenland.

(e) Murder and terrorism. Nazi conspirators provided the Henleinists, and particularly the FS, with money and arms with which to provoke incidents and to maintain a state of permanent unrest. Gendarmes, customs officers, and other Czech officials were attacked. A boycott was established against Jewish lawyers, doctors, and tradesmen.

The Henleinists terrorized the non-Henlein population and the Nazi Gestapo crossed into the border districts to carry Czechoslovak citizens across the border into Germany. In several cases, political foes of the Nazis were murdered on Czech soil. Nazi agents murdered Professor Theodor Lessing in 1933, and engineer Formis in 1935. Both men were anti-Nazis who had escaped from Germany after Hitler came to power and had sought refuge in Czechoslovakia.

Sometime afterwards, when there was no longer need for pretense and deception, Konrad Henlein made a clear and frank statement of the mission assigned to him by the Nazi conspirators. I offer in evidence Document Number 2863-PS, an excerpt from a lecture by Konrad Henlein quoted in the book Four Fighting Years, a publication of the Czechoslovak Ministry of Foreign Affairs; and I quote from Page 29. This book has been marked for identification Exhibit USA-92, but without offering it in evidence, I ask the Tribunal to take judicial notice of it. I shall read from Page 29. This lecture was delivered by Henlein on 4 March 1941, in the auditorium of the University of Vienna, under the auspices of the Wiener Verwaltungsakademie. During a thorough search of libraries in Vienna and elsewhere, we have been unable to find a copy of the German text. This text, this volume that I have here, is an English version. The Vienna newspapers the following day carried only summaries of the lecture. This English version, however, is an official publication of the Czech Government and is, under the circumstances, the best evidence that we can produce of the Henlein speech.

In this lecture on "The Fight for the Liberation of the Sudetens" Henlein said:

"National Socialism soon swept over us Sudeten Germans. Our struggle was of a different character from that in Germany. Although we had to behave differently in public we were, of course, secretly in touch with the National Socialist revolution in Germany so that we might be a part of it. The struggle for Greater Germany was waged on Sudeten soil, too. This struggle could be waged only by those inspired by the spirit of National Socialism, persons who were true followers of our Fuehrer, whatever their outward appearance. Fate sought me out to be the leader of the national group in its final struggle. When in the autumn of 1933, the leader of the NSDAP asked me to take over the political leadership of the Sudeten Germans, I had a difficult problem to solve. Should the National Socialist Party continue to be carried on illegally or should the movement, in the interest of the selfpreservation of the Sudeten Germans and in order to prepare their return to the Reich, wage its struggle under camouflage and by methods which appeared quite legal to the outside world? For us Sudeten Germans only the second alternative seemed possible, for the preservation of our national group was at stake. It would certainly have been easier to exchange this hard and mentally exhausting struggle for the heroic gesture of confessing allegiance to National Socialism and entering a Czechoslovak prison. But it seemed more than doubtful whether, by this means, we could have fulfilled the political task of destroying Czechoslovakia as a bastion in the alliance against the German Reich."

The account of Nazi intrigue in Czechoslovakia which I have just presented to the Tribunal is the outline of this conspiracy as it had been pieced together by the Czechoslovak Government early this summer. Since then, captured documents and other information made available to us since the defeat of Germany have clearly and conclusively demonstrated the implication, which hitherto could only be deduced, of the Nazi conspirators in the agitation in the Sudetenland.

I offer in evidence Document Number 3060-PS, Exhibit USA-93. This is the original, handwritten draft of a telegram sent from the German Legation in Prague on 16 March 1938 to the Foreign Minister in Berlin. It is presumably written by the German Minister Eisenlohr. It proves conclusively that the Henlein movement was an instrument, a puppet of the Nazi conspirators. The Henlein party, it appears from this document, was directed from Berlin and from the German Legation in Prague. It could have no policy of its own. Even the speeches of its leaders had to be co-ordinated with the German authorities.

I will read this telegram:

"Prague, 16 March 1938.

"Foreign (Office), Berlin; (cipher cable-secret); No. 57 of 16 March.

"With reference to cable order No. 30 of 14 March.

"Rebuff to Frank has had a salutary effect. Have thrashed out matters with Henlein, who recently had shunned me, and with Frank separately and received following promises:

"1. The line of German foreign policy as transmitted by the German Legation is exclusively decisive for policy and tactics of the Sudeten German Party. My directives are to be complied with implicitly.

"2. Public speeches and the press will be co-ordinated uniformly with my approval. The editorial staff of Zeit" Time- "is to be improved.

"3. Party leadership abandons the former intransigent line, which in the end might lead to political complications, and adopts a line of gradual promotion of Sudeten German interests. The objectives are to be set in every case with my participation and to be promoted by parallel diplomatic action.

Laws for the protection of nationalities (Volksschutzgesetze) and territorial autonomy are no longer to be stressed.

"4. If consultations with Berlin agencies are required or desired before Henlein issues important statements on his program, they are to be applied for and prepared through the Legation.

"5. All information of the Sudeten German Party for German agencies is to be transmitted through the Legation.

"6. Henlein will establish contact with me every week, and will come to Prague at any time if requested.

"I now hope to have the Sudeten German Party under firm control, as this is more than ever necessary for coming developments in the interest of foreign policy. Please inform Ministries concerned and Mittelstelle (Central Office for Racial Germans) and request them to support this uniform direction of the Sudeten German Party."

The initials are illegible.

The dressing down administered by Eisenlohr to Henlein had the desired effect. The day after the telegram was dispatched from Prague, Henlein addressed a humble letter to Ribbentrop, asking an early personal conversation.

I offer in evidence Document Number 2789-PS as Exhibit USA-94. This is the letter from Konrad Henlein to Defendant Ribbentrop, captured in the German Foreign Office files, dated 17 March 1938.

"Most honored Minister of Foreign Affairs:

"In our deeply felt joy over the fortunate turn of events in Austria we feel it our duty to express our gratitude to all those who had a share in this new grand achievement of our Fuehrer.

"I beg you, most honored Minister, to accept accordingly the sincere thanks of the Sudeten Germans herewith.

"We shall show our appreciation to the Fuehrer by doubled efforts in the service of the Greater German policy.

"The new situation requires a re-examination of the Sudeten German policy. For this purpose I beg to ask you for the opportunity of a very early personal talk.

"In view of the necessity of such a clarification I have postponed the nation-wide Party Congress, originally scheduled for 26th and 27th of March 1938, for 4 weeks.

"I would appreciate it if the Ambassador, Dr. Eisenlohr, and two of my closest associates would be allowed to participate in the requested talks.

"Heil Hitler. Loyally yours" - signed - "Konrad Henlein."

You will note that Henlein was quite aware that the seizure of Austria made possible the adoption of a new policy towards Czechoslovakia. You will also note that he was already in close enough contact with Ribbentrop and the German Minister in Prague to feel free to suggest early personal talks.

Ribbentrop was not unreceptive to Henlein's suggestion. The conversations Henlein had proposed took place in the Foreign Office in Berlin on the 29th of March 1938. The previous day Henlein had conferred with Hitler himself.

I offer in evidence Document Number 2788-PS as Exhibit USA-95, captured German Foreign Office notes of the conference on the 29th of March. I read the first two paragraphs:

"In this conference the gentlemen enumerated in the enclosed list participated.

"The Reich Minister started out by emphasizing the necessity to keep the conference which had been scheduled strictly a secret. He then explained, in view of the directives which the Fuehrer himself had given to Konrad Henlein personally yesterday afternoon, that there were two questions which were of outstanding importance for the conduct of policy of the Sudeten German Party."

I will omit the discussion of the claims of the Sudeten Germans and resume the minutes of this meeting in the middle of the last paragraph of the first page of the English translation, with the sentence beginning, "The aim of the negotiations."

"The aim of the negotiations to be carried out by the Sudeten German Party with the Czechoslovakian Government is finally this: To avoid entry into the Government by the extension and gradual specification of the demands to be made. It must be emphasized clearly in the negotiations that the Sudeten German Party alone is the party to the negotiations with the Czechoslovakian Government, not the Reich Cabinet. The Reich Cabinet itself must refuse to appear toward the government in Prague or toward London and Paris as the advocate or pacemaker of the Sudeten German demands. It is a self-evident prerequisite that during the impending discussion with the Czechoslovak Government the Sudeten Germans should be firmly controlled by Konrad Henlein, should maintain quiet and discipline, and should avoid indiscretions. The assurances already given by Konrad Henlein in this connection were satisfactory.

"Following these general explanations of the Reichsminister, the demands of the Sudeten German Party from the Czechoslovak Government, as contained in the enclosure, were discussed and approved in principle. For further co-operation, Konrad Henlein was instructed to keep in the closest possible touch with the Reichsminister and the head of the Central Office for Racial Germans, as well as the German Minister in Prague, as the local representative of the Foreign Minister. The task of the German Minister in Prague would be to support the demand of the Sudeten German Party as reasonable-not officially, but in more private talks with the Czechoslovak politicians, without exerting any direct influence on the extent of the demands of the Party.

"In conclusion, there was a discussion whether it would be useful if the Sudeten German Party would co-operate with other minorities in Czechoslovakia, especially with the Slovaks. The Foreign Minister decided that the Party should have the discretion to keep a loose contact with other minority groups if the adoption of a parallel course by them might appear appropriate.

"Berlin, 29 March 1938, "R" - for Ribbentrop.

Not the least interesting aspect of this secret meeting is the list of those who attended: Konrad Henlein; his principal deputy, Karl Hermann Frank; and two others represented the Sudeten German Party. Professor Haushofer, the geopolitician, and SS Obergruppenfuehrer Lorenz represented the Volksdeutsche Mittelstelle (the Central Office for Racial Germans). The Foreign Office was represented by a delegation of eight. These eight included Ribbentrop, who presided at the meeting and did most of the talking; Von Mackensen; Weizsacker and Minister Eisenlohr from the German Legation at Prague.

In May, Henlein came to Berlin for more conversations with the Nazi conspirators. At this time the plans for Case Green, for the attack on the Czechs, were already on paper, and it may be assumed that Henlein was briefed on the role he was to play during the summer months.

I again quote from General Jodl's diary, Document 1780-PS, the entry for 22 May 1938: "Fundamental conference between the Fuehrer and K. Henlein (see enclosure)." The enclosure unfortunately is missing from Jodl's diary.

The Tribunal will recall that in his speech in Vienna Henlein had admitted that he had been selected by the Nazi conspirators in the fall of 1933 to take over the political leadership of the Sudeten Germans. The documents I have just read show conclusively the nature of Henlein's mission. They demonstrate that Henlein's policy, his propaganda, even his speeches, were controlled by Berlin.

I will now show that from the year 1935 the Sudeten German Party was secretly subsidized by the German Foreign Office. I offer in evidence Document 3059-PS as Exhibit USA-96, another secret memorandum captured in the German Foreign Office file.

This memorandum, signed by Woermann and dated Berlin, 19 August 1938, was occasioned by the request of the Henlein Party for additional funds. I read from that document:

"The Sudeten German Party has been subsidized by the Foreign Office regularly since 1935 with certain amounts, consisting of a monthly payment of 15,000 marks; 12,000 marks of this are transmitted to the Prague Legation for disbursement and 3,000 marks are paid out to the Berlin representation of the Party (Bureau Burger). In the course of the last few months the tasks assigned to the Bureau Burger have increased considerably due to the current negotiations with the Czech Government. The number of pamphlets and maps which are produced and disseminated has risen; the propaganda activity in the press has grown immensely; the expense accounts have increased especially because due to the necessity for continuous good information, the expenses for trips to Prague, London, and Paris (including the financing of travels of Sudeten German deputies and agents) have grown considerably heavier. Under these conditions the Bureau Burger is no longer able to get along with the monthly allowance of 3,000 marks if it is to do everything required. Therefore Herr Burger has applied to this office for an increase of this amount from 3,000 marks to 5,500 marks monthly. In view of the considerable increase in the business transacted by the bureau, and of the importance which marks the activity of the bureau in regard to the co-operation with the Foreign Office, this desire deserves the strongest support.

"Herewith submitted to the personnel department with a request for approval. Increase of payments with retroactive effect from 1 August is requested." - signed - "Woermann."

Under this signature is a footnote:

"Volksdeutsche Mittelstelle" -Central Office for Racial Germans- "will be informed by the Political Department" handwritten marginal note.

We may only conjecture what financial support the Henlein movement received from other agencies of the German Government. As the military preparations to attack Czechoslovakia moved forward in the late summer and early fall, the Nazi command made good use of Henlein and his followers. About the 1st of August, the Air Attache in the German Legation in Prague, Major Moericke, acting on instructions from Luftwaffe headquarters in Berlin, visited the Sudeten German leader in Freudenthal. With his assistance and in the company of the local leader of the FS, the Henlein equivalent of the SS, he reconnoitered the surrounding countryside to select possible airfield sites for German use. The FS leader, a Czech reservist then on leave, was in the uniform of the Czech Army, a fact which, as the Attache noted, served as excellent camouflage.

I now read from the enclosure to Document 1536-PS, which I offered in evidence earlier and which bears United States Exhibit Number 83. I have already read the first four paragraphs of the enclosure:

"The manufacturer M. is the head of the Sudeten German Glider Pilots in Fr." -that's Freudenthal- "and said to be absolutely reliable by my trusted man. My personal impression fully confirmed this judgment. No hint of my identity was made to him, although I had the impression that M. knew who I was.

"At my request, with which he complied without any question, M. travelled with me over the country in question. We used M.'s private car for the trip.

"As M. did not know the country around Beneschau sufficiently well, he took with him the local leader of the FS, a Czech reservist of the Sudeten German Racial Group, at the time on leave. He was in uniform. For reasons of camouflage, I was entirely in agreement with this-without actually saying so.

"As M., during the course of the drive, observed that I photographed large open spaces out of the car, he said. 'Aha, so you're looking for airfields!' I answered that we supposed that in the case of any serious trouble, the Czechs would put their airfields immediately behind the line of fortifications. I had the intention of looking over the country from that point of view."

In the latter part of the Air Attache's report, reference is made to the presence of reliable agents and informers, which he called "V-Leute" (V-people), apparently drawn from the ranks of the Henlein party in this area. It was indicated that these agents were in touch with the "Abwehr Stelle" (the Intelligence Office) in Breslau.

In September, when the Nazi propaganda campaign was reaching its height, the Nazis were not satisfied with playing merely on the Sudeten demands for autonomy. They attempted to use the Slovaks as well. On the 19th of September the Foreign Office in Berlin sent a telegram to the German Legation in Prague. I offer the document in evidence, Number 2858-PS, Exhibit USA-97, another captured German Foreign Office document-a telegram:

"Please inform Deputy Kundt that Konrad Henlein requests to get in touch with the Slovaks at once and induce them to start their demands for autonomy tomorrow." - signed - "Altenburg."

Kundt was Henlein's representative in Prague.

As the harassed Czech Government sought to stem the disorders in the Sudetenland, the German Foreign Office turned to threatening diplomatic tactics in a deliberate effort to increase the tension between the two countries. I offer in evidence Documents 2855-PS, 2854-PS, 2853-PS, and 2856-PS, as United States Exhibits respectively 98, 99, 100, and 101. Four telegrams from the Foreign Office in Berlin to the Legation in Prague were dispatched between the 16th and 24th of September 1938. They are self-explanatory. The first is dated 16 September.

"Tonight 150 subjects of Czechoslovakia of Czech blood were arrested in Germany. This measure is an answer to the arrest of Sudeten Germans since the Fuehrer's speech of 12 September. I request you to ascertain as soon as possible the number of Sudeten Germans arrested since 12 September as far as possible. The number of those arrested there is estimated conservatively at 400 by the Gestapo. Cable report."

A handwritten note follows:

"Impossible for me to ascertain these facts as already communicated to the charge d'affaires."

The second telegram is dated September 17: "Most urgent.

"I. Request to inform the local government immediately of the following:

"The Reich Government has decided that:

"(a) Immediately as many Czech subjects of Czech descent, Czech-speaking Jews included, will be arrested in Germany as Sudeten Germans have been in Czechoslovakia since the beginning of the week; (b) If any Sudeten Germans should be executed pursuant to a death sentence on the basis of martial law, an equal number of Czechs will be shot in Germany."

The third telegram was sent on 24 September. I read it:

"According to information received here, Czechs have arrested two German frontier policemen, seven customs officials, and 30 railway officials. As counter measure all the Czech staff in Marschegg were arrested. We are prepared to exchange the arrested Czech officials for the German officials. Please approach Government there and wire result."

On the same day the fourth telegram was dispatched, and I read the last paragraph:

"'Confidential'. Yielding of Czech hostages arrested here for the prevention of the execution of any sentences passed by military courts against Sudeten Germans is, of course, out of question."

In the latter half of September, Henlein devoted himself and his followers wholeheartedly to the preparations for the coming German attack. About 15 September, after Hitler's provocative Nuremberg speech in which he accused Benes of torturing and planning the extermination of the Sudeten Germans, Henlein and Karl Hermann Frank, one of his principal deputies, fled to Germany to avoid arrest by the Czech Government. In Germany Henlein broadcast over the powerful Reichsener radio station his determination to lead the Sudeten Germans home to the Reich and denounced what he called the Hussites-Bolshevist criminals of Prague. From his headquarters in a castle at Donndorf, outside Bayreuth, he kept in close touch with the leading Nazi conspirators, including Hitler and Himmler. He directed activities along the border and began the organization of the Sudeten German Free Corps, an auxiliary military organization. You will find these events set forth in the Czechoslovak official government report, 998-PS, which has already been offered as Exhibit USA-91.

Henlein's activities were carried on with the advice and assistance of the German Nazi leaders. Lieutenant Colonel Kochling was assigned to Henlein in an advisory capacity to assist with the Sudeten German Free Corps. In a conference with Hitler on the night of September 17, Kochling received far-reaching military powers.

At this conference, the purpose of the Free Corps was frankly stated-the maintenance of disorder and clashes. I read from Item 25, a handwritten note labelled "most secret," on Page 49 of the Schmundt file, Document 388-PS:

"Most secret. Last night conference took place between Fuehrer and Lieutenant Colonel Kochling. Duration of conference 7 minutes. Lieutenant Colonel Kochling remains directly responsible to OKW. He will be assigned to Konrad Henlein in an advisory capacity. He received far-reaching military plenary powers from the Fuehrer. The Sudeten German Free Corps remains responsible to Konrad Henlein alone. Purpose: Protection of the Sudeten Germans and maintenance of disturbances and clashes. The Free Corps will be established in Germany. Armament only with Austrian weapons. Activities of Free Corps to begin as soon as possible."

THE PRESIDENT: Would that be a good place to break off for 10 minutes?

[A recess was taken]

MR. ALDERMAN: May it please the Tribunal, General Jodl's diary again gives a further insight into the position of the Henlein Free Corps. At this time, the Free Corps was engaged in active skirmishing along the Czech border, furnishing incidents and provocation in the desired manner. I quote from the entries in the Jodl diary, for the 19th and 20th September 1938, at Page 6 of the Document 1780-PS, which is Exhibit USA-72.

"19 September: Order is given to the Army High Command to take care of the Sudeten German Free Corps.

"20 September: England and France have handed over their demands in Prague, the contents of which are still unknown. The activities of the Free Corps start assuming such an extent that they may bring about, and already have brought about, consequences harmful to the plans of the Army. (Transferring rather strong units of the Czech Army to the proximity of the border.) By checking with Lieutenant Colonel Kochling, I attempt to lead these activities into normal channels.

"Toward the evening the Fuehrer also takes a hand and gives permission to act only with groups up to 12 men each, after the approval of the corps headquarters."

A report from Henlein's staff, which was found in Hitler's headquarters, boasted of the offensive operations of the Free Corps. It is Item 30 of the Schmundt file, Page 54 of Document 388-PS. I read the last two paragraphs:

"Since 19 September, in more than 300 missions, the Free Corps has executed its task with an amazing spirit of attack," now, that word "attack" was changed by superimposition to "defense" - "and with a willingness often reaching a degree of unqualified self-sacrifice. The result of the first phase of its activities: More than 1500 prisoners, 25 MG's" -which I suppose means machine guns- "and a large amount of other weapons and equipment, aside from serious losses in dead and wounded suffered by the enemy." - and there was superimposed in place of "enemy", "the Czech terrorists."

In his headquarters in the castle at Donndorf, Henlein was in close touch with Admiral Canaris of the Intelligence Division of the OKW and with the SS and the SA. The liaison officer between the SS and Henlein was Oberfuehrer Gottlob Berger (SS).

I now offer in evidence Document 3036-PS as Exhibit USA-102, which is an affidavit executed by Gottlob Berger; and in connection with that affidavit, I wish to submit to the Tribunal that it presents, we think, quite a different question of proof from the Schuschnigg affidavits which were not admitted in evidence by the Court. Schuschnigg, of course, was a neutral and non-Nazi Austrian. He was not a member of this conspiracy, and I can well understand that the Court rejected his affidavit for these reasons.

This man was a Nazi. He was serving in this conspiracy. He has made this affidavit. We think the affidavit has probative value and should be admitted by the Tribunal under the pertinent provision of the Charter, which says that you will accept in evidence any evidence having probative value. We think it would be unfair to require us to bring here as a witness a man who would certainly be a hostile witness, who is to us a member of this conspiracy, and it seems to us that the affidavit should be admitted with leave to the defendants, if they wish, to call the author of the affidavit as their witness. I should have added that this man was a prominent member of the SS which is charged before you as being a criminal organization, and we think the document is perfectly competent in evidence as an admission against interest by a prominent member of the SS organization.

DR. STAMHER: Mr. President, the Defense objects to the use of this document. This document was drawn up as late as 22 November 1945, here in Nuremberg, and the witness Berger could, therefore, be brought to Court without any difficulty. We must insist that he be heard here on the subjects on which the Prosecution wishes to introduce his testimony. That would be the only way in which the Defense could have an opportunity of crossexamining the witness and thereby contribute to obtaining objective truth.

[Pause in the proceedings while the Tribunal consulted.]

THE PRESIDENT: The Tribunal upholds the objection and will not hear this affidavit. It is open to either the Prosecution or the defendants, of course, to call the man who made the affidavit. That is all I have to say. We have upheld your objection.

MR. ALDERMAN: If the Tribunal please, I had another affidavit by one Alfred Helmut Naujocks which, I take it, will be excluded under this same ruling, and which, therefore, I shall not offer.

THE PRESIDENT: If the circumstances are the same.

MR. ALDERMAN: Yes, I might merely refer to it for identification because it is in your document books

THE PRESIDENT: Very well.

MR. ALDERMAN: It is Document 3029-PS.

THE PRESIDENT: Very well. That also will be rejected as evidence.

MR. ALDERMAN: Yes. Offensive operations along the Czechoslovakian border were not confined to skirmishes carried out by the Free Corps. Two SS-Totenkopf (Deathhead) battalions were operating across the border in Czech territory near Asch.

I quote now from Item 36 in the Schmundt file, an OKW most secret order, signed by Jodl, and dated 28 September. This appears at Page 61 of the Schmundt file:

"Supreme Command of the Armed Forces, Berlin, 28 September 1938; 45 copies, 16th copy; most secret.

"Subject: Four SS-Totenkopf battalions subordinate to the Commander-in-Chief Army.

"To: Reichsfuehrer SS and Chief of the German Police (SS Central Office) (36th copy).

"By order of the Supreme Command of the Armed Forces the following battalions of the SS Deathhead organization will be under the command of the Commander-in-Chief of the Army with immediate effect.

"Second and Third Battalions of the 2d SS-Totenkopf Regiment Brandenburg at present in Brieg (Upper Silesia).

"First and Second Battalions of the 3d SS-Totenkopf Regiment Thuringia, at present in Radebeul and Kotzschenbroda near Dresden.

"Commander-in-Chief of the Army is requested to deploy these battalions for the West, (Upper Rhine) according to the Fuehrer's instructions.

"These SS-Totenkopf units now operating in the Asch promontory (I and II Battalions of the SS-Totenkopf Regiment Oberbayern) will come under the Commander-in-Chief of the Army only when they return to German Reich territory, or when the Army crosses the German-Czech frontier.

"It is requested that all further arrangements be made between Commander-in-Chief of the Army and Reichsfuehrer SS (SS Central Office).

"For the Chief of the Supreme Command of the Armed Forces, Jodl."

According to the 25 September entry in General Jodl's diary, these SS-Totenkopf battalions were operating in this area on direct orders from Hitler. As the time X-Day approached, the disposition of the Free Corps became a matter of dispute.

On 26 September Himmler issued an order to the Chief of Staff of the Sudeten German Free Corps, directing that the Free Corps come under control of the Reichsfuehrer SS in the event of German invasion of Czechoslovakia. This document is Item 37 in the Schmundt file, on Page 62.

On 28 September Defendant Keitel directed that as soon as the German Army crosses the Czech border, the Free Corps will take orders from the OKH. In this most-secret order of the OKW, Keitel discloses that Henlein's men are already operating in Czechoslovak territory.

I read now from Item 34 of the Schmundt file on Page 58, the last three paragraphs of this most-secret order:

"For the Henlein Free Corps and units subordinate to it the principle remains valid, that they receive instructions direct from the Fuehrer and that they carry out their operations only in conjunction with the competent corps headquarters. The advance units of the Free Corps will have to report to the local commander of the frontier guard immediately before crossing the frontier.

"Those units remaining forward of the frontier should, in their own interests, get into communication with the frontier guard as often as possible.

"As soon as the Army crosses the Czechoslovak border the Henlein Free Corps will be subordinate to the OKH. Thus it will be expedient to assign a sector to the Free Corps, even now, which can be fitted into the scheme of army boundaries later."

On 30 September, when it became clear that the Munich Settlement would result in a peaceful occupation of the Sudetenland the Defendant Keitel ordered that the Free Corps Henlein, in its present composition, be placed under the command of Himmler.

I read from Item 38, at Page 63, of the Schmundt file:

"1. Attachment of the Henlein Free Corps. The Supreme Commander of the Armed Forces has just ordered that the Henlein Free Corps in its present composition be placed under command of Reichsfuehrer SS and the Chief of German Police. It is therefore not at the immediate disposal of OKH as field unit for the invasion, but is to be later drawn in, like the rest of the police forces, for police duties in agreement with the Reichsfuehrer SS."

I have been able, if the Tribunal please, to ascertain the date the Tribunal asked about before the recess.

The first visit of Chamberlain to Germany in connection with this matter was 15 September 1938. Chamberlain flew to Munich and arrived at 12:30 o'clock on 15 September. He went by train from Munich to Berchtesgaden, arriving at 1600 hours, by car at Berghof, arriving about at 1650, for three talks with Hitler. On 16 September Chamberlain returned by air to London.

The second visit was on 22 September. Chamberlain met with Hitler at Bad Godesberg at 1700 hours for a 3-hour discussion, and it was a deadlock. On 23 September discussions were resumed a 2230 hours. On 24 September Chamberlain returned to London.

The third visit was on 29 September. Chamberlain flew to Munich and the meeting of Chamberlain, Mussolini, Daladier, and Hitler took place at the Brown House at 1330 and continued until 0230 hours on 30 September 1938, a Friday, when the Munich Agreement was signed. Under the threat of war by the Nazi conspirators, and with war in fact about to be launched, the United Kingdom and France concluded the Munich Pact with Germany and Italy at that early morning hour of 30 September 1938. This Treaty will be presented by the British prosecutor. It is sufficient for me to say of it at this point that it was the cession of the Sudetenland by Czechoslovakia to Germany. Czechoslovakia was required to acquiesce.

The Munich Pact will be TC-23 of the British documents.

On 1 October 1938 German troops began the occupation of the Sudetenland. During the conclusion of the Munich Pact the Wehrmacht had been fully deployed for the attack, awaiting only the word of Hitler to begin the assault.

With the cession of the Sudetenland new orders were issued. On 30 September the Defendant Keitel promulgated Directive Number 1 on occupation of territory separated from Czechoslovakia. This is Item 39 at Page 64 of the Schmundt file. This directive contained a timetable for the occupation of sectors of former Czech territory between 1 and 10 October and specified the tasks of the German Armed Forces.

I read now the fourth and fifth paragraphs of that document:

"2. The present degree of mobilized preparedness is to be maintained completely, for the present also in the West.

Order for the rescinding of measures taken, is held over.

"The entry is to be planned in such a way that it can easily be converted into operation Grun."

It contains one other important provision about the Henlein forces, and I quote from the list under the heading "a. Army":

"Henlein Free Corps. All combat action on the part of the Volunteer Corps must cease as from 1st October."

The Schmundt file contains a number of additional secret OKW directives giving instructions for the occupation of the Sudetenland. I think I need not read them, as they are not essential to the proof of our case. They merely indicate the scope of the preparations of the OKW.

Directives specifying the occupational area of the Army, the units under its command, arranging for communication facilities, supply, and propaganda, and giving instructions to the various departments of the Government were issued over Defendant Keitel's signature on 30 September. These are Items 40, 41, and 42 in the Schmundt file. I think it is sufficient to read the caption and the signature.

THE PRESIDENT: What page?

MR. ALDERMAN: Page 66 of the English version. This is the Supreme Commander of the Armed Forces, most secret:

"Special Orders Number 1 to Directive Number 1. Subject: Occupation of Territory Ceded by Czechoslovakia." -Signature- "Keitel."

Item 41 is on Page 70 of the Schmundt file.

"Supreme Command of the Armed Forces; most secret IV a. Most secret; subject: Occupation of Sudeten-German Territory." - signed - "Keitel."

Item 42 in the Schmundt file is on Page 75, again most secret.

"Subject: Occupation of the Sudeten-German Area.", Signed "Keitel."

By 10 October Von Brauchitsch was able to report to Hitler that German troops had reached the demarcation line and that the order for the occupation of the Sudetenland had been fulfilled. The OKW requested Hitler's permission to rescind Case Green, to withdraw troops from the occupied area, and to relieve the OKH of executive powers in the Sudeten-German area as of 15 October. These are Items 46, 47, and 48 in the Schmundt file.

Item 46, which appears at Page 77, is a letter from Berlin, dated October 10, 1938, signed by Von Brauchitsch:

"My Fuehrer:

"I have to report that the troops will reach the demarcation line as ordered, by this evening. Insofar as further military operations are not required, the order for the occupation of the country which was given to me will thus have been fulfilled. The guarding of the new frontier line will be taken over by the reinforced frontier supervision service in the next few days.

"It is thus no longer a military necessity to combine the administration of the Sudetenland with the command of the troops of the Army under the control of one person.

"I therefore ask you, my Fuehrer, to relieve me, with effect from 15 October 1938, of the charge assigned to me: That of exercising executive powers in Sudeten-German Territory.

"Heil, my Fuehrer, Von Brauchitsch."

Item 47 of the Schmundt file, appearing on Page 78, is a secret telegram from the OKW to the Fuehrer's train, Lieutenant Colonel Schmundt:

"If evening report shows that occupation of Zone 5 has been completed without incident, OKW intends to order further demobilization.

"Principle: 1). To suspend operation Grun but maintain a sufficient state of preparedness on part of Army and Luftwaffe to make intervention possible if necessary. 2) All units not needed to be withdrawn from the occupied area and reduced to peacetime status, as population of occupied area is heavily burdened by the massing of troops."

Skipping to below the OKW signature, this appears, at the left:

"Fuehrer's decision:

"1. Agreed.

"2. Suggestion to be made on the 13 October in Essen by General Keitel. Decision will then be reached."

On the same date additional demobilization of the forces in the Sudetenland was ordered by Hitler and Defendant Keitel. Three days later the OKW requested Hitler's consent to the reversion of the RAD (Labor Corps) from the control of the Armed Forces. These are Items 52 and 53 in the Schmundt file.

As the German forces entered the Sudetenland, Henlein's Sudetendeutsche Partei was merged with the NSDAP of Hitler. The two men who had fled to Hitler's protection in mid-September, Henlein and Karl Hermann Frank, were appointed Gauleiter and Deputy Gauleiter, respectively, of the Sudetengau. In the parts of the Czechoslovak Republic that were still free the Sudetendeutsche Partei constituted itself as the National Socialistic German Worker Party in Czechoslovakia, NSDAP in Czechoslovakia, under the direction of Kundt, another of Henlein's deputies.

The Tribunal will find these events set forth in the Czechoslovak official report, Document 998-PS.

The stage was now prepared for the next move of the Nazi conspirators, the plan for the conquest of the remainder of Czechoslovakia. With the occupation of the Sudetenland and the inclusion of German-speaking Czechs within the Greater Reich, it might have been expected that the Nazi conspirators would be satisfied. Thus far in their program of aggression the defendants had used as a pretext for their conquests the union of the Volksdeutsche, the people of German descent, with the Reich. Now, after Munich, the Volksdeutsche in Czechoslovakia have been substantially all returned to German rule.

On 26 September, at the Sportpalast in Berlin, Hitler spoke to the world. I now refer and invite the notice of the Tribunal to the Volkischer Beobachter, Munich edition, special edition for 27 September 1938, in which this speech is quoted. I read from Page 2, Column 1, quoting from Hitler:

"And now we are confronted with the last problem which must be solved and will be solved. It is the last territorial claim"...

THE PRESIDENT: Is this document in our documents?

MR. ALDERMAN: No. I am asking the Court to take judicial notice of that.

THE PRESIDENT: Very well.

MR. ALDERMAN: It is a well-known German publication.

"It is the last territorial claim which I have to make in Europe, but it is a claim from which I will not swerve and which I will satisfy, God willing." (Document Number 2358-PS.) And further:

"I have little to explain. I am grateful to Mr. Chamberlain for all his efforts, and I have assured him that the German people want nothing but peace; but I have also told him that I cannot go back beyond the limits of our patience."

This is Page 2, Column 1.

"I assured him, moreover, and I repeat it here, that when this problem is solved there will be no more territorial problems for Germany in Europe. And I further assured him that from the moment, when Czechoslovakia solves its other problems that is to say, when the Czechs have come to an arrangement with their other minorities peacefully and without oppression, I will no longer be interested in the Czech State. And that, as far as I am concerned, I will guarantee it. We don't want any Czechs!"

47

The major portion of the passage I have quoted will be contained in Document TC-28, which I think, will be offered by the British prosecutor.

Yet two weeks later Hitler and Defendant Keitel were preparing estimates of the military forces required to break Czechoslovak resistance in Bohemia and Moravia.

I now read from Item 48, at Page 82, of the Schmundt file. This is a top-secret telegram sent by Keitel to Hitler's headquarters on 11 October 1938 in answer to four questions which Hitler had propounded to the OKW. I think it is sufficient merely to read the questions which Hitler had propounded:

"Question 1. What reinforcements are necessary in the situation to break all Czech resistance in Bohemia and Moravia?

"Question 2. How much time is requested for the regrouping or moving up of new forces?

"Question 3. How much time will be required for the same purpose if it is executed after the intended demobilization and return measures?

"Question 4. How much time would be required to achieve the state of readiness of 1 October?"

On 21 October, the same day on which the administration of the Sudetenland was handed over to the civilian authorities, a directive outlining plans for the conquest of the remainder of Czechoslovakia was signed by Hitler and initialed by the Defendant Keitel.

I now offer in evidence Document C-136 as Exhibit USA-104, a top-secret order of which 10 copies were made, this being the first copy, signed in ink by Keitel.

In this order, issued only 3 weeks after the winning of the Sudetenland, the Nazi conspirators are already looking forward to new conquests. I quote the first part of the body of the document: "The future tasks for the Armed Forces and the preparations for the conduct of war resulting from these tasks will be laid down by me in a later directive. Until this directive comes into force the Armed Forces must be prepared at all times or the following eventualities:

"1) The securing of the frontiers of Germany and the protection against surprise air attacks.

"2) The liquidation of the remainder of Czechoslovakia.

"3) The occupation of the Memel."

And then proceeding, the statement following Number 2:

"Liquidation of the remainder of Czechoslovakia: It must be possible to smash at any time the remainder of Czechoslovakia if her policy should become hostile towards Germany.

"The preparations to be made by the Armed Forces for this contingency will be considerably smaller in extent than those for Grun; they must, however, guarantee a continuous and considerably higher state of preparedness, since planned mobilization measures have been dispensed with. The organization, order of battle, and state of readiness of the units earmarked for that purpose are in peacetime to be so arranged for a surprise assault that Czechoslovakia herself will be deprived of all possibility of organized resistance. The object is the swift occupation of Bohemia and Moravia and the cutting off of Slovakia. The preparations should be such that at the same time

'Grenzsicherung West' "-the measures of frontier defense in the West-"can be carried out.

"The detailed mission of Army and Air Force is as follows: "a. Army: The units stationed in the vicinity of Bohemia-Moravia and several motorized divisions are to be earmarked for a surprise type of attack. Their number will be determined by the forces remaining in Czechoslovakia; a quick and decisive success must be assured. The assembly and preparations for the attack must be worked out. Forces not needed will be kept in readiness in such a manner that they may be either committed in securing the frontiers or sent after the attack army.

"b. Air Force: The quick advance of the German Army is to be assured by early elimination of the Czech Air Force. For this purpose the commitment in a surprise attack from peacetime bases has to be prepared. Whether for this purpose still stronger forces may be required can be determined from the development of the military-political situation in Czechoslovakia only. At the same time a simultaneous assembly of the remainder of the offensive forces against the West must be prepared."

And then Part 3 goes on under the heading, "Annexation of the Memel District."

It is signed by Adolf Hitler and authenticated by Defendant Keitel. It was distributed to the OKH, to Defendant Goering's Luftwaffe, and to Defendant Raeder at Navy headquarters.

Two months later, on 17 December 1938, Defendant Keitel issued an appendix to the original order, stating that by command of the Fuehrer preparations for the liquidation of Czechoslovakia are to continue.

I offer in evidence Document C-138 as Exhibit USA-105, and other captured OKW documents classified top secret.

Distribution of this order was the same as for the 21 October order. I shall read the body of this order.

"Corollary to Directive of 21. 10. 38.

"Reference: 'Liquidation of the Rest of Czechoslovakia.' The Fuehrer has given the following additional order:

"The preparations for this eventuality are to continue on the assumption that no resistance worth mentioning is to be expected.

"To the outside world too it must clearly appear that it is merely an action of pacification, and not a warlike undertaking.

"The action must therefore be carried out by the peacetime Armed Forces only, without reinforcements from mobilization. The necessary readiness for action, especially the ensuring that the most necessary supplies are brought up, must be effected by adjustment within the units.

"Similarly the units of the Army detailed for the march in must, as a general rule, leave their stations only during the night prior to the crossing of the frontier, and will not previously form up systematically on the frontier. The transport necessary for previous organization should be limited to the minimum and will be camouflaged as much as possible. Necessary movements, if any, of single units and particularly of motorized forces, to the troop training areas situated near the frontier, must have the approval of the Fuehrer.

49

"The Air Force should take action in accordance with the similar general directives.

"For the same reasons the exercise of executive power by the Supreme Command of the Army is laid down only for the newly occupied territory and only for a short period."

- signed - "Keitel."

I invite the attention of the Tribunal to the fact that this particular copy of this order, an original carbon signed in ink by Keitel, was the one sent to the OKM, the German Naval headquarters. It bears the initials of Fricke, head of the Operation Division of the naval war staff; Schniewind, Chief of Staff; and of Defendant Raeder.

As the Wehrmacht moved forward, with plans for what it clearly considered would be an easy victory, the Foreign Office played its part. In a discussion of means of improving German-Czech relations with the Czech Foreign Minister Chvalkovsky in Berlin on 31 January 1939, Defendant Ribbentrop urged upon the Czech Government a quick reduction in the size of the Czech Army. I offer in evidence Document 2795-PS as Exhibit USA-106, captured German Foreign Office notes of this discussion. I will read only the footnote, which is in Ribbentrop's handwriting:

"I mentioned to Chvalkovsky especially that a quick reduction in the Czech Army would be decisive in our judgment."

Does the Court propose sitting beyond 4:30?

THE PRESIDENT: No, I think not. The Tribunal will adjourn.

[The Tribunal adjourned until 4 December 1945 at 1000 hours.]

Twelfth Day:
Tuesday, 4 December 1945

THE PRESIDENT: I will call on the Chief Prosecutor for Great Britain and Northern Ireland.

SIR HARTLEY SHAWCROSS (Chief Prosecutor for the United Kingdom): May it please the Tribunal, on an occasion to which reference has and will be made, Hitler, the leader of the Nazi conspirators who are now on trial before you, is reported as having said, in reference to their warlike plans:

"I shall give a propagandist cause for starting the war, never mind whether it be true or not. The victor shall not be asked later on whether he told the truth or not. In starting and making a war, not the right is what matters, but victory -the strongest has the right."

The British Empire with its Allies has twice, within the space of 25 years, been victorious in wars which have been forced upon it, but it is precisely because we realize that victory is not enough, that might is not necessarily right, that lasting peace and the rule of international law is not to be secured by the strong arm alone, that the British nation is taking part in this Trial. There are those who would perhaps say that these wretched men should have been dealt with summarily without trial by "executive action"; that their power for evil broken, they should have been swept aside into oblivion without this elaborate and careful investigation into the part which they played in bringing this war about: Vae Victis! Let them pay the penalty of defeat. But that was not the view of the British Government. Not so would the rule of law be raised and strengthened on the international as well as upon the municipal plane; not so would future generations realize that right is not always on the side of the big battalions; not so would the world be made aware that the waging of aggressive war is not only a dangerous venture but a criminal one.

Human memory is very short. Apologists for defeated nations are sometimes able to play upon the sympathy and magnanimity of their victors, so that the true facts, never authoritatively recorded, become obscured and forgotten. One has only to recall the circumstances following upon the last World War to see the dangers to which, in the absence of any authoritative judicial pronouncement, a tolerant or a credulous people is exposed. With the passage of time the former tend to discount, perhaps because of their very horror, the stories of aggression and atrocity that may be handed down; and the latter, the credulous, misled by perhaps fanatical and perhaps dishonest propagandists, come to believe that it was not they but their opponents who were guilty of that which they would themselves condemn. And so we believe that this Tribunal, acting, as we know it will act notwithstanding its appointment by the victorious powers, with complete and judicial objectivity, will provide a contemporary touchstone and an authoritative and impartial record to which future historians may turn for truth, and future politicians for warning. From this record shall future generations know not only what our generation suffered, but also that our suffering was the result of crimes, crimes against the laws of peoples which the peoples of the world upheld and will continue in the future to uphold-to uphold by international co-operation, not based merely on military alliances, but grounded, and firmly grounded, in the rule of law.

Nor, though this procedure and this Indictment of individuals may be novel, is there anything new in the principles which by this prosecution we seek to enforce. Ineffective though, alas, the sanctions proved and showed to be, the nations of the world had, as it will be my purpose in addressing the Tribunal to show, sought to make aggressive war an international crime, and although previous tradition has sought to punish states rather than individuals, it is both logical and right that, if the act of waging war is itself an offense against international law, those individuals who shared personal responsibility for bringing such wars about should answer personally for the course into which they led their states. Again, individual war crimes have long been recognized by international law as triable by the courts of those states whose nationals have been outraged, at least so long as a state of war persists. It would be illogical in the extreme if those who, although they may not with their own hands have committed individual crimes, were responsible for systematic breaches of the laws of war affecting the nationals of many states should escape for that reason. So also in regard to Crimes against Humanity. The rights of humanitarian intervention on behalf of the rights of man, trampled upon by a state in a manner shocking the sense of mankind, has long been considered to form part of the recognized law of nations. Here too, the Charter merely develops a pre-existing principle. If murder, rapine, and robbery are indictable under the ordinary municipal laws of our countries, shall those who differ from the common criminal only by the extent and systematic nature of their offenses escape accusation?

It is, as I shall show, the view of the British Government that in these matters, this Tribunal will be applying to individuals, not the law of the victor, but the accepted principles of international usage in a way which will, if anything can, promote and fortify the rule of international law and safeguard the future peace and security of this war-stricken world.

By agreement between the chief prosecutors, it is my task, on behalf of the British Government and of the other states associated in this Prosecution, to present the case on Count Two of the Indictment and to show how these defendants, in conspiracy with each other, and with persons not now before this Tribunal, planned and waged a war of aggression in breach of the treaty obligations by which, under international law, Germany, as other states, has thought to make such wars impossible.

The task falls into two parts. The first is to demonstrate the nature and the basis of the Crime against Peace, which is constituted under the Charter of this Tribunal, by waging wars of aggression and in violation of treaties; and the second is to establish beyond all possibility of doubt that such wars were waged by these defendants.

As to the first, it would no doubt be sufficient just to say this. It is not incumbent upon the Prosecution to prove that wars of aggression and wars in violation of international treaties are, or ought to be, international crimes. The Charter of this Tribunal has prescribed that they are crimes and that the Charter is the statute and the law of this Court. Yet, though that is the clear and mandatory law governing the jurisdiction of this Tribunal, we feel that we should not be discharging our task in the abiding interest of international justice and morality unless we showed to the Tribunal, and indeed to the world, the position of this provision of the Charter against the general perspective of international law. For, just as in the experience of our country, some old English statutes were merely declaratory of the common law, so today this Charter merely declares and creates a jurisdiction in respect of what was already the law of nations.

Nor is it unimportant to emphasize that aspect of the matter, lest there may be some, now or hereafter, who might allow their judgment to be warped by plausible catchwords or by an uninformed and distorted sense of justice towards these defendants. It is not difficult to be misled by such criticisms as that resort to war in the past has not been a crime; that the power to resort to war is one of the prerogatives of the sovereign state; even that this Charter, in constituting wars of aggression a crime, has imitated one of the most obnoxious doctrines of National Socialist jurisprudence, namely post factum legislation-that the Charter is in this respect reminiscent of bills of attainder - and that these proceedings are no more than a measure of vengeance, subtly concealed in the garb of judicial proceedings which the victor wreaks upon the vanquished. These things may sound plausible -yet they are not true. It is, indeed, not necessary to doubt that some aspects of the Charter bear upon them the imprint of significant and salutary novelty. But it is our submission and our conviction, which we affirm before this Tribunal and the world, that fundamentally the provision of the Charter which constitutes wars, such wars as these defendants joined in waging and in planning a crime, is not in any way an innovation. This provision of the Charter does no more than constitute a competent jurisdiction for the punishment of what not only the enlightened conscience of mankind but the law of nations itself had constituted an international crime before this Tribunal was established and this Charter became part of the public law of the world.

So first let this be said:

Whilst it may be quite true that there is no body of international rules amounting to law in the Austinian sense of a rule imposed by a sovereign upon a subject obliged to obey it under some definite sanction, yet for 50 years or more the people of the world, striving perhaps after that ideal of which the poet speaks:

"When the war drums throb no longer
And the battle flags are furled,
In the parliament of man,

The federation of the world sought to create an operative system of rules based upon the consent of nations to stabilize international relations, to avoid war taking place at all and to mitigate the results of such wars as took place. The first treaty was of course the Hague Convention of 1899 for the Pacific Settlement of International Disputes. That Convention was, indeed, of no more than precatory effect, and we attach no weight to it for the purposes of this case, but it did establish agreement that, in the event of serious disputes arising between the signatory powers, they would as far as possible submit to mediation That Convention was followed in 1907 by another convention reaffirming and slightly strengthening what had previously been agreed. These early conventions fell, indeed, very far short of outlawing war, or of creating any binding obligation to arbitrate. I shall certainly not ask the Tribunal to say any crime was committed by disregarding those conventions.

But at least they established that the contracting powers accepted the general principle that, if at all possible, war should be resorted to only if mediation failed.

Although these conventions are mentioned in this Indictment, I am not relying on them save to show the historical development of the law, and it is unnecessary, therefore, to argue about their precise effect, for the place which they once occupied has been taken by far more effective instruments. I mention them now merely for this, that they were the first steps towards that body of rules of law which we are seeking here to enforce.

There were, of course, other individual agreements between particular states, agreements which sought to preserve the neutrality of individual countries, as, for instance, that of Belgium, but those agreements were inadequate, in the absence of any real will to comply with them, to prevent the first World War in 1914.

Shocked by the occurrence of that catastrophe, the Nations of Europe, not excluding Germany, and of other parts of the world, came to the conclusion that, in the interests of all alike, a permanent organisation of the Nations should be established to maintain the peace. And so the Treaty of Versailles was prefaced by the Covenant of the League of Nations.

Now, I say nothing at this moment of the general merits of the various provisions of the Treaty of Versailles. They have been criticised, some of them perhaps justly criticised, and they were certainly made the subject of much bellicose propaganda in Germany. But it is unnecessary to inquire into the merits of the matter, for, however unjust one might for this purpose assume the provisions of the Treaty of Versailles to have been, they contained no kind of excuse for the waging of war to secure an alteration in their terms. Not only was that Treaty a settlement, by agreement, of all the difficult territorial questions which had been left outstanding by the war itself, but it established the League of Nations which, if it had been loyally supported, could so well have resolved those international differences which might otherwise have led, as indeed they eventually did lead, to war. It set up in the Council of the League, in the Assembly and in the Permanent Court of International Justice, a machine not only for the peaceful settlement of international disputes, but also for the frank ventilation of all international questions by open and free discussion. At that time, in those years after the last war, the hopes of the world stood high. Millions of men in all countries - perhaps even in Germany herself - had laid down their lives in what they hoped and believed was a war to end war. Germany herself entered the League of Nations and was given a permanent seat on the Council, and on that Council, as in the Assembly of the League, German Governments which preceded that of the defendant von Papen in 1932 played their full part. In the years from 1919 to that time in 1932, despite some comparatively minor incidents in the heated atmosphere which followed the end of the war, the peaceful operation of the League continued. Nor was it only the operation of the League which gave ground, and good ground, for hope that at long last the rule of law would replace that of anarchy in the international field.

The statesmen of the world deliberately set out to make wars of aggression an international crime. These are no new terms invented by the victors to embody in this Charter. They have figured, and they have figured prominently, in numerous treaties, in governmental pronouncements, and in the declarations of statesmen in the period preceding the second World War. In treaties concluded between the Union of Soviet Socialist Republics and other states, such as Persia in 1927, France in 1935, China in 1937, the contracting parties undertook to refrain from any act of aggression whatever against the other party. In 1933 the Soviet Union became a party to a large number of treaties containing a detailed definition of aggression, and the same definition appeared in the same year in the authoritative report of the Committee on Questions of Security set up in connection with the Conference for the Reduction and Limitation of Armaments. But at this time states were going beyond commitments to refrain from wars of aggression and to assist states which were victims of aggression. They were condemning aggression in unmistakable terms. Thus in the Anti-War Treaty of Non-Aggression and Conciliation, which was signed on the 10th of October 1933, by a number of American states, subsequently joined by practically all the states of the American continents and a number of European countries as well, the contracting parties solemnly declared that "they condemn wars of aggression in their mutual relations or in those of other states." And that treaty was fully incorporated into the Buenos Aires convention of December 1936, signed and ratified by a large number of American countries, including, of course, the United States. And previously, in 1928, the 6th Pan-American Conference had adopted a resolution declaring that, as "war of aggression constitutes a crime against the human species . . . all aggression is illicit and as such is declared prohibited." A year earlier, as long ago as September 1927, the Assembly of the League of Nations adopted a resolution affirming the conviction that "a war of aggression can never serve as a means of settling international disputes and is, in consequence, an international crime" and going on to declare that "all wars of aggression are, and shall always be prohibited."

The first article of the draft Treaty for Mutual Assistance of 1923 read in these terms:

"The High Contracting Parties, affirming that aggressive war is an international crime, undertake the solemn engagement not to make themselves guilty of this crime against any other nation."

In the Preamble to the Geneva Protocol of 1924, it was stated that "offensive warfare constitutes an infraction of solidarity and an international crime." These instruments that I have just last mentioned remained, it is true, unratified for various reasons, but they are not without significance or value.

These repeated declarations, these repeated condemnations of wars of aggression, testified to the fact that with the establishment of the League of Nations, with the legal developments which followed it, the place of war in International Law had undergone a profound change. War was ceasing to be the unrestricted prerogative of sovereign States. The Covenant of the League of Nations did not totally abolish the right of war. It left, perhaps, certain gaps which were probably larger in theory than in practice. But in effect it surrounded the right of war by procedural and substantive checks and delays, which, if the Covenant had been faithfully observed, would have amounted to an elimination of war, not only between Members of the League, but also, by reason of certain provisions of the Covenant, in the relations of non-Members as well. And thus, the Covenant of the League restored the position as it existed at the dawn of International Law, at the time when Grotius was laying the foundations of the modern Law of Nations, and established the distinction, a distinction accompanied by profound legal consequences in the sphere, for instance, of neutrality, between a just war and an unjust war.Nor was that development arrested with the adoption of the Covenant of the League. The right of war was further circumscribed by a series of treaties, numbering-it is an astonishing figure but it is right-nearly a thousand, of arbitration and conciliation embracing practically all the nations of the world. The so-called Optional Clause of Article 36 of the Statute of the Permanent Court of International Justice, the clause which conferred upon the Court compulsory jurisdiction in regard to the most comprehensive categories of disputes, and which constituted in effect by far the most important compulsory treaty of arbitration in the postwar period, was widely signed and ratified. Germany herself signed it in 1927 and her signature was renewed, and renewed for a period of 5 years by the Nazi government in July of 1933. (Significantly, that ratification was not again renewed on the expiration of its 5 years' validity in March of 1938 by Germany). Since 1928 a considerable number of states signed and ratified the General Act for the Pacific Settlement of International Disputes which was designed to fill the gaps left by the Optional Clause and by the existing treaties of arbitration and conciliation.

And all this vast network of instruments of pacific settlement testified to the growing conviction throughout the civilized world that war was ceasing to be the normal or the legitimate means of settling international disputes. The express condemnation of wars of aggression, which I have already mentioned, supplies the same testimony. But there was, of course, more direct evidence pointing in the same direction. The Treaty of Locarno of the 16th October 1925, to which I shall have occasion to refer presently, and to which Germany was a party, was more than a treaty of arbitration and conciliation in which the parties undertook definite obligations with regard to the pacific settlement of disputes which might arise between them. It was, subject to clearly specified exceptions of self-defense in certain contingencies, a more general undertaking in which the parties to it agreed that "they would in no case attack or invade each other or resort to war against each other." And that constituted a general renunciation of war, and it was so considered to be in the eyes of international jurists and in the public opinion of the world. The Locarno Treaty was not just another of the great number of arbitration treaties which were being concluded at this time. it was regarded as a kind of cornerstone in the European settlement and in the new legal order in Europe in partial, just, and indeed, generous substitution for the rigors of the Treaty of Versailles. And with that treaty, the term "outlawry of war" left the province of mere pacifist propaganda. It became current in the writings on international law and in the official pronouncements of governments. No one could any longer say, after the Locarno Treaty -no one could any longer associate himself with the plausible assertion that at all events, as between the parties to that treaty, war remained an unrestricted right of sovereign states.

But, although the effect of the Locarno Treaty was limited to the parties to it, it had wider influence in paving the way towards that most fundamental, that truly revolutionary enactment in modern international law, namely, the General Treaty for the Renunciation of War of 27 August 1928, the Pact of Paris, the Kellogg-Briand Pact. That treaty, a most deliberate and carefully prepared piece of international legislation, was binding in 1939 on more than 60 nations, including Germany. It was, and it has remained, the most widely signed and ratified international instrument. It contained no provision for its termination, and it was conceived, as I said, as the cornerstone of any future international order worthy of the name. It is fully part of international law as it stands today, and it has in no way been modified or replaced by the Charter of the United Nations. It is right, in this solemn hour in the history of the world, when the responsible leaders of a state stand accused of a premeditated breach of this great treaty which was, which remains, a source of hope and of faith for mankind, to set out in detail its two operative articles and its Preamble. Let me read them to the Tribunal-first the Preamble, and it starts like this:

"The President of the German Reich" - and the other states associated . . .

THE PRESIDENT: Shall we find it among the documents?

SIR HARTLEY SHAWCROSS: It will be put in. I don't think you have it at the moment.

"The President of the German Reich . . . deeply sensitive of their solemn duty to promote the welfare of mankind; persuaded that the time has come when a frank renunciation of war as an instrument of international policy should be made to the end that the peaceful and friendly relations now existing between their peoples may be perpetuated; convinced that all changes in their relations with one another should be sought only by pacific means and be the result of a peaceful and orderly progress, and that any signatory power which shall hereafter seek to promote its national interests by resort to war, should be denied the benefits furnished by this Treaty; hopeful that, encouraged by their example, all the other nations of the world will join in this humane endeavor and by adhering to the present treaty as soon as it comes into force bring their peoples within the scope of its beneficent provisions, thus uniting civilized nations of the world in a common renunciation of war as an instrument of their national policy ...."

Then, Article I:

"The High Contracting Parties solemnly declare in the names of their respective peoples that they condemn recourse to war for the solution of international controversies and renounce it as an instrument of national policy in their relations with one another."

And Article II:

"The High Contracting Parties agree that the settlement or solution of all disputes or conflicts of whatever nature or of whatever origin they may be, which may arise among them, shall never be sought except by pacific means."

In that Treaty, that General Treaty for the Renunciation of War, practically the whole civilised world abolished war as a legally permissible means of enforcing the law or of changing it. The right of war was no longer of the essence of sovereignty. Whatever the position may have been at the time of the Hague Convention, whatever the position may have been in 1914, whatever it may have been in 1918 - and it is not necessary to discuss it - no International lawyer of repute, no responsible statesman, no soldier concerned with the legal use of Armed Forces, no economist or industrialist concerned in his country's war economy, could doubt that, with the Pact of Paris on the Statute Book, a war of aggression was contrary to International Law. Nor have the repeated violations of the Pact by the Axis Powers in any way affected its validity. Let this be firmly and clearly stated. Those very breaches, except perhaps to the cynic and the malevolent, have added to the strength of the Treaty; they provoked the sustained wrath of peoples angered by the contemptuous disregard of this great Statute and determined to vindicate its provisions. The

Pact of Paris is the Law of Nations. This Tribunal will declare it. The world must enforce it.

Let this also be said, that the Pact of Paris was not a clumsy instrument likely to become a kind of signpost for the guilty. It did not enable Germany to go to war against Poland and yet rely, as against Great Britain and France, on any immunity from warlike action because of the very provisions of the Pact. For the Pact laid down expressly in its Preamble that no State guilty of a violation of its provisions might invoke its benefits. And when, on the outbreak of the Second World War, Great Britain and France communicated to the League of Nations that a state of war existed between them and Germany as from the 3rd September, 1939, they declared that by committing an act of aggression against Poland, Germany had violated her obligations assumed not only towards Poland but also towards the other signatories of the Pact. A violation of the Pact in relation to one signatory was an attack upon all the other signatories and they were entitled to treat it as such. I emphasise that point lest any of these defendants should seize upon the letter of the Particulars of Count Two of the Indictment and seek to suggest that it was not Germany who initiated war with the United Kingdom and France on 3rd September, 1939. The declaration of war came from the United Kingdom and from France; the act of war and its commencement came from Germany in violation of the fundamental enactment to which she was a party.

The General Treaty for the Renunciation of War, this great constitutional instrument of an international society awakened to the deadly dangers of another Armageddon, did not remain an isolated effort soon to be forgotten in the turmoil of recurrent international crises. It became, in conjunction with the Covenant of the League of Nations or independently of it, the starting point for a new orientation of governments in matters of peace, war, and neutrality. It is of importance, and I wish to quote just one or two of the statements which were being made by Governments at that time in relation to the effect of the Pact. In 1929, His Majesty's Government in the United Kingdom said, in connection with the question of conferring upon the Permanent Court of International justice, jurisdiction with regard to the exercise of belligerent rights in relation to neutral States - and it illustrates the profound change which was being accepted as having taken place, as a result of the Pact of Paris, in International Law:

> "But the whole situation .... rests, and international law on the subject has been entirely built up, on the assumption that there is nothing illegitimate in the use of war as an instrument of national policy, and, as a necessary corollary, that the position and rights of neutrals are entirely independent of the circumstances of any war which may be in progress. Before the acceptance of the Covenant, the basis of the law of neutrality was that the rights and obligations of neutrals were identical as regards both belligerents, and were entirely independent of the rights and wrongs of the dispute which had led to the war, or the respective position of the belligerents at the bar of world opinion."

Then the Government went on:

> "Now it is precisely this assumption which is no longer valid as regards states which are members of the League of Nations and parties to the Peace Pact. The effect of those instruments, taken together, is to deprive nations of the right to employ war as an instrument of

national policy, and to forbid the states which have signed them to give aid or comfort to an offender."

This was being said in 1929, when there was no war upon the horizon.

"As between such States, there has been in consequence a fundamental change in the whole question of belligerent and neutral rights. The whole policy of His Majesty's present Government (and, it would appear, of any alternative government) is based upon a determination to comply with their obligations under the Covenant of the League and the Peace Pact. This being so, the situation which we have to envisage in the event of a war in which we were engaged is not one in which the rights and duties of belligerents and neutrals will depend upon the old rules of war and neutrality, but one in which the position of the Members of the League will be determined by the Covenant and by the Pact."

The Chief Prosecutor for the United States of America referred in his opening speech before this Tribunal to the weighty pronouncement of Mr. Stimson, the Secretary of War, in which, in 1932, he gave expression to the drastic change brought about in international law by the Pact of Paris, and it is perhaps convenient to quote the relevant passage in full:

"War between nations was renounced by the signatories of the Kellogg-Briand Pact. This means that it has become illegal throughout practically the entire world. It is no longer to be the source and subject of rights. It is no longer to be the principle around which the duties, the conduct, and the rights of nations revolve. It is an illegal thing. Hereafter, when two nations engage in armed conflict, either one or both of them must be wrongdoers-violators of this general treaty law. We no longer draw a circle about them and treat them with the punctilios of the duelist's code. Instead we denounce them as law-breakers."

And nearly 10 years later, when numerous independent states lay prostrate, shattered or menaced in their very existence before the impact of the war machine of the Nazi State, the Attorney General of the United States, subsequently a distinguished member of the highest Tribunal of that great country, gave significant expression to the change which had been effected in the law as the result of the Pact of Paris in a speech for which the freedom-loving peoples of the world will always be grateful. On the 27th of March 1941 - and I mention it now not as merely being the speech of a statesman, although it was certainly that, but as being the considered opinion of a distinguished lawyer, - he said this:

"The Kellogg-Briand Pact of 1928, in which Germany, Italy and Japan covenanted with us, as well as with other nations, to renounce war as an instrument of policy, made definite the outlawry of war and of necessity altered the dependent concept of neutral obligations.

"The Treaty for the Renunciation of War and the Argentine Anti-War Treaty deprived their signatories of the right of war as an instrument of national policy or aggression and rendered unlawful wars undertaken in violation of these provisions. In consequence these treaties destroyed the historical and juridical foundations of the doctrine of neutrality conceived as an attitude of absolute impartiality in relation to aggressive wars ....

"It follows that the state which has gone to war in violation of its obligations acquires no right to equality of treatment from other states, unless treaty obligations require different handling of affairs. It derives no rights from its illegality. "In flagrant cases of aggression where the facts speak so unambiguously that world opinion takes what may be the equivalent of judicial notice, we may not stymie international law and allow these great treaties to become dead letters. The intelligent public opinion of the world which is not afraid to be vocal, and the action of the American States, has made a determination that the Axis Powers are the aggressors in the wars today, which is an appropriate basis in the present state of international organizations for our policy."

Thus, there is no doubt that by the time the National Socialist State of Germany had embarked upon the preparation of the war of aggression against the civilized world and by the time it had accomplished that design, aggressive war had become, in virtue of the Pact of Paris and the other treaties and declarations to which I have referred, illegal and a crime beyond all uncertainty and doubt. And it is on that proposition' and fundamentally on that universal treaty, the Kellogg-Briand Pact, that Count Two of this Indictment is principally based.

The Prosecution has deemed it necessary-indeed, imperative-to establish beyond all possibility of question, at what I am afraid may appear to be excessive length, that only superficial learning or culpable sentimentality can assert that there is any significant element of retroactivity in the determination of the authors of this Charter to treat aggressive war as conduct which international law has prohibited and stigmatized as criminal. We have traced the progressive limitation of the rights of war, the renunciation and condemnation of wars of aggression, and above all, the total prohibition and condemnation of all wars conceived as an instrument of national policy. What statesman or politician in charge of the affairs of nations could doubt, from 1928 onwards, that aggressive war, or that all war, except in self-defense or for the collective enforcement of the law, or against a state which had itself violated the Pact of Paris, was unlawful and outlawed? What statesman or politician embarking upon such a war could reasonably and justifiably count upon an immunity other than that of a successful outcome of the criminal venture? What more decisive evidence of a prohibition laid down by positive international law could any lawyer desire than that which has been adduced before this Tribunal?

There are, it is true, some small town lawyers who deny the very existence of any international law; and indeed, as I have said, the rules of the law of nations may not satisfy the Austinian test of being imposed by a sovereign. But the legal regulation of international relations rests upon quite different juridical foundations. It depends upon consent, but upon a consent which, once given, cannot be withdrawn by unilateral action. In the international field the source of law is not the command of a sovereign but the treaty agreement binding upon every state which has adhered to it. And it is indeed true, and the recognition of its truth today by all the great powers of the world is vital to our future peace-it is indeed true that, as M. Litvinov once said, and as Great Britain fully accepts:

"Absolute sovereignty and entire liberty of action only belong to such states as have not undertaken international obligations. Immediately a state accepts international obligations it limits its sovereignty."

In that way and that way alone lies the future peace of the world. Yet it may be argued that although war itself was outlawed and forbidden, it was not criminally outlawed and criminally forbidden. International law, it may be said, does not attribute criminality to states and still less to individuals. But can it really be said on behalf of these defendants that the offense of these aggressive wars, which plunged millions of people to their death, which by dint of War Crimes and Crimes against Humanity brought about the torture and extermination of countless thousands of innocent civilians, which devastated cities, which destroyed the amenities-nay, the most rudimentary necessities of civilization in many countries -which has brought the world to the brink of ruin from which it will take generations to recover-will it seriously be said by these defendants that such a war is only an offense, only an illegality, only a matter of condemnation perhaps sounding in damages, but not a crime justiciable by any Tribunal? No law worthy of the name can allow itself to be reduced to an absurdity in that way, and certainly the great powers responsible for this Charter were not prepared to admit it. They draw the inescapable conclusion from the renunciation, the prohibition, the condemnation of war which had become part of the law of nations, and they refuse to reduce justice to impotence by subscribing to the outworn doctrines that a sovereign state can commit no crime and that no crime can be committed on behalf of the sovereign state by individuals acting in its behalf. They refuse to stultify themselves, and their refusal and their decision has decisively shaped the law for this Tribunal.

If this be an innovation, it is an innovation long overdue-a desirable and beneficent innovation fully consistent with justice, fully consistent with common sense and with the abiding purposes of the law of nations. But is it indeed an innovation? Or is it no more than the logical development of the law? There was indeed a time when international lawyers used to maintain that the liability of the state, because of its sovereignty, was limited to a contractual responsibility. International tribunals have not accepted that view. They have repeatedly affirmed that a state can commit a tort; that it may be guilty of trespass, of nuisance, and of negligence. And they have gone further. They have held that a state may be bound to pay what are in effect penal damages. In a recent case decided in 1935 between the United States and Canada, an arbitral tribunal, with the concurrence of its American member, decided that the United States were bound to pay what amounted to penal damages for an affront to Canadian sovereignty. And on a wider plane, the Covenant of the League of Nations, in providing for sanctions, recognized the principle of enforcement of the law against collective units, such enforcement to be, if necessary, of a penal character. And so there is not anything startlingly new in the adoption of the principle that the state as such is responsible for its criminal acts. In fact, save for reliance on the unconvincing argument of sovereignty, there is in law no reason why a state should not be answerable for crimes committed on its behalf. A hundred years ago Dr. Lushington, a great English Admiralty judge, refused to admit that a state could not be a pirate. History-very recent history-does not warrant the view that a state cannot be a criminal. On the other hand, the immeasurable potentialities for evil, inherent in the state in this age of science and organization would seem to demand, quite imperatively, means of repression of criminal conduct even more drastic and more effective than in the case of individuals. And insofar, therefore, as this Charter has put on record the principle of the criminal responsibility of the state, it must be applauded as a wise and far-seeing measure of international legislation.

[A recess was taken.]

SIR HARTLEY SHAWCROSS: *[Continuing.]* I was saying before the recess that there could be no doubt about the principle of criminal responsibility on the part of the state which engaged in aggressive war.

Admittedly, the conscience shrinks from the rigors of collective punishment, which may fall upon the guilty and the innocent alike, although, it may be noted, most of these innocent victims would not have hesitated to reap the fruits of the criminal act if it had been successful. Humanity and justice will find means of mitigating any injustice in collective punishment. Above all, much hardship can be obviated by making the punishment fall upon the individuals who were themselves directly responsible for the criminal conduct of their state. It is here that the powers who framed this Charter took a step which justice, sound legal sense, and an enlightened appreciation of the good of mankind must acclaim without cavil or reserve. The Charter lays down expressly that there shall be individual responsibility for the crimes, including the crimes against the peace, committed on behalf of the state. The state is not an abstract entity. Its rights and duties are the rights and duties of men. Its actions are the actions of men. It is a salutary principle, a principle of law, that politicians who embark upon a particular policy-as here-of aggressive war should not be able to seek immunity behind the intangible personality of the state. It is a salutary legal rule that persons who, in violation of the law, plunge their own and other countries into an aggressive war should do so with a halter around their necks.

To say that those who aid and abet, who counsel and procure a crime are themselves criminals, is a commonplace in our own municipal law. Nor is the principle of individual international responsibility for offenses against the law of nations altogether new. It has been applied not only to pirates. The entire law relating to war crimes, as distinct from the crime of war, is based upon the principle of individual responsibility. The future of international law, and indeed, of the world itself, depends on its application in a much wider sphere, in particular, in that of safeguarding the peace of the world. There must be acknowledged not only, as in the Charter of the United Nations, fundamental human rights, but also, as in the Charter of this Tribunal, fundamental human duties, and of these none is more vital, none is more fundamental, than the duty not to vex the peace of nations in violation of the clearest legal prohibitions and undertakings. If this be an innovation, it is an innovation which we are prepared to defend and to justify, but it is not an innovation which creates a new crime. International law had already, before the Charter was adopted, constituted aggressive war a criminal act.

There is thus no substantial retroactivity in the provisions of the Charter. It merely fixes the responsibility for a crime already clearly established as such by positive law upon its actual perpetrators. It fills a gap in international criminal procedure. There is all the difference between saying to a man, "You will now be punished for what was not a crime at all at the time you committed it," and in saying to him, "You will now pay the penalty for conduct which was contrary to law and a crime when you executed it, although, owing to the imperfection of the international machinery, there was at that time no court competent to pronounce judgment against you." It is that latter course which we adopt, and if that be retroactivity, we proclaim it to be most fully consistent with that higher justice which, in the practice of civilized states, has set a definite limit to the retroactive operation of laws. Let the defendants and their protagonists complain that the Charter is in this matter an ex parse fiat of the victors. These victors, composing, as they do, the overwhelming majority of the nations of the world, represent also the world's sense of justice, which would be outraged if the crime of war, after this second world conflict, were to remain unpunished. In thus interpreting, declaring, and supplementing the existing law, these states are content to be judged by the verdict of history. Securus judicat orbis terrarum. Insofar as the Charter of this Tribunal introduces new law, its authors have established a precedent for the future-a precedent operative against all, including themselves, but in essence that law, rendering recourse to aggressive war an international crime, had been well established when the Charter was adopted. It is only by way of corruption of language that it can be described as a retroactive law.

There remains the question, with which I shall not detain the Tribunal for long, whether these wars which were launched by Germany and her leaders in violation of treaties or agreements or assurances were also wars of aggression. A war of aggression is a war which is resorted to in violation of the international obligation not to have recourse to war, or, in cases in which war is not totally renounced, which is resorted to in disregard of the duty to utilize the procedure of pacific settlement which a state has bound itself to observe. There was, as a matter of fact, in the period between the two world wars, a divergence of opinion among jurists and statesmen whether it was preferable to attempt in advance a legal definition of aggression, or to leave to the states concerned and to the collective organs of the international community freedom of appreciation of the facts in any particular situation that might arise. Those holding the latter view argued that a rigid definition might be abused by an unscrupulous state to fit in with its aggressive design; they feared, and the British Government was for a time among those who took this view, that an automatic definition of aggression might become "a trap for the innocent and a signpost for the guilty." Others held that in the interest of certainty and security a definition of aggression, like a definition of any crime in municipal law, was proper and useful. They urged that the competent international organs, political and judicial, could be trusted to avoid in any particular case a definition of aggression which might lead to obstruction or to an absurdity. In May of 1933 the Committee on Security Questions of the Disarmament Conference proposed a definition of aggression on these lines:

"The aggressor in an international conflict shall, subject to the agreements in force between the parties to the dispute, be considered to be that state which is the first to commit any of the following actions:

"(1) Declaration of war upon another state;

"(2) Invasion by its armed forces, with or without a declaration of war, of the territory of another state;

"(3) Attack by its land, naval, or air forces, with or without a declaration of war, on the territory, vessels, or aircraft of another state;

"(4) Naval blockade of the coasts or ports of another state;

"(5) Provision of support to armed bands formed in its territory which have invaded the territory of another state, or refusal, notwithstanding the request of the invaded state, to take in its own territory all the measures in its power to deprive those bands of all assistance or protection."

The various treaties concluded in 1933 by the Union of Soviet Socialist Republics and other states followed closely that definition.

So did the draft convention submitted in 1933 by His Majesty s Government to the Disarmament Conference.

However, it is unprofitable to elaborate here the details of the problem or of the definition of aggression. This Tribunal will not allow itself to be deflected from its purpose by attempts to ventilate in this Court what is an academic and, in the circumstances, an utterly unreal controversy as to what is the nature of a war of aggression, for there is no definition of aggression, general or particular, which does not cover and cover abundantly and irresistibly in every detail, the premeditated onslaught by Germany on the territorial integrity and political independence of so many sovereign states.

This, then, being the law as we submit it to be to this Tribunal that the peoples of the world by the Pact of Paris had finally outlawed war and made it criminal-I turn now to the facts to see how these defendants under their leader and with their associates destroyed the high hopes of mankind and sought to revert to international anarchy. First, let this be said, for it will be established beyond doubt by the documents which you will see, from the moment Hitler became Chancellor in 1933, with the Defendant Von Papen as Reich Chancellor, and with the Defendant Von Neurath as his Foreign Minister, the whole atmosphere of the world darkened.

The hopes of the people began to recede. Treaties seemed no longer matters of solemn obligation but were entered into with complete cynicism as a means for deceiving other states of Germany's warlike intentions. International conferences were no longer to be used as a means for securing pacific settlements but as occasions for obtaining by blackmail demands which were eventually to be enlarged by war. The world came to know the "war of nerves", the diplomacy of the fait accompli, of blackmail and bullying.

In October 1933 Hitler told his Cabinet that as the proposed Disarmament Convention did not concede full equality to Germany, "It would be necessary to torpedo the Disarmament Conference. It was out of the question to negotiate: Germany would leave the Conference and the League". On the 21st of October 1933 Germany did so, and by so doing struck a deadly blow at the fabric of security which had been built up on the basis of the League Covenant. From that time on the record of their foreign policy became one of complete disregard of international obligations, and indeed not least of those solemnly concluded by themselves. Hitler himself expressly avowed to his confederates, "Agreements are kept only so long as they serve a certain purpose." He might have added that again and again that purpose was only to lull an intended victim into a false sense of security. So patent, indeed, did this eventually become that to be invited by the Defendant Ribbentrop to enter a nonaggression pact with Germany was almost a sign that Germany intended to attack the state concerned. Nor was it only the formal treaty which they used and violated as circumstances seemed to make expedient. These defendants are charged, too, with breaches of the less formal assurances which, in accordance with diplomatic usage, Germany gave to neighboring states. You will hear the importance which Hitler himself publicly attached to assurances of that kind. Today, with the advance of science, the world has been afforded means of communication and intercourse hitherto unknown, and as Hitler himself expressly recognized in his public utterances, international relations no longer depend upon treaties alone. The methods of diplomacy change. The leader of one nation can speak directly to the government and peoples of another, and that course was not infrequently adopted by the Nazi conspirators. But, although the methods change, the principles of good faith and honesty, established as the fundamentals of civilized society, both in the national and international spheres, remain unaltered. It is a long time since it was said that we are part one of another, and if today the different states are more closely connected and thus form part of a world society more than ever before, so also, more than before, is there that need for good faith and honesty between them.

Let us see how these defendants, ministers and high officers of the Nazi Government, individually and collectively comported themselves in these matters.

On the 1st of September 1939 in the early hours of the morning under manufactured and, in any event, inadequate pretexts, the Armed Forces of the German Reich invaded Poland along the whole length of her frontiers and thus launched the war which was to bring down so many of the pillars of our civilization.

It was a breach of the Hague Conventions. It was a breach of the Treaty of Versailles which had established the frontiers between Germany and Poland. And however much Germany disliked that treaty-although Hitler had expressly stated that he would respect its territorial provisions-however much she disliked it, she was not free to break it by unilateral action. It was a breach of the Arbitration Treaty between Germany and Poland concluded at Locarno on the 16th of October 1925. By that treaty Germany and Poland expressly agreed to refer any matters of dispute not capable of settlement by ordinary diplomatic machinery to the decision of an arbitral tribunal or of the Permanent Court of International Justice. It was a breach of the Pact of Paris. But that is not all. It was also a breach of a more recent and, in view of the repeated emphasis laid upon it by Hitler himself, in some ways a more important engagement into which Nazi Germany had entered with Poland. After the Nazi Government came into power, on the 26th of January 1934 the German and Polish Governments had signed a 10 year pact of non-aggression. It was, as the signatories themselves stated, to introduce a new era into the political relations between Poland and Germany. It was said in the text of the pact itself that "the maintenance and guarantee of lasting peace between the two countries is an essential prerequisite for the general peace of Europe." The two governments therefore agreed to base their mutual relations on the principles laid down in the Pact of Paris, and they solemnly declared that:

"In no circumstances ... will they proceed to the application of force for the purpose of reaching a decision in such disputes."

That declaration and agreement was to remain in force for at least 10 years and thereafter it was to remain valid unless it was denounced by either Government 6 months before the expiration of the 10 years, or subsequently by 6 months' notice. Both at the time of its signature and during the following 4 years Hitler spoke of the German-Polish agreement publicly as though it were a cornerstone of his foreign policy. By entering into it, he persuaded many people that his intentions were genuinely pacific, for the re-emergence of a new Poland and an independent Poland after the war had cost Germany much territory and had separated East Prussia from the Reich. And that Hitler should, of his own accord, enter into friendly relations with Poland-that in his speeches on foreign policy he should proclaim his recognition of Poland and of her right to an exit to the sea, and the necessity for Germans and Poles to live side by side in amity-these facts seemed to the world to be convincing proof that Hitler had no "revisionist" aims which would threaten the peace of Europe; that he was even genuinely anxious to put an end to the age-old hostility between the Teuton and the Slav. If his professions were, as embodied in the treaty and as contained in these declarations, genuine, his policy excluded a renewal of the "Drang nach Osten", as it had been called, and was thereby going to contribute to the peace and stability of Europe. That was what the people were led to think. We shall have occasion enough to see how little truth these pacific professions in fact contained.

The history of the fateful years from 1934 to 1939 shows quite clearly that the Germans used this treaty, as they used other treaties, merely as an instrument of policy for furthering their aggressive aims. It is clear from the documents which will be presented to the Tribunal that these 5 years fall into two distinct phases in the realization of the aggressive aims which always underlay the Nazi policy. There was first the period from the Nazi assumption of power in 1933 until the autumn of 1937. That was the preparatory period. During that time there occurred the breaches of the Versailles and Locarno Treaties, the feverish rearmament of Germany, the reintroduction of conscription, the reoccupation and remilitarization of the Rhineland, and all those other necessary preparatory measures for future aggression which my American colleagues have already so admirably put before the Tribunal.

During that period-the preparatory period-Germany was lulling Poland into a false sense of security. Not only Hitler, but the Defendant Goering and the Defendant Ribbentrop made statements approbating the non-aggression pact. In 1935 Goering was saying that, "The pact was not planned for a period of 10 years but forever; there need not be the slightest fear that it would not be continued." Even though Germany was steadily building up the greatest war machine that Europe had ever known, and although, by January 1937, the German military position was so strong and so secure that, in spite of the treaty breaches which it involved, Hitler could openly refer to his strong Army, he took pains, at the same time, to say - and again I quote - that:

> "By a series of agreements we have eliminated existing tensions and thereby contributed considerably to an improvement in the European atmosphere. I merely recall the agreement with Poland which has worked out to the advantage of both sides."

And so it went on: abroad, protestations of pacific intentions; at home, "guns before butter."

In 1937 this preparatory period drew to a close and Nazi policy moved from general preparation for future aggression to specific planning for the attainment of certain specific aggressive aims. And there are two documents in particular which mark that change.

The first of these was called "Directive for Unified Preparation for War", issued in June 1937-June 29, 1937-by the Reich Minister for War, who was then

Von Blomberg, Commander-in-Chief of the Armed Forces. That document is important, not only for its military directions, but for the appreciation it contained of the European situation and for the revelation of the Nazi attitude towards it.

> "The general political position" -Von Blomberg stated, and I am quoting from the document- "justifies the supposition that Germany need not consider an attack from any side. Grounds for this are, in addition to the lack of desire for war in almost all nations, particularly the Western Powers, the deficiencies in the preparedness for war of a number of states, and of Russia in particular."

It is true, he added, "The intention of unleashing a European war is held just as little by Germany." And it may be that that phrase was carefully chosen because, as the documents will show, Germany hoped to conquer Europe, perhaps to conquer the world in detail; to fight on one front at a time, against one power at a time, and not to unleash a general European conflict.

But Von Blomberg went on:

> "The politically fluid world situation, which does not preclude surprising incidents, demands a continuous preparedness for war of the German Armed Forces (a) to counter attack at any time" - yet he had just said that there was no fear of any attack - and "(b)" - and I invite the Tribunal again to notice this phrase - "to enable the military exploitation of politically favorable opportunities, should they occur."

That phrase is no more than a euphemistic description of aggressive war. It reveals the continued adherence of the German military leaders to the doctrine that military might, and if necessary war, should be an instrument of policy-the doctrine which had been explicitly condemned by the Kellogg Pact, which was renounced by the pact with Poland, and by innumerable other treaties.

The document goes on to set out the general preparations necessary for a possible war in the mobilization period of 1937-1938. It is evidence at least for this, that the leaders of the German Armed Forces had it in mind to use the military strength which they were building up for aggressive purposes. No reason, they say, to anticipate attack from any side-there is a lack of desire for war. Yet they prepare to exploit militarily favorable opportunities.

Still more important as evidence of the transition to planned aggression is the record of the important conference which Hitler held at the Reich Chancellery on the 5th of November 1937, at which Von Blomberg, Reich Minister for war; Von Fritsch, the Commander-in-Chief of the Army; Goering, Commander-in-Chief of the Luftwaffe; Raeder, the Commander-in-Chief of the Navy; and Von Neurath, then the Foreign Minister, were present. The minutes of that conference have already been put in evidence. I refer to them now only to emphasize those passages which make apparent the ultimate intention to wage an aggressive war. You will remember that-the burden of Hitler's argument at that conference was that Germany required more territory in Europe. Austria and Czechoslovakia were specifically envisaged. But Hitler realized that the process of conquering those two countries might well bring into operation the treaty obligations of Great Britain and of France. He was prepared to take the risk. You remember the passage:

> "The history of all times: Roman Empire, British Empire has proved that every space expansion can be effected only by breaking resistance

and taking risks. Even setbacks are unavoidable Neither formerly nor today has space been found without an owner. The attacker always comes up against the proprietor. The question for Germany is where the greatest possible conquest can be made at the lowest possible cost."

In the course of that conference Hitler had foreseen and discussed the likelihood that Poland would be involved if the aggressive expansionist aims which he put forward brought about a general European war in the course of their realization by the Nazi State. And when, therefore, on that very day on which that conference was taking place, Hitler assured the Polish Ambassador of the great value of the 1934 Pact with Poland, it can only be concluded that its real value in Hitler's eyes was that of keeping Poland quiet until Germany had acquired such a territorial and strategic position that Poland was no longer a danger.

That view is confirmed by the events which followed. At the beginning of February of 1938 the change from Nazi preparation for aggression to active aggression itself took place. It was marked by the substitution of Ribbentrop for Neurath as Foreign Minister, and of Keitel for Blomberg as head of the OKW. Its first fruits were the bullying of Schuschnigg at Berchtesgaden on February 12, 1938 and the forcible absorption of Austria in March. Thereafter the Green Plan for the destruction of Czechoslovakia was steadily developed in the way which you heard yesterday-the plan partially foiled, or final consummation at least delayed, by the Munich Agreement.

With those aspects, those developments of Nazi aggression, my American colleagues have already dealt. But it is obvious that the acquisition of these two countries, their resources in manpower, their resources in the production of munitions of war, immensely strengthened the position of Germany as against Poland. And it is, therefore, perhaps not surprising that, just as the Defendant Goering assured the Czechoslovak Minister in Berlin, at the time of the Nazi invasion of Austria, that Hitler recognized the validity of the German-Czechoslovak Arbitration Treaty of 1925, and that Germany had no designs against Czechoslovakia herself you remember, "I give you my word of honor," the Defendant Goering said-just as that is not surprising, so also it is not perhaps surprising that continued assurances should have been given during 1938 to Poland in order to keep that country from interfering with the Nazi aggression on Poland's neighbors.

Thus, on the 20th of February of 1938, on the eve of his invasion of Austria, Hitler, referring to the fourth anniversary of the Polish Pact, permitted himself to say this to the Reichstag - and I quote:

"... and so a way to a friendly understanding has been successfully paved, an understanding which, beginning with Danzig, has today in spite of the attempt of some mischief makers, succeeded in finally taking the poison out of the relations between Germany and Poland and transforming them into a sincere friendly co-operation ... Relying on her friendships, Germany will not leave a stone unturned to save that ideal which provides the foundation for the task ahead of us-peace."

Still more striking, perhaps, are the cordial references to Poland in Hitler's speech in the Sportpalast at Berlin on the 26th of September 1938. He then said:

"The most difficult problem with which I was confronted was that of our relations with Poland. There was a danger that Poles and Germans would regard each other as hereditary enemies. I wanted to prevent this. I know well enough that I should not have been successful if Poland had had a democratic constitution. For these democracies which indulge in phrases about peace are the most bloodthirsty war agitators. In Poland there ruled no democracy, but a man. And with him I succeeded, in precisely 12 months, in coming to an agreement which, for 10 years in the first instance, removed in principle the danger of a conflict. We are all convinced that this agreement will bring lasting pacification. We realize that here are two peoples which must live together and neither of which can do away with the other. A people of 33 millions will always strive for an outlet to the sea. A way for understanding, then, had to be found, and it will be further extended. But the main fact is that the two governments, and all reasonable and clear-sighted persons among the two peoples within the two countries, possess the firm will and determination to improve their relations. It was a real work of peace, of more worth than all the chattering in the League of Nations palace at Geneva."

And so flattery of Poland preceded the annexation of Austria and renewed flattery of Poland preceded the projected annexation of Czechoslovakia. The realities behind these outward expressions of good will are clearly revealed in the documents relating to the Fall Grun (*), which are already before the Tribunal. They show Hitler as fully aware that there was a risk of Poland, England, and France being involved in war to prevent the German annexation of Czechoslovakia and that this risk, although it was realized, was also accepted. On 25 August of 1938 top-secret orders to the German Air Force in regard to the operations to be conducted against England and France, if they intervened, pointed out that, as the French-Czechoslovak Treaty provided ' for assistance only in the event of an "unprovoked" attack, it would take a day or two for France and England, and I suppose for their legal advisors to decide whether legally the attack had been unprovoked or not, and consequently a Blitzkrieg, accomplishing its aims before there could be any effective intervention by France or England, was the object to be aimed at.

On the same day an Air Force memorandum on future organization was issued, and to it there was attached a map on which the Baltic States, Hungary, Czechoslovakia, and Poland were all shown as part of Germany, and preparations for expanding the Air Force, and I quote, "as the Reich grows in area," as well as dispositions for a two-front war against France and Russia, were discussed. And on the following day Von Ribbentrop was being minuted about the reaction of Poland towards the Czechoslovak problem. I quote: "The fact that after the liquidation of the Czechoslovakian question it will be generally assumed that Poland will be next in turn is not to be denied," is recognized, but it is stated, "The later this assumption sinks in, the better."

I will pause for a moment at the date of the Munich Agreement and ask the Tribunal to remind itself of what the evidence of documents and historical facts shows up to that day. It has made undeniable both the fact of Nazi aggressiveness and of active and actual aggression. Not only does that conference of 1937 show Hitler and his associates deliberately considering the acquisition of Austria and Czechoslovakia, if necessary by war, but the first of the operations had been carried through in March of 1938; and a large part of

69

the second, under threat of war-a threat which as we now see was much more than a bluff-a threat of actual and real war, although without the actual need for its initiation, secured, as I said, a large part of the second objective in September of 1938. And, more ominous still, Hitler had revealed his adherence to the old doctrines of Mein Kampf-those essentially aggressive doctrines to the exposition of which in Mein Kampf, long regarded as the Bible of the Nazi Party, we shall draw attention in certain particular passages. Hitler is indicating quite clearly not only to his associates, but indeed to the world at this time, that he is in pursuit of Lebensraum and that he means to secure it by threat of force, or if threat of force fails, by actual force-by aggressive war.

So far actual warfare had been avoided because of the love of peace, the lack of preparedness, the patience, the cowardice-call it what you will-of the democratic powers; but after Munich the question which filled the minds of all thinking people with acute anxiety was "where will this thing end? Is Hitler now satisfied as he declared himself to be? Or is his pursuit of Lebensraum going to lead to future aggressions, even if he has to embark on open, aggressive war to secure it?"

It was in relation to the remainder of Czechoslovakia and to Poland that the answer to these questions was to be given. So far, up to the time of the Munich Agreement, no direct and immediate threat to Poland had been made. The two documents from which I have just quoted, show of course, that high officers of the Defendant Goering's air staff already regarded the expansion of the Reich and, it would seem, the destruction and absorption of Poland, as a foregone conclusion. They were already anticipating, indeed, the last stage of Hitler's policy as expounded in Mein Kampf-war to destroy France and to secure Lebensraum in Russia. And the writer of the minute to Ribbentrop already took it for granted that, after Czechoslovakia, Poland would be attacked. But more impressive than those two documents is the fact that, as I have said, at the conference of 5 November 1937, war with Poland, if she should dare to prevent German aggression against Czechoslovakia, had been quite coolly and calmly contemplated, and the Nazi leaders were ready to take the risk. So also had the risk of war with England and France under the same circumstances been considered and accepted. As I indicated, such a war would, of course, have been aggressive war on Germany's part, and they were contemplating aggressive warfare. For to force one state to take up arms to defend another state against aggression, in other words, to fulfill its treaty obligations is undoubtedly to initiate aggressive warfare against the first state. But in spite of those plans, in spite of these intentions behind the scenes, it remains true that until Munich the decision for direct attack upon Poland and her destruction by aggressive war had apparently not as yet been taken by Hitler and his associates. It is to the transition from the intention and preparation of initiating aggressive war, evident in regard to Czechoslovakia, to the actual initiation and waging of aggressive war against Poland that I now pass. That transition occupies the 11 months from the 1st of October 1938 to the actual attack on Poland on the 1st of September 1939.

Within 6 months of the signature of the Munich Agreement the Nazi leaders had occupied the remainder of Czechoslovakia, which by that Agreement they had indicated their willingness to guarantee. On the 14th of March 1939 the aged and infirm president of the "rump" of Czechoslovakia, Hacha and his Foreign Minister were summoned to Berlin. At a meeting held between 1 o'clock and 2:15 in the small hours of the 15th of March in the presence of Hitler, of the Defendants Ribbentrop, Goering, and Keitel, they were bullied and threatened and even bluntly told that Hitler "had issued the orders for the German troops to move into Czechoslovakia and for the incorporation of Czechoslovakia into the German Reich."

It was made quite clear to them that resistance would be useless and would be crushed "by force of arms with all available means," and it was thus that the Protectorate of Bohemia and Moravia was set up and that Slovakia was turned into a German satellite, though nominally independent state. By their own unilateral action, on pretexts which had no shadow of validity, without discussion with the governments of any other country, without mediation, and in direct contradiction of the sense and spirit of the Munich Agreement, the Germans acquired for themselves that for which they had been planning in September of the previous year, and indeed much earlier, but which at that time they had felt themselves unable completely to secure without too patent an exhibition of their aggressive intentions. Aggression achieved whetted the appetite for aggression to come. There were protests. England and France sent diplomatic notes. Of course, there were protests. The Nazis had clearly shown their hand. Hitherto they had concealed from the outside world that their claims went beyond incorporating into the Reich persons of German race living in bordering territory. Now for the first time, in defiance of their solemn assurances to the contrary, non-German territory and non-German people had been seized. This acquisition of the whole of Czechoslovakia, together with the equally illegal occupation of Memel on the 22d of March 1939, resulted in an immense strengthening of the German positions, both politically and strategically, as Hitler had anticipated it would, when he discussed the matter at that conference in November of 1937.

But long before the consummation by the Nazi leaders of their aggression against Czechoslovakia, they had begun to make demands upon Poland. The Munich settlement achieved on the 25th of October 1938, that is to say within less than a month of Hitler's reassuring speech about Poland to which I have already referred, and within, of course, a month of the Munich Agreement, M. Lipski, the Polish Ambassador in Berlin, reported to M. Beck, the Polish Foreign Minister, that at a luncheon at Berchtesgaden the day before, namely, on the 24th of October 1938, the Defendant Ribbentrop had put forward demands for the reunion of Danzig with the Reich and for the building of an extra-territorial motor road and railway line across Pomorze, the province which the Germans called "The Corridor". From that moment onwards until the Polish Government had made it plain, as they did during a visit of the Defendant Ribbentrop to Warsaw in January 1939, that they would not consent to hand over Danzig to German sovereignty, negotiations on these German demands continued. And even after Ribbentrop's return from the visit to Warsaw, Hitler thought it worthwhile, in his Reichstag speech on the 30th of January 1939, to say:

"We have just celebrated the fifth anniversary of the conclusion of our non-aggression pact with Poland. There can scarcely be any difference of opinion today among the true friends of peace as to the value of this agreement. One only needs to ask oneself what might have happened to Europe if this agreement, which brought such relief, had not been entered into 5 years ago. In signing it, the great Polish marshal and patriot rendered his people just as great a service as the leaders of the National Socialist State rendered the German people. During the troubled months of the past year, the friendship between Germany and Poland has been one of the reassuring factors in the political life of Europe."

But that utterance was the last friendly word from Germany to Poland, and the last occasion on which the Nazi Leaders mentioned the German-Polish Agreement with approbation. During February 1939 silence fell upon German demands in relation to Poland. But as soon as the final absorption of Czechoslovakia had taken place and Germany had also occupied Memel, Nazi pressure upon Poland was at once renewed. In two conversations which he and the Defendant Ribbentrop held on the 21st of March and the 26th of March, respectively, with the Polish Ambassador, German demands upon Poland were renewed and were further pressed. And in view of the fate which had overtaken Czechoslovakia, in view of the grave deterioration in her strategical position towards Germany, it is not surprising that the Polish Government took alarm at the developments. Nor were they alone. The events of March 1939 had at last convinced both the English and the French Governments that the Nazi designs of aggression were not limited to men of German race, and that the specter of European war resulting from further aggressions by Nazi Germany had not, after all, been exorcised by the Munich Agreement.

As a result, therefore, of the concern of Poland and of England and of France at the events in Czechoslovakia, and at the newly applied pressure on Poland, conversations between the English and Polish Governments had been taking place, and, on the 31st of March 1939, Mr. Neville Chamberlain, speaking in the House of Commons, stated that His Majesty's Government had given an assurance to help Poland in the event of any action which clearly threatened Polish independence and which the Polish Government accordingly considered it vital to resist. On the 6th of April 1939 an Anglo-Polish communique stated that the two countries were prepared to enter into an agreement of a permanent and reciprocal character to replace the present temporary and unilateral assurance given by His Majesty's Government.

The justification for that concern on the part of the democratic powers is not difficult to find. With the evidence which we now have of what was happening within the councils of the German Reich and its Armed Forces during these months, it is manifest that the German Government were intent on seizing Poland as a whole, that Danzig-as Hitler himself was to say in time, a month later "was not the subject of the dispute at all." The Nazi Government was intent upon aggression and the demands and negotiations in respect to Danzig were merely a cover and excuse for further domination.

Would that be a convenient point to stop?

THE PRESIDENT: We will adjourn now until 2 o'clock.

[A recess was taken until 1400 hours.]

THE PRESIDENT: Before the Attorney General continues his opening statement, the Tribunal wishes me to state what they propose to do as to time of sitting for the immediate future. We think it will be more convenient that the Tribunal shall sit from 10:00 o'clock in the morning until 1:00 o'clock, with a break for 10 minutes in the middle of the morning; and that the Tribunal shall sit in the afternoon from 2:00 o'clock until 5:00 o'clock with a break for 10 minutes in the middle of the afternoon; and that there shall be no open sitting of the Tribunal on Saturday morning, as the Tribunal has a very large number of applications by the defendants' counsel for witnesses and documents and other matters of that sort which it has to consider.

SIR HARTLEY SHAWCROSS: May it please the Tribunal, when we broke off I had been saying that the Nazi Government was intent upon aggression, and all that had been taking place in regard to Danzig-the negotiations, the demands that were being made were really no more than a cover, a pretext and excuse for further domination.

As far back as September 1938 plans for aggressive war against Poland, England, and France were well in hand. While Hitler, at Munich, was telling the world that the German people wanted peace, and that having solved the Czechoslovakian problem, Germany had no more territorial problems in Europe, the staffs of his Armed Forces were already preparing their plans. On the 26th of September 1938 he had stated:

> "We have given guarantees to the states in the West. We have assured all our immediate neighbors of the integrity of their territory as far as Germany is concerned. That is no mere phrase. It is our sacred will. We have no interest whatever in a breach of the peace. We want nothing from these peoples."

And the world was entitled to rely on those assurances. International co-operation is utterly impossible unless one can assume good faith in the leaders of the various states and honesty in the public utterances that they make. But, in fact, within 2 months of that solemn and apparently considered undertaking, Hitler and his confederates were preparing for the seizure of Danzig. To recognize those assurances, those pledges, those diplomatic moves as the empty frauds that they were, one must go back to inquire what was happening within the inner councils of the Reich from the time of the Munich Agreement.

Written some time in September 1938 is an extract from a file on the reconstruction of the German Navy. Under the heading "Opinion on the Draft Study of Naval Warfare against England," this is stated:

> "1. If, according to the Fuehrer's decision, Germany is to acquire a position as a world power, she needs not only sufficient colonial possessions but also secure naval communications and secure access to the ocean.
>
> "2. Both requirements can be fulfilled only in opposition to Anglo-French interests and would limit their position as world powers. It is unlikely that they can be achieved by peaceful means. The decision to make Germany a world power, therefore, forces upon us the necessity of making the corresponding preparations for war.
>
> "3. War against England means at the same time war against the Empire, against France, probably against Russia as well, and a large number of countries overseas, in fact, against one-third to one-half of the world.

"It can only be justified and have a chance of success" - and it was not moral justification which was being looked for in this document - "It can only be justified and have a chance of success if it is prepared economically as well as politically and militarily, and waged with the aim of conquering for Germany an outlet to the ocean."

THE PRESIDENT: I think the Tribunal would like to know at what stage you propose to put the documents, which you are citing, in evidence.

SIR HARTLEY SHAWCROSS: Well, Sir, my colleagues, my American and my British colleagues, were proposing to follow up my own address by putting these documents in. The first series of documents, which will be put in by my noted colleague, Sir David Maxwell-Fyfe, will be the treaties.

THE PRESIDENT: I suppose that what you quote will have to be read again.

SIR HARTLEY SHAWCROSS: Well, I am limiting my quotations as far as I possibly can. I apprehend that technically you may wish it to be quoted again, so as to get it on the record when the document is actually put into evidence. But I think it will appear, when the documents themselves are produced, that there will be a good deal more in most of them than I am actually citing now.

THE PRESIDENT: Yes. Very well.

SIR HARTLEY SHAWCROSS: This document on naval warfare against England is something which is both significant and new. Until this date the documents in our possession disclose preparations for war against Poland, England, and France, purporting on the face of them at least to be defensive measures to ward off attacks which might result from the intervention of those states in the preparatory German aggressions in Central Europe. Hitherto aggressive war against Poland, England, and France has been contemplated only as a distant objective. Now, in this document for the first time, we find a war of conquest by Germany against France and England openly recognized as the future aim, at least of the German Navy.

On 24 November 1938 an appendix was issued by Keitel to a previous order of the Fuehrer. In that appendix were set out the future tasks for the Armed Forces and the preparation for the conduct of the war which would result from those tasks.

"The Fuehrer has ordered" - I quote - "that besides the three eventualities mentioned in the previous directive . . . preparations are also to be made for the surprise occupation by German troops of the Free State of Danzig.

> "For the preparation the following principles are to be borne in mind." - This is the common pattern of aggression - "The primary assumption is the lightning seizure of Danzig by exploiting a favorable political situation, and not war with Poland. Troops which are going to be used for this purpose must not be held at the same time for the seizure of Memel, so that both operations can take place simultaneously, should such necessity arise."

Thereafter, as the evidence which is already before the Tribunal has shown, final preparations were taking place for the invasion of Poland. On the 3rd of April 1939, 3 days before the issue of the Anglo-Polish communique, the Defendant Keitel issued to the High Command of the Armed Forces a directive in which it was stated that the directive for the uniform preparation of war by the Armed Forces in 1939-40, was being re-issued and that part relating to Danzig would be out in April. The basic principles were to remain the same as in the previous directive. Attached to this document were the orders Fall Weiss, the code name for the proposed invasion of Poland. Preparation for that invasion was to be made, it was stated, so that the operation could be carried out at any time from the 1st of September 1939 onwards.

On the 11th of April Hitler issued his directive for the uniform preparation of the war by the Armed Forces, 1939-40, and in it he said:

"I shall lay down in a later directive future tasks of the Armed Forces and the preparations to be made in accordance with these for the conduct of war. Until that directive comes into force the Armed Forces must be prepared for the following eventualities:

"1. Safeguarding of the frontiers

"2. Fall Weiss,

"3. The annexation of Danzig."

Then, in an annex to that document which bore the heading "Political Hypotheses and Aims," it was stated that quarrels with Poland should be avoided. But should Poland change her policy and adopt a threatening attitude towards Germany, a final settlement would be necessary, notwithstanding the Polish Pact. The Free City of Danzig was to be incorporated in the Reich at the outbreak of the conflict at the latest. The policy aimed at limiting the war to Poland, and this was considered possible at that time with the internal crises in France and resulting British restraint.

The wording of that document- and the Tribunal will study the whole of it- does not directly involve the intention of immediate . aggression. It is a plan of attack "if Poland changes her policy and adopts a threatening attitude." But the picture of Poland, with her wholly inadequate armaments, threatening Germany, now armed to the teeth, is ludicrous enough, and the real aim of the document emerges in the sentence- and I quote: "The aim is then to destroy Polish military strength and to create, in the East, a situation which satisfies the requirements of defense" -a sufficiently vague phrase to cover designs of any magnitude. But even at that stage, the evidence does not suffice to prove that the actual decision to attack Poland on any given date had yet been taken. All the preparations were being set in train. All the necessary action was being proceeded with, in case that decision should be reached.

It was within 3 weeks of the issue of that last document that Hitler addressed the Reichstag on the 28th of April 1939. In that speech he repeated the demands which had already been made upon Poland, and proceeded to denounce the German-Polish Agreement of 1934. Leaving aside, for the moment, the warlike preparations for aggression, which Hitler had set in motion behind the scenes, I will ask the Tribunal to consider the nature of this denunciation of an agreement to which, in the past, Hitler had attached such importance.

In the first place, of course, Hitler's denunciation was per se ineffectual. The text of the agreement made no provision for its denunciation by either party until a period of 10 years had come to an end. No denunciation could be legally effective until June or July of 1943, and here was Hitler speaking in April of 1939, rather more than 5 years too soon.

In the second place, Hitler's actual attack upon Poland, when it came on 1 September was made before the expiration of the 6 months' period after denunciation required by the agreement before any denunciation could be operative. And in the third place, the grounds for the denunciation stated by Hitler in his speech to the Reichstag were entirely specious. However one reads its terms, it is impossible to take the view that the Anglo-Polish guarantee of mutual assistance against aggression could render the German-Polish Pact null and void, as Hitler sought to suggest. If that had been the effect of the Anglo-

Polish assurances, then certainly the pacts which had already been entered into by Hitler himself with Italy and with Japan had already invalidated the treaty with Poland. Hitler might have spared his breath. The truth is, of course, that the text of the English-Polish communique, the text of the assurances, contains nothing whatever to support the contention that the German-Polish Pact was in any way interfered with.

One asks: Why then did Hitler make this trebly invalid attempt to denounce his own pet diplomatic child? Is there any other possible answer but this:

That the agreement having served its purpose, the grounds which he chose for its denunciation were chosen merely in an effort to provide Germany with some kind of justification-at least for the German people-for the aggression on which the German leaders were intent.

And, of course, Hitler sorely needed some kind of justification, some apparently decent excuse, since nothing had happened, and nothing seemed likely to happen, from the Polish side, to provide him with any kind of pretext for invading Poland. So far he had made demands upon his treaty partner which Poland, as a sovereign state, had every right to refuse. If dissatisfied with that refusal, Hitler was bound, under the terms of the agreement itself, "To seek a settlement" -I am reading the words of the pact:

"To seek a settlement through other peaceful means, without prejudice to the possibility of applying those methods of procedure, in case of necessity, which are provided for such a case in the other agreements between them that are in force."

And that presumably was a reference to the German-Polish Arbitration Treaty, signed at Locarno in 1925.

The very facts, therefore, that as soon as the Nazi leaders cannot get what they want but are not entitled to from Poland by merely asking for it and that, on their side, they made no further attempt to settle the dispute "by peaceful means" - in accordance with the terms of the agreement and of the Kellogg Pact, to which the agreement pledged both parties-in themselves constitute a strong presumption of aggressive intentions against Hitler and his associates. That presumption becomes a certainty when the documents to which I am about to call the attention of the Tribunal are studied.

On the 10th of May Hitler issued an order for the capture of economic installations in Poland. On the 16th of May the Defendant Raeder, as Commander-in-Chief of the Navy, issued a memorandum setting out the Fuehrer's instructions to prepare for the operation Fall Weiss at any time from the 1st of September.

But the decisive document is the record of the conference held by Hitler on the 23rd of May 1939, in conference with many high-ranking officers, including the Defendants Goering, Raeder, and Keitel. The details of the whole document will have to be read to the Tribunal later and I am merely summarizing the substantial effect of this part of it now. Hitler stated that the solution of the economic problems with which Germany was beset at first, could not be found without invasion of foreign states and attacks on foreign property. "Danzig" - and I am quoting:

"Danzig is not the subject of the dispute at all. It is a question of expanding our living space in the East. There is, therefore, no question of sparing Poland, and we are left with the decision to attack Poland at the earliest opportunity. We cannot expect a repetition of the Czech affair. There will be fighting. Our task is to isolate Poland. The success of this isolation will be decisive. The isolation of Poland is a matter of skillful politics."

So he explained to his confederates. He anticipated the possibility that war with England and France might result, but a two-front war was to be avoided if possible. Yet England was recognized - and I say it with pride - as the most dangerous enemy which Germany had. "England", he said I quote, "England is the driving force against Germany... the aim will always be to force England to her knees." More than once he repeated that the war with England and France would be a life and death struggle. "But all the same," he concluded, "Germany will not be forced into war but she would not be able to avoid it."

On the 14th of June 1939 General Blaskowitz, then Commander-in-Chief of the 3rd Army group, issued a detailed battle plan for the Fall Weiss. The following day Von Brauchitsch issued a memorandum in which it was stated that the object of the impending operation was to destroy the Polish Armed Forces. "High policy demands," he said, "High policy demands that the war should be begun by heavy surprise blows in order to achieve quick results." The preparations proceeded apace. On the 22d of June the Defendant Keitel submitted a preliminary timetable for the operation, which Hitler seems to have approved, and suggested that the scheduled maneuver must be camouflaged, "in order not to disquiet the population." On the 3rd of July, Brauchitsch wrote to the Defendant Raeder urging that certain preliminary naval moves should be abandoned, in order not to prejudice the surprise of the attack. On the 12th and 13th of August Hitler and Ribbentrop had a conference with Ciano, the Italian Foreign Minister.

It was a conference to which the Tribunal will have to have regard from several points of view. I summarize now only one aspect of the matter: At the beginning of the conversation Hitler emphasized the strength of the German position, of Germany's Western and Eastern Fortifications, and of the strategic and other advantages they held in comparison with those of England, France, and Poland. Now I quote from the captured document itself. Hitler said this:

"Since the Poles through their whole attitude had made it clear that, in any case, in the event of a conflict, they would stand on the side of the enemies of Germany and Italy, a quick liquidation at the present moment could only be of advantage for the unavoidable conflict with the Western Democracies. If a hostile Poland remained on Germany's eastern frontier, not only would the 11 East Prussian divisions be tied down, but also further contingents would be kept in Pomerania and Silesia. This would not be necessary in the event of a previous liquidation."

Then this:

"Generally speaking, the best thing to happen would be to liquidate the false neutrals one after the other. This process could be carried out more easily if on every occasion one partner of the Axis covered the other while it was dealing with an uncertain neutral. Italy might well regard Yugoslavia as a neutral of that kind."

Ciano was for postponing the operation. Italy was not ready. She believed that a conflict with Poland would develop into a general European war. Mussolini was convinced that conflict with the Western Democracies was inevitable, but he was making plans for a period 2 or 3 years ahead. But the

Fuehrer said that the Danzig question must be disposed of, one way or the other, by the end of August. I quote: "He had, therefore, decided to use the occasion of the next political provocation which has the form of an ultimatum ...."

On the 22d of August Hitler called his Supreme Commanders together and gave the order for the attack. In the course of what he said he made it clear that the decision to attack had, in fact, been made not later than the previous spring. He would give a spurious cause for starting the war. And at that time the attack was timed to take place in the early hours of the 26th of August. On the day before, on the 25th of August, the British Government, in the hope that Hitler might still be reluctant to plunge the world into war, and in the belief that a formal treaty would impress him more than the informal assurances which had been given previously, entered into an agreement, an express agreement for mutual assistance with Poland, embodying the previous assurances that had been given earlier in the year. It was known to Hitler that France was bound by the Franco-Polish Treaty of 1921, and by the Guarantee Pact signed at Locarno in 1925 to intervene in Poland's favor in case of aggression. And for a moment Hitler hesitated. The Defendants Goering and Ribbentrop, in the interrogations which you will see, have agreed that it was the Anglo-Polish Treaty which led him to call off, or rather postpone, the attack which was timed for the 26th. Perhaps he hoped that after all there was still some chance of repeating what he had called the Czech affair. If so, his hopes were short-lived. On the 27th of August Hitler accepted Mussolini's decision not at once to come into the war; but he asked for propaganda support and for a display of military activity on the part of Italy, so as to create uncertainty in the minds of the Allies. Ribbentrop on the same day said that the armies were marching.

In the meantime, and, of course, particularly during the last month, desperate attempts were being made by the Western Powers to avert war. You will have details of them in evidence, of the intervention of the Pope, of President Roosevelt's message, of the offer by the British Prime Minister to do our utmost to create the conditions in which all matters in issue could be the subject of free negotiations, and to guarantee the resultant decisions. But this and all the other efforts of honest men to avoid the horror of a European conflict were predestined to failure. The Germans were determined that the day for war had come. On the 31st of August Hitler issued a top-secret order for the attack to commence in the early hours of the 1st of September.

The necessary frontier incidents duly occurred. Was it, perhaps, for that, that the Defendant Keitel had been instructed by Hitler to supply Heydrich with Polish uniforms? And so without a declaration of war, without even giving the Polish Government an opportunity of seeing Germany's final demands- and you will hear the evidence of the extraordinary diplomatic negotiations, if one can call them such, that took place in Berlin-without giving the Poles any opportunity at all of negotiating or arbitrating on the demands which Nazi Germany was making, the Nazi troops invaded Poland.

On the 3rd of September Hitler sent a telegram to Mussolini thanking him for his intervention but pointing out that the war was inevitable and that the most promising moment had to be picked after cold deliberation. And so Hitler and his confederates now before this Tribunal began the first of their wars of aggression for which they had prepared so long and so thoroughly. They waged it so fiercely that within a few weeks Poland was overrun.

On the 23rd of November 1939 Hitler reviewed the situation to his military commanders and in the course of what he said he made this observation:

"One year later Austria came; this step was also considered doubtful. It brought about an essential reinforcement of the Reich. The next step was Bohemia, Moravia, and Poland. This step also was not possible to accomplish in one move. First of all the Western Fortifications had to be finished.... Then followed the creation of the Protectorate, and with that the basis for action against Poland was laid. But I was not quite clear at the time whether I should start first against the East and then in the West, or vice versa.... The compulsion to fight with Poland came first. One might accuse me of wanting to fight again and again. In struggle, I see the fate of all beings."

He was not sure where to attack first. But that sooner or later he would attack, whether it were in the East or in the West, was never in doubt. And he had been warned, not only by the British and French Prime Ministers but even by his confederate Mussolini, that an attack on Poland would bring England and France into the war. He chose what he thought was the opportune moment, and he struck.

Under these circumstances the intent to wage war against England and France, and to precipitate it by an attack on Poland, is not to be denied. Here was defiance of the most solemn treaty obligations. Here was neglect of the most pacific assurances. Here was aggression, naked and unashamed, which was indeed to arouse the horrified and heroic resistance of all civilized peoples, but which, before it was finished, was to tear down much of the structure of our civilization.

Once started upon the active achievement of their plan to secure the domination of Europe, if not of the world, the Nazi Government proceeded to attack other countries, as occasion offered. The first actually to be attacked, actually to be invaded, after the attack upon Poland, were Denmark and Norway.

On the 9th of April 1940 the German Armed Forces invaded Norway and Denmark without any warning, without any declaration of war. It was a breach of the Hague Convention of 1907. It was a breach of the Convention of Arbitration and Conciliation signed between Germany and Denmark on 2 June 1926. It was, of course, a breach of the Kellogg-Briand Pact of 1928. It was a violation of the Non-Aggression Treaty between Germany and Denmark made on the 31st of May 1939. And it was a breach of the most explicit assurances which had been given. After his annexation of Czechoslovakia had shaken the confidence of the world, Hitler attempted to reassure the Scandinavian states. On the 28th of April 1939 he affirmed that he had never made any request to any of them which was incompatible with their sovereignty and independence. On the 31st of May 1939 he signed a non-aggression pact with Denmark.

On the 2d of September 1939, the day after he had invaded Poland and occupied Danzig, he again expressed his determination, so he said, to observe the inviolability and integrity of Norway in an aide-memoire which was handed to the Norwegian Foreign Minister by the German Minister in Oslo on that day.

A month later, in a public speech on the 6th of October 1939, he said:

"Germany has never had any conflicts of interest or even points of controversy with the northern states, neither has she any today. Sweden and Norway have both been offered non-aggression pacts by Germany, and have both refused them, solely because they do not feel themselves threatened in any way."

When the invasion of Denmark and Norway was already begun in the early morning of 9 April 1940, a German memorandum was handed to the governments of those countries attempting to justify the German action. Various allegations against the governments of the invaded countries were made. It was said that Norway had been guilty of breaches of neutrality. It was said that she had allowed and tolerated the use of her territorial waters by Great Britain. It was said that Britain and France were themselves making plans to invade and occupy Norway and that the Government of Norway was prepared to acquiesce in such an event.

I do not propose to argue the question whether or not these allegations were true or false. That question is irrelevant to the issues before this Court. Even if the allegations were true- and they were patently false-they would afford no conceivable justification for the action of invading without warning, without declaration of war, without any attempt at mediation or conciliation.

Aggressive war is none the less aggressive war because the state which wages it believes that other states might, in the future, take similar action. The rape of a nation is not justified because it is thought she may be raped by another. Nor even in self-defense are warlike measures justified except after all means of mediation have been tried and failed and force is actually being exercised against the state concerned.

But the matter is irrelevant because, in actual fact, with the evidence which we now possess, it is abundantly clear that the invasion of these two countries was undertaken for quite different purposes. It had been planned long before any question of breach of neutrality or occupation of Norway by England could ever have occurred. And it is equally clear that the assurances repeated again and again throughout 1939 were made for no other purpose than to lull suspicion in these countries and to prevent them taking steps to resist the attack against them which was all along in active preparation.

For some years the Defendant Rosenberg, in his capacity as Chief of the Foreign Affairs Bureau-APA-of the NSDAP, had interested himself in the promotion of Fifth Column activities in Norway and he had established close relationship with the Nasjonal Samling, a political group headed by the now notorious traitor, Vidkun Quisling. During the winter of 1938-39, APA was in contact with Quisling, and later Quisling conferred with Hitler and with the Defendants Raeder and Rosenberg. In August 1939 a special 14-day course was held at the school of the Office of Foreign Relations in Berlin for 25 followers whom Quisling had selected to attend. The plan was to send a number of selected and "reliable" men to Germany for a brief military training in an isolated camp. These "reliable men" were to be the area and language specialists to German special troops who were taken to Oslo on coal barges to undertake political action in Norway. The object was: a coup in which Quisling would seize his leading opponents in Norway, including the King, and prevent all military resistance from the beginning. Simultaneously with those Fifth Column activities Germany was making her military preparations. On the 2d of September 1939, as I said, Hitler had assured Norway of his intention to respect her neutrality. On 6 October he said that the Scandinavian states were not menaced in any way. Yet on the 3rd October the Defendant Raeder was pointing out that the occupation of bases, if necessary by force, would greatly improve the German strategic position. On the 9th of October Doenitz was recommending Trondheim as the main base, with Narvik as an alternative base for fuel supplies. The Defendant Rosenberg was reporting shortly afterwards on the possibility of a coup d'etat by Quisling, immediately supported by German military and naval forces. On the 12th of December 1939 the Defendant Raeder advised Hitler, in the presence of the Defendants Keitel and Jodl, that if Hitler was favorably impressed by Quisling, the OKW should prepare for the occupation of Norway, if possible with Quisling's assistance, but if necessary entirely by force. Hitler agreed, but there was a doubt whether action should be taken against the Low Countries or against Scandinavia first.

Weather conditions delayed the march on the Low Countries. In January-1940 instructions were given to the German Navy for the attack on Norway. On the 1st of March a directive for the occupation was issued by Hitler. The general object was not said to be to prevent occupation by English forces but, in vague and general terms, to prevent British encroachment in Scandinavia and the Baltic and "to guarantee our ore bases in Sweden and to give our Navy and Air Force a wider start line against Britain." But the directive went on (and here is the common pattern):

" .. . on principle we will do our utmost to make the operation appear as a peaceful occupation, the object of which is the military protection of the Scandinavian states .... It is important that the Scandinavian-states as well as the western opponents should be taken by surprise by our measures.... In case the preparations for embarkation can no longer be kept secret, the leaders and the troops will be deceived with fictitious objectives."

The form and success of the invasion are well known. In the early hours of the 9th of April, seven cruisers, 14 destroyers, and a number of torpedo boats and other small craft carried advance elements of six divisions, totalling about 10,000 men, forced an entry and landed troops in the outer Oslo Fjord, Kristiansand, Stavanger, Bergen, Trondheim, and Narvik. A small force of troops was also landed at Arendal and Egersund on the southern coast. In addition, airborne troops were landed near Oslo and Stavanger in airplanes. The German attack came as a complete surprise. All the invaded towns along the coast were captured according to plan and with only slight losses. Only the plan to capture the King and Parliament failed. But brave as was the resistance, which was hurriedly organized throughout the country -nothing could be done in the face of the long-planned surprise attack- and on the 10th of June military resistance ceased. So another act of aggression was brought to completion.

Almost exactly a month after the attack on Norway, on the 10th of May 1940, the German Armed Forces, repeating what had been done 25 years before, streamed into Belgium, the Netherlands, and Luxembourg according to plan-a plan that is, of invading without warning and without any declaration of war.

What was done was, of course, a breach of the Hague Convention, and is so charged. It was a violation of the Locarno Agreement of 1925, which the Nazi Government affirmed in 1935, only illegally to repudiate it a couple of years later. By that agreement all questions incapable of settlement by ordinary diplomatic means were to be referred to arbitration. You will see the comprehensive terms of all those treaties. It was a breach of the Treaty of Arbitration and Conciliation signed between Germany and the Netherlands on the 20th of May 1926. It was a breach of a similar treaty with Luxembourg of 11 September 1929. It was a breach of the Kellogg-Briand Pact. But those treaties, perhaps, had not derived in the minds of the Nazi rulers of Germany any added sanctity from the fact that they had been solemnly concluded by the governments of pre-Nazi Germany. Let us then consider the specific assurances and undertakings which the Nazi rulers themselves gave to these states which lay in the way of their plans against France and England and which they had always intended to attack. Not once, not twice, but 11 times the clearest possible assurances were given to Belgium, the Netherlands, and Luxembourg. On those assurances, solemnly given and formally expressed, these countries were entitled to rely and did rely. In respect of the breach of those assurances these defendants are charged. On the 30th of January 1937, for instance, Hitler had said:

"As for the rest, I have more than once expressed the desire and the hope of entering into similar good and cordial relations with our neighbors. Germany has, and here I repeat this solemnly, given the assurance time and time again that, for instance, between her and France there cannot be any humanly conceivable points of controversy. The German Government has further given the assurance to Belgium and Holland that it is prepared to recognize and to guarantee the inviolability and neutrality of these territories."

After Hitler had remilitarized the Rhineland and had repudiated the Locarno Pact, England and France sought to re-establish the position of security for Belgium which Hitler's action had threatened. And they, therefore, gave to Belgium on the 24th of April 1937 a specific guarantee that they would maintain, in respect of Belgium, the undertakings of assistance which they had entered into with her both under the Locarno Pact and under the Covenant of the League. On the 13th of October 1937 the German Government also made a declaration assuring Belgium of its intention to recognize the integrity of that country.

It is, perhaps, convenient to deal with the remaining assurances as we review the evidence which is available as to the preparations and intentions of the German Government prior to their actual invasion of Belgium on the 10th of May 1940.

As in the case of Poland, as in the case of Norway and Denmark, so also here the dates speak for themselves.

As early as August of 1938 steps were being taken to utilize the Low Countries as bases for decisive action in the West in the event of France and England opposing Germany in the aggressive plan which was on foot at that time against Czechoslovakia.

In an Air Force letter dated the 25th of August 1938 which deals with the action to be taken if England and France should interfere in the operation against Czechoslovakia, it is stated:

"It is not expected for the moment that other states will intervene against Germany. The Dutch and the Belgian area assumes in this connection much more importance for the conduct of war in Western

Europe than during the World War, mainly as advance base for the air war."

In the last paragraph of that order it is stated:

"Belgium and the Netherlands, when in German hands, represent an extraordinary advantage in the prosecution of the air war against Great Britain as well as against France . . ."

That was in August 1938. Eight months later, on the 28th of April 1939, Hitler is declaring again:

"I was pleased that a number of European states availed themselves of this declaration by the German Government to express and emphasize their desire to have absolute neutrality."

A month later, on the 23rd of May 1939, Hitler held that conference in the Reich Chancellery, to which I already referred. The minutes of that meeting report Hitler as saying:

"The Dutch and Belgian air bases must be occupied by armed forces. Declarations of neutrality cannot be considered of any .value. If England and France want a general conflict on the occasion of the war between Germany and Poland they will support Holland and Belgium in their neutrality .... Therefore, if England intends to intervene at the occasion of the Polish war, we must attack Holland with lightning speed. It is desirable to secure a defense line on Dutch soil up to the Zuider Zee."

Even after that he was to give his solemn declarations that he would observe the neutrality of these countries. On the 26th of August 1939, when the crisis in regard to Danzig and Poland was reaching its climax, on the very day he had picked for the invasion of Poland, declarations assuring the governments concerned of the intention to respect their neutrality were handed by the German Ambassadors to the King of the Belgians, the Queen of the Netherlands, and to the Government of the Grand Duchy of Luxembourg in the most solemn form. But to the Army Hitler was saying:

"If Holland and Belgium are successfully occupied and held, a successful war against England will be secured."

On the 1st of September Poland was invaded, and 2 days later England and France came into the war against Germany, in pursuance of the treaty obligations already referred to. On the 6th of October Hitler renewed his assurances of friendship to Belgium and Holland, but on the 9th of October, before any kind of accusation had been made by the German Government of breaches of neutrality, Hitler issued a directive for the conduct of the war. And he said this:

"1) If it becomes evident in the near future that England and France, acting under her leadership, are not disposed to end the war, I am determined to take firm and offensive action without letting much time elapse.

"2) A long waiting period results not only in the ending of Belgian and perhaps also of Dutch neutrality to the advantage of the Western Powers, but also strengthens the military power of our enemies to an increasing degree, causes confidence of the neutrals in final German victory to wane, and does not help to bring Italy to our aid as brothers-in-arms.

"3) I therefore issue the following orders for the further conduct of military operations:

"(a) Preparations should be made for offensive action on the northern flank of the Western Front crossing the area of Luxembourg, Belgium, and Holland. This attack must be carried out as soon and as forcefully as possible.

"(b) The object of this attack is to defeat as many strong sections of the French fighting army as possible, and her ally and partner in the fighting, and at the same time to acquire as great an area of Holland, Belgium, and northern France as possible, to use as a base offering good prospects for waging aerial and sea warfare against England and to provide ample coverage for the vital district of the Ruhr."

Nothing could state more clearly or more definitely the object behind the invasion of these three countries than that document expresses it.

On the 15th of October 1939 the Defendant Keitel wrote a most secret letter concerning "Fall Gelb" which was the name given to the operation against the Low Countries. In it he said that:

"The protection of the Ruhr area by moving aircraft reporting service and the air defense as far forward as possible in the area of Holland is significant for the whole conduct of the war. The more Dutch territory we occupy, the more effective can the defense of the Ruhr area be made. This point of view must determine the choice of objectives of the Army, even if the Army and Navy are not directly interested in such territorial gain. It must be the object of the Army's preparations, therefore, to occupy, on receipt of a special order, the territory of Holland, in the first instance in the area of the Grebbe-Maas line. It will depend on the military and political attitude of the Dutch, as well as on the effectiveness of their flooding, whether objectives can and must be further extended."

The Fall Gelb operation had apparently been planned to take place at the beginning of November 1939. We have in our possession a series of 17 letters, dated from 7th November until the 9th May postponing almost from day to day the D-Day of the operation, so that by the beginning of November all the major plans and preparations had in fact been made.

On the 10th of January 1940 a German airplane force-landed in Belgium. In it was found the remains of an operation order which the pilot had attempted to burn; setting out considerable details of the Belgian landing grounds that were to be captured by the Air Force. Many other documents have been found which illustrate the planning and preparation for this invasion in the latter half of 1939 and early 1940, but they carry the matter no further, and they show no more clearly than the evidence to which I have already referred, the plans and intention of the German Government and its Armed Forces.

On the 10th of May 1940 at about 0500 hours in the morning, the German invasion of Belgium, Holland, and Luxembourg began.

And so once more the forces of aggression moved on. Treaties, assurances, the rights of sovereign states meant nothing. Brutal force, covered by as great an element of surprise as the Nazis could secure, was to seize that which was deemed necessary for striking the mortal blow against England, the main

84

enemy. The only fault of these three unhappy countries was that they stood in the path of the German invader, in his designs against England and France. That was enough, and they were invaded.

[A recess was taken.]

SIR HARTLEY SHAWCROSS: On the 6th of April 1941 German Armed Forces invaded Greece and Yugoslavia. Again the blow was struck without warning and with the cowardice and deceit which the world now fully expected from the self-styled "Herrenvolk". It was a breach of the Hague Convention. It was a breach of the Pact of Paris. It was a breach of a specific assurance given by Hitler on the 6th of October 1939.

He had then said this:

"Immediately after the completion of the Anschluss, I informed Yugoslavia that from now on the frontier with this country will also be an unalterable one and that we desire only to live in peace and friendship with her."

But the plan for aggression against Yugoslavia had, of course, been in hand well before that. In the aggressive action eastward towards the Ukraine and the Soviet territories, security of the southern flank and the lines of communication had already been considered by the Germans.

The history of the events leading up to the invasion of Yugoslavia by Germany is well known. At 3 o'clock in the morning of the 28th of October 1940 a 3-hour ultimatum had been presented by the Italian Government to the Greek Government, and the presentation of that ultimatum was immediately followed by the aerial bombardment of Greek provincial towns and the advance of Italian troops into Greek territory. The Greeks were not prepared. They were at first forced to withdraw. But later the Italian advance was at first checked, then driven towards the Albanian frontier, and by the end of 1940 the Italian Army had suffered severe reverses at Greek hands.

Of the German position in the matter there is, of course, the evidence of what occurred when, on the 12th of August 1939, Hitler had this meeting with Ciano.

You will remember that Hitler said then:

"Generally speaking, the best thing to happen would be to liquidate false neutrals one after the other. This process could be carried out more easily if, on every occasion, one partner of the Axis covered the other while it was dealing with an uncertain neutral. Italy might well regard Yugoslavia as a neutral of this kind."

Then the conference went on and it met again on the 13th of August, and in the course of lengthy discussions, Hitler said this:

"In general, however, on success by one of the Axis partners, not only strategical but also psychological strengthening of the other partner and also of the whole Axis would ensue. Italy carried through a number of successful operations in Abyssinia, Spain, and Albania, and each time against the wishes of the democratic entente. These individual actions have not only strengthened Italian local interests, but have also ... reinforced her general position. The same was the case with German action in Austria and Czechoslovakia .... The strengthening of the Axis by these individual operations was of the greatest importance for the unavoidable clash with the Western Powers."

85

And so once again we see the same procedure being followed. That meeting had taken place on the 12th and the 13th of August of 1939. Less than 2 months later, Hitler was giving his assurance to Yugoslavia that Germany only desired to live in peace and friendship with her, with the state, the liquidation of which by his Axis partner, he had himself so recently suggested.

Then came the Italian ultimatum to Greece and war against Greece and the Italian reverse.

We have found, amongst the captured documents, an undated letter from Hitler to Mussolini which must have been written about the time of the Italian aggression against Greece:

"Permit me' -Hitler said- "at the beginning of this letter to assure you that within the last 14 days my heart and my thoughts have been more than ever with you. Moreover, Duce, be assured of my determination to do everything on your behalf which might ease the present situation for you. When I asked you to receive me in Florence, I undertook the trip in the hope of being able to express my views prior to the beginning of the threatening conflict with Greece, about which I had received only general information. First, I wanted to request you to postpone the action, if at all possible, until a more favorable time of the year, at all events until after the American presidential election. But in any case, however, I wanted to request you, Duce, not to undertake this action without a previous lightning-like occupation of Crete and, for this purpose, I also wanted to submit to you some practical suggestions in regard to the employment of a German parachute division and a further airborne division ... Yugoslavia must become disinterested, if possible, however, from our point of view, interested in co-operating in the liquidation of the Greek question. Without assurances from Yugoslavia, it is useless to risk any successful operation in the Balkans. . . Unfortunately, I must stress the fact that waging a war in the Balkans before March is impossible. Hence it would also serve to make any threatening influence upon Yugoslavia of no purpose, since the Serbian General Staff is well aware of the fact that no practical action could follow such a threat before March. Hence, Yugoslavia must, if at all possible, be won over by other means and in other ways."

On the 12th of November 1939, in his top-secret order, Hitler ordered the OKH to make preparations to occupy Greece and Bulgaria, if necessary. Apparently 10 divisions were to be used in order to prevent Turkish intervention. I think I said 1939; it should, of course, have been the 12th of November 1940. And to shorten the time, the German divisions in Romania were to be increased.

On the 13th of December Hitler issued an order to OKW, OKL, OKH, OKM, and the General Staff on the operation Marita, as the invasion of Greece was to be called. In that order it was stated that the invasion of Greece was planned and was to commence as soon as the weather was advantageous. A further order was issued on the 11th of January of 1941.

On the 28th of January of 1941 Hitler saw Mussolini. The Defendants Jodl, Keitel, and Ribbentrop were present at the meeting. We know about it from Jodl's notes of what took place. We know that Hitler stated that one of the purposes of German troop concentrations in Romania was for use in the plan

Marita against Greece.

On the 1st of March 1941 German troops entered Bulgaria and moved towards the Greek frontier. In the face of this threat of an attack on Greece by German as well as Italian forces, British troops were landed in Greece on the 3rd of March, in accordance with the declaration which had been given by the British Government on the 13th of April 1939; that Britain would feel bound to give Greece and Romania, respectively, all the support in her power in the event of either country becoming the victim of aggression and resisting such aggression. Already, of course, the Italian operations had made that pledge operative.

On the 25th of March of 1941, Yugoslavia, partly won over by the "other means and in other ways" to which Hitler had referred, joined the Three Power Pact which had already been signed by Germany, Italy, and Japan. The preamble of the pact stated that the three powers would stand side by side and work together.

On the same day the Defendant Ribbentrop wrote two notes to the Yugoslav Prime Minister assuring him of Germany's full intention to respect the sovereignty and independence of his country. That declaration was just another example of the treachery employed by German diplomacy. We have already seen the preparations that had been made. We have seen Hitler's attempts to tempt the Italians into an aggression against Yugoslavia. We have seen, in January, his own orders for preparations to invade Yugoslavia and then Greece. And now, on the 25th of March, he is signing a pact with that country and his Foreign Minister is writing assurances of respect for her sovereignty and territorial integrity.

As a result of the signing of that pact, the anti-Nazi element in Yugoslavia immediately accomplished a coup d'etat and established a new government. And thereupon, no longer prepared to respect the territorial integrity and sovereignty of her ally, Germany immediately took the decision to invade. On the 27th of March, 2 days after the Three Power Pact had been signed, Hitler issued instructions that Yugoslavia was to be invaded and used as a base for the continuance of the combined German and Italian operation against Greece.

Following that, further deployment and instructions for the action Marita were issued by Von Brauchitsch on the 30th of March 1941.

It was said- and I quote:

"The orders issued with regard to the operation against Greece remain valid so far as not affected by this order.... On the 5th April, weather permitting, the Air Forces are to attack troops in Yugoslavia, while simultaneously the attack of the 12th Army begins against both Yugoslavia and Greece."

And as we now know, the invasion actually commenced in the early hours of the 6th of April.

Treaties, pacts, assurances, obligations of any kind, are brushed aside and ignored wherever the aggressive interests of Germany are concerned.

I turn now to the last act of aggression in Europe-my American colleagues will deal with the position in relation to Japan-I turn now to the last act of aggression in Europe with which these Nazi conspirators are charged, the attack upon Russia.

In August of 1939 Germany, although undoubtedly intending to attack Russia at some convenient opportunity, concluded a treaty of non-aggression with the Union of Soviet Socialist Republics. When Belgium and the Low Countries were occupied and France collapsed in June of 1940, England-although with the inestimably valuable moral and economic support of the United States of America-was left alone in the field as the sole representative of democracy in the face of the forces of aggression. At that moment only the British Empire stood between Germany and the achievement of her aim to dominate the Western World. Only the British Empire- and England as its citadel. But it was enough. The first, and possibly the decisive, military defeat which the enemy sustained was in the campaign against England; and that defeat had a profound influence on the future course of the war.

On the 16th of July of 1940 Hitler issued to the Defendants Keitel and Jodl a directive-which they found themselves unable to obey-for the invasion of England. It started off- and Englishmen will forever be proud of it-by saying that:

> "Since England, despite her militarily hopeless situation, shows no signs of willingness to come to terms, I have decided to prepare a landing operation against England and if necessary to carry it out. The aim is... to eliminate the English homeland as a base for the carrying on of the war against Germany .... Preparations for the entire operation must be completed by mid-August."

But the first essential condition for that plan was, I quote: "... the British Air Force must morally and actually be so far overcome that it does not any longer show any considerable aggressive force against the German attack."

The Defendant Goering and his Air Force, no doubt, made the most strenuous efforts to realize that condition, but, in one of the most splendid pages of our history, it was decisively defeated. And although the bombardment of England's towns and villages was continued throughout that dark winter of 1940-41, the enemy decided in the end that England was not to be subjugated by these means, and, accordingly, Germany turned back to the East, the first major aim unachieved.

On the 22d of June 1941 German Armed Forces invaded Russia, without warning, without declaration of war. It was, of course, a breach of the usual series of treaties; they meant no more in this case than they had meant in the other cases. It was a violation of the Pact of Paris it was a flagrant contradiction of the Treaty of Non-Aggression which Germany and Russia had signed on the 23rd of August a year before.

Hitler himself said, in referring to that agreement, that "agreements were only to be kept as long as they served a purpose."

The Defendant Ribbentrop was more explicit. In an interview with the Japanese Ambassador in Berlin on the 23rd of February 1941, he made it clear that the object of the agreement had merely been, so far as Germany was concerned, to avoid a two-front war.

In contrast to what Hitler and Ribbentrop and the rest of them were planning within the secret councils of Germany, we know what they were saying to the rest of the world.

On the 19th of July, Hitler spoke in the Reichstag:

> "In these circumstances" -he said- "I considered it proper to negotiate as a first priority a sober definition of interest with Russia. It would be made clear once and for all what Germany believes she must regard as her sphere of interest to safeguard her future and, on the other hand,

what Russia considers important for her existence. From this clear delineation of the sphere of interest there followed the new regulation of Russian-German relations. Any hope that now, at the end of the term of the agreement, a new Russo-German tension could arise is childish. Germany has taken no step which would lead her outside her sphere of interest, nor has Russia. But England's hope to achieve an amelioration of her own position through the engineering of some new European crisis, is, insofar as it is concerned with Russo-German relations, an illusion.

"English statesmen perceive everything somewhat slowly, but they too will learn to understand this in the course of time."

The whole statement was, of course, a tissue of lies. It was not many months after it had been made that the arrangements for attacking Russia were put into hand. And the Defendant Raeder gives us the probable reason for the decision in a note which he sent to Admiral Assmann:

"The fear that control of the air over the Channel in the Autumn of 1940 could no longer be attained, a realization which the Fuehrer no doubt gained earlier than the Naval War Staff, who were not so fully informed of the true results of air raids on England (our own losses), surely caused the Fuehrer, as far back as August and September" -this was August and September of 1940- "to consider whether, even prior to victory in the West, an Eastern campaign would be feasible, with the object of first eliminating our last serious opponent on the Continent .... The Fuehrer did not openly express this fear, however, until well into September."

He may not have spoken to the Navy of his intentions until later in September, but by the beginning of that month he had undoubtedly told the Defendant Jodl about them.

Dated the 6th of September 1940, we have a directive of the OKW signed by the Defendant Jodl, and I quote:

"Directions are given for the occupation forces in the East to be increased in the following weeks. For security reasons" - and I quote - "this should not create the impression in Russia that Germany is preparing for an Eastern offensive."

Directives are given to the German Intelligence Service pertaining to the answering of questions by the Russian Intelligence Service, and I quote:

"The respective strength of the German troops in the East is to be camouflaged by ... frequent changes in this area .... The impression is to be created that the bulk of the troops is in the south of the Government General and that the occupation in the North is relatively small."

And so we see the beginning of the operations.

On the 12th of November 1940 Hitler issued a directive, signed by the Defendant Jodl, in which it was stated that the political task to determine the attitude of Russia had begun, but that without reference to the result of preparations against the East, which had been ordered orally.

It is not to be supposed that the U.S.S.R. would have taken part in any conversations at that time if it had been realized that on the very day orders were being given for preparations to be made for the invasion of Russia, and that the order for the operation, which was called "Plan Barbarossa", was in active preparation. On the 18th of December the order was issued, and I quote:

> "The German Armed Forces have to be ready to defeat Soviet Russia in a swift campaign before the end of the war against Great Britain."

And later, in the same instruction- and I quote again:

> "All orders which shall be issued by the High Commanders in accordance with this instruction have to be clothed in such terms that they may be taken as measures of precaution in case Russia should change her present attitude towards ourselves."

Germany kept up the pretense of friendliness and, on the 10th of January 1941, well after the Plan Barbarossa for the invasion of Russia had been decided upon, Germany signed the German-Russian Frontier Treaty. Less than a month later, on the 3rd of February of 1941, Hitler held a conference, attended by the Defendants Keitel and Jodl, at which it was provided that the whole operation against Russia was to be camouflaged as if it was part of the preparation for the "Plan Seelowe", as the plan for the invasion of England was described.

By March of 1941 plans were sufficiently advanced to include provision for dividing the Russian territory into nine separate states to be administered under Reich Commissars, under the general control of the Defendant Rosenberg; and at the same time detailed plans for the economic exploitation of the country were made under the supervision of the Defendant Goering, to whom the responsibility in this matter- and it is a serious one-had been delegated by Hitler.

You will hear something of the details of these plans. I remind you of one document which has already been referred to in this connection.

It is significant that on the 2d of May of 1941 a conference of State Secretaries took place in regard to the Plan Barbarossa, and in the course of that it was noted:

> "1. The war can be continued only if all Armed Forces are fed out of Russia in the third year of the war.
>
> "2. There is no doubt that, as a result, many millions of people will be starved to death if we take out of the country the things necessary for us."

But that apparently caused no concern. The "Plan Oldenbourg", as the scheme for the economic organization and exploitation of

Russia was called, went on. By the 1st of May 1941, the D-Day of the operation had been fixed. By the 1st of June preparations were virtually complete and an elaborate timetable was issued. It was estimated that, although there would be heavy frontier battles, lasting perhaps 4 weeks, after that no serious opposition was to be expected.

On the 22d of June, at 3:30 in the morning, the German armies marched again. As Hitler said in his proclamation to them, "I have decided to give the fate of the German people and of the Reich and of Europe again into the hands of our soldiers."

The usual false pretexts were, of course, given. Ribbentrop stated on the 28th of June that the step was taken because of the threatening of the German frontiers by the Red Army. It was a lie, and the Defendant Ribbentrop knew it was a lie.

On the 7th of June 1941 Ribbentrop's own Ambassador in Moscow was reporting to him, and I quote, that, "All observations show that Stalin and Molotov, who are alone responsible for Russian foreign policy, are doing everything to avoid a conflict with Germany." The staff records which you will see make it clear that the Russians were making no military preparations and that they were continuing their deliveries under the Trade Agreement to the very last day. The truth is, of course, that the elimination of Russia as a political opponent and the incorporation of the Soviet territory in the German Lebensraum had been one of the cardinal features of Nazi policy for a very long time, subordinated latterly for what the Defendant Jodl called diplomatic reasons.

And so, on the 22d of June, the Nazi armies were flung against the power with which Hitler had so recently sworn friendship, and Germany embarked upon that last act of aggression in Europe, which, after long and bitter fighting, was eventually to result in Germany's own collapse.

That, then, is the case against these defendants, as amongst the rulers of Germany, under Count Two of this Indictment.

It may be said that many of the documents which have been referred to were in Hitler's name, and that the orders were Hitler's orders, and that these men were mere instruments of Hitler's will. But they were the instruments without which Hitler's will could not be carried out; and they were more than that. These men were no mere willing tools, although they would be guilty enough if that had been their role. They are the men whose support had built Hitler up into the position of power he occupied; these are the men whose initiative and planning often conceived and certainly made possible the acts of aggression done in Hitler's name; and these are the men who enabled Hitler to build up the Army, the Navy, the Air Force, the war economy, the political philosophy, by which these treacherous attacks were carried out, and by which he was able to lead his fanatical followers into peaceful countries to murder, to loot, and to destroy. They are the men whose cooperation and support made the Nazi Government of Germany possible.

The government of a totalitarian country may be carried on without representatives of the people, but it cannot be carried on without any assistance at all. It is no use having a leader unless there are also people willing and ready to serve their personal greed and ambition by helping and following him. The dictator who is set up in control of the destinies of his country does not depend on himself alone either in acquiring power or in maintaining it. He depends upon the support and the backing which lesser men, themselves lusting to share in dictatorial power, anxious to bask in the adulation of their leader, are prepared to give.

In the criminal courts of our countries, when men are put on their trial for breaches of the municipal laws, it not infrequently happens that of a gang indicted together in the dock, one has the master mind, the leading personality. But it is no excuse for the common thief to say, "I stole because I was told to steal", for the murderer to plead, "I killed because I was asked to kill." And these men are in no different position, for all that it was nations they sought to rob, and whole peoples which they tried to kill. "The warrant of no man excuseth the doing of an illegal act." Political loyalty, military obedience are excellent things, but they neither require nor do they justify the commission of patently wicked acts. There comes a point where a man must refuse to answer to his leader if he is also to answer to his conscience. Even the common soldier, serving in the ranks of his army, is not called upon to obey illegal orders. But these men were no common soldiers: They were the men whose skill and cunning, whose labor and activity made it possible for the German Reich to tear up existing treaties, to enter into new ones and to flout them, to reduce international negotiations and diplomacy to a hollow mockery, to destroy all respect for and effect in international law and, finally, to march against the peoples of the world to secure that domination in which, as arrogant members of their self-styled master race, they professed to believe. If these crimes were in one sense the crimes of Nazi Germany, they also are guilty as the individuals who aided, abetted, counselled, procured, and made possible the commission of what was done.

The total sum of the crime these men have committed-so awful in its comprehension-has many aspects. Their lust and sadism, their deliberate slaughter and degradation of so many millions of their fellow creatures that the imagination reels, are but one side of this matter. Now that an end has been put to this nightmare, and we come to consider how the future is to be lived, perhaps their guilt as murderers and robbers is of less importance and of less effect to future generations of mankind than their crime of fraud-the fraud by which they placed themselves in a position to do their murder and their robbery. That is the other aspect of their guilt. The story of their "diplomacy", founded upon cunning, hypocrisy, and bad faith, is a story less gruesome no doubt, but no less evil and deliberate. And should it be taken as a precedent of behavior in the conduct of international relations, its consequences to mankind will no less certainly lead to the end of civilized society.

Without trust and confidence between nations, without the faith that what is said is meant and that what is undertaken will be observed, all hope of peace and security is dead. The Governments of the United Kingdom and the British Commonwealth, of the United States of America, of the Union of Soviet Socialist Republics, and of France, backed by and on behalf of every other peace-loving nation of the world, have therefore joined to bring the inventors and perpetrators of this Nazi conception of international relationship before the bar of this Tribunal. They do so, so that these defendants may be punished for their crimes. They do so, also, that their conduct may be exposed in all its naked wickedness and they do so in the hope that the conscience and good sense of all the world will see the consequences of such conduct and the end to which inevitably it must always lead. Let us once again restore sanity and with it also the sanctity of our obligations towards each other.

THE PRESIDENT: Mr. Attorney, would it be convenient to the prosecutors from Great Britain to continue?

SIR HARTLEY SHAWCROSS: The proposal was that my friend, Mr. Sidney Alderman, should continue with the presentation of the case with regard to the final acts of aggression against Czechoslovakia and that that being done, my British colleagues would continue with the presentation of the British case. As the Tribunal will appreciate, Counts One and Two are in many respects complementary, and my American colleagues and ourselves are working in closest cooperation in presenting the evidence affecting those counts.

THE PRESIDENT: Mr. Alderman, would it be convenient for you to go on until 5 o'clock?

MR. ALDERMAN: Yes. May it please the Tribunal, it is quite convenient for me to proceed. I can but feel that it will be quite anticlimactic after the address which you just heard.

When the Tribunal rose yesterday afternoon, I had just completed an outline of the plans laid by the Nazi conspirators in the weeks immediately following the Munich Agreement. These plans called for what the German officials called "the liquidation of the remainder of Czechoslovakia." You will recall that 3 weeks after Munich, on 21 October, the same day on which the administration of the Sudetenland was handed over to the civilian authorities, Hitler and Keitel had issued an order to the Armed Forces. This document is C-136, Exhibit USA-104.

In this order Hitler and Keitel ordered the beginning of preparations by the Armed Forces for the conquest of the remainder of Czechoslovakia. You will also recall that 2 months later, on 17 December, the Defendant Keitel issued an appendix to the original order directing the continuation of these preparations. This document is C-138, Exhibit USA-105, and both these documents have already been introduced.

Proceeding on the assumption that no resistance worth mentioning was to be expected, this order emphasized that the attack on Czechoslovakia was to be well camouflaged so that it would not appear to be a warlike action. "To the outside world," it said, and I quote, "it must appear obvious that it is merely an action of pacification and not a warlike undertaking."

Thus, in the beginning of 1939 the basic planning for military action against the mutilated Czechoslovak Republic had already been carried out by the German High Command.

I turn now to the underhand and criminal methods used by the Nazi conspirators to ensure that no resistance worth mentioning would, in fact, be met by the German Army. As in the case of Austria and the Sudetenland, the Nazi conspirators did not intend to rely on the Wehrmacht alone to accomplish their calculated objective of liquidating Czechoslovakia. With the German minority separated from Czechoslovakia, they could no longer use the cry, "Home to the Reich." One sizable minority, the Slovaks, still remained within the Czechoslovak state.

I should mention at this point that the Czechoslovak Government had made every effort to conciliate Slovak extremists in the months after the cession of the Sudetenland. Autonomy had been granted to Slovakia, with an autonomous Cabinet and Parliament at Bratislava. Nevertheless, despite these concessions, it was in Slovakia that the Nazi conspirators found fertile ground for their tactics. The picture which I shall now draw of Nazi operations in Slovakia is based on the Czechoslovak official Government Report, Document Number 998-PS, already admitted in evidence as Exhibit USA-91, and of which the Court has already taken judicial notice.

Nazi propaganda and research groups had long been interested in maintaining close connection with the Slovak autonomist opposition. When Bela Tuka, who later became Prime Minister of the puppet state of Slovakia, was tried for espionage and treason in 1929, the evidence established that he had already established connections with Nazi groups within Germany. Prior to 1938 Nazi aides were in close contact with the Slovak traitors living in exile and were attempting to establish more profitable contacts in the semi-fascist Slovak Catholic People's Party of Monsignor Andrew Hlinka. In February and July 1938 the leaders of the Henlein movement conferred with top men of Father Hlinka's party and agreed to furnish one another with mutual assistance in pressing their respective claims to autonomy. This understanding proved useful in the September agitation when at the proper moment the Foreign Office in Berlin wired the Henlein leader, Kundt, in Prague to tell the Slovaks to start their demands for autonomy.

This telegram, our Document Number 2858-PS, Exhibit USA-97, has already been introduced in evidence and read.

By this time-midsummer 1938-the Nazis were in direct contact with figures in the Slovak autonomist movement and had paid agents among the higher staff of Father Hlinka's party. These agents undertook to render impossible any understanding between the Slovak autonomists and the Slovak parties in the government at Prague.

Hans Karmasin, later to become Volksgruppenfuehrer, had been appointed Nazi leader in Slovakia and professed to be serving the cause of Slovak autonomy while actually on the Nazi payroll. On 22 November the Nazis indiscreetly wired Karmasin to collect his money at the German Legation in Prague, and I offer in evidence Document 2859-PS as Exhibit USA-107, captured from the German Foreign Office files. I read this telegram which was sent from the German Legation at Prague to Pressburg:

"Delegate Kundt asks to notify State Secretary Karmasin he would appreciate it if he could personally draw the sum which is being kept for him at the treasury of the Embassy." - signed - "Hencke"

Karmasin proved to be extremely useful to the Nazi cause. Although it is out of its chronological place in my discussion, I should like now to offer in evidence Document 2794-PS, a captured memorandum of the German Foreign Office which I offer as Exhibit USA-108, dated Berlin, 29 November 1939.

This document, dated 8 months after the conquest of Czechoslovakia, throws a revealing light both on Karmasin and on the German Foreign Office, and I now read from this memorandum:

"On the question of payments to Karmasin.

"Karmasin receives 30,000 marks monthly from the VDA "Peoples' League for Germans Abroad- "until 1 April 1940; from then on 15,000 marks monthly.

"Furthermore, the Central Office for Racial Germans" -Volksdeutsche Mittelstelle- "has deposited 300,000 marks for Karmasin with the German Mission in Bratislava" -Pressburg- "on which he could fall back in an emergency.

"Furthermore, Karmasin has received money from Reich Minister Seyss-Inquart; for the present it has been impossible to determine what amounts had been involved, and whether the payments still continue.

"Therefore, it appears that Karmasin has been provided with sufficient money; thus one could wait to determine whether he would put up new demands himself.

"Herewith presented to the Reich Foreign Minister." - signed - "Woermann."

This document shows the complicity of the German Foreign Office in the subsidization of illegal organizations abroad. More important, it shows that the Germans still considered it necessary to supply their undercover representatives in Pressburg with substantial funds, even after the declaration of the so-called Independent State of Slovakia.

Sometime in the winter of 1938-39, the Defendant Goering conferred with Durkansky and Mach, two leaders in the Slovak extremist group, who were accompanied by Karmasin. The Slovaks told Goering of their desire for what they called independence, with strong political, economic, and military ties to Germany. They promised that the Jewish problem would be solved as it had been solved in Germany; that the Communist Party would be prohibited. The notes of the meeting report that Goering considered that the Slovak efforts towards independence were to be supported, but as the document will show, his motives were scarcely altruistic.

I now offer in evidence Document 2301-PS as Exhibit USA-109, undated minutes of a conversation between Goering and Durkansky. This document was captured among the files of the German Foreign Office.

I now read these minutes, which are jotted down in somewhat telegraphic style. To begin with:

"Durkansky (Deputy Prime Minister) reads out declaration. Contents: 'Friendship for the Fuehrer; gratitude, that through the Fuehrer, autonomy has become possible for the Slovaks: The Slovaks never want to belong to Hungary. The Slovaks want full independence with strongest political, economic, and military ties to Germany. Bratislava to be the capital. The execution of the plan only possible if the army and police are Slovak.

"An independent Slovakia to be proclaimed at the meeting of the first Slovak Diet. In the case of a plebiscite the majority would favor a separation from Prague. Jews will vote for Hungary. The area of the plebiscite to be up to the March, where a large Slovak population lives.

"The Jewish problem will be solved similarly to that in Germany. The Communist Party to be prohibited.

"The Germans in Slovakia do not want to belong to Hungary but wish to stay in Slovakia.

"The German influence with the Slovak Government considerable; the appointment of a German Minister (member of the Cabinet) has been promised.

"At present negotiations with Hungary are being conducted by the Slovaks. The Czechs are more yielding towards the Hungarians than the Slovaks.

"The Field Marshal" -that is Field Marshal Goering- "considers that the Slovak negotiations towards independence are to be supported in a suitable manner. Czechoslovakia without Slovakia is still more at our mercy.

"Air bases in Slovakia are of great importance for the German Air Force for use against the East."

On 12 February a Slovak delegation journeyed to Berlin. It consisted of Tuka, one of the Slovaks with whom the Germans had been in contact, and Karmasin, the paid representative of the Nazi conspirators in Slovakia. They conferred with Hitler and the Defendant Ribbentrop in the Reich Chancellery in Berlin on Sunday, 12 February 1939.

I now offer in evidence Document 2790-PS as Exhibit USA-110, the captured German Foreign Office minutes of that meeting:

"After a brief welcome Tuka thanks the Fuehrer for granting this meeting. He addresses the Fuehrer with 'My Fuehrer' and he voices the opinion that he, though only a modest man himself, might well claim to speak for the Slovak nation. The Czech courts and prison gave him the right to make such a statement. He states that the Fuehrer had not only opened the Slovak question but that he had been also the first one to acknowledge the dignity of the Slovak nation. The Slovakian people will gladly fight under the leadership of the Fuehrer for the maintenance of European civilization. Obviously future association with the Czechs had become an impossibility for the Slovaks from a moral as well as an economic point of view."

Then skipping to the last sentence: " 'I entrust the fate of my people to your care." - addressing that to the Fuehrer!

During the meeting the Nazi conspirators apparently were successful in planting the idea of insurrection with the Slovak delegation. I refer to the final sentence of the document, which I have just read, the sentence spoken by Tuka, "I entrust the fate of my people to your care."

It is apparent from these documents that in mid-February 1939 the Nazis had a well-disciplined group of Slovaks at their service, many of them drawn from the ranks of Father Hlinka's party. Flattered by the personal attention of such men as Hitler and the Defendant Ribbentrop and subsidized by German representatives, these Slovaks proved willing tools in the hands of the Nazi conspirators.

In addition to Slovaks, the conspirators made use of the few Germans still remaining within the mutilated Czechoslovak Republic. Kundt, Henlein's deputy who had been appointed leader of this German minority, created as many artificial "focal points of German culture" as possible. Germans from the districts handed over to Germany were ordered from Berlin to continue their studies at the German University in Prague and to make it a center of aggressive Nazism.

With the assistance of German civil servants, a deliberate campaign of Nazi infiltration into Czech public and private institutions was carried out, and the Henleindists gave full co-operation to Gestapo agents from the Reich who appeared on Czech soil. The Nazi political activity was designed to undermine and to weaken Czech resistance to the commands from Germany.

In the face of continued threats and duress on both diplomatic and propaganda levels, the Czech Government was unable to take adequate measures against these trespassers upon its sovereignty.

I am using as the basis of my remarks the Czechoslovak official Government report, Document Number 998-PS.

In early March, with the date for the final march into Czechoslovakia already close at hand, Fifth Column activity moved into its final phase. In Bohemia and Moravia the FS, Henlein's equivalent of the SS, were in touch with the Nazi conspirators in the Reich and laid the groundwork of the events of 14 and 15 March.

I now offer in evidence Document 2826-PS as Exhibit USA-lll. This is an article by SS Group Leader Karl Hermann Frank, published in the publication Boehmen and Maehren, the official periodical of the Reich Protector of Bohemia and Moravia, edition May 1941, Page 179.

This is an article written by one of the Nazi leaders in Czechoslovakia at the moment of Germany's greatest military successes. It is a boastful article and reveals with a frankness rarely found in the Nazi press both the functions which the FS and the SS served and the pride the Nazi conspirators took in the activities of these organizations. It is a long quotation.

THE PRESIDENT: Are you going on with this tomorrow, Mr. Alderman?

MR. ALDERMAN: Yes.

THE PRESIDENT: Will you take the whole day?

MR. ALDERMAN: No, not more than an hour and a half.

THE PRESIDENT: And after that the British prosecutors will go on?

MR. ALDERMAN: Yes.

[The Tribunal adjourned until 5 December 1945 at 1000 hours.]

Thirteenth Day:
Wednesday, 5th December, 1945

MR. ALDERMAN: May it please the Tribunal: When the Tribunal rose yesterday afternoon, I had just offered in evidence Document 2826-PS, Exhibit USA 111. This was an article by S.S. Group Leader Karl Hermann Frank, published in Bohmen und Mahren, or Bohemia and Moravia, the official periodical of the Reich Protector of Bohemia and Moravia, the issue of March, 1941, at Page 79. It is an article which reveals with considerable frankness the functions which the F. S. and the S. S. had, and shows the pride which the Nazi conspirators took in the activities of these organisations. I read from that article, under the heading "The S.S. on 15th March, 1939":

"A modern people and a modern State are today unthinkable without political troops. To these are allotted the special task of being the advance guard of the political will and the guarantor of its unity. This is especially true of the German folk-groups, which have their home in some other people's State. Accordingly the Sudeten German Party had formerly also organised its political troop, the "Voluntary Vigilantes" or, in German, "Freiwilliger Selbstschutz " called F.S. for short. This troop was trained especially in accordance with the principles of the S.S., so far as these could be used in this region at that time. The troop was likewise assigned here the special task of protecting the homeland actively, if necessary. It stood up well in its first test in this connection, whenever, in the autumn crisis of 1938, it had to assist in the protection of the homeland, arms in hand.

After the annexation of the Sudeten Gau, the tasks of the F.S. were transferred essentially to the German student organisations as compact troop formations in Prague and Brunn, apart from the isolated German communities which remained in the Second Republic. This was also natural because many students from the Sudeten Gau were already active members of the S.S. The student organisations then had to endure this test, in common with other Germans, during the crisis of March, 1939.

In the early morning hours of 15th March, after the announcement of the planned entry of German troops into various localities, German men had to act in some localities in order to assure a quiet course of events, either by assumption of the police authority, as for instance in Brunn, or by corresponding instruction of the police president. In some Czech offices, men had likewise, in the early hours of the morning, begun to burn valuable archives and the material of political files. It was also necessary to take measures here in order to prevent foolish destruction. How significant the many-sided and comprehensive measures were considered by the competent German agencies, follows from the fact that many of the men either on 15th March itself or on the following days were admitted into the S.S. with fitting acknowledgement, in part even through the Reich leader of the S.S. himself or through S.S. Group Leader Heydrich. The activities and deeds of these men were thereby designated as accomplished in the interest of the S.S.

Immediately after the corresponding divisions of the S.S. had marched in with the first columns of the German Army and had assumed responsibility in the appropriate sectors, the men here placed themselves at once at their further disposition, and became valuable auxiliaries and collaborators.

I now ask the Court to take judicial notice, under Article 21 of the Charter, of three official documents. These are identified by us as Documents D-571, D-572 and 2943-PS. I offer them in evidence, respectively, D-571 Exhibit USA 112; D-572 as Exhibit USA 113; and 2943-PS which is the French Official Yellow Book, at Pages 66 and 67, as Exhibit USA 114.

THE PRESIDENT: Have you cited 572?

MR. ALDERMAN: D-572 was Exhibit USA 113. The first two documents are British diplomatic dispatches, properly certified to by the British Government, which give the background of intrigue in Slovakia - German intrigue in Slovakia. The third Document, 2943-PS or Exhibit USA 114, consists of excerpts from the French Yellow Book, principally excerpts from dispatches signed by M. Coulondre, the French Ambassador in Berlin, to the French Foreign Office, between 13th and 18th March, 1939. I expect to draw on these three dispatches rather freely in the further course of my presentation, since the Tribunal will take judicial notice of each of these documents, I think; and, therefore, it may not be necessary to read them at length into the transcript. In Slovakia the long-anticipated crisis came on 10th March. On that day the Czechoslovakian Government dismissed those members of the Slovak cabinet who refused to continue negotiations with Prague, among them Foreign Minister Tiso and Durcansky. Within twenty-four hours the Nazis seized upon this act of the Czechoslovak Government as an excuse for intervention. On the following day, 11th March, a strange scene was enacted in Bratislava, the Slovak capital. I quote from Document D-571, which is Exhibit USA 112. That is the report of the British Minister in Prague to the British Government.

"Herr Burckel, Herr Seyss-Inquart, and five German generals came at about 10 p.m. in the evening of Saturday, the 11th March, into a cabinet meeting in progress in Bratislava, and told the Slovak Government that they should proclaim the independence of Slovakia. When M. Sidor, the Prime Minister, showed hesitation, Herr Burckel took him on one side and explained that Herr Hitler had decided to settle the question of Czechoslovakia definitely. Slovakia ought, therefore, to proclaim her independence, because Herr Hitler would otherwise disinterest himself in her fate. M. Sidor thanked Herr Burckel for this information, but said that he must discuss the situation with the Government at Prague"

- a very strange situation that he should have to discuss such a matter with his own Government before obeying instructions of Herr Hitler delivered by five German generals and Herr Burckel and Herr Seyss-Inquart.

Events went on moving rapidly, but Durcansky, one of the dismissed ministers, escaped with Nazi assistance to Vienna, where the facilities of the German broadcasting station were placed at his disposal. Arms and ammunition were brought from German offices in Engerau across the Danube into Slovakia, where they were used by the F.S. and the Hlinka Guards to create incidents and disorder of the type required by the Nazis as an excuse for military action. The German Press and radio launched a violent campaign against the Czechoslovak Government; and, significantly, an invitation from Berlin was delivered in Bratislava. Tiso, the dismissed Prime Minister, was summoned by Hitler to an audience in the German capital. A plane was awaiting him in Vienna.

At this point, in the second week of March, 1939, preparations for what the Nazi leaders liked to call the liquidation of Czechoslovakia were progressing with what to them must have been very satisfying smoothness. The military, diplomatic and propaganda machinery of the Nazi conspirators was moving in close co-ordination. As during the process of the Fall Grun, or Case Green, of the preceding summer, the Nazi conspirators had invited Hungary to participate in this new attack. Admiral Horthy, the Hungarian Regent, was again greatly flattered by this invitation.

I offer in evidence Document 2816-PS, as Exhibit USA 115. This is a letter which the distinguished Admiral of Hungary - a country which, incidentally, had no navy - wrote to Hitler on 13th March, 1939, and which we captured in the German Foreign Office files.

"Your Excellency,

My sincere thanks,

I can hardly tell you how happy I am because this Head Water Region - I dislike using big words - is of vital importance to the life of Hungary" - I suppose he needed some head waters for the non-existent navy of which he was admiral.

"In spite of the fact that our recruits have been serving for only five weeks we are going into this affair with eager enthusiasm. The dispositions have already been made. On Thursday, the 16th of this month, a frontier incident will take place which will be followed by the big blow on Saturday" - He does not like to use big words. "Big Blow" is sufficient.

"I shall never forget this proof of friendship, and your Excellency may rely on my unshakeable gratitude at all times.

Your devoted friend,

HORTHY".

From this cynical and callous letter from the distinguished Admiral -

THE PRESIDENT: Was that letter addressed to the Hungarian Ambassador at Berlin ?

MR. ALDERMAN: I thought it was addressed to Hitler, if the President please.

THE PRESIDENT: There are some words at the top which look like a Hungarian name.

MR. ALDERMAN: That is the letter heading. As I understand it, the letter was addressed to Adolf Hitler.

THE PRESIDENT: All right.

MR. ALDERMAN: And I should have said it was - it ended with the -

THE PRESIDENT: Is there anything on the letter which indicates that?

MR. ALDERMAN: Only the fact that it was found in the Berlin Foreign Office, and the wording of the letter and the address, "Your Excellency" we may be drawing a conclusion as to whom it was addressed; but it was found in the Berlin Foreign Office.

From that cynical and callous letter it may be inferred that the Nazi conspirators had already informed the Hungarian Government of their plans for further military action against Czechoslovakia. As it turned out the timetable was advanced somewhat. I would draw the inference that His Excellency, Adolf Hitler, informed his devoted friend Horthy of this change in good time.

On the diplomatic level the defendant Ribbentrop was quite active. On 13th March, the same day on which Horthy wrote his letter, Ribbentrop sent a cautionary telegram to the German minister in Prague outlining the course of conduct he should pursue during the coming diplomatic pressure. I offer in evidence Document 2815-PS as Exhibit USA 116. This is the telegram sent by Ribbentrop to the German Legation in Prague on 13th March.

"Berlin, 13th March, 1939. Prague. Telegram in secret code.

With reference to telephone instructions given by Kordt today, in case you should get any written communication from President Hacha, please do not make any written or verbal comments or take any other action on them, but pass them on here by cipher telegram. Moreover, I must ask you and the other members of the Embassy to make a point of not being available if the Czech Government wants to communicate with you during the next few days.

Signed Ribbentrop."

On the afternoon of 13th March, Tiso, accompanied by Durcansky and Herr Meissner, the local Nazi leader, arrived in Berlin in response to the summons from Hitler to which I have heretofore referred. Late that afternoon Tiso was received by Hitler in his study in the Reich Chancellery and presented with an ultimatum. Two alternatives were given him: either declare the independence of Slovakia or be left without German assistance; or, what were referred to as the mergers of Poland and Hungary. This decision, Hitler said, was not a question of days, but of hours. I now offer in evidence Document 2802-PS as Exhibit USA 117, again a document captured in the German Foreign Office; German Foreign Office minutes of the meeting between Hitler and Tiso on 13th March. I read the bottom paragraph on Page 2 and the top paragraph on Page 3 of the English translation. The first paragraph I shall read is a summary of Hitler's remark. You will note that in the inducements he held out to the Slovaks, Hitler displayed his customary disregard for the truth. I quote:

"Now he had permitted Minister Tiso to come here in order to make this question clear in a very short time. Germany had no interest East of the Carpathian mountains. It was indifferent to him what happened there. The question was whether Slovakia wished to conduct her own affairs or not. He did not wish for anything from Slovakia. He would not pledge his people or even a single soldier to something which was not in any way desired by the Slovak people. He would like to secure final confirmation as to what Slovakia really wished. He did not wish that reproaches should come from Hungary that he was preserving something which did not wish to be preserved at all. He took a liberal view of unrest and demonstration in general, but in this connection unrest was only an outward indication of interior instability. He would not tolerate it and he had for that reason permitted Tiso to come in order to hear his decision. It was not a question of days, but of hours. He bad stated at that time that if Slovakia wished to make herself independent he would support this endeavour and even guarantee it. He would stand by his word so long as Slovakia would make it clear that she wished for independence. If she hesitated or did not wish to dissolve the connection with Prague, he would leave the destiny of Slovakia to the mercy of events, for which he would be no longer responsible. In that case he would only intercede for German interests, and those did not lie East of the Carpathians. Germany had nothing to do with Slovakia. She had never belonged to Germany.

The Fuehrer asked the Reich Foreign Minister (the defendant Ribbentrop) if he had any remarks to add. The Reich Foreign Minister also emphasised for his part the conception that in this case a decision was a question of hours not of days. He showed the Fuehrer a message he had just received which reported Hungarian troop movements on the Slovak frontiers. The Fuehrer read this report, mentioned it to Tiso, and expressed the hope that Slovakia would soon decide clearly for herself."

A most extraordinary interview. Germany had no interest in Slovakia; Slovakia had never belonged to Germany; Tiso was invited there; and this is what happened: those present at that meeting included the defendant Ribbentrop, the defendant Keitel, State Secretary Dietrich, State Secretary Keppler, the German Minister of State Meissner. I invite the attention of the Tribunal to the presence of the defendant Keitel on this occasion as on so many other occasions where purely political measures in furtherance of Nazi aggression were under discussion, and where apparently there was no need for technical military advice.

While in Berlin the Slovaks also conferred separately with the defendant Ribbentrop and with other high Nazi officials. Ribbentrop very solicitously handed Tiso a copy already drafted in Slovak language of the law proclaiming the independence of Slovakia. On the night of the 13th a German plane was conveniently placed at Tiso's disposal to carry him home. On 14th March, pursuant to the wishes of the Nazi conspirators, the diet of Bratislava proclaimed the independence of Slovakia. With Slovak extremists acting at the Nazi bidding in open revolt against the Czechoslovak Government, the Nazi leaders were now in a position to move against Prague. On the evening of the 14th, at the suggestion of the German Legation in Prague, M. Hacha, the President of the Czechoslovak Republic and M. Chvalkowsky, his Foreign Minister, arrived in Berlin. The atmosphere in which they found themselves might be described as somewhat hostile. Since the preceding week-end, the Nazi Press had accused the Czechs of using violence against the Slovaks, and specially against the members of the German minority and citizens of the Reich. Both Press and radio proclaimed that the lives of Germans were in danger. Such a situation was intolerable. It was necessary to smother as quickly as possible the focus of trouble, which Prague had become, in the heart of Europe - these peacemakers.

After midnight on the 15th at 1.15 in the morning, Hacha and Chvalkowsky were ushered into the Reich Chancellery. They found there Adolf Hitler, the defendants Ribbentrop, Goering, and Keitel and other high Nazi officials.

I now offer in evidence Document 2798-PS as Exhibit USA 118. This document is the captured German Foreign Office account of this infamous meeting. It is a long document. Parts of it are so revealing and give so clear a picture of Nazi behaviour and tactics that I should like to read them in full.

It must be remembered that this account of the fateful conference on the night of March 14th-15th comes from German sources, and of course it must be read as an account biased by its source, or as counsel for the defendants said last week "a tendentious account." Nevertheless, even without too much discounting of the report on account of its source, it constitutes a complete condemnation of the Nazis, who by pure and simple international banditry forced the dissolution of Czechoslovakia. And I interpolate to suggest that international banditry has been a crime against International Law for centuries.

I will first read the headings to the minutes. In the English mimeographed version in the document books the time given is an incorrect translation of the original. It should read 0115 to 0215. Conversation between the Fuehrer and Reich Chancellor and the President of Czechoslovakia, Hacha, in the presence of the Reich Foreign Minister, von Ribbentrop, and of the Czechoslovakian Foreign Minister, Chvalkowsky, in the Reich Chancellery on 15th March, 1939, 0115 to 0215 hours. Others present were General Field Marshal Goering, General Keitel, Secretary of the State, von Weizsaecker, Minister of the State, Meissner, Secretary of the State, Dietrich, Counsellor of the Legation, Hewel. Hacha opened the conference. He was conciliatory - even humble, though the President of a sovereign State. He thanked Hitler for receiving him and he said he knew that the fate of Czechoslovakia rested in the Fuehrer's hands. Hitler replied that he regretted that he had been forced to ask Hacha to come to Berlin, particularly because of the great age of the President. Hacha was then, I believe, in his seventies. But this journey, Hitler told the President, could be of great advantage to his country because, and I quote "It was only a matter of hours before Germany would intervene." I quote now from the top of page three of the English translation. You will bear in mind that what I am reading are rough notes or minutes of what Adolf Hitler said - "Czechoslovakia was a matter of indifference to him."

"If Czechoslovakia had kept closer to Germany it would have been an obligation to Germany, but he was glad that he did not have this obligation now. He had no interests whatsoever in the territory East of the little Carpathian Mountains. He did not want to draw the final consequences in the autumn - "

THE PRESIDENT: Mr. Alderman, do you not think you ought to read the last sentence on page two ?

MR. ALDERMAN: Perhaps so; yes. The last sentence from the preceding page was:

"For the other countries Czechoslovakia was nothing but a means to an end. London and Paris were not in a position really to stand up for Czechoslovakia. Czechoslovakia was a matter of indifference to him."

Then I had read down to -

"But even at that time and also later in his conversations with Chvalkowsky he made it clear that they would ruthlessly smash this State if Benes's tendencies were not completely revised. Chvalkowsky understood this and asked the Fuehrer to have patience. (He often bragged of his patience.) The Fuehrer saw this point of view, but the months went by without any change. The new regime did not succeed in eliminating the old one psychologically. He observed this from the Press, mouth-to-mouth propaganda, dismissals of Germans, and many other things which, to him, were a symbol of the total position.

At first he had not understood this but when it became clear to him he drew his conclusions because, had the development continued in this way, the relations with Czechoslovakia would in a few years have become the same as six months ago. Why did Czechoslovakia not immediately reduce its army to a reasonable size? Such an army was a tremendous burden for such a State because it only makes sense if it supports the foreign political mission of the State. Since Czechoslovakia no longer has a foreign political mission such an army is meaningless. He enumerates several examples which proved to him that the spirit in the army had not changed. This symptom convinced him that the army also would be a source of a severe political burden in the future. Added to this were the inevitable development of economic necessities, and, further, the protests of national groups which could no longer endure life as it was."

I now interpolate, if the Tribunal please, to note the significance of that language of Adolf Hitler to the President of a supposed sovereign State and its Prime Minister, having in his presence General Field Marshal Goering, the Commander of the Air Force, and General Keitel. Continuing the quotation -

"Thus it is that the die was cast on the past Sunday. I sent for the Hungarian Ambassador and told him that I was withdrawing my hands from this country. We were now confronted with this fact. He had given the order to the German troops to march into Czechoslovakia and to incorporate Czechoslovakia into the German Reich. He wanted to give Czechoslovakia fullest autonomy and a life of her own to a larger extent than she ever had enjoyed during Austrian rule. Germany's attitude towards Czechoslovakia would be determined tomorrow and the day after tomorrow and depended on the attitude of the Czechoslovakian people and the Czechoslovakian military towards the German troops. He no longer trusts the government. He believed in the honesty and straightforwardness of Hacha and Chvalkowsky, but doubted that the Government would be able to assert itself in the entire nation. The German Army had already started out today, and at one barracks where resistance was offered, it was ruthlessly broken; another barracks had given in at the deployment of heavy artillery.

At six o'clock in the morning the German Army would invade Czechoslovakia from all sides and the German Air Force would occupy the Czech airfields. There existed two possibilities. The first one was that the invasion of the German troops would lead to a battle. In this case the resistance would be broken by all means with physical force. The other possibility was that the invasion of the German troops would be tolerated. In that case it would be easy for the Fuehrer to give Czechoslovakia, in the new organisation of Czech life, a generous life of her own autonomy, and a certain national liberty.

We were witnessing at the moment a great historical turning-point. He would not like to torture and de- nationalise the Czechs. He also did not do all that because of hatred but in order to protect Germany. If Czechoslovakia in the fall of last year would not have yielded" - I suppose that is a bad translation for "had not yielded" -"the Czech people would have been exterminated. Nobody could have prevented him from doing- that. It was his will that the

Czech people should live a full national life and he believed firmly that a way could be found which would make far-reaching concessions to the Czech desires. If fighting should break out tomorrow, the pressure would result in counter-pressure. One would annihilate another and it would then not be possible any more for him to give the promised alleviations. Within two days the Czech Army would not exist any more. Of course, Germans would also be killed and this would result in a hatred which would force him" - that is, Hitler - "because of his instinct of self- preservation, not to grant autonomy any more. The world would not move a muscle. He felt pity for the Czech people when he was reading the foreign Press. It would leave the impression on him which could be summarised in a German proverb: 'The Moor has done his duty, the Moor may go'.

That was the state of affairs. There existed two trends in Germany, a harder one which did not want any concessions and wished in memory to the past that Czechoslovakia would be conquered with blood, and another one, the attitude of which corresponded with the suggestions which he had just mentioned.

That was the reason why he had asked Hacha to come there. This invitation was the last good deed which he could do for the Czech people. If it should come to a fight, the bloodshed would also force us to hate. But the visit of Hacha could perhaps prevent the extreme. Perhaps it would contribute to finding a form of construction which would be more far-reaching for Czechoslovakia than she could ever have hoped for in the old Austria. His aim was only to create the necessary security for the German people.

The hours went past. At 6 o'clock the troops would march in. He was almost ashamed to say that there was one German division to each Czech battalion. The military action was no small one, but planned with all generosity. He would advise him" - that is, Adolf Hitler would advise Paul Hacha - "now to retire with Chvalkowsky in order to discuss what should be done."

In his reply to this long harangue, Hacha, according to the German minutes, said that he agreed that resistance would be useless. He expressed doubt that he would be able to issue the necessary orders to the Czech Army in the four hours left to him, before the German Army crossed the Czech border. He asked if the object of the invasion was to disarm the Czech Army. If so, he indicated that might possibly be arranged. Hitler replied that his decision was final; that it was well known what a decision of the Fuehrer meant. He turned to the circle of Nazi conspirators surrounding him, for their support, and you will remember that the defendants Goering, Ribbentrop and Keitel were all present. The only possibility of disarming the Czech Army, Hitler said, was by the intervention of the German Army.

I read now one paragraph from Page 4 of the English version of the German minutes of this infamous meeting. It is the next to the last paragraph on Page 4.

"The Fuehrer states that his decision was irrevocable. It was well known what a decision of the Fuehrer meant. He did not see any other possibility for disarmament and asked the other gentlemen" - that is, including Goering, Ribbentrop, and Keitel - "whether they shared his opinion, a question which was answered in the affirmative. The only possibility of disarming the Czech Army was by the German Army".

At this sad point Hacha and Chvalkowsky retired from the room.

I now offer in evidence Document 2861-PS, an excerpt from the official British War Blue Book, at Page 24, and I offer it as Exhibit USA 119. This is an official document of the British Government, of which the Tribunal will take judicial notice under the provisions of Article 21 of the Charter. The part from which I read is a dispatch from the British Ambassador, Neville Henderson, describing a conversation with the defendant Goering, in which the events of this early morning meeting are set forth.

"From: Neville Henderson. To: Viscount Halifax. Berlin, 28th May, 1939. My Lord: I paid a short visit to Field Marshal Goering at Karinhall yesterday."

Then I skip two paragraphs and begin reading with paragraph four. I am sorry, I think I had better read all of those paragraphs.

"Field Marshal Goering, who had obviously just been talking to someone else on the subject, began by inveighing against the attitude which was being adopted in England towards everything German and particularly in respect of the gold held there on behalf of the National Bank of Czechoslovakia. Before, however, I had had time to reply, he was called to the telephone and on his return did not revert to this specific question. He complained, instead, of British hostility in general, of our political and economic encirclement of Germany, and the activities of what he described as the war party in England ...

I told the Field Marshal that before speaking of British hostility, he must understand why the undoubted change of feeling, in England towards Germany had taken place. As he knew quite well, the basis of all the discussions between Mr. Chamberlain and Herr Hitler last year had been to the effect that, once the Sudetens were allowed to enter the Reich, Germany would leave the Czechs alone and would do nothing to interfere with their independence. Herr Hitler had given a definite assurance to that effect in his letter to the Prime Minister of the 27th September. By yielding to the advice of his 'wild men' and deliberately annexing Bohemia and Moravia, Herr Hitler had not only broken his word to Mr. Chamberlain but had infringed the whole principle of self-determination on which the Munich agreement rested.

At this point, the Field Marshal interrupted me with a description of President Hacha's visit to Berlin. I told Field Marshal Goering that it was not possible to talk of free will when I understood that he himself had threatened to bombard Prague with his aeroplanes, if Doctor Hacha refused to sign. The Field Marshal did not deny the fact but explained how the point had arisen. According to him, Doctor Hacha had from the first been prepared to sign everything but had said that constitutionally he could not do so without reference first to Prague. After considerable difficulty, telephonic communication with Prague was obtained and the Czech Government had agreed, while adding that they could not guarantee that one Czech battalion at least would not fire on German troops. It was, he said, only at that stage that he had warned Doctor Hacha that, if German lives were lost, he would bombard Prague. The Field Marshal also repeated, in reply to some comment of mine, the story that the advance occupation of Vitkovice had been effected solely in order to forestall the Poles who, he said, were known to have the intention of seizing this valuable area at the first opportunity."

I also invite the attention of the Tribunal and the judicial notice of the Tribunal, to dispatch No. 77, in the French Official Yellow Book, at Page 7 of the book, identified as our Document 2943-PS, appearing in the document book under that number, and I ask that it be given an identifying number Exhibit USA 114. This is a dispatch from M. Coulondre, the French Ambassador, and it gives another well- informed version of this same midnight meeting. The account, which I shall present to the Court, of the remainder of this meeting is drawn from these two sources, the British Blue Book and the French Yellow Book. I think the Court may be interested to read somewhat further at large in those two books, which furnish a great deal of the background of all of these matters.

When President Hacha left the conference room in the Reich Chancellery, he was in such a state of exhaustion that he needed medical attention from a physician who was conveniently on hand for that purpose, a German physician. When the two Czechs returned to the room, the Nazi conspirators again told them of the power and invincibility of the Wehrmacht. They reminded them that in three hours, at six in the morning -

THE PRESIDENT: You are not reading?

MR. ALDERMAN: I am not reading, I am summarising.

THE PRESIDENT: Go on.

MR. ALDERMAN: They reminded him that in three hours - at six in the morning - the German Army would cross the border. The defendant Goering boasted of what the Wehrmacht would do if the Czech forces dared to resist the invading Germans.

If German lives were lost, defendant Goering said, his Luftwaffe would blast half of Prague into ruins in two hours and that, he said, would be only the beginning.

Under this threat of imminent and merciless attack by land and air, the aged President of Czechoslovakia, at four- thirty in the morning, signed the document with which the Nazi conspirators confronted him and which they had already had prepared. This Document is TC-49, the declaration of 15th March, 1939, one of the series of documents which will be presented by the British Prosecutor, and from it I quote this, on the assumption that it will subsequently be introduced:

"The President of the Czechoslovakian State entrusts with entire confidence the destiny of the Czech people and the Czech country to the hands of the Fuehrer of the German Reich" - really a rendezvous with destiny.

While the Nazi officials were threatening and intimidating the representatives of the Czech Government, the Wehrmacht had in some areas already crossed the Czech border.

I offer in evidence Document 2860-PS, another excerpt from the British Blue Book, of which I ask the Court to take judicial notice. This is a speech by Lord Halifax, the Secretary of State for Foreign Affairs, from which I quote one passage. This is Document 2860-PS, which I have already offered and had identified:

"It is to be observed" - and the fact is surely not without significance -
"that the towns of Maehrisch-Ostrau and Vitkovice were actually,

107

occupied by German S.S. detachments on the evening of the 14th March, while the President and the Foreign Minister of Czechoslovakia were still on their way to Berlin and before any discussion had taken place."

At dawn on March 15th, German troops poured into Czechoslovakia from all sides. Hitler issued an order of the day to the Armed Forces and a proclamation to the German people, which stated distinctly "Czechoslovakia has ceased to exist."

On the following day, in contravention of Article 81 of the Treaty of Versailles, Czechoslovakia was formally incorporated into the German Reich under the name of "The Protectorate of Bohemia and Moravia." The decree is Document TC-51, another of the documents which the British delegation will present to the Tribunal later in this week. It was signed in Prague on 16th March, 1939, by Hitler, Lammers and the defendants Frick and von Ribbentrop.

I should like to quote the first sentence of this decree. "The Bohemian and Moravian countries belonged for a millennium to the Lebensraum 'living space' of the German people." The remainder of the decree sets forth in bleak detail the extent to which Czechoslovakia henceforth would be subjected to Germany. A German Protector was to be appointed by the German Fuehrer for the so-called "Protectorate," the defendant von Neurath. God deliver us from such protectors!! The German Government assumed charge of their foreign affairs and of their customs and of their excise. It was specified that German garrisons and military establishments would be maintained in the Protectorate. At the same time the extremist leaders in Slovakia who, at German Nazi insistence, had done so much to undermine the Czech State found that the independence of their week-old State was itself in effect qualified.

I offer in evidence Document 1439-PS as Exhibit USA - I need not offer that. I think it is a decree in the Reichsgesetzblatt, of which I ask the Tribunal to take judicial notice, and it is identified as our Document 1439- PS. It appears at Page 606, 1939, Reichsgesetzblatt, Part II.

The covering declaration is signed by the defendant Ribbentrop, Minister of Foreign Affairs; and then there is a heading: "Treaty of Protection to be extended by the German Reich to the State of Slovakia."

"The German Government and the Slovakian Government have agreed, after the Slovakian State has placed itself under the protection of the German Reich, to regulate by treaty the consequences resulting from this fact. For this purpose, the undersigned representatives of the two Governments have agreed on the following provisions:

Article 1. The German Reich undertakes to protect the political independence of the State of Slovakia and the integrity of its territory.

Article 2. For the purpose of making effective the protection undertaken by the German Reich, the German Armed Forces shall have the right, at all times, to construct military installations and to keep them garrisoned in the strength they deem necessary, in an area delimited on its Western side by the frontiers of the State of Slovakia, and on its Eastern side by a line formed by the Eastern rims of the Lower Carpathians, the White Carpathians, and the Javernik Mountains."

Then I skip.

"The Government of Slovakia will organise its military forces in close agreement with the German Armed Forces."

I also offer in evidence Document 2793-PS.

THE PRESIDENT: Would not that be a convenient time to break off? I understand, too, that it would be for the convenience of the defence counsel if the Tribunal adjourn for an hour and a quarter rather than for an hour at midday, and accordingly, the Tribunal will retire at 12.45 and sit again at 2 o'clock.

(A recess was taken.)

MR. ALDERMAN: May it please the Tribunal, this secret protocol between Germany and Slovakia provided for close economic and financial collaboration between them. Mineral resources and sub-soil rights were placed at the disposal of the German Government.

I offer in evidence Document 2793-PS, Exhibit USA 120, and from it I read paragraph 3:

"Investigation, development and utilisation of the Slovak natural resources. In this respect the basic principle is that, in so far as they are not needed to meet Slovakia's own requirements, they should be placed in the first place at Germany's disposal. The entire soil research" - Bodenforschung is the German word - "will be placed under the Reich Agency for soil- research." That is the Reichsstelle fur Bodenforschung. "The Government of the Slovak State will soon start an investigation to determine whether the present owners of concessions and privileges have fulfilled the industrial obligations prescribed by law, and it will cancel concessions and privileges in cases where these duties have been neglected."

In their private conversations the Nazi conspirators gave abundant evidence that they considered Slovakia a mere puppet State - in effect a German possession.

I offer in evidence Document R-100 as Exhibit USA 121. This document is a memorandum of information given by Hitler to von Brauchitsch on 25th March, 1939. Much of it deals with problems arising from recently occupied Bohemia and Moravia and Slovakia. I quote, beginning at the sixth paragraph:

"Col. Gen. Keitel will inform Slovak Government via Foreign Office that it would not be lawful to keep or garrison armed Slovak units (Hlinka Guards) on this side of the border formed by the river Waag. They shall be transferred to the new Slovak territory. Hlinka Guards should be disarmed.

Slovakia shall be requested via Foreign Office to deliver to us against payment any arms we want and which are still kept in Slovakia. This request is to be based upon agreement made between army and Czech troops. For this payment these millions should be used which we will pour anyhow into Slovakia.

Czech Protectorate:

H. Gr." - the translator's note indicates that that probably means army groups, but I cannot vouch for it - "shall be asked again whether the request shall be repeated for the delivery of all arms within a stated time limit and under the threat of severe penalties.

We take former Czechoslovakian war material without paying for it. The guns bought by contract before 15th February, though, shall be paid for. Bohemia and Moravia have to make annual contributions to the German Treasury. Their amount shall be fixed on the basis of the expenses earmarked formerly for the Czech army."

The German conquest of Czechoslovakia, in direct contravention of the Munich Agreement, was the occasion for the formal protests by the British and French Governments. These Documents, TC-52 and TC-53, dated 17th March, 1939, will be presented to the Tribunal by the British Prosecutor.

On the same day, 1939, 17th March, the Acting Secretary of State of the United States Government issued a statement, which I will offer in evidence, and I invite the Court to take judicial notice of the entire volume, Document 2862 - PS-as Exhibit USA 122, which is an excerpt from the official volume entitled Peace and War: United States Foreign Policy, 1931-1941 issued under the seal of the Department of State of the United States of America. Incidentally, this volume, which happens to be my own copy and I hope I can get another one-I am placing in evidence, because I am quite certain that in its study of the background of this whole case the Court will be very much interested in this volume, which is a detailed chronological history of all the diplomatic events leading up to and through the Second World War to 1941. But what I am actually offering in evidence at the moment appears on Pages 454 and 455 of the volume, a statement by the Acting Secretary of State Sumner Welles, dated 17th March, 1939:

"The Government of the United States has on frequent occasions stated its conviction that only through international support of a programme of order based upon law can world peace be assured.

This Government, founded upon and dedicated to the principles of human liberty and of democracy, cannot refrain from making known this country's condemnation of the acts which have resulted in the temporary extinguishment of the liberties of a free and independent people with whom, from the day when the Republic of Czechoslovakia attained its independence, the people of the United States have maintained specially close and friendly relations.

The position of the Government of the United States has been made consistently clear. It has emphasised the need for respect for the sanctity of treaties and of the pledged word, and for non-intervention by any nation in the domestic affairs of other nations; and it has on repeated occasions expressed its condemnation of a policy of military aggression.

It is manifest that acts of wanton lawlessness and of arbitrary force are threatening the world peace and the very structure of modern civilisation. The imperative need for the observance of the principles advocated by this Government has been clearly demonstrated by the developments which have taken place during the past three days."

With Czechoslovakia in German hands, the Nazi conspirators had accomplished the programme they had set themselves in the meeting in Berlin on 5th November, 1938. You will recall that this programme of conquest was intended to shorten their frontiers, to increase their industrial and food reserves, and to place them in a position, both industrially and strategically, from which they could launch more ambitious and more devastating campaigns of aggression. In less than a year and a half this programme had been carried through to the satisfaction of the Nazi leaders, and at that point I would again invite the Court's attention to the large chart on the wall. I think it is no mere figure of speech to make reference to the wolf's head, what is known in Anglo-American law as caput lupinum.

The lower jaw formed near Austria was taken - the red part on the first chart - 12th March, 1938. Czechoslovakia thereby was encircled, and the next step was the absorption of the mountainous part, the Sudetenland, indicated on the second chart in red. On 1st October, 1938, Czechoslovakia was further encircled and its defences weakened, and then the jaws clamped in, or the pincers, as I believe General Keitel or General Jodl called them - I believe it was General Jodl's diary - and you see what they did to Czechoslovakia. On 15th March, 1939 the borders were shortened, new bases were acquired, and then Czechoslovakia was destroyed. Bohemia and Moravia are in black, and Slovakia in what might be called light tan. But I have read to you the documents which showed in what condition Slovakia was left; and with the German military installations in Slovakia, you see how completely the Southern border of Poland was flanked, as well as the Western border, the stage being set for the next aggression, which the British Prosecutor will describe to you.

Of all the Nazi conspirators the defendant Goering was the most aware of the economic and strategic advantages which would accrue from the possession by Germany of Czechoslovakia.

I now offer in evidence Document 1301-PS, which is a rather large file, and we offer particularly Item 10 of the document, at Page 25 of the English translation. I offer it as Exhibit USA 123. Page 25 of the English translation contained the Top Secret minutes of a conference with Goering in the Luftwaffe Ministry, the Air Ministry. The meeting which was held on 14th October, 1938, just two weeks after the occupation of the Sudetenland, was devoted to the discussion of economic problems. As of that date, the defendant Goering's remarks were somewhat prophetic. I quote from the third paragraph, from the bottom of Page 26 of the English translation:

"The Sudetenland has to be exploited with all the means. General Field Marshal Goering counts upon a complete industrial assimilation of Slovakia. Czechoslovakia would become a German dominion. Everything possible must be taken out. The Oder-Danube canal has to be speeded up. Searches for oil and ore have to be conducted in Slovakia, notably by State Secretary Keppler."

In the summer of 1939, after the incorporation of Bohemia and Moravia into the German Reich, defendant Goering again revealed the great interest of the Nazi leaders in Czech economic potential.

I offer in evidence Document R-133 as exhibit USA 124. This document is a minute, dated Berlin - 27th July, 1939 signed by Muller, of a conference between Goering and a group of officials from the O.K.W. and from other agencies of the German Government concerned with war production. This meeting had been held two days previously, on 25th July. I read the first part of the account of this meeting.

"In a rather long statement the Field Marshal explained that the incorporation of Bohemia and Moravia into the, German economy had taken place, in order among other reasons, to increase the

German war potential, by exploitation of the industry there. Letters, such as the decree of the Reich Minister for Economics - S-10 402/39 of 10th July 1939 - as well as a letter with similar meaning to the Junkers firm, which might possibly lower the kind and extent of the armament measures in the Protectorate, are contrary to this principle. If it is necessary to issue such directives, this should be done only with his consent. In any case, he insists" - that is defendant Goering insists - "in agreement with the directive by Hitler, that the war potential of the Protectorate is definitely to be exploited in part or in full and is to be directed towards mobilisation as soon as possible."

In addition to strengthening the Nazi economic potential for the following wars of aggression, the conquest of Czechoslovakia provided the Nazis with new bases from which to wage their next war of aggression, the attack on Poland.

You will recall the minutes of the conference between Goering and a pro-Nazi Slovak delegation in the winter of 1938-1939. Those minutes are Document 2801-PS, which I introduced into evidence earlier, as Exhibit USA 109. You will recall the last, sentence of those minutes, a statement of defendant Goering's conclusions. I quote this sentence again:

"Air bases in Slovakia are of great importance for the German Air Force for use against the East."

I now offer in evidence Document 1874-PS, as Exhibit USA 125. This document is the German minutes of a conference between defendant Goering and Mussolini and Ciano on 15th April, 1939, one month after the conquest of Czechoslovakia.

In this conference, Goering told his junior partners in the Axis of the progress of German preparations for war. He compared the strength of Germany with the strength of England and France. Not unnaturally, he mentioned the German occupation of Czechoslovakia, in this connection. I read two paragraphs of these thoughts, on Page 4, paragraph 2, of the German minutes.

THE PRESIDENT: Which document is this?

MR. ALDERMAN: It is 1874-PS

"However, the heavy armament of Czechoslovakia shows, in any case, how dangerous it could have been, even after Munich, in the event of a serious conflict. By German action, the situation of both Axis countries was ameliorated because, among other reasons, of the economic possibilities which resulted from the transfer to Germany of the great production capacity of Czechoslovakia. That contributes toward a considerable strengthening of the Axis against the Western Powers.

Furthermore, Germany now need not keep ready a single division for protection against that country in case of bigger conflict. This too, is an advantage by which both Axis countries will, in the last analysis, benefit."

Then on Page 5, paragraph 2, of the German version:-

"The action taken by Germany in Czechoslovakia is to be viewed as an advantage for the Axis in case Poland should finally join the enemies of the Axis powers. Germany could then attack this country from two flanks, and would be within only twenty-five minutes flying distance from the new Polish industrial centre, which had been moved further into the interior of the country, nearer to the other Polish industrial districts, because of its proximity to the border."

Now, by the turn of events, it is located again in the proximity of the border. And that flanking on two fronts is illustrated on the four segment chart.

I think the chart itself demonstrates, better than any oral argument, the logic, the cold calculation, the deliberation of each step to this point of the German aggression. More than that, it demonstrates what I might call the master stroke of the aggressive war case, that is that each conquest of the Nazi conspirators was deliberately planned as a stepping-stone to new and more ambitious aggression. You will recall the words of Hitler, at the conference in the Reich Chancellery on 23rd May, 1939, when he was planning the Polish campaign, Document L-79, Exhibit USA 27. I quote from it.

"The period which lies behind us has indeed been put to good use. All measures have been taken in the correct sequence and in harmony with our aims."

It is appropriate to refer to two other speeches of the Nazi leaders. In his lecture in Munich on 7th November, 1943, the defendant Jodl spoke as follows, and I quote from Page 5 of Document L-172, already received in evidence as Exhibit USA 34; on Page 8 of the German text:

"The bloodless solution of the Czech conflict in the autumn of 1938 and spring of 1939, and the annexation of Slovakia, rounded off the territory of Greater Germany in such a way that it now became possible to consider the Polish problem on the basis of more or less favourable strategic premises."

In the speech to his military commanders on 23rd November, 1939, Hitler described the process by which he had rebuilt the military power of the Reich; this is our Document 789- PS, Exhibit USA 23. I quote one passage from the second paragraph:

"The next step was Bohemia, Moravia and Poland. This step too it was not possible to accomplish in one campaign. First of all, the Western fortifications had to be finished. It was not possible to reach the goal in one effort. It was clear to me, from the first moment, that I could not be satisfied with the Sudeten- German territory. That was only a partial solution. The decision to march into Bohemia was made. Then followed the erection of the Protectorate and with that, the basis for the action against Poland was laid."

Before I leave the subject of the aggression against Czechoslovakia, I should like to submit to the Court a document which became available to us too late to be included in our document book. It reached me on Saturday, late in the afternoon or late at night. This is an official document, again from the Czechoslovakian Government, a supplement to the Czechoslovakian report, which I had previously offered in evidence. I now offer it, identified as Document 3061-PS, as Exhibit USA 126.

The document was furnished us, if the Court please, in the German text with an English translation, which did not seem to us quite adequate, and we have had it re-translated into English, and the translation has just been passed up, I believe, to the Tribunal. That mimeographed translation should be appended to our document book "O".

I shall not read the report; it is about twelve pages long. The Court will take judicial notice of it, under the Provisions of the Charter. I merely summarise. This document gives confirmation and corroboration to the other evidence which I presented to the Tribunal. In particular, it offers support to the following allegations:

First, the close working relationship between Henlein and the S.D.P., on the one hand, and Hitler and defendants, Hess and Ribbentrop, on the other.

Second, the use of the German Legation in Prague to direct the German Fifth Column activities.

Third, the financing of the Henlein Movement by agencies of the German Government, including the German diplomatic representatives at Prague.

Fourth, the use of the Henlein Movement to conduct espionage on direct orders from the Reich.

In addition, this document gives further details of the circumstances of the visit of President Hacha to Berlin on the night of 14th March. It substantiates the fact that President Hacha required the medical attention of Hitler's physician and it supports the threat, which the defendant Goering made to the Czech delegation.

Now, if it please the Tribunal, that concludes my presentation of what, to me, has always seemed one of the saddest chapters in human history, the rape and destruction of the frail little nation of Czechoslovakia.

SIR DAVID MAXWELL FYFE: May it please the Tribunal: Before I tender the evidence which I desire to place before the Tribunal, it might be convenient if I explained how the British case is to be divided up and who will present the different parts.

I shall deal with the general treaties. After that, my learned friend, Colonel Griffith-Jones, will deal with Poland. Thirdly, Major Elwyn Jones will deal with Norway and Denmark. Fourthly, Mr. Roberts will deal with Belgium, Holland, and Luxembourg. Fifthly, Colonel Phillimore will deal with Greece and Yugoslavia. After that, my friend, Mr. Alderman, of the American Delegation, will deal on behalf of both delegations with the aggression against the U.S.S.R. and the U.S.A.

May I also, with the Tribunal's permission, say one word about the arrangements that we have made as to documents. Each of the defendants' counsel will have a copy of the document book, of the different document books, in English. In fact, 30 copies of the first four of our document books have already been placed in the defendants' Information Centre. We hope that the last document book, dealing with Greece and Yugoslavia, will have the 30 copies placed there today.

In addition, the defendants' counsel have at least six copies in German of every document.

With regard to my own part of the case, the first section on general treaties, all the documents on this phase are in the Reichsgesetzblatt or Die dokumente der Deutschen Politik, of which ten copies have been made available to the defendants' counsel, so that with regard to the portion with which the Tribunal is immediately concerned, the defendants' counsel will have at least 16 copies in German of every document referred to.

Finally, there is a copy of the Reichsgesetzblatt and Die Dokumente available for the Tribunal, other copies if they so desire, but one is placed ready for the

Tribunal if any member wishes to refer to a German text.

THE PRESIDENT: Do you propose to call any oral witnesses?

SIR DAVID MAXWELL FYFE: No, my Lord, no oral witnesses.

If the Tribunal please, before I come to the first treaty I want to make three quotations to deal with a point which was mentioned in the speech of my learned friend, The Attorney General, yesterday.

It might be thought from the melancholy story of broken treaties and violated assurances, which the Tribunal has already heard, that Hitler and the Nazi Government did not even profess it necessary or desirable to keep the pledged word. Outwardly, however, the professions were very different. With regard to treaties, on the 18th October, 1933, Hitler said, "Whatever we have signed we will fulfil to the best of our ability."

The Tribunal will note the reservation, "Whatever we have signed."

But, on the 21st May, 1935, Hitler said:

> "The German Government will scrupulously maintain every treaty voluntarily signed, even though it was concluded before their accession to power and office."

On assurances Hitler was even more emphatic. In the same speech, the Reichstag Speech on 21st May, 1935, Hitler accepted assurances as being of equal obligation, and the world at that time could not know that that meant of no obligation at all. What he actually said was:

> "And when I now hear from the lips of a British statesman that such assurances are nothing, and that the only proof of sincerity is the signature appended to collective pacts, I must ask Mr. Eden to be good enough to remember that it is a question of an assurance in any case. It is sometimes much easier to sign treaties with the mental reservations that one will reconsider one's attitude at the decisive hour, than to declare before an entire nation and with full opportunity one's adherence to a policy which serves the course of peace because it rejects anything which leads to war."

And then he proceeds with the illustration of his assurance to France.

Never having seen the importance which Hitler wished the world to believe he attached to treaties, I shall ask the Tribunal, in my part of the case, to look at fifteen only of the treaties which he and the Nazis broke. The remainder of the sixty-nine broken treaties shown on the chart and occurring between 1933 and 1941 will be dealt with by my learned friends.

There is one final point as to the position of a treaty in German law, as I understand it. The appearances of a treaty in the Reichsgesetzblatt makes it part of the statute law of Germany, and that is by no means an uninteresting aspect of the breaches which I shall put before the Tribunal.

The first treaty to be dealt with is the Convention for the Pacific Settlement of International Disputes, signed at The Hague on the 29th July, 1899. I ask that the Tribunal take judicial notice of the Convention, and for convenience I hand in as Exhibit GB I the British Document, TC-1. The German reference is to the Reichsgesetzblatt for 1901, No. 44, Sections 401 to 404, and 482 and 483. The Tribunal will find the relevant charge in Appendix C as Charge 1.

As the Attorney General said yesterday, these Hague Conventions are only the first gropings towards the rejection of the inevitability of war. They do not render the making of aggressive war a crime, but their milder terms were as readily broken as the more severe agreements.

On the 19th July, 1899, Germany, Greece, Serbia and twenty-five other nations signed a convention. Germany ratified the convention on 4th September, 1900, Serbia on the 11th May, 1901, Greece on the 4th April, 1901.

By Article 12 of the treaty between the Principal Allied and Associated Powers and the Serb-Croat-Slovene State, signed at St. Germaine-en-Laye on the 10th September, 1919, the new Kingdom succeeded to all the old Serbian treaties, and later, as the Tribunal know, changed its name to Yugoslavia.

I think it is sufficient, unless the Tribunal otherwise wish, for me to read the first two articles only.

"Article 1. With a view to obviating as far as possible recourse to force in the relations between States, the signatory powers agree to use their best efforts to ensure the pacific settlement of international differences.

Article 2. In case of serious disagreement or conflict, before an appeal to arms the signatory powers agree to have recourse, as far as circumstances allow, to the good offices or mediation of one or more friendly powers."

After that the Convention deals with machinery, and I do not think, subject to any wish of the Tribunal, that it is necessary for me to deal with it in detail.

The second treaty is the Convention for the Pacific Settlement of International Disputes, signed at The Hague on the 18th October, 1907. Again I ask the Tribunal to take judicial notice of this, and for convenience hand in as Exhibit GB 2 the Final Act of the Conference at The Hague, which contains British Documents TC-2, 3 and 4. The reference to this convention in German is to the Reichsgesetzblatt for 1910, Number 52, Sections 22 to 25, and the relevant charge in Charge 2.

This Convention was signed at The Hague by forty-four nations, and it is in effect as to thirty-one nations, twenty-eight signatories, and three adherents. For our purpose it is in force as to the United States, Belgium, Czechoslovakia, Denmark, France, Germany, Luxembourg, Japan, Netherlands, Norway, Poland, and Russia.

By the provisions of Article 91 it replaces the 1899 Convention as between the contracting powers. As Greece and Yugoslavia are parties to the 1899 Convention and not to that of 1907, the 1899 Convention is in effect with regard to them, and that explains the division of countries in Appendix C.

Again I only desire that the Tribunal should look at the first two articles.

"Article 1. With a view to obviating as far as possible recourse to force in the relations between States, the contracting powers agree to use their best efforts to ensure the pacific settlement of international differences."

Then I do not think I need trouble to read Article 2. It is the same article as to mediation, and again, there are a number of machinery provisions.

The third treaty is The Hague Convention relative to the opening of hostilities, signed at the same time. It is contained in the exhibit which I put in. Again I ask that judicial notice be taken of it. The British Document is TC- 3. The German reference is the Reichsgesetzblatt for 1910, Number 2, Sections 82 to 102, and the reference in Appendix C to Charge 3.

This Convention applies to Germany, Poland, Norway, Denmark, Belgium, the Netherlands, Luxembourg, and Russia. It relates to a procedural step in notifying one's prospective opponent before opening hostilities against him. It appears to have had its immediate origin in the Russo-Japanese war, 1904, when Japan attacked Russia without any previous warning. It will be noted that it does not fix any particular lapse of time between the giving of notice and the commencement of hostilities, but it does seek to maintain an absolutely minimum standard of international decency before the outbreak of war.

Again, if I might refer the Tribunal to the first article: "The contracting powers recognise that hostilities between them must not commence without a previous and explicit warning in the form of either a declaration of war, giving reasons, or an ultimatum with a conditional declaration of war."

Then there are a number again of machinery provisions, with which I shall not trouble the Tribunal.

The fourth treaty is the Hague Convention 5, respecting the rights and duties of neutral powers and persons in case of war on land, signed at the same time. That is British Document TC-4, and the German reference is Reichsgesetzblatt 1910, Number 2, Sections 168 and 176. Reference in Appendix C is to Charge 4.

THE PRESIDENT: Is it necessary to give the German reference? If it is necessary for defendants' counsel, all right, but if not it need not be done.

SIR DAVID MAXWELL FYFE: If I may omit them it will save some time.

THE PRESIDENT: Yes.

SIR DAVID MAXWELL FYFE: If any of the defendants' counsel want any specific reference perhaps they will be good enough to ask me.

THE PRESIDENT: Yes.

SIR DAVID MAXWELL FYFE: Germany was an original signatory to the Convention, and the Treaty is in force as a result of ratification or adherence between Germany and Norway, Denmark, Belgium, Luxembourg, the Netherlands, the U.S.S.R. and the United States.

I call the attention of the Tribunal to the short contents of Article I:

"The territory of neutral powers is inviolable."

A point does arise, however, on this Convention. I want to make this clear at once. Under Article 20 the provisions of the present Convention do not apply except between the contracting powers, and then only if all the belligerents are parties to the Convention.

As Great Britain and France entered the war within two days of the outbreak of the war between Germany and Poland, and one of these powers had not ratified the Convention, it is arguable that its provisions did not apply to the Second World War.

I do not want the time of the Tribunal to be occupied by an argument on that point when there are so many more important treaties to be considered. Therefore, I do not press that as a charge of a breach of treaty. I merely call the attention of the Tribunal to the terms of Article I as showing the state of international opinion at that time and as an element in the aggressive character of the war which we are considering.

THE PRESIDENT: Perhaps this would be a good time to break off.

[A recess was taken]

SIR DAVID MAXWELL FYFE: As the Tribunal adjourned I had come to the fifth treaty, the Treaty of Peace between the Allied and Associated Powers and Germany, signed at Versailles the 28th June, 1919. I again ask the Tribunal to take judicial cognisance of this treaty, and I again hand in for convenience, Exhibit GB 3, which is a copy of the treaty, including British Documents TC-5 to TC-10 inclusive. The reference in Appendix C is to Charge 5.

Before I deal with the relevant portions, may I explain very briefly the lay-out of the treaty.

Part I contains the Covenant of the League of Nations, and Part II sets the boundaries of Germany in Europe. These boundaries are described in detail.

Part II makes no provision for guaranteeing these boundaries.

Part III, Articles 31 to 117, with which the Tribunal is concerned, contains the political clauses for Europe. In it, Germany guarantees certain territorial boundaries in Belgium, Luxembourg, Austria, Czechoslovakia, France, Poland, Memel, Danzig, etc.

It might be convenient for the Tribunal to note, at the moment, the interweaving of this treaty with the next, which is the Treaty for the Restoration of Friendly Relations between the United States and Germany.

Parts I, II and III of the Versailles Treaty are not included in the United States Treaty. Parts IV, V, VI, VIII, IX, X, XI, XII, XIV and XV are all repeated verbatim in the United States Treaty from the Treaty of Versailles.

The Tribunal is concerned with Part V, the military, naval, and air clauses. Parts VII and XIII are not included in the United States Treaty.

I do not think there is any reason to explain what the parts are, but if the Tribunal wishes to know about any specific part, I shall be very happy to explain it.

The first part that the Tribunal is concerned with is that contained in the British Document TC-5, and which consists of Articles 42 to 44 dealing with, the Rhineland. These are very short, and repeated in the Locarno Treaty. Perhaps I had better read them once, so that the Tribunal will keep them in mind.

> "Article 42. Germany is forbidden to maintain or construct any fortifications either on the left bank of the Rhine or on the right bank 1 to the West of a line drawn 50 kilometres to the East of the Rhine.
>
> Article 43. In the area defined above, the maintenance and the assembly of armed forces, either permanently or temporarily, and military manoeuvres of any kind, as well as the upkeep of all permanent works for mobilisation, are in the same way forbidden.
>
> Article 44. In case Germany violates in any manner whatever the provisions of Articles 42 and 43, she shall be regarded as committing a hostile act against the powers signatory of the present treaty, and as calculated to disturb the peace of the world."

I am not going to put in evidence, but I simply draw the Tribunal's attention to a document of which they can take judicial notice, as it has been published by the German State, the Memorandum Of 7th March, 1936, giving their account of the breach. The matters regarding the breach have been dealt with by my friend Mr. Alderman, and I do not propose to go over the ground again.

The next part of the Treaty is in the British Document TC-6, dealing with Austria:

> "Article 80. Germany acknowledges and will respect strictly the independence of Austria within the frontiers which may be fixed in a treaty between that State and the principal allied and associated powers; she agrees that this independence shall be inalienable, except with the consent of the Council of the League of Nations."

Again, in the same way, the proclamation of Hitler, dealing with Austria, the background of which has been dealt with by my friend Mr. Alderman, is attached as TC-47. I do not intend to read it because the Tribunal can again take judicial notice of the public proclamation.

Next is Document TC-8, dealing with Memel.

"Germany renounces, in favour of the principal allied and associated powers, all rights and title over the territories included between the Baltic, the North- eastern frontier of East Prussia as defined in Article 28 of Part II (Boundaries of Germany) of the present treaty, and the former frontier between Germany and Russia. Germany undertakes to accept the settlement made by principal allied and associated powers in regard to these territories, particularly in so far as concerns the nationality of inhabitants."

I do not think that the Tribunal has had any reference to the formal document of incorporation of Memel, of which again the Tribunal can take judicial notice; and I put in, for convenience, a copy as GB 4. It is British Document TC- 53A, and it appears in our book. It is very short, so perhaps the Tribunal will bear with me while I read it:

"The transfer Commissioner for the Memel territory, Gauleiter und Oberpresident Erich Koch, effected on 3rd April, 1939, during a conference at Memel, the final incorporation of the late Memel territory into the National Socialist Party Gau of East Prussia and into the State administration of the East Prussian Regierungsbezirk of Gumbinnen."

Then, we next come to TC-9, which is the article relating to Danzig, Article 100, and I shall only read the first sentence, because the remainder consists of geographical boundaries:

"Germany renounces, in favour of the principal allied and associated powers, all rights and title over the territory comprised within the following limits," and then the limits are set out and are described in a German map attached to the Treaty.

Lieutenant-Colonel Griffith-Jones, who will deal with this part of the case, will formally prove the documents relating to the occupation of Danzig, and I shall not trouble the Tribunal with them now.

If the Tribunal would go on to British Document TC-7 - that is Article 81, dealing with the Czechoslovak pledge.

"Germany, in conformity with the action already taken by the allied and associated powers, recognises the complete independence of the Czechoslovak State, which will include the autonomous territory of the Ruthenians to the South of the Carpathians. Germany hereby recognises the frontiers of this State as determined by the principal allied and associated powers and other interested States."

Mr. Alderman has dealt with this matter only this morning, and he has already put in an exhibit giving in detail the conference between Hitler and President Hacha, and the Foreign Minister Chvalkowsky, at which the defendants Goering and Keitel were present. Therefore, I am not going to put in to the Tribunal the British translation of the captured foreign office minutes, which occurs in TC-48; but I put it formally, as Mr. Alderman asked me to this morning, as GB 6, the Document TC-49, which is the agreement signed by Hitler and the defendant Ribbentrop for Germany and Dr. Hacha and Dr. Chvalkowsky for Czechoslovakia. It is an agreement of which the Tribunal will take judicial notice. I am afraid I cannot quite remember whether Mr. Alderman read that this morning; it is Document TC-49. He certainly referred to it.

THE PRESIDENT: No, he did not read it.

SIR DAVID MAXWELL FYFE: Then perhaps I might read it:

"Text of the Agreement between the Fuehrer and Reich Chancellor Adolf Hitler and the President of the Czechoslovak State, Dr. Hacha.

The Fuehrer and Reich Chancellor today received in Berlin, at their own request, the President of the Czechoslovak State, Dr. Hacha, and the Czechoslovak Foreign Minister, Dr. Chvalkowsky, in the presence of Herr von Ribbentrop, the Foreign Minister of the Reich. At this meeting the serious situation which had arisen within the previous territory of Czechoslovakia owing to the events of recent weeks, was subjected to a completely open examination. The conviction was unanimously expressed on both sides that the object of all their efforts must be to assure quiet, order and peace in this part of Central Europe. The President of the Czechoslovak State declared that, in order to serve this end and to reach a final pacification, he confidently placed the fate of the Czech people and of their country in the hands of the Fuehrer of the German Reich. The Fuehrer accepted this declaration and expressed his decision to assure to the Czech people, under the protection of the German Reich, the autonomous development of their national life, in accordance with their special characteristics. In witness whereof this document is signed in duplicate."

The signatures I have mentioned appear.

The Tribunal will understand that it is not my province to make any comment; that has been done by Mr. Alderman, and I am not putting forward any of the documents I have read as having my support; they merely put forward factually as part of the case.

The next document, which I put in as GB 7, is the British Document TC-50. That is Hitler's proclamation to the German people, dated 15th March, 1939. Again, I do not think that Mr. Alderman read that document.

THE PRESIDENT: No, he did not read it.

SIR DAVID MAXWELL FYFE: Then I shall read it.

"Proclamation of the Fuehrer to the German people, 15th March, 1939.

To the German People:

Only a few months ago Germany was compelled to protect her fellow-countrymen, living in well-defined settlements, against the unbearable Czechoslovakian terror regime; and during the last weeks the same thing has happened on an ever-increasing scale. This is bound to create an intolerable state of affairs within an area inhabited by citizens of so many nationalities.

These national groups, to counteract the renewed attacks against their freedom and life, have now broken away from the Prague Government. Czechoslovakia has ceased to exist.

Since Sunday, at many places, wild excesses have broken out, amongst the victims of which are again many Germans. Hourly the number of oppressed and persecuted people crying for help is increasing. From areas thickly populated by German-speaking inhabitants, which last autumn Czechoslovakia was allowed by German generosity to retain, refugees robbed of their personal belongings are streaming into the Reich.

Continuation of such a state of affairs would lead to the destruction of every vestige of order in an area in which Germany is vitally interested, particularly as for over one thousand years it formed a part of the German Reich.

In order definitely to remove this menace to peace and to create the conditions for a necessary new order in this living space, I have today resolved to allow German troops to march into Bohemia and Moravia. They will disarm the terror gangs and the Czechoslovakian forces supporting them, and protect the lives of all who are menaced. Thus they will lay the foundations for introducing a fundamental reordering of affairs which will be in accordance with the thousand-year-old history and will satisfy the practical needs of the German and Czech peoples.

Signed: Adolf Hitler, Berlin, 15th March, 1939."

Then there is a footnote, which is an order of the Fuehrer to the German Armed Forces of the same date, in which the substance is that they are told to march in to safeguard lives and property of all inhabitants, and not to conduct themselves as enemies, but as an instrument for carrying out the German Reich Government's decision.

I put in, as GB 8, the decree establishing the Protectorate, which is TC-51.

I think again, as these are public decrees, the Tribunal can take judicial notice of them. Their substance has been fully explained by Mr. Alderman. With the permission of the Tribunal, I will not read them in full now.

Then again, as Mr. Alderman requested, I put in, as GB 9, British Document TC-52, the British protest. If I might just read that to the Tribunal - it is from Lord Halifax to Sir Neville Henderson, our Ambassador in Berlin:

"Foreign Office, 17th March, 1939

Please inform the German Government that his Majesty's Government desires to make it plain to them that they cannot but regard the events of the past few days as a complete repudiation of the Munich Agreement, and a denial of the spirit in which the negotiators of that Agreement bound themselves to co-operate for a peaceful settlement.

His Majesty's Government must also take this occasion to protest against the changes effected in Czechoslovakia by German military action, which are, in their view, devoid of any basis of legality."

And again at Mr. Alderman's request, I put in as GB 10 the Document TC-53, which is the French protest of the same date, and I might read the third paragraph:

"The French Ambassador has the honour to inform the Minister for Foreign Affairs of the Reich, of the formal protest made by the Government of the French Republic against the measures which the communication of Count de Welzeck records.

The Government of the Republic consider, in fact, that in face of the action directed by the German Government against Czechoslovakia, they are confronted with a flagrant violation of the letter and the spirit of the agreement signed at Munich on 9th September, 1938.

The circumstances in which the agreements of March 15th have been imposed on the leaders of the Czechoslovak Republic do not, in the eyes of the Government of the Republic, legalise the situation registered in that agreement.

The French Ambassador has the honour to inform His Excellency, the Minister for Foreign Affairs of the Reich, that the Government of the Republic cannot recognise under these conditions the legality of the new situation created in Czechoslovakia by the action of the German Reich."

I now come to Part 5 of the Versailles Treaty, and the relevant matters are contained in the British Document TC- 10. As considerable discussion is centred around them, I read the introductory words:

"Part 5, Military, Naval and Air Clauses:

In order to render possible the initiation of a general limitation of the armaments of all nations, Germany undertakes strictly to observe the military, naval and air clauses which follow.

Section 1. Military Clauses. Effectives and Cadres of the German Army.

Article 159. The German military forces shall be demobilised and reduced as prescribed hereinafter.

Article 160. By a date which must not be later than 31st March, 1920, the German Army must not comprise more than seven divisions of infantry and three divisions of cavalry.

After that date, the total number of effectives in the Army of the States constituting Germany must not exceed 100,000 men, including officers and establishments of depots. The army shall be devoted exclusively to the maintenance of order within the territory and to the control of the frontiers.

The total effective strength of officers, including the personnel of staffs, whatever their composition, must not exceed 4,000.

Divisions and Army Corps headquarters staffs shall be organised in accordance with Table Number 1 annexed to this Section. The number and strength of units of infantry, artillery, engineers, technical services and troops laid down in the aforesaid table constitute maxima which must not be exceeded."

Then there is a description of units that can have their own depots, and the divisions under corps headquarters, and then the next two provisions are of some importance.

"The maintenance or formation of forces differently grouped, or of other organisations for the command of troops or for preparation for war is forbidden.

The great German General Staff and all similar organisations shall be dissolved and may not be reconstituted in any form."

I do not think I need trouble the Tribunal with Article 161, which deals with administrative services.

Article 163 provides the steps by which the reduction will take place, and then we come to Chapter 2, dealing with armament, and that provides that up till the time at which Germany is admitted as a member of the League of Nations, the armaments shall not be greater than the amount fixed in Table Number 11.

If the Tribunal will notice the second part, Germany agrees that after she has become a member of the League of Nations, the armaments fixed in the said table shall remain in force until they are modified by the Council of the League of Nations. Furthermore, she hereby agrees strictly to observe the decisions of the Council of the League on this subject.

Then Article 165 deals with guns, machine guns, etc., and 167 deals with notification of guns, and 168, the first part, says:-

"The manufacture of arms, munitions or any war material shall only be carried out in factories or works, the location of which shall be communicated to and approved by the governments of the Principal Allied and Associated Powers, and the number of which they retain the right to restrict."

Article 169 deals with the surrender of material.

Article 170 prohibits importation.

171 prohibits gas, and 172 provides for disclosure. Then 173, under the heading "Recruiting and Military Training," deals with one matter, the breach of which is of great importance:

"Universal compulsory military service shall be abolished in Germany.
The German Army may only be reconstituted and recruited by means of voluntary enlistment."

Then the succeeding articles deal with the method of enlistment, in order to prevent a quick rush through the army of men enlisted for a short time.

I think that all I need do is draw the attention of the Tribunal to the completeness and detail with which all these points are covered in Articles 174 to 179.

Then, passing on to TC-10, Article 180. That decrees the prohibition of fortress works beyond a certain line and the Rhineland. The first sentence is:

"All fortified works, fortresses and field works situated in German territory to the West of a line drawn 50 kilometres to the East of the Rhine shall be disarmed and dismantled."

I shall not trouble the Tribunal with the tables which show the amounts.

Then we come to the naval clauses, and I am sorry to say that the pages are out of order. If the Tribunal will go on four pages, they will come to Article 181, and I will read just that to show the way in which the naval limitations are imposed, and refer briefly to the others.

Article 181 says:

"After a period of two months from the coming into force of the present Treaty the German naval forces in commission must not exceed:
Six battleships of the Deutschland or Lothringen type.
Six light cruisers.
Twelve destroyers.
Twelve torpedo boats
or an equal number of ships constructed to replace them as provided in Article 190.
No submarines are to be included."

All other warships, except where there is provision to the contrary in the present Treaty, must be placed in reserve or devoted to commercial purposes.

Then 182 simply deals with the mine sweeping necessary to clean up the mines, and 183 limits the personnel to fifteen thousand, including officers and men of all grades and corps, and 184 deals with surface ships not in German ports, and the succeeding clauses deal with various details, and I pass at once to Article 191, which says:

"The construction or acquisition of any submarines, even for commercial purposes, shall be forbidden in Germany."

194 makes corresponding obligations of voluntary engagements for longer service, and 196 and 197 deal with naval fortifications and wireless stations.

Then, if the Tribunal please, would they pass on to Article 198, the first of the Air Clauses. The essential, important sentence is the first:

"The Armed Forces of Germany must not include any Military or Naval Air Forces."

I do not think I need trouble the Tribunal with the detailed provisions which occur in the next four clauses, which are all consequential.

Then, the next document, which for convenience is put next to that, is British Document TC-44, which for convenience I put in as GB 11, but this again is merely auxiliary to Mr. Alderman's argument. It is the report of the formal statement made at the German Air Ministry about the restarting of the Air Corps, and I respectfully suggest that the Tribunal can take judicial notice of that.

Similarly, without proving formally the long document, TC-45, the Tribunal can again take judicial notice of the public proclamation, which is a well-known public document in Germany, the proclamation of compulsory military service. Mr. Alderman has again dealt with this fully in his address.

I now come to the sixth treaty, which is the treaty between the United States and Germany restoring friendly relations, and I put in a copy as Exhibit GB 12. It is Document TC-11, and the Tribunal will find it as the second last document in the document book. The purpose of this Treaty was to complete the official cessation of hostilities between the United States of America and Germany, and I have already explained to the Tribunal that it incorporated certain parts of the Treaty of Versailles. The relevant portion for the consideration of the Tribunal is Part 5, and I have just concluded going through the clauses of the Treaty of Versailles which are repeated verbatim in this Treaty. I therefore, with the approval of the Tribunal, will not read them again, but at Page 11 of my copy, they will see the clauses are repeated in exactly the same way.

THE TRIBUNAL (Mr. Biddle): We have not a copy in our book. We have one with Austria.

SIR DAVID MAXWELL FYFE: It ought to be the second last document in the book. May I pass mine up. Does that apply to other than the American Associate judges? I am so sorry.

Then I pass to the seventh treaty, which is the Treaty of Mutual Guarantee between Germany, Belgium, France, Great Britain and Italy, done at Locarno, 16th October, 1925. I ask the Tribunal to take judicial notice of that, and I put in as Exhibit GB 13, the British Document TC-12.

THE PRESIDENT: At some later stage, you will have all the members furnished with a copy of this treaty between the United States and Germany?

SIR DAVID MAXWELL FYFE: Oh, I thought it was only two that were deficient.

THE PRESIDENT: No, I think the Soviet member and my alternate, Mr. Justice Birkett, have the Austrian one. I think I am the only one that has the German one. I am not quite sure about the French member.

SIR DAVID MAXWELL FYFE: I am so sorry, my Lord. I will see that the American Treaty is sent in.

THE PRESIDENT: Very well.

SIR DAVID MAXWELL FYFE: It will be done at once, but so far as reference is concerned, the Tribunal will appreciate that the clauses are word for word the same as the Versailles clauses. If they wish to refer to it in the meantime, it is the same as the clauses in the Versailles Treaty. That will not make any difference, my Lord, in procuring a copy of the treaty.

I was dealing with the Treaty of Locarno, and it might be convenient if I just reminded the Tribunal of the treaties that were negotiated at Locarno, because they do all go together and are to a certain extent mutually dependent.

At Locarno, Germany negotiated five treaties: (a) The Treaty of Mutual Guarantee between Germany, Belgium, France, Great Britain and Italy; (b) the Arbitration Convention between Germany and France; (c) the Arbitration Convention between Germany and Belgium; (d) the Arbitration Treaty between Germany and Poland; and (e) an Arbitration Treaty between Germany and Czechoslovakia.

Article 10 of the Treaty of Mutual Guarantee provided that it should come into force as soon as ratifications were deposited at Geneva in the archives of the League of Nations, and as soon as Germany became a member of the League of Nations. The ratifications were deposited on the 14th September, 1926, and Germany became a member of the League of Nations.

The two arbitration conventions and the two arbitration treaties which I mentioned provided that they should enter into force under the same conditions as the Treaty of Mutual Guarantee. That is Article 21 of the Arbitration Conventions and Article 22 of the Arbitration Treaties.

The most important of the five agreements is the Treaty of Mutual Guarantee. One of the purposes was to establish in perpetuity the borders between Germany and Belgium and Germany and France. It contains no provision for denunciation or withdrawal therefrom, and provides that it shall remain in force until the Council of the League of Nations decides that the League of Nations ensures sufficient protection to the parties to the Treaty - an event which never happened - in which case the Treaty of Mutual Guarantee shall expire one year later.

The general scheme of the Treaty of Mutual Guarantee is that Article I provides that the parties guarantee three things: the border between Germany and France, the border between Germany and Belgium, and the demilitarisation of the Rhineland.

Article 2 provides that Germany and France, and Germany and Belgium agree that they will not attack or invade each other, with certain inapplicable exceptions, and Article 3 provides that Germany and France, and Germany and Belgium agree to settle all disputes between them by peaceful means.

The Tribunal will remember, because this point was made by my friend, Mr. Alderman, that the first important violation of the Treaty of Mutual Guarantee appears to have been the entry of German troops into the Rhineland on 7th March, 1936. The day after France and Belgium asked the

League of Nations Council to consider the question of the German reoccupation of the Rhineland and the purported repudiation of the treaty, and on the 12th March, after a protest from. the British Secretary for Foreign Affairs, Belgium, France, Great Britain and Italy recognised unanimously that the re-occupation was a violation of this treaty, and on the 14th March, the League Council duly and properly decided that it was not permissible, and that the Rhineland clauses of the pact were not voidable by Germany, because of the alleged violation by France in the Franco-Soviet Mutual Assistance Pact.

That is the background to the treaty with the International Organisations that were then in force, and if I might suggest them to the Tribunal, without adding to the summary which I have given, the relevant articles are 1, 2 and 3, which I have mentioned, 4, which provides for the bringing of violations before the Council of the League, as was done, and 5 I ask the Tribunal to note, because it deals with the clauses of the Versailles Treaty which I have already mentioned. It says:

"The provisions of Article 3 of the present Treaty are placed under the guarantee of the High Contracting Parties as provided by the following stipulations:

If one of the Powers referred to in Article 3 refuses to submit a dispute to peaceful settlement or to comply with an arbitral or judicial decision and commits a violation of Article 2 of the present Treaty or a breach of Article 42 or 43 of the Treaty of Versailles, the provisions of Article 4 of the present Treaty shall apply."

That is the procedure of going to the League in the case of a flagrant breach or of taking more stringent action.

I remind the Tribunal of this provision because of the quotations from Hitler which I mentioned earlier, where he said that the German Government would scrupulously maintain their treaties voluntarily signed, even though they were concluded before their accession to power; that includes the Treaty of Versailles. No one has ever argued, for a moment, to the best of my knowledge, that Stresemann was in any way acting involuntarily when he signed the pact on behalf of Germany, along with the other representatives. Germany signed not only by Stresemann, but by Herr Hans Luther, so that there you have a treaty freely entered into, which repeats the violation provisions of the Versailles, and binds Germany in that regard. I simply call the attention of the Tribunal to Article 8, which deals with the preliminary enforcement of the Treaty by the League, which perhaps I should read because of the fact I told the Tribunal, that all the other treaties had the same lasting qualities, the same provision contained therein as the Treaty of Mutual Guarantee:

"Article 8

The present Treaty shall be registered at the League of Nations in accordance with the Covenant of the League. It shall remain in force until the Council, acting on a request of one or other of the High Contracting Parties notified to the other signatory Powers three months in advance, and voting at least by a two-thirds majority, decides that the League of Nations ensures sufficient protection to the High Contracting Parties; the Treaty shall cease to have effect on the expiration of a period of one year from such decision."

Thus, in signing this Treaty, the German representative clearly placed the question of repudiation or violation of the Treaty in the hands of others, as they were at the time, of course, members of the League, and members in the Council of the League; thus they then left the repudiation or violations to the decision of the League.

Then the next Treaty I mention is the Arbitration Treaty between Germany and Czechoslovakia, which was one of the Locarno groups to which I already referred my remarks, but, for convenience, I am quoting GB 14, which is British Document TC-14. As a breach to this Treaty, as charged in Charge 8, Appendix C, I mentioned the background of the Treaty, and I shall not go into it again. I think a good part that the Tribunal should look at is Article I, which is the governing clause, and sets out the dispute in Document TC-14:

"All disputes of every kind between Germany and Czechoslovakia with regard to which the Parties are in conflict as to their respective rights, and which it may not be possible to settle amicably by the normal methods of diplomacy, shall be submitted for decision either to an arbitrary Tribunal, or to the Permanent Court of International justice as laid down hereafter. It is agreed that the disputes referred to above include, in particular, those mentioned in Article 13 of the Covenant of the League of Nations. This provision does not apply to disputes arising out of, or prior to the present Treaty and belonging to the past. Disputes for the settlement of which a special procedure is laid down in other conventions in force between the High Contracting Parties, shall be settled in conformity with the provisions of those Conventions."

Articles 2 to 21. This Treaty was registered with the Secretariat in accordance with its Article 22. The second sentence shows that the present Treaty was entered into and the terms in force under the same conditions as the said Treaty, which is the Treaty of Mutual Guarantee.

Now I think that is all I shall mention about this Treaty. I think I am right in saying that my friend, Mr. Alderman, referred to it. It is certainly the Treaty to which President Benes unsuccessfully appealed during the crisis in the autumn of 1938. Now the ninth Treaty, with which I should deal, is not in this document book, and I merely put it in formally, because my friend, Mr. Roberts, is dealing with it, and will read the appropriate parts of it verbatim. It will be enough to put in, as I first mentioned, the Arbitration Convention between Germany and Belgium at Locarno, of which I hand in a copy for the convenience of the Tribunal, GB 15. This Arbitration Convention is made in the same form, but I thought I would leave the essential parts until the case concerned with Belgium, the Low Countries and Luxembourg, which my friend, Mr. Roberts, will present. I only ask the Tribunal to accept the foremost document for the moment. And the same applies to the tenth Treaty, which is mentioned in Charge 10 of Appendix C. That is the Arbitration Treaty between Germany and Poland, of which I ask the Tribunal to take judicial notice, and which I hand in as GB 16. That again will be dealt with by my friend, Colonel Griffith-Jones, when he is dealing with the Polish case.

Now I can take the Tribunal straight to the matter which is not a treaty, but is a solemn declaration, and that is TC- 18, which I now put in as Exhibit GB 17, and ask that the Tribunal take judicial notice of, as the Declaration of the Assembly of the League of Nations. The importance is the date, which was 24th September, 1927. The Tribunal may remember that I asked them to take judicial notice of the fact that Germany had become a member of the League

127

of Nations on 10th September, 1926, a year before.

The importance of this Declaration lies not only in its effect on International Law, to which I will say my learned friend referred, but in the fact that it was unanimously adopted by the Assembly of the League of Nations, of which Germany was a free, and I might say, an active member at the time. I think that I will read TC-18, that is, if the Tribunal will be good enough to look at the speech made by M. Sokal, the Polish Rapporteur, and this is the translation after the Rapporteur had dealt with the formalities. Referring to the committee's declaration being unanimously adopted, M. Sokal, the Rapporteur, said in the second paragraph:

"The Committee was of opinion that, at the present juncture, a solemn resolution passed by the Assembly, declaring that wars of aggression must never be employed as a means of settling disputes between States, and that such wars constituted an International Crime, would have a salutary effect on public opinion, and would help to create an atmosphere favourable to the League's future work in the matter of security and disarmament.

While recognising that the draft resolution does not constitute a regular legal instrument, which would be adequate in itself and represent a concrete contribution towards security, the Third Committee unanimously agreed as to its great moral and educative value."

Then he asked the Assembly to adopt the draft resolution, and I read simply the terms of the resolution, which shows what so many nations, including Germany, had in mind at that time; The Assembly, recognising the solidarity which unites the community of nations, being inspired by a firm desire for the maintenance of general peace, being convinced that a war of aggression can never serve as a means of settling international disputes, and is in consequence an International Crime; considering that the solemn renunciation of all wars of aggression would tend to create an atmosphere of general confidence calculated to facilitate the progress of the work undertaken with a view to disarmament:

Declares: 1. That all wars of aggression are and shall always be prohibited.

2. That every pacific means must be employed to settle disputes of every description, which may arise between States.

3. That the Assembly declares that the States Members of the League are under an obligation to conform to these principles."

The fact of the solemn renunciation of war was taken in the form of a roll-call, and the President announced, you will see, at the end of the extract:

"All the delegations having pronounced in favour of the declaration submitted by the Third Committee, I declare it unanimously adopted."

THE TRIBUNAL (Mr. Biddle): What is the date of that?

SIR DAVID MAXWELL FYFE: 24th September, 1927. Germany joined the League on 10th September, 1926.

The last general Treaty which I have to place before the Tribunal is the Kellogg-Briand Pact. The Pact took effect in 1928; my learned friend the Attorney General in opening this part of the case read it, and on coming to it fully I hand in as Exhibit GB 18 the British Document TC-19, which is a copy of that Pact. I did not intend, unless the Tribunal desires otherwise, to read it again, as the Attorney General yesterday read it in full, and I leave the document before the Tribunal in that form.

Now what remains for me to do is to place before the Tribunal certain documents which Mr. Alderman mentioned in the course of his address, and left to me. I am afraid I have not placed them in special order, because they do not relate to the Treaties, but to Mr. Alderman's address. The first of these I hand in as Exhibit GB 19. This is British Document TC-26, and comes just after that resolution of the League of Nations, to which the Tribunal had just been giving attention, TC-26. It is the assurance contained in Hitler's speech on 21st May, 1935, and it is very short, and unless the Tribunal has it in mind from Mr. Alderman's speech, I should like to read it again - I am not sure that it was read before - as follows:

"Germany neither intends nor wishes to interfere in the domestic affairs of Austria, to annex Austria, or to attach that country to her. The German people and the German Government have, however, the very comprehensible desire, arising out of the simple feeling of solidarity due to a common national descent, that the right to self-determination should be guaranteed not only to foreign nations, but to the German people everywhere.

I myself believe that no regime which is not anchored in the people, supported by the people, and desired by the people, can exist permanently."

The next Document which is TC-22, and which is on the next page, I now hand in as Exhibit GB 20, and it is the official copy of the official proclamation of the Agreement between the German Government and the Government of the Federal State of Austria, on 11th July, 1936, and I am almost certain that Mr. Alderman did read this document, but I refer the Tribunal to paragraph one of the agreement and to what it essentially contains:

"The German Government recognises the full sovereignty of the Federal State of Austria in the sense of the pronouncements of the German Leader and Chancellor of the 21st May, 1935."

That I hand in as GB 20. I now have three documents which Mr. Alderman asked me to hand in with regard to Czechoslovakia. The first is TC-27, which the Tribunal will find two documents farther on from the one about agreement with Austria, to which I have just been referring. That is the German Assurance to Czechoslovakia, and what I am handing in as GB 21, is the letter from M. Masaryk, T. G. Masaryk's son, to Lord Halifax, dated the 12th March, 1938, and again I think that if Mr. Alderman did not read this, he certainly quoted the statement made by the defendant Goering, which appears in the third paragraph. In the first statement Field Marshal Goering used the expression "ich gebe Ihnen mein Ehrenwort," which I understand means, "I give you my word of honour," and, if you will look down three paragraphs, after the defendant Goering had asked that there would not be a mobilisation of the Czechoslovak Army, the communication continues:

"M. Masaryk was in a position to give him definite and binding assurances on this subject, and today spoke with Baron von Neurath" - the defendant von Neurath - "who, among other things, assured him on behalf of Herr Hitler, that 'Germany still considers herself bound by the German-Czechoslovak Arbitration Convention concluded at

Locarno in October, 1925'."

So there I remind the Tribunal that in 1925 Herr Stresemann was speaking on behalf of Germany in an agreement voluntarily concluded; had there been the slightest doubt of that question, the defendant Neurath was giving the assurance on behalf of Hitler that Germany still considered herself bound by the German-Czechoslovak Arbitration Convention on the 12th March, 1938, six months before Dr. Benes made a hopeless appeal to it, before the crisis in the autumn of 1938.

There is also the difficult position of the Czechoslovakian Government, which is set out in the last paragraph that M. Masaryk wrote, and which the Tribunal may think is put with great force in this last sentence:

"They cannot however fail to view with great apprehension the sequel of events in Austria between the date of the bilateral agreement between Germany and Austria, on the 11th July, 1936, and yesterday, the 11th March, 1938."

To refrain from comment, I venture to say that is one of the most pregnant sentences relating to this period.

Now the next document, which is on the next page, is British Document TC-28, which I hand in as Exhibit GB 22. And that is an Assurance of the 26th September, 1938, which Hitler gave to Czechoslovakia, and again the Tribunal will check my memory; I do not think that Mr. Alderman read this document.

THE PRESIDENT: No, I do not recall it.

SIR DAVID MAXWELL FYFE: If he did not, the Tribunal ought to have it before them, because it contains very important points as to the alleged governing principle of getting Germans back to the Reich, on which the Nazi conspirators purported for a considerable time to rely. It said:-

"I have little to explain. I am grateful to Mr. Chamberlain for all his efforts, and I have assured him that the German people want nothing but peace; but I have also told him that I cannot go back beyond the limits of our patience."

The Tribunal will remember this is between the Godesberg Treaty meeting and the Munich Pact:-

"I assured him, moreover, and I repeat it here, that when this problem is solved there will be no more territorial problems for Germany in Europe. And I further assured him that from the moment when Czechoslovakia solves its other problems, that is to say, when the Czechs have come to an arrangement with their other minorities peacefully, and without oppression, I will no longer be interested in the Czech State. And that, as far as I am concerned, I will guarantee it. We do not want any Czechs. But I must also declare before the German people that in the Sudeten- German problem my patience is now at an end. I made an offer to M. Benes which was no more than the realisation of what he had already promised. He now has peace or war in his hands. Either he will accept this offer and at length give the Germans their freedom, or we shall get this freedom for ourselves."

Less than six months before the 15th March, Hitler was saying in the most violent terms, that "He did not want any Czechs." The Tribunal has heard it said by my friend Mr. Alderman this morning. The last document which I shall ask to put in, which I now ask the Tribunal to take notice of, and hand in is

Exhibit GB 23, which is the British Document TC-23 and a copy of the Munich Agreement Of 29th September, 1938. That was signed by Hitler, the late Neville Chamberlain, M. Daladier and Mussolini, and it is largely a procedural agreement by which the entry of German troops into Sudeten-German territory is regulated. That is shown by the preliminary clause: "Germany, the United Kingdom, France and Italy " taking into consideration the agreement, which has been already reached in principle, for the cession to Germany of the Sudeten-German territory as agreed on the following terms and conditions governing the said cession and the measures consequent thereon, and by this agreement they each hold themselves responsible for the steps necessary to secure fulfilment."

And I do not think, unless the Tribunal wants it, I need go through the steps. In Article 4, it states that:

"The occupation by stages of the predominantly German territory by German troops will begin on the 1st October. The four territories marked on the attached map," and in article 6, "The final determination of the frontiers will be carried out by the international commission."

And it provides also that there is the right of option and the release from the forces the Czech forces of Sudeten Germans.

That was what Hitler was asking for in the somewhat rhetorical passage which I have just read out, and it will be observed that there is an annex to the Agreement which is most significant.

"Annex to the Agreement.

His Majesty's Government in the United Kingdom and the French Government have entered into the above Agreement on the basis that they stand by the offer contained in Paragraph 6 of the Anglo-French Proposal of the 19th September, relating to an international guarantee of the new boundaries of the Czechoslovak State against unprovoked aggression.

When the question of the Polish and Hungarian minorities in Czechoslovakia has been settled, Germany and Italy, for their part, will give a guarantee to Czechoslovakia."

"The Polish and Hungarian minorities," not the question of Slovakia which the Tribunal heard this morning. That is why Mr. Alderman submitted, and I respectfully joined him in his submission, that the action of the 15th March was a flagrant violation of the letter and spirit of that Agreement.

That, my Lord, is the part of the case which I desired to present.

THE PRESIDENT: We will now recess for ten minutes.

SIR DAVID MAXWELL FYFE: Thank you.

(A recess was taken.)

LIEUTENANT-COLONEL GRIFFITH-JONES: May it please the Tribunal, Count 2 of the Indictment charges participation in the planning, the preparation, the initiation and waging of various wars of aggression, and it charges that those wars are also in breach of international treaties. It is our purpose now to present to the Tribunal the evidence in respect of those aggressive wars against Poland and against the United Kingdom and France.

Under Paragraph B. of the particulars to that Count 2, reference is made to Count I in the Indictment for the allegations charging that those wars were wars of aggression, and Count I also sets out the particulars of the

131

preparations and planning for those wars, and in particular those allegations will be found in Paragraph F-4. But, my Lord, with the Tribunal's approval

I would propose first to deal with the allegations of breach of treaties which are mentioned in Paragraph C. of the particulars, and of which the details are set out in Appendix C. The section of Appendix C. which relates to the war against Poland is Section 2, which charges a violation of the Hague Convention in respect of the pacific settlement of international disputes, on which Sir David has already addressed the Court, and I do not propose, with the Court's approval, to say more than that.

Section 3 of Appendix C. and Section 4 charges breaches of the other Hague Conventions of 1907. Section 5 (Subsection 4) charges a breach of the Versailles Treaty in respect of the Free City of Danzig, and Section 13 a breach of the Kellogg-Briand Pact.

All those have already been dealt with by Sir David Maxwell Fyfe, and it remains, therefore, for me only to deal with two other sections of Appendix C Section 10, which charges a breach of the Arbitration Treaty between Germany and Poland, signed at Locarno on the 16th October, 1925, and Section 15 Of Appendix C., which charges a violation of the Declaration of Non-Aggression which was entered into between Germany and Poland on the 26th January, 1934.

If the Tribunal would take Part I of the British document book No. 2, I will describe in a moment how the remaining parts are divided. The document book is divided into six parts. The Tribunal will look at Part I for the moment. The document books which have been handed to the defence counsel are in exactly the same order, except that they are bound in one and not in six separate covers, in which the Tribunal's documents are bound for convenience.

The German-Polish Arbitration Treaty, the subject of Section 10 of Appendix C. is Document TC-15 and it is the end document in the book. It has already been put in under the number GB 16.

My Lord, I would quote the preamble and Articles I and 2 from that Treaty.

"THE PRESIDENT OF THE GERMAN EMPIRE AND THE PRESIDENT OF THE POLISH REPUBLIC:

Equally resolved to maintain peace between Germany and Poland by assuring the peaceful settlement of differences which might arise between the two countries;

Declaring that respect for the rights established by treaty or resulting from the law of nations is obligatory for international tribunals;

Agreeing to recognise that the rights of a State cannot be modified save with its consent;

And considering that sincere observance of the methods of peaceful settlement of international disputes permits of resolving, without recourse to force, questions which may become the cause of division between States;

Have decided ."

Then going on to Article I:

"All disputes of every kind between Germany and Poland with regard to which the Parties are in conflict as to their respective rights, and which it may not be possible to settle amicably by the normal methods of diplomacy, shall be submitted for decision either to an arbitral tribunal or to the Permanent Court of International justice, as laid down hereafter."

I go straight to Article 2:-

"Before any resort is made to arbitral procedure before the Permanent Court of International Justice, the dispute may, by agreement between the Parties, be submitted, with a view to amicable settlement, to a permanent international commission, styled the Permanent Conciliation Commission, constituted in accordance with the present Treaty."

Thereafter the Treaty goes on to lay down the procedure for arbitration and for conciliation.

THE PRESIDENT: It is in the same terms, is it not, as the arbitration treaty between Germany and Czechoslovakia and Germany and Belgium?

LIEUTENANT-COLONEL GRIFFITH-JONES: Well - yes, it is, my Lord, both signed at Locarno.

THE PRESIDENT: Yes.

LIEUTENANT-COLONEL GRIFFITH-JONES: The wording, however, of the charge in Section 10, it will be noted, is that Germany did, on or about the 1st September, 1939, unlawfully attack and invade Poland without having first attempted to settle its disputes with Poland by peaceful means.

The only other treaty to which I refer, the German-Polish Declaration of the 26th January, 1934, will be found as the last document in Part 1 of the Tribunal's document book, which is the subject of Section 10 of Appendix C.

"The German Government and the Polish Government" - This, of course, was signed on the 26th January, 1934.

"The German Government and the Polish Government consider that the time has come to introduce a new era in the political relations between Germany and Poland by a direct understanding between the States. They have therefore decided to establish by the present declaration a basis for the future shaping of those relations.

The two Governments assume that the maintenance and assurance of a permanent peace between their countries is an essential condition for general peace in Europe."

THE PRESIDENT: Do you think it is necessary to read all this? We are taking judicial notice of it.

LIEUTENANT-COLONEL GRIFFITH-JONES: I am very much obliged. I am willing to shorten this, if I can.

In view of what is later alleged by the Nazi Government, I will particularly draw attention to the last paragraph in that declaration:

"The declaration shall remain in effect for a period of ten years counting from the day of exchange of instruments of ratification. In case it is not denounced by one of the two governments six months before the expiration of that period of time, it shall continue in effect, but can then be denounced by either government after six months and at any time six months in advance."

My Lord, I pass then from the breach of treaties to present to the Court the evidence upon the planning and preparation of these wars, and in support of the allegations that they were wars of aggression. For convenience, as I say, the documents have been divided into separate parts and if the Tribunal would look at the index, the total index to their documents, which is a separate book, on the front page it will be seen how these documents have been divided. Part 1 is the "Treaties"; Part 2 is entitled "Evidence of German Intentions Prior to March, 1939." It might perhaps be more accurately described as "Pre-March, 1939, Evidence", and it will be with that part that I would now deal.

It has been put to the Tribunal that the actions against Austria and Czechoslovakia were in themselves part of the preparation for further aggression, and I now - dealing with the early history of this matter - wish to draw the Court's particular attention only to those parts of the evidence which show that even at that time, before the Germans had seized the whole of Czechoslovakia, they were perfectly prepared to fight England, Poland and France, if necessary, to achieve those aims; that they appreciated the whole time that they might well have to do so. And, what is more, that, although not until after March, 1939, did they begin their immediate and specific preparations for a specific war against Poland, nevertheless, they had, for a considerable time before, had it in mind specifically to attack Poland, once Czechoslovakia was completely theirs.

During this period also - and this happens throughout the whole story of the Nazi regime in Germany - as afterwards, while they are making their preparations and carrying out their plans, they are giving to the outside world assurance after assurance so as to lull them out of any suspicion of their real object.

The dates - as I think the Attorney General said, addressing you yesterday - the dates in this case, almost more than the documents, speak for themselves. The documents in this book are arranged in the order in which I will refer to them, and the first that I would refer to is Document TC-70, which will go in as GB 25.

It is only interesting to see what Hitler said of the agreement with Poland when it was signed in January, 1934.

"When I took over the Government on the 30th January, the relations between the two countries seemed to me more than unsatisfactory. There was a danger that the existing differences which were due to the territorial Clauses of the Treaty of Versailles, and the mutual tension resulting therefrom, would gradually crystallise into a state of hostility which, if persisted in, might too easily acquire the character of a dangerous traditional enmity."

I go down to the last paragraph:-

"In the spirit of this Treaty the German Government is willing and prepared to cultivate economic relations with Poland in such a way that here, too, the state of unprofitable suspicion can be succeeded by a period of useful co-operation. It is a matter of particular satisfaction to us that in this same year the National Socialist Government of Danzig has been enabled to effect a similar clarification of its relations with its Polish neighbour."

That was in 1934. Three years later, again on the 30th January, speaking in the Reichstag, Hitler said - this is Document PS-2368, which will be GB 26. I will, if I may, avoid so far as possible repeating passages which the Attorney General quoted in his speech the other day. The first paragraph, in fact, he quoted to the Tribunal. It is a short paragraph but perhaps I might read it now, but I will, dealing with this evidence, so far as possible avoid repetition - Hitler said, on that occasion:

"By a series of agreements we have eliminated existing tension and thereby contributed considerably to an improvement in the European atmosphere. I merely recall an agreement with Poland which has worked out to the advantage of both sides. True statesmanship will not overlook realities but consider them. The Italian nation and the new Italian State are realities. The German nation and the German Reich are equally realities, and to my own fellow citizens I would say that the Polish nation and the Polish State have also become a reality."

That was on the 30th January, 1937.

On the 24th June, 1937, we have a "Top Secret Order ", C- 175, which has already been put in as Exhibit USA 69. It is a "Top Secret Order" issued by the Reich Minister for War and Commander-in-Chief of the Armed Forces, signed "von Blomberg". There is at the top, "Written by an Officer. Outgoing documents in connection with this matter and dealing with it in principle are to be written by an officer." So it is obviously highly secret, and with it is enclosed a Directive for the Unified Preparation for War of the Armed Forces to come into force on the 1st August, 1937. The directive enclosed with it is divided into Part 1, "General Guiding Principle"; Part 2, "Likely Warlike Eventualities"; Part 3, "Special Preparations".

The Tribunal will remember that the Attorney General quoted the opening passages. The general position justifies the supposition that Germany need not consider an attack from any side.

It goes on - the second paragraph:

"The intention to unleash a European war is held just as little by Germany. Nevertheless, the politically fluid world situation, which does not preclude surprising incidents, demands a continuous preparedness for war of the German Armed Forces.

To counter attacks at any time, and to enable the military exploitation of politically favourable opportunities should they occur."

It then goes on to set out the preparations which are to he made, and I would particularly draw the Tribunal's attention to paragraph 2b:

"The further working on mobilisation without public announcement, in order to put the Armed Forces in a position to begin a war suddenly and by surprise both as regards strength and time."

On the next page, under Paragraph 4:

"Special preparations are to be made for the following eventualities:

Armed intervention against Austria; warlike entanglement with Red Spain."

Thirdly, and this shows so clearly how they appreciated at that time that their actions against Austria and Czechoslovakia might well involve them in war, "England, Poland, Lithuania take part in a war against us."

If the Tribunal would turn over to Part 2 of that directive, Page 5 of that document: "Probable warlike eventualities-

Concentrations ":-

1. War on two fronts with focal point in the West.

Suppositions. In the West, France is the opponent. Belgium may side with France, either at once, or later, or not at all. It is also possible that France may violate Belgium's neutrality if the latter is neutral. She will certainly violate that of Luxembourg."

135

I pass to Part 3, which will be found on Page 9 of that exhibit, and I particularly refer to the last paragraph on that page under the heading "Special Case-Extension Red- Green." It will he remembered that Red was Spain and Green was Czechoslovakia.

"The military political starting point used as a basis for concentration plans Red and Green can be aggravated if either England, Poland or Lithuania join on the side of our opponents. Thereupon our military position would be worsened to an unbearable, even hopeless extent. The political leaders will therefore do everything to keep these countries neutral, above all England and Poland."

Thereafter it sets out the conditions which are to be the basis for the discussion. Before I leave that document, the date will be noted, June, 1937, and it shows clearly that at that date, anyway, the Nazi Government appreciated the likelihood, if not the probability of fighting England and Poland and France, and were prepared to do so if they had to. On the 5th November, 1937, the Tribunal will remember that Hitler held his conference in the Reich Chancellery, the minutes of which have been referred to as the Hoszbach notes. I will refer to one or two lines of that document for the attention of the Tribunal to what Hitler said in respect of England, Poland, and France. On page 1 of that exhibit, the middle of the page

"The Fuehrer then stated: 'The aim of German policy is the security and preservation of the nation and its propagation. This is consequently a problem of space'."

He then went on, you will remember, to discuss what he described as "participation in world economy", and at the bottom of Page 2 he said:

"The only way out, and one which may appear imaginary, is the securing of greater living space, an endeavour which at all times has been the cause of the formation of States and movements of nations."

And at the end of that first paragraph, on Page 3:

"The history of all times, Roman Empire, British Empire, has proved that every space expansion can only be effected by breaking resistance and taking risks. Even setbacks are unavoidable. Neither formerly nor today has space been found without an owner. The attacker always comes up against the proprietor."

My Lord, it is clear that that reference was not only -

THE PRESIDENT: (interposing) It has been read already.

LIEUTENANT-COLONEL GRIFFITH-JONES: But my object was only to try to collect, so far as England and Poland were concerned, everything that has been given. If the Tribunal thought that it was unnecessary, I would welcome the opportunity -

THE PRESIDENT: I think the Tribunal would wish you not to read anything that has been read already.

LIEUTENANT-COLONEL GRIFFITH-JONES: I would pass then to the next document in that part of the document book. I put that document in. It was referred to by the Attorney General in his address yesterday, and it shows that on the same day as the Hoszbach meeting was taking place, a communique was being issued as a result of the Polish Ambassador's audience with Hitler, in which it was said in the course of the conversation, "It was confirmed that Polish-German relations should not meet with difficulty because of the Danzig question." That document is TC-73. I put it in as GB 27. On the 2nd of January -

THE PRESIDENT: That has not been read before, has it?

LIEUTENANT-COLONEL GRIFFITH-JONES: It was read by the Attorney General in his opening.

THE PRESIDENT: In his opening? Very well.

LIEUTENANT-COLONEL GRIFFITH-JONES: On the 2nd January, 1938, some unknown person wrote a memorandum for the Fuehrer. This document was one of the seven foreign office documents of which a microfilm was captured by Allied troops when they came into Germany. It is headed, "Very Confidential - Personal Only", and is called "Deduction on the report, German Embassy, London, regarding the future form of Anglo- German relations":

> "With the realisation that Germany will not tie herself to a status quo in Central Europe, and that sooner or later a military conflict in Europe is possible, the hope of an agreement will slowly disappear among Germanophile British politicians, in so far as they are not merely playing a part that has been given to them. Thus the fateful question arises: Will Germany and England eventually be forced to drift into separate camps and will they march against each other one day? To answer this question, one must realise the following -
>
> Change of the status quo in the East in the German sense can only be carried out by force. So long as France knows that England, which so to speak has taken on a guarantee to aid France against Germany, is on her side, France's fighting for her Eastern allies is probable in any case, always possible, and thus with it war between Germany and England. This applies then even if England does not want war. England, believing she must defend her borders on the Rhine, would be dragged in automatically by France. In other words, peace or war between England and Germany rests solely in the hands of France, who could bring about such a war between Germany and England by way of a conflict between Germany and France. It follows therefore that war between Germany and England on account of France can be prevented only if France knows from the start that England's forces would not be sufficient to guarantee their common victory. Such a situation might force England, and thereby France, to accept a lot of things that a strong Anglo-French coalition would never tolerate.
>
> This position would arise for instance if England, through insufficient armament or as a result of threats to her Empire by a superior coalition of powers, e.g. Germany, Italy, Japan, thereby tying down her military forces in other places, were not able to assure France of sufficient support in Europe."

The next page goes on to discuss the possibility of a strong partnership between Italy and Japan, and I would pass from my quotation to the next page where the writer is summarising his ideas.

Paragraph 5: Therefore, conclusions to be drawn by us.

1. Outwardly, further understanding with England in regard to the protection of the interests of our friends.

2. Formation under great secrecy, but with whole-hearted tenacity of a coalition against England, that is to say, a tightening of our friendship

137

with Italy and Japan; also the winning over of all nations whose interests conform with ours directly or indirectly.

3. Close and confidential co-operation of the diplomats of the three great powers towards this purpose. Only in this way can we confront England, be it in a settlement or in war. England is going to be a hard, astute opponent in this game of diplomacy.

4. The particular question whether in the event of a war by Germany in Central Europe - I am afraid the translation of this is not very good - "The particular question whether, in the event of a war in Central Europe France and thereby England would interfere, depends on the circumstances and the time at which such a war commences and ceases, and on military considerations which cannot be gone into here."

And whoever it was who wrote that document, he appears to be on a fairly high level, because he concludes by saying, "I should like to give the Fuehrer some of these viewpoints verbally." That document is GB 28. I am afraid the next two documents have got into your books in the wrong order. If you will refer to 2357-PS - you will remember that the document to the Fuehrer, which I have just read, was dated the 2nd January.

On 20th January, 1938, Hitler spoke in the Reichstag.

THE PRESIDENT: February, you said?

LIEUTENANT-COLONEL GRIFFITH-JONES: I beg your pardon, February 1938. That is 2357-PS, and will be Exhibit GB 30. In that speech he said:

"In the fifth year following the first great foreign political agreement with the Reich, it fills us with sincere gratification to be able to affirm that in our relations with the State, with which we had had perhaps the greatest difference, not only has there been a 'detente,' but in the course of the years there has been a constant improvement. This good work, which was regarded with suspicion by so many at the time, has stood the test, and I may say that since the League of Nations finally gave up its continual attempts to unsettle Danzig, and appointed a man of great personal attainments as the new Commissioner, this most dangerous spot from the point of view of European peace has entirely lost its menacing character. The Polish State respects the national conditions in this State, and both the city of Danzig and Germany respect Polish rights. And so the way to an understanding has been successfully paved, an understanding which beginning with Danzig has today, in spite of the attempts of certain mischief- makers, succeeded in finally taking the poison out of the relations between Germany and Poland, and transforming them into a sincere, friendly co-operation.

To rely on her friendships, Germany will not leave a stone unturned to save that ideal which provides the foundation for the task which is ahead of us - peace."

I turn back to the next - to the document which was in our document books, the one before that, L-43, which will be Exhibit GB 29. This is a document to which the Attorney General referred yesterday. It is dated the 2nd May, 1938, and is entitled, "Organisational Study, 1950." It comes from the office of the Chief of the Organisational Staff of the General Staff of the Air Force, and its purpose is said to be:

138

"The task is to search, within a framework of very broadly conceived conditions, for the most suitable type of organisation of the Air Force. The result gained is termed, 'Distant Objective.' From this shall be deduced the goal to be reached in the second phase of the setting-up process in 1942; this will be called, 'Final Objective, 1942.' This in turn yields what is considered the most suitable proposal for the reorganisation of the staffs of the Air Force Group Commands, Air Gaus, Air Divisions, etc."

The Table of Contents, the Tribunal will see, is divided into various sections, and Section I is entitled, "Assumptions." Under the heading "Assumption 1, frontier of Germany ", see map, enclosure one.

The Tribunal sees a reproduction of that map on the wall and it will be seen that on the 2nd May, 1938, the Air Force was in Estonia, Latvia, Lithuania, Poland, Czechoslovakia, Austria and Hungary, all coming within the boundaries of the Reich. The original map is here attached to this file and if the Tribunal will look at the original exhibit, it will be seen that this organisational study has been prepared with the greatest care and authority, with a mass of charts attached to the appendices.

I would refer also to the bottom of the second page, in the Tribunal's copy of the translation.

"Consideration of the principles of organisation on the basis of the assumptions for war and peace made in Section 1;
1. Attack Forces:-
Principal adversaries: England, France and Russia."

It then goes on to show all the one hundred and forty-four Geschwader employed against England, very much concentrated in the Western half of the Reich; that is to say, they must be deployed in such a way that they, by making full use of their range, can reach all English territory down to the last corner.

THE PRESIDENT: Perhaps it is involved in the map. I think you should refer to the organisation of the Air Forces, with group commands at Warsaw and Konigsberg.

LIEUTENANT-COLONEL GRIFFITH-JONES: I am much obliged. Under the paragraph "Assumption" double heading 2, "Organisation of Air Force in peacetime", seven group commands: - 1 Berlin, 2 Brunswick, 3 Munich, 4 Vienna, 5 Budapest, 6 Warsaw, and 7 Konigsberg."

THE PRESIDENT: Yes.

LIEUTENANT-COLONEL GRIFFITH-JONES: I am very much obliged. Lastly, in connection with that document, on Page 4 of the Tribunal's translation, the last paragraph:

"The more the Reich grows in area and the more the Air Force grows in strength, the more imperative it becomes to have locally bound commands."

I only emphasise the opening, "The more the Reich grows in area, the more the Air Force grows in strength" but I would say one word on that document. The original, I understand, is signed by an officer who is not of the top rank in the Air Force and I, therefore, do not want to over-emphasise the inferences that can be drawn from it, but it is submitted that it at least shows the lines upon which the General Staff of the Air Force were thinking at that time.

The Tribunal will remember that in February, 1938, the defendant Ribbentrop succeeded von Neurath as Foreign Minister. We have another document from that captured microfilm, which is dated 26th August, 1938, when Ribbentrop had become Foreign Minister, and it is addressed to him, as "The Reich Minister, via the State Secretary." It is a comparatively short document and I will read the whole of it.

The most pressing problem of German policy, the Czech problem, might easily, but must not lead to a conflict with the Entente. (TC-76 - GB 31.) Neither France nor England are looking for trouble regarding Czechoslovakia. Both would perhaps leave Czechoslovakia to herself, if she should, without direct foreign interference and through internal signs of disintegration, due to her own faults, suffer the fate she deserves. This process, however, would have to take place step by step and would have to lead to a loss of power in the remaining territory by means of a plebiscite and an annexation of territory.

The Czech problem is not yet politically acute enough for any immediate action, which the Entente would watch inactively, and not even if this action should come quickly and surprisingly. Germany cannot fix any definite time, and this fruit could be plucked without too great a risk. She can only prepare the desired developments."

I pass to the last paragraph on that page. I think I can leave out the intervening lines, Paragraph 5.

THE PRESIDENT: Should you not read the next paragraph "for this purpose."

LIEUTENANT-COLONEL GRIFFITH-JONES:

"For this purpose the slogan emanating from England at present of the 'right for autonomy of the Sudeten Germans,' which we have intentionally not used up to now, is to be taken up gradually. The international conviction that the choice of nationality was being withheld from these Germans will do useful spadework, notwithstanding the fact that the chemical process of dissolution of the Czech form of States may or may not be finally speeded up by mechanical means as well. The fate of the actual body of Czechoslovakia, however, would not as yet be clearly decided by this: but would nevertheless be definitely sealed.

This method of approach towards Czechoslovakia is to be recommended because of our relationship with Poland. It is unavoidable that the German departure from the problems of boundaries in the South-east and their transfer to the East and Northeast must make the Poles sit up. The fact is" - I put in an "is" because I think it is obviously left out of the copy I have in front of me. - "The fact is that after the liquidation of the Czech question, it will be generally assumed that Poland will be the next in turn.

But the later this assumption sinks into international politics as a firm factor, the better. In this sense, however, it is important for the time being to carry on the German policy, under the well known and proved slogans of 'The right to autonomy' and 'Racial unity'. Anything else might be interpreted as pure imperialism on our part, and create the resistance to our plan by the Entente at an earlier date and more energetically, than our forces could stand up to."

That was on 26th August, 1938, just as the Czech crisis was leading up to a Munich settlement. While at Munich, or rather a day or two before the Munich agreement was signed, Herr Hitler made a speech. On the 26th

September, he said: - I think I will read just two lines -

"I assured him, moreover, and I repeat it here, that when this problem is solved there will be no more territorial problems for Germany in Europe."

And again, the last document in your book, which is another extract from that same speech, I will not read unless the Tribunal desire because the Attorney General quoted it in his address yesterday. These two documents precede TC-28, which is already in as GB 2, and TC-29, which is the second extraction of that same speech, and is Exhibit GB 32.

I would refer the Tribunal to one more document under this part which has already been put in by my American colleagues. It is C-23, now Exhibit USA 49, and it appears before TC-28 in your document book. The particular passage of the exhibit, to which I would refer, is a letter from Admiral Carl, which appears at the bottom of the second page. It is dated some time in September, with no precise date, and is entitled "Opinion on the 'Draft Study of Naval Warfare against England'".

There is full agreement with the main theme of the Study. Again, the Attorney General quoted the remainder of that letter yesterday, which the Tribunal will remember.

"If, according to the Fuehrer's decision, Germany is to acquire a position as a world power, she needs not only sufficient colonial possessions but also naval communications and secure access to the ocean."

That, then, was the position at the time of the Munich agreement in September, 1938.

The gains of Munich were not, of course, so great as the Nazi Government had hoped and had intended and, as a result, they were not prepared straight away to start any further aggressive action against Poland or elsewhere: but, as we have heard this morning, when Mr. Alderman dealt, in his closing remarks, with the advantages that were gained by the seizure of Czechoslovakia, Jodl and Hitler said on subsequent occasions, that Czechoslovakia was only setting the stage for this attack on Poland. It is, of course, obvious now that they intended and indeed had taken the decision to proceed against Poland as soon as Czechoslovakia had been entirely occupied.

We know that now from what Hitler said in talking to his military commanders at a later date. The Tribunal will remember the speech-where he said that from the first he never intended to abide by the Munich agreement, but that he had to have the whole of Czechoslovakia. As a result, although not ready to proceed in full force against Poland, after September, 1938, they did at once begin to approach the Poles on the question of Danzig. Until, as the Tribunal will see, the whole of Czechoslovakia had been taken in March, no pressure was put on, but immediately after the Sudetenland had been occupied preliminary steps were taken to stir up trouble with Poland, which would and was eventually to lead to the excuse or so-called justification for their attack on that country.

If the Tribunal would turn to part 3.

THE PRESIDENT: I think it is time to adjourn now until 10 o'clock tomorrow morning.

[The Tribunal adjourned until 6th December, 1945, at 1000 hours.]

Fourteenth Day:
Thursday, 6 December 1945

THE PRESIDENT: The Tribunal has received an urgent request from the defendants' counsel that the Trial should be adjourned at Christmas for a period of 3 weeks. The Tribunal is aware of the many interests which must be considered in a trial of this complexity and magnitude, and, as the Trial must inevitably last for a considerable time, the Tribunal considers that it is not only in the interest of the defendants and their counsel but of every one concerned in the Trial that there should be a recess. On the whole it seems best to take that recess at Christmas rather than at a later date when the Prosecution's case has been completed. The Tribunal will therefore rise for the Christmas week and over the 1st of January, and will not sit after the session on Thursday, the 20th of December, and will sit again on Wednesday, the 2d of January.

MR. JUSTICE JACKSON: I should like, in justice to my staff, to note the American objection to the adjournment for the benefit of the defendants.

LT. COL. GRIFFITH-JONES: May it please the Tribunal, the tribunal will return to Part III of that document book in which included the documents relating to the earlier discussions between the German and Polish Governments on the question of Danzig. Those discussions, the Tribunal will remember, started almost immediately after the Munich crisis in September 1938, and started, in the first place, as cautious and friendly discussions until the remainder of Czechoslovakia had finally been seized in March of the following year.

I would refer the Tribunal to the first document in that part, TC-73, Number 44. That is a document taken from the official *Polish White Book*, which I put in as Exhibit GB-27 (a). It gives an account of a luncheon which took place at the Grand Hotel, Berchtesgaden, on the 24th of October, where Ribbentrop saw Mr. Lipski, the Polish ambassador to Germany:

> "In a conversation of the 29th of October, over a luncheon at the Grand Hotel, Berchtesgaden, at which M. Hewel was present, Von Ribbentrop put forward a proposal for a general settlement of issues between Poland and Germany. This included the reunion of Danzig with the Reich, while Poland would be assured the retention of railway and economic facilities there. Poland would agree to the building of an extraterritorial motor road and a railway line across Pomorze (northern part of the corridor).In exchange Von Ribbentrop mentioned the possibility of an extension of the Polish-German Agreement to 25 years and a guarantee of Polish-German frontiers."

I do not think I need read the following lines. I go to the last but one paragraph:

> "Finally, I said to Von Ribbentrop that I could see no possibility of an agreement involving the reunion of the Free City with the Reich. I concluded by promising to communicate the substance of this conversation to you."

I would emphasize the submission of the Prosecution as to this part of the case and that it is that the whole question of Danzig was indeed, as Hitler has himself said, no question at all. Danzig was raised simply as an excuse, as so-called justification, not for the seizure of Danzig, but for the invasion and seizure of the whole of Poland, and we see it starting now. As we progress with the story it will become ever more apparent that that is what the Nazi government were really aiming at only providing themselves with some kind of crisis which would provide some kind of justification for walking into the rest of Poland.

I turn to the next document. It is again a document taken from the *Polish White Book*, T-73, Number 45, which will be GB-27 (b). TC-73 will be the *Polish White Book*, which I shall put in later. That document sets out the instructions that Mr. Beck, the Polish Foreign Minister, gave to Mr. Lipski to hand to the German Government in reply to the suggestion put forward by Ribbentrop at Berchtesgaden on the 24th of October. I need not read the first page. The history of Polish-German relationship is set out, and the needs of Poland in respect of Danzig are emphasized. I turn to the second page of that exhibit, to Paragraph 6:

"In the circumstances, in the understanding of the Polish Government, the Danzig question is governed by two factors: The right of the German population of the city and the surrounding villages to freedom of life and development, and fee fact that in all matters appertaining to the Free City as a port it is connected with Poland. Apart from the national character of the majority of the population, everything in Danzig is definitely bound up with Poland."

It then sets out the guarantees to Poland under the existing statute, and I pass to Paragraph 7:

"Taking all the foregoing factors into consideration, and desiring to achieve the stabilization of relations by way of a friendly understanding with the Government of the German Reich, the Polish Government proposes the replacement of the League Nations guarantee and its prerogatives by a bilateral Polish-German agreement. This agreement should guarantee the existence of the Free City of Danzig so as to assure freedom of national and cultural life to its German majority, and also should guarantee all Polish rights. Notwithstanding the complications involved in such a system, the polish Government must state that any other solution, and in particular any attempt to incorporate the Free City into the Reich, must inevitably lead to a conflict. This would not only take the form of local difficulties, but also would suspend all possibility of Posh-German understanding in all its aspects."

And then finally in Paragraph 8:

"In face of the weight and cogency of these questions, I already to have final conversations personally with the governing circles of the Reich. I deem it necessary, however, that you should first present the principles to which we adhere, so that my eventual contact should not end in a breakdown, which would be dangerous for the future."

The first stage in those negotiations had been entirely successful from the German point of view. They had put forward a proposal, the return of the City of Danzig to the Reich, which they might well have known would have been unacceptable. It was unacceptable, and the Polish Government had

143

warned the Nazi Government that it would be. They had offered to enter into negotiations, but they had not agreed, which is exactly what the German Government had hoped. They had not agreed to the return of Danzig to the Reich. The first stage in producing the crisis had been accomplished.

Shortly afterward, within a week or so of that taking place, after the Polish Government had offered to enter into discussions with the German Government, we find another top-secret order, issued by the Supreme Command of the Armed Forces, signed by the Defendant Keitel. It goes to the OKH, OKM, and OKW and it is headed, "The First Supplement to the Instruction Dated the 21st of October 1938":

> "The Fuehrer has ordered: Apart from the three contingencies mentioned in the instructions of that date of 21 October 1938, preparations are also to be made to enable the Free State of Danzig to be occupied by German troops by surprise ...."The preparations will be made on the following basis: Condition is a quasi-revolutionary occupation of Danzig, exploiting a politically favorable situation, not a war against Poland."

We remember, of course, that at that moment the remainder of Czechoslovakia had not been seized and therefore they were not ready to go to war with Poland. That document does show how the German Government answered the proposal to enter into discussions. That is C-137 and will become GB-33.

On the 5th of January 1939 Mr. Beck had a conversation with Hitler. It is unnecessary to read the first part of that document, which is the next in the Tribunal's book, TC-73, Number 48, which will become GB-34. In the first part of that conversation, of which that document is an account, Hitler offers to answer any questions. He says he has always followed the policy laid down by the 1934 agreement. He discusses the Danzig question and emphasizes that in the German view it must sooner or later return to Germany. I quote the last but one paragraph of that page:

> "Mr. Beck replied that the Danzig question was a very difficult problem. He added that in the Chancellor's suggestion he did not see any equivalent for Poland, and that the whole of Polish opinion, and not only people thinking politically but the widest spheres of Polish society, were particularly sensitive on this matter.

> "In answer to this the Chancellor stated that to solve this problem it would be necessary to try to find something quite new, some new form, for which he used the term Korperschaft, which on the one hand would safeguard the interests of the German population, and on the other the Polish interests. In addition, the Chancellor declared that the Minister could be quite at ease, there would be no *faits accomplis* in Danzig, and nothing would be done to render difficult the situation of the Polish Government."

The Tribunal will remember that in the very last document we looked at, on the 24th of November, orders had already been received, or issued, for preparations to be made for the occupation of Danzig by surprise; yet here he is assuring the Polish Foreign Minister that there is to be no *fait accompli* and he can be quite at his ease.

I turn to the next step, Document TC-73, Number 49, which will become GB-35, conversation between Mr. Beck and Ribbentrop, on the day after the one to which I have just referred between Beck and Hitler.

THE PRESIDENT: Did you draw attention to the fact that the last conversation took place in the presence of the Defendant Ribbentrop?

LT. COL. GRIFFITH-JONES: I am very obliged to you. No, I did not. As I say, it was on the next day, the 6th of January. The date in actual fact does not appear on the copy I have got in my book. It does appear in the *White Book* itself.

"Mr. Beck asked Ribbentrop to inform the Chancellor that whereas previously, after all his conversations and contacts with German statesmen, he had been feeling optimistic, today, for the first time he was in a pessimistic mood. Particularly in regard to the Danzig question, as it had been raised by the Chancellor, he saw no possibility whatever of agreement."

I emphasize this last paragraph:

"In answer Ribbentrop once more emphasized that Germany was not seeking any violent solution. The basis of their policy towards Poland was still a desire for the further building upon friendly relations. It was necessary to seek such a method of clearing away the difficulties as would respect the rights and interests of the two parties concerned."

The Defendant Ribbentrop apparently was not satisfied with that one expression of good faith. On the 25th of the same month, January 1939, some fortnight or three weeks later, he was in Warsaw and made another speech, of which an extract is set out in PS-2530, which will become GB-36:

"In accordance with the resolute will of the German national leader, the continual progress and consolidation of friendly relations between Germany and Poland, based upon the existing agreement between us, constitute an essential element in German foreign policy. The political foresight and the principles worthy of true statesmanship, which induced both sides to take the momentous decision of 1934, provide a guarantee that an other problems arising in the course of the future evolution of events will also be solved in the same spirit, with due regard to the respect and understanding of the rightful interests of both sides. Thus Poland and Germany can look forward to the future with full confidence in the solid basis of their mutual relations."

And even so, the Nazi Government must have been still anxious that the Poles were beginning to sit up_Your Lordship will remember the expression "sit up" used in the note to the Fuehrer_and to assume they would be the next in turn, because on the 30th of January Hitler again spoke in the Reichstag, 30th of January 1939, and gave further assurances of their good faith.

That document, that extract, was read by the Attorney General in his address, and therefore, I only put it in now as an exhibit. That is TC-73, Number 57, which will become GB-37.

That, then, brings us up to the March 1939 seizure of the remainder of Czechoslovakia and the setting up of the Protectorate of Bohemia and Moravia.

If the Tribunal will now pass to the next part, Part IV, of that document book, I had intended to refer to three documents where Hitler and Jodl were setting out the advantage gained through the seizure of the remainder of Czechoslovakia. But the Tribunal will remember that Mr. Alderman, in his closing remarks yesterday morning, dealt very fully with that matter showing what advantages they did gain by that seizure and showing on the chart that he had on the wall the immense strengthening of the German position against Poland. Therefore, I leave that matter. The documents are already in evidence, and if the Tribunal should wish to refer to them, they are found in their correct order in the story in that document book.

As soon as that occupation had been completed, with a week of marching into the rest of Czechoslovakia, the heat was beginning to be turned on against Poland.

If the Tribunal would pass to Document TC-73, which is about half way through that document book_it follows after Jodl's lecture, which is a long document - TC-73, Number 61. It is headed: "Official documents concerning Polish-German Relations." This will be GB-38. On the 21st of March Mr. Lipski again saw Ribbentrop and the nature of the conversation was generally very much sharper than that that had been held a little time back at the Grand Hotel, Berchtesgaden:

"I saw Ribbentrop today. He began by saying he had asked me to call in order to discuss Polish-German relations in their entirety.

"He complained about our press, and the Warsaw students' demonstrations during Count Ciano's visit."

I think I can go straight on to the larger paragraph, which commences with "further"

"Further, Ribbentrop referred to the conversation at Berchtesgaden between you and the Chancellor, in which Hitler put forward the idea of guaranteeing Poland's frontiers in exchange for a motor road and the incorporation of Danzig into the Reich. He said that there had been further conversations between you and him in Warsaw" - that is, between him, of course, and Mr. Beck - "He said that there had been further conversations between you and him in Warsaw on the subject, and that you had pointed out the great difficulties in the way of accepting these suggestions. He gave me to understand that all this had made an unfavorable impression on the Chancellor, since so far he had received no positive reaction whatever on our part to his suggestions. Ribbentrop had talked to the Chancellor, only yesterday. He stated that the Chancellor was still in favor of good relations with Poland, and had expressed a desire to have a thorough conversation with you on the subject of our mutual relations. Ribbentrop indicated that he was under the impression that difficulties arising between us were also due to some misunderstanding of the Reich's real aims. The problem needed to be considered on a higher plane. In his opinion, our two States were dependent on each other."

I think it unnecessary that I should read the next page. Briefly, Ribbentrop emphasizes the German argument as to why Danzig should return to the Reich, and I turn to the first paragraph on the following page:

"I stated" - that is Mr. Lipski - "I stated that now, during the settlement of the Czechoslovakian question, there was no understanding whatever between us. The Czech issue was already hard enough for the Polish public to swallow, for, despite our disputes with the Czechs, they were after all a Slav people. But in regard to Slovakia, the position was far worse. I emphasized our community of race, language, and religion, and mentioned the help we had given in their achievement of independence. I pointed out our long frontier with Slovakia. I indicated that the Polish man in the street could not understand why the Reich had assumed the protection of Slovakia, that protection being directed against Poland I said emphatically that this question was a serious blow to our relations.

"Ribbentrop reflected for a moment, and then answered that this could be discussed.

"I promised to refer to you the suggestion of a conversation between you and the Chancellor. Ribbentrop remarked that I might go to Warsaw during the next few days to talk the matter over. He advised that the talk should not be delayed, lest the Chancellor should come to the conclusion that Poland was rejecting all his offers.

"Finally, I asked whether he could tell me anything about his conversation with the Foreign Minister of Lithuania. Ribbentrop answered vaguely that he had seen Mr. Urbszyson the latter's return from Rome, and that they had discussed the Memel question, which called for a solution."

That conversation took place on the 21st of March. It teas not very long before the world knew what the solution to Memel was. On the next day German Armed Forces marched in.

If the Tribunal would turn over - I think the next document is unnecessary - turn over to TC-72, Number 17, which becomes GB-39. As a result of these events, not unnaturally, considerable anxiety teas growing both in the government of Great Britain and the Polish Government, and the two governments therefore had been undertaking conversations with each other.

On the 31st of March, the Prime Minister, Mr. Chamberlain, spoke in the House of Commons, and he explained that as a result of the conversations that had been taking place between the British and Polish Governments - I quote from the last but one paragraph of his statement:

"As the House is aware, certain consultations are now proceeding with other governments. In order to make perfectly clear the position of His Majesty's Government in the meantime, before those consultations are concluded, I now have to inform the House that during that period, in the event of any action which clearly threatened Polish independence and which the Polish Government accordingly considered it vital to resist with their national forces, His Majesty's Government would feel themselves bound at once to lend the Polish Government all support in their power. They have given the Polish Government an assurance to this effect.

"I may add that the French Government have authorized me to make it plain that they stand in the same position in this matter as do His Majesty's Government."

On the 6th of April, a week later, a formal communique was issued by the Anglo-Polish Governments which repeated the assurance the Prime Minister had given a week before and in which Poland assured Great Britain of her support should she, Great Britain, be attacked. I need not read it all. In fact, I need not read any of tit. I put it in. It is TC-72, Number 18. I put it in as GB-40.

The anxiety and concern that the governments of Poland and Great Britain were feeling at that time appear to have been well justified. During the same week, on the 3rd of April, the Tribunal will See in the next document an order signed by Keitel. It emanates from the High Command of the Armed Forces. It is dated Berlin, 3rd of April 1939. Its subject is: "Directive for the Armed Forces 1939-40":

"Directive for the Uniform Preparation of War by the Armed Forces for 1939-40 is being reissued.

"Part I (Frontier Defense) and Part II (Danzig) will be issued in the middle of April. Their basic principles remain unchanged.

"Part II, Case White" - which is the code name for the operation against Poland - "Part II, Case White, is attached herewith. The signature of the Fuehrer will be appended later.

"The Fuehrer has added the following directives to Case White:

"1. Preparations must be made in such a way that the operation can be carried out at any time from 1st of September 1939 onwards." - This is in April, the beginning of April.

"2. The High Command of the Armed Forces has been directed to draw up a precise timetable for Case White and to arrange by conferences the synchronized Tunings among the three branches of the Armed Forces.

"3. The plans of the branches of the Armed Forces and the details for the timetable must be submitted to the OKW by the 1st of May."

That document, as the Tribunal will see on the following page under the heading "Distribution", went to the OKH, OKM, OKW.

THE PRESIDENT: Are those words at the top part of the document, or are they just notes?

LT. COL. GRIFFITH-JONES: They are part of the document.

THE PRESIDENT: Directives from Hitler and Keitel, preparing for war.

LT. COL. GRIFFITH-JONES: I beg your pardon; no, they are not. The document starts from under the words "Translation of a document signed by Keitel."

THE PRESIDENT: Yes, I see.

LT. COL. GRIFFITH-JONES: The first words being "top-secret."

If the Tribunal will look at the second page, following after "Distribution", it will be seen that there follows a translation of another document, dated the 11th of April, and that document is signed by Hitler:

"I shall lay down in a later directive the future tasks of the Armed Forces and the preparations to be made in accordance with these for the conduct of the war." - No question about war - "conduct of the war."

"Until that directive comes into force, the Armed Forces must be prepared for the following eventualities:

"I. Safeguarding the frontiers of the German Reich, and protection against surprise air attacks;

"II. Case White;

"III. The Annexation of Danzig.

"Annex IV contains regulations for the exercise of military authority in East Prussia in the event of a warlike development."

Again that document goes to the OKH, OKM, OKW.

On the next page of the copy the Tribunal have, the translation of Annex I is set out, which is the safeguarding of the frontiers of the German Reich, and I would quote from Paragraph (2) under "Special Orders":

"Legal Basis. It should be anticipated that a state of defense or a state of war, as defined in the Reich defense law of the 4th of September 1938, will not be declared. All measures and demands necessary for carrying out a mobilization are to be based on the laws valid in peacetime."

My Lord, that document is C-120. It becomes GB-41. It contains some other later documents to which I shall refer in chronological order.

The statement of the Prime Minister in the House of Commons, followed by the Anglo-Polish communiquÃ© of the 6th of April, was seized upon by the Nazi Government to urge on, as it were, the crisis which they were developing in Danzig between themselves and Poland.

On the 28th of April the German Government issued a memorandum in which they alleged that the Anglo-Polish Declaration was incompatible With the 1934 agreement between Poland and Germany, and that as a result of entering into or by reason of entering into that agreement, Poland had unilaterally renounced the 1934 agreement

I would only quote three short passages, or four short passages, from that document. It is TC-72, Number 14. It becomes GB-42. Some of these passages are worth quoting, if only to show the complete dishonesty of the whole document on the face of it:

"The German Government have taken note of the Polish British declaration regarding the progress and aims of the negotiations recently conducted between Poland and Great Britain. According to this declaration there has been concluded between the Polish Government and the British Government a temporary understanding, to be replaced shortly by a permanent agreement, which will provide for the giving of mutual assistance by Poland and Great Britain in the event of the independence of one of the two states being directly or indirectly threatened."

Thereafter, the document sets out in the next three paragraphs the history of German friendship towards Poland. I quote from the last paragraph, Paragraph 5, on that page:

"The agreement which has now been concluded by the Polish Government with the British Government is in such obvious contradiction to these solemn declarations of a few months ago that the German Government can take note only with surprise and astonishment of such a violent and fundamental reversal of Polish policy.

"Irrespective of the manner in which its final formulation may be determined by both parties, the new Polish-British agreement is intended as a regular pact of alliance which, by reason of its general sense and of the present state of political relations, is directed exclusively against Germany. From the obligation now accepted by the Polish Government, it appears that Poland intends, in certain circumstances, to take an active part in any possible German-British conflict, in the event of aggression against Germany, even should this conflict not affect Poland and her interest. This is a direct and open blow against the renunciation of an use of force contained in the 1934 declaration."

I think I can omit Paragraph 6. Paragraph 7:

"The Polish Government, however, by their recent decision to accede to an alliance directed against Germany, have given it to be understood that they prefer a promise of help by a third power to the direct guarantee of peace by the German Government. In view of this, the German Government are obliged to conclude that the Polish Government do not at present attach h any importance to seeking a solution of German-Polish problems by means of direct, friendly discussion with the German Government. The Polish Government have thus abandoned the path, traced out in 1934, to the shaping of German-Polish relations."

All this would sound very well, if it had not been for the fact that orders for the invasion of Poland had already been issued and the Armed Forces had been told to draw up a precise timetable.

The document goes on to set out the history of the last negotiations and discussions. It sets out the demands of the 21st, which the German Government had made; the return of Danzig, the Autobahn, the railway, the promise by Germany of the 25 years' guarantee, and I go down to the last but one paragraph on Page 3 of the Exhibit, under the heading (1):

"The Polish Government did not avail themselves of the opportunity offered to them by the German Government for a just settlement of the Danzig question; for the final safeguarding of Poland's frontiers with the Reich and thereby for permanent strengthening of the friendly, neighborly relations between the two countries. The Polish Government even rejected German proposals made with this object.

"At the same time the Polish Government accepted, with regard to another state, political obligations which are not compatible either with the spirit, the meaning, or the text of the German-Polish declaration of the 26th of January 1934. Thereby, the Polish Government arbitrarily and unilaterally rendered this declaration null and void."

In the last paragraph the German Government says that, nevertheless, they are prepared to continue friendly relations with Poland.

On the same day as that memorandum was issued Hitler made a speech in the Reichstag, 28 April, in which he repeated, in effect, the terms of the memorandum. This is Document T - 72, Number 13, which becomes GB-43. I would only refer the Tribunal to the latter part of the second page of the translation. He has again repeated the demands and offers that Germany made in March, and he goes on to say that the Polish Government have rejected his offer and lastly:

"I have regretted greatly this incomprehensible attitude of the Polish Government. But that alone is not the decisive fact. The worst is that now Poland, like Czechoslovakia a year ago, believes under the pressure of a lying international campaign, that it must call up troops although Germany, other part, has not called up a single man and had not thought of proceeding in any way against Poland. As I have said, this is, in itself, very regrettable and posterity will one day decide whether it was really right to refuse the suggestion made this once by me. This, as I have said, was an endeavor on my part to solve a question which intimately affects the German people by a truly unique compromise and to solve it to the advantage of both countries. According to my conviction, Poland was not a giving party in this solution at all, but only a receiving party, because it should be beyond all doubt that Danzig will never become Polish. The intention to attack, ton the part of Germany, which was merely invented by the international press, led, as you know, to the so-called guarantee offer and to an obligation on the part of the Polish Government for mutual assistance...."

It is unnecessary, My Lord, to read more of that. It shows us, as I say, how completely dishonest was everything that the German Government was saying at that time. There was Hitler, probably with a copy of the orders for Fall Weiss in his pocket as he spoke, saying that the intention to attack, by Germany, was an invention of the international press.

In answer to that memorandum and that speech the Polish Government issued a memorandum on the 28th of April. It is set out in the next exhibit, TC-72, Number 16, which becomes GB-44. It is unnecessary to read more than . . .

THE PRESIDENT: It is stated as the 8th of May, not the 28th of April.

LT. COL. GRIFFITH-JONES: I beg your pardon, yes, on the 5th of May.

It is unnecessary to read more than two short paragraphs from that reply. I can summarize the document in a word. It sets out the objects of the 1934 agreement: to renounce the use of force and to carry on friendly relationship between the two countries, to solve difficulties by arbitration and other friendly means. The Polish Government appreciate that there are difficulties about Danzig and have long been ready to carry out discussions. They set out again their part in the recent discussions, and I turn to the second page of the document, the one but last paragraph or, perhaps, I should go back a little to the top of that page, the first half of that page. The Polish Government allege that they wrote, as indeed they did, to the German Government on the 26th of March giving their point of view, that they then proposed joint guarantees by the Polish and German Governments of the City of Danzig based on the principles of freedom for the local population in internal affairs. They said they were prepared to examine the possibilities of a motor road and railway facilities and that they received no reply to these proposals:

"It is clear that negotiations in which one state formulates demands and the other is to be obliged to accept those demands unaltered, are not negotiations in the spirit of the declaration of 1934 and are incompatible with the vital interests and dignity of Poland."

Which, of course, in a word summarizes the whole position of the Polish point of view. And thereafter they reject the German accusation that the Anglo-Polish agreement is incompatible with the 1934 German-Polish agreement. They state that Germany herself has entered into similar agreements with other nations and lastly, on the next page, they too say that they are still willing to entertain a new pact with Germany, should Germany wish to do so.

If the Tribunal would turn back to the Document C-120, to the first two letters, to which I referred only a few minutes ago, it becoming GB-41. On the bottom of the page there is a figure 614, on the first page of that exhibit, "Directives from Hitler and Keitel Preparing for War and the Invasion of

Poland". I would refer to page 6 of that particular exhibit. The page number will be found at the bottom of the page, in the center. It is a letter from the Supreme Commander of the Armed Forces, signed by Hitler and dated the 10th of May. It goes to OKW, OKH, OKM, various branches of the OKW and with it apparently were enclosed "instructions for the Economic War and the Protection of Our Own economy." I only mention it now to show better that throughout this time preparations for the immediate aggression were continuing. That document will still be part of the same exhibit.

Again on the next page, which is headed Number C-120(1), I am afraid this is a precis only, not a full translation and therefore, perhaps, I will not read it. But it is the annex, showing the "Directives for the War against the Enemy Economy and Measures of Protection for Our Own Economy."

As we will see later, not only were the military preparations being carried out throughout these months and weeks, but economic and every other kind of preparation was being made for war at the earliest moment.

I think this period of preparation, translated up to May 1939, finishes really with that famous meeting or conference in the Reich Chancellery on the 23rd of May about which the Tribunal has already heard. It was L-79 and is now Exhibit USA-27; and it was referred to, I think, and has been known as the "Schmundt minutes." It is the last document which is in the Tribunal's document book of this part and I do not propose to read anything of it. It has been read already and the Tribunal will remember that it was the speech in which Hitler was crying out for Lebensraum and said that Danzig was not the dispute at all. It was a question of expanding their living space in the East, where he said that the decision had been taken to attack Poland.

THE PRESIDENT: Would you remind me of the date of it?

LT. COL. GRIFFITH-JONES: The 23rd of May 1939. Your Lordship will remember that Goering, Raeder, and Keitel, among many others, were present. It has three particular lines of which I want to remind the Tribunal, where he said:

"If there were an alliance of France, England, and Russia against Germany, Italy, and Japan, I would be constrained to attack England and France with a few annihilating blows. The Fuehrer doubts the possibility of a peaceful settlement with England."

So that, not only haste decision been taken definitely to attack Poland, but almost equally definitely to attack England and France, also.

I pass to the next period, which I have described as the final preparations taken from June up to the beginning of the war, at the beginning of September - Part V of the Tribunal's document book. If the Tribunal Will glance at the index to the document book, they will find I have, for convenience, divided the evidence up under four subheadings:

Final preparations of the Armed Forces; economic preparation; the famous Obersalzberg speeches; and the political or diplomatic preparations urging on the crisis and the justification for the invasion of Poland.

I refer the Tribunal to the first document in that book, dealing with the final preparations of the Armed Forces. It again is an exhibit containing various documents, and I refer particularly to the second document, dated the 22d of June 1939. This is Document C-126, which will become GB-45.

It will be remembered that a precise timetable had been called for. Now, here it is:

"The Supreme Command of the Armed Forces has submitted to the Fuehrer and Supreme Commander, a 'preliminary timetable' for Case White based on the particulars so far available from the Navy, Army, and Air Force. Details concerning the days preceding the attack and the start of the attack were not included in this timetable.

"The Fuehrer and Supreme Commander is, in the main, in agreement with the intentions of the Navy, Army, and Air Force and made the following comments on individual points:

"1. In order not to disquiet the population by calling up reserves on a larger scale than usual for the maneuvers scheduled for 1939, as is intended, civilian establishments, employers or other private persons who make inquiries should be told that men are being called up for the autumn maneuvers and for the exercise units it is intended to form for these maneuvers.

"It is requested that directions to this effect be issued to subordinate establishments."

All this became relevant, particularly relevant, later when we find the German Government making allegations of mobilization on the part of the Poles. Here we have it in May, or rather June - they are mobilizing, only doing so secretly:

"2. For reasons of security, the clearing of hospitals in the area of the frontier must not be carried out."

If the Tribunal will turn to the top of the following page, it will be seen that that order is signed by the Defendant Keitel. I think it is unnecessary to read any further from that document. There is - which perhaps will save turning back, if I might take it rather out of date now - the first document on that front page of that exhibit, a short letter dated the 2d of August. It is only an extract, I am afraid, as it appears in the translation:

"Attached are operational directions for the employment of U-boats which are to be sent out to the Atlantic, by way of precaution, in the event of the intention to carry out Case White remaining unchanged. Commander, U-boats is handing in his operation orders by the 12th of August to the operations staff of the Navy."

One must assume that the Defendant Doenitz knew that his U-boats were to go out into the Atlantic "by way of precaution in the event of the intention to carry out Case White remaining unchanged."

I turn to the next document in the Tribunal's book, C-30, which becomes GB-46. That is a letter dated the 27th of July. It contains orders for the air and sea forces for the occupation of the German Free City of Danzig:

"The Fuehrer and Supreme Commander of the Armed Forces has ordered the reunion of the German Free State of Danzig with the Greater German Reich. The Armed Forces must occupy Danzig Free State immediately in order to protect the German population. There will be no hostile intention on the part of Poland so long as the occupation takes place without the force of arms."

It then sets out how the occupation is to be effected. All this again becomes more relevant when we discuss the diplomatic action of the last few days before the war, when Germany was purporting to make specious offers for the settlement of the question by peaceful means. I would like to offer this as evidence that the decision had been taken and nothing was going to move him from that decision. That document, as set out, says that, "There will be no hostile intention on the part of Poland so long as the occupation takes place without the force of arms." Nevertheless, that was not the only condition upon which the occupation was to take place and we find that during July, right up to the time of the war, steps were being taken to arm the population of Danzig and to prepare them to take part in the coming occupation.

I refer the Tribunal to the next Document, TC-71, which becomes GB-47, where there are set out a few only of the reports which were coming back almost daily during this period from Mr. Shepherd, the Consul-General in Danzig, to the British Foreign Minister. The sum total of those reports can be found in the *British Blue Book.*I now would refer to only two of them as examples of the kind of thing that was happening.

I refer to the first that appears on that exhibit, dated the 1st of July 1939.

"Yesterday morning four German army officers in mufti arrived here by night express from Berlin to organize Danzig Heimwehr. All approaches to hills and dismantled forts, which constitute a popular public promenade on the western fringe of the city, have been closed with barbed wire and 'verboten' notices. The walls surrounding the shipyards bear placards: 'Comrades keep your mouths shut lest you regret consequences.'

"Master of British steamer *High Commissioner Wood,* while he was roving Konigsberg from the 28th of June to 30th of June, observed considerable military activity, including extensive shipment of camouflaged covered lorries and similar material, by small coasting vessels. On the 28th of June four medium-sized steamers, loaded with troops, lorries, field kitchens, and so forth, left Konigsberg ostensibly returning to Hamburg after maneuvers, but actually proceeding to Stettin. Names of steamers...."

And again, as another example, the report Number 11, on the next page of the exhibit, dated the 10th of July, states:

"The same informant, whom I believe to be reliable, advises me that on the 8th of July, he personally saw about 30 military lorries with East Prussian license numbers on the Bischofsberg, where numerous field kitchens had been placed along the hedges. There were also eight large antiaircraft guns in position, which he estimated as being of over 3-inch caliber, and three six-barreled light antiaircraft machine guns. There were about 500 men, drilling with rifles, and the whole place is extensively fortified with barbed wire."

I do not think it is necessary to occupy the Tribunal's time in reading more. Those, as I say, are two reports only, of a number of others that can be found in the *British Blue Book,* which sets out the arming and preparation of the Free City of Danzig.

On the 12th of August and the 13th of August, when preparations were practically complete - and it will be remembered that they had to be complete for an invasion of Poland on the 1st of September - we find Hitler and the Defendant Ribbentrop at last disclosing their intentions to their allies, the Italians.

One of the passages in Hitler's speech of the 23rd of May, it will be remembered - I will not quote it now because the document has been read before. However, in a passage in that speech Hitler, in regard to his proposed attack on Poland, had said, "Our object must be kept secret even from the Italians and the Japanese."

Now, when his preparations are complete, he discloses his intentions to his Italian comrades, and does so in hope that they will join him.

The minutes of that meeting are long, and it is not proposed to read more than a few passages. The meeting can be summarized generally by saying, as I have, that Hitler is trying to persuade the Italians to come into the war with him. The Italians, or Ciano, rather, is most surprised. He had no idea, as he says, of the urgency of the matter; and they are not prepared. He, therefore, is trying to dissuade Hitler from starting off so soon until the Duce can have had a little more time to prepare himself.

The value - perhaps the greatest value - of the minutes of that meeting is that they show quite clearly the German intention to attack England and France ultimately, anyway, if not at the same time as Poland.

I refer the Tribunal to the second page of the exhibit. Hitler is trying to show the strength of Germany, the certainty of winning the war; and, therefore, he hopes to persuade the Italians to come in:

"At sea, England had for the moment no immediate reinforcements in prospect." - I quote from the top of the second page. - "Some time would elapse before any of the ships now under construction could be taken into service. As far as the land army was concerned, after the introduction of conscription 60,000 men had been called to the colors."

I quote this passage particularly to show the intention to attack England. We have been concentrating rather on Poland, but here his thoughts are turned entirely towards England:

"If England kept the necessary troops in her own country- she could send to France, at the most, two infantry divisions anyone armored division. For the rest she could supply a few bomber squadrons, but hardly any fighters, since, at the outbreak of war, the German Air Force would at once attack England and the English fighters would be urgently needed for the defense of their own country.

"With regard to the position of France, the Fuehrer said that in the event of a general war, after the destruction of Poland - which would not take long - Germany would be in a position to assemble a hundred divisions along the West Wall and France would then be compelled to concentrate all her available forces from the colonies, from the Italian frontier and elsewhere, on her own Maginot Line for the life and death struggle which would then ensue. The Fuehrer also thought that the French would find it no easier to overrun the Italian fortifications than to overrun the West Wall. Here Count Ciano showed signs of extreme doubt." - Doubts which, perhaps, in view of the subsequent performances, were well justified.

"The Polish Agony was most uneven in quality. Together with a few parade divisions, there were large numbers of troops of less value. Poland was very weak in antitank and antiaircraft defense and at the moment neither France nor England could help her in this respect."

What this Tribunal will appreciate, of course, is that Poland formed such a threat to Germany on Germany's eastern frontier.

"If, however, Poland were given assistance by the Western Powers over a longer period, she could obtain these weapons and German superiority would thereby be diminished. In contrast to the fanatics of Warsaw and Krakow, the population of their areas is indifferent. Furthermore, it was necessary to consider the position of the Polish State. Out of 34 million inhabitants, one and one-half million were German, about four million were Jews, and approximately nine million Ukrainians, so that genuine Poles were much less in number than the total population and, as already said, their striking power was to be valued variably. In these circumstances Poland could be struck to the ground by Germany in the shortest time.

"Since the Poles, through their whole attitude, had made it clear that in any case, in the event of a conflict, they would stand on the side of the enemies of Germany and Italy, a quick liquidation at the present moment could only be of advantage for the unavoidable conflict with the Western Democracies. If a hostile Poland remained on Germany's eastern frontier, not only would the 11 East Prussian divisions be tied down; but also further contingents would be kept in Pomerania and Silesia. This would not be necessary in the event of a previous liquidation."

The argument goes on on those lines.

I pass on to the next page, at the top of the page:

"Coming back to the Danzig question, the Fuehrer said to Count Ciano that it was impossible for him to go back now. He had made an agreement with Italy for the withdrawal of the Germans from South Tyrol, but for this reason he must take the greatest care to avoid giving the impression that this Tyrolese withdrawal could be taken as a precedent for other areas. Furthermore, he had justified the withdrawal by pointing to a general easterly and northeasterly direction of a German policy. The east and northeast, that is to say the Baltic countries, had been Germany's undisputed sphere of influence since time immemorial, as the Mediterranean had been the appropriate sphere for Italy. For economic reasons also, Germany needed the foodstuffs and timber from these eastern regions."

Now we get the truth of this matter. It is not the persecution of German minorities on the Polish frontiers, but the economic reasons, the need for foodstuffs and timber from Poland:

"In the case of Danzig, German interests were not only material, although the city had the greatest harbor in the Baltic - the transshipment by tonnage was 40 percent of that of Hamburg - but Danzig was a Nuremberg of the north, an ancient German city awaking sentimental feelings for every German, and the Fuehrer was bound to take account of this psychological element in public opinion. To make a comparison with Italy, Count Ciano should suppose that Trieste was in Yugoslav hands and that a large Italian minority was being treated brutally on Yugoslav soil. It would be difficult to assume that Italy would long remain quiet over anything of this kind.

"Count Ciano, in replying to the Fuehrer's statement, first expressed the great surprise on the Italian side over the completely unexpected seriousness of the position. Neither in the conversations in Milan nor in those which took place during his Berlin visit had there been any sign, from the German side, that the position with regard to Poland was so serious. On the contrary, the Minister of Foreign Affairs had said that in his opinion the Danzig question would be settled in the course of time. On these grounds, the Duce, in view of his conviction that a conflict with the Western Powers was unavoidable, had assumed that he should make his preparations for this event; he had made plans for a period of 2 or 3 years. If immediate conflict was unavoidable, the Duce, as he had told Ciano, would certainly stand on the German side; but for various reasons he would welcome the postponement of a general conflict until a later time."

No question of welcoming the cancellation of a general conflict; the only concern of anybody is as to time.

"Ciano then showed, with the aid of a map, the position of Italy in the event of a general war. Italy believed that a convict with Poland would not be limited to that country but would develop into a general European war."

Thereafter, during the meeting, Ciano goes on to try to dissuade Hitler from any immediate action. I quote two lines from the argument at the top of Page 5 of the exhibit:

"For these reasons the Duce insisted that the Axis Powers should make a gesture which would reassure people of the peaceful intentions of Italy and Germany."

Then we get the Fuehrer's answer to those arguments, half-way down Page 5:

"The Fuehrer answered that for a solution of the Polish problem no time should be lost; the longer one waited until the autumn, the more difficult would military operations in eastern Europe become. From the middle of September weather conditions made air operations hardly possible in these areas, while the conditions of the roads, which were quickly turned into a morass by the autumn rains, would be such as to make them impossible for motorized forces. From September to May, Poland was a great marsh and entirely unsuited for any kind of military operations. Poland could, however, occupy Danzig in October . . . and Germany would not be able to do anything about it since they obviously could not bombard or destroy the place."

They couldn't possibly bombard or destroy any place where there happened to be Germans living. Warsaw, Rotterdam, England, London - I wonder whether any sentiments of that kind were held in consideration in regard to those places.

"Ciano asked how soon, according to the Fuehrer's view, the Danzig question must be settled. The Fuehrer answered that this settlement must be made one way or another by the end of August. To the question of Ciano as to what solution the Fuehrer proposed, Hitler answered that Poland must give up political control of Danzig, but that Polish economic interests would obviously be reserved and that Polish general behavior must contribute to a general lessening of the tension. He doubted whether Poland was ready to accept this solution since, up to the present, the German proposals had been refused. The Fuehrer had made this proposal personally to Beck, at his visit to Obersalzberg. They were extremely favorable to Poland. In return for the political surrender of Danzig, under a complete guarantee of Polish interests, and the establishment of a connection between East Prussia and the Reich, Germany would have given a frontier guarantee, a 25-year pact of friendship, and the participation of Poland in influence over Slovakia. Beck had received the proposal with the remark that he was willing to examine it. The plain refusal of it came only as a result of English intervention. The general Polish aims could be seen clearly from the press. They wanted the whole of East Prussia, and even proposed .to advance to Berlin ...." - That was something quite different.

The meeting was held over that night, and it continued on the following day. On Page 7, in the middle of the page, it will be seen:

"The Fuehrer had therefore come to two definite conclusions: (1) in the event of any further provocation, he would immediately attack; (2) if Poland did not clearly and plainly state her political intention, she must be forced to do so."

I go to the last line on that page:

"As matters now stand, Germany and Italy would simply not exist further in the world through the lack of space; not only was there no more space, but existing space was completely blockaded by its present possessors; they sat like misers with their heaps of gold and deluded themselves about their riches .... The Western Democracies were dominated by the desire to rule the world and would not regard Germany and Italy as in their class. This psychological element of contempt was perhaps the worst thing about the whole business. It could only be settled by a life death struggle which the two Axis partners could meet more easily because their interests did not clash on any point.

"The Mediterranean was obviously the most ancient domain for which Italy had claim to predominance. The Duce himself . . . had summed up the position to him in the words that Italy, because of its geographic location, was already the dominant power in the Mediterranean. On the other hand, the Fuehrer said that Germany must take the old German road eastwards and that this road was also desirable for economic reasons, and that Italy had geographical and historical claims to permanency in the Mediterranean. Bismarck . . . had recognized it and had said as much in his well-known letter to Mazzini. The interests of Germany and Italy went in quite different directions and there never could be a conflict between them.

"The Minister of Foreign Affairs added that if the two problems mentioned in yesterday's conversations were settled, Italy and Germany would have their backs free for work against the West. The Fuehrer said that Poland must be struck down so that for 10 years" - there appears to have been a query raised in the translation - "for so many years long she would have been incapable of fighting. In such a case, matters in the west could be settled.

"Ciano thanked the Fuehrer for his extremely clear explanation of the situation. He had, one his side, nothing to add and would give the Duce full details. He asked for more definite information on one point, in order that the Duce might have all the facts before him. The Duce might indeed have to make no decision because the Fuehrer believed that the conflict with Poland could be localized. On the basis of lone experience decision of the Fuehrer, and German reaction would follow in a moment. The second condition required certain decisions as to time. Ciano therefore asked what was the date by which Poland must have satisfied Germany about her political condition. He realized that this date depended upon climatic conditions.

"The Fuehrer answered that the decision of Poland must be made clear at the latest by the end of August. Since, however, the decisive part of military operations against Poland could be carried out within a period of 14 days, and the final liquidation would need another . . . 4 weeks, it could be finished at the end of September or the beginning of October. These could be regarded as the dates. It followed, therefore, that the last date on which he could begin to take action was the end of August.

"Finally, the Fuehrer reassured Ciano that since his youth he had favored German-Italian co-operation, and that To other view was expressed in his publications. He had always thought that Germany and Italy were naturally suited for collaboration, since there were no conflicts of interest between them. He was personally fortunate to live at a time in which, apart from himself, there was one other statesman who would stand out great and unique in history; that he could be this man's friend was for him a matter of great personal satisfaction, and if the hour of common battle struck, he would always be found on the side of the Duce for better or for worse."

THE PRESIDENT: We might adjourn now for 10 minutes.

[A recess was taken.]

LT. COL. GRIFFITH-JONES: If the Tribunal please, I never actually put that last document that I was referring to in as an exhibit. It is Document TC-77, which becomes GB-48.

Having referred the Tribunal to those documents showing that the military preparations were throughout the whole period in hand and nearing their completion, I would refer to one letter from the defendant Funk, showing that at the same time the economists had not been idle. It is a letter dated the 26th of August 193g, in which Funk is writing to his FOhrer. He says:

"My Fuehrer! I thank you sincerely and heartily for your most friendly and kind wishes on the occasion of my birthday. How happy and how grateful to you we ought to be for being granted the favor of experiencing these overwhelmingly great and world-changing times and taking part in the mighty events of these days.

"The information given to me by Field Marshal Goering, that you, my Fuehrer, yesterday evening approved in principle the measures prepared by me for financing the war and for shaping the relationship between wages and prices and for carrying through emergency sacrifices, made me deeply happy. I hereby report to you, with all respect, that I have succeeded by means of precautions taken during the last few months, in making the Reich Bank internally so strong and externally so unassailable that even the most serious shocks in the international money and credit market cannot affect us in the least. In the meantime, I have quite inconspicuously changed into gold all the assets of the Reich Bank and of the whole of the German economy abroad on which it was possible to lay hands. Under the proposals I have prepared for a ruthless elimination of all consumption which is not of vital importance and of all public expenditure and public works which hare not of importance for the war effort, we will be in a position to cope with all demands on finance and economy without any serious shocks. I have considered it my duty as the general plenipotentiary for economy, appointed by you, to make this report and solemn promise to you, my Fuehrer. Heil my Fuehrer" - signed - "Walter Funk."

That document is PS-699, and it goes in as GB-49.

It is difficult in view of that letter to see how the Defendant Funk can say that he did not know of the preparations and of the intentions of the German Government to wage war.

I come now to the speech which Hitler made on the 22d of August at Obersalzberg to his commanders-in-chief. By the end of the third week of August, preparations were complete. That speech has already been read to the Tribunal. I would, perhaps, ask the Tribunal's patience if I quoted literally half a dozen lines so as to carry the story on in sequence.

On the first page of PS-1014, which is already USA-30, the fourth line:

"Everybody shall have to make a point of it that we were determined from the beginning to fight the Western Powers."

The second paragraph:

"Destruction of Poland is in the foreground. The aim is the elimination of living forces, not the arrival at a certain line. Even if war should break out in the West, the destruction of Poland shall be the primary objective."

Again, the famous sentence in the third paragraph:

"I shall give a propagandistic cause for starting the war, never mind whether it be plausible or not. The victor shall not be asked later on whether he told the truth or not. In starting and making a war, not the right is what matters but victory."

We are going to see only too clearly how that propagandistic cause, which already had been put in hand, was brought to its climax.

I turn to the next page (798-PS, USA-29), the third paragraph:

"It was clear to me that a conflict with Poland had to come sooner or later. I had already made this decision in the spring, but I thought that I would first turn against the West in a few years, and only afterwards against the East."

I refer to these passages again particularly to emphasize the intention of the Nazi Government, not only to conquer Poland, but ultimately, in any event, to wage aggressive war against the Western Democracies.

I refer lastly to the last page, a passage which becomes more and more significant as we continue the story of the last few days: I quote from the fourth paragraph:

"We need not be afraid of a blockade. The East will supply us with grain, cattle, coal, lead, and zinc. It is a big aim, which demands great efforts. I am, only afraid that at the last minute some 'Schweinehund' will make a proposal for mediation.

"The political aim is set farther. A beginning has been made for the destruction of England's hegemony. The way is open for the soldier, after I have made the political preparations."

And, again, the very last line becomes significant later:

"Goering answers with thanks to the Fuehrer and the assurance that the Armed Forces will do their duty."

We pass from the military-economic preparations and his exhortations to his generals to see how he was developing the position in the diplomatic and political field.

On the 23rd of August 1939 the Danzig Senate passed a decree whereby Gauleiter Forster was appointed head of the State of the Free City of Danzig, a position which did not exist under the statute setting up the constitution of the Free City. I put in the next document, which is taken from the *British Blue Book,* only as evidence of that event, an event that was, of course, aimed at stirring up the feeling in the Free City at that time. That is TC-72, Number 62, which becomes GB-50.

At the same time, frontier incidents were being manufactured by the Nazi Government with the aid of the SS. The Tribunal has already heard the evidence of General Lahousen the other day in which he referred to the provision of Polish uniforms to the SS

forces for these purposes, so that dead Poles could be found lying about the German side of the frontier. I refer the Tribunal now to three short reports which corroborate the evidence that that gentleman came and gave before you, and they are found in the *British Blue Book.* They are reports from the British Ambassador in Warsaw.

The first of them, TC-72, Number 53, which becomes GB-51, is dated 26th of August.

"A series of incidents again occurred yesterday on German frontier.

"Polish patrol met a party of Germans one kilometer from the East Prussian frontier near Pelta. Germans opened fire. Polish patrol replied, killing leader, whose body is being returned.

"German bands also crossed Silesian frontier near Szczyglo, twice near Bybnik, and twice elsewhere, firing shots and attacking blockhouses and customs posts with machine guns and hand grenades. Poles have protested vigorously to Berlin. *Gazeta Polska,* in an inspired lead article today, says these are more than incidents. They are clearly prepared acts of aggression of pare-military disciplined detachments, supplied with regular army's arms, and in one case it was a regular army detachment. Attacks more or less continuous.

"These incidents did not cause Poland to forsake calm and strong attitude of defense. Facts spoke for themselves and acts of aggression came from German side. This was the best answer to the ravings of German press.

"Ministry for Foreign Affairs state uniformed German detachment has since shot a Pole across frontier and wounded another."

I pass to the next report, TC-72, Number 54, which becomes GB-52. It is dated the same date, the 26th of August.

"Ministry for Foreign Affairs categorically deny story recounted by Hitler to the French Ambassador that 24 Germans were recently killed at Lodz and eight at Bielsko. The story is without any foundation whatever."

And lastly, TC-72, Number 55, which becomes GB-53, the report of the next day, the 27th of August.

"So far as I can judge, German allegations of mass ill-treatment of German minority by Polish authorities are gross exaggeration, if not complete falsification. There is no sign of any loss of control of situation by Polish civil authorities. Warsaw, and so far as I can ascertain, the rest of Poland is still completely calm.

"3. Such allegations are reminiscent of Nazi propaganda methods regarding Czechoslovakia last year.

"4. In any case it is purely and simply deliberate German provocation in accordance with fixed policy that has since March" - since the date when the rest of Czechoslovakia was seized and they were ready to go against Poland - "that has since March exacerbated feeling between the two nationalities. I suppose this has been done with the object:

"(a) Creating war spirit in Germany, (b) impressing public opinion abroad, (c) provoking either defeatism or apparent aggression in Poland.

"5. It has signally failed to achieve either of the two latter objects.

"6. It is noteworthy that Danzig was hardly mentioned by Herr Hitler.

"7. German treatment of Czech Jews and Polish minority is apparently negligible factor compared with alleged sufferings of Germans in Poland where, be it noted, they do not amount to more than 10 per cent of the population in any commune.

"8. In the face of these facts it can hardly be doubted that, if Herr Hitler decided on war, it is for the sole purpose of destroying Polish independence.

"9. I shall lose no opportunity of impressing on Minister for Foreign Affairs necessity of doing everything possible to prove that Hitler's allegations regarding German minority are false."

And yet, again, we have further corroboration of General Lahousen's evidence in a memorandum, which has been captured, of a conversation between the writer and Keitel. It is 795-PS, and it becomes GT-54. That conversation with Keitel took place on the 17th of August, and from the memorandum I quote the first paragraph:

"I reported my conference with Jost to Keitel He said that he would not pay any attention to this action, as the Fuehrer had not informed him, and had only let him know that we were to furnish Heydrich with Polish uniforms. He agrees that I instruct The General Staff. He says he does not think much of actions of this kind. However, there is nothing else to be done if they have been ordered by the Fuehrer; that he could not ask the Fuehrer how he had planned the execution of this special action. In regard to Dirsehau, he has decided that this action would be executed only by the Army."

That then, My Lord, was the position at the end of the first week in August - I mean at the end of the third week in August. On the 22d of August the Russian-German Non-Aggression Pact was signed in Moscow, and we have heard in Hitler's speech of that date to his commanders-in-chief how it had gone down as a shock to the rest of the world. In fact, the orders to invade Poland were given immediately after the signing of that treaty, and the H-hour was actually to be in the early morning of the 25th of August. Orders were given to invade Poland in the early hours of the 25th of August, and that I shall prove in a moment.

On the same day - the 23rd of August - that the German-Russian Agreement was signed in Moscow, news reached England that it was being signed. And of course the significance of it from a military point of view as to Germany, particularly in the present circumstances, was obvious; and the British Government immediately made their position clear in one last hope - and that one last hope was that if they did so the German Government might possibly think better of it. And I refer to Document TC-72, Number 56; it is the first document in the next to the last part of the Tribunal document book, in which the Prime Minister wrote to Hitler. That document becomes GB-55:

"Your Excellency:

"Your Excellency will have already heard of certain measures taken by His Majesty's Government, and announced in the press and on the wireless this evening.

"These steps have, in the opinion of His Majesty's Government, been rendered necessary by the military movements which have been reported from Germany and by the fact that apparently the announcement of a German-Soviet Agreement is taken in some quarters in Berlin to indicate that intervention by Great Britain on behalf of Poland is no longer a contingency that need be reckoned with. No greater mistake could be made. Whatever may prove to be the nature of the German-Soviet agreement, it cannot alter Great Britain's obligation to Poland, which His Majesty's Government have stated in public repeatedly and plainly and which they a redetermined to fulfill.

"It has been alleged that, if His Majesty's Government had made their position more clear in 1914, the great catastrophe would have been avoided. Whether or not there is any force in that allegation, His Majesty's Government are resolved that on this occasion there shall be no such tragic misunderstanding.

"If the case should arise, they are resolved and prepared to employ without delay all the forces at their command; and it is impossible to foresee the end of hostilities once engaged. It would be a dangerous delusion to think that, if war once starts, it will come to an early end even if a success on any one of the several fronts on which it will be engaged should have been secured."

Thereafter the Prime Minister urged the German Government to try and resolve the difficulty without recourse to the use of force; and he suggested that a truce should be declared while direct discussions between the two Governments, the Polish and German Governments, might take place. I quote in Prime Minister Chamberlain's language:

"At this moment I confess I can see no other way to avoid a catastrophe that will involve Europe in war. In view of the grave consequences to humanity which may follow from the action of their rulers, I trust that Your Excellency will weigh with the utmost deliberation the considerations which I have put before you "

On the following day, the 23rd of August, Hitler replied to Prime Minister Chamberlain, and that document is TC-72, Number 60, and it becomes

GB-56. He starts off by saying that Germany has always wanted England's friendship, and has always done everything to get it; on the other hand, she has some essential interests which it is impossible for Germany to renounce. I quote the third paragraph:

> "Germany was prepared to settle the questions of Danzig and of the corridor by the method of negotiation on the basis of a proposal of truly unparalleled magnanimity. The allegation which is disseminated by England regarding a German mobilization against Poland" - we see here the complete dishonesty of the whole business - "the assertion of aggressive designs towards Ptomania, Hungary, and so forth as well as these-called guarantee declarations, which were subsequently given, had, however, dispelled Polish inclination to negotiate on a basis of this kind which would have been tolerable for Germany also.
>
> "The unconditional assurance given by England to Poland, that she would render assistance to that country in all circumstances regardless of the causes from which a conflict might spring, could only be interpreted in that country as an encouragement thenceforward to unloosen, under cover of such a charter, a wave of appalling terrorism against the one and a half million German inhabitants living in Poland."

Again I cannot help remembering the report by the British Ambassador, to which I just referred:

> "The atrocities which since then have been taking place in that country are terrible for the victims but intolerable for a great power such as the German Reich, which is expected to remain a passive onlooker during these happenings. Poland has been guilty of numerous breaches of her obligations towards the Free City of Danzig, has made demands in the character of ultimata, and has initiated a process of economic strangulation."

It goes on to say that "Germany will not tolerate a continuance of the persecution" and the fact that there is a British guarantee to Poland makes no difference to her determination to end this state of affairs. from Paragraph 7:

> "The German Reich Government has received information to the effect that the British Government has the intention to carry out measures of mobilization which, according to the statements contained in your own letter, are clearly directed against Germany alone. This is said to be true of France as well. Since Germany has never had the intention of taking military measures other than those of a defensive character against England or France and, as has already been emphasized, has never intended, and does not in the future intend, to attack England or France, it follows that this announcement as confirmed by you, Mr. Prime Minister, in your own letter, can only refer to a contemplated act of menace directed against the Reich. I, therefore, inform your Excellency that in the event of these military announcements being carried into effect, I shall order immediate mobilization of the German forces."

If the intention of the German Government had been peaceful, if they really wanted peace and not war, what was the purpose of these lies; these lies saying that they had never intended to attack England or France, carried out no mobilization, statements which, in view of what we now have, we know to be lies?. What can have been their object if their intention had always been for a peaceful settlement of the Danzig question only? Then I quote again from the last paragraph:

"The question of the treatment of European problems on a peaceful basis is not a decision which rests on Germany, but primarily on those who since the crime committed by the Versailles dictate have stubbornly and consistently opposed any peaceful revision. Only after a change of the spirit on the part of the responsible powers can there be any real change in the relationship between England and Germany. I have all my life fought for Anglo-German friendship; the attitude adopted by British diplomacy - at any rate up to the present - has, however, convinced me of the futility of such an attempt. Should there be any change in this respect in the future, nobody could be happier than I."

On the 25th of August the formal Anglo-Polish Agreement of mutual assistance was signed in London. It is unnecessary to read the document. The Tribunal will be well aware of its contents where both Governments undertake to give assistance to the other in the event of aggression against either by any third power. I point to Document TC-73; it is Number 91 and it becomes GB-57. I shall refer to the fact of its signing again in a moment but perhaps it is convenient while we are dealing with a letter between the British Prime Minister and Hitler to refer also to a similar correspondence which took place a few days later between the French Prime Minister M. Daladier and Hitler. I emphasize these because it is desired to show how deliberately the German Government was set about their pattern of aggression. "The French Ambassador in Berlin has informed me of your personal communication," written on the 26th of August:

"In the hours in which you speak of the greatest responsibility which two heads of the Governments can possibly take upon themselves, namely, that of shedding the blood of two great nations who long only for peace and work I feel I owe it to you, personally, and to both our peoples to say that the fate of peace still rests in your hands alone.

"You cannot doubt but what are my own feelings towards Germany nor France's peaceful feelings towards your nation. No Frenchman has done more than myself to strengthen between our two nations not only peace but also sincere co-operation in their own interests as well as in those of Europe and of the whole world. Unless you credit the French people with a lower sense of honor than I credit to the German nation, you cannot doubt that France loyally fulfills her obligations toward other powers, such as Poland, which, as I am fully convinced, wants to live in peace with Germany. These two convictions are fully compatible.

"Till now there has been nothing to prevent a peaceful solution of the international crisis with all honor and dignity for all nations, if the same will for peace exists on all sides.

"Together with the good will of France I proclaim that of all her allies. I take it upon myself to guarantee Poland's readiness, which she has always shown, to submit to the mutual application of a method of open settlement as it can be imagined between the governments of two sovereign nations. With the clearest conscience I can assure you that, among the differences which have arisen between Germany and Poland over the question of Danzig, there is not one which could not be submitted to such a method with a purpose of reaching a peaceful and just solution.

"Moreover, I can declare on my honor that there is nothing in France's clear and loyal solidarity with Poland and her allies, which could in any way prejudice the peaceful attitude of my country. This solidarity has never prevented us, and does not prevent us today, from keeping Poland in the same friendly state of mind.

"In so serious an hour I sincerely believe that no high-minded human being could understand it if a war of destruction were started without a last attempt being made to reach a peaceful settlement between Germany and Poland. Your desire for peace could, in all certainty, work for this aim without any prejudice to German honor. I, who desire good harmony between the French and the German people, and who am, on the other hand, bound to Poland by bonds of friendship and by a promise, am prepared, as head of the French Government, to do everything an upright man can do to bring this attempt to a successful conclusion.

"You and I were in the trenches in the last war. You knows, as I do, what horror and condemnation the devastations of that war have left in the conscience of the people without any regard to its outcome. The picture I can see in my mind's eye of your outstanding role as the leader of the German people on the road of peace, toward the fulfillment of its task in the common work of civilization, leads me to ask for a reply to this suggestion.

"If French and German blood should be shed again as it was shed 25 years ago in a still longer and more murderous war, then each of the two nations will fight believing in its own victory. But the most certain victors will be destruction and barbarity."

THE PRESIDENT: I think we will adjourn now until 2 o'clock.

[A recess was taken until 1400 hours.]

COLONEL ROBERT G. STOREY (Executive Trial Counsel for the United States): If it please the Tribunal, with the consent of Lieutenant Colonel Griffith-Jones, may I make an announcement to the Defense Counsel.

At 7:30 in the courtroom this evening, the remainder of the motion pictures which the United States will over in evidence will be shown for the Defense Counsel. We urge that all of them come at 7:30.

DR. DIX: I believe I can say on behalf of all members of the Defense that they do not consider it necessary that the films be shown to them before the proceedings, that is, shown to them twice. We fully and with gratitude appreciate the courtesy and readiness to facilitate our work; but our evenings are very much taken up by the preparation of our cases and by the necessary consultations with our clients.

The question of films is on a level different from that of documents. Documents one likes to read in advance or simultaneously or later; but since we can hear and take note of the testimony of witnesses only during the main proceedings, we are, of course, to an even greater degree in a position and prepared to become acquainted with the felons submitted as evidence only during the proceedings. We believe the Prosecution need not take the trouble of showing every film to us on some evening before it is shown again in the proceedings. We hope this will not be construed as, shall I say, a sort of demonstration in some respect, for the reason really is that our time is so fully taken up by our preparations that all superfluous work might well be spared both the Prosecution and us. I repeat and emphasize that we fully and gratefully appreciate the Prosecution's manifest readiness to facilitate our work, and I ask that my words be understood in this light.

THE PRESIDENT: Do I understand that you think it will be unnecessary for the defendants' counsel to have a preview of the films, to see them before they are produced in evidence? Is that what you are saying?

DR. DIX: Yes, that is what I said.

THE PRESIDENT: Colonel Storey, I am not sure that you were here when Dr. Dix began his observation; but I understand that what he says is that in view of the amount of preparation which the defendants' counsel have to undertake, they do not consider it necessary to have a view of these films before they are produced in evidence, but at the same time he wishes to express his gratification at the co-operation of the Counsel for the Prosecution.

COL. STOREY: Very agreeable. It's all right with us. We were doing it for their benefit.

THE PRESIDENT: Very well.

LT. COL. GRIFFITH-JONES: When the Tribunal rose for the adjournment, I had just read the letter from M. Daladier to Hitler, of the 26th of August. On the 27th of August Hitler replied to that letter, and I think it unnecessary to read the reply. The sense of it was very much the same as that which he wrote to the British Prime Minister in answer to the letter that he had received earlier in the week.

Those two letters are taken from the *German White Book* which I put in evidence as GB-58, so perhaps the Tribunal would treat both those letters as of the same number. After that, nobody could say that the German Government could be in any doubt as to the position that was to be taken up by both the British and French Governments in the event of a German aggression against Poland.

But the pleas for peace did not end there. On the 24th of August President Roosevelt wrote to both Hitler and the President of the Polish Republic. I quote only the first few paragraphs of his letter:

"In the message which I sent you on April the 14th, I stated that it appeared to be that the leaders of great nations had it in their power to liberate their peoples from the disaster that impended, but that, unless the effort were immediately made, with goodwill on an sides, to find a peaceful and constructive solution to existing controversies, the crisis which the world was confronting must end in catastrophe. Today that catastrophe appears to be very near at hand indeed.

"To the message which I sent you last April I have received no reply, but because my confident belief that the cause of world peace - which is the cause of humanity itself - rises above all other considerations, I am again addressing myself to you, with the hope that the war which impends, and the consequent disaster to all peoples, may yet be averted.

"I therefore urge with all earnestness - and I am likewise urging the

President of the Republic of Poland - that the Governments of Germany and Poland agree by common accord to refrain from any positive act of hostility for a reasonable, stipulated period; and that they agree, likewise by common accord, to solve the controversies which have arisen between them by one of the three following methods:

"First, by direct negotiation; second, by the submission of these controversies to an impartial arbitration in which they can both have confidence; third, that they agree to the solution of these controversies through the procedure of conciliation."

I think it is unnecessary to read any more of that letter. As I have already indicated to the Tribunal, the answer to that was the order to his armed forces to invade Poland on the following morning.

That document is Exhibit TC-72, Number 124, which becomes GB-59.

I put in evidence also the next document, TC-72, Number 126, GB-60, which is the reply to that letter from the President of the Polish Republic, in which he accepts the offer to settle the differences by any of the peaceful methods suggested.

On the 25th of August, no reply having been received from the German Government, President Roosevelt wrote again:

"I have this hour received from the President of Poland a reply to the message which I addressed to Your Excellency and to him last night."

The text of the Polish reply is then set out.

"Your Excellency has repeatedly publicly stated that the aims and objects sought by the German Reich were just and reasonable.

"In his reply to my message the President of Poland has made it plain that the Polish Government are waling, up on the basis set forth in my message, to agree to solve the controversy which has arisen between the Republic of Poland and the German Reich by direct negotiation or the processor conciliation.

"Countless human lives can yet be saved, and hope may still be restored that the nations of the modern world may even now construct the foundation for a peaceful and happier relationship, if you and the Government of the German Reich will agree to the pacific means of settlement accepted by the Government of Poland. All the world prays that Germany, too, will accept."

But, My Lord, Germany would not accept, nor would she accept the appeals by the Pope which appear in the next document.

I am sorry - the President of Poland's reply, TC-72 becomes Number 127, GB-61.

They would not agree to those proposals, nor would they pay heed to the Pope's appeal, which is TC-72, Number 139 on the same date, the 24th of August, which becomes GB-62. I do not think it is necessary to read that. It is an appeal in similar terms. And there is yet a further appeal from the Pope on the 31st of August, TC-72, Number 14, which becomes GB-63. It is 141; I beg your pardon. It is TC-72, Number 141. I think the printing is wrong in the Tribunal's translation:

"The Pope is unwilling to abandon hope that pending negotiations may lead to a just pacific solution, such as the whole world continues to pray for."

I think it is unnecessary to read the remainder of that. If the Pope had realized that those negotiations to which he referred as the "pending negotiations" in the last days of August, which we are about to deal with now, were completely bogus negotiations, bogus insofar as Germany was concerned, and put forward, as indeed they were - and as I hope to illustrate to the Tribunal in a moment - simply as an endeavor to dissuade England either by threat or by bribe from meeting her obligations to Poland, then perhaps he would have saved himself the trouble in ever addressing that last appeal

It will be seen quite clearly that those final German offers, to which I now turn, were no offers in the accepted sense of the word at all; that there was never any intention behind them of entering into discussions, negotiation, arbitration, or any other form of peaceful settlement with Poland. They were just an attempt to make it rather easier to seize and conquer Poland than appeared likely if England and France observed the obligations that they had undertaken.

Perhaps I might, before dealing with the documents, summarize in a word those last negotiations.

On the 22d of August, as we have seen, the German-Soviet Pact was signed. On the 24th of August, orders were given to his armies to march the following morning. After those orders had been given, the news apparently reached the German Government that the British and Polish Governments had actually signed a formal pact of non-aggression and of mutual assistance. Until that time, it will be remembered, the position was that the Prime Minister had made a statement in the House and a joint communiqué had been issued - I think on the 6th of April - that they would in fact assist one another if either were attacked, but no formal agreement had been signed.

Now, on the 24th of August after those orders had been given by him, the news came that such a formal document had been signed; and the invasion was postponed for the sole purpose of making one last effort to keep England and France out of the war - not to end the war, not to cancel the war, but to keep them out.

And to do that, on the 25th of August, having postponed the invasion, Hitler issued a verbal communiqué to Sir Nevile Henderson which, as the Tribunal will see, was a mixture of bribe and threat with which he hoped to persuade England to keep out.

On the 28th of August Sir Nevile Henderson handed the British Government's reply to that communiqué to Hitler. - That reply stressed that the difference ought to be settled by agreement. The British Government put forward the view that Danzig should be guaranteed and, indeed, any agreement come to should be guaranteed by other powers, which, of course, in any event would have been quite unacceptable to the German Reich.

As I say, one really need not consider what would have been acceptable and not acceptable because once it had been made clear - as indeed it was in that British Government's reply of the 28th of August - that England would not be put off assisting Poland in the event of German aggression, the German Government really had no concern with further negotiation but were concerned only to afford themselves some kind of justification and to prevent themselves appearing too blatantly to turn down all the appeals to reason that were being put forward.

On the 29th of August, in the evening at 7:15, Hitler handed to Sir Nevile Henderson the German Government's answer to the British Government's reply of the 28th. And here again in this document it is quite clear that the whole object of it was to put forward something which was quite unacceptable. He agrees to enter into direct conversations as suggested by the British Government, but he demands that those conversations must be based up on the return of Danzig to the Reich and also of the whole of the Corridor.

It will be remembered that hitherto, even when he alleged that Poland had renounced the 1934 agreement, even then he had put forward as his demands the return of Danzig alone and the arrangement for an extra-territorial Autobahn and railroad running through the Corridor to East Prussia. That was unacceptable then. To make quite certain, he now demands the whole of the Corridor; no question of an Autobahn or railway. The whole thing must become German.

Even so, even to make doubly certain that the offer would not be accepted, he says:

". . . on those terms I am prepared to enter into discussion; but to do so, as the matter is urgent, I expect a plenipotentiary with full powers from the Polish Government to be here in Berlin by Wednesday, the 30th of August 1939."

This offer was made at 7:15 p.m. on the evening of the 29th. That offer had to be transmitted first to London, and from London to Warsaw; and from Warsaw the Polish Government had to give authority to their Ambassador in Berlin. So that the timing made it quite impossible to get authority to their Ambassador in Berlin by midnight the following night. It allowed them no kind of opportunity for discussing the matters at all. As Sir Nevile Henderson described it, the offer amounted to an ultimatum.

At midnight on the 30th of August at the time by which the Polish Plenipotentiary was expected to arrive, Sir Neville Henderson saw Ribbentrop; and I shall read to you the account of that interview, in which Sir Nevile Henderson handed a further message to Ribbentrop in reply to the message that had been handed to him the previous evening, and at which Ribbentrop read out in German a two- or three-page document which purported to be the German proposal to be discussed at the discussions between them and the Polish Government. He read it out quickly in German. He refused to hand a copy of it to the British Ambassador. He passed no copy of it at all to the Polish Ambassador. So that there was no kind of possible chance of the Poles ever having before them the proposals which Germany was so graciously and magnanimously offering to discuss.

On the following day, the 31st of August, Mr. Lipski saw Ribbentrop and could get no further than to be asked whether he came with full powers. When he did not - when he said he did not come with full powers, Ribbentrop said that he would put the position before the Fuehrer. But, in actual fact, it was much too late to put any position to the Fuehrer by that time, because on the 31st of August - I am afraid I am unable to give you the exact time - but on the 31st of August, Hitler had already issued his Directive Number 1 for the conduct of the war, in which he laid down H-Hour as being a quarter to five the following morning, the 1st of September. And on the evening of the 31st of August at 9 o'clock the German radio broadcast the proposals which Ribbentrop had read out to Sir Nevile Henderson the night before, saying that these were the proposals which had been made for discussion but that, as no Polish Plenipotentiary had arrived to discuss them, the German Government assumed that they were turned down. That broadcast at 9 o'clock on the evening of the 31st of August was the first that the Poles had ever heard of the proposals, and the first, in fact, that the British Government or their representatives in Berlin knew about them, other than what had been heard when Ribbentrop had read them out and refused to give a written copy, on the evening of the 30th.

After that broadcast at 9:15, perhaps when the broadcast was in its course, a copy of those proposals was handed to Sir Nevile Henderson, for the first time.

Having thus summarized for the convenience, I hope, of the Tribunal, the timing of events during that last week, I would ask the Tribunal to refer briefly to the remaining documents in that document book. I first put in evidence an extract from the interrogation of the Defendant Goering, which was taken on the 29th of August 1945.

DR. STAHMER: As defense counsel for the Defendant Goering, I object to the use of this document which is an extract from testimony given by the Defendant Goering. Since the defendant is present here in court, he can at any time be called to the stand and give direct evidence on this subject before the Tribunal.

THE PRESIDENT: Is that your objection?

DR. STAHMER: Yes.

THE PRESIDENT: The Tribunal does not understand the ground of your objection, in view of Article 15 (c) and Article 16 (b) and (c) of the Charter. Article 15 (c) provides that the Chief Prosecutors shall undertake, among others, the duty of "the preliminary examination of all necessary witnesses and of the defendants"; and Article 16 provides that:

"In order to ensure fair trial for the defendants, the following procedure shall be followed: . . . (b) During any preliminary examination . . . of a defendant he shall have the right to give any explanation relevant to the charges made against him; (c) A preliminary examination of a defendant. . . shall be conducted in, or translated into, a language which the defendant understands."

Those provisions of the Charter, in the opinion of the Tribunal, show that the defendants may be interrogated and that their interrogations may be put in evidence.

DR. STAHMER: I was prompted by the idea that when it is possible to call a witness, direct examination in court is preferable, since the evidence thus obtained is more concrete.

THE PRESIDENT: You certainly have the opportunity of summoning the defendant for whom you appear to give evidence himself, but that has nothing to do with the admissibility of his interrogation - his preliminary examination.

LT. COL. GRIFFITH-JONES: This extract is TC-90, which I put in as GB-64. I quote from the middle of the first answer. It is at the end of the 7th line. The Defendant Goering says there:

"On the day when England gave her official guarantee to Poland, the Fuehrer called me on the telephone and told me that he had stopped the planned invasion of Poland. I asked him then whether this was just temporary or for good. He said 'No, I will have to see whether we can eliminate British intervention."

THE PRESIDENT: Ought you not read the question before the answer?

LT. COL. GRIFFITH-JONES: I go back to the question:

"When the negotiations of the Polish Foreign Minister in London brought about the Anglo-Polish Treaty, at the end of March or the beginning of April 1939, was it not fairly obvious that a peaceful solution was impossible?"

"Answer: 'Yes, it seemed impossible after my conviction.'

I think that must be a bad translation - "according to my conviction."

THE PRESIDENT: Yes.

LT. COL. GRIFFITH-JONES:

But not according to the convictions of the Fuehrer. When it was mentioned to the Fuehrer that England had given her guarantee to Poland, he said that England was also guaranteeing Romania, but then when the Russians took Bessarabia, nothing happened; and this made a big impression on him. I made a mistake here. At this time Poland only had the promise of a guarantee. The guarantee itself was only given shortly before the beginning of the war. On the day when England gave her official guarantee to Poland, the Fuehrer called me on the telephone and told me that he had stopped the planned invasion of Poland. I asked him then whether this was just temporary, or for good. lie said, 'No, I will have to see whether we can eliminate British intervention.'So, then I asked him, 'Do you think that it will be any different within 4 or 5 days?' At this same time - I do not know whether you know about that, Colonel - I was in communication with Lord Halifax by a special courier, outside the regular diplomatic channels, to do everything to stop war with England. After the guarantee, I held an English declaration of war inevitable. I already told him in the spring of 1939, after occupying Czechoslovakia, I told him that from now on, if he tried to solve the Polish question, he would have to count on the enmity of England - 1939, that is, after the Protectorate.

"Question: 'Is it not a fact that preparations for the campaign against Poland were originally supposed to have been completed by the end of August 1939?'

"Answer: 'yes.'

"Question: 'And that the final issuance of the order for the campaign against Poland came sometime between the15th and 20th of August 1939, after the signing of the treaty with Soviet :Russia?'" - The dates obviously are wrong there.

"Answer: 'Yes, that is true.'

"Question: 'Is it not also a fact that the start of the campaign was ordered for the 25th of August but on the24th of August in the afternoon it was postponed until September the 1st in order to await the results of new diplomatic maneuvers with the English Ambassador?'

"Answer: 'Yes.' "

My only comment upon that document is in respect to the second paragraph where Goering is purporting not to want war with England. The Court will remember how it was Goering, after the famous speech of the 22d of August to his commanders-in-chief, who got up and thanked the Fuehrer for his exhortation and assured him that the Armed Forces would play their part.

I omit the next document in the document book, which carries the matter a little further, and we go on to Hitler's verbal communique, as it is called in the *British Blue Book*, that Remanded to Sir Nevile Henderson on the 25th of August, after he had heard of the signing of the Anglo-Polish agreement, in an endeavor to keep England from meeting her obligations. He states in the first paragraph, after hearing the British Ambassador, that he is anxious to make one more effort to save war. In the second paragraph, he asserts again that Poland's provocations were unbearable; and I quote Paragraph 2:

"Germany was in all circumstances determined to abolish these Macedonian conditions on her eastern frontier and, what is more, to do so in the interests of quiet and order and also in the interests of European peace.

"The problem of Danzig and the Corridor must be solved. The British Prime Minister had made a speech which was not in the least calculated to induce any change in the German attitude. At the most, the result of this speech could be a bloody and incalculable war between Germany and England. Such a war would be bloodier than that of 1914 to 1918. In contrast to the last war, Germany would no longer have to fight on two fronts." - One sees the threats, veiled threats, appearing in this paragraph - "Agreement with Russia was unconditional and signified a change in foreign policy of the Reich which would last a very longtime. Russia and Germany would never again take up arms against each other. Apart from this, the agreements reached with Russia would also render Germany secure economically for the longest possible period of war.

"The Fuehrer had always wanted Anglo-German understanding. War between England and Germany could at best bring some profit to Germany, but none at all to England."

Then we come to the bribe:

"The Fuehrer declared the German-Polish problem must be solved and will be solved. He is, however, prepared and determined, after the solution of this problem, to approach England once more with a large, comprehensive offer. He is a man of great decisions; and in this case also, he will be capable of being great in his action." - and then, magnanimously - "He accepts the British Empire and is ready to pledge himself personally for its continued existence and to place the power of the German Reich at its disposal on condition that his colonial demands, which are limited, should be negotiated by peaceful means .... His obligations to Italy remain untouched."

Again he stresses irrevocable determination never to enter into war with Russia. I quote the last two paragraphs:

"If The British Government would consider these ideas, a blessing for Germany..."

THE PRESIDENT: Why do you not read the first few lines of Paragraph 3?

LT. COL. GRIFFITH-JONES: Yes; I did summarize it - Paragraph 3:

"He also desired to express the irrevocable determination of Germany never again to enter into conflict with Russia."

THE PRESIDENT: Yes.

LT. COL. GRIFFITH-JONES: I quote the last two paragraphs:"If the British Government would consider these ideas, a blessing for Germany and also for the British Empire might result. If they reject these ideas, there will be war. In no case will Great Britain emerge stronger; the last war proved it. The Fuehrer repeats that he himself is a man of far-reaching decisions by which he is bound, and that this is his last offer...."

THE PRESIDENT: The Tribunal will adjourn and then the matter can be investigated.

[A recess was taken.]

LT. COL. GRIFFITH-JONES: I had just finished reading the offer from Hitler to the British Government, which was TC-72, Number 68, and which becomes GB-65.

The British Government were not, of course, aware of the real object that lay behind that message; and, taking it at its face value and desirous to enter into discussions, they wrote back on the 28th of August saying that they were prepared to enter into discussions. They agreed with Hitler that the differences must be settled, and I quote from Paragraph 4:

> "In the opinion of His Majesty's Government, a reasonable solution of the differences between Germany and Poland could and should be effected by agreement between the two countries on lines which would include the safeguarding of Poland's essential interests; and they recall that in his speech of the 28th of April, the German Chancellor recognized the importance of these interests to Poland.

> "But, as was stated by the Prime Minister in his letter to the German Chancellor of the 22d of August, His Majesty's Government consider it essential for the success of the discussions, which would precede the agreement, that it should be understood beforehand that any settlement arrived at would be guaranteed by other powers. His Majesties Government would be ready, if desired, to make their contribution to the effective operation of such a guarantee." I go to the last paragraph on that page, Paragraph 6:

> "His Majesty's Government have said enough to make their own attitude plain in the particular matters at issue between Germany and Poland. They trust that the German Chancellor will not think that, because His Majesty's Government are scrupulous concerning their obligations to Poland, they are not anxious to use all their influence to assist the achievement of a solution which may commend itself both to Germany and to Poland."

That, of course, knocked the German hopes on the head. They had failed by their tricks and their bribes to dissuade England from observing her obligations to Poland, and it was now only a matter of getting out of their embarrassment as quickly as possible and saving their face as much as possible. me last document becomes GB-66. And I put in also Sir Nevile Henderson's account of that interview, TC-72, Number 75, which becomes GB-67.During that interview, the only importance of it is that Sir Nevile Henderson again emphasized the British attitude and that they were determined in any event to meet their obligations to Poland. One paragraph I would quote, which is interesting in view of the letters that were to follow, paragraph 10:

> "In the end I asked him two straight questions: 'Was he willing to

negotiate directly with the Poles?' and Divas he ready to discuss the question of an exchange of population?' He replied in the affirmative as regards the latter, although there I have no doubt that he was thinking at the same time of a rectification of frontiers. As regards the first, He said he could not give me an answer until after he had given the reply of His Majesty's Government the careful consideration which such a document deserved. In this connection he turned to Ribbentrop and said, 'We must summon Field Marshal Goering to discuss it with him.' "

Then in the next paragraph, again Sir Nevile Henderson finally repeated to him very solemnly the main note of the whole conversation, so fat as he was concerned.

I pass to the next document, which is TC-72, Number 78, which becomes GB-68.

The German reply, as I outlined before, was handed to Sir Nevile Henderson at 7:15 p.m. on the 29th of August. The reply sets out the suggestion submitted by the British Government in their previous note; and it goes on to say that the German Government are prepared to enter into discussion on the basis that the whole of the Corridor, as well as Danzig, are returned to the Reich. I quote particularly the next to the last paragraph on the first page of that document:

"The demands of the German Government are in conformity with the revision of the Versailles Treaty, which has always been recognized as being necessary, in regard to this territory, namely: return of Danzig and the Corridor to Germany, the safeguarding-of the existence of the German national group in the territories remaining to Poland."

It is only just now, as I emphasized before, that that right has been recognized for so long. On the 28th of April his demands consisted only of Danzig, of an Autobahn, and of the railway.

The Tribunal will remember the position which he is trying to get out of now' He is trying to manufacture justification by putting forth proposals which under no possible circumstances could either Poland or Great Britain accept. But, as I said before, he wanted to make doubly certain.

I go to the second page, and start with the third paragraph:

"The British Government attach importance to two considerations:. (1) That the existing danger of an imminent explosion, should be eliminated as quickly as possible by direct negotiations; and (2) that the existence of the Polish State, in the form in which it would then continue to exist, should be adequately safeguarded in the economic and political sphere by means of international guarantees.

"On this subject the German Government make the following declaration:

"Though skeptical as to the prospects of a successful outcome, they are nevertheless, prepared to accept the English proposal and to enter into direct discussion. They do so, as has already been emphasized, solely as the result of the impression made upon them by the written statement received from the British Government that they, too, desire a pact of friendship in accordance with the general lines indicated to the British Ambassador."

And then, to the last but one paragraph:

"For the rest, in making these proposals, the German Government have never had any intention of touching Poland's. vital interests. or questioning the existence of an independent Polish State."

These letters really sound like the letters of some common swindler rather than of the government of a great nation.

> "The German Government; accordingly, in these circumstances agree to accept the British Government's offer of their good offices in securing the dispatch to Berlin of a Polish Emissary with full powers. Hey count on the arrival of this Emissary on Wednesday, the 30th August 1939.

> "The German Government will immediately draw up proposals for a solution acceptable to themselves and will, if possible, place these at the disposal of the British Government before the arrival of the Polish negotiator."

That was at 7:15 in the evening of the 29th of August and as I have explained, it allowed little time in order to get the Polish Emissary there by midnight the following night. That document was GB-68.

The next document, Sir Nevile Henderson's account of the interval, summarizes what had taken place; and I quote particularly paragraph 4:

> "I remarked that this phrase" - that is the passage about the Polish Emissary being there by midnight the following night - "sounded like an ultimatum, but after some heated remarks both Herr Hitler and Herr Von Ribbentrop assured me that it was only intended to stress the urgency of the moment when the two fully mobilized armies were standing face to face."

That was the interview on the evening of the 29th of August. The last document becomes GB-69.

Again the British Government replied, and Sir Nevile Henderson handed this reply to Ribbentrop at the famous meeting on midnight of the 30th of August at the time the Polish Emissary had been expected. I need not read at length. The British Government reciprocate the desire for improved relations They stress again that they cannot sacrifice the interest. of other friends in order to obtain an improvement in the situation. They understand, they say, that the German Government accept the condition that The settlement should be subject to international guarantee. Whey make a reservation as to the demands that the germane put forward in their last letter and they are informing the Polish Government immediately; and lastly, they understand that the German Government are drawing up the proposals. That Document TC-72, Number 89, will be GB-70. For the account of the interview, we go to the next document in the Tribunal's book, TC-72, Number 92, which becomes GB-71. It is not a very long document. It is perhaps worth reading in full:

> "I told Herr Ribbentrop this evening that His Majesty's Government found it difficult to advise the Polish Government to accept the procedure adumbrated in the German reply and suggested that he should adopt the normal contact, 'i.e. that when German proposals were ready, to invite the Polish Ambassador to call and to hand him proposals for transmission to his Government with a view to immediate opening of negotiations. I added that if this basis afforded prospect of settlement, His Majesty's Government could be counted upon to do their best in Warsaw to temporize negotiations.

> "Ribbentrop's reply was to produce a lengthy document which he read

out in German, aloud, at top speed. Imagining that he would eventually hand it to me, I did not attempt to follow too closely the 16 or more articles which it contained. Though I cannot, therefore, guarantee the accuracy, the main points were ...." - and I need not read out the main points.

I go to Paragraph 3:

"When I asked Ribbentrop for text of these proposals in accordance with undertaking in the German reply of yesterday, he asserted that it was now too late as Polish representative had not arrived in Berlin by midnight.

"I observed that to treat the matter in this way meant that the request for Polish representative to arrive in Berlin on the 30th of August constituted in fact an ultimatum, in spite of what he and Herr Hitler had assured me yesterday. This he denied, saying that the idea of an ultimatum was a figment of my imagination. Why then, I asked, could he not adopt the normal procedure and give me a copy of the proposals, and ask the Polish Ambassador to call on him just as Hitler had summoned me a few days ago, and hand them to him for communication to the Polish Government? In the most violent terms Ribbentrop said that he would never ask the Ambassador to visit him. He hinted that if the, Polish Ambassador asked him for interview it might be different. I said that I would, naturally, inform my Government so at once. Whereupon he said, while those were his personal views, he would bring all that I had said to Hitler's notice. It was for the Chancellor to decide.

"We parted on that note, but I must tell you that Von Ribbentrop's demeanor during an unpleasant interview was aping Hitler at his worst. He inveighed incidentally against the Polish mobilization, but I retorted that it was hardly surprising since Germany had also mobilized as Herr Hitler himself had admitted to me yesterday."

Nevertheless, Sir Nevile Henderson did not know at that time that Germany had also already given the orders to attack Poland some days before. The following day, the 31st of August at 6:30in the evening, Mr. Lipski, the Polish Ambassador, had an interview with Ribbentrop. This document, the next Document TC-73, Number 112, becomes GB-72, and is a short account in a report to Mr. Beck:

"I carried out my instructions. Ribbentrop asked if I had special plenipotentiary powers to undertake negotiations. I said, 'No'. He then asked whether I had been informed that on London's suggestion the German Government had expressed their readiness to negotiate directly with a delegate of the Polish Government, furnished with the requisite full powers, who was to have arrived on the preceding day, the 30th of August. I replied that I had no direct information on the subject. In conclusion, Ribbentrop repeated that he had thought I would be empowered to negotiate. He would communicate my *demarche* to the Chancellor."

As I have indicated already, it was too late. The orders had already been given on that day to the German Army to invade.

I turn to C-126. It is already in as GB-45. Other portions of it were put in, and I refer now to the letter on the second page, for the order (most-secret order). It is signed by Hitler and is described as his "Directive Number 1 for the Conduct of the War," dated. 31st of August 1939. Paragraph 1:

"(1) Now that all the political possibilities of disposing by peaceful means of a situation on the eastern frontier, which is intolerable for Germany, are exhausted, I have determined on a solution by force.

"(2) me attack on Poland is to be carried out in accordance with the preparations made for Case White with the alterations which result, where the Army is concerned, from the fact that it has in the meantime almost completed its dispositions.

"Allotment of tasks and the operational target remain unchanged.

"The date of attack: 1st of September 1939; time of attack:4.45" - inserted in red pencil - "this time also applies to the Operation at Gdynia, Bay of Danzig and-the Dirschau Bridge."'(3) In the West it is important that the responsibility for the opening of hostilities should rest unequivocally with England and France. At first, purely local action should be taken against insignificant frontier violations."

There it sets out the details of the order which, for the purpose of this Court, it is unnecessary to read. That evening at 9 o'clock the German radio broadcast the terms of the German proposals about which-they were so willing to enter into discussions with the Polish Government. It sets out the proposals at length. It will be remembered that by this time neither Sir Nevile Henderson nor the Polish Government nor their Ambassador had yet been given their written copy of them, and it is indeed a document which is tempting to read - or to read extracts of it simply as an exhibition or an example of pure hypocrisy. I refer to the second paragraph Document TC-72, Number 98, exhibit GB-39:

"Further, the German Government pointed out that they felt able to make the basic points regarding the offer of an understanding available to the British Government by the time the Polish negotiator arrived in Berlin."

Now, we have heard the manner in which they did that. They then say that:

"Instead of a statement regarding the arrival of authorized Polish personage, the first answer the Government of the- Reich received of their readiness for an understanding was the news of the Polish mobilization; and only toward-12 o'clock on the night of the 30th of August 1939, did they receive a somewhat general assurance of British readiness to help .towards the commencement of negotiations.

"Although the fact that the Polish negotiator expected by the Government of the Reich did not arrive removed the necessary conditions for informing His Majesty Government of the views of the German Government as regards a possible basis for negotiation, since His Majesty's Government themselves had pleaded for direct negotiations between Germany and Poland, the German Minister for Foreign Affairs Ribbentrop-gave the British Ambassador, on the occasion of the presentation of the last British note, precise information as to the text of the German proposals which will be regarded as a basis of negotiation in the event of the arrival of the Polish Plenipotentiary."

And, thereafter, they go on to set out the story, or rather their version of the story, of the negotiations over the last few days.

I pass to the next but one document in the Tribunal's book, TC-54, which becomes GB-73. On the 1st of September when his armies were already crossing the frontier and the whole of the frontier, he issued this proclamation to his Armed Forces:

"The Polish Government, unwilling to establish good neighborly relations as aimed at by me, want to force the issue byway of arms.

"The Germans in Poland are being persecuted with bloody terror and driven from their homes. Several acts of frontier violation, which cannot be tolerated by a great power,-show that Poland is no longer prepared to respect the Reich's frontiers. To put an end to these mad acts, I can see no other way but from now onwards to meet force with force.

"The German Armed Forces will with firm determination take up the struggle for the honor and the vital rights of the resuscitated German people.

"I expect every soldier to be conscious of the high tradition of the eternal German soldierly qualities and to do his duty to the last.

"Remember always and in any circumstances that you are the representatives of National Socialist Greater Germany.

"Long live our people and the Reich."

And so we see that at last Hitler had kept his word to his generals. He had afforded them their propagandistic justification; and at that time, anyway, it did not matter what people said about it afterwards. "The victor shall not be asked later on, whether he told the truth or not." Might is what counts - or victory is what counts and not right.

On that day, the 1st of September, when news came of this violation of Polish ground, the British Government in accordance with their treaty obligations sent an ultimatum to the German Government in which they stated - I quote from the last-paragraph:

"I am accordingly to inform your Excellency that unless the German Government are prepared to give His Majesty's Government satisfactory assurances that the German Government have suspended all aggressive action against Poland and are prepared promptly to withdraw their forces from Polish territory, His Majesty's Government in the United Kingdom will without hesitation fulfil their obligations to Poland."

By the 3rd of September no withdrawal had taken place, and so at g o'clock - the document, TC-72, Number 110, I have just referred to will be GB-74 at 9 o'clock on the 3rd of September, a final ultimatum was handed to the German Minister of Foreign Affairs. I quote from the third paragraph:

"Although this communication was made more than 24 hours ago, no reply has been received but German attacks upon Poland have been continued and intensified. I have accordingly the honor to inform you that, unless not later than 11 o'clock British summer time today, the 3rd of September, satisfactory assurances to the above effect have been given by the German Government and have reached His Majesty's Government in London, a state of war will exist between the two countries as from that hour."

And so it was that at 11 o'clock on the 3rd of September a state of war existed between Germany end England and between Germany and France. All the appeals to peace, all the appeals to reason we now see completely stillborn; stillborn when they were made. Plans, preparations, intentions, determination to carry out this assault upon Poland, had been going on for months, for years before. It mattered not what anybody but the German Government had in mind or whatever rights anybody else but the German nation thought they had; and, if there is any doubt left at all after what we have seen, I would ask you to look at two more documents.

If you would look at the last document first of all, in your document book - 1831-PS, which becomes GB-75. Even now on the3rd of September, Mussolini offers some chance of peace.

We have here a telegram. It is timed 6:30 hours, and I am afraid I am unable to say whether that is 6:30 in the morning or evening; but it is dated the 3rd of September, and I quote:

"The Italian Ambassador handed to the State Secretary at the Duce's order the following copy for the Fuehrer and Reich Chancellor and for the Reich Minister for Foreign Affairs:

" Italy sends the information, leaving, of course, every decision to the Fuehrer, that it still has a chance to call a conference with France, England, and Poland on the following basis:

> An armistice which would leave the army corps where they are at present" - and it will be remembered that on the3rd of September they had advanced a considerable way over the frontier -
>
> 2. calling a conference within 2 or 3 days;
>
> 3. solution of the Polish-German controversy would be certainly favorable for Germany as matters stand today.

"This idea, which originated from the Duce, has its foremost exponent in France.

"Danzig is already German and Germany is holding already securities which guarantee most of her demands. Besides, Germany has had already her "moral satisfaction." If she would accept the plan for a conference, it will achieve all her aims and at the same time prevent a war which already today has the aspect of being universal and of extremely long duration.'"

But, My Lord, perhaps even Mussolini did not appreciate what all Germany's aims were; and, of course, the offer was turned down in the illuminating letter which Hitler was to write in reply. I refer you back to the document before that. It is still part of the same Exhibit GB-75.

THE PRESIDENT: As I understand it, the "GB" references you give are not on the documents at all; they are the exhibit numbers themselves, which are to be put on the document after they have been put in.

LT. COL. GRIFFITH-JONES: Yes. That is correct. They will, be put in by the Court, of course.

THE PRESIDENT: Will you try to make clear the references which are on the document so that the Tribunal could find the document itself?

LT. COL. GRIFFITH-JONES: Yes. The last document was 1831-PS, and it is the very last one in the document book. That is the one I have just referred to - the telegram from Mussolini. The document to which I am about to refer is the one but last in the Tribunal's book but it has the same number on it as the last because it forms part of the same exhibit.

THE PRESIDENT: I think if you would just explain the system in which the exhibits are numbered, it would help us.

LT. COL. GRIFFITH-JONES: The exhibits are numbered at the present moment before they are put in evidence with a variety of serial numbers, such as "PS", "TC", "L" and other letters. There is no significance attached to that at all. It depends on whom they have been found by and what files they have come from. When the documents are put in as exhibits, they are marked by the Court with a court number. The documents put in by the United States representatives were all prefixed with the letters "USA." The documents which have been put in by the British prosecutors have all been prefixed with the letters "GB." If it would be of any assistance to members of the Tribunal, I will have their document books marked up this evening with the new court numbers that have been put upon them by the Court officials, during the course of the day.

THE PRESIDENT: We will talk about that later.

LT. COL GRIFFITH-JONES: If there is any document missing from any of these books, I have a copy.

THE PRESIDENT: You are going to read 1831-PS?

LT. COL. GRIFFITH-JONES: Yes, that is GB-75.

"Duce:

"I first want to thank you for your last attempt at a mediation: I would have been. ready to accept, but only under condition that there would be a possibility to give me certain guarantees that the conference would be successful. Because for the last 2 days the German troops are engaged in an extraordinarily rapid advance in Poland, it would have been impossible to devaluate the bloody sacrifices made thereby by diplomatic intrigues. Nevertheless, I believe that a way could have been found if England would not have been determined to wage war under all circumstances. I have not given in to the English because, Duce, I do not believe that peace could have been maintained for more than one-half a year or a year. Under these circumstances I thought that, in spite of everything, the present moment was better for resistance. At present the superiority of the German Armed Forces in Poland is so overwhelming in all the fields that the Polish Army will collapse in a very short time. I doubt whether this fast success could have been achieved in 1 or 2 years. England and France would have armed their allies to such an extent that the crushing technical superiority of the German Armed Forces could not have become so apparent any more. I am aware, Duce, that the fight which I enter is one for life and death. My own fate does not play any role in it at all. But I am also aware that one cannot avoid such a struggle permanently and that one has to choose, after cold deliberation, the moment for resistance in such away that the probability of success is guaranteed; and I believe in this success, Duce, with the firmness of a rock. Recently you have given me the kind assurance that you think you will be able to help me in a few fields. I acknowledge this in advance, with sincere thanks. But I believe also - even if we march now over different roads - that fate will finally join us. If the National Socialistic Germany were destroyed by the Western Democracies, the Fascist Italy would also have to face a grave future. I was personally always aware of this community of the future of our two governments and I know that you, Duce, think the same way. To the situation in Poland, I would like to make the brief remark that we lay aside, of course, all unimportant things, that we do not waste any man on unimportant tasks' but direct all on acts in the light of great operational considerations. The northern Polish Army, which is in the Corridor, has already been completely encircled by our action. It will be either wiped out or will surrender. Otherwise, all operations proceed according to plan. The daily achievements of the troops are far beyond all expectations. The superiority of our Air Force is complete, although scarcely one-third of it is in Poland. To the West, I will be on the defensive. France can here sacrifice its blood first. Then the moment will come when we can confront the enemy. also there with the Cull power of the nation. Accept my; thanks, Duce, for all your assistance which you have given to me in the past; and I ask you not to deny it to me in the future."

That completes the evidence which I propose to offer upon this part of the case in respect of the war of aggression against Poland, England, and France, which is charged in Count Two.

MAJOR F. ELWYN JONES (Junior Counsel for the United Kingdom): May it please the Tribunal, in the early hours of the morning of the 9th of April 1940 Nazi Germany invaded Norway and Denmark. It is my duty to present to. the Tribunal the Prosecution's evidence which has been prepared in collaboration with my American colleague, Major Finely, with regard to these brutal wars of aggression, which were also wars in violation of international treaties, agreements, and assurances. With the Court's permission I would like, first of all, to deal with the treaties and agreements and assurances that were in fact violated by. these two invasions of Norway and Denmark.

The invasions were, of course, in the first instance violations of the Hague Convention and of the Kellogg-Briand Pact. My learned friend, Sir David Maxwell-Fyfe, has already dealt with those matters in the course of his presentation of the evidence. In addition to these general treaties, there were specific agreements between Germany and Norway and Denmark. In the first instance there was the Treaty of Arbitration and Conciliation between Germany and Denmark, which was signed at Berlin on 2 June 1926. The Court will find that treaty, TC-17, on the first page of British Document Book Number 3; and to that exhibit it may be convenient to give the Number GB-76. I am proposing to read only the first article of that treaty, which is in these terms:

"The contracting parties undertake to submit to the procedure of arbitration or conciliation, in conformity with the present treaty, all disputes of any nature whatsoever which may arise between Germany and Denmark, and which it has not been possible to settle within a reasonable period by diplomacy or to bring with the consent of both parties, before the Permanent Court of International Justice.

"Disputes for the solution of which a special procedure has been laid down in other conventions in force between the contracting parties shall be settled in accordance with the provisions of such conventions."

Then there follows in the remaining articles the establishment of the machinery for arbitration.

182

I would next refer to the Treaty of Non-Aggression between Germany and Denmark, which was signed by the Defendant Ribbentrop on the 31st of May 1939 which, as the Tribunal will recollect, was 10 weeks after the Nazi seizure of Czechoslovakia. The Court will find that as Document TC-24 in the document book and it will now bear the Exhibit Number GB-77.

With the Court's permission, in view of the identity of the signatory of that treaty, I would like to read the Preamble and Articles 1 and 2.

"The Chancellor of the German Reich and His Majesty, King of Denmark and Iceland, being firmly resolved to maintain peace between Denmark and Germany in all circumstances, have agreed to confirm this resolve by means of a treaty and have appointed as their Plenipotentiaries: The Chancellor of the German Reich . . . and His Majesty, the Tog of Denmark and Iceland ...."

Article 1 reads as follows:

"The German Reich and the Kingdom of Denmark shall in no case resort to war or to any other use of force, one against the other.

"Should action of the kind referred to in Paragraph 1 be taken by a third power against one of the contracting parties, the other contracting party shall not support such action in any way."

Then Article 2 deals with the ratification of the treaty, and the second paragraph states:

"The treaty shall come into force on the exchange of the instruments of ratification and shall remain in force for a period of 10 years from that date .... "

As the Tribunal will observe, the treaty is dated the 31st of May 1939. At the bottom of the page there appears the signature of the Defendant Ribbentrop. The Tribunal will shortly see that less than a year after the signature of this treaty the invasion of Denmark by the Nazi forces was to show the utter worthlessness of treaties to white the Defendant Ribbentrop put his signature.

With regard to Norway, the Defendant Ribbentrop and the Nazi conspirators were party to a similar perfidy. In the first instance I would refer to Document TC-30, which is the next document in the British Document Book 3 and which will bear the Exhibit Number GB-78. The Tribunal will observe that that is an assurance given to Denmark, Norway, Belgium, and the Netherlands on the 28th of April 1939. That, of course, was after the annexation of Czechoslovakia had shaken the confidence of the world; and this was presumably an attempt, now submitted by the Prosecution to be a dishonest attempt, to try to reassure the Scandinavian States. The assurance is in a speech by Hitler and reads:

". . . I have given binding declarations to a large number of states. None of these states can complain that even a trace of a demand contrary thereto has ever been made to them by Germany. None of the Scandinavian statesmen, for example, can contend that a request has ever been put to them by the German Government or by German public opinion which was incompatible with the sovereignty and integrity of their state.

"I was pleased that a number of European states availed themselves of these declarations by the German Government to express and emphasize their desire too for absolute neutrality. This applies to the Netherlands, Belgium, Switzerland, Denmark, *et cetera.* "

A further assurance was given by the Nazi Government on the 2d of September 1939 which, as the Tribunal will recollect, was the day after the Nazi invasion of Poland. The Court will observe the next document in British Document Book 3 is the Document TC-31,which will be Exhibit GB-79. That is an *aide-memoire* that was handed to the Norwegian Foreign Minister by the German Minister in Oslo on the 2d of September 1939. It reads:

"The German Reich Government are determined, in view of the friendly relations which exist between Norway and Germany, under no circumstances to prejudice the inviolability and integrity of Norway and to respect the territory of the Norwegian State. In making this declaration, the Reich Government naturally expect on their side that Norway will observe an unimpeachable neutrality towards the Reich and will not tolerate any breaches of Norwegian neutrality by any third party. Should the attitude of the Royal Norwegian Government differ from this so that any such breach of neutrality by a third party occurs, the Reich Government would then obviously be compelled to safeguard the interest of the Reich in such a way as the resulting situation might dictate."

There follows, finally, the further German assurance to Norway, which appears as the next document in the book, TC-32, which will be Exhibit GB-80. That is a speech by Hitler on the 6th of October 1939; and if the Court win observe Paragraph 2 at the top of the page, the extract from the speech reads as follows:

"Germany has never had any conflicts of interest or even points of controversy with the Northern States; neither has she any today. Sweden and Norway have both bee in offered. non-aggression pacts by Germany and have both refused them solely because they did not feel themselves threatened in any way."

Those are clear and positive assurances which Germany gave. The Court will see that violation of those assurances is charged in paragraph XXII of Appendix C of the Indictment at Page 43. The Court will notice that there is a minor typographical error in The date of the first assurance which is alleged in the Indictment to have been given on the 3rd of September 1939. The Court will see from Document TC-31, which is Exhibit GB-79, that the assurance was in fact given on the 2d of September 1939.

Now those treaties and. assurances were the diplomatic background too the brutal Nazi aggression on Norway and Denmark, and the evidence which the Prosecution winnow place before the Court will in any submission establish beyond reasonable doubt that these assurances were simply given to lull suspicion and cause the intended victims of Nazi aggression to be unprepared to meet the Nazi attack.: for we now know that as early as October 1939 these conspirators and their confederates were plotting the invasion of Norway, and the evidence will indicate that the most active conspirators in that plot were the Defendants Raeder and Rosenberg.

The Norwegian invasion is, in one respect, not a typical Nazi aggression in that Hitler had to be persuaded to embark upon it, The chief instruments of persuasion were Raeder and Rosenberg. Raeder because he thought Norway strategically important and because he coveted glory for his Navy, Rosenberg because of his political connections in Norway which he sought to develop.

As the Tribunal will shortly see, in the Norwegian Vidkun Quisling the

184

Defendant Rosenberg found a very model of the Fifth column agent, the very personification of perfidy.

The evidence as to the early stages of the Nazi conspiracy to invade Norway is found in a letter which the Defendant Raeder wrote on the 10th of January 1944 to Admiral Assmann, the official German naval historian.

I put in this letter, the document C-66, which will be Exhibit GB-81, and which the Court will find further on in this book of documents. I should explain that in this book of documents the document s are inserted in the numerical order of the series to which they belong and not in the order of their submission to the court. I am trusting that that Will be a more convenient form of bundling them together than to set them down in the order of presentation.

THE PRESIDENT: 66?

MAJOR JONES: C-66. It is headed, "memorandum to Admiral Assmann; for his own information; not to be used for publication."

The Court will observe that the first page deals with Barbarossa; If the Tribunal turns to the next page headed."(b) Weserubung,"the Tribunal will find from documents which I shall shortly be submitting to the Court that Weserubung was the code name for the invasion of Norway and Denmark.

I will omit the first sentence. The document which, as I have said, is a communication from the Defendant Raeder to Assmann reads as follows:

"During the weeks preceding the report on the 10th of October 1939, I was in correspondence with Admiral Carls, who, in a detailed letter to me, first pointed out the Importance of an occupation of the Norwegian coast by Germany. I passed this letter on to C/SKL" - which is the Chief of Staff of the Naval War Staff - "for their information and prepared some notes based on this letter . . . for my report to the Fuehrer; which I made on the 10th of October 1939, since my opinion was absolutely identical with that of Admiral Carls, while at that time SKL was more dubious about the matter. In these notes I stressed the disadvantages which an occupation of Norway by the British would have for us: Control of the approaches to the Baltic, outflanking of our naval operations and our air attacks on Britain, pressure on Sweden. I also stressed the advantages for us of the occupation of the Norwegian coast: Outlet to the North Atlantic, no possibility of a British mine barrier, as in the years 1917-18. Naturally, at the time,. only the coast and bases were considered; I included Narvik, though admiral Carls, in the course of our correspondence, thought that Narvik could be excluded .... The Fuehrer saw at once the significance of the Norwegian problem, he asked me to leave the notes and stated that he wished to consider the question himself."

I will pause in the reading of that document at that point and return to it later so that the story may be revealed to the Court in a chronological order.

That report of Raeder, in my submission, shows that the whole evolution of this Nazi campaign against Norway affords a good example of the participation of the German High Command in the Nazi conspiracy to attack inoffensive neighbors:

This letter, an extract from which I have just read, has revealed that Raeder reported to Hitler on the 10th of October 1939 . . .

THE TRIBUNAL (Mr. Biddle): When was that report?

MAJOR JONES: The report, C-66, was made in January 1944 by the

Defendant Raeder to Assmann, who was the German naval historian, and so, presumably, was for the purposes of history.

Before Raeder's report of 10 October 1939 was made to the Fuehrer, Raeder got a second opinion on the Norwegian invasion. On the 3rd of October Raeder made out the questionnaire to which I now invite the Court's attention. It is Document C-122 and The Court will find it next but one to C-66 in the document book. That will now be Exhibit GB-82.

That, as the Tribunal will observe, is headed "Gaining of Bases in Norway (extract from War Diary)" and bears the date of the 3rd of October 1939. It reads:

"The Chief of the Naval Operations Staff" - who was the Defendant Raeder - "considers it necessary that the Fuehrer be informed as soon as possible of the opinions of the Naval Operations Staff on the possibilities of extending the operational base to the north. It must be ascertained whether it is possible to gain bases in Norway under the combined pressure of Russia and Germany, with the basic aim of improving our strategic and operational position. The following questions must be given consideration:

"(a) What places in Norway can be considered as bases?

"(b) Can bases be gained by military force against Norway's will if it is impossible to carry this out without fighting?

"(c) What are the possibilities of defense after the occupation?

"(d) Will the harbors have to be developed completely as bases or have they already decisive advantages suitable for supply position?"

Then there follows in parenthesis:

'The Commander of the U-boat Fleet" - which is a reference, of course, to the Defendant Doenitz". . . considers such harbors already extremely useful as equipment and supply bases at which Atlantic U-boats can call temporarily."

And then Question (e):

"What decisive advantages would exist for the conduct of the war at sea in gaining bases in north Denmark, e.g. Skagen?"

There is, in our possession, a document C-5, to find which it will be necessary for the Court to go back in the document book to the first of the C exhibits. This will be Exhibit GB-83.

This is a memorandum written by the Defendant Doenitz on Norwegian bases. It presumably relates to the questionnaire of the Defendant Raeder which, as I have indicated, was in circulation at about that time. The document is headed, "Commander of the U-boat Fleet; Operations Division," and is marked "most secret." The subject is "Base in Norway."

Then there are set out "suppositions," "advantages and disadvantages," and, over one page, "conclusions". I am proposing to read the last paragraph, III

"The following is therefore proposed:

"(1) Establishment of a base in Trondheim, including:

"a) Possibility of supplying fuel, compressed air, oxygen, provisions;

"b)Repair opportunities for normal overhaul work after an encounter;

186

"c) Good opportunities for accommodating U boat crews;

"d) Flak protection, L.A. antiaircraft armament, patrol and M/S units.

"(2) Establishment of the possibility of supplying fuel in Narvik as an alternative."

That is a Doenitz memorandum.

Now, as the Tribunal saw in the report of Raeder to Assmann, in October 1939, Hitler was merely considering the Norwegian aggression and had not yet committed himself to it, although, as the Tribunal will see very shortly, Hitler was most susceptible to any suggestions of aggression against the territory of another country.

The documents will show that the Defendant Raeder persevered in pressing his point of view with regard to Norway, and at this stage he found a powerful ally in the Defendant Rosenberg.

The Nazi employment of traitors and the stimulation of treachery as a political weapon are now unhappily proven historical facts, but should proof be required of that statement it is found in the remarkable document which I now invite the Court to consider. I refer to Document 007-PS, which is after the TC and D series in the document book. That will be Exhibit GB-84.

That is headed on Page 1, "Brief Report on Activities of the Foreign Affairs Bureau of the Party" - Aussenpolitisches Amt der NSDAP - "from 1933 to 1943." It reads:

"When the Foreign Affairs Bureau" (Aussenpolitisches Amt) was established on the 1st of April 1933, the Fuehrer directed that it should not be expanded to a large bureaucratic agency; but should rather develop its effectiveness through initiative and suggestions.

"Corresponding to the extraordinarily hostile attitude adopted by the Soviet Government in Moscow from the beginning, the newly-established bureau devoted particular attention to internal conditions in the Soviet Union as well as to the effects of world Bolshevism, primarily in other European countries. It entered into contact with the most variegated groups inclining towards National Socialism in combatting Bolshevism, focussing its main attentions on nations and states bordering on the Soviet Union. On the one hand those nations and states constituted an insulating ring encircling the Bolshevist neighbor; on the other hand they were the laterals of German living space and took up a flanking position towards the Western Powers, especially Great Britain in order to wield the desired influence by one means or another" - and the Court win shortly see the significance of that phrase - "the bureau was compelled to use the most varying methods, taking into consideration the completely different living conditions, the ties of blood and intellect, and historical dependence of the movements observed by the bureau in those countries.

"In Scandinavia a progressively more outspoken pro-Anglo Saxon attitude based on economic considerations had become more dominant after the World War of 1914-18. There the bureau put the entire emphasis on influencing general cultural relations with the Nordic peoples. For this purpose it took the Nordic Society in Lubeck under its protection. The Reich conventions of this society were attended by many outstanding personalities, especially from Finland.

While there were no openings for purely political co-operation in Sweden and Denmark, an association based on Greater Germanic ideology was found in Norway. Very close relations, which led to further consequences, were established with its founder."

If the Court will turn to the end of the main part of the statement which is 4 pages forward - in the intervening pages, I may say, there is an account of the activity of Rosenberg's bureau in various parts of Europe, and indeed of the world, which I am not proposing to call the Tribunal's attention to at this stage - but if the Tribunal will look at the last paragraph of the main body of the report which bears the signature of the Defendant Rosenberg, The last two sentences read:

"With the outbreak of war it was entitled to consider its task as terminated. The exploitation of the many personal connections in many lands can be resumed under a different guise."

If the Tribunal will turn to the annex to the document, which is on the next page, the Tribunal will appreciate what "exploitation of personal connections" involved.

Annex I to the document is headed, "Brief Report on Activities of the Foreign Affairs Bureau of the Nazi Party from 1933 to 1943."

It is headed, "The Political Preparation of the Military Occupation of Norway during the War Years 1939-40," and it reads:

"As previously mentioned, of all political groupings in Scandinavia only Nasjonal Sampling, led in Norway by the former Minister of War and retired major, Vidkun Quisling, deserved serious political attention. This was a fighting political group possessed by the idea of a Greater Germanic community. Naturally all ruling powers were hostile and attempted to prevent by any means its success among the population. The bureau maintained constant relation with Quisling and attentively observed the attacks he conducted with tenacious energy on the middle class, which had been taken in tow by the English. From the beginning it appeared probable that without revolutionary events which would stir the population from their forms. attitude no successful progress of Nasjonal Samling was to be expected. During the winter1938-39 Quisling was privately visited by a member of the bureau. When the political situation in Europe came to ahead in 1939, Quisling made an appearance at the convention of the Nordic Society in Lubes in June. He expounded his conception of the situation and his apprehensions concerning Norway. He emphatically drew attention to the geopolitically decisive importance of Norway in the Scandinavian area and to the advantages that would accrue to the power dominating the Norwegian coast in case of a convict between the Greater German Reich and Great Britain.

"Assuming that his statements would be of special interest to the Marshal of the Reich, Goering, for aero-strategical reasons, Quisling was referred to State Secretary Korner by the bureau. The Staff Director of the bureau handed the (Chief of the Reich Chancellery a memorandum for transmission to the Fuehrer ...."

In a later part of the document, which I shall read at a later stage of my presentation of the evidence, if I may, the Court will see how Quisling came into contact with Raeder. The Prosecution's submission with regard to this document is that it is another illustration of the close interweaving between the political and the military leadership of the Nazi State, of the close link between the professional soldiers and the professional thugs.

The Defendant Raeder, in his report to Admiral Assmann, admitted his collaboration with Rosenberg; and I will invite The Court's attention once more to Document C-66, which is Exhibit GB-81. In the page headed "Weserubung," the second paragraph of the Raeder report reads as follows:

"In the further developments, I was supported by Commander Schreiber, Naval Attache in Oslo, and the M-Chief personally - in conjunction with the Rosenberg organization. Thus we got in touch with Quisling and Hagelin, who came to Berlin in the beginning of December and were taken to the Three by me - with the approval of Reichsleiter Rosenberg... ,"

I will later draw the attention of the Tribunal to the developments in December.

The details of the manner in which the Defendant Raeder did make contact personally with Quisling are not very clear. But I would draw the Court's attention to the Document C-65, which precedes . . .

THE PRESIDENT: Would you read the end of that paragraph?

MAJOR JONES: With your Lordship's permission, I would like to revert to that in a later stage in my unfolding of the evidence.

In the Document C-65, which will be Exhibit GB-85, we have a report of Rosenberg to Raeder in which the full extent of Quisling's preparedness for treachery and his potential usefulness to the Nazi aggressors was reported and disclosed to the Defendant Raeder.

Paragraph 1 of that report deals with matters which I have already dealt with in reading Rosenberg's statement, 007-PS. But if the Court win look at the second paragraph of Exhibit GB-85, C-65, it reads as follows:

"The reasons for a coup, on which Quisling made a report, would be provided by the fact that the Storthing" - that is to say the Norwegian parliament - "had, in defiance of the constitution, passed a resolution prolonging its own life which is to become operative on January 12th. Quisling still retains in his capacity as a long-standing officer and a former Minister of War the closest relations with the Norwegian Army. He showed me the original of a letter which he had received only a short time previously from the commanding officer in Narvik, Colonel Sunlo. In this letter Colonel Sunlo frankly lays emphasis on the fact that if things went on as they were going at present, Norway was finished."

If the Court will turn to the next page of that document, The last two paragraphs, the details of a treacherous plot to overthrow the government of his own country, by the traitor Quisling in collaboration with the Defendant Rosenberg, will be indicated to the Court.

"A plan has been put forward which deals with the possibility of a coup and which provides for a number of selected Norwegians to be trained in Germany with all possible speed for such a purpose, being allotted their exact tasks and provided with experienced and die-hard National Socialists who are practiced in such operations. These trained men should then proceed with all speed to Norway where details would then require to be further discussed. Some important centers in Oslo would have to be taken over forthwith, and at the same time, the German Fleet together with suitable contingents of the German Army would go into operation when summoned specially by the new Norwegian Government in a specified bay at the approaches to Oslo. Quisling has no doubts that such a *coup*, having teem carried out with instantaneous success, would immediately bring him the approval of those sections of the army with which he at present has connections; and thus it goes without saying that he has never discussed a political fight with them. As far as the King is concerned, he believes that he would respect it as an accomplished fact."

How wrong Quisling was in that anticipation was shown, of course, by subsequent developments. The last sentence reads:

"Quisling gives figures of the number of German troops required which accord with German calculations."

The Tribunal may think that there are no words in the whole vocabulary of abuse sufficiently strong to describe that degree of treachery.

THE PRESIDENT: Is that document dated?

MAJOR JONES: That document does not bear a date.

THE PRESIDENT: We will break off now.

[The Tribunal adjourned until 7 December 1945 at 1000 o'clock.]

Fifteenth Day:
Friday, 7th December, 1945

MAJOR ELWYN JONES: May it please the Tribunal, yesterday afternoon when the Tribunal adjourned I was dealing with the stage of the Nazi conspiracy against Norway at which the activities of the defendants Raeder and Rosenberg converged. And the Court will remember that I submitted in evidence Document C-65, which was a report from the defendant Rosenberg to Raeder regarding Quisling, and ending with the infamous words: "Quisling gives figures of the number of German troops required which accord with German calculations."

The Court has already received in evidence and heard read material parts of Document C-66, which was the report of Raeder to Admiral Assmann, which disclosed how, in December, 1939, the defendant Raeder did in fact meet Quisling and Hagelin.

I now invite the Court to look at Document C-64 which, for the purpose of the record, will be Exhibit GB 86. The Court will observe that that is a report by Raeder of the meeting of the Naval Staff with Hitler on 12th December, 1939, at 1200 hours, in the presence of the defendants Keitel and Jodl and Puttkammer, who at this time was adjutant to Hitler.

The report is headed "Norwegian Question", and the first sentence reads:

"C.-in-C. Navy" - who of course was the defendant Raeder - "has received Quisling and Hagelin. Quisling creates the impression of being reliable."

And then there follows, in the next two paragraphs, a statement of Quisling's views, views with which the Court is by now familiar because of my reading of extracts from the Document 007-PS; but I draw the Court's attention to the fourth paragraph in Document C-64, beginning:

"The Fuehrer thought of speaking to Quisling personally so that he might form an impression of him. He wanted to see Rosenberg once more first, as the latter had known Quisling for a long while. C.-in-C. Navy" - that is, of course, Raeder - "suggests that if the Fuehrer formed a favourable impression, the O.K.W. should obtain permission to make plans with Quisling for the preparation and carrying out of the occupation.

(a) By peaceful means: that is to say, German Forces summoned by Norway;

(b) To agree to do so by force."

That was 12th December, the meeting at which Raeder made this report to Hitler.

If the Court will now look at Document C-66, which is Raeder's record of these transactions for the purpose of history, the Court will observe, in the last sentence of the second paragraph of the section of C-66 headed

"(b) Weserubung", these words:

"Thus we got in touch with Quisling and Hagelin, who came to Berlin at the beginning of December and were taken to the Fuehrer - "

THE PRESIDENT: I have not got it.

MAJOR ELWYN JONES: I beg your Lordship's pardon; it is Document C-66, the second page, headed "Weserubung", in the second paragraph.

"Thus we got in touch with Quisling and Hagelin, who came to Berlin at the beginning of December and were taken to the Fuehrer by me, with the approval of Reichsleiter Rosenberg."

And then the Court will observe a note at the end of the page:-

"At the crucial moment, R" - presumably Rosenberg - "hurt his foot, so that I visited him in his house on the morning of 14th December."

That is, of course, Raeder's note, and it indicates the extent of his complicity in this conspiracy.

The report continues

"On the grounds of the Fuehrer's discussion with Quisling and Hagelin on the afternoon Of 14th December, the Fuehrer gave the order that preparations for the Norwegian operation were to be made by the Supreme Command of the Armed Forces.

Until that moment the Naval War Staff had taken no part in the development of the Norwegian question, and continued to be somewhat sceptical about it. The preparations, which were undertaken by Captain Crank in Supreme Command of the Armed Forces, were founded, however, on a memorandum of the Naval War Staff."

The Court may well think that the note of the defendant Raeder referring to "the crucial moment" was an appropriate one, because the Court will see that on that day, 14th December, Hitler gave the order that preparations for the Norwegian operation were to be begun by the Supreme Command of the Armed Forces.

If the Court will now turn to Document 007-PS, which is further on in the document book, and which the Court will remember is Rosenberg's report on the activities of his organisation - it is after the "D" documents - if the Court will turn to about ten lines from the bottom of the first page of Annex 1, dealing with Norway, the Court will see that there were further meetings between Quisling and the Nazi chiefs in December, and I am going to read now the section beginning:

"Quisling was granted a personal audience with the Fuehrer on 16th December, and once more on the 18th December. In the course of this audience the Fuehrer emphasised repeatedly that he personally would prefer a completely neutral attitude of Norway, as well as of the whole of Scandinavia. He did not intend to enlarge the theatre of war and to draw still other nations into the conflict."

As I have said in opening the presentation of this part of the case, here was an instance where pressure had to be brought to bear on Hitler to induce him to take part in these operations.

The report continues

"Should the enemy attempt" - there is a mis-translation here - "to extend the war, however, with the aim of achieving further throttling and intimidation of the Greater German Reich, he would be compelled to gird himself against such an undertaking. In order to counterbalance increasing enemy propaganda activity, he promised Quisling financial support of his movement, which was based on

Greater Germanic ideology. Military exploitation of the question now raised was assigned to the special military staff, which transmitted special missions to Quisling. Reichsleiter Rosenberg was to take over political exploitation. Financial expenses were to be defrayed by the Ministry for Foreign Affairs" - that is to say, by Ribbentrop's organisation - "the Minister for Foreign Affairs" - that is to say, Ribbentrop - "being kept continuously informed by the Foreign Affairs Bureau" - which, of course, was Rosenberg's organisation.

Chief of Section Scheidt was charged with maintaining liaison with Quisling. In the course of further developments he was assigned to the Naval Attache in Oslo. Orders were given that the whole matter be handled with strictest secrecy".

Here again the Court will note the close link between the Nazi politicians and the Nazi service chiefs.

The information that is available to the prosecution as to the events of January, 1940, is not full, but the Court will see that the agitation of the defendants Raeder and Rosenberg did bear fruit, and I now invite the Court to consider a letter of Keitel's, Document C-63, which, for the purposes of the record, will be Exhibit GB 87. The Court will observe that that is an order - a memorandum - signed by the defendant Keitel, dated the 27th January, 1940. It is marked "Most Secret, five copies; reference, Study 'N'" - which was another code name for the Weserubung Preparations - "Access only through an officer".

It is headed: "C.-in-C. of the Navy" - that is to say, the defendant Raeder - "has a report on this."

The document reads:

"The Fuehrer and Supreme Commander of the Armed Forces wishes that Study 'N' should be further worked on under my direct and personal guidance, and in the closest conjunction with the general war policy. For these reasons the Fuehrer has commissioned me to take over the direction of further preparations.

A working staff has been formed at the Supreme Command of the Armed Forces Headquarters for this purpose, and this represents, at the same time, the nucleus of a future operational staff."

Then, at the end of the memorandum:

"All further plans will be made under the cover name 'Weserubung'."

I should like respectfully to draw the Tribunal's attention to the importance of that document, to the signature of Keitel upon it, and to the date of this important decision.

Prior to this date, 27th January, 1940, the planning of the various aspects of the invasion of Norway and Denmark had been confined to a relatively small group, whose aim had been to persuade Hitler of the desirability of undertaking this Norwegian operation. The issuance of this directive of Keitel's on 27th January, 1940, was the signal that the Supreme Command of the German Armed Forces, the O.K.W., had accepted the proposition of the group that was pressing for this Norwegian adventure, and turned the combined resources of the German military machine to the task of producing practical and co-ordinated plans for the Norwegian operation.

The Court will observe that from January onward the operational planning for the invasion of Norway and Denmark was started through the normal channels.

And now I would refer the Court to some entries in the diary of the defendant Jodl, to see how the preparations progressed. That is Document 1809-PS, which will be, for the purposes of the record, Exhibit GB 88. That, the Court will observe, is the last document in the document book.

There is a slight confusion in the order in which the entries are set out in the diary, because the first three pages relate to entries which will be dealt with in another part of the case.

I invite the Court's attention to Page 3 of these extracts from Jodl's diary, beginning at the bottom, 6th February. The entry under the date line of 6th February, 1940 starts: "New idea: Carry out 'H' and Weser Exercise only and guarantee Belgium's neutrality for the duration of the war."

I would like to repeat that entry, if I may be permitted to do so

"New idea: Carry out 'H' and Weser Exercise only, and guarantee Belgium's neutrality for the duration of the war."

The next entry to which I invite the Court's attention is the entry of the 21st February.

THE TRIBUNAL (Mr. Biddle): What does that mean: "To carry out 'H'"?

MAJOR ELWYN JONES: That is a reference to another code word, "Hartmut", which the Court will see disclosed in a subsequent document. That is another code word for this Norwegian and Danish operation.

The entry of 21st February in Jodl's diary reads: "Fuehrer has talked with General von Falkenhorst and charges him with preparation of 'Weser Exercise'. Falkenhorst accepts gladly. Instructions issued to the three branches of the Armed Forces."

Then the next entry, on the next page -

THE PRESIDENT: "Weser Exercise" - is that Norway too?

MAJOR ELWYN JONES: That is Norway too, my Lord, yes. That is a translation of "Weserubung".

The entry on the next page, under the date of 28th February:

"I propose, first to the Chief of O.K.W. and then to the Fuehrer, that Case Yellow" - which, as the Court knows, is the code name for the invasion of the Netherlands - "and Weser Exercise" - the invasion of Norway and Denmark - "must be prepared in such a way that they will be independent of one another as regards both time and forces employed. The Fuehrer completely agrees, if this is in any way possible."

So the Court will observe that the new idea of 6th February, that the neutrality of Belgium might be observed, had been abandoned by 28th February.

The next entry is of 29th February - I am not troubling the Court with further entries of 28th February, which relate to the forces to be employed in the invasion of Norway and Denmark.

29th February, the second paragraph

"Fuehrer also wishes to have a strong task force in Copenhagen and a plan, elaborated in detail, showing how individual coastal batteries are to be captured by shock troops. Warlimont, Chief of Landesverteidigung, instructed to make out immediately the order of the Army, Navy, and Air Force, and Director of Armed Forces to make out a similar order regarding the strengthening of the staff."

And there, for the moment, I will leave the entries in Jodl's diary and refer the Court to the vital Document C-174, which, for the purposes of the record, will be Exhibit GB 89. The Court will see, from that document, that it is Hitler's operation order to complete the preparations for the invasion of Norway and Denmark. It bears the date of 1st March, 1940, and it is headed: "The Fuehrer and Supreme Commander of the Armed Forces, most Secret."

Then, "Directive for Fall Weserubung."

> "The development of the situation in Scandinavia requires the making of all preparations for the occupation of Denmark and Norway by a part of the German Armed Forces-Fall Weserubung. This operation should prevent British encroachment on Scandinavia and the Baltic; further, it should guarantee our ore base in Sweden and give our Navy and Air Force a wider start line against Britain."

The second part of Paragraph 1 reads:

> "In view of our military and political power in comparison with that of the Scandinavian States, the force to be employed in the Fall Weserubung will be kept as small as possible. The numerical weakness will be balanced by daring actions and surprise execution. On principle we will do our utmost to make the operation appear as a peaceful occupation, the object of which is the military protection of the neutrality of the Scandinavian States. Corresponding demands will be transmitted to the Governments at the beginning of the occupation. If necessary, demonstrations by the Navy and the Air Force will provide the necessary emphasis. If, in spite of this, resistance should be met with, all military means will be used to crush it."

There follows, in Paragraph 2 on the next page:

> "I put in charge of the preparations and the conduct of the operation against Denmark and Norway the Commanding General of the 21st Army Corps, General von Falkenhorst."

Paragraph 3:

> "The crossing of the Danish border and the landings in Norway must take place simultaneously. I emphasise that the operations must be prepared as quickly as possible. In case the enemy seizes the initiative against Norway, we must be able to apply immediately our own counter- measures.
>
> It is most important that the Scandinavian States as well as the Western opponents should be taken by surprise by our measures. All preparations, particularly those of transport and of readiness, drafting and embarkation of the troops, must be made with this factor in mind.
>
> In case the preparations for embarkation can no longer be kept secret, the leaders and the troops will be deceived with fictitious objectives."

Then Paragraph 4 on the next page. "The Occupation of Denmark which is given the code name of "Weserubung Sud".

> "The task of Group XXI: Occupation by surprise of Jutland and of Fyen immediately after occupation of Seeland.
>
> Added to this, having secured the most important places, the Group will break through as quickly as possible from Fyen to Skagen and to the East coast."

Then there follow other instructions with regard to the operation.

Paragraph 5: "Occupation of Norway, Weserubung Nord. The task of Group XXI: Capture by surprise of the most important places on the coast by sea and airborne operations.

The Navy will take over the preparation and carrying out of the transport by sea of the landing troops."

And there follows a reference to the part of the Air Force, and I would like particularly to draw the Court's attention to that reference.

This is Paragraph 5 on Page 3 of Hitler's directive:-

"The Air Force, after the occupation has been completed, will ensure air defence and will make use of Norwegian bases for air warfare against Britain."

I am underlining that entry at this stage, because I shall be referring to it in connection with a later document.

Whilst these preparations were being made and just prior to the final decision of Hitler -

THE PRESIDENT: Did you draw our attention to the defendant by whom it was initialled, Fricke, on the first page of that document.

MAJOR ELWYN JONES: That is an initial by Fricke, who is a different person altogether from the defendant Frick. This is a high functionary in the German Admiralty and has no connection with the defendant who is before the Tribunal.

As I was saying, my Lord, while these decisions were being made, reports were coming in through Rosenberg's organisation from Quisling, and if the Court will again turn, for the last time, to Document 007-PS, which is Rosenberg's report, the Tribunal will observe the kind of information which Rosenberg's organisation was supplying at this time. The third paragraph, "Quisling's reports" - that is in Annex I in Rosenberg's report, the section dealing with Norway, the paragraph beginning with:-

"Quisling's reports, transmitted to his representative in Germany, Hagelin, and dealing with the possibility of intervention by the Western Powers in Norway with tacit consent of the Norwegian Government, became more urgent by January. These increasingly better substantiated communications were in the sharpest contrast to the views of the German Legation in Oslo, which relied on the desire for neutrality of the then Norwegian Nygaardsvold Cabinet and was convinced of that Government's intention and readiness to defend Norway's neutrality. No one in Norway knew that Quisling's representative for Germany maintained the closest relations to him; he therefore succeeded in gaining a foothold within governmental circles of the Nygaardsvold Cabinet and in listening to the Cabinet members' views. Hagelin transmitted what he had heard to the Bureau" - Rosenberg's bureau - "which conveyed the news to the Fuehrer through Reichsleiter Rosenberg. During the night of 16th to 17th February, English destroyers attacked the German steamer 'Altmark' in Josingfjord."

The Tribunal will remember that that is a reference to the action by the British destroyer "Cossack" against the German naval auxiliary vessel "Altmark", which was carrying three hundred British prisoners, captured on the high seas, to Germany through Norwegian territorial waters. The position of the British delegation with regard to that episode is that the use that was being made by the "Altmark" of Norwegian territorial waters was in fact a flagrant abuse in itself of Norwegian neutrality, and the action taken by H.M.S. "Cossack", which was restricted to rescuing the three hundred British prisoners on board-no attempt being made to destroy the "Altmark" or to capture the armed guards on board her - was fully justified under International Law.

Now the Rosenberg report, the reading of which I interrupted to give that statement of the British view on the "Altmark" episode - the Rosenberg report continues:

> "The Norwegian Government's reaction to this question permitted the conclusion that certain agreements had been covertly arrived at between the Norwegian Government and the Allies. Such assumption was confirmed by reports of Section Leader Scheidt, who in turn derived his information from Hagelin and Quisling. But even after this incident the German Legation in Oslo championed the opposite view, and went on record as believing in the good intentions of the Norwegians."

So the Tribunal will see that the Nazi Government preferred the reports of the traitor Quisling to the considered judgement of German diplomatic representatives in Norway. The result of the receipt of reports of that kind was the Hitler decision to invade Norway and Denmark. The culminating details in the preparations for the invasion are again found in Jodl's diary, which is the last document in the document book. I will refer the Court to the entry of the 3rd March:

> "The Fuehrer expressed himself very sharply on the necessity of a swift entry into N" - which is Norway - "with strong forces.
> No delay by any branch of the Armed Forces. Very rapid acceleration of the attack necessary".

Then the last entry on 3rd March:

> "Fuehrer decides to carry out 'Weser Exercise' before case 'Yellow' with a few days interval."

So that the important issue of strategy, which had been concerning the German High Command for some time, had been decided by this date, and the fate of Scandinavia was to be sealed before the fate of the Low Countries; and the Court will observe from those entries Of 3rd March, that, by that date, Hitler had become an enthusiastic convert to the idea of a Norwegian aggression.

The next entry in Jodl's diary of 5th March:

> "Big conference with the three Commanders-in-Chief about 'Weser Exercise'; Field Marshal in a rage because not consulted till now. Will not listen to anyone and wants to show that all preparations so far made are worthless.
> Result:
> (a) Stronger forces to Narvik.
> (b) Navy to leave ships in the ports (Hipper or Lutzow in Trondheim).
> (c) Christiansand can be left out at first.
> (d) Six divisions envisaged for Norway.
> (e) A foothold to be gained immediately in Copenhagen."

Then the next entry to which I desire to draw the Court's attention is the entry of 13th March, which the Court may think is one of the most remarkable in the whole documentation of this case.

"Fuehrer does not give order yet for 'W'." - Weser Exercise - "He is still looking for an excuse."

The entry of the next day, 14th March, shows a similar pre- occupation on the part of Hitler with seeking an excuse for the flagrant aggression. It reads:-

"English keep vigil in the North Sea with fifteen to sixteen submarines; doubtful whether reason to safeguard own operations or prevent operations by Germans. Fuehrer has not yet decided what reason to give for Weser Exercise."

Then I would like the Court to look at the entry for 21St March, which, by inadvertence, has been included in the next page - the bottom of Page 6.

"Misgivings of Task Force 21 ."

The Court has seen from documents that I have put in already that Task Force 21 was Falkenhorst's Force, which was detailed to conduct this invasion.

"Misgivings of Task Force 21 about the long interval between taking up readiness positions at 0530 hours and close of diplomatic negotiations. Fuehrer rejects any earlier negotiations, as otherwise calls for help go out to England and America. If resistance is put up it must be ruthlessly broken. The political plenipotentiaries must emphasise the military measures taken, and even exaggerate them."

Comment upon that entry is, I think, unnecessary. The next entry, if the Court will turn to Page 5, of 28th March, the third sentence:

"Individual naval officers seem to be lukewarm concerning the Weser Exercise and need a stimulus. Also Falkenhorst and the other two commanders are worrying about matters which are none of their business. Franke sees more disadvantages than advantages.

In the evening the Fuehrer visits the map room and roundly declares that he will not stand for the Navy clearing out of the Norwegian ports right away. Narvik, Trondheim and Oslo will have to remain occupied by naval forces."

There the Court will observe that Jodl, as ever, is the faithful collaborator of Hitler.

Then on 2nd April:

"Commander-in-Chief of the Air Force, Commander-in-Chief of the Navy, and General von Falkenhorst with the Fuehrer. All confirm preparations completed. Fuehrer orders carrying out of the Weser Exercise for 9th April."

Then the last entry in the next page, the 4th April.

"Fuehrer drafts the proclamation. Piepenbrock, Chief of Military Intelligence 1, returns with good results from the talks with Quisling in Copenhagen."

Until the very last the treachery of Quisling continued to be most active.

The prosecution has in its possession a large number of operation orders that were issued in connection with the aggression against Norway and Denmark, but I propose to draw the Court's attention to only two of them to illustrate the extent of the secrecy and the deception that was used by the defendants and their confederates in the course of that aggression. I would now draw the Court's attention to Document C-115 which, for the purpose of the record, will be Exhibit GB 90. First of all I will draw the Court's attention to the second paragraph, "General Orders", with a date, "4th April, 1940":

"The barrage-breaking vessels, Sperrbrecher, will penetrate inconspicuously, and with lights on, into Oslo Fjord disguised as merchant steamers.

Challenge from coastal signal stations and look-outs are to be answered by the deceptive use of the names of English steamers. I lay particular stress on the importance of not giving away the operation before zero hour."

Then the next entry is an order for reconnaissance forces, dated 24th March, 1940: "Behaviour during entrance into the harbour." The third paragraph is the part that I wish to draw the Court's attention to.

"The disguise as British craft must be kept up as long as possible. All challenges in Morse by Norwegian ships will be answered in English. In answer to questions a text with something like the following content will be chosen:

'Calling at Bergen for a short visit; no hostile intent.'

Challenges to be answered with names of British warships:-

'Koln' -- H.M.S.'Cairo';

'Konigsberg' -- H.M.S. 'Calcutta';

'Bromsoe' -- H.M.S. 'Faulkner';

'Karl Peters' -- H.M.S. 'Halcyon';

'Leopard' -- British destroyer;

'Wolf' -- British destroyer;

E-boats -- British motor torpedo boats.

Arrangements are to be made enabling British war flags to be illuminated. Continual readiness for making smoke."

And then finally the next order dated the 24th March, 1940, Annex 3 "To Flag Officer Reconnaissance Forces; most secret."

Next page, Page 2:-

"Following is laid down as guiding principle should one of our own units find itself compelled to answer the challenge of passing craft; to challenge in case of the 'Koln': H.M.S. 'Cairo'; then to order to stop; (1) Please repeat last signal; (2) Impossible to understand your signal; in case of a warning shot: Stop firing. British ship. Good friend. In case of an inquiry as to destination and purpose: Going Bergen. Chasing German steamers."

Then I would draw the Court's attention to Document C-151, which for the purposes of the record will be Exhibit GB 91, which is a Donitz; order in connection with this operation. If the Court will observe, it is headed:

"Top Secret, Operation Order' Hartmut'. Occupation of Denmark and Norway. This order comes into force on the code word 'Hartmut'. With its coming into force the orders hitherto valid for the boats taking part lose their validity.

The day and hour are designated as 'Weser-Day' and 'WeserHour', and the whole operation is known as 'Weserubung'.

The operation ordered by the code word has as its objective the rapid surprise-landing of troops in Norway. Simultaneously Denmark will be occupied from the Baltic and from the land side."

There is at the end of that paragraph another contribution by Donitz to this process of deception:

"The naval force will, as they enter the harbour, fly the British flag until the troops have landed, except presumably at Narvik."

The Tribunal now knows as a matter of history that on 9th April, 1940, the Nazi onslaught on the unsuspecting and almost unarmed people of Norway and Denmark was launched. When the invasions had already begun a German memorandum was handed to the Governments of Norway and Denmark attempting to justify the German action, and I would like to draw the Court's attention to Document TC-55, Exhibit GB 92. That is at the beginning of the book of documents, the sixth document of the book. I am not proposing to read the whole of that memorandum. I have no doubt the defending counsel will deal with any parts which they consider relevant to the defence. The Court will observe that it is alleged that Britain and France were guilty in their maritime warfare of breaches of International Law, and that Britain and France were making plans themselves to invade and occupy Norway, and that the Government of Norway was prepared to acquiesce in such a situation.

The memorandum states -and I would now draw the Court's attention to Page 3 of the memorandum, to the paragraph just below the middle of the page beginning "The German Troops":-

"The German troops, therefore, do not set foot on Norwegian soil as enemies. The German High Command does not intend to make use of the points occupied by German troops as bases for operations against England, as long as it is not forced to do so by measures taken by England and France. German military operations aim much more exclusively at protecting the North against proposed occupation of Norwegian strong points by English-French forces."

In connection with that statement I would remind the Court that in his operation order of 1st March, Hitler had then given orders to the Air Force to make use of Norwegian bases for air warfare against Britain. That is 1st March. And this is the memorandum which was produced as an excuse on 9th April. The last two paragraphs of the German memorandum to Norway and Denmark, the Court may think, are a classic Nazi combination of diplomatic hypocrisy and military threat. They read:-

"The Reich Government thus expects that the Royal Norwegian Government and the Norwegian people will respond with understanding to the German measures, and offer no resistance to it. Any resistance would have to be and would be broken by all possible means by the German forces employed, and would therefore lead only to absolutely useless bloodshed. The Royal Norwegian Government is therefore requested to take all measures with the greatest speed to ensure that the advance of the German troops can take place without friction and difficulty. In the spirit of the good German-Norwegian relations that have always existed, the Reich Government declares to the Royal Norwegian Government that Germany has no intention of infringing by her measures the territorial integrity and political independence of the Kingdom of Norway, now or in the future."

What the Nazis meant by the protection of the Kingdom of Norway was shown by their conduct on 9th April. I now refer the Court to Document TC-56, which will be Exhibit GB 93, which is a report by the Commander-in-

Chief of the Royal Norwegian Forces. It is at the beginning of the document book, the last of the TC. documents.

I will not trouble the Court with the first page of the report. If the Tribunal will turn to the second page, it reads:-

"The Germans, considering the long lines of communications and the threat of the British Navy, clearly understood the necessity of complete surprise and speed in the attack. In order to paralyse the will of the Norwegian people to defend their country and, at the same time, to prevent Allied intervention, it was planned to capture all the more important towns along the coast simultaneously. Members of the Government and Parliament and other military and civilian people occupying important positions were to be arrested before organised resistance could be put into effect, and the King was to be forced to form a new government with Quisling as its head."

The next paragraph was read by the learned British Attorney General in his speech and I will refer only to the last paragraph but one:

"The German attack came as a surprise and all the invaded towns along the coast were captured according to plan with only slight losses. In the Oslofjord, however, the cruiser 'Blucher', carrying General Engelbrecht and parts of his division, technical staffs and specialists, who were to take over the control of Oslo, was sunk. The plan to capture the King and members of the Government and Parliament failed. In spite of the surprise of the attack, resistance was organised throughout the country."

That is a brief picture of what occurred in Norway.

What happened in Denmark is described in a memorandum prepared by the Danish Royal Government, a copy of which I hand in as Exhibit GB 94, and an extract from which is in Document D-628, which follows the TC documents.

"Extracts from the memorandum concerning Germany's attitude towards Denmark before and during the occupation, prepared by the Royal Danish Government.

On 9th April, 1940 at 0420 hours" - in the morning that is - "the German Minister appeared at the private residence of the Danish Minister for Foreign Affairs accompanied by the Air Attache of the Legation. The appointment had been made by a telephone call from the German Legation to the Secretary General of the Ministry for Foreign Affairs at 4 o'clock the same morning. The Minister said at once that Germany had positive proof that Great Britain intended to occupy bases in Denmark and Norway. Germany had to safeguard Denmark against this. For this reason German soldiers were now crossing the frontier and landing at various points in Zealand, including the port of Copenhagen; in a short time German bombers would be over Copenhagen; their orders were not to bomb until further notice. It was now up to the Danes to prevent resistance, as any resistance would have the most terrible consequences. Germany would guarantee Denmark territorial integrity and political independence. Germany would not interfere with the internal government of Denmark, but wanted only to make sure of the neutrality of the country. For this purpose the presence of the German Wehrmacht in

Denmark was required during the war.

The Minister for Foreign Affairs declared in reply, that the allegation concerning British plans to occupy Denmark was completely without foundation; there was no possibility of anything like that. The Minister for Foreign Affairs protested against the violation of Denmark's neutrality which, according to the German Minister's statement, was in progress. The Minister for Foreign Affairs declared further that he could not give a reply to the demands, which had to be submitted to the King and the Prime Minister, and further observed that the German Minister knew, as everybody else, that the Danish Armed Forces had orders to oppose violations of Denmark's neutrality, so that fighting presumably had already taken place. In reply, the German Minister stated that the matter was very urgent, especially to avoid air bombardment."

What happened thereafter is described in a dispatch from the British Minister in Copenhagen to the British Foreign Secretary, which the Tribunal will find in D-627, the document preceding the one which I have just read. That document, for the purposes of the record, will be Exhibit GB 95.

That dispatch reads:

"The actual events of the 9th April have been pieced together by members of my staff either from actual eye- witnesses or from reliable information subsequently received, and are given below. Early in the morning towards 5 o'clock, three small German transports steamed into the approach to Copenhagen harbour, while a number of aeroplanes circled overhead. The Northern battery, guarding the harbour approach, fired a warning shot at these planes when it was seen that they carried German markings. Apart from this, the Danes offered no further resistance, and the German vessels fastened alongside the quays in the Free Harbour. Some of these aeroplanes proceeded to drop leaflets over the town, urging the population to keep calm and co-operate with the Germans. I enclose a specimen leaflet, which is written in a bastard Norwegian-Danish, a curiously un-German disregard of detail, together with a translation. Approximately 800 soldiers landed with full equipment and marched to Kastellet, the old fortress of Copenhagen, and now barracks. The door was locked, so the Germans promptly burst it open with explosives and rounded up all the Danish soldiers within, together with the womenfolk employed in the mess. The garrison offered no resistance, and it appears that they were taken completely by surprise. One officer tried to escape in a motor car, but his chauffeur was shot before he could get away. He died in hospital two days later. After seizing the barracks, a detachment was sent to Amalienborg, the King's palace, where they engaged the Danish sentries on guard, wounding three, one of them fatally .. Meanwhile, a large fleet of bombers flew over the city at low altitude."

Then, the last paragraph of the dispatch reads:

"It has been difficult to ascertain exactly what occurred in Jutland. It is clear, however, that the enemy invaded Jutland from the South at dawn on 9th April, and were at first resisted by the Danish forces, who suffered casualties. The chances of resistance were weakened by the extent to which the forces appear to have been taken by surprise. The chief permanent official of the Ministry of War, for instance, motored into Copenhagen on the morning of 9th April, and drove blithely past a sentry who challenged him, in blissful ignorance that this was not one of his own men. It took a bullet, which passed through the lapels of his coat, to disillusion him."

The German memorandum to the Norwegian and Danish Governments spoke of the German desire to maintain the territorial integrity and political independence of those two small countries.

I will close by drawing the Court's attention to two documents which indicate the kind of territorial integrity and political independence the Nazi conspirators contemplated for the victims of their aggression. I will first draw the Court's attention to an entry in Jodl's diary, which is the last document in the book, on the last page of the book, the entry dated 19th April:

"Renewed crisis. Envoy Brauer" - that is the German Minister to Norway - "is recalled: since Norway is at war with us, the task of the Foreign Office is finished. In the Fuehrer's opinion force has to be used. It is said that Gauleiter Terboven will be given a post. Field Marshal" - which, as the Court will see from the other entries, is presumably a reference to the defendant Goering - "is moving in the same direction. He criticises as defects that we did not take sufficiently energetic measures against the civilian population, that we could have seized electrical plant, that the Navy did not supply enough troops. The Air Force cannot do everything."

The Court will see from that entry and the reference to Gauleiter Terboven that already, by 19th April, rule by Gauleiters had replaced rule by Norwegians.

The final document is Document C-41, which will be Exhibit GB 96, which is a memorandum dated 3rd June, 1940, signed by Fricke, who, of course, has no connection with the defendant Frick. Fricke was, at that date, the head of the Operations Division of the German Naval War Staff, which was a key appointment in the very nerve centre of German naval operations. That is why, as the Tribunal noticed, he came to be initialling the important Naval documents.

That memorandum is, as I have said, dated 3rd June, 1940, and relates to questions of territorial expansion and bases.

"These problems are pre-eminently of a political character and comprise an abundance of questions of a political type, which it is not the Navy's province to answer, but they also materially affect the strategic possibilities open - according to the way in which this question is answered - for the subsequent use and operation of the Navy.

It is too well known to need further mention that Germany's present position in the narrows of the Heligoland Bight and in the Baltic - bordered as it is by a whole series of States and under their influence is an impossible one for the future of Greater Germany. If, over and above this, one extends these strategic possibilities to the point that Germany shall not continue to be cut off for all time from overseas by natural geographical facts, the demand is raised that somehow or other an end shall be put to this state of affairs at the end of the war.

The solution could perhaps be found among the following possibilities.

1. The territories of Denmark, Norway and Northern France acquired during the course of the war continue to be so occupied and organised that they can in future be considered as German possessions.

This solution will recommend itself for areas where the severity of the decision tells, and should tell, on the enemy and where a gradual 'Germanising' of the territory appears practicable.

2. The taking over and holding of areas which have no direct connection with Germany's main body, and which, like the Russian solution in Hangoe, remain permanently as an enclave in the hostile State. Such areas might be considered possibly around Brest and Trondheim.

3. The power of Greater Germany in the strategic areas acquired in this war should result in the existing population of these areas feeling themselves politically, economically and militarily to be completely dependent on Germany. If the following results are achieved - that expansion is undertaken (on a scale I shall describe later) by means of the military measures for occupation taken during the war, that French powers of resistance (popular unity, mineral resources, industry, armed forces) are so broken that a revival must be considered out of the question, that the smaller States such as the Netherlands, Denmark and Norway are forced into a dependence on us which will enable us in any circumstances and at any time easily to occupy these countries again, then in practice the same, but psychologically much more, will be achieved."

Then Fricke recommends:-

"The solution given in 3, therefore, appears to be the proper one, that is, to crush France, to occupy Belgium, part of North and East France, and to allow the Netherlands, Denmark and Norway to exist on the basis indicated above."

Then, the culminating paragraph of this report of Fricke reads as follows:-

"Time will show how far the outcome of the war with England will make an extension of these demands possible."

The submission of the prosecution is that this and other documents which have been submitted to the Court tear apart the veil of the Nazi pretences. These documents reveal the menace behind the good will of Goering; they expose as fraudulent the diplomacy of Ribbentrop; they show the reality behind the ostensible political ideology of tradesmen in treason like Rosenberg, and finally, and above all, they render sordid the professional status of Keitel and of Raeder.

THE PRESIDENT: The Tribunal will now adjourn.

[A recess was taken.]

MR. ROBERTS: May it please the Tribunal: it is my duty to present that part of Count 2 which relates to the allegations with regard to Belgium, the Netherlands, and Luxembourg. In Charges 2, 3, 4, 9, 11, 13, 14, 18, 19 and 23 there are charges of violating certain treaties and conventions and violating certain assurances. So far as the treaties are concerned, some of them have been put in evidence already, and I will indicate that when I come to them.

May I, before I come to the detail, remind the Tribunal of the history of these unfortunate countries, the Netherlands and Belgium; Belgium especially, which for so many centuries was the cockpit of Europe.

The independence of Belgium was guaranteed, as the Tribunal wilt remember, in 1839 by the great European powers. That guarantee was observed for seventy-five years, until it was shamelessly broken by the Germans in 1914, who brought all the horrors of war to Belgium, and all the even greater horrors of a German occupation of Belgium. History was to repeat itself in a still more shocking fashion some twenty-five years after, in 1940, as the Tribunal already knows.

The first treaty which was mentioned in these charges is The Hague Conventions of 1907. That has been put in by my learned friend, Sir David, and I think I need say nothing about it.

The second treaty is the Locarno Convention, the Arbitration and Conciliation Convention of 1935. My Lord, that was between Germany and Belgium. That was put in by Sir David. It is Exhibit GB 15, and I think I need say nothing more about that either.

Belgium's independence and neutrality was guaranteed by Germany in that document.

My Lord, the next treaty is The Hague Arbitration Convention of May, 1926, between Germany and the Netherlands. That document I ought formally to put in. It is in the Reichsgesetzblatt, which perhaps I may call R.G.B. in the future, for brevity; and it, no doubt, will be treated as a public document. But in my bundle of documents, which goes in the order in which I propose to refer to them, I think it is more convenient for the presentation of my case. That is the second or third document, TC-16.

THE PRESIDENT: It is Book 4 is it?

MR. ROBERTS: It is Book 4, my Lord. This is the Convention of Arbitration and Conciliation between Germany and the Netherlands, signed at The Hague in May, 1926. Your Lordships have the document; perhaps I need only read Article 1:

> "The contracting parties" - those are the Netherlands and the German Reich - "undertake to submit all disputes of any nature whatever, which may arise between them which it has not been possible to settle by diplomacy and which have not been referred to the Permanent Court of International justice, to be dealt with by arbitration or conciliation as provided."

And then, my Lord, there follow all the clauses which deal merely with the machinery of conciliation, and which are unnecessary for me to read. May I just draw attention to the first article, Article 21, which provides that the Convention shall be valid for ten years, and then shall remain in force for successive periods of five years until denounced by either party. This treaty never was denounced by Germany at all.

The Treaty I put in is Document TC-16, which will be Exhibit GB 97; and a certified copy is put in and a translation for the Court.

As the Tribunal already knows, in 1928 the Kellogg-Briand Pact was made at Paris, by which all the powers renounced recourse to war. That is put in as Exhibit GB 18, and I need not, I think, put it in or refer to it again.

Then the last of these treaties, all of which, of course, belong to the days of the Weimar Republic, is the Arbitration Treaty between Germany and

Luxembourg, executed in 1929. That is Document TC-20 in the bundle. It is two documents further on than the one the Tribunal has referred to last. This is the Treaty of Arbitration and Conciliation between Germany and Luxembourg, signed at Geneva in 1929. May I just read the first few words of Article I, which are familiar:

"The Contracting parties undertake to settle by peaceful means all disputes of any nature whatever which may arise between them and which it may not be possible to settle by diplomacy."

And then there follow the clauses dealing with the machinery for peaceful settlement of disputes, which follow the common form.

My Lord, those were the treaty obligations. May I put in that last treaty, TC-20, which will be Exhibit GB 98.

My Lord, those were the treaty obligations between Germany and Belgium at the time when the Nazi Party came into power in 1933, and, as you have heard from my learned friend, Hitler adopted and ratified the obligations of Germany under the Weimar Republic with regard to the treaties which had been entered into. My Lord, nothing more occurred to alter the position of Belgium until in March, 1936, Germany reoccupied the Rhineland and announced, of course, the resumption of conscription and so on. And Hitler, on 7th March, 1936, purported, in a speech, to repudiate the obligations of the German Government under the Locarno Pact, the reason given being the execution of the Franco-Soviet Pact of 1935. Sir David has dealt with that and has pointed out that there was no legal foundation for this claim to be entitled to renounce obligations under the Locarno Pact. But Belgium was, of course, left in the air in the sense that she had entered into various obligations under the Locarno Pact in return for the liabilities which other nations acknowledged, and now one of those liabilities, namely, the liability of Germany to observe the Pact, had been renounced.

So, on 30th January, 1937, perhaps because Hitler realised the position of Belgium and of the Netherlands, in the next document in the bundle (TC-33 and 35, which I hand in and will be Exhibit GB 99) he gave the solemn assurance - he used the word "solemn". That has already been read by the Attorney General, and so I do not want to read it again. But the Tribunal will see that it is a full guarantee. In April, 1937, in a document which is not before the Court, France and England released Belgium from her obligations under the Locarno Pact. It is a matter of history and it does occur in an exhibit, but it has not been copied. Belgium, of course, gave guarantees of strict independence and neutrality, and France and England gave guarantees of assistance should Belgium be attacked. And it was because of that that Germany, on 13th October, 1937, in the next document, gave a very clear and unconditional guarantee to Belgium-Document TC-34, which I offer in evidence as Exhibit GB 100 - the German declaration of 13th October, 1937, which shows the minutes:

"I have the honour on behalf of the German Government to make the following communication to Your Excellency: The German Government has taken cognisance with particular interest of the public declaration in which the Belgian Government defines the international position of Belgium. For its part, the German Government has repeatedly given expression, especially through the declaration of the Chancellor of the German Reich in his speech of

30th January, 1937, to its own point of view. The German Government has also taken cognisance of the declaration made by the British and French Governments on 24th April, 1937" - that is a document to which I have previously referred - "since the conclusion of a treaty - "

THE PRESIDENT: When you are reading a document to which you attach importance, would you go a little bit slower?

MR. ROBERTS: I certainly will. A little bit slower or faster?

THE PRESIDENT: Slower in the documents to which you attach great importance.

MR. ROBERTS: Yes.

"Since the conclusion of a treaty to replace the Treaty of Locarno may still take some time, and being desirous of strengthening the peaceful aspirations of the two countries, the German Government regards it as appropriate to define now its own attitude towards Belgium. To this end, it makes the following declaration: First, the German Government has taken note of the views which the Belgian Government has thought fit to express. That is to say, (a) of the policy of independence which it intends to exercise in full sovereignty; (b) of its determination to defend the frontiers of Belgium with all its forces against any aggression or invasion, and to prevent Belgian territory from being used for purposes of aggression against another State as a passage or as a base of operation by land, by sea, or by air, and to organise the defence of Belgium in an efficient manner for this purpose. Secondly: The German Government considers that the inviolability and integrity of Belgium are common interests of the Western Powers. It confirms its determination that in no circumstances will it impair this inviolability and integrity, and that it will at all times respect Belgian territory except, of course, in the event of Belgium's taking part in a military action directed against Germany in an armed conflict in which Germany is involved. The German Government, like the British and French Governments, is prepared to assist Belgium should she be subjected to an attack or to invasion."

Then, on the following page:

"The Belgian Government has taken note with great satisfaction of the declaration communicated to it this day by the German Government.
It thanks the German Government warmly for this communication."

My Lord, may I pause there to emphasise that document. There, in October, 1937, is Germany giving a solemn guarantee to this small nation of its peaceful aspiration towards her, and its assertion that the integrity of the Belgian frontier was a common interest between it and Belgium and the other Western Powers.

You have before you to try, the leaders of the German Government and the leaders of the German Armed Forces. One does not have to prove, does one, that everyone of those accused must have known perfectly well of that solemn undertaking given by his government? Every one of these accused, in their various spheres of activity - some more actively than the others - was a party to the shameless breaking of that treaty two and a-half years afterwards, and I submit that, on the ordinary laws of inference and justice, all those men must be fixed as active participators, in that disgraceful breach of faith which brought misery and death to so many millions.

Presumably it will be contended on the part, for instance, of Keitel and Jodl that they were merely honourable soldiers carrying out their duty. This Tribunal, no doubt, will inquire what code of honour they observe which permits them to violate the pledged word of their country.

That this declaration of October, 1937, meant very little to the leaders, and to the High Command of Germany can be seen by the next document which is Document PS-375 in the bundle. It is Exhibit USA 84, and has already been referred to many times. May I just refer or remind the Tribunal of one sentence or two. The document comes into existence on 24th August, 1938, at the time when the Czechoslovakian drama was unfolding, and it was uncertain at that time whether there would be war with the Western Powers. It is top secret, addressed to the General Staff of the 5th section of the German Air Force. The subject: "Extended Case Green - Estimate of the Situation." Probably the more correct word would be "Appreciation of the Situation with Special Consideration of the Enemy." Apparently some staff officer had been asked to prepare this appreciation. In view of the fact that it has been read before, I think I need only read the last paragraph, which is Paragraph H, and it comes at the bottom of Page 6, the last page but one of the document:-

"Requests to Armed Forces Supreme Command, Army and Navy."

This, you see, was an appreciation addressed by an Air Force staff officer. So these are requests to the Army and Navy. And then, if one turns over the page, No. 4: "Belgium and the Netherlands would, in German hands, represent an extraordinary advantage in the prosecution of the air war against Great Britain as well as against France. Therefore it is held to be essential to obtain the opinion of the Army as to the conditions under which an occupation of this area could be carried out and how long it would take. And in this case it would be necessary to reassess the commitment against Great Britain." The point that the prosecution desires to make on that document is that it is apparently assumed by the staff officer who prepared this, and assumed quite rightly, that the leaders of the German nation and the High Command, would not pay the smallest attention to the fact that Germany had given her word not to invade Holland or Belgium. They are recommending it as a militarily advantageous thing to do, strong in the knowledge that, if the Commanders and the Fuehrer agree with that view, treaties are to be completely ignored. Such, I repeat, was the honour of the German Government and of its leaders.

Now, in March, 1939, as has been proved, the remainder of Czechoslovakia was peacefully annexed, and then came the time for further guarantees; in the next documents TC-35 and 39, the assurances, which were given to Belgium and the Netherlands on 28th April, 1939.

These have been read by my learned friend, Major Elwyn Jones. They are Exhibit GB 78. I need not read them again.

There is also a guarantee to Luxembourg, which is on the next page, TC-42A. That was given in the same speech by Hitler in the Reichstag, and this 42A was where Hitler was dealing with a communication from Mr. Roosevelt, who was feeling a little uneasy on the other side of the Atlantic as to Hitler's intentions, and may I, before I read this document, say that I believe the Tribunal will be seeing a film of the delivery by Hitler of this part of this speech, and you will have the privilege of seeing Hitler in one of his jocular moods, because this was greeted and was delivered in a jocular vein, and you will see in the film that the defendant Goering, who sits above Hitler in the Reichstag, appreciates very much the joke, the joke being this - that it is an absurd suggestion to make that Germany could possibly go to war with any of her neighbours - and that was the point of the joke that everybody appears to have appreciated very much.

Now, if I may read this document:

"Finally, Mr. Roosevelt demands the readiness to give him an assurance that the German fighting forces will not attack the territory or possessions of the following independent nations and, above all, that they will not march into them. And he goes on to name the following as the countries in question: Finland, Latvia, Lithuania, Estonia, Norway, Sweden, Denmark, Holland, Belgium, Great Britain, Ireland, France, Portugal, Spain, Switzerland, Lichtenstein, Luxembourg, Poland, Hungary, Roumania, Yugoslavia, Russia, Bulgaria, Turkey, Iraq, Arabia, Syria, Palestine, Egypt and Iran.

A. I started off by taking the trouble to find out in the case of the countries listed, firstly, whether they feel themselves threatened, and secondly and particularly, whether this question Mr. Roosevelt has asked us was put as the result of a demarche by them or at least with their consent.

The answer was a general negative, which in some cases took the form of a blunt rejection. Actually this counter- question of mine could not be conveyed to some of the States and nations listed, since they are not at present in possession of their liberty (as for instance Syria), but are occupied by the military forces of democratic States, and therefore, deprived of all their rights.

Thirdly, apart from that, all the States bordering on Germany have received much more binding assurances and, above all, much more binding proposals than Mr. Roosevelt asked of me in his peculiar telegram."

You will see that, although that is sneering at Mr. Roosevelt, it is suggesting in the presence, certainly, of the accused Goering as being quite absurd that Germany should nurture any warlike feeling against its neighbours. But the hollow falsity of that and the preceding guarantee is shown by the next document. May I put this Document, TC- 42A, in as Exhibit GB 101.

The next document, which is Hitler's conference of 23rd May, has been referred to many times and is Exhibit USA 27. Therefore, I need only very shortly remind the Tribunal of two passages. First of all, on the first page, it is interesting to see who was present: The Fuehrer, Goering, Admiral Raeder, Brauchitsch, Colonel General Keitel, and various others who are not accused. Colonel Warlimont was there. He, I understand, was Jodl's deputy.

Well, now, the purpose of the conference was an analysis of the situation. Then, may I refer to the third page, down at the bottom. The stencil number is 819:

"What will this struggle be like?"

And then these words:

"The Dutch and Belgian air bases must be occupied by armed force.
Declarations of neutrality must be ignored."

Then, at the bottom:-

"Therefore, if England intends to intervene in the Polish war, we must occupy Holland with lightning speed. We must aim at securing a new defence line on Dutch soil up to the Zuider Zee."

There is this decision made: "Declarations of neutrality must be ignored," and there is the Grand Admiral present, and there is the Air Minister and Chief of the German Air Force, and there is General Keitel present. They all appear, and all their subsequent actions show that they acquiesced in that: "Give your word and then break it." That is their code of honour, and you will see that at the end of the meeting, the very last page - the stencil number is 823 - Field Marshal Goering asked one or two questions.

There was the decision of 23rd May. Is it overstating the matter to submit that any syllable of guarantee, any assurance given after that, is just purely hypocrisy, is just the action - apart from the multiplicity of the crimes here - of the common criminal?

THE PRESIDENT: Mr. Roberts, I think we would like you, so far as possible, to confine yourself to the document.

MR. ROBERTS: Yes, my Lord. Then we go to 22nd August, 798- PS. That has already been put in and is Exhibit USA 29. My Lord, that was Hitler's speech Of 22nd August. It has been read and re-read. I only, my Lord, refer to one passage, and that is at the bottom of the second page:-

"Attack from the West from the Maginot Line: I consider this impossible.

Another possibility is the violation of Dutch, Belgian and Swiss neutrality. I have no doubt that all these States as well as Scandinavia will defend their neutrality by all available means."

My Lord, I desire to emphasise the next sentence:-

"England and France will not violate the neutrality of these countries."

Then I desire to comment, I ask your Lordship to bear that sentence in mind, that correct prophecy, when remembering the excuses given for the subsequent invasion of Belgium and the Netherlands.

My Lord, the next documents are TC-36, 40 and 42. Those are three assurances. TC-36 is by the Ambassador of Germany to the Belgium Government.

"In view of the gravity of the international situation, I am expressly instructed by the Head of the German Reich to transmit to Your Majesty the following communication:-

Though the German Government is at present doing everything in its power to arrive at a peaceful solution of the questions at issue between the Reich and Poland, it nevertheless desires to define clearly, here and now, the attitude which it proposes to adopt towards Belgium should a conflict in Europe become inevitable.

The German Government is firmly determined to abide by the terms of the declaration contained in the German Note of 13th October, 1937. This provides in effect that Germany will, in no circumstances, impair the inviolability and integrity of Belgium, and will at all times respect Belgian territory. The German Government renews this undertaking however, in the expectation that the Belgian Government, for its part, will observe an attitude of strict neutrality and that Belgium will tolerate no violations on the part of a third power, but that, on the contrary, she will oppose it with all the forces at her disposal. It goes without saying that, if the Belgian Government were to adopt a different attitude, the German Government would naturally be compelled to defend its interests in conformity with the new situation thus created."

My Lord, may I make one short comment on the last part of that document? I submit it is clear that the decision having been made to violate the neutrality as we know, those last words were put in to afford some excuse in the future.

That document will be Exhibit GB 102.

My Lord, the next document is a similar document, communicated to Her Majesty, the Queen of the Netherlands, on the same day, 26th August, 1939. Subject to the Tribunal's direction, I do not think I need read it. It is a public document in the German document book, and it has exactly the same features.

That will be Exhibit GB 103

Then, my Lord, TC-42, the next document (Exhibit GB 104), is a similar document in relation to Luxembourg. That is dated 26th August, the same day. I am not certain; it has two dates. I think it is 26th August. My Lord, that is, in the same terms, a complete guarantee with the sting in the tail as in the other two documents. Perhaps I need not read it.

My Lord, as the Tribunal knows, Poland was occupied by means of the lightning victory, and in October German Armed Forces were free for other tasks. The first step that was taken, so far as the Netherlands and Belgium are concerned, is shown by the next document, which is, I think, in as GB 80, but the true, essential portions refer to Belgium and the Netherlands. It is the next document in your Lordships' bundle, No. 4

THE PRESIDENT: TC-32?

MR. ROBERTS: Yes. It begins with TC-32, and then if you go to the next one, my Lords will see TC-37 on the same page - and then TC-41; both 37 and 41 refer to this matter. Now, this is a German assurance on the 6th October, 1939:-

"Belgium.

Immediately after I had taken over the affairs of the State I tried to create friendly relations with Belgium. I renounced any revision or any desire for revision. The Reich has not made any demands which would in any way be likely to be considered in Belgium as a threat."

My Lord, there is a similar assurance to the Netherlands, the next part of the document:

"The new Reich has endeavoured to continue the traditional friendship with the Netherlands. It has not taken over any existing differences between the two countries and has not created any new ones."

I submit it is impossible to over emphasise the importance of those assurances of Germany's good faith.

My Lord, the value of that good faith is shown by the next document, which refers to the very next day, 7th October. Those two guarantees were 6th October. Now we come to Document 2329-PS, dated 7th October. It is from the Commander-in-Chief of the Army, von Brauchitsch, and it is addressed to various Army Groups. He said, third paragraph:

"The Dutch Border between Ems and Rhine is to be observed only.

At the same time Army Group B has to make all preparations, according to special orders, for immediate invasion of Dutch and Belgian territory, if the political situation so demands."

"If the political situation so demands" - the day after the guarantee! I put in the last document; that bears an original typewritten signature of von Brauchitsch, and it will be Exhibit GB 105.

My Lord, the next document is in two parts. Both are numbered C-62. The first part is dated 9th October, 1939, two days after the document I have read. My Lord, that was all read by the Attorney General in opening, down to the bottom of Paragraph (c). Therefore, I will not read it again. May I remind the Tribunal of just one sentence.

> "Preparations should be made for offensive action on the Northern flank of the Western Front crossing the area of Luxembourg, Belgium and the Netherlands. This attack must be carried out as soon and as forcefully as possible."

In the next paragraph, may I just read six words:

> "The object of this attack is to acquire as great an area of Holland, Belgium and Northern France as possible."

That document is signed by Hitler himself. It is addressed to the three accused: the Supreme Commander of the Army, Keitel; Navy, Raeder; and Air Minister, Commander-in-Chief of the Air Force, Goering. That is the distribution.

I will hold that document over and put that other one in with it.

My Lord, the next document refers to 15th October, 1939. It is from the Supreme Command of the Armed Forces. It is signed by Keitel in what is to some of us his familiar red pencil signature, and it is again addressed to Raeder and Goering and to the General Staff of the Army.

Now, that also has been read by the Attorney General; may I just remind the Tribunal that at the bottom of the page there is:

> "It must be the object of the Army's preparations, therefore, to occupy - on receipt of a special order - the territory of Holland, in the first instance as far as the Grebbe-Maas" - or Meuse - "line."

The second paragraph deals with the taking possession of the West Frisian Islands.

It is clear beyond discussion, in my submission, that, from that moment, the decision to violate the neutrality of these three countries had been made. All that remained was to work out the details, to wait until the weather became favourable, and, in the meantime, to give no hint that Germany's word was about to be broken again. Otherwise these small countries might have had some chance of combining with themselves and their neighbours.

It will be Exhibit GB 106.

The next document is a Keitel directive. It is Document 440- PS, Exhibit GB 107. It is again sent to the Supreme Commander of the Army, the Navy and the Air Forces, and it gives details of how the attack is to be carried out. I want to read only a very few selected passages.

Paragraph 2 on the first page:-

> "Contrary to previously issued instructions, all action intended against Holland may be carried out without a special order as to when the general attack will start.
> The attitude of the Dutch Armed Forces cannot be anticipated ahead of time."

Then may I comment here, will your Lordships note here that this is a German concession:-

"Wherever there is no resistance, the entry should carry the character of a peaceful occupation."

Paragraph (b) of the next paragraph:-

"At first the Dutch area, including the West Frisian Islands situated just off the coast, for the present without Texel, is to be occupied up to the Grebbe-Maas line."

The next two paragraphs I need not read. They deal with action against the Belgians, however, and in Paragraph 5:

"The 7th Airborne Division" - they were parachutists - "will be committed for the airborne operation only after the possession of bridges across the Albert Canal" - which is in Belgium, as the Court knows - "has been assured."

Then, in Paragraph 6 (b), Luxembourg is mentioned. It is mentioned in Paragraph 5 as well. The signature is "Keitel", but that is typed. It is authenticated by a staff officer.

Then the next Document is C-10, Exhibit GB 108, and it is dated 28th November, 1939. That has the signature of Keitel, in his red pencil, and it is addressed to the Army, Navy and Air Force. It deals with the fact that, if a quick break- through should fail North of Liege, other machinery for carrying out the attack will be used.

Paragraph 2 shows clearly that the Netherlands is to be violated. It speaks of "(a) The occupation of Walcheren Island and thereby Flushing harbour, or of some other southern Dutch island especially valuable for our sea and air warfare" and "(b) Taking of one or more Maas crossings between Namur and Dinant."

My Lord, the documents show that from November until March, 1940, the High Command and the Fuehrer were waiting for favourable weather before A-day, as they called it. That was the attack on Luxembourg, Belgium and the Netherlands.

My Lord, the next Document, C-72, consists of 18 documents which range in date from 7th November until 9th May, 1940. They are certified photostats I put in, and they are all signed either by Keitel personally or by Jodl personally, and I do not think it is necessary for me to read them. The defence, I think, have all had copies of them, but they show successively that A-day is being postponed for about a week, having regard to the weather reports. That will be Exhibit GB 109.

My Lord, on 10th January, 1940, as the Attorney General informed the Tribunal, a German aeroplane made a forced landing in Belgium. The occupants attempted to burn the orders of which they were in possession, but they were only partially successful. The next document I offer is Document TC-58a; it will be Exhibit GB 110. The original is a photostat certified by the Belgian Government who, of course, came into possession of the original.

My Lord, I can summarise it. They are orders to the Commander of the Second Air Force Fleet - Luftflotte - clearly for offensive action against France, Holland and Belgium. One looks at the bottom of the first page. It deals with the disposition of the Belgian Army. The Belgian Army covers the Liege-Antwerp Line with its main force, its lighter forces in front of the Meuse-Schelde Canal. Then it deals with the disposition of the Dutch Army; and then, if you turn over to Page 3, you see that the German Western Army directs its attack between the North Sea and the Moselle, with the strongest possible air-force support, through the Belgian-Luxembourg region.

My Lord, I think I need read no more. The rest are operational details as to the bombing of the various targets in Belgium and in Holland.

My Lord, as to the next document, my learned friend, Major Elwyn Jones, put in Jodl's diary, which is GB 88, and I desire to refer very, very briefly to some extracts which are printed first in Bundle No. 4.

If one looks at the entry for 1st February, 1940, and then some lines down -

THE PRESIDENT: 1809-PS?

MR. ROBERTS: Yes, that is right, my Lord.

THE PRESIDENT: We have not got the GB numbers on the documents.

MR. ROBERTS: I am sorry, my Lord.

If your Lordship will look eight lines down it says: "1700 hours General Jeschennek" and then:-

> "1.Behaviour of parachute units. In front of The Hague they have to be strong enough to break in if necessary by sheer brute force. The 7th Division intends to drop units near the town.
>
> 2. Political mission contrasts to some extent with violent action against the Dutch Air Force."

My Lord, I think I need not read the rest: it is operational detail.

> "2nd February." I refer again to Jodl's entry under "a" as to "landings can be made in the centre of The Hague."

THE PRESIDENT: Which date?

MR. ROBERTS: That was 2nd February, my Lord, the bottom of the same page, under "a". I was endeavouring not to read more than a word or two.

THE PRESIDENT: Quite right.

MR. ROBERTS: If your Lordship will turn over the page - I omit 5th February - you come to "26th February. Fuehrer raises the question whether it is better to undertake the Weser Exercise before or after case 'Yellow'."

Then on 3rd March, the last sentence:-

> "Fuehrer decides to carry out Weser Exercise before case 'Yellow', with a few days' interval".

Then, my Lord, there is an entry to which I desire to call your Lordship's attention, on 8th May, that is, two days before the invasion, the top of the page:-

> "Alarming news from Holland, cancelling of furloughs, evacuations, road-blocks, other mobilisation measures. According to reports of the intelligence service the British have asked for permission to march in, but the Dutch have refused."

My Lord, may I make two short comments on that? The first is that the Germans are rather objecting because the Dutch are actually making some preparation for resistance. "Alarming news " they say. The second point is that Jodl is there recording that the Dutch armies according to their intelligence reports, are still adhering properly to their neutrality. But I need not read any more of the diary extracts.

My Lord, that is the story except for the documents which were presented to Holland and to Belgium and to Luxembourg after the invasion was a fait accompli, because, as history now knows, at 4.30 a.m. on 10th May these three small countries were violently invaded with all the fury of modern warfare. No warning was given to them by Germany and no complaint was made by Germany of any breaches of any neutrality before this action was taken.

THE PRESIDENT: Perhaps this will be a convenient place to break off until 2 o'clock.

MR. ROBERTS: Yes, my Lord.

[A recess was taken until 1400 hours.]

MR. ROBERTS: May it please the Tribunal, when the Court adjourned, I had just come to the point at 4.30 a.m. on 10th May, 1940, when the Germans invaded these three small countries without any warning - a violation which, the prosecution submits it is clear from the documents, had been planned and decided upon months before.

My Lord, before I close this part of the case, may I refer to three documents in conclusion. My Lord, the invasion having taken place at 4.30 in the morning, in each of the three countries, the German Ambassadors called upon representatives of the three governments some hours later, and handed in a document which was similar in each case and which is described as a "Memorandum" or an "Ultimatum". My Lord, an account of what happened in Belgium is set out in our Document TC-58, which is about five documents from the end of the bundle. It is headed "Extract From 'Belgium - The Official Account of What Happened 1939-1940'", and I hand in an original copy, certified by the Belgian Government, which is Exhibit GB 111.

My Lord, might I read short extracts? I read the third paragraph:-

"From 4.30 information was received which left no shadow of doubt: the hour had struck. Aircraft were first reported in the East. At 5 o'clock came news of the bombing of two Netherlands aerodromes, the violation of the Belgian frontier, the landing of German soldiers at the Eben-Emael Fort, the bombing of the Jemelle station."

My Lord, then I think I can go to two paragraphs lower down:-

"At 8.30 a.m. the German Ambassador came to the Ministry of Foreign Affairs. When he entered the Minister's room, he began to take a paper from his pocket. M. Spaak" - that is the Belgian Minister - "stopped him: 'I beg your pardon, Mr. Ambassador. I will speak first.' And in an indignant voice, he read the Belgian Government's protest: 'Mr. Ambassador, the German Army has just attacked our country. This is the second time in 25 years that Germany has committed a criminal aggression against a neutral and loyal Belgium. What has just happened is perhaps even more odious than the aggression of 1914. No ultimatum, no note, no protest of any kind has ever been placed before the Belgian Government. It is through the attack itself that Belgium has learned that Germany has violated the undertakings given by her on 13th October, 1937, and renewed spontaneously at the beginning of the war. The act of aggression committed by Germany, for which there is no justification whatever, will deeply shock the conscience of the world. The German Reich will be held responsible by history. Belgium is resolved to defend herself. Her cause, which is the cause of Right, cannot be vanquished'."

Then I think I shall omit the next paragraph: "The Ambassador read the note" - and in the last paragraph: "In the middle of this communication M. Spaak, who had by his side the Secretary-General, interrupted the

Ambassador: 'Hand me that document', he said. 'I should like to spare you so painful a task.' After studying the note, M. Spaak confined himself to pointing out that he had already replied by the protest he had just made."

THE PRESIDENT: The Tribunal would like you to read what the Ambassador read.

MR. ROBERTS: I am sorry. I was thinking of the next document I was going to read. I read the last paragraph on the first page:

"The Ambassador was then able to read the note he had brought:

'I am instructed by the Government of the Reich,' he said, 'to make the following declaration: In order to forestall the invasion of Belgium, Holland, and Luxembourg, for which Great Britain and France have been making preparations clearly aimed at Germany, the Government of the Reich is compelled to ensure the neutrality of the three countries mentioned, by means of arms. For this purpose, the Government of the Reich will bring up an Armed Force of the greatest size, so that resistance of any kind will be useless. The Government of the Reich guarantees Belgium's European and Colonial territory, as well as her dynasty, on condition that no resistance is offered. Should there be any resistance, Belgium will risk the destruction of her country and loss of her independence. It is, therefore, in the interests of Belgium that the population be called upon to cease all resistance and that the authorities be given the necessary instructions to make contact with the German Military Command'."

My Lord, the so-called ultimatum, handed in some hours after the invasion had started, is Document TC-57, which is the last document but three in the bundle. It is the document I handed in and it becomes Exhibit GB 112. My Lord, it is a long document and I will read to the Tribunal such parts as the Tribunal thinks advisable:

"The Reich Government" - it begins - "has for a long time had no doubts as to what was the chief aim of British and French war policy. It consists of the spreading of the war to other countries, and of the misuse of their peoples as auxiliary and mercenary troops for England and France.

The last attempt of this sort was the plan to occupy Scandinavia with the help of Norway, in order to set up a new front against Germany in this region. It was only Germany's last minute action which upset this project. Germany has furnished documentary evidence of this before the eyes of the world.

Immediately after the English-French action in Scandinavia miscarried, England and France took up their policy of war expansion in another direction. In this respect, while the retreat from Norway was still going on, the English Prime Minister announced that, as a result of the altered situation in Scandinavia, England was once more in a position to go ahead with the transfer of the full weight of her Navy to the Mediterranean, and that English and French units were already on the way to Alexandria. The Mediterranean now became the centre of English-French war propaganda. This was partly to gloss over the Scandinavian defeat and the big loss of prestige before their own people and before the world, and partly to make it appear that the Balkans had been chosen for the next theatre of war against Germany.

In reality, however, this apparent shifting to the Mediterranean of English-French war policy had quite another purpose. It was nothing but a diversion manoeuvre in grand style, to deceive Germany as to the direction of the next English-French attack. For, as the Reich Government has long been aware, the true aim of England and France is the carefully prepared and now immediately imminent attack on Germany in the West, so as to advance through Belgium and Holland to the region of the Ruhr.

Germany had recognised and respected the inviolability of Belgium and Holland, it being, of course, understood that these two countries, in the event of a war of Germany against England and France, would maintain the strictest neutrality.

Belgium and the Netherlands have not fulfilled this condition."

THE PRESIDENT: Mr. Roberts, do you think it is necessary to read this in full?

MR. ROBERTS: No, I do not. I was going to summarise these charges. If your Lordship would be good enough to look at the bottom of the first page, you will see the so-called ultimatum complaining of the hostile expressions in the Belgian and Netherlands Press; and then, my Lord, in the second paragraph, over the page, there is an allegation of the attempts of the British Intelligence to bring a revolution into Germany with the assistance of Belgium and the Netherlands.

Then, my Lord, in Paragraph 3, reference is made to military preparation by the two countries; and in Paragraph 4 it is pointed out that Belgium has fortified the Belgian-German frontier.

A complaint is made in regard to Holland in Paragraph 5, that British aircraft have flown over the Netherlands country.

There are, my Lord, other charges made against the neutrality of these two countries, although no instances are given. I do not think I need refer to anything on Page 3 of the document.

Page 4, my Lord, I would like, if I might, to read the middle paragraph:-

"In this struggle for existence forced upon the German people by England and France the Reich Government is not disposed to await submissively the attack by England and France and to allow them to carry the war over Belgium and the Netherlands into German territory."

My Lord, I just emphasise the following sentence, and then I read no further:-

"It has therefore now issued the command to German troops to ensure the neutrality of these countries by all the military means at the disposal of the Reich."

My Lord, it is unnecessary, in my submission, to emphasise the falsity of that statement. The world now knows that for months preparations had been made to violate the neutrality of these three countries. This document is saying "The orders to do so have now been issued."

My Lord, a similar document, similar in terms altogether, was handed to the representatives of the Netherlands Government; This is TC-60, and will be Exhibit GB 113, which is the last document but one in the bundle. My Lord,

217

that is a memorandum to the Luxembourg Government, which enclosed with it a copy of the document handed to the Governments of Belgium and the Netherlands.

My Lord, I only desire to emphasise the second paragraph of TC-60.

"In defence against the imminent attack, the German troops have now received the order to safeguard the neutrality of these two countries."

My Lord, the last document, TC-59, which I formerly put in, that is Exhibit GB 111.

My Lord, that is the dignified protest of the Belgian Government against the crime which was committed against her. My Lord, those are the facts supporting the charges of the violation of treaties and assurances against these three countries and supporting the allegation of the making of an aggressive war against them. My Lord, in the respectful submission of the prosecution here, the story is a very plain, a very simple one, a story of perfidy, dishonour, and shame.

COLONEL PHILLIMORE: May it please the Tribunal, it is my task to present the evidence on the wars of aggression and wars in breach of treaties against Greece and Yugoslavia. The evidence which I shall put in to the Tribunal has been prepared in collaboration with my American colleague, Lieutenant-Colonel Krucker.

The invasions of Greece and Yugoslavia by the Germans, which took place in the early hours of the morning of 6th April, 1941, constituted direct breaches of The Hague Convention of 1899 on the Pacific Settlement of International Disputes and of the Kellogg-Briand Pact Of 1928. Those breaches are charged, respectively, at Paragraphs 1 and 13 of Appendix C of the Indictment. Both have already been put in by my learned friend, Sir David Maxwell Fyfe, who also explained the obligation of the German Government to the Governments of Yugoslavia and Greece under those Pacts.

In the case of Yugoslavia the invasion further constituted a breach of an express assurance by the Nazis, which is charged at Paragraph 26 of Appendix C. This assurance was originally given in a German Foreign Office release, made in Berlin on 28th April, 1938, but was subsequently repeated by Hitler himself on 6th October, 1939, in a speech he made in the Reichstag, and it is in respect of this last occasion that the assurance is specifically pleaded in the Indictment.

May I ask the Tribunal to turn now to the first document in the document book, which is Book No. 5. The first document is PS-2719, which is part of the document which has already been put in as Exhibit GB 58. This is the text of the German Foreign Office release, on 28th April, 1938, and I would read the beginning and then the last paragraph but one on the page:-

"Berlin, 28th April, 1938. The State Secretary of the German Foreign Office to the German Diplomatic Representatives.

As a consequence of the re-union of Austria with the Reich, we have now new frontiers with Italy, Yugoslavia, Switzerland, Liechtenstein and Hungary. These frontiers are regarded by us as final and inviolable. On this point the following special declarations have been made ."

And then to the last paragraph:-

"3. Yugoslavia.

The Yugoslav Government have been informed by authoritative

German quarters that German policy has no aims beyond Austria, and that the Yugoslav frontier would, in any case, remain untouched. In his speech made at Graz on 3rd April, the Fuehrer and Chancellor stated that, in regard to the re-union of Austria, Yugoslavia and Hungary had adopted the same attitude as Italy. We were happy to have frontiers there which relieved us of all anxiety about providing military protection for them."

Then, if I may, I will pass to the second document in the book, TC-92, and offer that as Exhibit GB 114. This is an extract from a speech made by Hitler on the occasion of the dinner in honour of the Prince Regent of Yugoslavia on 1st June, 1939. I will read the extract in full:

"The German friendship for the Yugoslav nation is not only a spontaneous one. It gained depth and durability in the midst of the tragic confusion of the world war. The German soldier then learned to appreciate and respect his extremely brave opponent. I believe that this feeling was reciprocated. This mutual respect finds confirmation in common political, cultural and economic interests. We therefore look upon your Royal Highness's present visit as a living proof of the accuracy of our view, and, at the same time, on that account we derive from it the hope that German-Yugoslav friendship may continue further to develop in the future and to grow ever closer.

In the presence of your Royal Highness, however, we also perceive a happy opportunity for a frank and friendly exchange of views which, and of this I am convinced, in this sense can only be fruitful to our two peoples and States. I believe this all the more because a firmly established reliable relationship of Germany and Yugoslavia now that, owing to historical events, we have become neighbours with common boundaries fixed for all time, will not only guarantee lasting peace between our two peoples and countries, but can also represent an element of calm to our nerve-wracked continent. This peace is the goal of all who are disposed to perform really constructive work."

As we now know, this speech was made at the time when Hitler had already decided upon the European war. I think I am right in saying it was a week after the Reich Chancellery conference, known as the Schmundt note, to which the Tribunal has been referred more than once. The reference to "nerve-wracked continent" might perhaps be attributed to the war of nerves which Hitler had himself been conducting for many months.

Now I pass to a document which is specifically pleaded at Paragraph 26 as the Assurance breached; it is the next document in the bundle, TC-43 - German Assurance to Yugoslavia of 6th October, 1939, It is part of the document which has already been put in as Exhibit GB 8o. This is an extract from the "Dokumente der Deutschen Politik":

"Immediately after the completion of the Anschluss I informed Yugoslavia that, from now on, the frontier with this country would also be an unalterable one, and that we only desired to live in peace and friendship with her."

Despite the obligations of Germany under the Convention of 1899, and the Kellogg-Briand Pact, and under the assurances which I have read, the fate of both Greece and Yugoslavia had, as we now know, been sealed ever since the meeting between Hitler and the defendant Ribbentrop, and Ciano at

Obersalzberg on 12th and 13th August, 1939.

We will pass to the next document in the bundle, which is TC- 77. That document has already been put in as Exhibit GB 48, and the passages to which I would draw your Lordship's attention have been already quoted, I think, by my learned friend, the Attorney General; those passages are on Page 2 in the last paragraph: From "Generally speaking" until "neutral of this kind", and then again on Pages 7 and 8, the part quoted by the Attorney General, and emphasised particularly by Lieutenant-Colonel Griffith-Jones. At the foot of Page 7, on the second day of the meeting, the words beginning "In general, however, success by one of the Axis partners -" to "their backs free for work against the West."

THE PRESIDENT: Is that quoted?

COLONEL PHILLIMORE: Yes, sir.

THE PRESIDENT: Was not Page 7 quoted before?

COLONEL PHILLIMORE: Both of those passages have been quoted before; and if I might sum up the effect of the meeting as revealed by the document as a whole, it shows Hitler and the defendant Ribbentrop, only two months after the dinner to the Prince Regent, seeking to persuade the Italians to make war on Yugoslavia at the same time that Germany commences hostilities against Poland, as Hitler had decided to do in the very near future. Ciano, whilst evidently in entire agreement with Hitler and Ribbentrop as to the desirability of liquidating Yugoslavia, and himself anxious to secure Salonika, stated that Italy was not yet ready for a general European war. Despite all the persuasion which Hitler and the defendant Ribbentrop exerted at the meeting, it became necessary for the Nazi conspirators to reassure their intended victim, Yugoslavia, since in fact Italy did maintain its position and did not enter the war when Germany invaded Poland, whilst the Germans themselves were not yet ready to strike in the Balkans. It was just for this reason that on 6th October, through Hitler's speech, they repeated the assurance they had given in April, 1938. It is, of course, a matter of history that, after the defeat of the Allied Armies in May and June, 1940, the Italian Government declared war on France, and that subsequently at 3 o'clock in the morning on 28th October, 1940, the Italian Minister at Athens presented the Greek Government with a 3 hours' ultimatum, upon the expiry of which Italian troops were already invading the soil of Greece.

If I may quote to the Tribunal the words in which His Majesty's Minister reported that event:

"The President of the Council has assured himself an outstanding -"

THE PRESIDENT: You have referred to a document?

COLONEL PHILLIMORE: It is not in any of my documents. It is merely carrying the story to the next document:

"The President of the Council has assured himself an outstanding place in Greek history, and, whatever the future may bring, his foresight in quietly preparing his country for war, and his courage in rejecting without demur the Italian ultimatum when delivered in the small hours of that October morning will surely obtain an honourable mention in the story of European statecraft. He means to fight until Italy is completely defeated, and this reflects the purpose of the whole Greek nation."

I turn now to the next document in the bundle, that is, PS- 2762, a letter from Hitler to Mussolini, which I put in as Exhibit GB 115. Although not dated, I think it is clear from the contents that it was written shortly after the Italian invasion of Greece. It has been quoted in full by the Attorney General, but I think it would assist the Tribunal if I read just the last two paragraphs of the extract:-

"Yugoslavia must become disinterested. If possible however, from our point of view, interested in co- operating in the liquidation of the Greek question. Without assurances from Yugoslavia, it is useless to risk any successful operation in the Balkans.

Unfortunately I must stress the fact that waging a war in the Balkans before March is impossible. Therefore any threatening move towards Yugoslavia would be useless since the impossibility of a materialisation of such threats before March is well known to the Serbian General Staff. Therefore Yugoslavia must, if at all possible, be won over by other means and other ways."

You may think the reference in the first two lines to his thoughts having been with Mussolini for the last 14 days probably indicates that it was written in about the middle of November, shortly after the Italian attack.

THE PRESIDENT: Could you give us the date of the Italian attack?

COLONEL PHILLIMORE: 28th October, 1940.

THE PRESIDENT: Thank you.

COLONEL PHILLIMORE: As the Tribunal will see from the succeeding document, it was at this time that Hitler was making his plans for the offensive in the spring of 1941, which included the invasion of Greece from the North. This letter shows that it was an integral part of those plans that Yugoslavia should be induced to co-operate in them or at least to maintain a disinterested attitude towards the liquidation of the other Balkan States.

I pass now to the next document in the bundle, PS-444, which becomes Exhibit GB 116. It is a "Top Secret Directive" issued from the Fuehrer's Headquarters, signed by Hitler, initialled by the defendant Jodl, and dated i2th November, 1940. I will read the first two lines and then pass to Paragraph 4 on the third page:-

"Directive No. 18.

The preparatory measures of Supreme H.Q. for the prosecution of the war in the near future are to be made along the following lines."

Omitting the section which deals with operations against Gibraltar and an offensive against Egypt, I will read Paragraph 4 on the third page:-

"Balkans.

The Commander-in-Chief of the Army will make preparations for occupying the Greek mainland North of the Aegean Sea, in case of need entering through Bulgaria, and thus make possible the use of German Air Force units against targets in the Eastern Mediterranean, in particular against those English air bases which are threatening the Roumanian oil area.

In order to be able to face all eventualities and to keep Turkey in check, the use of an army group of an approximate strength of ten divisions is to be the basis for the planning and the calculations of deployment. It will not be possible to count on the railway leading through Yugoslavia for moving these forces into position.

So as to shorten the time needed for the deployment, preparations will be made for an early increase in the German Army mission in Roumania, the extent of which must be submitted to me.

The Commander-in-Chief of the Air Force will make preparations for the use of German Air Force units in the South-east Balkans and for aerial reconnaissance on the Southern border of Bulgaria, in accordance with the intended ground. operations."

I do not think I need trouble the Tribunal with the rest. The next document in the bundle, PS-1541, which I offer in evidence as Exhibit GB 117, is the directive issued for the actual attack on Greece. Before reading it, it might be convenient if I summarised the position of the Italian invading forces at that time, as this is one of the factors mentioned by Hitler in the directive. I can put it very shortly. I again use the words in which H.M. Minister reported:-

"The morale of the Greek Army throughout has been of the highest, and our own naval and land successes at Taranto and in the Western Desert have done much to maintain it.

With relatively poor armaments and the minimum of equipment and modern facilities they have driven back or captured superior Italian forces, more frequently than not at the point of the bayonet. The modern Greeks have thus shown that they are not unworthy of the ancient traditions of their country and that they, like their distant forbears, are prepared to fight against odds to maintain their freedom."

In fact, the Italians were getting the worst of it, and it was time that Hitler came to the rescue. Accordingly, this directive was issued on 13th December, 1940; it is Top Secret, Directive Number 20, for the Operation Marita. The distribution included one to the Commander of the Navy, which, of course, would be the defendant Raeder; one to the Commander of the Air Force, which would be the defendant Goering; one to the Supreme Command of the Armed Forces, Keitel; and one to the Command Staff, which, I take it, would be the defendant Jodl. I shall read the first two paragraphs and then summarise the next two, if I may:-

"The result of the battles in Albania is not yet decisive. Because of a dangerous situation in Albania it is doubly necessary that the British attempt to create air bases under the protection of a Balkan front be foiled, as this would be dangerous above all to Italy as well as to the Roumanian oil fields.

My plan, therefore, is (a) to form a slowly increasing task force in Southern Roumania within the next few months, (b) after the setting in of favourable weather, probably in March, to send this task force for the occupation of the Aegean North coast by way of Bulgaria, and (c) if necessary, to occupy the entire Greek mainland (Operation Marita). The support of Bulgaria is to be expected."

The next paragraph gives the forces for the operation, and Paragraph 4 deals with the operation Marita itself. Paragraph 5 states:-

"The military preparations, which will produce exceptional political results in the Balkans, demand the exact control of all the necessary measures by the General Staff. The transport through Hungary and the arrival in Roumania will be reported step by step by the General Staff of the Armed Forces, and are to be explained, at first, as a strengthening of the German Army mission in Roumania. Consultations with the Roumanians or the Bulgarians which may point to our intentions, as well as notification to the Italians, are each subject to my consent, as also are the sending of scouting missions and advanced parties."

I think I need not trouble the Tribunal with the rest. The next document, PS-448, which I put in as Exhibit GB 118, is again a "Top Secret Directive" carrying the plan a little further; it deals with decisive action in support of the Italian forces in Tripoli and in Albania. I read, if I may, the first short paragraph, and then the paragraph at the foot of the page.

"The situation in the Mediterranean theatre of operations demands, for strategical, political and psychological reasons, German assistance, due to employment of superior forces by England against our allies."

And in Paragraph 3, after dealing with the forces to be transferred to Albania, the directive sets out what the duties of the German forces will be:-

(a) To serve in Albania for the time being as a reserve for an emergency case, should new crises arise there.

(b) To ease the burden of the Italian Army group when later attacking with the aim of tearing open the Greek defence front at a decisive point for a far-reaching operation.

(c) To open up the Straits West of Salonika from the rear, in order to support thereby the frontal attack of List's Army."

That directive was signed by Hitler, and, as can be seen on the original which I have put in, it was initialled by both the defendant Keitel and the defendant Jodl. Here again, of course, a copy went to the defendant Raeder, and I take it that the copy sent to Foreign Intelligence would probably reach the defendant Ribbentrop.

I pass to C-134, the next document in the bundle, which becomes Exhibit GB 119. This records a conference which took place on 19th and 2oth January between the defendant Keitel and the Italian General, Guzzoni, and which was followed by a meeting between Hitler and Mussolini, at which the defendants Ribbentrop, Keitel and Jodl were present.

I need not trouble the Tribunal with the meeting with the Italians, but if you would pass to Page 3 of the document, there is a paragraph there in the speech which the Fuehrer made, which is perhaps just worth reading - the speech by the Fuehrer on 20th January, 1941, in the middle of Page 3. It sets out that the speech was made after the conference with the Italians, and then shows who was present.

On the German side I would call your attention to the presence of the Minister for Foreign Affairs, the Chief of the Supreme Command of the Armed Forces, and the Chief of the Armed Forces Operational Staff. These are, of course, the defendants Ribbentrop, Keitel and Jodl; and on the Italian side, the Duce, Ciano and the three Generals.

It is the last paragraph that I would wish to read:-

"The massing of troops in Roumania serves a threefold purpose:

(a) An operation against Greece.

(b) Protection of Bulgaria against Russia and Turkey.

(c) Safeguarding the guarantee to Roumania.

Each of these tasks requires its own group of forces, altogether, therefore, very strong forces whose deployment far from our base requires a long time.

Desirable that this deployment is completed without interference from the enemy. Therefore disclose the game as late as possible. The tendency will be to cross the Danube at the last possible moment and to line up for attack at the earliest possible moment."

I pass to the next document, PS-1746, which I offer as Exhibit GB 120. That document is in three parts. It consists, in the first place, of a conference between Field Marshal List and the Bulgarians, on 8th February.

The second part and the third part deal with later events, and I will, if I may, come back to them at an appropriate time.

I would read the first and the last paragraphs on the first page of this document.

"Minutes of questions discussed between the representatives of the Royal Bulgarian General Staff and the German Supreme Command - General Field Marshal List - in connection with the possible movement of German troops through Bulgaria and their commitment against Greece and possibly against Turkey, if she should involve herself in the war."

And then the last paragraph on the page shows the plan being concerted with the Bulgarians:-

Paragraph 3: "The Bulgarian and the German General Staffs will take all measures in order to camouflage the preparation of the operations, and to assure in this way the most favourable conditions for the execution of the German operations as planned.

The representatives of the two General Staffs consider it suitable to inform their Governments that it will be advisable, of necessity, to take secrecy and surprise into consideration when the Three Power Treaty is signed by Bulgaria, in order to assure the success of the military operations."

I pass then to the next Document, C-59. I offer that as Exhibit GB 121. It is a further Top Secret Directive of 19th February. I need not, I think, read it. All that is set out of importance is the date for the Operation Marita. It sets out that the bridge across the Danube is to be begun on 28th February, the river crossed on 2nd March, and the final orders to be issued on the 26th February at the latest.

It is perhaps worth noting that on the original, which I have put in, the actual dates are filled in the handwriting of the defendant Keitel.

It is perhaps just worth setting out the position of Bulgaria at this moment, Bulgaria adhered to the Three-Power Pact on 1st March -

THE PRESIDENT: What year?

COLONEL PHILLIMORE: 1941. And on the same day the entry of German troops into Bulgaria began in accordance with the Plan Marita and the directives to which I have referred the Tribunal.

The landing of British troops in Greece on 3rd March, in accordance with the guarantee given in the spring of 1939 by His Majesty's Government, may have accelerated the movement of the German forces; but, as the Tribunal will have seen, the invasion of Greece had been planned long beforehand and was already in progress at this time.

I pass now to the next document in the bundle, C-167, which I put in as

224

Exhibit GB 122. 1 am afraid it is not a very satisfactory copy, but the original, which I have put in, shows that both the defendants, Keitel and Jodl, were present at the interview with Hitler which this extract records. It is a short extract from a report by the defendant Raeder on an interview with Hitler, in the presence of the defendants Keitel and Jodl. It is perhaps interesting as showing the ruthless nature of the German intention.

"The C.-in-C. of the Navy asks for confirmation that the whole of Greece will have to be occupied even in the event of a peaceful settlement.

Fuehrer: The complete occupation is a prerequisite of any settlement."

The above document-

THE PRESIDENT: Is it dated ?

COLONEL PHILLIMORE: It took place on the 18th March at 1600 hours.

THE PRESIDENT: Is that on the original document?

COLONEL PHILLIMORE: Yes, on the original document.

THE PRESIDENT: Yes.

COLONEL PHILLIMORE: The document I have referred to shows, it is submitted, that the Nazi conspirators, in accordance with their principle of liquidating any neutral who did not remain disinterested, had made every preparation by the end of January and were, at this date, in the process of moving the necessary troops to ensure the final liquidation of Greece, which was already at war with and getting the better of their Italian allies.

They were not, however, yet ready to deal with Yugoslavia, towards which their policy accordingly remained one of lulling the unsuspecting victim. On 25th March, 1941, in accordance with this policy, the adherence of Yugoslavia to the Three-Power Pact was secured. This adherence followed a visit on 15th February, 1941, by the Yugoslav Premier Cvetkovic and the Foreign Minister Cinkar-Markovic to the defendant Ribbentrop at Salzburg and subsequently to Hitler at Berchtesgaden, after which these ministers were induced to sign the Pact at Vienna on 25th March. On this occasion the defendant Ribbentrop wrote the two letters of assurance, which are set out in the next document in the bundle, PS- 2450, which I put in as Exhibit GB 123. If I might read from half-way down the page:-

"Notes of the Axis Governments to Belgrade.

At the same time, when the protocol on the entry of Yugoslavia to the Tri-Partite, Pact was signed, the governments of the Axis Powers sent to the Yugoslavian Government the following identical notes:

'Mr. Prime Minister.

In the name of the German Government and at its behest I have the honour to inform Your Excellency of the following:

On the occasion of the Yugoslavian entry today into the Tri-Partite Pact the German Government confirms its determination to respect the sovereignty and territorial integrity of Yugoslavia at all times.'"

That letter was signed by the defendant Ribbentrop, who, you will remember, was present at the meeting in August, 1939, when he and Hitler tried to persuade the Italians to invade Yugoslavia. In fact it was 11 days after this letter was written that the Germans did invade Yugoslavia and two days after the letter was written that they issued the necessary order.

If I might read the second letter

"Mr. Prime Minister.

With reference to the conversations that occurred in connection with the Yugoslavian entry into the Tri- Partite Pact, I have the honour to confirm to Your Excellency herewith in the name of the Reich Cabinet (Reichsregierung), that in the agreement between the Axis Powers and the Royal Yugoslavian Government, the Governments of the Axis Powers during this war will not direct a demand to Yugoslavia to permit the march or transportation of troops through Yugoslavian national territory."

The position at this stage, the 25th March, 1941, was, therefore, that German troops were already in Bulgaria moving towards the Greek frontier, while Yugoslavia had, to use Hitler's own term in his letter to Mussolini, "become disinterested" in the cleaning-up of the Greek question.

The importance of the adherence of Yugoslavia to the Three- Power Pact appears very clearly from the next document in the bundle, PS-2765, which I put in as GB 124. It is an extract from the minutes of a meeting between Hitler and Ciano, and, if I might just read the first paragraph

"The Fuehrer first expressed his satisfaction with Yugoslavia's joining the Tri-Partite Pact and the resulting definition of her position. This is of special importance in view of the proposed military action against Greece, for, if one considers that for 350 to 4oo kilometres the important line of communication through Bulgaria runs within 20 kilometres of the Yugoslav border, one can judge that with a dubious attitude of Yugoslavia an undertaking against Greece would have been militarily an extremely foolhardy venture."

Again it is a matter of history that on the night of 26th March, when the two Yugoslav ministers returned to Belgrade, General Simovic and his colleagues effected their removal by a coup d'etat, and Yugoslavia emerged on the morning of 27th March, ready to defend, if need be, its independence. The Yugoslav people had found itself.

The Nazis reacted to this altered situation with lightning rapidity, and the immediate liquidation of Yugoslavia was decided on.

I ask the Tribunal to turn back to PS-1746, which I put in as GB 120, to the second part on Page 3 of the document, consisting of a record of a conference of Hitler and the German High Command on the situation in Yugoslavia, dated 27th March, 1941.

It shows that those present included the Fuehrer; the Reich Marshal, that is of course, the defendant Goering; Chief of the O.K.W., that is the defendant Keitel; Chief of the Wehrmacht Fuehrungstab, that is the defendant Jodl. Then - over the page - "later on the following persons were added." I call the Tribunal's attention to the fact that those who came in later included the defendant Ribbentrop.

If I might read the part of Hitler's statement set out on Page 4

"The Fuehrer describes Yugoslavia's situation after the coup d'etat. Statement that Yugoslavia was an uncertain factor in regard to the coming Marita action and even more in regard to the Barbarossa undertaking later on. Serbs and Slovenes were never pro-Germans."

I think I can pass on to the second paragraph:

"The present moment, is for political and military reasons favourable for us to ascertain the actual situation in the country and the country's attitude towards us. For, if the overthrow of the Government would have happened during the Barbarossa action, the consequences for us probably would have been considerably more serious."

And then the next paragraph, to which I would particularly draw the Tribunal's attention:

"The Fuehrer is determined, without waiting for possible loyalty declarations of the new government, to make all preparations in order to destroy Yugoslavia militarily and as a national unit. No diplomatic inquiries will be made nor ultimatums presented. Assurances of the Yugoslav Government, which cannot be trusted anyhow in the future, will be taken note of. The attack will start as soon as the means and troops suitable for it are ready.

It is important that action be taken as soon as possible. An attempt will be made to let the bordering States participate in a suitable way. Actual military support against Yugoslavia is to be requested of Italy, Hungary, and in certain respects of Bulgaria too. Roumania's main task is the protection against Russia. The Hungarian and the Bulgarian ambassadors have already been notified. During the day a message will be addressed to the Duce.

Politically it is especially important that the blow against Yugoslavia is carried out with unmerciful harshness and that the military destruction is done in a lightning-like undertaking. In this way Turkey would become sufficiently frightened and the campaign against Greece later on would be influenced in a favourable way. It can be assumed that the Croats will come to our side when we attack. A corresponding political treatment (autonomy later on) will be assured to them. The war against Yugoslavia should be very popular in Italy, Hungary and Bulgaria, as territorial acquisitions are to be promised to these states; the Adriatic coast for Italy, the Banat for Hungary, and Macedonia for Bulgaria.

This plan assumes that we speed up the schedule of all preparations and use such strong forces that the Yugoslav collapse will take place within the shortest time."

Well, of course, the Tribunal will have noted that in that third paragraph - two days after the pact had been signed and the assurances given - because there has been a coup d'etat, and it is just possible that the operations against Greece may be affected - the destruction of Yugoslavia is decided upon without any question of taking the trouble to ascertain the views of the new Government.

Then there is one short passage on Page 5, the next page of the document, which I would like to read.

"5. The main task of the Air Force is to start as early as possible with the destruction of the Yugoslavian Air Force ground installations and to destroy the capital Belgrade in attacks by waves."

I pause there to comment; we now know, of course, how ruthlessly this bombing was done, when the residential areas of Belgrade were bombed at 7 o'clock on the following Sunday morning, the morning of the 6th.

THE PRESIDENT: The 6th April?

COLONEL PHILLIMORE: The 6th April.

Then again, still in the same document, the last part of it, Part V, at Page 5; a tentative plan is set out, drawn up by the defendant Jodl, and I would read one small paragraph at the top of the following page, Page 6:

"In the event of the political development requiring an armed intervention against Yugoslavia, it is the German intention to attack Yugoslavia in a concentric way as soon as possible, to destroy her armed forces and to dissolve her national territory."

I read that because the plan is issued from the office of the defendant Jodl.

Now, passing to the next document in the bundle, C-127, I put that in as Exhibit GB 125. It is an extract from the order issued after the meeting, from the minutes of which I have just read, that is, the meeting of 27th March, recorded in PS-1746, Part II. It is worth reading the first paragraph:

"The military putsch in Yugoslavia has altered the political situation in the Balkans. Yugoslavia must, in spite of her protestations of loyalty, for the time being be considered as an enemy and therefore be crushed as speedily as possible."

I pass to the next document, PS-1835, which I put in evidence as Exhibit GB 126. It is an original telegram, containing a letter from Hitler to Mussolini, forwarded through the German Ambassador in Rome by Hitler and the defendant Ribbentrop. It is written to advise Mussolini of the course decided on and under the guise of somewhat fulsome language the Duce is given his orders. If I might read the first five paragraphs:

"Duce, events force me to give you, Duce, by this the quickest means, my estimation of the situation and the consequences which may result from it.

(1) From the beginning I have regarded Yugoslavia as a dangerous factor in the controversy with Greece. Considered from the purely military point of view, German intervention in the war in Thrace would not be at all justified as long as the attitude, of Yugoslavia remained ambiguous, and she could threaten the left flank of the advancing columns on our enormous front.

(2) For this reason I have done everything and honestly have endeavoured to bring Yugoslavia into our community bound together by mutual interests. Unfortunately these attempts did not meet with success, or they were begun too late to produce any definite result. Today's reports leave no doubt as to the imminent turn in the foreign policy of Yugoslavia.

(3) I do not consider this situation as being catastrophic, but nevertheless it is a difficult one, and we on our part must avoid any mistake if we do not want, in the end, to endanger our whole position.

(4) Therefore I have already arranged for all necessary measures in order to meet a critical development with necessary military means. The change in the deployment of our troops has been ordered also in Bulgaria. Now I would cordially request you, Duce, not to undertake any further operations in Albania in the course of the next few days. I consider it necessary that you should cover and screen the most important passes from Yugoslavia into Albania with all available forces. These measures should not be considered as designed for a long period of time, but as auxiliary measures designed to prevent for at

least fourteen days to three weeks a crisis arising.

I also consider it necessary, Duce, that you should reinforce your forces on the Italian-Yugoslav front with all available means and with utmost speed.

(5) I also consider it necessary, Duce, that everything which we do and order be shrouded in absolute secrecy and that only personalities who necessarily must be notified know anything about them. These measures will completely lose their value should they become known."

Then he goes on to emphasise further the importance of secrecy.

I pass to R-95, the next document in the bundle, which I put in as Exhibit GB 127. It was referred to by my learned friend, the Attorney General. It is an operational order, signed by General von Brauchitsch, which is merely passing to the Armies the orders contained in Directive No. 25, which was the Document C-127, an extract of which I put in as Exhibit GB 125. I will not trouble the Tribunal with reading it.

I pass to TC-93, which has already been put in with TC-92 as Exhibit GB 114. The invasion of Greece and Yugoslavia took place on this morning, 6th April, on which Hitler issued the proclamation from which this passage is an extract:-

"From the beginning of the struggle it has been England's steadfast endeavour to make the Balkans a theatre of war. British diplomacy did, in fact, using the model of the World War, succeed in first ensnaring Greece by a guarantee offered to her and then finally in misusing her for Britain's purposes.

The documents published today afford" - that refers to the German 'White Book' which they published of all the documents leading up to the invasion - "The documents published today afford a glimpse of a practice which, in accordance with very old British recipes, is a constant attempt to induce others to fight and bleed for British interests.

In the face of this I have always emphasised that:

(1) The German people have no antagonism to the Greek people but that

(2) We shall never, as in the first World War, tolerate a power establishing itself on Greek territory with the object, at a given time, of being able to advance thence from the South-east into German living space. We have swept the Northern flank free of the English; we are resolved not to tolerate such a threat inn the South."

Then the paragraph to which I would draw the Tribunal's particular attention:-

"In the interests of a genuine consolidation of Europe it has been my endeavour since the day of my assumption of power above all to establish a friendly relationship with Yugoslavia. I have consciously put out of mind everything that once took place between Germany and Serbia, I have not only offered the Serbian people the hand of the German people, but in addition have made efforts as an honest broker to assist in bridging all difficulties which existed between the Yugoslav State and various nations allied to Germany."

One can only think that when he issued that proclamation Hitler must momentarily have forgotten the meeting with Ciano in August, 1939, and the meeting with the defendant Ribbentrop and the others on 27th March a few days earlier.

I pass to the last document in the bundle. It is a document which has already been put in, L-172, and it was put in as Exhibit USA 34. It is a record of a lecture delivered by the defendant Jodl on 7th November, 1943. At Page 4 there is a short passage which sets out his views two and a-half years later on the action taken in April, 1941. I refer to Paragraph 11 on Page 4:-

> "What was, however, less acceptable was the necessity of affording our assistance as an ally in the Balkans in consequence of the 'extra-turn' of the Italians against Greece. The attack which they launched in the autumn of 1940 from Albania with totally inadequate means was contrary to all agreement, but in the end led to a decision on our part which-taking a long view of the matter-would have become necessary, in any case, sooner or later. The planned attack on Greece from the North was not executed merely as an operation in aid of an ally. Its real purpose was to prevent the British from gaining a foothold in Greece and from menacing our Roumanian oil area from that country."

If I might summarise the story: The invasion of Greece was decided on at least as early as November or December, 1940, and planned for the end of March or the beginning of April, 1941 No consideration was at any time given to any obligations under treaties or conventions which might make such invasion a breach of International Law. Care was taken to conceal the preparations so that the German forces might have an unsuspecting victim.

In the meanwhile Yugoslavia, though to be liquidated in due course, was clearly better left for a later stage. Every effort was made to secure her co-operation for the offensive against Greece or, at least, to ensure that she would abstain from any interference.

The coup d'etat of General Simovic upset this plan and it was then decided that, irrespective of whether or not his government had any hostile intentions towards Germany, or even of supporting the Greeks, Yugoslavia must be liquidated.

It was not worth while to take any steps to ascertain Yugoslavia's intentions when it would be so little trouble, now that the German troops were deployed, to destroy her militarily and as a national unit. Accordingly, in the early hours of Sunday morning, 6th April, German troops marched into Yugoslavia without warning, and into Greece simultaneously with the formality of handing a note to the Greek Minister in Berlin, informing him that the German forces were entering Greece to drive out the British. M. Koryzis, the Greek Minister, in replying to information of the invasion from the German Embassy, replied that history was repeating itself and that Greece was being attacked by Germany in the same way as by Italy. Greece returned, he said, the same reply as in the preceding October.

That concludes the evidence in respect of Greece and Yugoslavia. But, as I have the honour to conclude the British case, I would like, if the Tribunal would allow me, to draw their attention, very shortly indeed, to one common factor which runs through the whole of this aggression. I can do it, I think, in five minutes.

It is an element in the diplomatic technique of aggression, which was used with singular consistency, not only by the Nazis themselves but also by their

Italian friends. Their technique was essentially based upon securing the maximum advantage from surprise, even though only a few hours of unopposed military advance into the country of the unsuspecting victim could thus be secured. Thus there was, of course, no declaration of war in the case of Poland.

The invasion of Norway and of Denmark began in the small hours of the night of 8th-9th April, and was well under way as a military operation before the diplomatic explanations and excuses were presented to the Danish Foreign Minister, at 4.20 a.m. on the morning of the 9th, and to the Norwegian Minister, between 4.30 and 5 on that morning.

The invasion of Belgium, Luxembourg and Holland began not later than 5 o'clock, in most cases earlier, in the small hours of 10th May, whilst the formal ultimatum, delivered in each case with the diplomatic excuses and explanations, was not presented until afterwards. In the case of Holland, the invasion began between 3 and 4 o'clock in the morning. It was not until 6 o'clock, when The Hague had already been bombed, that the German Minister asked to see M. van Kleffens. In the case of Belgium, where the bombing began at 5 o'clock, the German Minister did not see M. Spaak until 8 o'clock. The invasion of Luxembourg began at 4 o'clock and it was at 7 o'clock when the German Minister asked to see M. Beck.

Mussolini copied this technique. It was 3 o'clock on the morning of 28th October, 1940, when his Minister in Athens presented a three-hour ultimatum to General Metaxas.

The invasions of Greece and Yugoslavia, as I have said, both began in the small hours of 6th April, 1941. In the case of Yugoslavia, no diplomatic exchange took place even after the event, but a proclamation was issued by Hitler - a proclamation from which I read an extract - at 5 o'clock that Sunday morning, some two hours before Belgrade was bombed.

In the case of Greece, once again, it was at 5.20 a.m. that M. Koryzis was informed that German troops were entering Greek territory.

The manner in which this long series of aggressions was carried out is, in itself, further evidence of the essentially aggressive and treacherous character of the Nazi regime. Attack without warning at night to secure an initial advantage and proffer excuses or reasons afterwards. Their method of procedure is clearly the method of the barbarian, of the State which has no respect for its own pledged word, nor for the rights of any people but its own.

One is tempted to speculate whether this technique was evolved by the honest broker himself or by his honest clerk, the defendant Ribbentrop.

THE PRESIDENT: Mr. Alderman, will you be ready to go on after a short adjournment. That is what you were intending to do

MR. ALDERMAN: Yes.

THE PRESIDENT: We will adjourn for 10 minutes.

[A recess was taken.]

MR. ALDERMAN: May it please the Tribunal, before proceeding with the presentation of the evidence relating to the aggression against the Soviet Union, I shall take about 15 minutes to offer two further documents relating to the aggression against Austria.

These two documents are stapled in a supplementary book, supplement to document Book N.

Both documents are correspondence of the British Foreign Office. They have been made available to us through the courtesy of our British colleagues.

First, I offer in evidence Document 3045-PS as Exhibit USA 127. This is in two parts. The first is a letter dated 12th March, 1938, from Ambassador Neville Henderson, at the British Embassy, Berlin, to Lord Halifax. It reads:-

"My Lord,

With reference to your Telegram No. 79 of 11th March, I have the honour to transmit to your Lordship herewith a copy of a letter which I addressed to Baron von Neurath in accordance with the instructions contained therein and which was delivered on the same evening.

The French Ambassador addressed a similar letter to Baron von Neurath at the same time."

The enclosure is the note of 11th March, from the British Embassy to defendant von Neurath and it reads as follows

"Dear Reich Minister,

My Government are informed that a German ultimatum was delivered this afternoon at Vienna demanding, inter alia, the resignation of the Chancellor and his replacement by the Minister of the Interior, a new Cabinet of which two-thirds of the members were to be National Socialists, and the readmission of the Austrian Legion to the country with the duty of keeping order in Vienna. I am instructed by my Government to represent immediately to the German Government that if this report is correct H. M.G." - meaning His Majesty's Government - "in the U.K. feels bound to register a protest in the strongest terms against such use of coercion backed by force against an independent state in order to create a situation incompatible with its national independence.

As the German Minister for Foreign Affairs has already been informed in London, such action is bound to produce very great reactions, of which it is impossible to foretell the issues."

I now offer Document 3287-PS, as Exhibit USA 128.

This consists of a transmittal from the British Embassy, Berlin, to the British Foreign Office, of defendant von Neurath's letter of response dated 12th March, 1938. The letter is identified in the document with the letter "L".

First the defendant von Neurath objected to the fact that the British Government was undertaking the role of protector of Austria's independence. I quote from the second paragraph of his letter:-

"In the name of the German Government I must point out here that the Royal British Government has no right to assume the role of a protector of Austria's independence. In the course of diplomatic consultations on the Austrian question, the German Government never left any doubt with the Royal British Government that the formation of relations between Germany and Austria could not be considered anything but the inner concern of the German people and that it did not affect a third power."

Then, in response to the assertions regarding Germany's ultimatum, von Neurath set out what he stated to be the true version of events.

I quote the last two long paragraphs of the letter; in the English translation I start at the bottom of Page 1 of the letter:-

"Instead, the former Austrian Chancellor announced, on the evening of 9th March, the surprising and arbitrary resolution, decided on by himself, to hold an election within a few days which, under the prevailing circumstances, and especially according to the details provided for the execution of the election, could and was to have the sole purpose of oppressing politically the predominant majority of the population of Austria. As could have been foreseen, this procedure, being a flagrant violation of the agreement of Berchtesgaden, led to a very critical point in Austria's internal situation. It was only natural that the members of the then Austrian Cabinet who had not taken part in the decision for an election should have protested very strongly against it. Therefore, a Cabinet crisis occurred in Vienna which, on 11th March, resulted in the resignation of the former Chancellor and in the formation of a new Cabinet. It is untrue that the Reich used forceful pressure to bring about this development. In particular the assertion which was spread later by the former Chancellor, that the German Government had presented the Federal President with a conditional ultimatum, is a pure invention; according to the ultimatum he had to appoint a proposed candidate as Chancellor and to form a Cabinet conforming to the proposals of the German Government, otherwise the invasion of Austria by German troops was held in prospect. The truth of the matter is that the question of sending military or police forces from the Reich was brought up only when the newly formed Austrian Cabinet addressed a telegram, already published by the Press, to the German Government, urgently asking for the dispatch of German troops as soon as possible, in order to restore peace and avoid bloodshed. Faced with the immediately threatening danger of a bloody civil war in Austria, the German Government then decided to comply with the appeal addressed to it.

This being the state of affairs, it is impossible that the attitude of the German Government, as asserted in your letter, could lead to some unforeseeable reactions. A complete picture of the political situation is given in the proclamation which, at noon today, the German Reich Chancellor has addressed to the German people. Dangerous reactions to this situation can take place only if eventually a third party should try to exercise its influence, contrary to the peaceful intentions and legitimate aims of the German Government, on the shaping of events in Austria, a step which would be incompatible with the right of self-government of the German people."

That ends the quotation.

Now, in the light of the evidence which has already been presented to the Tribunal, this version of the events given by the defendant von Neurath is a hollow mockery of the truth.

We have learned, from the portions quoted from Document 1780- PS, which is Exhibit USA 72 - Jodl's diary - the entry for 10th March, 1938, the fact that von Neurath was taking over the duties of the Foreign Office while Ribbentrop was detained in London, that the Fuehrer wished to send an ultimatum to the Austrian Cabinet, that he had dispatched a letter to Mussolini of his reasons for taking action, and that army mobilisation orders were given.

We have seen the true facts about the ultimatum from two different documents. I refer to 812-PS, Exhibit USA 61, Report of Gauleiter Rainer to Reichskommissar Burckel, dated 6th July, 1939, which was transmitted to the defendant Seyss- Inquart on 22nd August, 1939. The portion reporting on the events of 11th March have already been read to the Tribunal.

I also refer to Document 2949-PS, Exhibit USA 76, the transcripts of Goering's telephone conversations, relevant portions of which I have already read to the Tribunal.

These documents emphatically show, and with unmistakable clarity, that the German Nazis did present an ultimatum to the Austrian Government that it would send troops across the border if Schuschnigg did not resign, and if defendant Seyss- Inquart were not appointed Chancellor.

These documents also show that the impetus of the famous telegram came from Berlin and not from Vienna, that Goering composed the telegram and Seyss-Inquart did not even have to send it, but merely said "agreed."

The transcript of Goering's telephone call to Ribbentrop, is indicated as Part W of that document. In it the formula was developed and recited for English consumption that there had been no ultimatum and that the German troops crossed the border in response only to the telegram.

And now, in this document from which I have just read, we find the same bogus formula coming from the pen of the defendant von Neurath. He was at the meeting of 5th November, 1937, of which we have the Hoszbach Minutes, Exhibit USA 25. And so he knew very well the firmly held Nazi ideas with respect to Austria and Czechoslovakia. Yet, in the period after 10th March, 1938, when he was handling the foreign affairs for this conspiracy, and particularly after the invasion of Austria, he played his part in making false representations. He gave an assurance to Mr. Mastny regarding the continued independence of Austria. I refer to the document introduced by Sir David Maxwell Fyfe, Document TC-27, which is Exhibit GB 21.

We see him here, still handling foreign affairs, although using the letterhead of the Secret Cabinet Council, as the exhibit shows, reciting this diplomatic fable with respect to the Austrian situation, a story also encountered by us in the transcript of the Goering-Ribbentrop telephone call, all in furtherance of the aims of what we call the conspiracy.

Now, if the Tribunal please, it might have been fitting and appropriate for me to present the case on collaboration with Japan and the attack on the United States on this 7th December, 1945, the fourth anniversary of the attack on Pearl Harbour. However, our plan was to proceed chronologically, so that part of the case must wait its turn for presentation next week.

We now come to the climax of this amazing story of wars of aggression, perhaps one of the most colossal misjudgements in history, when Hitler's intuition led him and his associates to launch an aggressive war against the Union of Soviet Socialist Republics.

In my last appearance before the Tribunal I presented an account of the aggression against Czechoslovakia. In the meantime, our British colleagues have given you the evidence covering the formulation of the plan to attack Poland and the preparations and initiation of actual aggressive war. In addition, they have laid before the Tribunal the story of the expansion of the war into a general war of aggression, involving the planning and execution of attacks on Denmark, Norway, Belgium and the Netherlands, Luxembourg, Yugoslavia, and Greece, and in doing so, the British prosecution has marshalled and presented to the Court various international treaties, agreements and assurances and the evidence establishing the breaching of those treaties and assurances.

I should like to present to the Tribunal now the account of the last but one of the defendants' acts of aggression, the invasion of the U.S.S.R. The section of the Indictment in which this crime is charged is Count 1, Section 4 (f), Paragraph 6, German invasion on 22nd June, 1941, of the U.S.S.R. Territory in violation of the Non-Aggression Pact of 23rd August, 1939. The first sentence of this paragraph is the one with which we shall be concerned today. It reads:-

"On 22nd June, 1941, the Nazi conspirators deceitfully denounced the Non-Aggression Pact between Germany and the U.S.S.R. and without any declaration of war invaded Soviet territory, thereby beginning a war of aggression against the U.S.S.R."

The documents having a bearing on this phase of the case are contained in document book marked "P", which we now hand to the Court.

First, if the Tribunal please, the inception of the plan. As a point of departure for the story of aggression against the Soviet Union, I should like to take the date 23rd August, 1939. On that date, just a week before the invasion of Poland, the Nazi conspirators caused Germany to enter into the Treaty of Non-Aggression with the U.S.S.R., which is referred to in this section of the Indictment which I have just quoted. This treaty, Document TC-25, will be introduced in evidence by our British colleagues, but it contains two articles which I should like to bring to the attention of the Tribunal. Article C 1 provided as follows:-

"The two contracting parties undertake to refrain from any act of violence, any aggressive action, or any attack against one another, whether individually or jointly with other Powers."

Article 5 provides that:

"Should disputes or conflicts arise between the contracting parties, regarding the questions of any kind whatsoever, the two parties would clear away these disputes or conflicts solely by friendly exchanges of view or, if necessary, by arbitration commissions."

It is well to keep these solemn pledges in mind during the course of the story which is to follow. This treaty was signed for the German Government by the defendant Ribbentrop. Its announcement came as somewhat of a surprise to the world, since it appeared to constitute a reversal of the previous trend of Nazi foreign policy. The explanation for this about-face has been provided, however, by no less eminent a witness than the defendant Ribbentrop himself in a discussion which he had with the Japanese Ambassador Oshima in Fuschl on 23rd February, 1941. A report of that conference was forwarded by Ribbentrop to certain German diplomats in the field for their strictly confidential and purely personal information. This report we now have. It is Document 1834-PS. I offer it in evidence as Exhibit USA 129, the original German document.

On Page 2 of the English translation, Ribbentrop tells Oshima the reason for the Pact with the U.S.S.R. That is Page 4 of the German document.

"Then when it came to war the Fuehrer decided on a treaty with Russia - as a necessity for avoiding a two- front war."

In view of the spirit of opportunism which motivated the Nazis in entering into this solemn pledge of arbitration and non-aggression, it is not very surprising to find that they regarded it, as they did all treaties and pledges, as binding on them only so long as it was expedient for them to be bound. That they did so regard it is evidenced by the fact that even while the campaign in the West was still in progress, they began to consider the possibility of launching a war of aggression against the U.S.S.R.

In a speech to the Reich and Gauleiters at Munich in November, 1943, which is set forth in our Document L-172, already in evidence as Exhibit USA 34, the defendant Jodl admitted - and I shall read from Page 7 of the English translation, which is at Page 15 of the original German text:-

> "Parallel with all these developments realisation was steadily growing of the danger drawing constantly nearer from the Bolshevik East - that danger which has been only too little perceived in Germany and of late, for diplomatic reasons, had deliberately to be ignored.

> However, the Fuehrer himself has always kept this danger steadily in view and even as far back as during the Western Campaign had informed me of his fundamental decision to take steps against this danger the moment our military position made it at all possible."

At the time this decision was made, however, the Western campaign was still in progress, and so any action in the East necessarily had to be postponed for the time being. On 22nd June, 1940, however, the Franco-German armistice was signed at Compiegne, and the campaign in the West, with the exception of the war against Britain, came to an end. The view that Germany's key to political and economic domination lay in the elimination of the U.S.S.R. as a political factor and in the acquisition of "Lebensraum" at her expense, had long been basic in Nazi ideology. As we have seen, this idea had never been completely forgotten even while the war in the West was in progress. Now, flushed with the recent success of their arms, and yet keenly conscious of both their failure to defeat Britain and the needs of their armies for food and raw, materials, the Nazis began serious consideration of the means for achieving their traditional ambition by conquering the Soviet Union.

The situation in which Germany now found herself made such action appear both desirable and practical. As early as August, 1940, General Thomas received a hint from the defendant Goering that planning for a campaign against the Soviet Union was already under way. Thomas at that time was the Chief of the Wirtschaftsruestungsamt of the O.K.W.

I should, perhaps, mention that this office is generally referred to in the German documents by the abbreviation WR. RUE.

General Thomas tells of receiving this information from Goering in his draft of a work entitled Basic Facts for a History of German War and Armament Economy, which he prepared during the summer of 1944. This book is our Document 2353-PS, and has already been admitted into evidence as Exhibit USA 35. I am sorry, it was marked that for identification purposes. I now offer it in evidence as Exhibit USA 35.

On Pages 313 to 315 of this work, Thomas discusses the Russo- German Trade Agreement of 1939 and relates how, since the Soviets were delivering quickly and well under this agreement and were requesting war materials in return, there was much pressure in Germany until early in 1940 for increased delivery on the part of the Germans. However, at Page 315, he has the following to say about the change of heart expressed by the German leaders in August, 1940. I read from Page 9 of the English translation:

> "On 14th August, the Chief of the Wirtschaftsruestungsamt, during a conference with Reichsmarshal Goering, was informed that the

Fuehrer desired punctual delivery to the Russians only until spring 1941. Later on we were to have no further interest in completely satisfying the Russian demands. This illusion moved the Chief of the Wirtschaftsruestungsamt to give priority to matters concerning Russian war economy."

I shall refer to this statement again later when I discuss the preparation for the economic exploitation of Soviet territory expected to be captured. At that time, too, I shall introduce evidence which will show that in November, 1940, Goering informed Thomas that a campaign was planned against the U.S.S.R.

Preparations for so large an undertaking as an invasion of the Soviet Union necessarily entailed, even these many months in advance of the date of execution, certain activity in the East in the way of construction projects and strengthening of forces. Such activity could not be expected to pass unnoticed by the Soviet Intelligence Service. Counter-intelligence measures were obviously called for.

In an O.K.W. directive signed by the defendant Jodl and issued to the Counter-Intelligence Service abroad on 6th September, 1940, such measures were ordered. This directive is Document 1229-PS and I offer it in evidence as Exhibit USA 130, a photostat of the captured German document. This directive pointed out that the activity in the East must not be permitted to create the impression in the Soviet Union that an offensive was being prepared, and outlined the line for the counter-intelligence people to take to disguise this fact. The text of the directive indicates by implication the extent of the preparations already under way, and I should like to read it to the Tribunal:-

"The Eastern territory will be manned more strongly in the weeks to come. By the end of October the status shown on the enclosed map is supposed to be reached.

These regroupings must not create the impression in Russia that we are preparing an offensive in the East. On the other hand, Russia will realise that strong and highly trained German troops are stationed in the Government General, in the Eastern Provinces, and in the Protektorat. She should draw the conclusion that we can at any time protect out interests - especially in the Balkans - with strong forces against Russian seizure.

For the work of our own intelligence service as well as for the answer to questions of the Russian Intelligence Service, the following directives apply:

1. The respective total strength of the German troops in the East is to be veiled as far as possible by giving news about a frequent change of the army units there. This change is to be explained by movements into training camps, regroupings.

2. The impression is to be created that the centre of the massing of troops is in the Southern part of the Government, in the Protektorat and in Austria, and that the massing in the North is relatively unimportant.

3. When it comes to the equipment situation of the units, especially of the armoured divisions, things are to be exaggerated, if necessary.

4. By suitable news the impression is to be created that the anti-aircraft protection in the East has been increased considerably

237

after the end of the campaign in the West, and that it continues to be increased with captured French material for all important targets.

5. Concerning improvements on railroads, roads, aerodromes, etc., it is to be stated that the work is kept within normal limits, is needed for the improvement of the newly-won Eastern territories, and serves primarily economical traffic.

The Supreme Command of the Army (O.K.H.) decides to what extent correct details, i.e., numbers of regiments, manning of garrisons, etc., will be made available to the defence for purposes of counter espionage.

The Chief of the Supreme Command of the Armed Forces. By order of

(signed) JODL".

Early in November, 1940, Hitler reiterated his previous orders, and called for a continuation of preparations, promising further and more definite instructions as soon as this preliminary work produced a general outline of the Army's operational plan. This order was contained in a top secret directive from the Fuehrer's headquarters, No. 18, dated 12th November, 1940, signed by Hitler and initialled by Jodl. It is Document 444-PS in our numbered series and is already in evidence as Exhibit GB 116.

The directive begins by saying:

"The preparatory measures of Supreme Headquarters for the prosecution of the war in the near future are to be made along the following lines .."

It then outlines plans for the various theatres and the policy regarding relations with other countries and says, regarding the U.S.S.R. - and I read now from Page 3, Paragraph No. 5, of the English translation:

"Political discussions have been initiated with the aim of clarifying Russia's attitude for the time being. Irrespective of the results of these discussions, all preparations for the East which have already been verbally ordered will be continued.

Instructions on this will follow as soon as the general outline of the army's operational plans have been submitted to, and approved, by me."

On 5th December, 1940, the Chief of the General Staff of the Army, at that time General Halder, reported to the Fuehrer concerning the progress of the plans for the coming operation against the U.S.S.R. A report of this conference with Hitler is contained in captured Document 1799-PS. This is a folder containing many documents, all labelled annexes and all bearing on "Fall Barbarossa," the plan against the U.S.S.R. This folder was discovered in the War Diary of the Wehrmacht Fuehrungstab and was apparently an enclosure to that diary.

The report I am here referring to is Annex No. I, and is dated December, 1940.

I now offer in evidence Document 1799-PS as Exhibit USA 131. I should also like to read into the record a few sentences from the report of 5th December, 1940, as they indicate the state of the planning for this act of aggression, six and a- half months before it occurred.

"Report to the Fuehrer on 5th December, 1940.

"The Chief of the General Staff of the Army then reported about the planned operation in the East. He expanded at first on the geographical fundamentals. The main war industrial centres are in the Ukraine, in Moscow and in Leningrad."

Then, omitting a few sentences.

"The Fuehrer declares that he has agreed with the discussed operational plans and adds the following:

The most important goal is to prevent the Russians withdrawing on a closed front. The Eastward advance should be combined until the Russian Air Force becomes unable to attack the territory of the German Reich and on the other hand the German Air Force will be enabled to conduct raids to destroy Russian war industrial territory. In this way, we should be able to achieve the annihilation of the Russian Army and to prevent its regeneration. The first commitment of the forces should take place in such a way as to make the annihilation of strong enemy units possible."

Then, again omitting some passages.

"It is essential that the Russians should not take up positions in the rear again. The number of 130 to 140 divisions as planned for the entire operation is sufficient."

THE PRESIDENT: Would that be a good time to break off?

MR. ALDERMAN: Very convenient, sir.

THE PRESIDENT: Then we shall not sit in open session tomorrow. We will sit again on Monday at 10 o'clock.

[The Tribunal adjourned until 10th December, 1945, at 1000 hours.]

Sixteenth Day:
Monday, 10 December 1945

THE PRESIDENT: The Tribunal has received a letter from Dr. Dix on behalf of the Defendant Schacht. In answer to that the Tribunal wishes the defendants' counsel to know that they will be permitted to make one speech only in accordance with Article 24 (h) of the Charter, and this speech will be at the conclusion of all the evidence.

At the conclusion of the case for the Prosecution, the defendants' counsel win be invited to submit to the Tribunal the evidence they propose to call; but they will be strictly confined to the names of the witnesses and the matters to which their evidence will be relevant, and this submission must not be in the nature of a speech. Is that clear? In case there should be any misunderstanding, what I have just said will be posted up on the board in the defendants' Counsel Room so that you can study it there.

MR. ALDERMAN: May it please the Tribunal, when the Tribunal rose Friday, I had just reached the point in my discussion of aggression against the U.S.S.R. where, with the campaign in the West at an end, the Nazi conspirators had begun the development of their plans to attack the Soviet Union. Preliminary high level planing and action was in progress. Hitler had indicated earlier in November that more detailed and definite instructions would be issued. These would be issued as soon as the general outline of the Army's operational plans had been submitted to him and approved by him. We had thus reached the point in the story indicated on the outline submitted last Friday as Part 3 of the Plan Barbarossa.

By the 18th of December 1940, the general outline of the Army's operational plan having been submitted to Hitler, the basic strategical directive to the High Command of the Army, Navy, and the Air Force for Barbarossa-Directive Number 21-was issued. This directive, which for the first time marks the plan to invade the Soviet Union, was specifically referred to in an order although the order was classified top secret. It also marked the first use of the code word Barbarossa to denote this operation.

The directive is Number 446-PS, and was offered in evidence in the course of my opening statement as Exhibit USA-31. Since it was fully discussed at that time, it is, I believe, sufficient now merely to recall to the Tribunal two or three of the most significant sentences in that document. Most of these sentences appear on Page 1 of the English translation. One of the most significant, I believe, is this sentence with which the order begins:

> "The German Armed Forces must be prepared to crush Soviet Russia in a quick campaign even before the end of the war with England."

On the same page it is stated:

> "Preparations requiring firing more time to start are, if this has not yet been done, to begin presently and are to be completed by 15 May 1941. Great caution has to be exercised that the intention of the attack mill not be recognized."

The directive then outlines the broad strategy on which the intended invasion was to proceed and the parts that the various services (Army, Navy, and Air Force) were to play therein, and calls for oral reports to Hitler by the Commanders-in-chief, closing as follows:

"V." - that is on Page 2 - "I am expecting the reports of the commanders-in-chief on their further plans based on this letter of instructions.

"The preparations planned by all branches of the Armed Forces are to be reported to me through the High Command, also in regard to their time."

Signed by Hitler, and initialed by Jodl, Keitel, Warlimont, and one illegible name.

It is perfectly clear both from the contents of the order itself as well as from its history, which I have outlined, that this directive was no mere planning exercise by the staff. It was an order to prepare for an act of aggression, which was intended to occur and which actually did occur.

The various services which received the order certainly understood it as an order to prepare for action, and did not view it as a hypothetical staff problem. This is plain from the detailed planning and preparation which they immediately undertook in order to implement the general scheme set forth in this basic directive.

So we come to the military planning and preparation for the implementation of Plan Barbarossa. The Naval war Diary for 13 January 1941 indicates the early compliance of the OKM with that part of Directive Number 21 which ordered progress in preparation to be reported to Hitler through the High Command of the Armed Forces. This entry in the War Diary is Document C-35 in our numbered series, and I offer it in evidence as Exhibit USA-132.

This document contains a substantial amount of technical information concerning the Navy's part in the coming campaign and the manner in which it was preparing itself to play the part. I feel, however, that it will be sufficient for the establishment of our point that the Navy was actively preparing for the attack at this early date, to read only a small portion of the entry into the record, beginning on Page 1 of the English translation, which is Page 401 of the Diary itself. The entry reads:

"30 January 1941. Page 401 of the diary. 7. Talk by Ia about the plans and preparations for the Barbarossa Case to be submitted to the High Command of Armed Forces." '

I should note that "Ia" is in this case the abbreviation for a deputy chief of naval operations. Then follows a list of the Navy's objectives in the war against Russia. Under the latter many tasks for the Navy are listed, but I think one is sufficiently typical to give the Tribunal an idea of all. I quote from the top of Page 2 of the English translation:

"II. Objectives of War Against Russia ....

"d) To harass the Russian fleet by surprise blows as: 1) Lightning-like actions at the outbreak of the war by air force units against strong points and combat vessels in the Baltic, Black Sea, and Polar Sea."

The purpose of the offer of this document is merely that it indicates the detailed thinking and planning which was being carried out to implement Barbarossa almost six months before the operation actually got under way. It is but another piece in the mosaic of evidence which demonstrates beyond question of doubt that the invasion of the Soviet Union was one of the most coldbloodedly premeditated attacks on a neighboring power in the history of the world. Similarly the Naval War Diary for the month of February contains at least several references to the planning and preparation for the coming campaign. Extracts of such references are contained in Document W33, which I am now offering in evidence as Exhibit USA-133.

I think it will be sufficient to quote for the record as typical the entry for 19 February 1941, which appears at Page 3 of the English translation and at Page 248 of the Diary itself.

"In regard to the impending operation Barbarossa for which all S-boats in the Baltic will be needed, a transfer -can only be considered after conclusion of the Barbarossa operations."

On the 3rd of February 1941 the Fuehrer held a conference to assess the progress thus far made in the planning for Barbarossa. The conference also discussed the plans for "Sonnenblume," which was the code name for. the North African operation-"Sunflower." Attending this conference were, in addition to Hitler: The Chief of the Supreme Command of the Armed Forces, the Defendant Keitel; the Chief of the Armed Forces Operations Staff, the Defendant Jodl; the Commander-in-Chief of the Army, Brauchitsch; the Chief of the Army General Staff, Halder; as well as several others, including Colonel Schmundt, Hitler's Adjutant.

A report of this conference is contained in our Document Number 872-PS, which I now offer as Exhibit USA-134.

During the course of this conference the Chief of the Army General Staff gave a long report about enemy strength as compared with their own strength and the general overall operational plans for the invasion. This report was punctuated at various intervals by comments from the Fuehrer.

At Page 4 of the English translation of the conference plan, which is at Page 6 of the German original, there is an interesting extract, which, although written in a semi-shorthand, is at least sufficiently clear to inform us that elaborate timetables had already been set out for the deployment of troops as well as for industrial operations. I quote:

"The intended time period was discussed with a plan: 1st Deployment Staffel (Aufmarschstaffel) transfer now, front Germany - East; 2nd Deployment Staffel (Aufmarschstaffel) from the middle of March will give up three divisions for reinforcement in the West. Army Groups and Army High Commands are being withdrawn from the West. There are already considerable reinforcements though still in the rear area. From now on, 'Attila'" - I might state here parenthetically that this was the code word for the operation for the occupation of Unoccupied France - "'Attila' can be carried out only under difficulties. Industrial traffic is hampered by transport movements. From the middle of April, Hungary will be approached about the march-through. Three deployment staffels from the middle of April. 'Felix' is now no longer possible, as the main part of the artillery is being entrained." - "Felix" was the name for the proposed operation against Gibraltar.

"In industry the full capacity timetable is in force. No more camouflage. Fourth Deployment Echelon, from 25. IV to 15. V, withdraws considerable forces from the West ('Seelowe' can no longer be carried out)."-"Seelowe" (or Sea Lion) was a code word for the planned operation against England and "Marita," which we shall see a little later in the quotation, was the code word for the action against Greece.-"The concentration of troops in the East is clearly apparent. The full capacity timetable is maintained. The complete picture of the disposition of forces on the map shows 8 Marita divisions.

"Commander-in-Chief, Army, requests that he no longer have to assign 5 control divisions for this; but might hold them ready as reserves for commander in the West.

"Fuehrer: 'When Barbarossa commences the world will hold its breath and make no comment.'"

This much, I believe, when read with the conference conclusions, which I shall read in a moment, is sufficient to show that the Army as well as the Navy regarded Barbarossa as an action directive and were far along with their preparations even as early as February 1941-almost 5 months prior to 22 June, the date the attack was actually launched. The conference report summarized the conclusions of the conference, insofar as they affected Barbarossa, as follows; I am now reading from Page 6 of the English translation, which is on Page 7 of the German:

"Conclusions:-

1. 'Barbarossa'

(a) The Fuehrer on the whole was in agreement with the operational plan. When it is being carried out, it must be remembered that the main aim is to gain possession of the Baltic States and Leningrad.

(b) The Fuehrer desires that the operation map and the plan of the disposition of forces be sent to him as soon as possible.

(c) Agreements with neighbouring States, who are taking part, may not be concluded until there is no longer any necessity for camouflage. The exception is Roumania with regard to the reinforcing of the Moldau.

(d) It must, at all costs, be possible to carry out 'Attila.'

(e) The strategic concentration for 'Barbarossa' will be camouflaged as a feint for 'Seeloewe' and the subsidiary measure 'Marita'."

On 13th March 1941 the Defendant Keitel signed an operational directive to Fuehrer Order Number 21, which was issued in the form of "Directives for Special Areas." This detailed operational order is Number 447-PS in our numbered series, and I now offer it in evidence as Exhibit USA-135.

This order which was issued more than 3 months in advance of the attack indicates how complete were the plans on practically every phase of the operation. Section I of the directive is headed, "Area of Operations and Executive Power," and outlines who was to be in control of what and where. It states that while the campaign is in progress in territory through which the Army is advancing, the Supreme Commander of the Army has the executive power. During this period, however, the Reichsfuehrer SS is entrusted with "special tasks." This assignment is discussed in Paragraph 2b, which appears on Page 1 of the English translation and reads as follows:

"b) In the area of operations of the Army the Reichsfuehrer SS is, on behalf of the Fuehrer, entrusted with special tasks for the preparation of the political administration-tasks which result from the struggle which has to be carried out between two opposing political systems. Within the realm of these tasks the Reichsfuehrer SS shall act independently and under his own responsibility. The executive power invested in the Supreme Commander of the Army (OKH) and in agencies determined by him shall not be affected by this. It is the responsibility of the Reichsfuehrer SS that through the execution of his tasks military operations shall not be disturbed. Details shall be arranged directly through the OKH with the Reichsfuehrer SS."

The order then states that in time political administration will be set up under Commissioners of the Reich, and discusses the relationship of these officials to the Army. This is contained in Paragraph 2c and Paragraph 3, parts of which I should like to read:

"c) As soon as the area of operations has reached sufficient depth, it is to be limited in the rear. The newly occupied territory in the rear of the area of operations is to be given its own political administration. For the present it is to be divided on the basis of nationality and according to the positions of the Army groups into North (Baltic countries), Center (White Russia), and South (Ukraine). In these territories the political administration is taken care of by Commissioners of the Reich who receive their orders from the Fuehrer.

"3) For the execution of all military tasks within the areas under the political administration in the rear of the area of operations, commanding officers who are responsible to the Supreme Commander of the Armed Forces (OKW) shall be in command.

"The commanding officer is the supreme representative of the Armed Forces in the respective areas and the bearer of the military sovereign rights. He has the tasks of a territorial commander and the rights of a supreme Army commander or a commanding general. In this capacity he is responsible primarily for the following tasks:

"a) Close co-operation with the Commissioner of the Reich in order to support him in his political tasks; b) exploitation of the Country and securing its economic values for use by German industry."

The directive also outlines the responsibility for the administration of economy in the conquered territory, a subject I will develop more fully later in my presentation. This provision is also in Section I, Paragraph 4, which I shall read:

"4) The Fuehrer has entrusted the uniform direction of the administration of economy in the area of operations and in the territories of political administration to the Reich Marshal, who has delegated the Chief of the 'Wi Ru Amt.' with the execution of the task. Special orders on that-will come from the O.K.W./Wi./Rue/Amt."

The second section deals with matters of personnel, supply, and . . .

THE PRESIDENT: Mr. Alderman, will you tell us at some time who these people are? Who is the Reich Marshal?

MR. ALDERMAN: The Reich Marshal is the Defendant Goering.

THE PRESIDENT: And who was the Reichsfuehrer of the SS at that time?

MR. ALDERMAN: Himmler.

THE PRESIDENT: Himmler?

MR. ALDERMAN: Yes.

The second section deals with matters of personnel, supply, and communication traffic, and I shad not read it here.

Section III of the order deals with the relations with certain other countries, and states in part as follows-I am reading from Page 3 of the English translation:

"III. Regulations regarding Romania, Slovakia, Hungary, and Finland.

"9) The necessary arrangements with these countries shall be made by the OKW together with the Foreign Office and according to the wish of the respective high commands. In case it should become necessary during the course of the operations to grant special rights, applications for this purpose are to be submitted to the OKW."

The document closes with a section regarding Sweden, which is also on Page 3 of the English Translation:

"IV. Directives regarding Sweden.

"12) Since Sweden can only become a transient area for troops, no special authority is to be granted to the commander of the German troops. However, he is entitled and compelled to secure the immediate protection of railroad transports against sabotage and attacks.

"The Chief of the High Command of the Armed Forces, '- signed -"Keitel."

As was hinted in the original Barbarossa order, Directive Number 21, which I discussed earlier, the plan originally contemplated that the attack would take place about the 15th of May 1941. In the meantime, however, the Nazi conspirators found themselves involved in a campaign in the Balkans, and were forced to delay Barbarossa for a few weeks. Evidence of this postponement is found in a document, which bears our Number C-170. This document has been identified by the Defendant Raeder as a compilation of official extracts from the Naval War Staff War Diary. It was prepared by naval archivists who had access to the Admiralty files, and contains file references to the papers which were the basis for each entry.

I offer that document in evidence as Exhibit USA-136.

Although I shall refer to this document again later, I should like at present to read only an item which appears in the second paragraph of Item 142 on Page 19 of the English translation and which is in the text in a footnote on Page 26 in the German original. This item is dated 3 April 1941, and reads as follows:

"Balkan operation delay; Barbarossa now in about 5 weeks. Ail measures which can be construed as offensive actions are to be stopped according to the Fuehrer's order."

By the end of April, however, things were sufficiently straightened out to permit the Fuehrer to definitely set D-Day as the 22d of June-more than 7 weeks away. Document Number 873-PS in our series is a top-secret report of a conference with the Chief of the Section "Landesverteidigung" of the "Wehrmacht Fuehrungsstab" on April 30, 1941. I now offer that document in evidence as Exhibit USA-137.

I think it will be sufficient to read the first two paragraphs of this report:

"1) Timetable Barbarossa. The Fuehrer has decided:

"Action Barbarossa begins on 22 June. From 23 May maximal troop movements performance schedule. At the beginning of operations the OKH reserves will have not yet reached the appointed areas.

"2) Proportion of actual strength in the Plan Barbarossa:

"Sector North, German and Russian forces approximately of the same strength; Sector Middle, great German superiority; Sector South, Russian superiority."

Early in June, practically 3 weeks before D-Day, preparations for the attack were so complete that it was possible for the High Command to issue an elaborate timetable showing in great detail the disposition and missions of the Army, Navy, and Air Force.

This timetable is Document Number C-39 in our series, and I offer it in evidence now as Exhibit USA-138.

This document was prepared in 21 copies, and the one offered here was the third copy which was given to the High Command of the Navy; Page 1 is in the form of a transmittal, and reads as follows:

"Top secret; Supreme Command of the Armed Forces; Or. 44842/41 top military secret WFSt/Abt. L (I Op.); Fuehrer's headquarters; for chiefs only, only through officer; 21 copies; I Op. 00845/41; received 6 June; no enclosures.

"The Fuehrer has authorized the appended timetable as a foundation for further preparations for Plan Barbarossa. If alterations should be necessary during execution, the Supreme Command of the Armed Forces must be informed.

"Chief of Supreme Command of the Armed Forces" - signed - Keitel."

I shall not bother to read to you the distribution list which indicates Mere the 21 copies went.

THE PRESIDENT: Mr. Alderman, the Tribunal does not think it necessary that you should read all those preliminary matters at the head of these documents, "top secret," "only through officer," and then the various reference numbers and file information when you give identification of a document.

MR. ALDERMAN: Yes, Sir.

The next two pages of the document are in the form of a text outlining the state of preparations as of the 1st of June 1941. The outline is in six paragraphs covering the status on that date under six headings: General, Negotiations with friendly states, Army, Navy, Air Force, and Camouflage.

I think it unnecessary to read into the record any of this textual material. The remainder of the paper is in tabular form with seven columns headed from left to right at the top of each page: Date, Serial number, Army, Air Force, Navy, OKW, Remarks. Most interesting among the items appearing on this chart . . .

THE PRESIDENT: Mr. Alderman, will you read the first paragraph, for that seems to be important. There are two lines there.

MR. ALDERMAN: Yes.

THE PRESIDENT: The heading "General" on Page 2.

MR. ALDERMAN: Yes, Sir.

"1. General. The timetable for the maximum massing of troops in the East mill be put into operation on the 22d of May."

THE PRESIDENT: Yes.

MR. ALDERMAN: Most interesting among the items appearing on this chart, in my opinion, are those appearing on Pages 9 and 10. These are at Page 8 of the German version. At the bottom of Page 9 it is provided in the columns for Army, Navy, and Air Force-and I quote:

"Up to 1300 hours is latest time at which operation can be cancelled."

Under the column headed OKW appears the note that-and again I quote:

"Cancelled by code word 'Altona' or further confirmation of start of attack by code word 'Dortmund' "

In the Remarks column appears the statement that:

"Complete absence of camouflage of formation of Army point of main effort, concentration of armor and artillery must be reckoned with."

The second entry on Page 10 of the chart for the 22d of June, under Serial number 31, gives a notation which cuts across the columns for the Army, Air Force, Navy, and OKW, and provides as follows, under the heading:

"Invasion Day. X-Hour for the start of the invasion by the Army and crossing of the frontier by the Air Forces: 0330 hours."

In the Remarks column, it states that:

"Amy assembly independent of any lateness in starting on the part of the Air Force owing to weather."

The other parts of the chart are similar in nature to those quoted and give, as I have said, great detail concerning the disposition and missions of the various components of the Armed Forces.

On 9 June 1941 the order of the Fuehrer went out for final reports on Barbarossa to be made in Berlin on 14 June 1941, which was just 8 days before D-Day. This order is signed by Hitler's Adjutant, Schmundt, and is C-78 in our numbered series of documents. I offer it in evidence now as Exhibit USA-139.

I read from Page 1 the matter under the heading "Conference Barbarossa":

"1. The Fuehrer and Supreme Commander of the Armed Forces has ordered reports on Barbarossa by the commanders of Army groups, armies, and naval and air commanders of equal rank.

"2. The reports will be made on Saturday, 14 June 1941, at the Reich Chancellery, Berlin.

"3. Timetable:

"a) 1100 hours, "Silver Fox"; b) 1200 hours-1400 hours, Army Group South; c) 1400 hours-1530 hours, lunch party for all participants in conference; d) from 1530 hours, Baltic, Army Group North, Army Group Center, in this order."

It is signed by Schmundt.

There is attached a list of participants and the order in which they will report which I shall not read. The list includes, however, a large number of the members of the Defendant High Command and General Staff group as of that date. Among those to participate were, of course, the Defendants Goering,

Keitel, Jodl, and Raeder.

I believe that the documents which I have introduced and quoted from are more than sufficient to establish conclusively the premeditation and cold-blooded calculation which marked the military preparations for the invasion of the Soviet Union. Starting almost a full year before the commission of the crime, the Nazi conspirators planned and prepared every military detail of their aggression against the Soviet Union with all of that thoroughness and meticulousness which has come to be associated with the German character. Although several of these defendants played specific parts in this military phase of the planning and preparation for the attack, it is natural enough that the leading roles were performed, as we have seen, by the military figures: the Defendants Goering, Keitel, Jodl, and Raeder.

Next, preparation for plunder-plans for the economic exploitation and spoliation of the Soviet Union.

Not only was there detailed preparation for the invasion from a purely military standpoint, but equally elaborate and detailed planning and preparation was undertaken by the Nazi conspirators to ensure that their aggression would prove economically profitable.

A little later in my presentation I shall discuss with the Tribunal the motives which led these conspirators to attack, without provocation, a neighboring power. I shall at that time show that the crime was motivated by both political and economic considerations. The economic basis, however, may be simply summarized at this point as the greed of the Nazi conspirators for the raw material, food, and other supplies which their neighbor possessed and which they conceived of themselves as needing for the maintenance of their war machine. To these defendants such a need was translated indubitably as a right, and they early began planning and preparing with typical care and detail to ensure that every bit of the plunder which it would be possible to reap in the course of their aggression would be exploited to their utmost benefit.

I have already put into the record evidence showing that as early as August of 1940 General Thomas, the chief of the B Group Army, received a hint from the Defendant Goering about a possible attack on the U.S.S.R. which prompted him to begin considering the Soviet war economy. I also said at that time that I would later introduce evidence that in November 1940-8 months before the attack-Thomas was categorically informed by Goering of the planned operation in the East and preliminary preparations were commenced for the economic plundering of the territories to be occupied in the course of such operation. Goering, of course, played the overall leading role in this activity by virtue of his position at the head of the Four Year Plan.

Thomas describes his receipt of the knowledge and this early planning at Page 369 of his draft, which is our Document 2353-PS Introduced earlier as Exhibit USA-35; the part I shall read is at Pages 10 and 11 of the English translation:

"In November 1940 the Chief of Wi Ru together with Secretaries of State Korner, Neumann, Backe, and General Von Hanneken were informed by the Reich Marshal of the action planned in the East.

"By reason of these directives the preliminary preparations for the action in the East were commenced by the office of Wi Ru at the end of 1940.

"The preliminary preparations for the action in the East included first of all the following tasks:

"1. Obtaining of a detailed survey of the Russian armament industry, its location, its capacity, and its associate industries.

"2. Investigation of the capacities of the different big armament centers and their dependency one on the other.

"3. Determining the power and transport system for the industry of the Soviet Union.

"4. Investigation of sources of raw materials and petroleum (crude oil).

"5. Preparation of a survey of industries other than armament industries in the Soviet Union.

"These points were concentrated in one big compilation, 'War Economy of the Soviet Union,' and illustrated with detailed maps."-I am still quoting.-"Furthermore a card index was made containing all the important factories in Soviet Russia and a lexicon of economy in the German-Russian language for the use of the German war economy organization.

"For the processing of these problems a task staff, 'Russia,' was created, first in charge of Lieutenant Colonel Luther and later on in charge of Major General Schubert. The work was carried out according to the directives from the chief of the office, respectively"-I suppose-"by the group of departments for foreign territories"-Ausland-"with the co-operation of all departments, economy offices, and any other persons possessing information on Russia. Through these intensive preparative activities an excellent collection of material was made which proved of the utmost value later on for carrying out the operations and for administering the territories."

That ends the quotation.

By the end of February 1941 this preliminary planning had proceeded to a point where a broader plan of organization was needed, and so General Thomas held a conference with his subordinates on 28 February 1941 to call for such a plan. A memorandum of this conference, classified top secret and dated 1 March 1941, was captured, and is our Document 1317-PS. I now offer it in evidence as Exhibit USA-140. The text of this memorandum reads as follows:

"The general ordered that a broader plan of organization be drafted for the Reich Marshal.

"Essential Points:

"1. The whole organization to be subordinate to the Reich Marshall Purpose: Support and extension of the measures of the Four Year Plan.

"2. The organization must include everything concerning war economy, excepting only food which is said to be made already a special mission of State Secretary Backe.

"3. Clear statement that the organization is to be independent of the military or civil administration. Close co-ordination, but instructions direct from the central office in Berlin.

"4. Scope of activities to be divided into two steps: a) Accompanying the advancing troops directly behind the front lines in order to avoid the destruction of supplies and to secure the removal of important goods; b) Administration of the occupied industrial districts and exploitation of economically complementary districts." I

And then, on the bottom of Page 1:

"5. In view of the extended field of activity the term 'war economy inspection' is to be used in preference to armament inspection.

"6. In view of the great field of activity the organization must be generously equipped and personnel must be correspondingly numerous. The main mission of the organization will consist of seizing raw materials and taking over all important exploitations. For the latter mission reliable persons from German concerns will be interposed suitably from the beginning, since successful operation from the beginning can only be performed by the aid of their experience. (For example: lignite, ore, chemistry, petroleum).

"After the discussion of further details Lieutenant Colonel Luther was instructed to make an initial draft of such an organization within a week.

"Close co-operation with the individual sections in the building is essential. An officer must still be appointed for the Wi and Ru with whom the operational staff can remain in constant contact. Wi is to give each section chief and Lieutenant Colonel Luther a copy of the new plan regarding Russia.

"Lieutenant General Schubert is to be asked to be in Berlin the second half of next week. Also, the four officers who are ordered to draw up the individual armament inspections are to report to the office chief at the end of the week. signed- Hamann."

Hamann, who signed the report, is listed among those attending as a captain and apparently the junior officer present, so presumably it fell naturally enough to Hamann to prepare the notes on the conference. The authority and mission of this organization which Thomas was organizing at the direction of Goering was clearly recognized by Keitel in his operational order of 13 March 1941. This order is Number 447-PS, and I have already offered it in evidence earlier as Exhibit USA-135. At that time I quoted the paragraph in The order in which it was stated that the Fuehrer had entrusted the uniform direction of the administration of economy in the areas of operation and political administration to the Reich Marshal who in turn had delegated his authority to the Chief of the Wi Ru Amt.

The organizational work called for by General Thomas at the meeting on 28 February apparently proceeded apace, and on 29 April 1941 a conference was held with various branches d the Armed Forces to explain the organizational set-up of the Economic Staff "Oldenburg.', Oldenburg was the code name given to this economic counterpart of Plan Barbarossa. A report of this conference is captured Document Number 1157-PS, and I now offer it in evidence as Exhibit USA-141. Section 1 of this memorandum deals with the general organization of Economic Staff Oldenburg as it had developed by this time, and I should like to read most of that section into the record. The report begins:

"Conference with the Branches of the Armed Forces at 1000 hours on Tuesday, 29th April 1941.

"1. Welcome. Purpose of the meting: Introduction to the

organizational structure of the economic section of the undertaking Barbarossa-Oldenburg.

"As already known, the Fuehrer, contrary to previous procedure, has ordered for this drive the uniform concentration in one hand of all economic operations and has entrusted the Reich Marshal with the overall direction of the economic administration in the area of operations and in the areas under political administration.

"The Reich Marshal has delegated this function to an Economic General Staff working under the director of the Economic Armament Office (Chief, Wi Ru Amt).

"Under the Reich Marshal and the Economic General Staff the supreme central authority in the area of the drive itself is the"-and then a heading-"Economic Staff Oldenburg for special duties under the command of Lieutenant General Schubert. His subordinate authorities, geographically subdivided, are: 5 economic inspectorates, 23 economic commands, and 12 district offices which are distributed among important places within the area of the economic command.

"These offices are used in the military rear area. The idea is that in the territory of each army group an economic inspectorate is to be established at the seat of the commander of the military rear area, and that this inspectorate will supervise the economic exploitation of the territory.

"A distinction must be made between the military rear area and the bathe area proper on the one hand, and the rear area of the army on the other hand. In the latter, economic matters are dealt with by the Group IV Economy"-IV Wi- "of the Army Headquarters Command, that is, the liaison officer of the Economic Armament Office within the Supreme Command of the Armed Forces assigned to the Army Headquarters Command. For the battle area he has attached to him technical battalions, reconnaissance and recovery troops for raw materials, mineral oil, agricultural machinery, in particular, tractors and means of production.

"In the rear area of the Army situated between the battle and the military rear area, Group IV Economy with the various field commands are placed at the disposal of the liaison officer of the Economic Armament Office for the support of the specialists of the Army Headquarters Command, who are responsible for supplying the troops from the country's resources and for preparing the subsequent general economic exploitation.

"While these units move with the troops, economic inspectorates, economic commands and their sub-offices remain established in the locality.

"The new feature inherent in the organization under the command of the Economic Staff Oldenburg is that it does not only deal with military industry but comprises the entire economic field. Consequently all offices are no longer to be designated as offices of the military industries or armaments but quite generally as economic inspectorates, economic commands, *et cetera*.

"This also corresponds with the internal organization of the individual offices which, from the Economic Staff Oldenburg down to the economic commands, requires a standard subdivision into three large groups, i. e. Group M, dealing with troop requirements, armaments, industrial transport organization; Group L, which concerns itself with all questions of feeding and agriculture, and Group W. which is in charge of the entire field of trade and industry, including raw materials and supplies; further, questions of forestry, finance and banking, enemy property, commerce and exchange of commodities, and manpower allocation.

"Secretary of State Backe is appointed Commissioner for Food and Agriculture in the General Stab; the problems falling within the field of activities of Group W are dealt with by General Von Hanneken."

The remainder of the document deals with local subdivisions, personnel and planing problems, and similar details, which I think it unnecessary to put into the record.

These documents portray vividly the coldly calculated method with which those Nazis prepared months in advance to rob and loot their intended victim. They show that the conspirators not only planned to stage a wanton attack on a neighbor to whom they had pledged security, but they also intended to strip that neighbor of his food, his factories, and all his means of livelihood.

As I shall point out more fully later when I discuss the question of motivation, these men made their plans for plunder being fully aware that to carry them out would necessarily involve ruin and starvation for millions of the inhabitants of the Soviet Union.

THE PRESIDENT: This would be a good time to adjourn.

[A recess was taken.]

MR. ALDERMAN: May the Tribunal please, I have been informed by the interpreters that I have been speaking at a great speed this morning, so I shall try to temper the speed.

Next, the politics of destruction; preparation for the political phase of the aggression. As I have already indicated and as I shall develop more fully later in this discussion, there were both economic and political reasons motivating the action of the conspirators in invading the Soviet Union. I have already discussed the extent of the planning and preparations for the economic side of the aggression. Equally elaborate planning and preparation were engaged in by the conspirators to ensure the effectuation of the political aims of their aggression. It is, I believe, sufficient at this point to describe that political aim as the elimination of the Union of Soviet Socialist Republics as a powerful political factor in Europe and the acquisition of Lebensraum.

For the accomplishment of this purpose the Nazi conspirators selected as their agent the Defendant Rosenberg. As early as the 2d of April 1941 Rosenberg or a member of his staff prepared a memorandum on the U.S.S.R. This memorandum speculates on the possibility of a disagreement with the U.S.S.R. which would result in a quick occupation of an important part of that country. This memorandum then considers what the political goal of such occupation should be and suggests ways for reaching such a goal.

The memorandum is Number 1017-PS in our series, and I offer it in evidence now as Exhibit USA-142.

Beginning with the second paragraph it reads, under the subject "U.S.S.R.":

"A military conflict with the U.S.S.R. will result in an extraordinarily rapid occupation of an important and large section of me U.S.S.R. It is very probable that military action on our part will very soon be followed by the military collapse of me U.S.S.R. The occupation of these areas would then present not so many military as administrative and economic difficulties. Thus arises the first question:

"Is the occupation to be determined by purely military or economic needs respectively, or is the laying of political foundations for a future organization of the area also a factor in determining how far the occupation shall be extended? If so, it is a matter of urgency to fix the political goal which is to be attained, for it will without doubt also have an effect on military operations.

"If the political overthrow of the eastern empire, in the weak condition it would be at the time, is set as the goal of military operations, one may conclude that:

"1) The occupation must comprise areas of vast proportions.

"2) From the very beginning the treatment of individual sections of territory should, in regard to administration as well as economics and ideology, be adapted to the political ends we are striving to attain.

"3) Again, extraordinary questions concerning these vast areas such as, in particular, the ensuring of essential supplies for the continuation of war against England, the maintenance of production which this necessitates, and the great directives for the completely separate areas, should best be dealt with all together in one place.

"It should again be stressed here that, in addition, all the arguments which follow only hold good, of course, once the supplies from the area to be occupied, which are essential to Greater Germany for the continuance of the war, have been assured.

"Anyone who knows the East sees in a map of Russia's population the following national or geographical units:

"(a) Greater Russia, with Moscow as its center; (b) White Russia, with Minsk or Smolensk as its capital; (c) Estonia, Latvia, and Lithuania; (d) The Ukraine and the Crimea, with Kiev as its center; (e) The Don area, with Rostov as its capital; (I) The area of the Caucasus; (g) Russian Central Asia or Russian Turkestan."

The memorandum then proceeds to discuss each of the areas or geographical units in some detail, and I shall not read those pages. At the end of the paper, however, the writer sums up his thoughts and briefly outlines his plan. I should like to read that portion into the record. It is at the bottom of Page 4 of the English translation under the heading "Summary":

"The following systematic constructional plan is evolved from the points briefly outlined here:

"(1) The creation of a central department for the occupied areas of the U.S.S.R. to be confined more or less to war time. Working in agreement with the higher and supreme Reich authorities, it would be the task of this department:

"(a), To issue binding political instructions to the separate administration areas, having in mind the situation existing at the time and the goal which is to be achieved;

"(b) To secure for the Reich supplies essential to the war from all the occupied areas;

"(c) To make preparations for, and to supervise the carrying out in main outline of, the primarily important questions for all areas, as for instance, those of finance and funds, transport, and the production of oil, coal, and food.

"(2) The carrying out of sharply defined decentralization in the separate administration areas, grouped together by race or by reason of political economy for the carrying out of the totally dissimilar tasks assigned to them.

"As against this, an administrative department regulating matters in principle and to be set up on a purely economic basis, as is at present envisaged, might very soon prove to be inadequate and fail in its purpose. Such a central office would be compelled to carry out a common policy for all areas, dictated only by economic considerations, and this might impede the carrying out of the political task and, in view of its being run on purely bureaucratic lines, might possibly even prevent it.

"The question therefore arises whether the opinions which have been set forth should not, purely for reasons of expediency, be taken into consideration from the very beginning when organizing the administration of the territory on a basis of war economy. In view of the vast spaces and the difficulties of administration which arise from that alone, and also in view of the living conditions created by Bolshevism, which are totally different from those of Western Europe, the whole question of the U.S.S.R. would require different treatment from that which has been applied in the individual countries of Western Europe."

THE TRIBUNAL (Mr. Biddle): Is that signed?

MR. ALDERMAN: It is not signed. No, Sir.

THE TRIBUNAL (Mr. Biddle): Is it in the Defendant Rosenberg's handwriting?

MR. ALDERMAN: It was in the Rosenberg file.

THE TRIBUNAL (Mr. Biddle): Is there anything to indicate that he wrote it?

MR. ALDERMAN: No. I said it was evidently prepared by Rosenberg or under his authority. We captured the whole set of Rosenberg files, which constitutes really a large library.

It is evident that the "presently envisaged administration operating on a purely economic basis" to which this memorandum described as having been set up under Goering and General Thomas.

Rosenberg's statement-if this be his statement-of the political purpose of the invasion and his analysis of the achieving of it apparently did not fall on deaf ears. By a Fuehrer order, dated 20 April 1941, Rosenberg was named commissioner for the central control of questions connected with the east European region. This order is part of the correspondence regarding Rosenberg's appointment, which has been given the Number 865-PS in our series. I ask that this file, ad relating to the same subject and consisting of four letters, all of which I shall read or refer to, be admitted in evidence as Exhibit USA-143.

The order itself reads as follows-it is the first item on the English translation of 865-PS:

"I name Reichsleiter Alfred Rosenberg as my commissioner for the central control of questions connected with the east European region. An office, which is to be furnished in accordance with his orders, is at the disposal of Reichsleiter Rosenberg for the carrying out of the duties thereby entrusted to him. The necessary money for this office is to be taken out of the Reich Chancellery Treasury in a lump sum.

"Fuehrer's headquarters, 20th April 1941. The Fuehrer, signed, Adolf Hitler; Reich Minister and Head of Reich Chancellery, signed, Dr. Lammers."

This particular copy of the Fuehrer's order was enclosed in a letter which Dr. Lammers wrote to the Defendant Keitel requesting his co-operation for Rosenberg and asking that Keitel appoint a deputy to work with Rosenberg. This letter reads as follows-it is on the stationery of the Reich Minister and the Head of the Reich Chancellery, Berlin, 21 April 1941. I omit the salutation:

"Herewith I am sending you a copy of the Fuehrer's decree of the 20th of this month by which the Fuehrer appointed Reichsleiter Alfred Rosenberg as his commissioner for the central control connected with the east European region. In this capacity Reichsleiter Rosenberg is to make the necessary preparations for the probable emergency with all speed. The Fuehrer wishes that Rosenberg shall be authorised for this purpose to obtain the closest co-operation of the highest Reich authorities, receive information from them, and summon the representatives of the highest Reich authorities to conferences. In order to guarantee the necessary secrecy of the commission and the measures to be undertaken, for the time being, only those of the highest Reich authorities should be informed on whose co-operation Reichsleiter Rosenberg will primarily depend. They are: The Commissioner for the Four Year Plan" -that is Goering-"the Reich Minister of Economics, and you yourself"-that is Keitel-"Therefore, may I ask you in accordance with the Fuehrer's wishes to place your co-operation at the disposal of Reichsleiter Rosenberg in the carrying out of the task imposed upon him. It is recommended in the interests of secrecy that you name a representative in your office with whom the office of the Reichsleiter can communicate and who, in addition to your usual deputy, should be the only one to whom you should communicate the contents of this letter.

"I should be obliged if you would acknowledge the receipt of this letter.

"Heil Hitler, Yours very sincerely, signed, Dr. Lammers."

In the next letter Keitel writes Lammers acknowledging receipt of his letter and telling of his compliance with the request. Keitel also writes Rosenberg teeing him of the action he has taken. Now, the letter to Dr. Hammers-I shall read the text:

"Dear Reich Minister:

"I acknowledge receipt of the copy of the Fuehrer's decree in which the Fuehrer appointed Reichsleiter Alfred Rosenberg as his commissioner for the central control of questions connected with the east European region. I have named General of the Artillery Jodl, head of the Armed Forces Operational Staff, as my permanent deputy, and Major General Warlimont as his deputy to Reichsleiter Rosenberg."

And the letter to Reichsleiter Rosenberg on the same date:

"The head of the Reich Chancellery has sent me a copy of the Fuehrer's decree, by which he has appointed you his commissioner for the central control of questions connected with the east European region. I have charged General of the artillery Jodl, head of the Armed Forces Operational Staff, and his deputy, Major General Warlimont, with the solving of these questions as far as they concern the Supreme Command of the Armed Forces. How I ask you, as far as your office is concerned, to deal with them only."

Immediately upon receipt of the order from Hitler Rosenberg began building his organization, coffering with the various ministries, issue his instructions, and generally making the detailed plats and preparations necessary to carry out his assigned mission. Although Rosenberg's files, which were captured intact, were crowded with documents evidencing both the extent of the preparation and its purpose, I believe that the citation of a small number white are typical should be sufficient for the Tribunal and the record. All of those I shall now discuss were found in the Defendant Rosenberg's files.

Our document numbered 1030-PS is a memorandum, dated 8 May 1941, entitled, "General Instructions for all Reich Commissioners in the Occupied Eastern Territories." I offer that in evidence as Exhibit USA-144.

In these instructions to his chief henchmen Rosenberg outlines the political aims and purposes of the attack. In the second and third paragraphs of the English translation, which appear on Page 2 of the German, the following remarks appear:

"the only possible political goal of war can be the aim to free the German Reich from the 'grossrussisch' pressure for centuries to come. This does not only correspond with German interests but also with historical justice, for Russian imperialism was in a position to accomplish its policy of conquest and oppression almost unopposed, whilst it threatened Germany again and again. Therefore, the German Reich has to beware of starting a campaign against Russia with a historical injustice, meaning the reconstruction of a great Russian empire, no matter of What kind. On the contrary, all historical struggles of the various nationalities against Moscow and Leningrad have to be scrutinized for their bearing on the situation today. This has been done on the part of the National Socialist movement to correspond to the Leader's political testament as laid down in his book, that now the military and political threat in the East shall be eliminated forever.

"Therefore this huge area must be divided according to its historical and racial conditions into Reich commissions each of which bears within itself a different political aim. The Reich Commission Eastland"-Ostland-"including White Ruthenia, will have the task to prepare, by way of development into a Germanized protectorate, a progressively closer cohesion with Germany. The Ukraine shall become an independent state in alliance with Germany, and Caucasia with the contiguous northern territories a federal state with a German plenipotentiary. Russia proper must put her own house in order for the future. These general viewpoints are explained in the following instructions for each Reich commissioner. Beyond that there are still a few general considerations which possess validity for all Reich commissioners."

The fifth paragraph of the English translation, Page 7 of the German, presents a fascinating rationalization of a contemplated robbery. It reads:

"The German people have achieved, in the course of centuries, tremendous accomplishments in the eastern European area. Nearly all its land and houses were confiscated without indemnification; hundreds of thousands (in the south on the Volga) starved or were deported or, as in the Baltic territories, deprived of the fruits of their cultural work during the past 700 years. The German Reich must proclaim the principle that after the occupation of the Eastern Territories the former German assets are the property of the people of Greater Germany, irrespective of the consent of the former individual proprietors, where the German Reich may reserve the right (assuming that it has not already been done during resettlement) to arrange a just settlement. The manner of compensation and restitution of this national property will be subject to different treatment by each Reich commission."

Document Number 1029-PS in our series is an "Instruction for a Reich Commissioner Ostland." It is typical of the type of instruction which was issued to each of the appointed commissioners (or Kommissars), and is amazingly frank in outlining intentions of the Nazi conspirators toward the country they intended to occupy in the course of their aggression. I offer this document in evidence as Exhibit USA-145. I should like to read into the record the first three paragraphs. It begins:

"All the regions between Narva and Tilsit have constantly been in close relationship with the German people. A 700 year-old history has moulded the inner sympathies of the majority of the races living there in a European direction and has in spite of all Russian threats added this region to the living space of Greater Germany.

"The aim of a Reich commissioner for Estonia, Latvia, Lithuania, and White Ruthenia"-last words added in pencil- "must be to strive to achieve the form of a German Protectorate and then transform the region into part of the Greater German Reich by germanizing racially possible elements, colonizing Germanic races, and banishing undesirable elements. The Baltic Sea must become a Germanic inland sea under the guardianship of Greater Germany.

"For certain cattle-raising products the Baltic region was a land of surplus; and the Reich commissioner must endeavor to make this surplus once more available to the German people and, if possible, to increase it. With regard to the process of germanizing or resettling, the Estonian people are strongly germanized to the extent of 50 percent by Danish, German, and Swedish blood, and can be considered as a kindred nation. In Latvia the section capable of being assimilated is considerably smaller than in Estonia. In this country stronger resistance will have to be rezoned with and banishment on a larger scale will have to be envisaged. A similar development may have to be reckoned with in Lithuania, for here too the immigration of racial Germans is called for In order to promote very extensive germanization (on the East Prussian border)."

Skipping a paragraph, the next paragraph is also interesting and reads as follows:

"The task of a Reich commissioner with his seat of office in Riga will therefore largely be an extraordinarily positive one. A country which 700 years ago was captured by German knights, built up by the Hanseatic League, and by reason of a constant influx of German blood together with Swedish elements was a predominantly germanized land, is to be established as a mighty German borderland. The preliminary cultural conditions are available everywhere; and the German Reich will be able to guarantee the right to a later settlement to all those who have distinguished themselves in this war, to the descendants of those who gave their lives during the war, and also to all who fought in the Baltic campaign, never once lost courage, fought on in the hour of despair, and delivered Baltic civilization from Bolshevism. For the rest the solution of the colonization problem is not a Baltic question but one whim concerns Greater Germany, and it must be settled on these lines."

These two directives are, I think, sufficiently typical of the lot to show the Tribunal the extent of the planning and preparation for this phase of the aggression as well as the political purpose it was hoped would be achieved thereby. However, on 28 June 1941, less than a week after the invasion, Rosenberg himself prepared a full report of his activities since his appointment on the 20th of April. One might almost think he had so meticulously recorded his activities in order to be of assistance to this prosecution.

This report is numbered 1039-PS, and I now offer it in evidence as Exhibit USA-146. To me the most interesting things about this report are its disclosures concerning the number of these defendants who worked with and assisted Rosenberg in the planning and preparation for this phase of the aggression and the extent to which practically all of the ministries and offices of both state and Party are shown to have been involved in this operation The report was found in the Defendant Rosenberg's files; and although it is rather long, it is of sufficient importance in implicating persons, groups, and organizations, that it must, I believe, be read in full in order that it may be made part of the record. It is headed, "Report on the Preparatory Work in Eastern European Territories":

"Immediately after the notification of individual supreme Reich offices regarding the Fuehrer's Decree of 20. 4. 41 a conference with the Chief of the OKW"-Armed Forces High Command-"took place"- That is the Defendant Keitel- "After presentation of the various political aims in the proposed Reich commissions and presentation of personal requirements for the East, the chief of the OKW explained that reservation"-UK-Stellung-"would be too complicated in this case and that this matter could be carried out best by direct assignment"- Abkommandierung-"by command of the Chief of the OKW. General Field Marshal Keitel then issued an appropriate command which established the basis for the coming requirements. He named as deputy and liaison officer General Jodl and Major General Warlimont.

The negotiations which then commenced relative in all questions of the Eastern territory including personal needs"-relative to, I suppose it is "were carried on by the gentlemen of the OKW in collaboration with officials of my office.

"A conference took place with Admiral Canaris to the effect that under the given confidential circumstances my office could in no way deal with any representatives of the people of the east European area. I asked him to do this insofar as the military intelligence required it and then to name persons to me who could count as political personalities, over and above the military intelligence, in order to arrange for their eventual commitment later. Admiral Canaris said that naturally also my wish not to recognize any political groups among the emigrants would be considered by him and that he was planning to proceed in accordance with my indications.

"Later on I informed General Field Marshal Von Brauchitsch and Grossadmiral Raeder about the historical and political conceptions of the Eastern problem. In further conferences we agreed to appoint a representative of my office to the Supreme Commander of the Army, respectively to the Chief Quartermaster, and to the Army groups for questions relative to political configuration and requests of the OKW. In the meantime this has been done.

"Already at the outset there was a discussion with Minister of Economics" -Reichswirtschaftsminister- "Funk"-the Defendant Funk-"who appointed as his permanent deputy Ministerial Director Dr. Schlotterer. Almost daily conferences were then held with Dr. Schlotterer with reference to the war economic intentions of the Economic Operational Staff East. In this connection I had conferences with General Thomas, State Secretary Korner, State Secretary Backe, Ministerial Director Riecke, General Schubert, and others.

"Far-reaching agreement was reached in the eastern questions as regards direct technical work now and in the future. A few problems regarding the general relationship of the proposed Reich ministry toward the Four Year Plan are still open and will be subject, after submission, to the decision of the Fuehrer. 1h principle I declared that I in no way intended to found an economic department in my office; economics would rather be handled substantially and practically by the Reich Marshal"-that is the Defendant Goering-"and the persons appointed by him. However, the two responsible department heads, namely, Ministerial Director Dr. Schlotterer for industrial economy and Ministerial Director Riecke for food economy, would be placed in my office as permanent liaison men to co-ordinate here political aims with the economic necessities in a department which would still have to unite with other persons for such co-ordinating work, depending on labor conditions as they may arise later on (political leadership of labor unions, construction, *et cetera*).

"After notification of the Reich Foreign Minister, the latter appointed Geheimrat Grosskopf as permanent liaison man to my office. For the requested representation in the political department of my of lice (headed by Reichsamtsleiter Dr. Leibbrandt), the Foreign Ministry released Consul General Dr. Brautigam, who is known to me for many years, speaks Russian, and worked for years in Russia. Negotiations, which if necessary will be placed before the Fuehrer, are under way with the Foreign Office regarding its wishes for the assignment of its representatives to the future Reich commissioners (or Kommissars).

"The Propaganda Ministry"-that is Goebbels "appointed State Secretary Gutterer as permanent liaison man, and a complete agreement was reached to the erect that the decisions on all political and other essays, speeches, proclamations, et cetera, would be made in my office; a great number of substantial works for propaganda would be delivered and the papers prepared by the Propaganda Ministry would be modified here, if necessary. The whole practical employment of propaganda will undisputedly be subject to the Reich Ministry of Public Enlightenment and Propaganda. For the sake of closer co-operation the Propaganda Ministry assigns yet another person directly under my department, 'Enlightenment and Press,' and in addition appoints a permanent press liaison man. All these activities have been going on for some time, and without attracting attention to my office in any way this co-ordination on contents and terminology takes place continually every day.

"Thorough discussions took place with Reich Minister Ohnesorge concerning future transmission of communication and setting up of all technical necessities in future occupied territories; with Reich Minister Seldte on the supply of labor forces, with Reich Minister Frick"-that is the Defendant Frick-"(State Secretary Stuckart) in detailed form on the assignment of numerous necessary officials for the commissions. According to the present estimate there will be four Reich commissions as approved by the Fuehrer. I shall propose to the Fuehrer for political and other reasons to set up a suitable number of general commissions (24), main commissions (about 80), and regional commissions (over 900). A general commission would correspond to a former general government; a main commission to a main government.

"A regional commission contains three or four districts"- Kreise-"In view of the huge spaces that is the minimum number which appears necessary for a future civil government or administration. A portion of the officials has already been requested on the basis of the above-named command of the Chief of the OKW."

THE PRESIDENT: Mr. Alderman, speaking for myself I don't understand why it is necessary to read this document in full. You have already shown that there was a plan for dividing Russia up into a number of commissions.

MR. ALDERMAN: Quite true. I should like merely to point out two of three other individual defendants who are referred to in this document and as to whom the document shows that they were in immediate complicity with this whole scheme. The first of those, about three paragraphs further down, the Reich Youth Leader-that is the Defendant Baldur Von Schirach. Then of course Gruppenfuehrer SS Heydrich, about the next paragraph . . .

THE PRESIDENT: Well, he is not a defendant.

MR. ALDERMAN: No, Sir. His organization is, however, if the Tribunal please, charged as a criminal organization.

In the next paragraph, the Defendant Ministerial Director Fritzsche, who worked under Goebbels.

Without a long discussion of further evidence I might summarize the individual implication in this fashion. Those of the individual defendants now on trial which this report personally involves are Keitel, Jodl, Seeder, Funk, Goering, Ribbentrop, Frick, Schirach, and Fritzsche. The organizations involved by this report include the following:

> OKW, OKH, OKM, Ministry of the Interior, Ministry of Economics, Reich Foreign Ministry, Propaganda Ministry, Ministry of Labor, Ministry of Communications, the Reich Physicians' Union, Ministry of Munitions and Armaments, Reich Youth Leadership, Reich Organization Leadership, German Labor Front, the SS, the SA, and the Reich Press Chief.

At a later stage in the Trial, and in other connections, I should like to ask the Tribunal to consider that that document with which I have just been dealing be considered a part of the record to the extent that it involves these individuals.

THE PRESIDENT: I think you can treat it as all being in evidence.

MR. ALDERMAN: At a later stage in the Trial and in other connections, evidence will be introduced concerning the manner in which all of this planing and preparation for the elimination of the Union of Soviet Socialist Republics as a political factor was actually carried out. The planned execution of intelligentsia and other Russian leaders was, for example, but a part of the actual operation of the program to destroy the Soviet Union politically and make impossible its early resurrection as a European power.

Having thus elaborately prepared on every side for the invasion of the Soviet Union, the Nazi conspirators proceeded to carry out their plans; and on 22 June 1941 hurled their armies across the borders of the U.S.S.R. In announcing this act of perfidy to the world Hitler issued a proclamation on the day of the attack. The text of this statement has already been brought to the Tribunal's attention by my British colleagues, and I should like merely to refer to it in passing here by quoting therefrom this one sentence, "I have therefore today decided to give the fate of Europe again into the hands of our soldiers."

This announcement told the world that the die had been cast -the plans darkly conceived almost a full year before and secretly and continuously developed since then, had now been brought to fruition. These conspirators, having carefully and completely planned and prepared this war of aggression, now proceeded to initiate and wage it.

That brings us to the consideration of the motives for the attack. Before going into the positive reasons I should like first to point out that not only was Germany bound by a solemn covenant not to attack the U.S.S.R., but throughout the entire period from August 1939 to the invasion in 1941 the Soviet Union was faithful to its agreements with Germany and displayed no aggressive intentions toward territories of the German Reich. General Thomas, for example, points out in his draft of "Basic Facts for a History of the German War and Armaments Economy," which is our Document Number 2353-PS and which I put in evidence earlier as Exhibit USA-35, that insofar as the German-Soviet Trade Agreement of 11 August 1939 was concerned, the Soviets carried out their deliveries thereunder up to the very end.

Thomas points out that deliveries by the Soviets were usually made quickly and well; and since the food and taw materials being thus delivered were considered essential to the German economy, efforts were made to keep up their side too. However, as preparations for the campaign proceeded, the Nazis cared less about complying with their obligations under that agreement. At Page 315 of his book Thomas says, and I read from Page 9 of the English translation:

"Later on the urgency of the Russian deliveries diminished, as preparations for the campaign in the East were already under way."

By that, clearly he speaks of German deliveries to Russia, not as to what the Russians delivered.

"The Russians carried out their deliveries as planned right up to the start of the attack; even during the last few days transports of indict-rubber from the Far East were completed by express transit trains."

Again at Page 404 this author brings this point out even more forcefully when he states-and I shall read the first paragraph on Page 14 of the English translation:

"In addition to the Italian negotiations until June 1941, the negotiations with Russia were accorded a great deal of attention.

"The Fuehrer issued the directive that, in order to camouflage German troop movements, the orders Russia has placed in Germany must be filled as promptly as possible. Since the Russians only made grain deliveries when the Germans delivered orders placed by the Russians and since, in the case of the individual firms, these deliveries to Russia made it impossible for them to fill orders for the German Armed Forces, it was necessary for the Wi Mu office to enter into numerous individual negotiations with German firms in order to coordinate Russian orders with those of the Germans from the standpoint of priority. In accordance with the wishes of the Foreign Office German industry was instructed to accept all Russian orders even if it were impossible to fill them within the limits of the time set for manufacture and delivery. Since, in May especially, large deliveries had to be made to the Navy, the firms were instructed. to allow the equipment to go through the Russian Acceptance Commission, then however, to make such a detour during its transportation as to make it impossible for it to be delivered over the frontier prior to the beginning of the German attack."

Not only was the Soviet Union faithful to the treaty obligations with Germany but the evidence shows that she had no aggressive intentions toward any German territory. Our Document Number C-170, which is in evidence as Exhibit USA-136, is as I have previously stated, a file on Russo-German relations found in the files of the Naval High Command covering the entire period from the treaty to the attack. The entries in this file demonstrate conclusively the point I have just stated. It will, I think, be sufficient to read to the Tribunal a few entries which include reports from the German Ambassador in Moscow as late as June 1941. I shall read the first entry, 165 on Page 21 of the English translation; that is 4 June:

"Outwardly, no change in the relationship Germany-Russia; Russian deliveries continue to full satisfaction. Russian Government is endeavoring to do everything to prevent a conflict with Germany."

In entry 167 on Page 22 of the English translation, it says: "6 June. Ambassador in Moscow reports . . . Russia will only fight if attacked by

Germany. Situation is considered in Moscow much more serious than up to now. All military preparations have been made quietly-as far as can be recognized, only defensive. Russian policy still strives as before to produce the best possible relationship to Germany." The next one is entry 169, also on Page 22; the date, 7 June: "From the report of the Ambassador in Moscow . . . all observations show that Stalin and Molotov, who alone are responsible for Russian foreign policy, are doing everything to avoid a conflict with Germany. The entire behavior of the Government as well as the attitude of the press, which reports all events concerning Germany in a factual, indisputable manner, support this view. The loyal fulfillment of the economic treaty with Germany proves the same thing."

Now, that is the German Ambassador talking to you.

The reasons, therefore, which led to the attack on the Soviet Union could not have been self-defense or treaty breaches. In truth, no doubt, as has been necessarily implied from the materials presented on planning and preparation, more than one motive entered into the decision of the Nazi conspirators to launch their aggression against the U.S.S.R. All of them, however, appear to blend into one grand motive of Nazi policy. The pattern into which these various reasons impelling the decision to attack may be said to fall is the traditional Nazi ambition for expansion to the East at the expense of the U.S.S.R. This Nazi version of an earlier imperial imperative -the "Drang nach Osten" (or the drive to the East)- had been a cardinal principle of the Nazi Party almost since its birth and rested on the twin bases of political strategy and economic aggrandizement. Politically such action meant the elimination of the powerful country to the east, white might constitute a threat to German ambitions, and acquisition of Lebensraum; while on the economic side, it offered magnificent opportunities for the plunder of vast quantities of food, raw materials, and other supplies, going far beyond any legitimate exploitation under the Geneva Convention principles for military purpose. Undoubtedly the demands of the German war economy for food and raw material served to revive the attractiveness on the economic side of this theory while the difficulties Germany was experiencing in defeating England reaffirmed for the Nazi conspirators the temporarily forgotten Nazi political imperative of eliminating, as a political factor, their one formidable opponent on the continent.

As early as 1923 Hitler outlined this theory in some detail in *Mein Kampf* where he stated, and I quote from Page 641 of the Houghton Mifflin English edition, as follows:

"There are two reasons which induce me to submit to a special examination the relation of Germany to Russia: (1) Here perhaps we are dealing with the most decisive concern of all German foreign affairs; and (2) this question is also the touchstone for the political capacity of the young National Socialist movement to think clearly and to act correctly."

And again at Page 654 of the same edition:

"And so we National Socialists consciously draw a line beneath the foreign policy tendency of our pre-war period. We take up where we broke off 600 years ago. We stop the endless German movement to the south and-west, and turn our gaze toward the land in the East. At long last we break off: the colonial and commercial policy of the pre-war period and shift to the soil policy of the future.

"If we speak of soil in Europe today, we can primarily have in mind only Russia and her vassal border states."

The political portion of this economy or purpose is clearly reflected in the stated purposes of the organization which the Defendant Rosenberg set up to administer the Occupied Eastern Territories. I have already discussed this material and need not repeat it now. In a speech, however, which he delivered 2 days before the attack to the people most interested in the problem of the East' Rosenberg re-stated in his usual somewhat mystic fashion the political basis for the campaign and its inter-relationship with the economic goal. I should like to read a short extract from that speech, which is Document Number 1058-PS and which I now offer in evidence as Exhibit USA-147. The part I read is from Page 9 of the German text:

"The job of feeding the German people stands this year, without a doubt, at the top of the list of Germany's claims in the East; and here the southern territories and the northern Caucasus will have to serve as a balance for the feeding of the German people. We see absolutely no reason for any obligation on our part to feed also the Russian people with the products of that surplus territory. We know that this is a harsh necessity, bare of any feelings. A very extensive evacuation will be necessary, without any doubt, and it is sure that the future will hold very hard years in store for the Russians. A later decision will have to determine to what extent industries can still be maintained there (wagon factories, et cetera). The consideration and execution of this policy in the Russian area proper is for the German Reich and its future a tremendous and by no means negative task, as might appear, if one takes only the harsh necessity of the evacuation into consideration. The conversion of Russian dynamics towards the East is a task which requires the strongest characters. Perhaps this decision will also be approved by a coming Russia later, not in 30 but in a 100 years."

As I have indicated, the failure of the Nazi conspirators to defeat Great Britain had served to strengthen them further in their belief of the political necessity of eliminating the Soviet Union as a European factor before Germany could completely achieve her role as the master of Europe.

The economic motive for the aggression was brought out clearly in our discussion of the organization set up under Goering and General Thomas to carry out the economic exploitation of the territories they occupied. The purely materialistic basis for the attack was unmistakable; and if any doubt existed that at least one of the main purposes of the invasion was to steal the food and raw material needed for the Nazi war machine regardless of the horrible consequences such robbery would entail, that doubt is dispelled by a memorandum, which bears our Number 2718-PS and which I introduced earlier during my opening statement as Exhibit USA-32, showing clear and conscious recognition that these Nazi plans would no doubt result in starving to death millions of people by robbing them of their food.

Along the similar line, on June 20, 1941 General Thomas wrote a memorandum in which he stated that General Keitel had confirmed to him Hitler's present conception of the German economic policy concerning raw material. This policy expressed the almost unbelievably heartless theory that less manpower would be used in the conquest of sources of raw materials than would be necessary to produce synthetics in lieu of such raw materials. This is our Document Number 1456-PS, and I offer it in evidence as Exhibit USA-148. I should like to read the first two paragraphs.

THE PRESIDENT: Perhaps we better do that after the adjournment.

[A recess was taken until 1400 hours.]

THE PRESIDENT: I understand that the Defendant Kaltenbrunner is now in court. Will you stand up, please?

[Whereupon the defendant Kaltenbrunner stands up in the defendants' box.]

THE PRESIDENT: In accordance with Article 24 of the Charter, you must now plead either guilty or not guilty

ERNST KALTENBRUNNER: I plead not guilty. I do not believe that I have made myself guilty.

MR. ALDERMAN: May it please the Tribunal, I had just put in evidence our Document 1456-PS as Exhibit USA-148. I now read from that document on Page 1:

"The following is a new conception of the Fuehrer, which Minister Todt has explained to me and which has been confirmed later on by Field Marshal Keitel:

"I. The course of the war shows that we went too far in our autarkical endeavors. It is impossible to try to manufacture everything we lack by synthetic procedures or other measures. For instance, it is impossible to develop our motor fuel economy to a point where we can entirely depend on it. All these autarkical endeavors demand a tremendous amount of manpower, and it is simply impossible to provide it. One has to choose another way. What one does not have but needs, one must conquer. The commitment of men which is necessary for one single action will not be as great as the one that is currently needed for the running of the synthetic factories in question. The aim must therefore be to secure all territories which are of special interest to us for the war economy by conquering them.

"At the time the Four Year Plan was established I issued a statement in which I made it clear that a completely autarkical economy is impossible for us because the need of men will be too great. My solution, however, has always been directed to securing the necessary reserves for missing stocks by concluding economic agreements which would guarantee delivery even in wartime."

On this macabre note I come to the end of the story of this aggression. We have seen these conspirators as they planned, prepared, and finally initiated their wanton attack upon the Soviet Union. Others will carry on the tale and describe the horrible manner in which they waged this war of aggression and the countless crimes they committed in its wake. When I consider the solemn pledge of non-aggression, the base and sinister motives involved, the months of secret planning and preparation, and the unbelievable suffering intentionally and deliberately wrought-when I consider all of this, I feel fully justified in saying that never before-and, God help us, never again-in the history of relations between sovereign nations has a blacker chapter been written than the one which tells-of this unprovoked invasion of the territory of the Soviet Union. For those responsible-and they are here before you, the defendants in this case-it might be just to let the punishment fit the crime.

I now turn to the final phase of the detailed presentation of the aggressive-war part of the case: German collaboration with Italy and Japan, and aggressive war against the United States. The relevant portions of the Indictment are set forth in Subsection 7 under Section IV (F) of Count One, appearing at Pages 9 and 10 of the printed English text of the Indictment. The materials relating to this unholy alliance of the three fascist powers and to the aggressive war against the United States have been gathered together in a document book, marked with the letter "Q." which I now submit to the Tribunal.

Before moving on to the subject matter of this tripartite collaboration, I should like to invite the attention of the Tribunal to the significance of this phase. In the course of the joint presentation by the British and American Prosecution in the past several days, we have seen the swastika carried forward by force of arms from a tightly controlled and remilitarized Germany to the four corners of Europe. The elements of a conspiracy that I am now about to discuss project the Nazi plan upon a universal screen, involving the older world of Asia and the new world of the United States of America. As a result, the wars of aggression that were planned in Berlin and launched across the frontiers of Poland ended some six years later, almost to the day, in surrender ceremonies upon a United States battleship riding at anchor in the Bay of Tokyo.

The first formal alliance between Hitler's Germany and the Japanese Government was the Anti-Comintern Pact signed in Berlin on 25 November 1936. This agreement, on its face, was directed against the activities of the Communist International. It was subsequently adhered to by Italy on 6 November 1937.

I ask the Tribunal to take judicial notice of these official state documents in accordance with Article 21 of the Charter. The German text of these treaties-the original German-Japanese Anti-Comintern Pact and the subsequent Protocol of Adherence by Italy- is to be found in Volumes 4 and 5 of the Dokumente der Deutschen Politik, respectively. The English translation of the German-Japanese Anti-Comintern Pact of 25 November 1936 is contained in our Document 2508-PS; the English translation of the Protocol of Adherence by Italy of 6 November 1937 is contained in our Document 2506-PS. Both of these documents are included in the document books which have just been handed up to the Tribunal. It is an interesting fact, especially in the light of the evidence I shall submit regarding the Defendant Ribbentrop's active participation in collaboration with the Japanese, that Ribbentrop signed the Anti-Comintern Pact for Germany at Berlin even though at that time, November 1936, Ribbentrop was not the German Foreign Minister but simply Hitler's special Ambassador Plenipotentiary.

On 27 September 1940 some four years after the Anti-Comintern Pact was signed and one year after the initiation of war in Europe, the German, Italian, and Japanese Governments signed another pact at Berlin, a 10-year military-economic alliance. Again I note that the Defendant Ribbentrop signed for Germany, this time in his capacity as Foreign Minister. The official German text of this pact, as well as the Japanese and Italian texts together with an English translation, is contained in our Document 2643-PS, which has been certified by the signature and seal of the United States Secretary of State. I now offer in evidence Document 2643-PS as Exhibit USA-149.

The Tripartite Pact pledged Germany, Italy, and Japan to support of; and collaboration with, one another in the establishment of a New Ordering Europe and East Asia. I should like to read into the record parts of this far-reaching agreement:

"The Governments of Germany, Italy, and Japan consider it as a condition precedent of a lasting peace, that each nation of the world be given its own proper place. They have, therefore, decided to stand together and to co-operate with one another in their efforts in Greater East Asia and in the regions of Europe, wherein it is their prime purpose to establish and maintain a new order of things calculated to promote the prosperity and welfare of the peoples there. Furthermore, it is the desire of the three Governments to extend this co-operation to such nations in other parts of the world as are inclined to give to their endeavors a direction similar to their own, in order that their aspirations towards world peace as the ultimate goal may thus be realized. Accordingly, the Governments of Germany, Italy, and Japan have agreed as follows:

"Article 1. Japan recognizes and respects the leadership of Germany and Italy in the establishment of a New Order in Europe.

"Article 2: Germany and Italy recognize and respect the leadership of Japan in the establishment of a New Order in Greater East Asia.

"Article 3. Germany, Italy, and Japan agree to co-operate in their efforts on the aforesaid basis. They further undertake to assist one another with all political, economic, and military means, if one of the three contracting parties is attacked by a power at present not involved in the European war or in the Chinese-Japanese conflict."

I now skip to the first sentence of Article 6.

"The present pact shall come into force immediately upon signature and remain in force for 10 years from the date of its coming into force."

The Tripartite Pact of 27 September 1940 thus was a bold announcement to the world that the fascist leaders of Germany, Japan, and Italy had cemented a full military alliance to achieve world domination and to establish a New Order presaged by the Japanese invasion of Manchuria in 1931, the ruthless Italian conquest of Ethiopia in 1935, and the Nazi overflow into Austria early in 1938. I might also comment that this fact introduces the Fuehrerprinzip into world politics.

I should like to read in this connection a statement by Cordell Hull, Secretary of State of the United States, at the time of the signing of this Tripartite Pact. This statement appears in the official United States publication, Peace and War, United States Foreign Policy, 1g31-1941, which has already been put in evidence as Exhibit USA-122. Mr. Hull's statement is Number 184 therein. It is also our Document Number 2944-PS, and both the English text and a German translation thereof are included in the document books. I now quote a statement by the Secretary of State, 27 September 1940:

"The reported agreement of alliance does not, in view of the Government of the United States, substantially alter a situation which has existed for several years. Announcement of the alliance merely makes clear to all a relationship which has long existed in effect, and to which this Government have repeatedly called attention. That such an agreement has been in process of conclusion has been well known for some time, and that fact has been fully taken into account by the Government of the United States, in the determining of this country's policies."

That ends the quotation.

I shall not attempt here to trace the relationships and negotiations leading up to the Tripartite Pact of 27 September 1940. I shall note, however, one example of the type of German-Japanese relationship existing before the formalization of the Tripartite Pact. This is the record of the conversation of 31 January 1939 between Himmler and General Oshima, Japanese Ambassador at Berlin, which was referred to by the United States Chief of Counsel in his opening address. This document, which is signed by Himmler in crayon, is our Document Number 2195-PS. I offer it in evidence as Exhibit USA-150. I now quote the file memorandum:

"Today I visited General Oshima. The conversation ranged over the following subjects:

"1) The Fuehrer speech, which pleased him very much, especially because it has been spiritually well founded in every respect.

"2) We discussed the conclusion of a treaty to consolidate the triangle Germany-Italy-Japan into an even firmer mold. He also told me that, together with German counter-espionage', -Abwehr-"he was undertaking long-range projects aimed at the disintegration of Russia and emanating from the Caucasus and the Ukraine. However, this organization was to become effective only in case of war.

"3) Furthermore, he had succeeded up to now in sending 10 Russians with bombs across the Caucasian frontier. These Russians had the mission to kill Stalin. A number of additional Russians whom he had also sent across had been shot at the frontier."

Whatever the beginning and the course of development of the fascist triplice, the Nazi conspirators, once their military and economic alliance with Japan had been formalized, exhorted the Japanese to aggression against those nations with whom they were at war and those with whom they contemplated war. In this the conspirators pursued a course strikingly parallel to that followed in their relationship with the other member of the European Axis. On 10 June 1940 in fulfillment of her alliance with Germany, Italy had carried out her "stab in the back" by declaring war against France and Great Britain. These Nazi conspirators set about to induce similar action by Japan on the other side of the world.

As I shall show, the nations against whom the German-Japanese collaboration was aimed at various times were the British Commonwealth of Nations, the Union of Soviet Socialist Republics, and the United States of America. I shall deal with each of these nations in the order named.

At least as early as 23 February 1941-on the basis of documents available to us-these conspirators undertook to exploit their alliance with Japan by exhortations to commit aggression against the British Commonwealth. Again the figure of the Defendant Ribbentrop appears. On that date, 23 February 1941, he held a conference with General Oshima, the Japanese Ambassador to Berlin, at which he urged that the Japanese open hostilities against the British in the Far East as soon as possible.

The report of that conference, our Document 1834-PS, has already been offered in connection with the presentation of the case on aggression against the Soviet Union as Exhibit USA-129. A part of it has already been read into the record and I now intend to read other portions. I shall again come back to this document when dealing with the German-Japanese collaboration as regards the United States.

As can be seen on the cover page of the English translation, Ribbentrop on 2 March sent copies of an extract of the record of this conference to his various ambassadors and ministers for their strictly confidential and purely personal information with the further note that-and I quote:

"These statements are of fundamental significance for orientation in the general political situation facing Germany in early spring 1941."

I shall now quote from the top of Page 2 of the English translation of 1834-PS, to the end of the first paragraph on that page, and then skip to the last three sentences of the second paragraph:

"Extract from the report of the conference of the Reich Foreign Minister with Ambassador Oshima in Fuschl on 13 February 1941.

"After particularly cordial mutual greetings the RAM (Reich Foreign Minister) declared that Ambassador Oshima had been proved right in the policy he had pursued regarding Germany in the face of the many doubters in Japan. By Germany's victory in the West these policies had been fully vindicated. He (the RAM)"-that is Ribbentrop-"regretted that the alliance between Germany and Japan, for which he had been working with the ambassador for many years already, had come into being only after various detours; but public opinion in Japan had not been ripe for it earlier. The main thing was, however, that they are together now."

Then, skipping:

'Now that the German-Japanese alliance has been concluded, Ambassador Oshima is the man who gets credit for it from the Japanese side. After conclusion of the alliance the question of its further development now stands in the foreground. How is the situation in this respect?"

Ribbentrop, thereafter in the conference, proceeded to shape the argument for Japanese intervention against the British. First outlining the intended air and U-boat warfare by Germany against England, he said-and I now quote the last two sentences in Paragraph 4, on Page 2, of the English translation:

"Thereby England's situation would take catastrophic shape overnight. The landing in England is prepared; its execution, however, depends on various factors, above all on weather conditions."

And then skipping and picking up at the first full paragraph on Page 3 of the English translation, I quote the Defendant Ribbentrop again:

"The Fuehrer will beat England wherever he encounters her. Besides, our strength is not only equal but superior to a combined English-American air force at any time. The number of pilots at our disposal is unlimited. The same is true of our airplane production capacity. As far as quality is concerned, ours always has been to the English-to say nothing about the American-and we are on the way to enlarge even this lead. Upon order of the Fuehrer the antiaircraft defense, too, will be greatly reinforced. Since the Army has been supplied far beyond its requirements and enormous reserves have been piled up-the ammunitions plants have been slowed down because of the immense stock of material- production now will be concentrated on submarines, airplanes, and antiaircraft guns.

"Every eventuality had been provided for; the war has been won today, militarily, economically, and politically. We have the desire to end the war quickly, and to force England to sue for peace soon. The Fuehrer is vigorous and healthy, fully convinced of victory, and determined to bring the war as quickly as possible to a victorious close. To this end the cooperation with Japan is of importance. However, Japan, in her own interest, should come in as soon as possible. This would destroy England's key position in the Far East. Japan, on the other hand, would thus secure her position in the Far East, a position which she could acquire only through war. There were three reasons for quick action:

"1) Intervention by Japan would mean a decisive blow against the center of the British Empire (threat to India, cruiser warfare, et cetera). The effect upon the morale of the British people would be very serious and this would contribute toward a quick ending of the war.

"2) A surprise intervention by Japan is bound to keep America out of the war. America, which at present is not yet armed and would hesitate greatly to expose her Navy to any risks west of Hawaii, could then less likely do this. If Japan would otherwise respect the American interests, there would not even be the possibility for Roosevelt to use the argument of lost prestige to make war plausible to the Americans. It is very unlikely that America would declare war if she then would have to stand by helplessly while Japan takes the Philippines without America being able to do anything about it.

"3) In view of the coming New World Order it seems to be in the interest of Japan also to secure for herself, even during the war, the position she wants to hold in the Far East at the time of a peace treaty. Ambassador Oshima agreed entirely with this line of thought and said that he would do everything to carry through this policy."

I should like to note at this point the subtlety of Ribbentrop's argument. First he told the Japanese Ambassador that Germany had already practically won the war by herself. Nevertheless he suggested that the war could be successfully terminated more quickly with Japan's aid and that the moment was propitious for Japan's entry. Then referring to the spoils of the conquest, he indicated that Japan would be best advised to pick up by herself during the war the positions she wanted, implying that she would have to earn her share of the booty, which is reminiscent of that statement I read to you earlier from the Fuehrer, that "those who wished to be in on the meal must take a part in the cooking."

Continuing Ribbentrop's argument to show the real nature of the German-Japanese alliance, I shall now read the top two paragraphs on Page 5 of the English translation of 1834-PS:

"The Reich Foreign Minister continued by saying that it was Japan's friendship which had enabled Germany to arm after the Anti-Comintern Pact was concluded. On the other hand, Japan had been able to penetrate deeply into the English sphere of influence in China. Germany's victory on the continent has brought now, after the conclusion of the Three Power Pact, great advantages for Japan. France, as a power, was eliminated in the Far East (Indo-China). England, too, was considerably weakened; Japan had been able to close in steadily on Singapore. Thus, Germany had already contributed enormously to the shaping of the future fate of the two nations. Due to our geographical situation, we should have to carry the main burden of the final battle in the future, too. If an unwanted conflict with Russia should arise, we should have to carry the main burden also in this case. If Germany should ever weaken, Japan would find herself confronted by a world coalition within a short time. We would all be in the same boat. The fate of both nations would be determined for centuries to come. The same was true for Italy. The interests of the three countries would never intersect. A defeat of Germany would also mean the end of the Japanese imperialistic idea.

"Ambassador Oshima definitely agreed with these statements and emphasized the fact that Japan was determined to keep her imperial position. The Reich Foreign Minister then discussed the great problems which would arise after the war for the parties of the Three Power Pact from the shaping of a new order in Europe and East Asia. The problems arising then would require a bold solution. Thereby no over-centralization should take place; but a solution should be found on a basis of parity, particularly in the economic realm. In regard to this the Reich Foreign Minister advanced the principle that a free exchange of trade should take place between the two spheres of influence on a liberal basis. The European-African hemisphere under the leadership of Germany and Italy, and the East Asian sphere of interest under the leadership of Japan. As he conceived it, for example, Japan would conduct trade and make trade agreements directly with the independent states in the European hemisphere as heretofore, while Germany and Italy would trade directly and make trade agreements with the independent countries within the Japanese orbit of power, such as China, Thailand, Indo-China, et cetera. Furthermore, as between the No economic spheres, each should fundamentally grant the other preferences with regard to third parties. The Ambassador expressed agreement with this thought."

In the document I have just quoted from we have seen the instigation to war by the Defendant Ribbentrop, the German Foreign Minister. I shall return to him again in this connection. I now wish to show, however, the participation of the so-called military representatives in the encouragement and provocation of further wars of aggression. I therefore offer in evidence our Document Number C-75 as Exhibit USA-151.

This document is a top-secret order signed by the Defendant Keitel as Chief of the OKW and entitled, "Basic Order Number 24 regarding Collaboration with Japan." It is dated 5 March 1941, about a week and a half after Ribbentrop's conference with Oshima that I have just discussed. It was distributed in 14 copies to the highest commands of the Army, Navy, and Air Force as well as to the Foreign Office. We have turned up two copies of this order, identical except for handwritten notations, presumably made by the

271

recipients. C-75, the document I have introduced, is copy Number 2 of the order distributed to the naval war staff of the Commander-in-Chief of the Navy, the OKM. We also have Copy number 4, designed for the Wehrmacht Fuehrungsstab (the Operations Staff of the High Command of the Armed Forces). The head of this Operations Staff was the Defendant Jodl. Copy Number 4 was found in the OKW files at Flensburg. It is our Document Number 384-PS, and was referred to by the United States Chief of Counsel in his opening address. I shall not burden the Tribunal and the record by introducing two identical copies of the same order.

Basic Order Number 24 was the authoritative Nazi policy on collaboration with Japan. I shall, therefore, propose to read it in its entirety, some two pages of English translation:

"The Fuehrer has issued the following order regarding collaboration with Japan:

"1. It must be the aim of the collaboration based on the Three Power Pact to induce Japan, as soon as possible, to take active measures in the Far East"-The underscoring is in the original document-"Strong British forces will thereby be tied down, and the center of gravity of the interests of the United States of America will be diverted to the Pacific. The sooner she intervenes, the greater will be the prospects of success for Japan in view of the still undeveloped preparedness for war . on the part of her adversaries. The Barbarossa operation will create particularly favorable political and military prerequisites for this."

Then there is a marginal note, "Slightly exaggerated."

THE PRESIDENT: Do you have any idea when that marginal notation was put in?

MR. ALDERMAN: I assume that was written by the recipient of this copy of the order.

THE PRESIDENT: By whom?

MR. ALDERMAN: By the recipient of this particular copy of the order, which was the naval war staff.

"2. To prepare the way for the collaboration it is essential to strengthen the Japanese military potential with all means available. For this purpose the High Commands of the branches of the Armed Forces will comply in a comprehensive and generous manner with Japanese desires for information regarding German war and combat experience, and for assistance in military economics and in technical matters. Reciprocity is desirable, but this factor should not stand in the way of negotiations. Priority should naturally be given to those Japanese requests which would have the most immediate application in waging war. In special cases the Fuehrer reserves the decisions for himself.

"3. The harmonizing of the operational plans of the No parties is the responsibility of the Naval High Command. This will be subject to the following guiding principles:

"a. The common aim of the conduct of war is to be stressed as forcing England to the ground quickly and thereby keeping the United States out of the war. Beyond this Germany has no political, military, or economic interests in the Far East which would give occasion for any reservations with regard to Japanese intentions.

"b. The great successes achieved by Germany in mercantile warfare make it appear particularly suitable to employ strong Japanese forces for the same purpose. In this connection every opportunity to support German mercantile warfare must be exploited.

"c. The raw material situation of the pact powers demands that Japan should acquire possession of those territories which it needs for the continuation of the war, especially if the United States intervenes. Rubber shipments must be carried out even after the entry of Japan into the war, since they are of vital importance to Germany.

"d. The seizure of Singapore as the key British position in the Far East would mean a decisive success for the entire conduct of war of the three powers.

"In addition, attacks on other systems of bases of British naval power-extending to those of American naval power only if the entry of the United States into the war cannot be prevented-will result in weakening the enemy's system of power in that region and also, just like the attack on sea communications, in tying down substantial forces of all kinds (Australia). A date for the beginning of operational discussions cannot yet be fixed.

"4. In the military commissions to be formed in accordance with the Three Power Pact, only such questions are to be dealt with as equally concern the three participating powers. These will include primarily the problems of economic warfare. The working out of the details is the responsibility of the main commission with the co-operation of the Armed Forces High Command.

"5. The Japanese must not be given any intimation of the Barbarossa operations."

It is signed by Keitel as Chief of the Armed Forces High Command.

If the Tribunal will glance at the distribution list, you will see that it went to the heads of all the Armed Forces, Armed Forces High Command: Joint Operation Staff, Intelligence divisions, and to the chief of foreign affairs, simultaneously for the Foreign Office.

It appears from what I have just read that the Nazis' cardinal operational principle in collaboration with Japan was, as early as March 1941, the inducement of Japan to aggression against Singapore and other British far eastern bases. I shall pass over, for the moment, other references to the United States in Basic Order Number 24 and take up that point later.

I now wish to refer to our Document Number C-152, which has already been introduced by the British prosecution as Exhibit GB-122. This document is the top-secret record of a meeting on 18 March 1941, about 2 weeks after the issuance of Basic Order Number 24; a meeting attended by Hitler, the Defendant Raeder, the Defendant Keitel, and the Defendant Jodl We are concerned only with Paragraph 11 in this phase, where Raeder, then Commander-in-Chief of the Navy, is speaking. I quote:

"Japan must take steps to seize Singapore as soon as possible, since the opportunity will never again be as favorable (tie-up of the whole English Fleet;

273

unpreparedness of U.S.A. for war against Japan; inferiority of the United States Fleet in comparison with the Japanese). Japan is indeed making preparations for this action; but according to all declarations made by Japanese officers, she will only carry it out if Germany proceeds to land in England. Germany must, therefore, concentrate all her efforts on spurring Japan to act immediately. It Japan has Singapore, all other East Asiatic questions regarding the U.S A. and England are thereby solved (Guam, Philippines, Borneo, Dutch East Indies).

> "Japan wishes, if possible, to avoid war against the U.S.A. She can do so if she determinedly takes Singapore as soon as possible."

The fact clearly appears from these minutes that military staff conferences had already been held with the Japanese to discuss the activation of Japanese military support against the British and to urge their immediate attack on Singapore. I quote again the second sentence in that paragraph:

> "Japan is indeed making preparations for this action; but according to all declarations made by Japanese officers, she will carry it out only if Germany proceeds to land in England."

Apparently the Nazis were subsequently able to persuade the Japanese to eliminate this condition precedent to their performance under the contract.

I now turn to further efforts by the Defendant Ribbentrop to induce the Japanese to aggression against the British Commonwealth. On the 29th of March 1941 he met with the Japanese Foreign Minister, Matsuoka, who was then in Berlin. A report of their conversations found in the German Foreign Office archives is contained in our Document 1877-PS, which I now offer in evidence as Exhibit USA-152.

Relevant portions of this document have been translated into English. I shall now read from the top of Page 1 of the English translation:

> "The RAM" - that is Ribbentrop - "resumed, where they had left off, the preceding conversation with Matsuoka about the latter's impending talks with the Russians in Moscow. He expressed the opinion that it would probably be best, in view of the whole situation, not to carry the discussions with the Russians too far. He did not know how the situation would develop. One thing was certain, however, namely that Germany would strike immediately, should Russia ever attack Japan. He was ready to give Matsuoka this positive assurance so that Japan could push forward to the south on Singapore without fear of possible complications with Russia. The largest part of the German Army was on the Eastern frontiers of the Reich anyway and fully prepared to open the attack at any time. He (the RAM), however, believed that Russia would try to avoid developments leading to war. Should Germany, however, enter into a conflict with Russia, the U.S.S.R. would be finished off within a few months. In this case Japan would have, of course, even less reason to be afraid than ever, if she wants to advance on Singapore. Consequently, she need not refrain from such an undertaking because of possible fears of Russia.
>
> "He could not know, of course, just how things with Russia would develop. It was uncertain whether or not Stalin would intensify his present unfriendly policy against Germany. He (the RAM) wanted to point out to Matsuoka in any case that a conflict with Russia was at least within the realign of possibility. In any case, Matsuoka could not

report to the Japanese Emperor, upon his return, that a conflict between Russia and Germany was impossible. On the contrary, the situation was such that such a conflict, even if it were not probable, would have to be considered possible.,

I now skip five pages of the German text and continue directly with the English translation:

"Next, the RAM turned again to the Singapore question. In view of the fears expressed by the Japanese of possible attacks by submarines based on the Philippines, and of the intervention of the British Mediterranean and home fleets, he had again discussed the situation with Grossadmiral Raeder. The latter had stated that the British Navy during this year would have its hands so full in the English home waters and in the Mediterranean that it would not be able to send even a single ship to the Far East. Grossadmiral Raeder had described the United States submarines as so poor that Japan need not bother about them at all.

"Matsuoka replied immediately that the Japanese Navy had a very low estimate of the threat from the British Navy. It also held the view that, in case of a clash with the American Navy, it would be able to smash the latter without trouble. However, it was afraid that the Americans would not take up the battle with their fleet; thus the conflict with the United States might perhaps be dragged out to 5 years. This possibility caused considerable worry in Japan.

"The RAM replied that America could not do anything against Japan in the case of the capture of Singapore. Perhaps for this reason alone, Roosevelt would think twice before deciding on active measures against Japan. For while on the one hand he could not achieve anything against Japan, on the other hand there was the probability of losing the Philippines to Japan; for the American President, of course, this would mean a considerable loss of prestige, and because of the inadequate rearmament, he would have nothing to offset such a loss.

"In this connection Matsuoka pointed out that he was doing everything to reassure the English about Singapore. He acted as if Japan had no intention at all regarding this key position of England In the past; Therefore it might be possible that his attitude toward the British would appear to be friendly in words and in acts. However, Germany should not be deceived by that. He assumed this attitude not only in order to reassure the British, but also in order to fool the pro-British and pro-American elements in Japan just so long, until one day he would suddenly open the attack on Singapore.

"In this connection Matsuoka stated that his tactics were based on the certain assumption that the sudden attack against Singapore would unite the entire Japanese nation with one blow. ('Nothing succeeds like success,' the RAM remarked.3 He followed here the example expressed in the words of a famous Japanese statesman addressed to the Japanese Navy at the outbreak of the Russo-Japanese war: 'You open fire, then the nation will be united.' The Japanese need to be shaken up to awaken. After all, as an Oriental, he believed in the fate which would come, whether you wanted it or not."

I then skip again in the German text, and continue with what appears in the

English translation:

"Matsuoka then introduced the subject of German assistance in the blow against Singapore, a subject which had been broached to him frequently, and mentioned the proposal of a German written promise of assistance.

"The RAM replied that he had already discussed these questions with Ambassador Oshima. He had asked him to procure maps of Singapore in order that the Fuehrer-who probably must be considered the greatest expert on military questions at the present time-could advise Japan on the best method of attack against Singapore. German experts on aerial warfare, too, would be at her disposal; they could draw up a report, based on their European experiences, for the Japanese on the use of dive-bombers from airfields in the vicinity against the British Fleet in Singapore.. Thus, the British Fleet would be forced to disappear from Singapore immediately.

"Matsuoka remarked that Japan was less concerned with the British Fleet than with the capture of the fortifications.

"The RAM replied that here, too, the Fuehrer had developed new methods for the German attacks on strongly fortified positions, such as the Maginot Line and Fort Eben-Emael, which he could make available to the Japanese.

"Matsuoka replied in this connection that some of the younger expert Japanese Naval officers, who were close friends of his, were of the opinion that the Japanese Naval forces would need 3 months until they could capture Singapore. As a cautious Foreign Minister, he had doubled this estimate. He believed he could stave off any danger which threatened from America for 6 months. If, however, the capture of Singapore required still more time and if the operations would perhaps even drag out for a year, the situation with America would become extremely critical; and he did not know as yet how to meet it.

"If at all avoidable, he would not touch the Netherlands East Indies, since he was afraid that in case of a Japanese attack on this area, the oil fields would be set afire. They could be brought into operation again only after 1 or 2 years. 'The RAM added that Japan would gain decisive influence over the Netherlands East Indies simultaneously with the capture of Singapore."

On the 5th of April, about a week after the conference from whose minutes I have just quoted, Ribbentrop again met with Matsuoka and again pushed the Japanese another step along the road to aggressive war. The notes of this conference, which were also found in the German Foreign Office archives, are contained in our Document 1882-PS, which I now offer as Exhibit USA-158. I shall read a few brief extracts from these notes, starting with the third paragraph on Page 1 of the English translation:

"In answer to a remark by Matsuoka that Japan was now awakened and, according to the Japanese temperament, would take action quickly after the previous lengthy deliberation, the Reich Foreign Minister replied that it was necessary, of course, to accept a risk in this connection just as the Fuehrer had done successfully with the occupation of the Rhineland, with the proclamation of sovereignty of armament and with the resignation from the League of Nations."

I now skip several pages of the German text and continue on with the English translation.

"The Reich Foreign Minister replied that the new German Reich would actually be built up on the basis of the ancient traditions of the Holy Roman Empire of the German nation, which in its time was the only dominant power on the European continent.

"In conclusion, the Reich Foreign Minister once again summarized the points he wanted Matsuoka to take back to Japan with him from his trips:

"1) Germany had already won the war. With the end of this year, the world would realize this. Even England would have to concede it, if she had not collapsed before then, and America would also have to resign herself to this fact.

"2) There were no conflicting interests between Japan and Germany. The future of both countries could be regulated for the long run on the basis that Japan should predominate in the Far East, Italy and Germany in Europe and Africa.

"3) Whatever might happen, Germany would win the war. But it would hasten victory if Japan would enter the war. Such an entry into the war was undoubtedly more in the interest of Japan than in that of Germany, for it offered a unique opportunity, which would hardly ever return, for the fulfillment of the national objectives of Japan-a chance which would make it possible for her to play a really leading role in East Asia."

Here again, in the portion just quoted, we see Ribbentrop pursuing the same track I have previously noted. Germany has already won the war for all practical purposes. Japan's entry will hasten the inevitable end. But Japan had better get the positions she wants during the war.

I also invite the Tribunal's attention to Ribbentrop's assurances, expressed in the quotation I read from 1877-PS previously, that Japan likewise had nothing to fear from the Soviet Union if Japan entered the conflict. The references to the weaknesses of the United States, scattered throughout the quotations I have read, were also an ingredient in this brew which was being so carefully prepared and brought to a boil.

I should like to introduce one more document on the part of the case dealing particularly with exhortation of the Japanese to aggression against the British Commonwealth. This is our Document 1538-PS, which I now over as Exhibit USA-154. This document is a top-secret report, dated 24 May 1941, from the German Military Attaché in Tokyo to the Intelligence Division of the Now. I wish merely to call attention, at this point, to the last sentence in the paragraph numbered 1, wherein it is stated-I quote: "The preparations for attack on Singapore and Manila stand."

I shall return to this document later. I point out here, however, the fact which appears from the sentence I have just read, that the German military were keeping in close touch with the Japanese operational plans against Singapore, which the Nazi conspirators had fostered.

Next, exhortations by the Nazis to Japanese aggression against the U.S.S.R.

I invite the Tribunal's attention, at this point, to the language of the Indictment on Page 10 of the English edition. I quote, beginning with the eighth line from the top of the page:

"The Nazi conspirators conceived that Japanese aggression would weaken and handicap those nations with whom they were at war and those with whom they contemplated war. Accordingly, the Nazi conspirators exhorted Japan to seek a 'new order of things'."

The evidence I have just adduced showed the Nazi exhortations with particular reference to the British Commonwealth of Nations. We now turn to their efforts to induce the Japanese to commit a "stab in the back" on the Union of Soviet Socialist Republics. Here again the Defendant Ribbentrop appears as the central figure.

For some months prior to the issuance of Basic Order Number 24 regarding collaboration with Japan, the conspirators had been preparing Fall Barbarossa, the plan for the attack on the U.S.S.R. Basic Order Number 24 decreed, however, that the Japanese "must not be given any intimation of the Barbarossa operation."

In his conference with the Japanese Foreign Minister Matsuoka, on 29 March 1941, almost 3 weeks after the issuance of Basic Order Number 2d, Ribbentrop nevertheless hinted at things to come. The report of this conference, contained in 1877-PS, has already been introduced as Exhibit USA-152 and read into the record. I wish to invite the Tribunal's attention again to the first two paragraphs of the English translation of 1877-PS, where Ribbentrop assured Matsuoka that the largest part of the German Army was on the eastern frontiers of the Reich fully prepared to open the attack at any time. Ribbentrop then added that although he believed that the U.S.S.R. would try to avoid developments leading to war, nevertheless a conflict with the Soviet Union, even if not probable, would have to be considered possible.

Whatever conclusion the Japanese Ambassador drew from these remarks in April of 1941 can only be conjectured. Once the Nazis had unleashed their aggression against the U.S.S.R. in June of 1941, the tenor of Ribbentrop's remarks left no room for doubt. On 10 July 1941 Ribbentrop dispatched a coded telegram to Ott, the German Ambassador in Tokyo. The telegram is our Document 2896-PS, which I now introduce as Exhibit USA-155. I quote from numbered Paragraph 4 of that telegram, which is the first paragraph of the English translation:

"Please take this opportunity to thank the Japanese Foreign Minister for conveying the cable report of the Japanese Ambassador in Moscow. It would be convenient if we could keep on receiving news from Russia this way. In summing up, I should like to say I have now, as in the past, full confidence in the Japanese policy and in the Japanese Foreign Minister; first of all because the present Japanese Government would really act inexcusably toward the future of their nation if they would not take this unique opportunity to solve the Russian problem, as well as to secure for all time its expansion to the south and settle the Chinese matter. Since Russia, as reported by the Japanese Ambassador in Moscow, is in effect close to collapse-a report which coincides with our own observations as far as we are able to judge the present war situation-it is simply impossible that Japan should not settle the matter of Vladivostok and the Siberian area as soon as her military preparations are completed."

Skipping now to the middle of the second paragraph on Page 1 of the English translation-the sentence beginning "However . . .":

"However, I ask you to employ all available means in further insisting upon Japan's entry into the war against Russia at the earliest possible date, as I have mentioned already in my note to Matsuoka. The sooner this entry is effected, the better. The natural objective still remains that we and Japan join hands on the trans-Siberian railroad before winter starts. After the collapse of Russia, however, the position of the Three-Power-Pact States in the world be so gigantic that the question of England's collapse or the total destruction of the British Isles will be only a matter of time. An America totally isolated from the rest of the world would then be faced with our taking possession of the remaining positions of the British Empire which are important for the Three Power-Pact countries. I have the unshakeable conviction that a carrying through of the New Order as desired by us will be a matter of course, and there would be no insurmountable difficulties if the countries of the Three Power Pact stand close together and encounter every action of the Americans with the same weapons. I ask you to report in the near future, as often as possible and in detail, on the political situation there."

We have Ott's reply to this telegram, dated 13 July 1941. This is our Document Number 2897-PS, which I offer in evidence as Exhibit USA-156. After reading the heading, I shall skip to the last paragraph on Page 3 of the German text, which is the paragraph appearing in the English translation:

"Telegram; secret cipher system"-Sent 14 July from Tokyo; arrived 14 July 1941-"As fast as possible.

"I am trying with all means to work toward Japan's entry into the war against Russia as soon as possible, especially using arguments of personal message of Foreign Minister and telegram cited above to convince Matsuoka personally, as well as the Foreign Office, military elements, nationalists, and friendly businessmen. I believe that according to military preparations, Japanese participation will soon take place. The greatest obstacle to this against which one has to fight is the disunity within the activist group which, without unified command, follows venous aims and only slowly adjusts itself to the changed situation."

On subsequent occasions Ribbentrop repeated his exhortations to induce the Japanese to aggression against the U.S.S.R. I shall present three documents covering July of 1942 and March and April of 1943. The first is our Document 2911-Ps which contains notes of a discussion between Ribbentrop and Oshima, Japanese Ambassador to Berlin, on 9 July 1942. As a matter of background I note that at this time German armies were sweeping forward in the U.S.S.R and the fall of Sevastopol had just been announced.

I now offer our Document 2911-PS as Exhibit USA-157, and I quote the relevant extracts appearing in the English translation thereof:

"He, the German Minister, had asked to see the Ambassador at this time, when the situation was as described, because now a question of fateful importance had arisen concerning the joint conduct of the war. If Japan felt herself sufficiently strong militarily, the moment for Japan to attack Russia was probably now. He thought it possible that if Japan attacked Russia at this time, it would lead to her (Russia) final moral collapse; at least it would hasten the collapse of her present system. In any case, never again would Japan have such an opportunity as existed at present to eliminate once and for all the Russian colossus in eastern Asia.

"He had discussed this question with the Fuehrer, and the Fuehrer was of the same opinion; but he wanted to emphasize one point right away: Japan should attack Russia only if she felt sufficiently strong for such an undertaking. Under no circumstances should Japanese operations against Russia be allowed to bog down at the half-way mark, and we do not want to urge Japan into an action that is not mutually profitable."

THE PRESIDENT: We will adjourn now, for 10 minutes.

[A recess was taken.]

MR. ALDERMAN: May it please the Tribunal, I now offer in evidence our Document Number 2954-PS as Exhibit USA-158. This is a record of a conference between Ribbentrop and Ambassador Oshima on 6 March 1943.

I note again for background that the strategic military situation in the broad expanses of the U.S.S.R. had changed somewhat.

In the previous month, February 1943, the Soviet armies had completely defeated the German forces at Stalingrad and inflicted very severe losses. Further north and west their winter offensive had removed large areas from the hands of the invader. Combined United States and British forces had already landed in North Africa.

You will remark as I read that the tone of Ribbentrop's argument at this time reflects the changed military situation. The familiar Japanese refrain of "So sorry, please," likewise appears to have crept in.

I note in this record that the month of February 1943 had also seen the end of the organized Japanese resistance on the Island of Guadalcanal .

I now quote the relevant extracts from the minutes of the discussion between Ribbentrop and Oshima on 6 March 1943, which appear in the English translation in the document book:

"Ambassador Oshima declared that he received a telegram from Tokyo, and he is to report by order of his Government to the Reich Minister for Foreign Affairs the following: The suggestion of the German Government to attack Russia was the subject of a common conference between the Japanese Government and the Imperial headquarters during which the question was discussed in detail and investigated exactly. The result is the following: The Japanese Government absolutely recognize the danger which threatens from Russia and completely understand the desire of their German ally that Japan on her part will also enter the war against Russia. However, it is not possible for the Japanese Government, considering the present war situation, to enter into the war. They are rather of the conviction that it would be in the common interest not to start the war against Russia now. On the other hand, the Japanese Government would never disregard the Russian question.

"The Japanese Government have the intention to become aggressive again in the future on other fronts.

"The RAM brought up the question, after the explanation by the Ambassador, how the continued waging of the war is envisaged in Tokyo. At present Germany wages the war against the common enemies, England and America, mostly alone, while Japan mostly behaves more defensively. However, it would be more correct that ad powers allied in the Three Power Pact would combine their forces not only to defeat England and America, but also Russia. It is not good when one part must fight alone. One cannot overstrain the German national strength. He was inwardly concerned about certain forces at work in Tokyo, who were of the opinion, and propagated the same, that doubtless, Germany could emerge from the battle victoriously and that Japan should proceed to consolidate her forces before she should further exert herself to the fullest extent."

I now skip several pages in the German text and resume the quotation:

"Then the RAM again brought up the question of the attack on Russia by Japan and he declared that, after all, the fight on the Burma front as wed as in the south is actuary more of a maritime problem; and on all fronts except those in China at best very few ground forces are stationed. Therefore the attack on Russia is primarily an Army affair, and he asked himself if the necessary forces for that would be available."

Ribbentrop kept on trying. He held another conference with Oshima about 3 weeks later on 18 April 1943. The top-secret notes of this conference are contained in our Document 2929-PS, which I now offer as Exhibit USA-159. I shall quote only one sentence:

"The Reich Minister for Foreign Affairs then stressed again that, without any doubt, this year presented the most favorable opportunity for Japan, if she felt strong enough and had sufficient anti-tank weapons at her disposal, to attack Russia, which certainly would never again be as weak as she was at the moment."

I now wish to come to that aspect of this conspiracy which is in a large measure responsible for the appearance of millions of Americans in uniform all over the world.

The Nazi preparations and collaboration with the Japanese against the United States, as noted by the United States Chief of Counsel in his opening statement, present a two-fold aspect; one of preparations by the Nazis themselves for an attack from across the Atlantic, and the other of fomenting war in the Pacific.

In the course of my presentation of the Nazi exhortations to the Japanese to war against the British Commonwealth and the U.S.S.R., I have referred to some documents and quoted some sentences relating to the United States. I shall take those documents up again in their relevant passages to show their particular application. I have also, in the treatment of Ribbentrop's urging the Japanese to war against the U.S.S.R., gone beyond the dates of 7 December and 11 December 1941, when the Japanese and German Governments respectively initiated and declared aggressive war against the United States.

Apart from the advantage and convenience of presentation, these documents have indicated the Nazi awareness and acceptance of the direction in which their actions were leading, as well as the universal aspects of their conspiracy and of their alliance with the Japanese. Their intentions against the United States must be viewed in the focus of both their over-all plan and their immediate commitments elsewhere. That their over-all plan involved ultimate aggressive war against the United States was intimated by the Defendant

Goering in a speech on 8 July 1938, when these conspirators had already forcibly annexed Austria and were perfecting their plans against Czechoslovakia.

This speech was delivered to representatives of the aircraft industry, and the copy that we have was transmitted as the enclosure to a secret memorandum from Goering's adjutant to General Udet, who was then in charge of experimental research for the Luftwaffe. It is contained in our Document R-140, which I now offer as Exhibit USA-160.

I invite the Tribunal's attention to the statement in the covering memorandum that the enclosure is a copy of the shorthand minutes of the conference. I shall not go through the long speech in which Goering caned for increased aircraft production and pointed to the necessity for full mobilization of German industrial capacity. I wish to quote just two sentences, which appear on Page 33 of the German text and Page 11 of the English translation. Quoting from the second full paragraph on Page 11 of the English translation, starting with the third sentence from the end of the paragraph:

"I still lack these rocket-motors which could make such flights . possible. I completely lack the bombers capable of round-trip Bights to New York with a 5-ton bomb load. I would be extremely happy to possess such a bomber which would at last stuff the mouth of arrogance across the sea."

Goering's fervent hope, of course, was not capable of realization at that time, either technically or in the fact of the Nazi conspirators' schedule of aggression that has been outlined here in the past several days.

During the period of their preparation for and the waging of aggressive war in Europe, up to the launching of the campaign against the U.S.S.R., it is only reasonable to believe that these conspirators were not disposed to involve the United States in war at that time. Nevertheless, even in the fall of 1940 the prosecution of war against the United States of America at a later date was on the military agenda. This is clearly shown in a document which we have found in the files of the OWL, the German Air Force files. It is Document 376-PS, which I now offer as Exhibit Number USA-161. This document is a memorandum marked "Chefsache," the German designation for top. secret, from a Major Von Falkenstein to an unspecified general, presumably a Luftwaffe general.

Falkenstein, who was a major of the General Staff, was at that time the Luftwaffe liaison officer with the Operations Stab of the OKW, which was the staff headed by the Defendant Jodl. His memorandum, which he characterizes as a "brief resume on the military questions current here," is dated the 29th of October 1940. It covers several questions. I shall quote to you numbered Paragraph 5, which appears at the bottom of the first page of the English translation and carries over to the reverse side of the one-sheet document:

"5) The Fuehrer is at present occupied with the question of the occupation of the Atlantic islands with a view to the prosecution of a war against America at a later date. Deliberations on this subject are being embarked upon here. Essential conditions are at the present:

"(a) No other operational commitment; (b) Portuguese neutrality; (c) support of France and Spain.

"A brief assessment of the possibility of seizing and holding air bases and of the question of supply is needed from the GAF." - or the

German Air Force.

The Nazis' military interest in the United States is further indicated by Paragraph 7 which I read:

"General Botticher has made repeated reference, especially in his telegram 2314, dated 26th of October, to the fact that in his opinion too many details of our knowledge of American aircraft industry are being published in the German press. The matter has been discussed at Armed Forces Supine Command. I pointed out that the matter was specifically a GAF one but have taken the liberty of referring the matter to you on its own merits."

Again, in July 1941, in his first flush of confidence resulting from early gains in the aggression against the U.S.S.R., the Fuehrer signed an order for further preliminary preparations for the attack on the United States. This top secret order, found in the files of the German Navy, is our Document C-74, which I now offer as Exhibit USA-162. I read from the first paragraph of that text just preceding the paragraph numbered (1):

"By virtue of the intentions announced in Directive Number 32, for the further conduct of the war, I lay down the following principles to govern the strength of personnel and of material supplies:

"(1) In general:

"The military domination of Europe after the defeat of Russia will enable the strength of the Army to be considerably reduced in the near future. As far as the reduced strength of the Army will allow, the armored units will be greatly increased.

"Naval armament must be restricted to those measures which have a direct connection with the conduct of the war against England and, should the case arise, against America.

"The main effort in armament will be shifted to the Air Force, which must be greatly increased in strength."

From these documents it appears that the Nazi conspirators were making at least preliminary plans of their own against the United States. The Nazis' over-all plan with regard to the United States was, however, a complex one involving, in addition, collaboration with the Japanese. In the course of their repeated representations to the Japanese to undertake an assault against British possessions in the Pacific Far mast, they again considered war against the United States.

I now refer again to Basic Order Number 24, regarding collaboration with Japan. This is our Document - 75, which I have put in as Exhibit USA--151. I have read it in its entirety into the record. The Tribunal will recall that in that basic order, which was issued on 5 March 1941, the Nazi policy was stated in Subparagraph (3) (a) as "forcing England to the ground quickly and thereby keeping the United States out of the war."

Nevertheless, the Nazi conspirators clearly contemplated, within the framework of that policy, the possibility of the United States' entry into the Far Eastern conflict which the Nazis were then instigating. This could result from an attack by Japan on possessions of the United States practically simultaneously with the assault on the British Empire, as actually happened Other possibilities of involvement of the United States were also discussed. This Basic Order Number 24 stated-and I am referring to Subparagraph (3) (c), on the top of Page 2 of the Document C-75:

"(c) The raw material situation of the pact powers demands that Japan should acquire possession of those territories which it needs for the continuation of the war, especially if the United States intervenes. Rubber shipments must be carried out even after the entry of Japan into the war, since they are of vital importance to Germany."

The order continues in an unnumbered paragraph, immediately below Subparagraph (3) (d):

"In addition, attacks on other systems of bases of British naval power extending to those of American naval power only if the entry of the United States into the war cannot be prevented-will result in weakening the enemy's system of power in that region and also, just like. the attack on sea communications, in tying down substantial forces of all kinds (Australia)."

In these passages there is a clear envisagement of United States involvement, as welt as a clear intent to attack. The vital threat to United States interests, if Japan were to capture Singapore, was also envisaged by the Defendant Raeder in his meeting of 18 March 1941 with Hitler and the Defendants Keitel and Jodl. These minutes are contained in our Document C-152, which has already been put in as Exhibit GB-122. I wish now to repeat the four sentences of Item 11 of the minutes of that conference, contained on Page 1 of the English translation. I am quoting the Defendant Raeder:

"Japan must take steps to seize Singapore as soon as possible, since the opportunity will never again be so favorable (tie-up of the whole English Fleet; unpreparedness of the US A. for war against Japan, inferiority of the United States Fleet in comparison with the Japanese). Japan is indeed making preparations for this action, but according to all declarations made by Japanese officers, she will carry it out only if Germany proceeds to land in England. Germany must, therefore, concentrate all her efforts on spurring Japan to act immediately. If Japan has Singapore, all other East Asiatic questions regarding the U.S.A. and England are thereby solved (Guam, the Philippines, Borneo, and the Dutch East Indies).

"Japan wishes, if possible, to avoid war against the U.S.A.. She can do so if she determinedly takes Singapore as soon as possible."

The Defendant Ribbentrop also recognized the possibility of United States involvement as a result of the course of aggression that he was urging on the Japanese. I refer again to his meeting of 23 February 1941 with the Japanese Ambassador Oshima, the notes of which are contained in our Document 1834-PS, which is in evidence as Exhibit USA-129.

The Tribunal will recall that in a passage I have already read, Subparagraph (2) near the bottom of Page 3 of the English translation, Ribbentrop assured Matsuoka that a surprise by Japan was bound to keep the United States out of the war since she was unarmed and could not risk either her fleet or the possibility of losing the Philippines as the result of a declaration of war. Two paragraphs later Ribbentrop practically dropped the pretense that the United States would not be involved. I quote here from the last paragraph at the bottom of Page 3 of the English translation:

"The Reich Foreign Minister mentioned further that if America should declare war because of Japan's entry into the war, this would mean that America had the intention to enter the war sooner or later anyway. Even though it would be preferable to avoid this, the entry into the war would, as explained above, be by no means decisive and would not endanger the final victory of the countries of the Three Power Pact. The Foreign Minister further expressed his belief that a temporary lift of the British morale caused by America's entry into the war would be canceled by Japan's entry into the war. If, however, contrary to all expectations, the Americans should be careless enough to send their navy, in spite of all, beyond Hawaii and to the Far East, this would represent the biggest chance for the countries of the Three Power Pact to bring the war to an end with the greatest rapidity. He-the Foreign Minister-is convinced that the Japanese Fleet would then do a complete job. Ambassador Oshima replied to this that unfortunately he does not think the Americans would do it, but he is convinced of a victory of his fleet in Japanese waters."

In the paragraphs that follow, some of which have already been read into the record, Ribbentrop again stressed the mutual inter-dependence of the Tripartite Pact powers and suggested coordinated action.

I want to quote now only the last paragraph on Page 5, a difficult bit of Nazi cynicism which by now is quite familiar.

"The Reich Foreign Minister then touched upon the question, explicitly designated as theoretical, that the contracting powers might be required, on the basis of new affronts by the U.S.A., to break off diplomatic relations. Germany and Italy were fundamentally determined on this. After signing of the Three Power Pact, we should proceed, if the occasion arises, also jointly in this matter. Such a lesson should open the eyes of the people in the United States, and under certain conditions swing public opinion towards isolation. Naturally a situation had to be chosen in which America found herself entirely in the wrong. The common step of the signatory powers should be exploited correspondingly in propaganda. The question, however, was in no way acute at the time."

Again, on 29 March 1941, Ribbentrop, this time in a conference with the Japanese Foreign Minister Matsuoka, discussed the possible involvement of the United States. Notes of this conference are contained in our Document 1877-PS, which I have already introduced as Exhibit USA-152; and I have read it into the record. The relevant statements appear in the bottom No paragraphs of Page 1 and the first full paragraph on Page 2 of the English translation. I shall not take the Tribunal's time to read them again.

I should like to refer to one more document to show that the Nazi conspirators knew that the aggressive war they were urging the Japanese to undertake both threatened the vital interests of the United States and could lead to the United States' involvement in the contemplated Far Eastern conflict. This document is our 1881-PS, report of the conference between Hitler and the Japanese Foreign Minister Matsuoka in Berlin on 4 April 1941. I have already offered, in my opening statement to the Tribunal 2 weeks ago, Document 1881-PS as Exhibit USA--33; and I read at that time a considerable portion of it into the record. Unless the Court prefers that I do not do so, it seems to me desirable at this point to re-read a few brief passages.

THE PRESIDENT: I think we might treat it as being in evidence.

MR. ALDERMAN: I wish to emphasize, however, that the passages which I read 2 weeks ago and which I had expected to re-read at this point show not only a realization of the probable involvement of the United States in the Far Eastern conflict that the Nazis were urging, but also a knowledge on their part that the Japanese Army and Navy were actually preparing war plans against the United States. Furthermore, we have a document that shows the Nazis knew at least a part of what those war plans were.

I now refer again to Document Number 1538-PS, which has been offered in evidence as Exhibit USA-154, the secret telegram from the German Military Attaché in Tokyo, dated 24 May 1941. He talks about the conferences he has had regarding Japan's entry in the war in the event Germany should become involved in war with the United States.

In the paragraph numbered 1 this sentence also appears-I quote the last sentence in numbered Paragraph Number 1, "Preparations for attack on Singapore and Manila stand."

May I at this point review the Nazi position with regard to the United States at this time, the spring of 1941. In view of their pressing commitments elsewhere and their aggressive plans against the U.S.S.R. set for execution in June of 1941, their temporary strategy was naturally a preference that the United States not be involved in the war at that time. Nevertheless, they had been considering their own preliminary plan against the United States, as seen in the Atlantic island document which I offered.

They were repeatedly urging the Japanese to aggression against the British Commonwealth just as they would urge them to attack the U.S.S.R. soon after the launching of the Nazi invasion of the Soviet Union. They were aware that the course along which they were pushing the Japanese in the Far East would probably lead to involvement of the United States. Indeed, the Japanese Foreign Minister had told Hitler this in so many words, and their own military men had fully realized the implications of the move against Singapore. They also knew that the Japanese Army and Navy were preparing operation plans against the U.S. They knew at least part of those plans.

The Nazi conspirators not only knew all these things; they accepted the risk of the aggressive course they were urging on the Japanese and pushed their eastern allies still further along that course.

In April 1941 Hitler told the Japanese Foreign Minister that in the event Japan would have become involved in the war with the United States, Germany would immediately take the consequences and strike without delay.

I refer to our Document 1881-PS, the notes of the Hitler-Matsuoka conference in Berlin on 4 April 1941, which has already been introduced as Exhibit Number USA-33. I refer particularly to the first four paragraphs on Page 2 of the English translation. I. think that has been read to you at least twice, and I perhaps need not repeat it.

Then, skipping two paragraphs, we see Hitler then encouraging Matsuoka in his decision to strike against the United States; and I invite your attention to the fourth paragraph on Page 2, which you have heard several times and which I shall not re-read.

Here in those passages were assurance, encouragement, and abetment by the head of the German State, the leading Nazi coconspirator, in April 1941. But the Nazi encouragement and promise of support did not end there.

I now offer our Document 2898-PS as Exhibit Number USA-163. This is another telegram from the German Ambassador in Tokyo regarding his conversation with the Japanese Foreign Minister. It is dated the 30th of November 1941, exactly 1 week before Pearl Harbor. I will read from the first four paragraphs on Page 2 of the German text, which is the first paragraph of the English translation; and this passage, I am sure, has not been read to the Tribunal. No part of this document has been read.

"The progress of the negotiations so far confirms his viewpoint that the difference of opinion between Japan and the U.S. is very great. The Japanese Government, since they sent Ambassador Kurusu, have taken a firm stand as he told me. He is convinced that this position is in our favor, and makes the United States think that her entry into the European war would be risky business. The new American proposal of 25 November showed great divergencies in the viewpoints of the two nations. These differences of opinion concern, for example, the further treatment of the Chinese question. The biggest"-and then the German text has the legend "one group missing," indicating that one group of the secret code was garbled on transmission. It would appear from the text that the missing words are "difference of opinion"-"The biggest (one group missing), however, resulted from the United States attempt to make the threepower agreement ineffective. The United States suggested to Japan that she conclude treaties of non-aggression with the United States, the British Empire, the Soviet Union, and other countries in order to prevent Japan's entry into the war on the side of the Axis Powers. Japan, however, insisted upon maintaining her treat' obligations, and for this reason American demands are the greatest obstacles for adjusting Japanese-American relations. He avoided discussing concessions promised by the United States and merely mentioned that grave decisions were at stake.

"The United States is seriously preparing for war and is about to operate a considerable part of its navy from southern Pacific bases. The Japanese Government are busy working out an answer in order to clarify their viewpoint. But he has no particulars at that moment. He thinks the American proposals as a whole unacceptable.

"Japan is not afraid of a breakdown of negotiations, and she hopes that if occasion arises Germany and Italy, according to the Three Power Pact, would stand at her side. I answered that there could be no doubt about Germany's future position. The Japanese Foreign Minister thereupon stated that he understood from my words that Germany, in such a case, would consider her relationship to Japan as that of a union by fate. I answered, according to my opinion, Germany was certainly ready to have mutual agreement between the two countries over this situation.

"The Minister of Foreign Affairs answered that it was possible that he would come back to this point soon. The conversation with the Minister of Foreign Affairs confirmed the impression that the United States note, in fact, is very unsatisfactory even for the compromise-seeking politicians here. For these circles America's position, especially in the China question, is very disappointing. The emphasis upon the Three Power Pact as being the main obstacle between successful Japanese-United States negotiations seems to point to the fact that the

Japanese Government are becoming aware of the necessity of close co-operation with the Axis Powers."

The time is now fast approaching for that day of infamy. I offer our Document 2987-PS as Exhibit USA-166. This document consists of extracts from the handwritten diary of Count Galeazzo Ciano during the period 3 December to 8 December 1941. It consists of notes he jotted down in the course of his daily business as Foreign Minister of Italy. The Italian has been translated into both English and German, and copies of both the English and the German are in the document books.

I now quote from the beginning of the entry of 3 December, Wednesday:

"Sensational move by Japan. The Ambassador asks for an audience with the Duce and reads him a long statement on the progress of the negotiations with America, concluding with the assertion that they have reached a dead end. Then invoking the appropriate clause in the Tripartite Pact, he asks that Italy declare war on America immediately after the outbreak of hostilities and proposes the signing of an agreement not to conclude a separate peace. The interpreter translating this request was trembling like a leaf. The Duce gave fullest assurances, reserving the right to confer with Berlin before giving a reply. The Duce was pleased with the communication and said, 'We are now on the brink of the inter-continental war which I predicted as early as September 1939.' What does this new event mean? In any case it means that Roosevelt has succeeded in his maneuver. Since he could not enter the war immediately and directly, he entered it indirectly by letting himself be attacked by Japan. Furthermore, this event also means that every prospect of peace is becoming further and further removed and that it is now easy-much too easy-to predict a long war. Who will be able to hold out longest? It is on this basis that the problem must be considered. Berlin's answer will be somewhat delayed because Hitler has gone to the southern Front to see General Kleist, whose armies continue to give way under the pressure of an unexpected Soviet of Pensive."

And then December 4, Thursday-that is 3 days before Pearl Harbor:

"Berlin's reaction to the Japanese move is extremely cautious. Perhaps they will accept because they cannot get out of it, but the idea of provoking America's intervention pleases the Germans less and less. Mussolini, on the other hand, is pleased about it." And December 5, Friday: "A night interrupted by Ribbentrop's restlessness. After delaying 2 days, now he cannot wait a minute to answer the Japanese; and at three in the morning he sent Mackensen to my house to submit a plan for a triple agreement relative to Japanese intervention and the pledge not to make a separate peace. He wanted me to awaken the Duce, but I did not do so, and the latter was very glad I had not."

It appears from the last entry I have read, that of December 5, that some sort of an agreement was reached.

On Sunday, 7 December 1941, Japan, without previous warning or declaration of war, commenced an attack against the United States at Pearl Harbor and against the British Commonwealth of Nations in the Southwest Pacific. On the morning of 11 December, 4 days after the Japanese assault in the Pacific, the German Government declared war on the United States, committing the last act of aggression which was to seal their doom. This declaration of war is contained in Volume IX of the *Dokumente der Deutschen Politik*, of which I now ask the Tribunal to take judicial notice as Exhibit USA-164. An English translation is contained in our document book, and for the convenience of the Tribunal is Number 2507-PS.

The same day, 11 December, the fourth anniversary of which is tomorrow, the Congress of the United States resolved:

"That the state of war between the United States and the Government of Germany which has thus been thrust upon the United States, is hereby formally declared."

This declaration is contained as Document 272 in the official publication *Peace and War*, of which the Tribunal has already taken judicial notice as Exhibit USA-122. The declaration itself has been reproduced for the document books as our Document 2945-PS.

It thus appears that, apart from their own aggressive intentions and declaration of war against the United States, the Nazi conspirators in their collaboration with Japan incited and kept in motion a force reasonably calculated to result in an attack on the United States. While maintaining their preference that the United States not be involved in war at the time, they nevertheless foresaw the distinct possibility, even probability, of such involvement as a result of the action they were encouraging. They were aware that the Japanese had prepared plans for attack against the United States, and they accepted the consequences by assuring the Japanese that they would declare war on the United States should a United States-Japanese conflict result.

In dealing with captured documents of the enemy the completeness of the plan is necessarily obscured, but those documents which have been discovered and offered in evidence before this Tribunal show that the Japanese attack was the proximate and foreseeable consequence of their collaboration policy and that their exhortations and encouragement of the Japanese as surely led to Pearl Harbor as though Pearl Harbor itself had been mentioned.

I should like to read the Ciano diary entry for 8 December, the day after Pearl Harbor:

"A night telephone call from Ribbentrop. He is overjoyed about the Japanese attack on America. He is so happy about it that I am happy with him, though I am not too sure about the final advantages of what has happened. One thing is now certain, that America will enter the conflict and that the conflict will be so long that she will be able to realize all her potential forces. This morning I told this to the Ding who had been pleased about the event. He ended by admitting that, in the long run, I may be right. Mussolini was happy, too. For a long time he has favored a definite clarification of relations between America and the Axis."

The final document consists of the top-secret notes of a conference between Hitler and Japanese Ambassador Oshima on 14 December 1941, from 1300 to 1400 hours, in the presence of the Reich Foreign Minister Ribbentrop. It is our Document 2932-PS, which I now offer as Exhibit USA-165. The immediate subject matter is the Pearl Harbor attack, but the expressions therein typify Nazi technique. I quote from the second paragraph of the English translation which has not been previously read:

"First the Fuehrer presents Ambassador Oshima with the Grand Cross of the Order of Merit of the German Eagle in gold. With cordial words he acknowledges his services in the achievement of German-Japanese co-operation, which has now obtained its culmination in a close brotherhood of arms. "General Oshima expresses his thanks for the great honor and emphasizes how glad he is that this brotherhood of arms has now come about between Germany and Japan.

"The Fuehrer continues: 'You gave the right declaration of war.' This method is the only proper one. Japan pursued it formerly and it corresponds with his own system, that is, to negotiate as long as possible. But if one sees the other is interested only in putting one oft, in shamming and humiliating one, and is not willing to come to an agreement, then one should strike as hard as possible, indeed, and not waste time declaring war. It was heart-warming to him to hear of the first operations of the Japanese. He himself negotiated with infinite patience at times, for example, with Poland and also with Russia. When he then realized that the other did not want to come to an agreement, he struck suddenly and without formality. He would continue to go on this way in the future."

If the Tribunal please, that ends my presentation of the various phases of aggressive warfare charged as Crimes against Peace in Count One of the Indictment. As I conclude this phase I hope the Tribunal will allow me to express my deep sense of obligation to Commander Sidney J. Kaplan, section chief, and to the members of his staff, who did the yeoman work necessary to assemble and prepare these materials that I have presented. These members of that stay, in the order in which the materials were presented, are: Major Joseph Dainow, Lieutenant Commander Harold Leventhal, Lieutenant John M. Woolsey, Lieutenant James A. Gorrell, Lieutenant Roy H. Steyer.

Commander Kaplan and his staff have fully measured up to the famous motto of his branch of the armed services, the United States Coast Guard, "Semper Paratus" (Always Prepared).

THE PRESIDENT: The Tribunal will now adjourn.

[The Tribunal adjourned until 11 December 1945 at 1000 hours.]

Seventeenth Day:
Tuesday, 11th December, 1945

COLONEL STOREY: If the Tribunal please, the United States next offers in evidence some captured moving pictures, through Commander Donovan, who had charge of taking them.

COMMANDER DONOVAN: May it please the Tribunal, the United States now offers in evidence Document 3054-PS, Exhibit USA 167, the motion picture entitled "The Nazi Plan". This document contains several affidavits with exhibits, copies of which have been furnished to defence counsel. I ask the Tribunal whether it believes it to be necessary for us formally to read the affidavits at this time. Since the motion pictures themselves will be presented to the Tribunal, and, therefore, will be a permanent record, I respectfully submit that the reading be waived.

In the past three weeks the prosecution has presented to this Tribunal a vast amount of evidence concerning the nature of the Nazi conspiracy and what we contend to be its deliberate planning, launching, and waging of wars of aggression. That evidence has consisted of documentary and some oral proof, but the Nazi conspirators did more than leave behind such normal kinds of evidence. German proficiency in photography has been traditional. Its use as a propaganda instrument was especially well known to these defendants, and as a result the United States in 1945 captured an almost complete chronicle of the rise and fall of National Socialism as documented in films made by the Nazis themselves. It is from excerpts of this chronicle that we have compiled the motion picture now to be presented, entitled "The Nazi Plan", which, in broad outline, sums up the case thus far presented under Counts i1 and 2 of the Indictment.

The motion picture has been divided into four parts. This morning we first offer to the Tribunal Parts 1 and 2, which are especially entitled "Rise of the N.S.D.A.P., 1921 to 1933", and "Acquiring Totalitarian Control of Germany, 1933 to 1935". This will be concluded by 11.20, at which time we assume the Tribunal will order its customary morning adjournment. At 11.30 we shall present Part 3, entitled "Preparation for Wars of Aggression, 1935 to 1939". This will be concluded shortly before 1 o'clock. At 2 o'clock we will offer Part 4, entitled "Wars of Aggression, 1939 to 1944", and this will be concluded by 3 o'clock.

Parts 1 and 2, now to be presented, enable us to re-live those years in which the Nazis fought for and obtained the power to rule all life in Germany. We see the early days of terrorism and propaganda, bearing final fruit in Hitler's accession to the Chancellery in 1933; then the consolidation of power within Germany, climaxed by the Parteitag in 1934, in which the Nazis proclaimed to the nation their plans for totalitarian control. It is in simple and dramatic form the story of how a nation forsook its liberty.

I wish again to emphasise that all film now presented to the Tribunal, including, for example, pictures of early Nazi newspapers, is original German film, to which we have added only the title in English. And now, if it please the

Tribunal, we shall present Parts 1 and 2 of "The Nazi Plan".

THE PRESIDENT: It may be convenient for the United States Prosecutor to know that the Tribunal proposes to rise this afternoon at 4 o'clock instead of 5 o'clock.

[The film "The Nazi Plan" was thus shown in the Court Room until 1125 hours, when a recess was taken.]

COMMANDER DONOVAN: May it please the Tribunal, in the films which have just been shown to the Tribunal, we have watched the Nazi rise to power. In Part 3 of our documentary motion picture now to be presented, we see the use they made of that power, and how the German Nation was led by militaristic regimentation to preparation for aggressive war as an instrument of national policy.

[The showing of the film then continued; at the end a recess was taken until 1400 hours.]

COMMANDER DONOVAN: This morning we presented photographic evidence of the history of National Socialism from 1921 to September, 1939. We saw the dignity of the individual in Germany destroyed by men dedicated to perverted nationalism, men who set forth certain objectives and then preached to a regimented people the accomplishment of those objectives by any means, including aggressive war.

In September, 1939, the Nazis launched the first of a series of catastrophic wars, terminated only by the military collapse of Germany. It is the final chapter in the history of National Socialism that the prosecution now presents.

May I again remind the Tribunal that all film presented and all German narration heard is in the original form as filmed by the Nazis.

[The showing of the film then continued.]

COMMANDER DONOVAN: The prosecution has concluded its presentation of the photographic summation entitled "The Nazi Plan". We shall deliver for the permanent records of the Tribunal, as soon as possible, the original films projected today.

COLONEL STOREY: If the Tribunal please, just a brief announcement about the presentation that will follow. The rest of the week will be consumed in the presentation of War Crimes and Crimes against Humanity, starting with exploitation of forced labour, concentration camps, persecution of the Jews, and Germanisation and spoliation in occupied countries. We should like to call the Tribunal's attention to the fact that many of these crimes will be crimes attributed to the criminal organisations. The programme following will be the criminal organisations, beginning with the Leadership Corps of the Nazi Party, the Reich Cabinet, the S.A., the S.S., and, finally, the S.D. and Gestapo.

Mr. Dodd will now present "Exploitation of Forced Labour".

MR. DODD: We propose to submit during the next several days evidence, as Colonel Storey has said a moment ago, concerning the conspirators' criminal deportation and enslavement of foreign labour, their illegal use of prisoners of war, their infamous concentration camps and their relentless persecution of the Jews. We will present evidence regarding the general [Page 288] aspects of these programmes, and our French and Soviet colleagues will present evidence of the specific application of these programmes in the West and the East, respectively.

These crimes were committed both before and after Nazi Germany had launched its series of aggressions. They were committed within Germany and in foreign countries as well. Although separated in time and space, these crimes had, of course, an inter-relationship which resulted from their having a common source in Nazi ideology; for within Germany the conspirators had made hatred and destruction of the Jew an official philosophy and a public duty; they had preached the concept of the master race with its corollary of slavery for others, they had denied and destroyed the dignity and the rights of the individual human being. They had organised force, brutality and terror into instruments of political power and had made them commonplaces of daily existence. We propose to prove that they had placed the concentration camp and a vast apparatus of force behind their racial and political myths, their laws and their policies. As every German Cabinet Minister or high official knew, behind the laws and decrees in the Reichsgesetzblatt was not the agreement of the people or their representatives, but the terror of the concentration camps and the Police State. The conspirators had preached that war was a noble activity and that force was the appropriate means of resolving international differences and, having mobilised all aspects of German life for war, they plunged Germany and the world into war.

We say that this system of hatred, savagery, and denial of individual rights, which the conspirators erected into a philosophy of government within Germany, into what we may call the Nazi Constitution, followed the Nazi armies as they swept over Europe. For the Jews of the occupied countries suffered the same fate as the Jews of Germany, and foreign labourers became the serfs of the master race - they were deported and enslaved by the millions. Many deported and enslaved labourers joined the victims of the concentration camps where they were literally worked to death in the course of the Nazi programme of extermination through work. We propose to show that this Nazi combination of the assembly line, the torture chamber and the executioner's rack in a single institution has a horrible repugnance to the twentieth century mind.

We say that it is plain that the programme of the concentration camp, the anti-Jewish programme, the forced labour programme, are all parts of a larger pattern, and this will become even more plain as we examine the evidence regarding these programmes and then test their legality by applying the relevant principles of International Law.

The evidence relating to the Nazi Slave Labour Programme has been assembled in a document book bearing the letter "R", and, in addition, there is an appendix to the document book consisting of certain photographs contained in a manila folder. Your Honours will observe that on some of the books we have placed some tabs, so that it will be easier for the Tribunal to locate the documents. Unfortunately, we did not have a sufficient number of tabs to do the work completely, and that will account for tabs missing on some of the document books.

It may illuminate the specific items of evidence which will be offered later if we first describe in rather general terms the elements of the Nazi foreign labour policy. It was a policy of mass deportation and mass enslavement, as I said a moment ago, and it was also carried out by force, by fraud, by terror, by arson, by means unrestrained by the laws of war, and laws of humanity, or the considerations of mercy. This labour policy was a policy as well of underfeeding and overworking foreign labourers, of subjecting them to every form of degradation, brutality and inhumanity. It was a policy which compelled foreign workers and prisoners of war to manufacture armaments and to engage in other operations of war directed against their own countries. It was a policy, as we propose to establish, which constituted a flagrant violation of the laws of war and the laws of humanity.

We shall show that defendants Sauckel and Speer are principally responsible for the formulation of the policy and for its execution, that defendant Sauckel, the Nazi Plenipotentiary General for Manpower, directed the recruitment, deportation and allocation of foreign civilian labour, that he sanctioned and directed the use of force as the instrument of recruitment, and that he was responsible for the care and treatment of the enslaved millions; that the defendant Speer, as Reich Minister for Armament and Munitions, Director of the Organisation Todt and member of the Central Planning Board, bears responsibility for the determination of the numbers of foreign slaves required by the German war machine responsible for the decision to recruit by force, and for the use under brutal, inhuman and degrading conditions, of foreign civilians and prisoners of war in the manufacture of armaments and munitions, the construction of fortifications, and in active military operations.

We shall also show in this presentation that the defendant Goering, as Plenipotentiary General for the Four Year Plan, is responsible for all of the crimes involved in the Nazi Slave Labour Programme. Finally, we propose to show that the defendant Rosenberg, as Reich Minister for the Eastern Occupied Territories, and the defendant Frank, as Governor of the Government General of Poland, and the defendant Seyss- Inquart, as Reich Commissar for the Occupied Netherlands, and the defendant Keitel, as Chief of the O.K.W., share responsibility for the recruitment by force and terror and for the deportation to Germany of the citizens of the areas overrun or subjugated by the Wehrmacht.

The use of vast numbers of foreign workers was planned before Germany went to war and was an integral part of the conspiracy for waging aggressive war. On 23rd May, 1939, a meeting was held in Hitler's study at the Reich Chancellery. Present were the defendants Goering , Raeder and Keitel.

I now refer to Document L-79 which has already been introduced in evidence as Exhibit USA 27. The document presents the minutes of this meeting, at which Hitler stated, as your Honours will recall, that he intended to attack Poland at the first suitable opportunity; but I wish to quote from Page 2 of the English text starting with Paragraph 13. In the German text the passage, by the way, appears at Page 4, Paragraphs 6 and 7. Quoting directly from the English text:

> "If fate brings us into conflict with the West, the possession of extensive areas in the East will be advantageous. We shall be able to rely upon record harvests even less in time of war than in peace.
>
> The population of non-German areas will perform no military service, and will be available as a source of labour."

We say the Slave Labour Programme of the Nazi conspirators was designed to achieve two purposes, both of which were criminal. The primary purpose, of course, was to satisfy the labour requirements of the Nazi war machine by compelling these foreign workers, in effect, to make war against their own countries and their allies. The secondary purpose was to destroy or weaken peoples deemed inferior by the Nazi racialists, or deemed potentially hostile by the Nazi planners of world supremacy.

These purposes were expressed by the conspirators themselves.

I wish to refer at this point and to offer in evidence Document 016-PS, which is Exhibit USA 168. This document was sent by the defendant Sauckel to the defendant Rosenberg on 20th April, 1942, and it describes Sauckel's Labour Mobilisation Programme. I wish to quote now from Page 2 of the English text, starting with the sixth paragraph, and in the German text, again, it appears at Page 2 of the second paragraph. Quoting from the text directly:

"The aim of this new, gigantic labour mobilisation is to use all the rich and tremendous sources, conquered and secured for us by our fighting Armed Forces under the Leadership of Adolf Hitler, for the armament of the Armed Forces and also for the nutrition of the Homeland. The raw materials as well as the fertility of the conquered territories and their human labour power are to be used completely and conscientiously to the profit of Germany and her allies."

The theory of the master race underlay the conspirators' labour policy in the East.

I now refer to Document 1130-PS, which is marked Exhibit USA 16q. This document consists of a statement made by one Erich Koch, Reich Commissar for the Ukraine, on 5th March, 1943, at a meeting of the National Socialist Party in Kiev. I quote from the first page of the English text, starting with the first paragraph, and in the German text it appears at Page 2, Paragraph 1. Quoting directly again from the English text, Koch said:-

"We are the master race and must govern hardly but justly..I will draw the very last out of this country. I did not come to spread bliss. I have come to help the Fuehrer. The population must work, work, and work again. for some people are getting excited, that the population may not get enough to eat. The population cannot demand that, one has only to remember what our heroes were deprived of in Stalingrad .. We definitely did not come here to give out manna. We have come here to create the basis for victory. We are a master race, which must remember that the lowliest German worker is racially and biologically a thousand times more valuable than the population here."

At this point I should like to offer in evidence Document 1919-PS, which is Exhibit USA 170. This is a document which contains a speech delivered by Himmler, the Reichsfuehrer S.S., to a group of S.S. Generals on 4th October, 1943, at Posen, and I am referring to the first page of the English text, starting with the third paragraph. For the benefit of the interpreters, in the German text it appears at Page 23 in the first paragraph. Quoting direct from this document, starting with the third paragraph:-

"What happens to a Russian, or to a Czech, does not interest me in the slightest. What the nations can offer in the way of good blood of our type, we will take, if necessary by kidnapping their children and raising them here with us. Whether nations live in prosperity or starve to death interests me only in so far as we need them as slaves for our Kultur: otherwise, it is of no interest to me. Whether 10,000 Russian females fall down from exhaustion while digging an anti-tank ditch interests me only in so far as the anti-tank ditch for Germany is finished--."

THE PRESIDENT: Who is the author of that document?

MR. DODD: The author of that quotation was the Reichsfuehrer S.S., Heinrich Himmler.

The next document to which I make reference is 031-PS, which is Exhibit USA 171. This document is a top secret memorandum prepared for the Ministry for the Eastern Occupied Territories on 12th June, 1944, and approved by the defendant Rosenberg; and from it I wish to quote from the English text, starting with the first paragraph, and in the German text the passage appears at Page 2 in the first paragraph. Quoting directly:-

"The Army Group Centre has the intention to apprehend 40,000 - 50,000 youths of the ages of 10 to 14 who are in the Army area, and to transport them to the Reich..."

I wish to pass now to line 21 of Paragraph 1, and quoting directly I read as follows:-

"It is intended to allot these juveniles primarily to the German trades as apprentices, to be used as skilled workers after 2 years' training. This is to be arranged through the Organisation Todt, which is especially equipped for such a task through its technical and other set-ups. This action is being greatly welcomed by the German trade since it represents a decisive measure for the alleviation of the shortage of apprentices."

Passing a little further on in that document, I wish to call to the attention of the Tribunal Paragraph 1 on Page 2, and to quote it directly:-

"This action is aimed not only at preventing a direct reinforcement of the enemy's military strength, but also at a reduction of his biological potentialities as viewed from the perspective of the future. These ideas have been voiced not only by the Reichsfuehrer of the S.S. but also by the Fuehrer. Corresponding orders were given during last year's withdrawals in the Southern Sector."

I call to your Honour's attention particularly, that the approval of the defendant Rosenberg is noted on Page 3 of the document. It is a note in ink in the original, and I quote it-:

"Regarding the above Obergruppenfuehrer Berger received the memorandum on 14th June. Consequently the Reich Minister has approved the action."

THE PRESIDENT: Mr. Dodd, did you mean to leave out the sentence at the bottom of Page 1?

MR. DODD: No, your Honour, I did not, but I did not want to refer to it at this time. I will refer to it a little later on.

THE PRESIDENT Is not it really a part of what follows at the top of Page 2, the words "Following are the arguments - ."

MR. DODD: I did omit that. I thought you were referring to the sentence above. I am sorry. "Following are the arguments against this decision of the minister"; and then, quoting:-

"This action is not only aimed at preventing direct reinforcement of any military - "

THE PRESIDENT: Yes, and you were telling us how the defendant Rosenberg was implicated.

MR. DODD: Yes. On the last page of that document, the original bears a note in ink, and in the mimeographed copy it is typewritten:

"Regarding the above Obergruppenfuehrer Berger received the memorandum on 14th June. Consequently the Reich Minister has approved the action."

One page back on that same document, from the first paragraph, four sentences down, the sentence begins:

"The Minister has approved the execution of the high action in the Army Territories, under the conditions and provisions arrived at in talks with Army Group Centre."

The purposes of the Slave Labour Programme which we have just been describing, namely the strengthening of the Nazi war machine and the destruction or weakening of peoples deemed inferior by the Nazi conspirators, were achieved, we repeat, by the impressment and deportation of millions of persons into Germany for forced labour. It involved the separation of husbands from their wives and children from their parents, and the imposition of conditions unfit for human existence, with the result that countless numbers were killed.

Poland was the first victim. The defendant Frank, as Governor of the Government General of Poland, announced that under his programme 1,000,000 workers were to be sent to Germany, and he recommended that police surround Polish villages and seize the inhabitants for deportation.

I wish to refer to Document 1375-PS, which is Exhibit USA 172. This document is a letter from the defendant Frank to the defendant Goering and it is dated the 25th January, 1940. I wish to quote from the first page of the English text, starting with the first paragraph, and in the German text, again, it appears at Page 1 of the first paragraph, and, quoting directly:-

"In view of the present requirements of the Reich for the defence industry, it is at present fundamentally impossible to carry on long term economic policy in the Government General. Rather, it is necessary so to steer the economy of the Government General that it will, in the shortest possible time, accomplish results representing the maximum that can be obtained from the economic strength of the Government General for the immediate strengthening of our capacity for defence.

In particular the following performances are expected of the total economy of the Government General."

I wish to pass on a little bit in this text to the second page and particularly to Paragraph (g) of the English text. In the German text, the same passage appears on Page 3 in Paragraph (g). I am quoting directly again:-

"Supply and transportation of at least one million male and female agricultural and industrial workers to the Reich - among them at least 750,000 agricultural workers of whom at least 50 per cent. must be women - in order to guarantee agricultural production in the Reich and as a replacement for industrial workers lacking in the Reich."

The methods by which these workers were to be supplied were considered by the defendant Frank, as revealed in the document to which we now refer.

It is an entry in the defendant Frank's own diary, to which we have assigned our Document 2233-PS-A, and which we offer as Exhibit USA 173. The portion which I shall read is the entry for Friday, 10th May, 1940. It appears in the document book as 2233-PS-A, on the third page, in the centre of the page. Just above are the words "Page 23", Paragraph 1, to the left, just above it:-

297

"Then the Governor General deals with the problem of the Compulsory Labour Service of the Poles. Upon the demands from the Reich it has now been decreed that compulsion may be exercised, in view of the fact that sufficient manpower was not voluntarily available for service inside the German Reich. This compulsion means the possibility of arrest of male and female Poles. Because of these measures a certain disquietude had developed which, according to individual reports, was spreading very much, and which might produce difficulties everywhere. General Field Marshal Goering some time ago pointed out in a long speech the necessity to deport into the Reich a million workers. The supply so far was 160,000. However, great difficulties had to be overcome. Therefore it would be advisable to consult the district and town chiefs in the execution of the compulsion, so that one could be sure from the start that this action would be reasonably successful. The arrest of young Poles when leaving church service or the cinema would bring about an increasing nervousness among them. Generally speaking, he had no objections at all if the rubbish, capable of work yet often loitering about, were snatched from the streets. The best method for this, however, would be the organisation of a raid, and it would be absolutely justifiable to stop a Pole in the street and to question him what he was doing, where he was working, etc."

I should like to refer to another entry in the diary of the defendant Frank, and I offer in evidence an extract from the entry made on 16th March, 1940, which appears in the document book as 2233-PS-B, and it is Exhibit USA 174. I wish particularly to quote from the third page of the English text:-

"The Governor General remarks that he had long negotiations in Berlin with the representatives of the Reich Ministry for Finance and the Reich Ministry for Food. An urgent demand was made there that Polish farm workers should be sent to the Reich in greater numbers. He has made the statement in Berlin that he, if it is demanded from him, could naturally exercise force in such a manner as to order the police to surround a village, and get the men and women in question out by force, and then send them to Germany. One can however also work in another way, besides these police measures, by retaining the unemployment compensation of those workers in question."

THE PRESIDENT: Why is it that this document is dated the 16th March, 1943

MR. DODD: That is clearly an error in the translation - I am sorry, your Honour. It is the 16th March, 1940. It is a mistake in the mimeographing.

The instruments of force and terror used to carry out this programme reached into many phases of Polish life. German labour authorities raided churches and theatres, seized those present and shipped them back to Germany. This appears in a memorandum to Himmler, which we offer in evidence as Document 2220-PS, and it becomes Exhibit USA 175. This memorandum is dated the 17th April, 1943, and it was written by Dr. Lammers, the Chief of the Reich Chancellery, and deals with the situation in the Government General of Poland.

DR. SERVATIUS (Counsel for defendant Sauckel): I should like to call the attention of the Court to the fact that the last three documents which have just been read were not made available to me beforehand. They did not appear in the original list of documents, and when checking the later list I could not find them either.

I therefore request that the reading of these documents be held in abeyance until I have had an opportunity to peruse them, and to discuss the matter with my client.

Perhaps I may, at the same time, lodge an additional complaint. I received some interrogation material in German the day before yesterday. My client, when asked, told me that they are not transcripts of the interrogation in the real sense of the word; that he was interrogated in German; that an interpreter translated his deposition into English, and that this was taken down.

THE PRESIDENT: I did not hear what you said last. I heard what you said about the three last documents not being available to you, and you went on to say something about interrogations.

DR. SERVATIUS: With regard to the interrogation document - as I shall call it - which was submitted to me I should like to make the following complaint. These documents cannot have the value of evidence as they were not presented to the defendant for approval; he did not sign them, nor were they read to him. They are transcripts in English, a language which the defendant understands but little or not at all.

I have also ascertained that another interrogation document, concerning the defendant Speer, contains statements detrimental to my client's interests, statements which are evidently incorrect too, as I established after talking to him.

I should like to have an opportunity of discussing the matter with the representatives of the prosecution, in order to clear up these differences and to decide whether I can agree to the use of these documents. For the time being I must object to use being made of these documents, which are to be presented by the prosecution today, or tomorrow at the latest.

THE PRESIDENT: As I understand it, you said to us that the last three documents were not available to you and that they were not in the original list. Is that right?

DR. SERVATIUS: Not available so far. I should like to have an opportunity to peruse these documents beforehand. They are being read here prior to my even having seen them.

THE PRESIDENT: And then you went on to deal with the interrogations which have not been put into evidence.

DR. SERVATIUS: It is, however, probable that the material will be put into evidence today, and I wish to take the opportunity of calling the Court's attention to the fact that I wish to discuss the matter with the prosecution beforehand, in case the material should be used during tomorrow's proceedings. Meanwhile I must object to this material being used as evidence.

THE PRESIDENT: Mr. Dodd, do you know what the circumstances are about these three documents which have not been supplied.

MR. DODD: I do not, your Honour. They have been placed in the defendants' Information Centre and they partly have been in the information list. It may be that through some oversight these entries of this diary were neglected.

DR. SERVATIUS: I have these documents in my hand; they are not numbered. The first document concerning Sauckel begins on Page 10, question and answer on Pages 11, 12. It is, therefore, not a coherent document, but consists of fragments of a transcript, the origin of which I should like to investigate.

THE PRESIDENT: Counsel for the prosecution will supply you with these documents at the adjournment this afternoon. With reference to the interrogation, if they propose to use any interrogation in the trial tomorrow, they can also supply you with any documents which are material to that interrogation.

DR. SERVATIUS: I agree to that.

MR. DODD: I believe I was referring to Document 2220-PS.

THE PRESIDENT: That is right. You have not begun to read it yet.

MR. DODD: I propose to read from the fourth page of the English text, Paragraph 2 at the top of the page, particularly the last two sentences of the paragraph; and in the German text the passage is found in Page 10, Paragraph 1. Quoting directly, it is as follows:-

> "As things were, the utilisation of manpower had to be enforced by means of more or less forceful methods, such as the instances when certain groups appointed by the Labour Offices caught churchgoers and cinema audiences here and there, and transported them into the Reich. That such methods undermine the people's willingness to work and the people's confidence to such a degree that it cannot be checked even with terror, is just as clear as the consequences brought about by a strengthening of the political resistance movement."

That is the end of the quotation. We say that Polish farmland was confiscated with the aid of the S.S. and was distributed to German inhabitants or held in trust for the German community, and the farm owners were employed as labourers, or transported to Germany against their will. We refer to Document 1352-PS, which becomes Exhibit USA 176. This document is a report of the S.S., and it bears the title "Achievement of Confiscations of Polish Agricultural Enterprises with the Purpose to Transfer the Poles to the Old Reich and to Employ Them as Agricultural Workers."

I wish to read from the first page of the English text beginning with the fifth paragraph; and in the German text it appears on Page 9, Paragraph 1. Quoting:-

> "It is possible without difficulty to accomplish the confiscation of small agricultural enterprises in the villages in which larger agricultural enterprises have been already confiscated, and are under the management of the East German Corporation for Agricultural Development."

And then passing down three sentences, there is this statement which I quote:-

> "The former owners of Polish farms, together with their families, will be transferred to the old Reich by the employment agencies, for employment as farm workers. In this way many hundreds of Polish agricultural workers can be placed at the disposal of agriculture in the old Reich in the shortest and simplest manner. In this way the most pressing shortage, that which is now felt especially in the root-crop districts, would be overcome."

Pursuant to the directions of the defendant Sauckel, his agents and the S.S. men deported Polish men to Germany without their families, thereby accomplishing one of the basic purposes of the programme, the supplying of labour for the German war effort, and at the same time, weakening the reproductive potential of the Polish people.

I wish to refer directly to Document L-61, which becomes Exhibit USA 177. This document is a letter from the defendant Sauckel to the Presidents of the "Landes" Employment Offices. It is dated 26th November, 1942, and I want to read from the first paragraph of that letter, which states as follows:-

"In agreement with the Chief of the Security Police and the S.D., Jews who are still in employment are, from now on, to be evacuated from the territory of the Reich and are to be replaced by Poles, who are being deported from the Government General."

Passing to the third paragraph of that same letter, we find this statement.

"The Poles who are to be evacuated as a result of this measure will be put into concentration camps and put to work whether they are criminal or asocial elements. The remaining Poles where they are suitable for labour will be transported without family into the Reich, particularly to Berlin, where they will be put at the disposal of the labour allocation offices, to work in armament factories instead of the Jews who are to be replaced."

THE PRESIDENT: Who is the Chief of the Security Police, mentioned in the second paragraph?

MR. DODD: The Chief of the Security Police was Heinrich Himmler. He was also the Reichsfuehrer of the S.S.

DR. SERVATIUS: I would like to add something with regard to this document. The defendant Sauckel denies knowledge of it, and the place of issue, not mentioned during the reading of this document, is relevant. This document, according to its letterhead, was written at 36 Saarland Strasse, a place which has never been the office of defendant Sauckel.

The second point is; this document was not signed by the defendant Sauckel, and contrary to the statement in the document list classifying it as an original letter, it is merely a copy marked "Signed Sauckel". The usual certification of the signature customary for all documents is missing. I should like the prosecution to take note of this, so that I can refer to this document in the defence later.

THE PRESIDENT: If the procedure which the Tribunal has laid down has been carried out, either the original document or a photostat copy will be in your Information Centre, and you can then compare or show to your client either the photostat or the original.

DR. SERVATIUS: I have done this, and only object to the fact that this document is being read with the exclusion of some parts which I consider important. If this letter is being read here it will have to be read in its entirety, and with parts considered essential by me, and, of course, we also attach importance to the kind of signature.

THE PRESIDENT: Will you repeat that.

DR. SERVATIUS: I beg that the letter be read in its entirety if it is to be used here; namely, with its complete heading and the signature of the defendant, such as it is. The certification of the signature is missing, a fact from which my client draws certain conclusions in his favour.

THE PRESIDENT: You will have an opportunity, after adjournment, of seeing this document, and you have been told already that you can refer, when your turn comes to present your defence, to the whole of any document. It is inconvenient to the Tribunal to have many interruptions of this sort, and if you wish to refer to the whole document, you will be able to do so at a later stage.

DR. SERVATIUS: I draw the conclusion therefrom that it is admissible to present parts of a document instead of a complete document. Do I understand the Court correctly ?

THE PRESIDENT: Yes, certainly. You can put in a part or the whole of the document when your turn comes. We will adjourn now; but, Mr. Dodd, you will satisfy this counsel for the defence as to the reason why he had not got these documents.

MR. DODD: Yes, I will.

THE PRESIDENT: And you will make them available to him and ensure that he has an opportunity of seeing the original of this document so that he can check the signature.

MR. DODD: We will have and furnish a photostat of the document, and I will see that the original is available to him.

THE PRESIDENT: All right, we will adjourn now.

[The Tribunal adjourned until 1000 hours, on 12th December, 1945.]

Eighteenth Day:
Wednesday, 12th December, 1945

THE PRESIDENT: The Tribunal will adjourn this morning at 12.30 for a closed session and sit again at 2 o'clock.

MR. DODD: May it please the Tribunal, I should like to report to the Tribunal this morning with reference to the questions which arose yesterday afternoon concerning three documents.

After adjournment we found that Document 2220-PS was in the defendants' Information Centre in photostatic form, and that the two other documents, being respectively two entries from the Frank diary, were also there but in a different form. The Frank diary consists of some 40 odd volumes which we, of course, were not able to photostat, so we had placed instead in the defendants' room the excerpts. As a matter of fact, we had placed the entire document book there.

DR. ALFRED SEIDL (Counsel for defendant Frank): Yesterday the prosecution showed documents concerning the defendant Frank. The documents concerned were 2233-PS-A and 2233-PS-B, Exhibits USA 173 and 174. These are not ordinary documents, but excerpts from the diary of Frank. Six weeks ago I applied in writing to have this diary, which consists Of 42 heavy, thick volumes, submitted to me. I first made this request on 2nd September, the second time on 16th November, the third time on 18th November and the fourth time on 3rd December.

In spite of this I have not received this diary, and I should like to ask the Tribunal that this diary be submitted to me as soon as possible, if for no other reason, because evidence is involved which the defendant Frank before his arrest handed over to the officer who was to arrest him so that it could be used as evidence for his defence.

I am not in a position to work through all this material in a few days, and I should like to ask the Tribunal that this diary be put at my disposal without delay.

In this connection I should like to call the attention of the Tribunal to another point. The Tribunal has already granted that the four long speeches delivered by defendant Frank in Germany in 1942, which led to his dismissal from his offices by Hitler, should be put at my disposal. The General Secretary of the Tribunal gave me notice of this as early as the 4th December. Unfortunately I have not received copies of these speeches up to this day. I should be very grateful therefore if the Tribunal will make certain that decisions of the Tribunal are being carried out and that the documents be submitted to me.

THE PRESIDENT: The Tribunal will look into these matters with the General Secretary of the Tribunal, and doubtless it will be able to arrange that you should have these documents submitted to you in the defendants' counsel Information Centre.

DR. SEIDL: Thank you.

THE PRESIDENT: Yes, Mr. Dodd.

MR. DODD: May I refer briefly to the discussion that we were engaged in yesterday in order to pick up the train of thought.

I wish to remind the Tribunal that we were discussing or had just completed a discussion of Document L-61, which had to do with a letter written by the defendant Sauckel to the residents of the "Landes" Employment Offices. I had read two excerpts from that letter.

Referring to the letter, we say that the Nazi campaign of force and terror and abduction was described in another letter to the defendant Frank, which we wish to refer to as Document 1526-PS.

THE PRESIDENT: Before you pass from that, Mr. Dodd, has either the original or the photostatic copy been shown to Sauckel's counsel?

MR. DODD: Oh, yes, sir. A photostatic copy was in the defendants' Information Centre, and after adjournment yesterday we got the original and handed it to him here in this room.

THE PRESIDENT: And he saw it?

MR. DODD: Yes, sir.

THE PRESIDENT: Very well.

MR. DODD: This Document, 1526-PS, Exhibit USA 178, is a letter written by the Chairman of the Ukrainian Main Committee, at Cracow, in February, 1943. I wish to read from the third page of the English text, beginning with the second paragraph. The same passage in the German text at Page 2, Paragraph 5. I quote:-

"The general nervousness is still more enhanced by the wrong methods of finding labour which have been used more and more frequently in recent months.

The wild and ruthless man-hunt as exercised everywhere in towns and country, in streets, squares, stations, even in churches, at night in houses, has badly shaken the feeling of security of the inhabitants. Everybody is exposed to the danger, to be seized anywhere and at any time by members of the police, suddenly and unexpectedly, and to be brought into an assembly camp. None of his relatives knows what has happened to him, and only months later one or the other gets news of his fate by a postcard."

I wish to turn to enclosure 5 on Page 8 of this document, which I quote:-

"In November of last year an inspection of all males of the age groups 1910 to 1920 was ordered in the area of Zaleschozyki (district of Czortkow). After the men had appeared for inspection, all those who were chosen were arrested at once, loaded into trains and sent to the Reich. Such recruiting of labourers for the Reich also took place in other areas of this district. Following some interventions the action was then stopped."

The resistance of the Polish people to this enslavement programme and the necessity for increased force were described by the defendant Sauckel's deputy, one Timm, at a meeting of the Central Planning Board, which was, by the way, Hitler's war-time planning agency. It was made up of the defendant Speer, Field Marshal Milch and State Secretary Korner. The Central Planning Board was the highest level economic planning agency, exercising production controls by allocating raw materials and labour to industrial users.

Now, Document R-124, Exhibit USA 179. This document consists of excerpts from minutes of the meetings of this Central Planning Board, and minutes of conferences between the defendant Speer and Hitler. Only the excerpts, of course, from these minutes upon which we rely are being offered in evidence. I would say to the Tribunal, however, that the balance of the minutes are available, or can or be made available if the Tribunal so desires.

This deputy of Sauckel, his name being Timm, made a statement at the 36th conference of the Central Planning Board, and it appears on Page 14, Paragraph 2, of the English text of Document R-124, and on Page 10, Paragraph 2, of the German text:-

"Especially in Poland the situation at the moment is extraordinarily serious. It is well known that violent battles occurred just because of these actions. The resistance against the administration established by us is very strong. Quite a number of our men have been exposed to increased dangers, and it was only in the last two or three weeks that some of them were shot dead, e.g., the head of the Labour Office of Warsaw who was shot in his office, and yesterday again, another man. This is how matters stand at present, and the recruiting itself, even if done with the best will, remains extremely difficult unless police reinforcements are at hand."

Deportation and enslavement of civilians reached unprecedented levels in the so-called Eastern Occupied Territories. These wholesale deportations resulted directly from labour demands made by the defendant Sauckel on the defendant Rosenberg, who was the Reich Minister for the Eastern Occupied Territories, and his subordinates, and also on the Armed Forces - a demand made directly on the Armed Forces by the defendant Sauckel.

On the 5th October, 1942, for example, the defendant Sauckel wrote to the defendant Rosenberg, stating that two million foreign labourers were required, and that the majority of these would have to be drafted from the recently Occupied Eastern Territories and especially from the Ukraine.

I wish to refer at this point to Document 017-PS, which will be Exhibit USA 180. This letter from the defendant Sauckel to the defendant Rosenberg I wish to quote in full. It begins by saying:-

"The Fuehrer has worked out new and most urgent plans for the armament industry which require the quick mobilisation of two million more foreign labour forces. The Fuehrer therefore has granted me, for the execution of my decree Of 21st March, 1942, new powers for my new duties, and has especially authorised me to take whatever measures I think are necessary in the Reich, the Protectorate, the General Government, as well as in the occupied territories, in order to assure at all costs an orderly mobilisation of labour for the German armament industry. The additional labour forces required will have to be drafted for the majority from the recently Occupied Eastern Territories, especially from the Reichskommissariat Ukraine. Therefore, the Reichskommissariat Ukraine must furnish:-

225,000 labour forces by 31st December, 1942, and 225,000 more by 1st May, 1943.

I ask you to inform Reichskommissar, Gauleiter, Party Member Koch about the new situation and requirements and especially to see to it that he will support personally in any way possible the execution of this new requirement.

I have the intention to visit Party Member Koch shortly and I would be grateful to you if you could inform me as to where and when I could meet him for a personal discussion. But I ask that the procurement be taken up at once with every possible pressure and the commitment of all powers, especially those of the experts of the labour offices. All the directives which had limited temporarily the procurement of Eastern labourers are annulled. The Reich procurement for the next months must be given priority over all other measures.

I do not ignore the difficulties which exist for the execution of this new requirement, but I am convinced that with the ruthless commitment of all resources, and with the full co-operation of all those interested, the execution of the new demands can be accomplished by the fixed date. I have already communicated the new demands to the Reichskommissar Ukraine by mail. In reference to our long-distance phone call of today I will send you the text of the Fuehrer's decree at the beginning of next week."

I should like to remind the Tribunal that we referred previously, yesterday afternoon, to this Reichskommissar, Gauleiter, Party Member Koch, and we quoted him as stating, the Tribunal will recall: "We are the master race. We must be hard," and so forth.

On the 17th March, 1943, the defendant Sauckel wrote again to the defendant Rosenberg, and on this occasion he demanded the importation of another 1,000,000 men and women from the Eastern territories within the following four months. I wish to refer at this point to Document 019-PS, which will be Exhibit USA 181. Quoting that letter in full:-

"After a protracted illness my Deputy for Labour Supply in the occupied Eastern territories, State Councillor Peuckert, is going there to regulate the supply both for Germany and the territories themselves.

I ask you sincerely, dear Party Member Rosenberg, to assist him to your utmost on account of the pressing urgency of his mission. I thank you for the hitherto good reception accorded to Peuckert. He himself has been charged by me with the absolute and completely unreserved co-operation with all bureaux of the Eastern territories. In particular the labour supply for German agriculture, and likewise for the most urgent armament production programmes ordered by the Fuehrer make the rapid importation of approximately one million men and women from the Eastern territories within the next four months imperative. Starting 15th March, the daily shipment must have reached 5,000 female and male workers respectively, while by the beginning of April this number has to be stepped up to 10,000. This is a requisite of the most urgent programmes, and the spring tillage and other agricultural tasks are not to suffer to the detriment of the nutrition and of the Armed Forces. I have foreseen the allotment of the draft quotas for the individual territories in agreement with your experts for the labour supply as follows:-

Daily quota starting 15th March, 1943 - .People
General Commissariat White Ruthenia - 500
Economic Inspection Centre - 500

Reichs Commissariat Ukraine - 3,000
Economic Inspection South - 1,000
Total - 5,000

Starting 1st April, 1943, the daily quota is to be doubled, corresponding to the doubling of the entire quota. I hope to visit personally the Eastern territories towards the end of the month, and ask you once more for your kind support."

The defendant Sauckel did travel to the East. He travelled to Kauen in Lithuania to press his demands. We offer in evidence Document 204-PS, which will be Exhibit USA 182. This document is a synopsis of a report of the City Commissioner of Kauen and minutes of a meeting in which the defendant Sauckel participated. I read from the second page of the English text, beginning with the first paragraph. The same passage appears in the German text at Page 5, Paragraph 2. Quoting directly as follows:-

"In a lecture in which the Plenipotentiary for the Arbeitseinsatz, Gauleiter Sauckel, made on 18th July, 1943, in Kauen, and in an official conference following it, between Gauleiter Sauckel and the General Commissar, the pool of labour in the Reich was again brought up urgently; Gauleiter Sauckel again demanded that Lithuanian labour be furnished in greater volume for the purpose of the Reich."

THE PRESIDENT: Who was the General Commissar, Rosenberg?

MR. DODD: The Plenipotentiary for the Arbeitseinsatz?

THE PRESIDENT: No, the General Commissar.

MR. DODD: His name is not known to us. He was apparently a local functionary in the Party.

THE PRESIDENT: Very well.

MR. DODD: The defendant Sauckel also visited Riga, in Latvia, to assert his demands, and the purpose of this visit is described in Document 2280-PS, which will be Exhibit USA 183. This document is a letter from the Reich Commissar for the Ostland to the Commissioner General in Riga and it is dated 3rd May, 1943. I wish to read from Page 1 of the English text, beginning with the first paragraph:-

"Following the basic statements of the Plenipotentiary General for manpower, Gauleiter Sauckel, on the occasion of his visit to Riga, on 21st April, 1943, it was decided in view of the critical situation and in disregard of all adverse considerations, that a total of 183,000 workers have to be supplied from the Eastern territories to the Reich territory. This task must definitely be accomplished within the next four months and at the latest must be completed by the end of August."

Here again we are not informed as to the name and identity of the Reich Commissar for the Ostland.

Sauckel asked the German Army for assistance in the recruitment and deportation of civilian labour from the Eastern territories. We refer now to Document 3010-PS, which will be Exhibit USA 184.

THE PRESIDENT: Mr. Dodd, were you saying that it was not known from whom that document emanated?

MR. DODD: No, sir. We say it is a letter from the Reichskommissar for the Ostland to the Commissioner General in Riga, but we do not know their names specifically at the time of the writing of the letter.

THE PRESIDENT: You do not know who the Reichskommissar of the Eastern territories was?

MR. DODD: We only know him by that title, "The Reichskommissar for the Ostland."

THE PRESIDENT: Very well.

MR. DODD: Lohse, I am now informed, was his name. I understood that we did not know it.

THE PRESIDENT: All right. **MR. DODD:** Referring to this Document 3010-PS, it is a secret organisation order of the Army Group South, dated 17th August, 1943. I wish to read from the first page of the English text, the first two paragraphs, as follows:-

> "The Plenipotentiary General for Labour Employment ordered the recruitment and employment of all born during the two years 1926 and 1927 for the whole of the newly occupied Eastern territory in Decree AZ. VI A 5780.28 (Enclosure I), copy of which is enclosed.
>
> The Reich Minister for Armament and Munitions approved this order. According to this order by the Plenipotentiary General for Labour Employment (B.G.A.) you have to recruit and to transport to the Reich immediately all labour force in your territory born during 1926 and 1927. The decree relative to labour duty and labour employment in the theatre of operations of the newly occupied Eastern territory of 6th February, 1943, and the executive orders therefore are the authority for the execution of this measure. Enlistment must be completed by 30th September, 1943, at the latest."

We say it is clear that the demands made by the defendant Sauckel resulted in the deportation of civilians from the occupied Eastern territories. The defendant Speer has recorded conferences with Hitler on 10th, 11th and 12th August, 1942, and this record is contained in Document R- 124, which is already in as Exhibit USA 179. I now wish to quote from Page 34, of that same document in Paragraph 1 of the English text. In the German text it appears at Page 23, Paragraph 2. Quoting directly:-

> "Gauleiter Sauckel promises to make Russian labour available for the fulfilment of the iron and coal programme and reports that - if required - he can supply a further million Russian labourers for the German armament industry up to and including October, 1942. He has already supplied 1,000,000 for the industry and 700,000 for agriculture. In this connection the Fuehrer states that the problem of providing labour can be solved in all cases and to any extent; he authorises Gauleiter Sauckel to take all measures required. He would agree to any necessary compulsion in the East as well as in the West if this question could not be solved on a voluntary basis."

In order to meet these demands of 1,700,000, 100,000 here and there, the Nazi conspirators made terror, violence and arson, as we said yesterday, fundamental instruments of their labour enslavement policy. Twenty days after the defendant Sauckel's demands Of 5th October, 1942, a top official in the defendant Rosenberg's Ministry described the measures taken to meet these demands. I wish to refer now to Document 294-PS, which is Exhibit USA 185. This document is a top secret memorandum dated 25th October, 1942, signed by one Braeutigam. I wish to quote from Page 4 Of the English text starting with the last paragraph, as follows. In the German text it appears at Page 8, Paragraph 2. Quoting directly:-

"We now experienced the grotesque picture of having to recruit millions of labourers from the Occupied Eastern Territories, after prisoners of war have died of hunger like flies, in order to fill the gaps that have formed within Germany. Now the food question no longer existed, In the prevailing limitless abuse of the Slavic humanity, 'recruiting' methods were used which probably have their origin in the blackest periods of the slave trade. A regular man-hunt was inaugurated. Without consideration of health or age the people were shipped to Germany where it turned out immediately that more than 100,000 had to be sent back because of serious illnesses and other incapabilities for work."

The defendant Rosenberg wrote concerning these brutalities to the instigator of them, the defendant Sauckel, and we refer now to Document 018-PS, which is Exhibit USA 186.

THE PRESIDENT: Mr. Dodd, from where did that top secret document come?

MR. DODD: It came from the files of the defendant Rosenberg.

This Document, 018-PS, is a letter from the defendant Rosenberg to the defendant Sauckel, and it is dated the 21st December, 1942, with attachments. I wish to quote from Page 1 of the English text starting at the middle of the second paragraph which reads as follows:-

"The report I have received shows that the increase of the guerrilla bands in the occupied Eastern Regions is largely due to the fact that the methods used for procuring labourers in these regions are felt to be forced measures of mass deportations, so that the endangered persons prefer to escape their fate by withdrawing into the woods or going to the guerrilla bands."

Passing now to Page 4 of the same English text, there is an attachment to Rosenberg's letter consisting of parts excerpted from letters of residents of the occupied Eastern territories, excerpted by Nazi censors apparently. In the German text it appears at Page 6, Paragraphs 1 and 2. Starting the quotation:-

"At our place, new things have happened. People are being taken to Germany. On 5th December, some people from the Kowkuski district were scheduled to go, but they did not want to and the village was set afire. They threatened to do the same thing in Borowytschi, as not all who were scheduled to depart wanted to go. Thereupon three truck loads of Germans arrived and set fire to their houses. In Wrasnytschi, twelve houses and in Borowytschi, three houses were burned.

On 1st October a new conscription of labour forces took place. I will describe the most important events to you. You cannot imagine the bestiality. You probably remember what we were told about the Soviets during their rule of the Poles. We did not believe it then, and now it seems just as incredible. The order came to supply 25 workers, but no one reported. All had fled. Then the German militia came and began to ignite the houses of those who had fled. The fire became very violent, since it had not rained for two months. In addition the grain stacks were in the farm yards. You can imagine what took place. The people who had hurried to the scene were forbidden to extinguish the flames and were beaten and arrested, so that seven homesteads burned down. The policemen meanwhile ignited other houses. The people fell on their knees and kissed the policemen's hands, but they beat them with rubber truncheons and threatened to burn down the whole village. I do not know how this would have ended if Sapurkany had not intervened. He promised that there would be labourers by morning. During the fire the militia went through the adjoining villages, seized the labourers, and put them under arrest. Wherever they did not find any labourers, they detained the parents, until the children appeared. That is how they raged throughout the night in Bieloserka. The workers who had not yet appeared by then were to be shot. All schools were closed and the married teachers were sent to work here, while the unmarried ones go to work in Germany. They are now catching humans like the dog-catchers used to catch dogs. They have already been hunting for one week and have not yet got enough. The imprisoned workers are locked in the schoolhouse. They cannot even go to perform their natural functions, but have to do it like pigs in the same room. People from many villages went on a certain day to a pilgrimage to the Monastery Potschaew. They were all arrested, locked in, and will be sent to work. Among them there are lame, blind and aged people."

Despite the fact that the defendant Rosenberg wrote this letter with this attachment, we say he nevertheless countenanced the use of force in order to furnish slave labour to Germany and admitted his responsibility for the "unusual and hard measures" that were employed. I refer to excerpts from the transcript of an interrogation under oath of the defendant Rosenberg on 6th October, 1945, which is Exhibit USA 187, and I wish to quote from Page 1 of the English text starting with the ninth paragraph.

THE PRESIDENT: You have not given us the PS number.

MR. DODD: It has no PS number.

THE PRESIDENT: I beg your pardon. Has a copy of it been given to Rosenberg's counsel?

MR. DODD: Yes, it has been. It is at the end of the document book, if your Honour pleases, the document book the Tribunal has.

THE PRESIDENT: I see.

DR. ALFRED THOMA (Counsel for defendant Rosenberg): In the name of my client, I object to the reading of this document for the following reasons. My client has been asked in the preliminary hearings several times about these questions concerning employment of labour. He declared that the defendant Sauckel, by virtue of plenary authority received from the Fuehrer and by order of the Plenipotentiary for the Four Year Plan, had the right to give him orders and that he (the defendant Rosenberg), despite this, demanded a recruitment of labour on a voluntary basis; that this was carried through, and that Sauckel agreed, providing the quota and the time limit could be met. Rosenberg further stated that his Ministry demanded in joint meetings that the quota be reduced and had in part been granted such a reduction.

This document which is going to be presented does not say anything about all these statements. The document which is to be presented contains only fragments of this declaration.

In order to give the Court a complete picture and in order to give the defence the possibility of a complete survey, I ask the Court to request the prosecution to present the record of the entire declaration and then, before this document is presented officially, to discuss the translation with the defence in order to prevent misunderstandings.

THE PRESIDENT: I am not sure that I understand your objection. You say, as I understood it, that Sauckel had authority from Hitler; is that right?

DR. THOMA: Yes.

THE PRESIDENT: And that Rosenberg was carrying out that authority.

DR. THOMA: Yes.

THE PRESIDENT: But all that counsel for the prosecution is attempting to do at the moment is to put in evidence an interrogation of Rosenberg. With reference to that, you ask that he should put in the whole interrogation?

DR. THOMA: Yes.

THE PRESIDENT: Well, we do not know yet whether he intends to put in the whole interrogation or a part of it.

DR. THOMA: I know only one thing. I have the document which the prosecution wishes to submit already in my hands, and I can see that it contains only fragments of the whole interrogation. What it particularly does not contain is the fact that Rosenberg always insisted that only voluntary recruitment be taken into consideration and that Rosenberg desired a reduction of the quotas, This is not contained in the document that is to be submitted.

THE PRESIDENT: If counsel for the prosecution reads a part of the interrogation, and you wish to refer to another part of the interrogation, in order that the part he has read should not be misleading, you will be at liberty to do so, when he has read his part of the interrogation; is that clear?

DR. THOMA: Yes. Then I will request the Tribunal to ask counsel for the prosecution if the document, which he intends to submit, contains the whole of Rosenberg's declaration.

THE PRESIDENT: Mr. Dodd, were you going to put in the whole of Rosenberg's interrogation?

MR. DODD: No, your Honour, I was not prepared to put in the whole of Rosenberg's interrogation, but only certain parts of it. These parts are available, and have been for some time, to counsel. The whole of the Rosenberg interrogation, in English, was given to Sauckel's counsel, however, and he has the entire text of it, the only available copy that we have.

THE PRESIDENT: Has counsel for Rosenberg not got the entire document?

MR. DODD: He has only the excerpt that we propose to read into the record here at this time.

DR. THOMA: May I please speak?

THE PRESIDENT: Mr. Dodd, the Tribunal considers that if you propose to put in a part of the interrogation, the whole interrogation ought to be submitted to the defendant's counsel, that then you may read what part you like of the interrogation, and then defendant's counsel may refer to any other part of the interrogation directly, if it is necessary for the purpose of explaining the part which has been read by counsel for the prosecution. So before you use this interrogation, Rosenberg's counsel must have a copy of the whole interrogation.

MR. DODD: I might say, your Honour, that we turned over the whole interrogation to counsel for the defendant Sauckel, and we understood that he would make it available to all other defence counsel. Apparently, that did not happen.

DR. THOMA: Thank you, my Lord.

DR. SERVATIUS (Counsel for defendant Sauckel): Last night I received from the prosecution these documents in English. That, of course, is sufficient for me, but counsel for the other defendants are not all in a position to follow the English text, so that certain difficulties have arisen, and I must have sufficient time to interpret these matters for my colleagues. Or perhaps the prosecution could give us the German text - for the interrogation took place in German and was translated into English - so that the original German text should be on hand.

Those are the difficulties, and I would like to have the German translation as soon as possible.

MR. DODD: With reference to the so-called German text, the original is an English text. These interrogations were made through an interpreter and they were transcribed in English, so that the original text is an English text, and that is what was turned over to the attorney for the defendant Sauckel with the understanding that it would be made available to all other counsel.

THE PRESIDENT: But of course that does not quite meet their difficulties because they do not all of them speak English, or are not all able to read English, so I am afraid you must wait until Rosenberg's counsel has got a copy of the entire interrogation in his own language.

MR. DODD: Very well.

Passing on beyond the document which we have just referred to, and which we now withdraw in view of the ruling, but which we will offer at a later date after we have complied with the ruling of the Court, we have a letter dated 21st December, 1942, which is Document 018-PS, and which will be Exhibit USA 186 - which, by the way, is a letter from the defendant Rosenberg to the defendant Sauckel - and I wish to quote from Page 1, Paragraph 3 of the English text. In the German text it appears at Page 4, Paragraph 1. Quoting directly:-

"Even if I do not close my eyes to the necessity that the numbers demanded by the Reich Minister for Armament and Munitions, as well as by the agricultural economy, justify unusual and hard measures, I have to ask, due to the responsibility for the occupied Eastern territories which lies upon me, that in the accomplishment of the ordered tasks such measures be excluded, the toleration and prosecution of which will some day be held against me, and my collaborators."

In the Ukraine area, arson was indeed used as a terror instrument to enforce these conscription measures, and we refer now to Document 254-PS, which is Exhibit USA 188. This document is from an official of the Rosenberg Ministry and was also found in the Rosenberg file. It is dated 29th June, 1943, and encloses a copy of a letter from one Paul Kaab, a district commissioner in the territory of Wassilkow, to the defendant Rosenberg. I wish to quote from Kaab's letter, Page 1, starting with Paragraph 1 of the English text which reads as follows:-

"According to a charge by the Supreme Command of the Armed

Forces - "

THE PRESIDENT: Mr. Dodd, I thought you said the date of it was 29th June, 1943.

MR. DODD: Yes, I did, your Honour. That was the date on the document.

THE PRESIDENT: The mimeographed copy of the document I have appears to have as date of the original document the 29th June, 1945, and the date below is 7th June, 1944.

MR. DODD: We will get the original document.

I am sorry, your Honour. There are two errors here. The document is dated the 29th June, 1944.

THE PRESIDENT: I see. And the enclosure is 7th June, 1944?

MR. DODD: Yes.

> "Answering to a charge by the Supreme Command of the Armed Forces that I burned down a few houses in the territory of Wassilkow, Ukraine, belonging to insubordinate people ordered for work-duty, this accusation is true."

Passing now to the third paragraph:-

> "During the year of 1942, the conscription of workers was accomplished by way of propaganda. Only very rarely was force necessary. Only in August, 1942, did measures have to be taken against two families in the villages Glewenka and Salisny/Chutter, each of which were to supply one person for labour. Both were requested in June for the first time, but did not obey, although requested repeatedly. They had to be brought up by force, but succeeded twice in escaping from the collecting camp, or when on transport. Before the second arrest, the fathers of both of the men were taken into custody, to be kept as hostages and to be released only when their sons should show up. When, after the second escape, rearrest of both the fathers and boys was ordered, the police patrols ordered to do so, found the houses to be empty."

Passing to Paragraph 4, it is stated, and I quote directly:-

> "That time I decided to take measures - "

THE PRESIDENT: Should not you read on at the top of that Page 2? You had read, had not you, "I ordered the burning down of the houses of the fugitives"?

MR. DODD: Yes, I have.

THE PRESIDENT: I thought you ought to go on after that "The result was ..." Do you see?

MR. DODD: "The result was that in the future the people obeyed willingly."

THE PRESIDENT: Wait a minute. My colleague doubts whether you have read the passage at the bottom of Page 1. I thought you had read it, beginning, "That time I decided to take measures - "

MR. DODD: No, I was just beginning to read it.

THE PRESIDENT: I beg your pardon.

MR. DODD: That is the fourth paragraph:

> "That time I decided to take measures to show the increasingly rebellious Ukrainian youth that our orders had to be followed. I ordered the burning down of the houses of the fugitives."

Would your Honour like to have the rest of that paragraph?

THE PRESIDENT: I think you should read the next few lines.

MR. DODD:

"The result was that in the future people willingly obeyed orders concerning labour obligations. However, the measure of burning houses has not become known for the first time by my actions, but was suggested in a secret letter from the commissioner for the commitment of labour as a forced measure in case other measures should fail. This harsh punishment was accepted by the population with satisfaction."

THE TRIBUNAL (Mr. Biddle): The Commissioner for Labour, Mr. Dodd - you just said, "an order from the Commissioner of Labour." Who was that?

MR. DODD: Well, we have discussed this matter previous to our appearance here today. The document does not identify him by name. We are not sure. The defendant Sauckel was called Plenipotentiary General for Labour, and we think we cannot go much further, and must say we do not know. It just does not appear.

THE TRIBUNAL (Mr. Biddle): Thank you.

MR. DODD: Reading that last sentence,

"This harsh punishment was accepted by the population with satisfaction previous to the measures, because both families ridiculed all the other duty-anxious families which sent their children partly voluntarily to the labour commitment."

Turning to Paragraph 2 on Page 2, beginning about two-thirds of the way through the paragraph, I wish to read as follows. In the German text it appears at Page 3, Paragraph 1:-

"After the initial successes, a passive resistance of the population started, which finally forced me to start again making arrests, confiscations, and transfers to labour camps. After a while a transport of people, obliged to work, overran the police in the railroad station in Wassilkow and escaped. I saw again the necessity for strict measures.

A few ring-leaders of course escaped before they were found in Plisseskoje and in Mitmitza. After repeated attempts to get hold of them, their houses were burned down."

Finally, I wish to pass to the last paragraph on Page 3 of that same document. In the German text it appears at Page 5, Paragraph 7. Quoting from that last paragraph on the third page:-

"My actions against fugitive people obliged to work were always reported to District Commissioner Dohrer, in office in Wassilkow; and to the general-commissioner (Generalkommissar) in Kiev. Both of them knew the circumstances and agreed with my measures because of their success."

That is the end of that part of the quotation.

That Generalkommissar in Kiev, as we indicated yesterday and again this morning, was the man Koch, concerning whom we quoted his statement about the master race.

Another document confirms the arson as an instrument of enforcing this labour programme in the village of Bieloserka in the Ukraine in cases of resistance to forced labour recruitment. Atrocities committed in this village are related in Document 118-PS, which is already in evidence as Exhibit USA 186. But in addition there is Document 290-PS which is Exhibit USA 189. This document consists of correspondence originating within the Rosenberg Ministry, which was, of course, the office headquarters of the defendant Rosenberg, and it is dated 12th November, 1943. I wish to quote from Page 1 of the English text, starting with the last line, as follows:-

"But even if Muller had been present at the burning of houses in connection with the national conscription in Bieloserka, this should by no means lead to his relief from office. It is mentioned specifically in a directive of the Commissioner General in Luck of 21st September, 1942, referring to the extreme urgency of the national conscription.

Estates of those who refuse to work are to be burned, and their relatives are to be arrested as hostages and to be brought to forced labour camps."

The S.S. troops were directed to participate in the abduction of these forced labourers and also in the raids on villages, burning of villages, and were directed to turn the entire population over for slave labour in Germany.

We refer to Document 3012-PS, which is Exhibit USA 19o. This document is a secret S.S. order and it is dated the 19th March, 1943. I wish to quote from Page 3 of the English text starting with the third paragraph. In the German text it appears at Page 2, Paragraph 3. It says and I quote it:-

"The activity of the labour offices, that is, of recruiting commissions, is to be supported to the greatest extent possible. It will not be possible always to refrain from using force. During a conference with the Chief of the Labour Commitment Staffs, an agreement was reached stating that whatever prisoners can be released, should be put at the disposal of the Commissioner of the Labour Office. When searching villages, when it has become necessary to burn down these villages, the whole population will be put at the disposal of the Commissioner by force."

THE PRESIDENT: Should not you read No. 4 which follows it?

MR. DODD: No. 4 says:

"As a rule, no more children will be shot."

I might say to your Honour that parts of these documents are going to be relied on for other purposes later and it sometimes may appear to the Tribunal that we are overlooking some of these excerpts, but nevertheless I am grateful to have them called to our attention because they are most pertinent to these allegations as well.

From the community of Zhitomir, where the defendant Sauckel appealed for more workers for the Reich, the Commissioner General reported on the brutality of the conspirators' programme, which he described as a programme of coercion and slavery. And I now refer to Document 266-PS, which is Exhibit USA 191. This document is a secret report of a conference between the Commissioner General of Zhitomir and the defendant Rosenberg in the community of Winniza on 17th June, 1943. The report itself is dated 30th June, 1943, and is signed by Leyser. I wish to quote from Page 1 of the English text, beginning with the last paragraph, and in the German text it appears at Page 2, Paragraph 3. Quoting it directly:-

"The symptoms created by the recruiting of workers are, no doubt, well known to the Reich Minister through reports and his own

315

observations. Therefore I shall not report them. It is certain that a recruitment of labour, in this sense of the word, can hardly be spoken of. In most cases it is nowadays a matter of actual conscription by force."

Passing now to Page 2 of that same document, and to Paragraph 1, Line 11 in the German text it appears at Page 3, Paragraph 2 - it says, and I quote it directly:-

"But as the Chief Plenipotentiary for the mobilisation of labour explained to us the gravity of the situation we had no other device. I consequently have authorised the commissioners of the areas to apply the severest measures in order to achieve the imposed quota. The deterioration of morale, in conjunction with this, does not need any further proof. It is nevertheless essential to win the war on this front too. The problem of labour mobilisation cannot be handled with gloves."

The recruitment measures which we have been discussing enslaved so many citizens of occupied countries that whole areas were depopulated.

I now wish to refer to our Document 3000-PS, which is Exhibit USA 192. This document is a partial translation of a report from the Chief of Main Office III with the High Command in Minsk, and it is dated 28th June, 1943. It was sent to Ministerialdirektor Riecke, who was a top official in the Rosenberg Ministry. I wish to read from Page 1 of the English text, starting with the second paragraph, as follows:-

"The recruitment of labour for the Reich, however necessary, had disastrous effects. The recruitment measures in the last months and weeks were absolute man- hunts, which have an irreparable political and economic effect. From White Ruthenia approximately 50,000 people have been obtained for the Reich so far. Another 130,000 are to be obtained. Considering the 2.4 million total population, these figures are impossible.

Due to the sweeping drives of the S.S. and police in November, 1942, about 115,000 hectares of farmland is not used, as the population is not there and the villages have been razed."

We have already referred to the conspirators' objective of permanently weakening the enemy through the enslavement of labour and the breaking up of families, and we invite the Tribunal's attention to Document 031-PS, which is in evidence as Exhibit USA 171, for we desire to emphasise that the policy was applied in the Eastern Occupied Territories, with the defendant Rosenberg's approval, of a plan for the apprehension and deportation of 40,000 to 50,000 youths of the ages of 10 to 14. Now, the stated purpose of this plan was to prevent a reinforcement of the enemy's military strength and to reduce the enemy's biological potentialities. We have already quoted from Page 3 of the English text of that document to establish that the defendant Rosenberg approved that plan, the so-called high action plan. We referred to it yesterday afternoon.

Further evidence of the conspirators' plan to weaken their enemies, in utter disregard of the rules of International Law, is contained in Document 1702-PS, which is Exhibit USA 193. This document is a secret order, issued by a Rear Area Military Commandant to the District Commissar at Kasatin, dated 25th December, 1943. I quote from Page 3 of the English text at Paragraph 1.

In the German text it appears at Page 12, Paragraph 1.

"1. The able-bodied male population between 15 and 65 years of age and the cattle are to be shipped back from the district East of the line Belilowka-Berditschen- Zhitomir."

This programme, which we have been describing, and the brutal measures that it employed, were not limited to Poland and the Occupied Eastern Territories but covered and cursed Western Europe as well. Frenchmen, Dutchmen, Belgians, Italians, all came to know the yoke of slavery and the brutality of their slave-masters.

In France these slave-masters intensified their programme in the early part of 1943, pursuant to instructions which the defendant Speer telephoned to the defendant Sauckel at 8 o'clock in the evening on the 4th January, 1943, from Hitler's headquarters. I now refer to Document 556-PS 13, which is Exhibit USA 194. This document, incidentally, is a note from his own files, signed by the defendant Sauckel, dated 5th January, 1943. I wish to quote from Page 1 of the English text, Paragraph 1 as follows:-

"1. On 4th January, 1943, at 8 p.m. Minister Speer telephones from the Fuehrer's headquarters and communicates that on the basis of the Fuehrer's decision, it is no longer necessary to give special consideration to Frenchmen in the further recruiting of specialists and helpers in France. The recruiting can proceed with emphasis and sharpened measures."

To overcome resistance to his slave labour programme, the defendant Sauckel improvised new impressment measures which were applied to both France and Italy by his own agents and which he himself labelled as grotesque. I now refer to Document R-124, which is Exhibit USA 179, and particularly Page 2 and Paragraph 2 of the English text; in the German text it appears at Page 2, Paragraph 1. Quoting directly from that page and that paragraph a statement made by Sauckel on 1st March, 1944, at a meeting of the Central Planning Board:-

"The most abominable point made by my adversaries is their claim that no executive had been provided within these areas in order to recruit in a sensible manner the Frenchmen, Belgians, and Italians and to dispatch them to work. Thereupon, I even proceeded to employ and train a whole batch of French male and female agents who for good pay, just as was done in olden times for "shanghai- ing", went hunting for men and made them drunk by using liquor as well as words, in order to dispatch them to Germany.

Moreover, I charged some able men with founding a special labour supply executive of our own, and this they did by training, and arming, with the help of the higher S.S. and Police Fuehrer a number of natives, but I still have to ask the Munitions Ministry for arms for the use of these men, for during the last year alone several dozens of very able labour executive officers have been shot dead. All these means I have to apply, grotesque as it sounds, to refute the allegation there was no executive to bring labour to Germany from these countries."

This same slave labour hunt proceeded in Holland as it did in France, with terror and abduction. I now refer to Document 1726-PS, which is Exhibit USA 195. This document is entitled "Statement of the Netherlands Government in view of the Prosecution and Punishment of the German Major War Criminals." I wish to quote from enclosure "h", entitled "Central Bureau for Statistics - The Deportation of Netherlands Workmen to Germany." It is Page 1 of the English text, starting with the first paragraph, and in the German text it appears at Page 1, also Paragraph 1. Quoting directly, it reads as follows:-

"Many large or reasonably large business concerns, especially in the metal industry, were visited by German commissions who appointed workmen for deportation. This combing out of the concerns was called the "Sauckel- action", so named after its leader, who was charged with the appointment of foreign workmen in Germany.

The employers had to cancel the contract with the appointed workmen temporarily, and the latter were forced to register at the labour offices, which then took care of the deportation under supervision of German "Fachberater'.

Workmen who refused - relatively few - were prosecuted by the 'Sicherheitsdienst' (S.D.). If captured by this service, they were mostly lodged for some time in one of the infamous prisoners' camps in the Netherlands and eventually put to work in Germany.

In this prosecution the Sicherheitsdienst (S.D.) was supported by the German Police Service, which was connected with the labour offices, and was composed of members of the N.S.D.A.P. and the like.

At the end of April, 1942, the deportation of working labourers started on a grand scale. Consequently, in the months of May and June, the number of deportees amounted to not less than 22,000 and 24,000 respectively of which number many were metal workers.

After that the action slackened somewhat, but in October, 1942, another top figure was reached (26,000). After the big concerns, the smaller ones had, in their turn, to give up their personnel.

This changed in November, 1944. The Germans then started a ruthless campaign for manpower, by-passing the labour offices. Without warning, they lined off whole quarters of the towns, seized people in the streets or in the houses and deported them.

Rotterdam and Schiedam, where these raids took place on 10th and 11th November, the number of people thus deported was estimated at 50,000 and 5,000 respectively.

In other places where the raids were held later, the numbers were much lower, because one was forewarned by what had happened. The exact figures are not known, as they have never been published by the occupants.

The people thus seized were put to work partly in the Netherlands, partly in Germany ..."

A document found in the O.K.H. files furnishes evidence of the seizure of workers in Holland and I refer to Document 3003-PS, which is Exhibit USA 196. This document is a partial translation of the text of a lecture delivered by one Lieutenant Haupt, of the German Wehrmacht, concerning the situation of the war economy in the Netherlands. I wish to quote from Page 1 of the English text, starting with the fourth line of Paragraph 1, quoting that directly, which reads as follows:-

"There had been some difficulties with the Arbeitseinsatz, that is, during the man-catching action, which became very noticeable because it was unorganised and unprepared. People were arrested in the streets and taken out of their homes. It had been impossible to carry out a unified release procedure in advance, because for security reasons, the time for the action had not been previously announced. Certificates of release, furthermore, were to some extent not recognised by the officials who carried out the action. Not only workers who had become available through the stoppage of industry but also those who were employed in our installations producing things for our immediate need, were apprehended or did not dare to go into the streets. In any case it proved to be a great loss to us ..."

I might say to the Tribunal, that the hordes of people displaced in Germany today indicate, to a very considerable extent, the length to which the conspirators' labour programme proceeded. The best available Allied and German data reveal that by January, 1945, approximately 4,795,000 foreign civilian workers had been put to work for the German war effort in the Old Reich, and among them were forced labourers of more than 14 different nationalities. I now refer to Document 2520-PS, Exhibit USA 197, which is an affidavit executed by Edward L. Duess, an economic analyst.

At the top of the first page there are tables setting forth the nationality and then the numbers of the various nations, and other groupings of prisoners of war and politicals, so- called. The workers alone total, according to Mr. Duess, who is an expert in this field, the 4,795,000 figure to which I have just referred. In the second paragraph of this statement of Duess, I should like to read for the record and quote directly:-

"I, Edward, L. Duess, for three years employed by the Foreign Economic Administration, Washington, as an economic analyst in London, Paris and Germany, specialising in labour and population problems of Germany during the war, do hereby certify that the figures of foreign labour employed in the Old Reich have been compiled on the basis of the best available material from German and Allied sources. The accompanying table represents a combination of German official estimates of foreigners working in Germany in January, 1945, and of American, British and French figures of the number of foreigners, actually discovered in the Old Reich since 10th May, 1945."

Only a very small proportion of these imported labourers came to Germany on a voluntary basis. At the 1st March, 1944, meeting of this same Central Planning Board, to which we have made reference before, the defendant Sauckel made clear himself the vast scale on which free men had been forced into this labour slavery. He made the statement, and I quote from Document R-124, which is in evidence as Exhibit USA 179, and from which I have quoted earlier this morning. I wish to refer to Page 11 of that document, the middle paragraph, Paragraph 3. In the German text it appears at Page 4, Paragraph 2 (the defendant Sauckel speaking), and I quote directly from that document:-

"Out of five million foreign workers who arrived in Germany, not even two hundred thousand came voluntarily."

The Nazi conspirators were not satisfied just to tear five million odd persons from their children, from their homes, from their native lands, but in addition, these defendants, who sit today in this Court room, insisted that this vast number of wretched human beings, who were in the so-called Old Reich as forced labourers, must be starved, given less than sufficient to eat, often beaten and mistreated, and permitted to die wholesale for want of food, for want of even the fundamental requirements of decent clothing, for the want of adequate shelter or indeed sometimes just because they produced too little.

Now, these conditions of deportation are vividly described in Document 054-PS, which is a report made to the defendant Rosenberg, concerning the treatment of Ukrainian labour. I wish to refer to Document 054-PS, which is Exhibit USA 198. Before quoting from it directly, according to this report the plight of these hapless victims was aggravated because many were dragged off without opportunity to collect their possessions. Indeed, men and women were snatched from bed and lodged in cellars, pending deportation. Some arrived in night clothing. Brutal guards beat them. They were locked in railroad cars for long periods without any toilet facilities at all, without food, without water, without heat. The women were subjected to physical and moral indignities and indecencies during medical examinations.

I refer now specifically to this Document 054-PS, which consists of a covering letter to the defendant Rosenberg, first of all, and is signed by one Theurer - a Lieutenant in the Wehrmacht-to which is attached a copy of a report by the Commandant of the Collecting Centre for Ukrainian Specialists at Charkow, and it also consists of a letter written by one of the specialists, in the Rosenberg office - no, by one of the workers, not in the Rosenberg office, but one of the specialists they were recruiting, by the name of Grigori. I wish to quote from the report at Page 2, starting at Paragraph 4 of the English text, and in the German text it appears at Page 3, Paragraph 4. Quoting directly from that page of the English text:-

"The starosts, that is the village elders, are frequently corruptible, they continue to have the skilled workers, whom they drafted, dragged from their beds at night to be locked up in cellars until they are shipped. Since the male and female workers often are not given any time to pick up their luggage, and so forth, many arrive at the Collecting Centre for Skilled Workers with entirely insufficient equipment (without shoes, only two dresses, no eating and drinking utensils, no blankets, etc.). In particularly extreme cases, new arrivals therefore have to be sent back again immediately to get the things most necessary for them. If people do not come along at once, threatening and beating of skilled workers by the above-mentioned militia is a daily occurrence and is reported from most of the communities. In some cases women were beaten until they could no longer march. One bad case in particular was reported by me to the commander of the civil police here (Colonel Samek) for severe punishment (place Sozokinkow, district Dergatschni). The encroachments of the starosts; and the militia are of a particularly grave nature because they usually justify themselves by claiming that all this is done in the name of the German Armed Forces. In reality, the latter have conducted themselves throughout in a highly understanding manner toward the skilled workers and the Ukrainian population. The same, however, cannot be said of some of the administrative agencies. To illustrate this, be it mentioned that a woman once arrived dressed in little more than a shirt."

Passing now to Page 4 of this same document, starting with the tenth line of the third paragraph and in the German text it appears at Page 5, Paragraph 2. Quoting directly again:-

"On the basis of reported incidents, attention must be called to the fact that it is irresponsible to keep workers locked in the cars for many hours so that they cannot even take care of the calls of nature. It is evident that the people of a transport must be given an opportunity from time to time, to get drinking water, to wash, and to relieve themselves. Cars have been shown in which people had made holes so that they could take care of the calls of nature. Persons should, if possible, relieve themselves well before reaching the larger stations."

Turning to Page 5 of the same document, Paragraph 12, in the German text it appears at Page 6, Paragraph 1:-

"The following abuses were reported from the delousing stations: In the women's and girls' shower rooms, services were partly performed by men, or men would join in or even help with the soaping and, on the other hand, there were female personnel in the men's shower rooms; men also for some time were taking photographs in the women's shower rooms. Since mainly Ukrainian peasants were transported in the last months, as far as the female portion of these are concerned, they were mostly of a high moral standard and used to strict decency, and they must have considered such a treatment as a national degradation. The above-mentioned abuses have been, according to our knowledge, settled by the intervention of the transport commanders. The reports of the photographing were made from Halle; the reports about the other incidents were made from Kiewerce. Such incidents, in complete disregard of honour and respect of the Greater German Reich, may still occur again here or there."

Sick and infirm people of the occupied countries were taken indiscriminately with the rest. Those who managed to survive the trip into Germany, but who arrived too sick to work, were returned like cattle together with those who fell ill at work, because they were of no further use to the Germans. The return trip took place under the same terrible conditions as the initial journey, and without any kind of medical supervision. Death came to many and their corpses were unceremoniously dumped out of the cars, with no provision for burial.

I quote from Page 3, Paragraph 3 of Document 054-PS. In the German text it appears at Page 2, Paragraph 3. Quoting directly:-

"Very depressing for the morale of the skilled workers and the population is the effect of those persons shipped back from Germany for having become disabled or not having been fit for labour commitment from the very beginning. Several times already transports of skilled workers on their way to Germany have crossed returning transports of such disabled persons, and have stood on the tracks alongside of each other for a long time. These returning transports are insufficiently cared for. Sick, injured or weak people, mostly 56 to 60 in a car, are usually escorted by only three to four men. There is neither sufficient care nor enough food. Those returning frequently made unfavourable - but surely exaggerated - statements about their treatment in Germany and on the way. As a result of all this and of what the people could see with their own eyes, a psychosis of fear was evoked among the specialist workers, that is, about the whole transport to Germany. Several transport leaders of the 62nd and 63rd in particular reported thereto in detail. In one case the leader of the transport of skilled workers observed with his own eyes how a person who died of hunger was unloaded from a returning transport on the side track. (First Lt. Hofman of the 63rd Transport Station, Darniza.) Another time it was reported that three dead had to be deposited by the side of the tracks on the way and had to be left behind unburied by the escort. It is also regrettable that these disabled persons arrive here without any identification. According to the reports of the transport commanders, one gets the impression that these persons unable to work, are assembled, penned into the wagons and sent off, provided with only a few male escorts, and without special care for food and medical or other attendance. The Labour Office at the place of arrival as well as the transport commanders confirm this impression."

Incredible as it may seem, mothers in the throes of childbirth shared cars with those infected with tuberculosis or venereal diseases. Babies, when born, were hurled out of these car windows and dying persons lay on the bare floors of freight cars without even the small comfort of straw.

I refer to Document 984-PS, which is Exhibit USA 199. This document is an inter-departmental report, prepared by Dr. Gutkelch, in the defendant Rosenberg's Ministry and it is dated 30th September, 1942. I wish to quote from Page 10 of the English text, starting with the fourth line from the top of the page. In the German text it appears at Page 22, Paragraph 1. Quoting directly from that paragraph:-

"How necessary this interference was is shown by the fact that this train with returning labourers had stopped at the same place where a train with newly recruited Eastern labourers had stopped. Because of the corpses in the trainload of returning labourers, a catastrophe might have been precipitated had it not been for the mediation of Mrs. Miller. In this train women gave birth to babies who were thrown out of the windows during the journey, people having tuberculosis and venereal diseases rode in the same car, dying people lay in freight cars without straw, and one of the dead was thrown on the railway embankment. The same must have occurred in other returning transports."

Some aspects of the Nazi transport were described by the defendant Sauckel himself in a decree which he issued on 20th July, 1942; and I refer specifically to Document 2241- PS 3, which is Exhibit USA 200. I ask that the Tribunal take judicial notice of the original decree, which is published in Section B 1 a, at Page 48 e, of a book entitled Die Beschaeftigung von Auslaendischen Arbeitskraeften in Deutschland. I quote from Page 1, Paragraph 2, of the English text, and I am quoting directly:-

"According to reports of transportation commanders (Transportleiter) presented to me, the special trains provided for this purpose have frequently been in a really deficient condition. Numerous window panes have been missing in the coaches. Old French coaches without lavatories have been partly employed so that the workers had to fit up an emptied compartment as a lavatory. In other cases, the coaches were not heated in winter so that the lavatories quickly became unusable because the water system was frozen and the flushing apparatus was therefore without water."

The Tribunal will unquestionably have noticed, or observed, that a number of the documents which we have referred to - and which we have offered - consist of complaints by functionaries of the defendant Rosenberg's Ministry, or by others, concerning the conditions under which foreign workers were recruited and lived. I think it is appropriate to say that these documents have been presented by the prosecution really for two purposes, or for a dual purpose, to establish, first, the facts recited therein, of course, but also to show that these conspirators had knowledge of these conditions, and that notwithstanding their knowledge of these conditions, these conspirators continued to countenance and assist in this enslavement programme of a vast number of citizens of occupied countries.

Once within Germany, slave labourers were subjected to almost unbelievable brutality and degradation by their captors; and the character of this treatment was in part made plain by the conspirators' own statements, as in Document 016-PS, which is in evidence as Exhibit USA 168, and I refer to Page 12, Paragraph 2 of the English text; in the German text it appears at Page 17, Paragraph 4. Quoting directly:-

"All the men must be fed, sheltered, and treated in such a way as to exploit them to the highest possible extent at the lowest conceivable degree of expenditure."

Force and brutality as instruments of production found a ready adherent in the defendant Speer who, in the presence of the defendant Sauckel, said at a meeting of the Central Planning Board - and I refer to Document R-124, which is already in evidence and which has been referred to previously. It is Exhibit USA 179. I refer particularly to Page 42 of that Document R-124, and Paragraph 2 of that Page 42. The defendant Speer, speaking at that meeting, stated:-

"We must also discuss the slackers. Ley has ascertained that the sick-list decreased to one-fourth or one-fifth in factories where there are doctors on the staff to examine the sick men. There is nothing to be said against S.S. and police taking drastic steps and putting those known as slackers into concentration camps. There is no alternative. Let it happen several times and the news will soon go around."

At a later meeting of the Central Planning Board, Field Marshal Milch agreed that so far as workers were concerned- and again I refer to Document R-124, and to Page 26, Paragraph 2 in the English text; and in the German text at Page 17, Paragraph 1. Field Marshal Milch, speaking at a meeting of the Central Planning Board when the defendant Speer was present, stated - and I am quoting directly:-

"The list of the shirkers should be entrusted to Himmler's trustworthy hands."

THE PRESIDENT: Page 17?

MR. DODD: No, your Honour; Page 26, Paragraph 2. The Page 17 was of the German text; in the English text it is at Page 26.

THE PRESIDENT: Thank you.

MR. DODD: Milch made particular reference to foreign workers - again in this Document R-124, at Page 26, Paragraph 3; in the German text it appears at Page 18, Paragraph 3 - when he said, and I am quoting him directly:-

"It is therefore not possible to exploit fully all the foreigners unless we put them on piece-work rates, or are authorised to take measures against those who are not doing their utmost."

The policy as actually executed was even more fearful than the policy as expressed by the conspirators. Indeed, these impressed workers were under-fed and overworked, and they were forced to live in grossly overcrowded camps where they were held as virtual prisoners, and were otherwise denied adequate shelter, adequate clothing, adequate medical care and treatment. As a consequence, they suffered from many diseases and ailments. They were generally forced to work long hours, up to and beyond the point of exhaustion. They were beaten and subjected to all manner of inhuman indignities.

An example of this mistreatment is found in the conditions which prevailed in the Krupp factories. Foreign labourers at the Krupp works were given insufficient food to enable them to perform the work required of them.

I refer to Document D-316, which is Exhibit USA 201. This document was found in the Krupp files. It is a memorandum upon the Krupp stationery to a Hert Hupe, a director of the Krupp Locomotive Factory in Essen, Germany, dated 14th March, 1942. I wish to refer to Page 1 of the English text, starting with Paragraph 1, as follows, and I am quoting directly:-

"During the last few days we established that the food for the Russians employed here is so miserable, that the people are getting weaker from day to day.

Investigations showed that single Russians are not able to place a piece of metal for turning into position, for instance, because of lack of physical strength. The same conditions exist in all places of work where Russians are employed."

The condition of foreign workers in Krupp workers' camps is described in detail in an affidavit executed in Essen, Germany, by Dr. Wilhelm Jaeger, who was the senior camp doctor. It is Document D-288, which is Exhibit USA 202.

"I, Dr. Wilhelm Jaeger, am a general practitioner in Essen, Germany, and its surroundings. I was born in Germany on 2nd December, 1888, and now live at Kettwig, Sengenholz, Germany. I make the following statement of my own free will. I have not been threatened in any way and I have not been promised any sort of reward.

On 1st October, 1942, I became senior camp doctor in Krupp's workers' camp, and was generally charged with the medical supervision of all Krupp's workers' camps in Essen. In the course of my duties it was my responsibility to report to my superiors in the Krupp works upon the sanitary and health conditions of the workers' camps. It was a part of my task to visit every Krupp camp which housed foreign civilian workers, and I am therefore able to make this statement on the basis of my personal knowledge.

My first official act as senior camp doctor was to make a thorough inspection of the various camps. At that time, in October, 1942, I found the following conditions:

The Eastern workers and Poles who worked in the Krupp works at Essen were kept at camps at Seumannstrasse, Spenlestrasse, Grieperstrasse, Heecstrasse, Germaniastrasse, Kapitan- Lehmannstrasse, Dechenschule, and Kramerplatz." (When the term "Eastern workers" is hereinafter used, it is to be taken as including Poles.) "All of the camps were surrounded by barbed wire and were closely guarded.

Conditions in all of these camps were extremely bad. The camps were greatly overcrowded. In some camps there were twice as many people in a barrack as health conditions permitted. At Kramerplatz, the inhabitants slept in treble-tiered bunks, and in the other camps they slept in double-tiered bunks. The health authorities prescribed a minimum space between beds Of 50 cm., but the bunks in these camps were separated by a maximum Of 20 to 30 cm.

The diet prescribed for the Eastern workers was altogether insufficient. They were given 1,000 calories a day less than the minimum prescribed for any German. Moreover, while German workers engaged in the heaviest work received 5,000 calories a day, the Eastern workers with comparable jobs received only 2,000 calories. These workers were given only two meals a day and their bread ration. One of these two meals consisted of a thin, watery soup. I had no assurance that they did in fact, receive the minimum which was prescribed. Subsequently, in 1943, when I undertook to inspect the food prepared by the cooks, I discovered a number of instances in which food was withheld from the workers.

The plan for food distribution called for a small quantity of meat per week. Only inferior meats, rejected by the veterinary, such as horse meat or tuberculin- infested, was permitted for this purpose. This meat was usually cooked into a soup.

The percentage of Eastern workers who were ill was twice as great as among the Germans. Tuberculosis was particularly widespread among these workers. The tuberculosis rate among them was four times the normal rate (2 per cent. Eastern workers, German, - 5 per cent.). At Dechenschule approximately 2.5 per cent. of the workers suffered from open tuberculosis. These were all active tuberculosis cases. The Tartars and Kirghises suffered most; as soon as they were overcome by this disease they collapsed like flies, The cause was bad housing, the poor quality and insufficient quantity of food, overwork, and insufficient rest.

These workers were likewise afflicted with spotted fever. Lice, the carrier of this disease, together with countless fleas, bugs and other vermin tortured the inhabitants of these camps. As a result of the filthy conditions, nearly all Eastern workers were afflicted with skin disease. The shortage of food also caused many cases of hunger-oedema, nephritis and shiga-kruse.

It was the general rule that workers were compelled to go to work unless a camp doctor had prescribed that they were unfit for work. At Seumannstrasse, Grieperstrasse, Germaniastrasse, Kapitan-Lehmannstrasse, and Dechenschule, there was no daily sick call. At these camps the doctors did not appear for two or three days. As a consequence, workers were forced to go to work despite illness.

I undertook to improve conditions as well as I could. I insisted upon the erection of some new barracks in order to relieve the overcrowded conditions of the camps. Despite this, the camps were still greatly overcrowded, but not as much as before. I tried to alleviate the poor sanitary conditions in Kramerplatz and Dechenschule by causing the installation of some emergency toilets, but the number was insufficient, and the situation was not materially altered.

With the onset of heavy air raids in March, 1943, conditions in the camps greatly deteriorated. The problem of housing, feeding, and medical attention became more acute than ever. The workers lived in the ruins of their former barracks. Medical supplies which were used up, lost or destroyed, were difficult to replace. At times the water supply at the camps was completely shut off for periods of eight to fourteen days. We installed a few emergency toilets in the camps, but there were far too few of them to cope with the situation.

During the period immediately following the March, 1943, raids, many foreign workers were made to sleep at the Krupp factories in the same rooms in which they worked. The day workers slept there at night, and the night workers slept there during the day, despite the noise which constantly prevailed. I believe that this condition continued until the entrance of American troops into Essen.

As the pace of air raids was stepped up, conditions became progressively worse. On 28th July, 1944, I reported to my superiors that:

The sick barrack in camp Rabenhorst is in such a bad condition that one cannot speak of a sick barrack any more. The rain leaks through in every corner. The housing of the sick is therefore impossible. The necessary labour for production is in danger because those persons who are ill cannot recover.

At the end of 1943, or the beginning of 1944 - I am not completely sure of the exact date - I obtained permission for the first time to visit the prisoner of war camps. My inspection revealed that conditions at these camps were worse than those I had found at the camps of the Eastern workers in 1942. Medical supplies at such camps were virtually non-existent. In an effort to cure this intolerable situation, I contacted the Wehrmacht authorities whose duty it was to provide medical care for the prisoners of war. My persistent efforts came to nothing. After visiting and pressing them over a period of two weeks, I was given a total of 100 aspirin tablets for over 3,000 prisoners of war.

The French prisoner of war camp in Nogerratstrasse had been destroyed in an air raid attack and its inhabitants were kept for nearly half a year in dog kennels, urinals, and old baking houses. The dog kennels were 3 ft. high, 9 ft. long, and 6 ft. wide. Five men slept in each of them. The prisoners had to crawl into these kennels on all fours. The camp contained no tables, chairs, or cupboards. The supply of blankets was inadequate. There was no water in the camp. That treatment which was extended was given in the open. Many of these conditions were mentioned to me in a report by Dr. Stinnesbeck dated 12th June, 1944, in which he said:-

Three hundred and fifteen prisoners are still accommodated in the camp. One hundred and seventy of these are no longer in barracks but in the tunnel in Grunertstrasse under the Essen-Muelheum railway line. This tunnel is damp and is not suitable for continued accommodation of human beings. The rest of the prisoners are accommodated in ten different factories in the Krupp works. The first medical attention is given by a French Military Doctor who takes great pains with his fellow countrymen. Sick people from Krupp factories must be brought to the sick parade. This parade is held in the lavatory of a burned-out public house outside the camp. The sleeping accommodation of the four French orderlies is in what was the men's room. In the sick bay there is a double tier wooden bed. In general, the treatment takes place in the open. In rainy weather it is held in the above-mentioned small room. These are insufferable conditions. There are no chairs, tables, cupboards, or water. The keeping of a register of sick people is impossible. Bandages and medical supplies are very scarce, all those badly hurt in the works are very often brought here for first aid and have to be bandaged here before being transported to hospital. There are many loud and lively complaints about food, which the guard personnel confirm as being correct.

Illness and loss of manpower must be reckoned with under these conditions.

In my report to my superiors at Krupps dated 2nd September, 1944, I stated-:

Camp Humboldtstrasse has been inhabited by Italian prisoners of war. After it had been destroyed by an air raid, the Italians were removed and 600 Jewish females from Buchenwald concentration camp were brought to work at the Krupp factories. Upon my first visit at Camp Humboldtstrasse, I found these females suffering from open festering wounds and other diseases.

I was the first doctor they had seen for at least a fortnight. There was no doctor in attendance at the camp. There were no medical supplies in the camp. They had no shoes and went about in their bare feet. The sole clothing of each consisted of a sack with holes for their arms and head. Their hair was shorn. The camp was surrounded by barbed wire and closely guarded by S.S. guards.

The amount of food in the camp was extremely meagre and of very poor quality. The houses in which they lived consisted of the ruins of former barracks and they afforded no shelter against rain and other weather conditions. I reported to my superiors that the guards lived and slept outside their barracks as one could not enter them without being attacked by 10, 20 and up to 50 fleas. One camp doctor employed by me refused to enter the camp again after he had been bitten very badly. I visited this camp with Dr. Grosne on two occasions and both times we left the camp badly bitten. We had great difficulty in getting rid of the fleas and insects which had attacked us. As a result of this attack by insects of this camp, I got large boils on my arms and the rest of my body. I asked my superiors at the Krupp works to undertake the necessary steps to delouse the camp so as to put an end to this unbearable vermin-infested condition. Despite this report, I did not find any improvement in sanitary conditions at the camp on my second visit a fortnight later.

When foreign workers finally became too sick to work or were completely disabled, they were returned to the Labour Exchange in Essen and from there they were sent to a camp at Friedrichsfeld. Among persons who were returned to the Labour Exchange were aggravated cases of tuberculosis, malaria, neurosis, cancer which could not be treated by operation, old age, and general feebleness. I know nothing about conditions at this camp because I have never visited it. I only know that it was a place to which workers who were no longer of any use to Krupp were sent.

My colleagues and I reported all of the foregoing matters to Herr Inn, Director of Friedrich Krupp A.G., Dr. Wiels, personal physician of Gustav Krupp von Bohlen and Halbach, Senior Camp Leader Kupke, and at all times to the health department. Moreover, I know that these gentlemen personally visited the camps.

Signed Dr. Wilhelm Jaeger."

THE PRESIDENT: We will adjourn now until 2 o'clock.

[A recess was taken until 1400 hours]

MR. DODD: May it please the Tribunal: We had just completed the reading of the affidavit executed by Dr. Wilhelm Jaeger at the noon recess. The conditions which were described in this affidavit were not confined to the Krupp factories alone but existed throughout Germany, and we turn to a report of the Polish Main Committee made to the Administration of the General Government of Poland, Document R-103, which is Exhibit USA 204. This document is dated 17th May, 1944, and describes the situation of the Polish workers in Germany, and I wish to refer particularly to Page 2 of the English translation, starting with Paragraph 2; in the German text it appears at Page 2, Paragraph 2, also. In quoting from the document, it reads:-

"The provision for cleanliness at many overcrowded camp rooms is contrary to the most elementary requirements. Often there is no opportunity to obtain warm water for washing; therefore, the cleanest parents are unable to maintain even the most primitive standard of hygiene for their children or, often, even to wash their only set of linen. A consequence of this is the spreading of scabies which cannot be eradicated.

We receive imploring letters from the camps of Eastern workers and their prolific families, beseeching us for food. The quantity and quality of camp rations mentioned therein - the so-called fourth grade of rations - is absolutely insufficient to maintain the energies spent in heavy work. 3.5 kg. of bread weekly and a thin soup at lunch time, cooked with swedes or other vegetables without any meat or fat, with a meagre addition of potatoes now and then is a hunger ration for a heavy worker.

Sometimes punishment consists of starvation which is inflicted, e.g. for refusal to wear the badge 'East'. Such punishment has the result that workers faint at work (Klosterteich Camp, Grunheim, Saxony). The consequence is complete exhaustion, an ailing state of health, and tuberculosis. The spreading of tuberculosis among the Polish factory workers is a result of the deficient food rations meted out in the community camps, because energy spent in heavy work cannot be replaced.

The call for help which reaches us brings to light starvation and hunger, severe stomach intestinal trouble, especially in the case of children, resulting from the insufficiency of food which does not take into consideration the needs of children. Proper medical treatment or care for the sick is not available in the mass camps."

We now refer to Page 3 of this same document, and particularly to the first paragraph. In the German text it appears at Page 5, Paragraph 1:-

"In addition to these bad conditions, there is lack of systematic occupation for and supervision of these hosts of children, which affects the life of prolific families in the camps. The children, left to themselves, without schooling or religious care, must run wild and grow up illiterate. Idleness in rough surroundings may and will create unwanted results in these children. An indication of the awful conditions this may lead to, is given by the fact that in the camps for Eastern workers (camp for Eastern workers, 'Waldlust', Post Office Lauf, Pegnitz) there are cases of 8-year-old delicate and undernourished children put to forced labour and perishing from such treatment.

The fact that these bad conditions dangerously affect the state of health and the vitality of the workers is proved by the many cases of tuberculosis found in very young people returning from the Reich to the General Government as unfit for work. Their state of health is usually so bad that recovery is out of the question. The reason is that a state of exhaustion resulting from overwork and a starvation diet is not recognised as an ailment until the illness betrays itself by high fever and fainting spells.

Although some hostels for unfit workers have been provided as a precautionary measure, one can only go there when recovery may no longer be expected (Neumarkt in Bavaria). Even there the incurables waste away slowly, and nothing is done even to alleviate the state of the sick by suitable food and medicines. There are children there with tuberculosis whose cure would not be hopeless and men in their prime who, if sent home in time to their families in rural districts, might still be able to recover. No less suffering is caused by the separation of families when wives and mothers of small children are away from their families and sent to the Reich for forced labour."

And finally, from Page 4 of the same document, starting with the first paragraph. In the German text it appears at Page 7, Paragraph 4:-

"If, under these conditions, there is no moral support such as is normally based on regular family life, then at least such moral support which the religious feelings of the Polish population require should be maintained and increased. The elimination of religious services, religious practice and religious care from the life of the Polish workers, the prohibition of church attendance, at a time when there is a religious service for other people, and other measures, show a certain contempt for the influence of religion on the feelings and opinions of the workers."

THE PRESIDENT: Can you tell us who the Polish Central Committee were; or, I mean, how they were founded?

MR. DODD: Well, so far as we are aware, it was a committee apparently set up by the Nazi State when it occupied Poland, to work in some sort of co-operation with it during the days of the occupation. We do not know the names of the members, and we have not any more specific information.

THE PRESIDENT: Is it a captured document?

MR. DODD: It is a captured document, yes, sir. All of the documents that I am presenting in connection with this case are, excepting the Netherlands Government's report and one or two other official reports, the Dois affidavit and such other matters. That particular document, it has just been called to my attention, was captured by the United States Third Army.

Particularly harsh and brutal treatment was reserved for workers imported from the conquered Eastern territories. As we have illustrated, they did indeed live in bondage, and they were subjected to almost every form of degradation, quartered in stables with animals, denied the right of free worship, and the ordinary pleasures of human society.

Illustrative of this treatment is Document EC-68, Exhibit USA 205. This Document, EC-68, bears the title "Directives on the Treatment of Foreign Farmworkers of Polish Nationality", issued by the Minister for Finance and Economy of Baden, Germany, on 6th March, 1941. We do not know his name, nor have we been able to ascertain it.

Quoting from the English text of this document from the beginning:-

"The agencies of the Reich Food Administration, State Peasant Association of Baden, have received the result of the negotiations with the Higher S.S. and Police Officers in Stuttgart on 14th February, 1941, with great satisfaction. Appropriate memoranda have already been turned over to the District Peasants Associations. Below, I promulgate the individual regulations, as they have been laid down during the conference, and how they are now to be applied accordingly:

1. Fundamentally, farmworkers of Polish nationality no longer have the right to complain, and thus no complaints may be accepted any more by any official agency.

2. The farmworkers of Polish nationality may not leave the localities in which they are employed, and have a curfew from 1st October to 31st March from 2000 hours to 0600 hours, and from 1st April to 30th September from 2100 hours to 0500 hours.

3. The use of bicycles is strictly prohibited. Exceptions are possible for riding to the place of work in the field if a relative of the employer or the employer himself is present.

4. The visit to churches, regardless of faith, is strictly prohibited, even when there is no service in progress. Individual spiritual care by clergymen outside of the church is permitted.

5. Visits to theatres, motion pictures, or other cultural entertainment are strictly prohibited for farmworkers of Polish nationality.

6. The visit to restaurants is strictly prohibited to farmworkers of Polish nationality, except for one restaurant in the village, which will be selected by the Rural Councillor's office (Landratsamt), and then only one day per week. The day to visit the restaurant will also be

determined by the Landratsamt. This regulation does not change the curfew regulation mentioned above under No. 2.

7. Sexual intercourse with women and girls is strictly prohibited, and wherever it is established, it must be reported.

8. Gatherings of farmworkers of Polish nationality after work is prohibited, whether it is on other farms, in the stables, or in the living quarters of the Poles.

9. The use of railroads, buses or other public conveyances by farmworkers of Polish nationality is prohibited.

10. Permits to leave the village may only be granted in very exceptional cases, by the local police authority (Mayor's office). However, in no case may it be granted if the applicant wants to visit a public agency on his own, whether it is a labour office or the District Peasants Association or whether he wants to change his place of employment.

11. Arbitrary change of employment is strictly prohibited. The farmworkers of Polish nationality have to work daily so long as the interests of the enterprise demand it, and as it is demanded by the employer. There are no time limits to the working time.

12. Every employer has the right to give corporal punishment to farmworkers of Polish nationality, if instructions and good words fail: The employer may not be held accountable in any such case by an official agency.

13. Farmworkers of Polish nationality should, if possible, be removed from the community of the home, and they can be quartered in stables, etc. No remorse whatever should restrict such action.

14. Report to the authorities is compulsory in all cases, when crimes have been committed by farmworkers of Polish nationality, such as sabotage of the enterprise or slowing down work, for instance, unwillingness to work, or impertinent behaviour; it is compulsory even in minor cases. An employer who loses his Pole through the latter having to serve a long prison sentence because of such a compulsory report, will receive another Pole from the competent labour office on preferential request.

15. In all other cases, only the State Police are still competent.

For the employer himself, severe punishment is contemplated if it is established that the necessary distance from farmworkers of Polish nationality has not been kept. The same applies to women and girls. Extra rations are strictly prohibited. Non-compliance with the Reich tariffs for farmworkers of Polish nationality will be punished by the competent labour office by the removal of the workers."

The women of the conquered territories were led away against their will to serve as domestics, and the defendant Sauckel described this programme in his own words, which appear in Document 016-PS, already offered in evidence as Exhibit USA 168, and particularly Page 7, fourth paragraph of the English text; in the German text it appears on Page 10, Paragraph 1, and I quote directly:-

"In order to relieve considerably the German housewife, especially the mother with many children, and the extremely busy farmwoman, and in order to avoid any further danger to their health, the Fuehrer also charges me with the procurement of 400,000-500,000 selected, healthy and strong girls from the territories of the East, for Germany."

Once captured, once forced to become labourers in Germany, or workers in Germany, these Eastern women, by order of the slavemaster, defendant Sauckel, were bound to the household to which they were assigned, permitted at the most three hours of freedom a week, and denied the right to return to their homes. I now refer to Document 3044 (b)-PS. That is Exhibit USA 2o6. The document is a decree issued by the defendant Sauckel containing instructions for housewives concerning Eastern household workers, and I ask that the Court take judicial notice of the original decree which appears on Pages 592 and 593 of the second volume of a publication of the Zentralverlag of the N.S.D.A.P., entitled "Verfuegungen, Anordnungen und Bekanntgaben", and I quote from the first paragraph of the English translation of a portion of the decree as follows:

"There is no claim for free time. Female domestic workers from the East may, on principle, leave the household only to take care of domestic tasks.

As a reward for good work, however, they may be given the opportunity to stay outside the home without work for three hours once a week. This leave must end with the onset of darkness, at the latest at 2000 hours.

It is prohibited to enter restaurants, movies, or other theatres, and similar establishments provided for German, or foreign workers. Attending church is also prohibited. Special events may be arranged for Eastern domestics in urban homes by the German Workers' Front, for Eastern domestics in rural homes by the Reich Food Administration with the German Women's League. Outside the home, the Eastern domestic must always carry her work card as a personal pass. Vacations, return to homes, are not granted as yet. The recruiting of Eastern domestics is for an indefinite period."

Always over these enslaved workers was the shadow of the Gestapo, and the torture of the concentration camps. Like other major programmes of the Nazi conspirators, the black- shirted guards of the S.S., and Himmler's methods of dealing with people were the instruments employed for enforcement.

On the subject of the slave labourers, a secret order dated 2oth February, 1942, issued by Reichsfuehrer S.S. Himmler to S.D. and Security Police Officers concerning Eastern workers, spells out the violence which was applied against them. I offer this order in evidence. It is our Document 3040-PS, which is Exhibit USA 207, and I ask this Court to take judicial notice of the original order, which is published in the "Allgemeine Erlassammlung," Part II, Section 2-A, III, small letter "f", Pages 15 to 24. I wish to quote from Page 3 of the English text starting with Paragraph III, in the German text it appears in Section 2-A, III, "f", at Page 19 of the publication as follows:-

"III. Combating violations against discipline. - (1) According to the equal status of labourers from the original Soviet Russian territory with prisoners of war, a strict discipline must be exercised in the quarters and at the working place. Violations against discipline, including work refusal and loafing at work, will be fought exclusively by the Secret State Police. The smaller cases will be settled by the leader of the guard according to instruction of the State Police administration offices, with measures as provided for in the enclosure. To break acute resistance, the guards shall be permitted to use also physical compulsion against the labourers. But this may be done only for a cogent cause. The manpower should always be informed about the fact that they will be treated decently when conducting themselves with discipline and accomplishing good work. In severe cases, that is in such cases where the measures at the disposal of the leader of the guard do not suffice, the State police office has to act with its means. Accordingly, they will be treated, as a rule, only with strict measures, that is, with transfer to a concentration camp, or with special treatment. The transfer to a concentration camp is to be done in the usual manner. In especially severe cases special treatment is to be requested at the Reich Security Main Office, stating personal data, and the exact facts.

Special treatment is hanging. It should not take place in the immediate vicinity of the camp. A certain number of labourers from the original Soviet Russian territory should attend the special treatment; they are then warned of the circumstances which lead to this treatment. Should special treatment be required within the camp for exceptional reasons of camp discipline, this is also to be requested."

And I turn now to Page 4 of the original text, Paragraph VI; in the German text it appears at Section 2-A, VI, "f", on Page 20.

"VI. Sexual intercourse. - Sexual intercourse is forbidden to labourers of the original Soviet Russian territory. By means of their closely confined quarters they have no opportunity for it. For every case of sexual intercourse with men or women of the German race, special treatment is to be requested for male labour from the original Soviet Russian territory, and, for female labour, transfer to a concentration camp."

And finally from Page 5 of the same document, Paragraph VIII, and in the German text it appears at Section 2-A, VIII, "f", at Page 21:-

"VIII. Search. - Fugitive workers from the original Soviet Russian territory are to be announced primarily in the German search book. Furthermore, search measures are to be decreed locally. When caught the fugitive must receive special treatment."

We have said to this Tribunal more than once that the primary purpose of the entire slave labour programme was, of course, to compel the people of the occupied country to work for German war economy. The decree by which defendant Sauckel was appointed Plenipotentiary General for manpower reveals that the purpose of the appointment was to facilitate acquisition of the manpower required for German war industries, and in particular the armaments industry, by centralising under Sauckel responsibility for the recruitment and allocation of foreign labour and prisoners of war in these industries. I refer to the document bearing our Number 1666-PS, Exhibit USA 208. This document is a decree signed by Hitler, Lammers, and the defendant Keitel, and it is dated 21st March, 1942, appointing the defendant Sauckel the Plenipotentiary General for the utilisation of labour. I ask that the Court take judicial notice of the original decree, which is published at Page 179, Part I, of the 194z Reichsgesetzblatt; referring to the English text starting at Paragraph

1, as follows, and quoting directly:-

"In order to secure the manpower requisite for war industries as a whole, and particularly for armaments, it is necessary that the utilisation of all available manpower, including that of workers recruited abroad, and of prisoners of war, should be subject to a uniform control, directed in a manner appropriate to the requirements of war industry, and further that all still incompletely utilised manpower in the Greater German Reich, including the Protectorate, and in the Government General, and in the occupied territories should be mobilised. Reichsstatthalter and Gauleiter Fritz Sauckel will carry out this task within the framework of the Four Year Plan, as Plenipotentiary General, for the utilisation of labour. In that capacity he will be directly responsible to the Commissioner for the Four Year Plan. Section III (Wages) and Section V (Utilisation of Labour) of the Reich Labour Ministry, together with their subordinate authorities, will be placed at the disposal of the Plenipotentiary General for the accomplishment of his task."

Sauckel's success can be measured from a letter which he himself wrote to Hitler on 15th April, 1943, and which contained his report on the one year of his activities. We refer to the Document 407-PS, VI, which will be Exhibit USA 209. I wish to quote from Paragraphs 6 and 9 on Page 1 of the English text; in the German text it appears at Page 2, Paragraphs 1 and 2:-

"After one year's activity as Plenipotentiary for the Direction of Labour, I can report that 3,638,056 new foreign workers were given to the German war economy from 1st April of last year to 31st March of this year. The 3,638,056 are distributed amongst the following branches of the German war economy. Armament- 1,568,801."

Still further evidence of this steady use of this enslaved foreign labour is found again in a report of the Central Planning Board, to which we have referred so many times this morning and yesterday. Another meeting of this Central Planning Board was held on 16th February, 1944, and I refer to our Document R-124, which contains the minutes of this meeting of the Central Planning Board, and which has been already offered in evidence as Exhibit USA 179, and I want to refer particularly to Page 26, Paragraph 1 of the English text of Document R-124. It is at Page 16, in Paragraph 2, of the German text:-

"The armament industry employs foreign workmen to a large extent; according to the latest figures-40 per cent."

Moreover, our Document 2520-PS, which is in evidence as Exhibit USA 197, records that, according to Speer Ministry tabulations, as Of 31st December, 1944, approximately two million civilian foreign workers were employed directly in the manufacture of armaments and munitions (end products or components). That the bulk of these workers had been forced to come to Germany against their will is made clear by Sauckel's statement which I previously quoted from Paragraph 3 of Page 11 of Document R-124. We quoted it this morning, the statement being that of five million foreign workers only two hundred thousand or less came voluntarily.

The defendants Sauckel, Speer and Keitel succeeded in the enforcement of foreign labour to construct military fortifications. Thus, citizens of France,

Holland and Belgium were compelled against their will to engage in the construction of the "Atlantic Wall", and we refer to our Document 556-PS-2, which is Exhibit USA 194. This is a Hitler order dated 8th September, 1942, and it is initialled by the defendant Keitel.

Quoting the order directly:-

"The extensive coastal fortifications which I have ordered to be erected in the area of Army Group West make it necessary that in the occupied territory all available workers should be committed and should give the fullest extent of their productive capacities. The previous allotment of domestic workers is insufficient. In order to increase it I order the introduction of compulsory labour and the prohibition of changing the place of employment without permission of the authorities in the occupied territories. Furthermore, the distribution of food and clothing ration cards to those subject to labour draft should in the future depend on the possession of a certificate of employment. Refusal to accept an assigned job, as well as abandoning the place of work without the consent of the authorities in charge, will result in the withdrawal of the food and clothing ration cards. The G.B.A. (Deputy General for Arbeitseinsatz) in agreement with the military commander, as well as the Reich Commissar, will issue the corresponding decrees for execution."

Indeed, the defendant Sauckel boasted to Hitler concerning the contribution of the forced labour programme to the construction of the Atlantic Wall by the defendant Speer's "Organisation Todt". And we refer to Document 407-PS VIII, which is Exhibit USA 210. This document is a letter from the defendant Sauckel to Hitler dated the 17th May, 1943. I refer to the second and last paragraphs:-

"In addition to the labour allotted to the total German economy by the Arbeitseinsatz since I took office, the Organisation Todt was supplied with new labour continually ". Thus: "The Arbeitseinsatz has done everything to help make possible the completion of the Atlantic Wall."

Similarly, Russian civilians were forced into labour battalions and compelled to build fortifications to be used against their own countrymen. In Document 031-PS, in evidence as Exhibit USA 171, which is a memorandum of the Rosenberg Ministry, it is stated in Paragraph 1 at Page 1 of that document:-

"The men and women in the theatres of operations have been-and will be conscripted into labour battalions to be used in the construction of fortifications."

In addition, the conspirators compelled prisoners of war to engage in operations of war against their own country and its allies. At a meeting of the Central Planning Board, again held on 19th February, 1943, attended by the defendant Speer and the defendant Sauckel and Field Marshal Milch, the following conversation occurred and is recorded in out Document R-124, at Page 32, Paragraph 5, of the English text. It is Page 20, the last paragraph, of the German text, and I quote it, the defendant Sauckel speaking:-

"Sauckel: If any prisoners are taken there, they will be needed.

Milch: We have made a request for an order that a certain percentage of men in the anti-aircraft artillery must be Russians. 50,000 will be taken altogether, 30,000 are already employed as gunners. This is an amusing thing that Russians must work the guns."

We refer now to Documents 3027 and 3028. They are respectively Exhibits USA 211 and 212. They will be found at the very back, I believe, of the document book, in a separate manila folder. They are official German Army photographs, and if your Honours will examine Document 3027- PS the caption states that Russian prisoners of war are acting as ammunition bearers during the attack upon Tschedowe. Document 3028-PS consists of a series of official German Army photographs taken in July and August, 1941, showing Russian prisoners of war in Latvia and the Ukraine being compelled to load and unload ammunition trains and trucks, and being required to stack ammunition, all, we say, in flagrant disregard of the rules of International Law, particularly Article 6 of the regulations annexed to The Hague Convention, No. IV of 1907, which provides that the tasks of prisoners of war shall have no connection with the operations of war. The use of prisoners of war in the German armament industry was as widespread and as extensive almost as in the use of the forced foreign civilian labour. We refer to Document 3005-PS, which is Exhibit USA 213. This document is a secret letter from the Reich Minister of Labour to the presidents of the Regional Labour Exchange Offices, which refers to an order of the defendant Goering to the effect that - I quote now from Paragraph 1 of that document - I am quoting it directly:-

"Upon personal order of the Reich Marshal 100,000 men are to be taken from among the French prisoners of war not yet employed in armament industry and are to be assigned to the armament industry (aeroplane industry). Gaps in manpower supply resulting therefrom will be filled by Soviet prisoners of war. The transfer of the above-named French prisoners of war is to be accomplished by 1st October." The Reich Marshal referred to in that quotation is, of course, the defendant Goering.

A similar policy was followed with respect to Russian, prisoners of war. The defendant Keitel directed the execution of Hitler's order to use prisoners of war in the German war economy, and I now make reference to our Document EC-194, which is Exhibit USA 24. This document is also a secret memorandum, according to its label, issued from Hitler's Headquarters on the 31st October, 1941, and I read from Page 1, Paragraphs 1 and 2, quoting it directly as follows:-

"The lack of workers is becoming an increasingly dangerous hindrance for the future German war and armament industry. The expected relief through discharges from the Armed Forces is uncertain as to the extent and date; however, even its greatest possible extent will by no means correspond to expectations and requirements in view of the great demand.

The Fuehrer has now ordered that even the working power of the Russian prisoners of war should be utilised to a large extent by large scale assignments for the requirements of the war industry. The prerequisite for production is adequate nourishment. Also very small wages are to be planned for the most modest supply, with a few consumers' goods for everyday life as eventual rewards for production."

And quoting now from the same document, Paragraph 2, II and III - I am quoting directly:-

"II. Construction and Armament Industry.

(a) Work units for construction of all kinds, particularly for the fortification of coastal defences (concrete workers unloading units for essential war plants.)

(b) Suitable armament factories which have to be selected in such a way that their personnel should consist in the majority of prisoners of war under guidance and supervision (eventually after withdrawal and other employment of the German workers).

III. Other War Industries.

(a) Mining as under 11 (b).

(b) Railroad construction units for building tracks, etc.

(c) Agriculture and forestry in closed units. The utilisation of Russian prisoners of war is to be regulated on the basis of the above examples by:

To I. The Armed Forces.

To II. The Reich Minister for Armament and Munitions and the Inspector General for the German Road System in agreement with the Reich Minister for Labour and Supreme Commander of the Armed Forces. Deputies of the Reich Minister for Armament and Munitions are to be admitted to the prisoner of war camps to assist in the selection of skilled workers."

The defendant Goering, at a conference at the Air Ministry on the 7th November, 1941, also discussed the use of prisoners of war in the armament industry. We refer now to our Document 1206-PS, which becomes Exhibit USA 215. This document consists of top secret notes on Goering's instructions as to the employment and treatment of prisoners of war in many phases of the German war industry. And I wish to quote from Paragraph 1 of Page 1 and Paragraph 4 of Page 2 of the English text, and from Paragraph 1, Page 1, and Paragraph 1, Page 3 of the German text as follows:-

"The Fuehrer's point of view as to employment of prisoners of war in war industries has changed basically. So far a total Of 5,000,000 prisoners of war- employed so far 2,000,000."

And on Page 2:-

"In the Interior and the Protectorate it would be ideal if entire factories could be manned by Russian prisoners of war except the employees necessary for direction. For employment in the Interior and the Protectorate the following are to have priority:-

(a) At the top, coal mining industry. Order by the Fuehrer to investigate all mines as to suitability for employment of Russians, at times manning the entire plant with Russian labourers.

(b) Transportation (construction of locomotives and cars, repair shops). Railroad repair and industry workers are to be sought out from the prisoners of war. Railroad is most important means of transportation in the East.

(c) Armament Industries. Preferably factories of armour and guns. Possibly also construction of parts for aeroplane engines. Suitable complete sections of factories to be manned exclusively by Russians. For the remainder, employment in columns. Use in factories of tool machinery, production of farm tractors, generators, etc. In emergency, erect in individual places barracks for occasional workers who are used as unloading details and for similar purposes. (Reich Minister of the Interior through communal authorities.)

O.K.W./ A.W.A. is competent for transporting Russian prisoners of war employment through 'Planning Board for Employment of all prisoners of war.' If necessary, offices of Reich Commissariats.

No employment where danger to men or their supply exists, that is, factories exposed to explosives, waterworks, powerworks, etc. No contact with German population, especially no 'solidarity'. German worker as a rule is foreman of Russians.

Food is a matter of the Four Year Plan. Supply their own food (cats, horses, etc.)

Clothes, billeting, messing somewhat better than at home where part of the people live in caverns.

Supply of shoes for Russians as a rule wooden shoes; if necessary install Russian shoe repair shops.

Examination of physical fitness in order to avoid importation of diseases.

Clearing of mines as a rule by Russians; if possible by selected Russian engineers."

The defendant Goering was not the only one of these defendants who sponsored and applied the policy for using prisoners of war in the armament industry. The defendant Speer also sponsored and applied this same policy of using prisoners of war in the armament industry. And we refer to Document 1435-PS, which is Exhibit USA 20. This document is a speech to the Nazi, Gauleiters delivered by the defendant Speer on 24th February, 1942, and I read from Paragraph 2 of that document:-

"I therefore proposed to the Fi1hrer at the end of December, that all my labour force, including specialists, be released for mass employment in the East. Subsequently the remaining prisoners of war, about 10,000, were put at the disposal of the armament industry by me."

He also reported at the 36th meeting of the Central Planning Board, held on 22nd April, 1943, that only 30 per cent. of the Russian prisoners of war were engaged in the armament industry. This the defendant Speer found unsatisfactory. Referring again to Document R-124, the minutes of the Central Planning Board, and particularly to Page 17 of that document, and to Paragraph 10 of the English text, and Page 14, Paragraph 7 of the German text, we find this statement by the defendant Speer: quoting directly:-

"There is a specified statement showing in what sectors the Russian prisoners of war have been distributed, and this statement is quite interesting. It shows that the armaments industry only received 30 per cent. I always complained about this."

At Page 20 of the same Document, R-124, Paragraph 11 on Page 20 of the English text, and Page 14, the last paragraph of the German text, the defendant Speer stated, and I quote from that paragraph directly:-

"The 90,000 Russian prisoners of war employed in the whole of the armament industry are for the greatest part skilled men."

The defendant Sauckel, who was appointed Plenipotentiary General for the utilisation of labour for the express purpose, among others, of integrating prisoners of war into the German war industry, made it plain that prisoners of war were to be compelled to serve the German armament industry. His labour mobilisation programme, which is Document 016-PS, already marked Exhibit USA 168, contains this statement on Page 6, Paragraph 10 of the English text, and Page 9, Paragraph 1 of the German text:-

"All prisoners of war, from the territories of the West as well as of the East, actually in Germany, must be completely incorporated into the German armament and nutrition industries. Their production must be brought to the highest possible level."

I wish to turn now from the exploitation of foreign labour in general to a rather special Nazi programme which appears to us to have combined the brutality and the purposes of the slave labour programme with those of the concentration camp. The Nazis placed all Allied nationals in concentration camps and forced them, along with the other inmates of the concentration camps, to work under conditions which were set actually to exterminate them. This was what we call the Nazi programme of "extermination through work".

In the spring of 1942 these conspirators turned to the concentration camps as a further source of slave labour for the armament industry. I refer to a new Document R-129, being Exhibit USA 217. This document is a letter to Himmler, the Reichsfuehrer S. S., dated the 30th April, 1942, from one of his subordinates, an individual named Pohl, S.S. Obergruppenfuehrer and General of the Waffen S.S.; and I wish to quote directly from the first page of that document.

"Today I report about the present situation of the concentration camps and about measures I have taken to carry out your order of 3rd March, 1942."

Then moving on from Paragraphs 1, 2 and 3 on Page 2 of the English text, and at Page 1 of the German text, I quote as follows:-

"1. The war has brought about a marked change in the structure of the concentration camps and has changed their duties with regard to the employment of the prisoners. The custody of prisoners for the sole reasons of security, education, or prevention is no longer the main consideration. The mobilisation of all prisoners who are fit for work for purposes of the war now, and for purposes of construction in the forthcoming peace, comes to the foreground more and more.

2. From this knowledge some necessary measures result with the aim of transforming the concentration camps into organisations more suitable for the economic tasks, whilst they were formerly merely politically interested.

3. For this reason I gathered together all the leaders of the former inspectorate of concentration camps, all camp commanders, and all managers and supervisors of work on 23rd and 24th April, 1942; I explained personally to them this new development. I compiled in the order attached the main essentials, which have to be brought into effect with the utmost urgency if the commencement of work for the purposes of the armament industry is not to be delayed."

Now, the order referred to in that third paragraph set the framework for a programme of relentless exploitation, providing in part as follows; and I now refer to the enclosure appended to the quoted letter which is also a part of Document R-129, found at Page 3, Paragraphs 4, 5 and 6 of the English text, and Page 3 of the German text:-

"4. The camp commander alone is responsible for the employment of the labour available. This employment must be, in the true meaning of the word, exhaustive, in order to obtain the greatest measure of performance. Work is allotted by the Chief of the Department D centrally and alone. The camp commanders themselves may not accept, on their own initiative, work offered by third parties, and may not negotiate about it.

5. There is no limit to working hours. Their duration depends on the kind of working establishments in the camps and the kind of work to be done. They are fixed by the camp commanders alone.

6 .Any circumstances which may result in a shortening of working hours (e.g. meals, roll-calls) have therefore to be restricted to the minimum which cannot be condensed any more. It is forbidden to allow long walks to work, and noon intervals are only for eating purposes."

The armament production programme we have just described was not merely a scheme for mobilising the manpower potential of the camps. It actually was integrated directly into the larger Nazi programme of extermination; and I wish to refer at this point to our Document 654-PS, being Exhibit USA 218.

THE PRESIDENT: Do you think it will be convenient to break off now for a few minutes?

MR. DODD: Very well.

[A recess was taken.]

MR. DODD: At the recess time I had made reference to Document 654-PS which is Exhibit USA 218. This document is a memorandum of an agreement between Himmler, Reichsfuehrer S.S., and the Minister of Justice, Thierack. It is dated 18th September, 1942. The concept of extermination to which I referred shortly before the recess, was embodied in this document and I wish to quote from Page 1, Paragraph 2.

"2. The transfer of anti-social elements from prison to the Reichsfuehrer for extermination through work. Persons under protective arrest, Jews, Gypsies, Russians and Ukrainians, Poles with more than three-year sentences, Czechs and Germans with more than eight-year sentences, according to the decision of the Reich Minister for justice. First of all the worst anti-social elements amongst those just mentioned are to be handed over. I shall inform the Fuehrer of this through Reichsleiter Bormann."

Now, this agreement further provided in Paragraph 12 on Page 2 of the English text, and Page 3, Paragraph 14 of the German text, as follows:-

"14. It is agreed that, in consideration of the intended aims of the Government for the clearing up of the Eastern problems, in future Jews, Poles, Gypsies, Russians and Ukrainians are no longer to be tried by the ordinary courts, so far as punishable offences are concerned, but are to be dealt with by the Reichsfuehrer S.S. This does not apply to civil lawsuits, nor to Poles whose names are announced or entered in the German Racial Lists."

Now, in September, 1942, the defendant Speer made arrangements to bring this new source of labour within his jurisdiction. Speer convinced Hitler that significant production could be obtained only if the concentration camp prisoners were employed in factories under the technical control of the Speer Ministry instead of the control in the camps. In fact, without defendant Speer's co-operation, we say it would have been most difficult to utilise the prisoners on any large scale for war production, since he would not allocate to Himmler the machine tools and other necessary equipment. Accordingly, it was agreed that the prisoners were to be exploited in factories under the defendant Speer's control. To compensate Himmler for surrendering this jurisdiction to Speer, the defendant Speer proposed, and Hitler agreed, that Himmler would receive a share of the armaments' output, fixed in relation to the man hours contributed by his prisoners. In the minutes of the defendant Speer's conference with Hitler on 20th, 21st, and the 22nd September, 1942, Document R-124, which is Exhibit USA 179, I wish to refer particularly to Page 34 of the English text. These are the defendant Speer's minutes on this conference. I am quoting from Page 34, Paragraph 36, beginning at the middle of the page, and it is at the top of Page 26 in the German text:-

"I pointed out to the Fuehrer that, apart from an insignificant amount of work, no possibility exists of organising armament production in the concentration camps, because: (1) the machine tools required are missing; (2) there are no suitable premises. Both these assets would be available in the armament industry, if use could be made of them by a second shift.

The Fuehrer agrees to my proposal that the numerous factories set up outside towns for A.R.P. reasons should release their workers for supplementing the second shift in town factories, and should in return be supplied with labour from the concentration camps - also two shifts.

I pointed out to the Fuehrer the difficulties which I expected to encounter if Reichsfuehrer S.S. Himmler should be able, as he requests, to exercise authoritative influence over these factories. The Fuehrer, too, does not consider such an influence necessary.

The Fuehrer, however, agrees that Reichsfuehrer S.S. Himmler should draw advantages from making his prisoners available; he should get equipment for his division.

I suggest giving him a share in kind (war equipment) in ratio to the working hours done by his prisoners. A 3 to 5 per cent. share is suggested, the equipment also being calculated according to working hours. The Fuehrer would agree to such a solution.

The Fuehrer is prepared to order the additional delivery of this equipment and weapons to the S. S., according to a list submitted to him."

After a demand for concentration camp labour had been created, and after a mechanism had been set up by the defendant Speer for exploiting this labour in armament factories, measures were evolved for increasing the supply of victims for extermination through work. A steady flow was assured by an agreement between Himmler and the Minister of Justice mentioned above, which was implemented by such programmes as the following, and I refer to Document L-61, Exhibit USA 177, and I wish to quote from Paragraph 3. That document, the Tribunal will recall, is the defendant Sauckel's letter dated

26th November, 1942, to the Presidents of the Landes Employment Offices, and I wish to quote from Paragraph 3 of that letter.

"The Poles who are to be evacuated as a result of this measure will be put into concentration camps and put to work whether they are criminal or asocial elements."

General measures were supplemented by special drives for persons who would not otherwise have been sent to concentration camps.

THE PRESIDENT: Did you not read that this morning?

MR. DODD: Yes, I did, your Honour. I was reading it again with particular reference to this feature of the proof.

For example, for "reasons of war necessity" Himmler ordered that at least 35,000 prisoners qualified for work should be transferred to concentration camps. I now offer in evidence Document 1063-PS D, which is Exhibit USA 219. This document is a Himmler order dated the 17th December, 1942. The order provides, and I quote in part, beginning with the first paragraph of that document:-

"For reasons of war necessity not to be discussed further here, the Reichsfuehrer S.S. and Chief of the German Police on 14th December, 1942, has ordered that until the end of January, 1943, at least 35,000 prisoners qualified for work, are to be sent to the concentration camps. In order to reach this number, the following measures are required:

(1) Up to this date (so far until 1st February, 1943) all Eastern workers or such foreign workers who have been fugitives, or who have broken contracts, and who do not belong to allied, friendly or neutral States are to be brought by the quickest means to the nearest concentration camps.

(2) The commanders and the commandants of the Security Police and the Security Service, and the chiefs of the State Police Headquarters will check immediately on the basis of a close and strict ruling:

(a) the prisons,

(b) the labour reformatory camps.

All prisoners qualified for work, if it is essentially and humanly possible, will be committed at once to the nearest concentration camp, according to the following instructions, for instance if penal procedures were to be established in the near future. Only such prisoners who in the interest of investigation procedures are to remain absolutely in solitary confinement can be left there.

Every single labourer counts!"

Measures were also adopted to ensure that this extermination through work was practised with maximum efficiency. Subsidiary concentration camps were established near important war plants. The defendant Speer has admitted that he personally toured Upper Austria and selected sites for concentration camps near various munitions factories in the area. I am about to refer to the transcript of an interrogation under oath of the defendant Albert Speer.

THE PRESIDENT: Mr. Dodd, do you understand the last document you read, 1063-PS to refer to prisoners of war or prisoners in ordinary prisons or what?

MR. DODD: We understood it to refer to prisoners in ordinary prisons. In view of the Tribunal's ruling this morning, I think I should state that, with respect to this interrogation of defendant Speer, we had provided the defendants' counsel with the entire text in German. It happens to be a brief interrogation, and so we were able to complete that translation, and it has been placed in their Information Centre.

DR. FLAECHSNER (Counsel for defendant Speer): In reference to the transcript of the interrogation the reading of which the prosecutor has just announced, I should like to say the following:-

"It is true that we have received the German transcript of the English protocol, if one may call it a protocol. A comparison of the English text with the German transcript shows that there are, both in the English text and in the German transcript, mistakes which change the meaning and which I believe are to be attributed to misunderstandings on the part of the certifying interpreter. I believe, therefore, that the so-called protocol, as well as the English text, does not actually give the contents of what defendant Speer tried to express during the interrogation. It would, therefore, not further the establishment of the truth should this protocol ever be used."

THE PRESIDENT: Mr. Dodd, when was the German translation given to counsel for the defendant?

MR. DODD: About four days ago, your Honour.

THE PRESIDENT: Mr. Dodd, is there any certification by the interrogator as to the English translation?

MR. DODD: There is, your Honour. There is a certification at the end of the interrogation by the interrogator and by the interpreter, and by the reporter as well. There are three certifications.

THE PRESIDENT: I think the best course will be in these circumstances to receive the interrogation now. You will have an opportunity, by calling the defendant, to show in what way he alleges, or you allege, that the interrogation is inaccurately translated.

DR. FLAECHSNER: Thank you, sir.

MR. DODD: May I respectfully refer your Honour to the last document in the document book, four pages from the end?

THE PRESIDENT: Which page do you refer to?

MR. DODD: I refer to the page bearing the number 16 of the English text of the transcript of the interrogation and Page 21 of the German text. The answer quoted is:-

"The fact that we were anxious to use workers from concentration camps in factories and to establish small concentration camps near factories in order to use the manpower that was then available there was a general one, but it did not come up only in connection with this trip." - Exhibit USA 270, i.e. Speer's trip to Austria.

THE PRESIDENT: I think I ought to say to defendant's counsel that if he had waited until he heard that piece of evidence read, he would have seen that it was quite unnecessary to make any objection.

MR. DODD: Defendant Goering endorsed this use of concentration camp labour and asked for more. We refer to our Document 1584-PS, Part I, which is Exhibit USA 221. This document is a teletype message from Goering to Himmler dated 14th February, 1944. I quote from the document beginning with the second sentence:-

"At the same time I ask you to put at my disposal as great a number of concentration-camp-(K.Z.) convicts as possible for air armament, as this kind of manpower proved to be very useful according to previous experience. The situation of the air war makes subterranean transfer of industry necessary. For work of this kind concentration-camp-(K.Z.) convicts can be especially well concentrated at work and in the camp."

Defendant Speer subsequently assumed responsibility for this programme and Hitler promised Speer that if the necessary labour for the programme could not be obtained, 100,000 Hungarian Jews would be brought in by the S.S.

Speer recorded his conferences with Hitler on 6th April and 7th April, 1944, in Document R-124, which is Exhibit USA 179, already in evidence. I quote from Page 36 of the English text, Page 29 of the German text as follows:-

"Suggested to the Fuehrer that, due to lack of builders and equipment, the second big building project should not be set up in German territory, but in close vicinity to the border on suitable soil (preferably on gravel base and with transport facilities) on French, Belgian or Dutch territory. The Fuehrer agrees to this suggestion if the works could be set up behind a fortified zone. For the suggestion of setting up works in French territory speaks mainly the fact that it would be much easier to procure the necessary workers. Nevertheless, the Fuehrer asks that an attempt be made to set up the second works in a safer area, namely, in the Protectorate. If it should prove impossible there, too, to get hold of the necessary workers, the Fuehrer himself will contact the Reichsfuehrer S.S. and will give an order that the required 100,000 men are to be made available by bringing in Jews from Hungary. Stressing the fact that the building organisation was a failure, the Fuehrer demands that these works must be built by the O.T. exclusively and that the workers should be made available by the Reichsfuehrer S.S. He wants to hold a meeting shortly in order to discuss details with all the men concerned."

The unspeakably brutal, inhuman, and degrading treatment inflicted on Allied nationals and other victims of concentration camps while they were indeed being literally worked to death is described in Document L-159, which is not in the document book. It is an official report prepared by a U.S. Congressional Committee, U.S. Senate Document 47. This Congressional Committee had inspected the liberated camps at the request of General Eisenhower. It will be Exhibit USA 222. 1 would like to quote from the document briefly, first. from Page 14, the last paragraph, and from the first two paragraphs of the English text.

"The treatment accorded to these prisoners in the concentration camps was generally as follows: They were herded together in some wooden barracks not large enough for one-tenth of their number. They were forced to sleep on wooden frames covered with wooden boards in tiers of two, three and even four, sometimes with no covering, sometimes with a bundle of dirty rags serving both as pallet and coverlet.

Their food consisted generally of about one-half of a pound of black bread per day and a bowl of watery soup at noon and night, and not always that. Owing to the great numbers crowded into a small space and to the lack of adequate sustenance, lice and vermin multiplied, disease became rampant, and those who did not soon die of disease or torture began the long, slow process of starvation. Notwithstanding the deliberate starvation programme inflicted upon these prisoners by lack of adequate food, we found no evidence that the people of Germany, as a whole, were suffering from any lack of sufficient food or clothing. The contrast was so striking that the only conclusion which we could reach was that the starvation of the inmates of these camps was deliberate.

Upon entrance into these camps, newcomers were forced to work either at an adjoining war factory or were placed 'in commando' on various jobs in the vicinity, being returned each night to their stall in the barracks. Generally a German criminal was placed in charge of each 'block' or shed in which the prisoners slept. Periodically he would choose the one prisoner of his block who seemed the most alert or intelligent or showed most leadership qualities. These would report to the guards' room and would never be heard of again. The generally accepted belief of the prisoners was that these were shot or gassed or hanged and then cremated. A refusal to work or an infraction of the rules usually meant flogging and other types of torture, such as having the fingernails pulled out, and in each case usually ended in death after extensive suffering. The policies described constituted a calculated programme of planned torture and extermination on the part of those who were in control of the German Government ..."

I quote next from Page 11 of the English text beginning with the second sentence of Paragraph 2, a description of Camp Dora at Nordhausen; Page 12, Paragraph 1 of the German text, quoting as follows:-

"On the whole, we found this camp to have been operated and administered much in the same manner as Buchenwald had been operated and managed. When the efficiency of the workers decreased as a result of the conditions under which they were required to live, their rations were decreased as punishment. This brought about a vicious circle in which the weak became weaker and were ultimately exterminated."

Such was the cycle of work, torture, starvation and death for concentration camp labour - labour which the defendant Goering, while requesting that more of it be placed at his disposal, said had proved very useful; labour which the defendant Speer was "anxious" to use in the factories under his control.

The policy underlying this programme, the manner in which it was executed, and the responsibility of the conspirators in connection with it has been dwelt upon at length. Therefore, we should like, at this point, to discuss the special responsibility of the defendant Sauckel.

The defendant Sauckel's appointment as Plenipotentiary General for Manpower is explained probably first of all by his having been an old and trusted Nazi. He certified in Document 2974-PS, dated 17th November, 1945, which is already in evidence before this Tribunal as Exhibit USA 15, that he held the following positions:

Starting with his membership in the N.S.D.A.P., he was thereafter a member of the Reichstag; he was Gauleiter of Thuringia; he was a member of the

Thuringian Legislature; he was Minister of Interior and head of the Thuringian State Ministry; he was Reichsstatthalter for Thuringia; he was an S.A. Obergruppenfuehrer, S. S. Obergruppenfuehrer; he was Administrator for the Berlin-Suhler Waffen and Fahrzeugwerke in 1935. He was head of the Gustloff Werke Nationalsozialistische Industrie-Stiftung, 1936, and the Honorary Head of the Foundation. And from 21st March, 1942, until 1945, he was the General Plenipotentiary for Labour Allocation.

Sauckel's official responsibilities are borne out by evidence. His appointment as Plenipotentiary General for Manpower was effected by a decree of 21st March, 1942, which we have read and which was signed by Hitler, Lammers, and the defendant Keitel. By that decree Sauckel was given authority as well as responsibility subordinate only to that of Hitler, and Goering, who was the head of the Four Year Plan, subordinate only to those two for all matters relating to recruitment, allocation, and handling of foreign and domestic manpower.

The defendant Goering, to whom Sauckel was directly responsible, abolished the recruitment and allocation agencies of his Four Year Plan and delegated their powers to the defendant Sauckel, and placed his far-reaching authority as deputy for the Four Year Plan at Sauckel's disposal.

In Document 1666-PS, a second 1666-PS, but of another date, the 27th March, 1942, I ask the Tribunal to take judicial notice of this original decree which is published in the 1942 Reichsgesetzblatt, Part 1, at Page 180:-

"In pursuance of the Fuehrer's Decree of 21st March, 1942, I decree as follows:-

1. My manpower sections are hereby abolished (circular letter of 22nd October, 1936). Their duties (recruitment and allocation of manpower, regulations for labour conditions) are taken over by the Plenipotentiary General for Arbeitseinsatz, who is directly under me.

2. The Plenipotentiary General for Arbeitseinsatz will be responsible for regulating the conditions of labour (wage policy) employed in the Reich territory, having regard to the requirements of Arbeitseinsatz.

3. The Plenipotentiary General for Arbeitseinsatz is part of the Four Year Plan. In cases where new legislation is required, or existing laws required to be modified, he will submit appropriate proposals to me.

4. The Plenipotentiary General for Arbeitseinsatz will have at his disposal for the performance of his task the right delegated to me by the Fuehrer for issuing instructions to the higher Reich authorities, their branches and the Party Offices, and their associated organisms and also the Reich Protector, the Governor General, the Commander-in-Chief, and heads of the civil administrations. In the case of ordinances and instructions of fundamental importance a report is to be submitted to me in advance."

Document 1903-PS is a Hitler Decree of 30th September, 1942, giving the defendant Sauckel extraordinary powers over the civil and military authority of the territories occupied by Germany. We ask that judicial notice be taken by this Tribunal of the original decree, which is published in Volume II, Page 510, of the "Verfuegungen/Anordnungen/Bekanntgaben", published by the Party Chancellery. This decree states as follows :-

"I herewith authorise the Deputy General for the Arbeitseinsatz, Reich Governor and District Leader (Gauleiter) Fritz Sauckel to take all necessary measures for the enforcement of my decree referring to a Deputy General for the Arbeitseinsatz of 21st March, 1942 (Reichsgesetzblatt I, Page 179) according to his own judgement in the Greater German Reich, in the Protectorate, and in the Government General as well as in the occupied territories, measures which will safeguard under all circumstances the regulated deployment of labour for the German war economy. For this purpose he may appoint commissioners to the bureaux of the military and civilian administration. These are subordinated directly to Deputy General for the Arbeitseinsatz. In order to carry out their tasks, they are entitled to issue directives to the competent military and civilian authorities in charge of the Arbeitseinsatz; and of wage policy.

More detailed directives will be issued by the Deputy General for the Arbeitseinsatz.

Fuehrer Headquarters, 30th September, 1942. The Fuehrer, signed Adolf Hitler."

Within one month after his appointment, the defendant Sauckel sent defendant Rosenberg his "Labour Mobilisation Programme". This programme - Document 016-PS, already in evidence as Exhibit USA 168 - envisaged a recruitment by force, and the maximum exploitation of the entire labour resources of the conquered areas and of prisoners of war, in the interests of the Nazi war machine at the lowest conceivable degree of expenditure to the German State.

The defendant Sauckel states - and I refer now to the bottom of Page 6 of the English text of that document. It is Page 9, Paragraph 2, of the German text, and I quote as follows:-

"It must be emphasised, however, that an additional tremendous number of foreign labourers has to be found for the Reich. The greatest pools for that purpose are the occupied territories of the East. Consequently, it is an immediate necessity to use the human reserves of the conquered Soviet territory to the fullest extent. Should we not succeed in obtaining the necessary amount of labour on a voluntary basis, we must immediately institute conscription of forced labour.

Apart from the prisoners of war still in the occupied territories, we must, therefore, requisition skilled or unskilled male and female labour from the Soviet territory, from the age of 15 up, for the labour mobilisation."

Passing to Page 11 of the English text, first paragraph, and Page 17, Paragraph 4 of the German text, I quote directly; as follows:

"The complete employment of all prisoners of war as well as the use of a gigantic number of new foreign civilian workers, men and women, has become an indisputable necessity for the solution of the mobilisation of labour programme in this war."

The defendant Sauckel proceeded to implement this plan, which he submitted with certain basic directives. He provided that if voluntary recruitment of foreign workers was unsuccessful, compulsory service should be instituted.

Document 3044-PS is the defendant Sauckel's Regulation No. 4, dated 7th May, 1942. We ask that the Tribunal take judicial notice of the original regulation published in Volume II, Pages 516 to 527 of the "Verfuegungen/ Anordnungen/Bekanntgaben", to which I have previously referred. Reading from Page 1, Paragraph 3, of the English text:-

"The recruitment of foreign labour will be carried out on the fundamental basis of volunteering. Where, however, in the occupied territories the appeal for volunteers does not suffice, obligatory service and drafting must, under all circumstances, be resorted to. This is an indisputable requirement of our labour situation."

Sauckel provided also for the allocation of foreign labour in the order of its importance to the Nazi war machine. We refer to Document 3044-(A)-PS, which is the defendant Sauckel's Regulation No. 10, and ask that the Court take judicial notice of the original regulation, published in Volume II, "Verfuegungen/Anordnungen/Bekanntgaben", at Pages 531 to 533 - Paragraph 3 of this regulation I quote as follows:

"The resources of manpower that are available in the occupied territories are to be employed primarily to satisfy the requirements of importance for the war in Germany itself. In allocating the said labour resources in the Occupied territories, the following order of priority will be observed:

(a) Labour required for the troops, the occupation authorities, and the civil authorities.

(b) Labour required for German armaments.

(c) Labour required for food and agriculture.

(d) Labour required for industrial work other than armaments.

(e) Labour required for industrial work in the interests of the population of the territory in question."

The defendant Sauckel, and agencies subordinate to him, exercised exclusive authority over the recruitment of workers from every area in Europe occupied by, controlled by, or friendly to the German nation. He affirmed - the defendant Sauckel himself did - this authority in a decree, Document 3044-PS, already in evidence as Exhibit USA 206. I refer to Paragraph 5 on Page 1 of the English text of that document, and I am quoting it directly:-

"The recruitment of foreign labour in the areas occupied by Germany, in allied, friendly or neutral States will be carried out exclusively by my Commissioners, or by the competent German military or civil agencies for the tasks of labour mobilisation."

THE PRESIDENT: Have not you read that already?

MR. DODD: No, I have not, if your Honour pleases. We have referred to that decree before, but we have not referred to this portion of it.

I am passing to Paragraph 2, 1-a on Page 2, and quoting, again, directly:-

"For the carrying out of recruitment in allied, friendly, or neutral foreign countries, my Commissioners are solely responsible."

In addition, the following defendant, who was informed by Sauckel of the quotas of foreign labourers which he required, collaborated with Sauckel and his agents in filling these quotas:-

The defendant Keitel, Chief of the O.K.W.-which was the Supreme

Command.

We refer to Document 3012-PS-I, which is Exhibit USA 190. This document is the record of a telephone conversation of the Chief of the Economic Staff East of the German Army, and it is dated 11th March, 1943. I wish to quote from the first two paragraphs of the document as follows:-

"The Plenipotentiary for the Arbeitseinsatz, Gauleiter Sauckel, points out to me, in an urgent teletype, that the Arbeitseinsatz in German agriculture, as well as all the most urgent armament programmes, ordered by the Fuehrer, make the most rapid procurement of approximately 1,000,000 women and men from the newly occupied territories an imperative necessity. For this purpose, Gauleiter Sauckel demands the daily shipment Of 5,000 workers beginning on 15th March; 10,000 workers, male and female, beginning 1st April, from the newly occupied territories."

I am passing down to the next paragraph:-

"In consideration of the extraordinary losses of workers, which occurred in German war industry because of the developments of the past months, it is now necessary that the recruiting of workers be taken up again everywhere with all emphasis. The tendency momentarily noticeable in that territory, to limit and/or entirely stop the Reich recruiting programme, is absolutely intolerable in view of this state of affairs. Gauleiter Sauckel, who is informed about these events, has, because of this, turned immediately to General Field Marshal Keitel on 10th March, 1943, in a teletype, and has emphasised on this occasion, that, as in all other occupied territories, where all other methods fail, a certain pressure must be used by order of the Fuehrer."

At this point we were prepared to offer a transcript of an interrogation under oath of the defendant Sauckel. The English only, of the transcript of the interrogation has been seen by the counsel for the defendant Sauckel. He has had it, however, for some time, and the excerpts on which we intended to rely were furnished to him as well in German.

If I understood the ruling of the Tribunal correctly, it would be necessary for us to have furnished the entire record in German.

THE PRESIDENT: I think you might use this interrogation, as the excerpts have been submitted in German.

MR. DODD: Yes, they have, your Honour, and the entire English text as well.

THE PRESIDENT: Very well.

MR. DODD: I refer to a transcript of an interrogation, under oath of the defendant Sauckel, held on the morning Of 5th October, 1945, Exhibit USA 224. That is the very last document in the document book. I wish to quote from the bottom of Page 1 of the English text, and Page 1, Paragraph 11 of the German text, as follows:-

Q. Was it necessary, in order to accomplish the completion of the quotas given, to have liaison with O.K.W.

A. I remember that the Fuehrer had given directives to Marshal Keitel, telling him that my task was a very important one, and I, too, have often conferred with Keitel after such discussions with the Fuehrer, when I asked him for his support.

Q. It was his task to supervise the proper performance of the military commanders in the occupied countries in carrying out their missions, was it not ?

A. Yes, the Fuehrer had told me that he would inform the Chief of the O.K.W., and the Chief of the Reich Chancellery, as to these missions. The same applies to the Foreign Minister."

We are also prepared to offer the transcript of an interrogation of the defendant Alfred Rosenberg. There is this distinction in so far as this record is concerned. While we have supplied the counsel with the German translation of those parts of it which we propose to use, we have not had an opportunity to supply the whole text to counsel. However, they have been supplied with the German of the parts which we propose to use and to offer to this Tribunal.

THE PRESIDENT: Well, you are prepared to do it hereafter, I suppose ?

MR. DODD: Yes, we will, your Honour, as soon as we can get these papers down to their Information Centre.

THE PRESIDENT: Yes.

MR. DODD: The next document is rather lengthy, and I wonder what the Tribunal's pleasure is. Do I understand that I may proceed with the interrogation ?

THE PRESIDENT: Yes.

MR. DODD: I wish to refer to the defendant Alfred Rosenberg, the Reich Minister for Eastern Occupied Territories, as one who also collaborated with the defendant Sauckel, and specifically, to refer to a transcript of an interrogation under oath of the defendant Rosenberg, on the afternoon of 6th October, 1945, Exhibit USA 187. That record may be found about the third from the last of the interrogation records in the document book, and I wish to read from Page 1 of the transcript:-

Q. Is not it a fact that Sauckel would allocate to the various areas under your jurisdiction the number of persons to be obtained for labour purposes?

A. Yes.

Q. And that, thereafter, your agents would obtain that labour in order to meet the quota which had been given; is that right?

A. Sauckel, normally, had very far-reaching desires, which one could not fulfil unless one looked very closely into the matter.

Q. Never mind about Sauckel's desires being far-reaching or not being far-reaching. That has nothing to do with it. You were given quotas for the areas over which you had jurisdiction, and it was up to you to meet that quota?

A. Yes; it was the responsibility of the administrative officials to receive this quota and to distribute the allotments over the districts in such a way, according to number and according to the age groups, that they would be most reasonably met.

Q. These administrative officials were part of your organisation, is not that right?

A. They were functionaries or officials of the Reichskommissar for the Ukraine, but, as such, they were placed in their office by the Ministry for the Eastern Occupied Territories.

Q. You recognised, did you not, that the quotas set by Sauckel could not be filled by voluntary labour, and you did not disapprove of the impressment of forced labour; is not that right?

A. I regretted that the demands of Sauckel were so urgent that they could not be met by a continuation of voluntary recruitments, and thus I submitted to the necessity of forced impressment."

Then, passing a little further down on that page:-

"Q. The letters that we have already seen between you and Sauckel do not indicate, do they, any disagreements on your part with the principle of recruiting labour against their will? They indicate, as I remember, that you were opposed to the treatment that was later accorded these workers, but that you did not oppose their initial impressment."

THE PRESIDENT: Mr. Dodd, I think you ought to read the next two answers, in fairness to the defendant Rosenberg, after the one where he said he submitted to the necessity of forced impressment.

MR. DODD: Very well, I will read those, your Honour.

THE PRESIDENT: Did you ever argue with Sauckel.

MR. DODD: Yes.

"Q. Did you ever argue with Sauckel that perhaps in view of the fact that quotas could not be met by voluntary labour, the labour recruiting programme be abandoned, except for such recruits as could be voluntarily enrolled?

A. I could not do that because the numbers or allotments that Sauckel had received from the Fuehrer to meet were absolutely binding for him, and I could not do anything about that."

And then, referring again to the question which I had just read, the answer is as follows:-

"That is right. In those matters I mostly discussed the possibility of finding the least harsh methods of handling the matter, though in no way placing myself in opposition to the orders that he was carrying out for the Fuehrer."

THE PRESIDENT: I think the Tribunal might adjourn now.

MR. DODD: Very well, your Honour.

[The Tribunal adjourned until 13th December, 1945, at 1000 hours.]

Nineteenth Day:
Thursday, 13th December, 1945

MR. DODD: May it please the Tribunal, at the close of yesterday's session, we were discussing and had just completed reading the excerpts from the interrogation of 6th October, 1945, wherein the defendant Alfred Rosenberg was questioned.

There have been introduced Documents 017-PS and 019-PS and I have read excerpts from them. The Tribunal will recall that they are letters written by the defendant Sauckel to the defendant Rosenberg, requesting the assistance of the defendant Rosenberg in the recruitment of additional foreign labourers. I refer to them in passing, by way of recapitulation, with respect to the defendant Sauckel's participation in this slave labour programme and also the assistance of the defendant Rosenberg. Also the defendant Sauckel received help from the defendant Seyss-Inquart, who was the Reichskommissar for the Occupied Netherlands.

I refer again to the transcript of the interrogation under oath of the defendant Sauckel, which was read from yesterday, and I now refer to another part of it. The transcript of this interrogation will be found at the back of the document book. It is the very last document and I wish to quote particularly from it.

"Q. For a moment, I want to turn our attention to Holland. It is my understanding that the quotas for the workers from Holland were agreed upon, and then the numbers given to the Reichskommissar Seyss-Inquart to fulfil, is that correct?

A. Yes, that is correct.

Q. After the quota was given to Seyss-Inquart, it was his mission to fulfil it - with the aid of your representatives; was it not?

A. Yes. This was the only possible thing for me to do and the same applied to other countries."

And the defendant Hans Frank, who was the Governor General of the Government General of Poland, participated in the filling of defendant Sauckel's quota requirements.

I refer again to the interrogation of the defendant Sauckel and to Page 1 of the excerpts from the transcript of this interrogation, as it appears in the document book:

"Q. Was the same procedure substantially followed of allocating quotas in the Government General of Poland?

A. Yes. I have to basically state again that the only possibility I had of carrying through these missions was to get in touch with the highest German military authorities in the respective country and to transfer to them the orders of the Fuehrer and ask them very urgently, as I have always done, to fulfil these orders.

Q. Such discussions in Poland, of course, were with the Governor General Frank?

A. Yes. I spent a morning and afternoon in Cracow two or three times

352

and I personally spoke to Governor General Frank. Naturally, there was also present Secretary Dr. Goebbels."

The S.S., as in most matters involving the use of force and brutality, also extended its assistance. We refer to Document 1292-PS, which is Exhibit USA 225. This Document, 1292-PS, is the report of the Reichschancellor Lammers of a conference with Hitler, which was attended by, among others, the defendant Sauckel, the defendant Speer, and Himmler, the Reichsfuehrer S.S. I turn to Page 2 of the document, beginning with the third line from the top of the page of the English text; and it is Page 4, Paragraph 2 of the German text. The quotation reads as follows:

"The Plenipotentiary for Employment and Labour, Sauckel, declares that he will attempt with fanatical determination to obtain these workers. Until now, he has always kept his promises as to the number of workers to be furnished. With the best of intentions, however, he is unable to make a definite promise for 1944. He will do everything in his power to furnish the requested manpower in 1944. Whether it will succeed depends primarily on what German enforcement agents will be made available. His project cannot be carried out with domestic enforcement agents."

There are additional quotations, as the Tribunal may observe, in this very part from which I have been reading, but I intend to refer to them again a little further on.

The defendant Sauckel participated in the formulation of the overall labour requirements for Germany, and passed out quotas to be filled by and with the assistance of the individuals and agencies referred to, in the certain knowledge that force and brutality were the only means whereby his demands could be met. Turning to Document 1292- PS again, and quoting from Page 1:-

"A conference took place with the Fuehrer today which was attended by: the Plenipotentiary for the Employment of Labour, Gauleiter Sauckel; the Secretary for Armament and War Production, Speer; the Chief of the Supreme Command of the Army, General Field Marshal Keitel; General Field Marshal Milch; the Minister of the Interior, Reichsfuehrer of the S.S. Himmler; and myself. (The Minister for Foreign Affairs and the Minister of National Economy had repeatedly asked to be permitted to participate prior to the Conference, but the Fuehrer did not wish their attendance.)

The Fuehrer declared in his introductory remarks:

I want a clear picture:

1. How many workers are required for the maintenance of German War Economy?

(a) For the maintenance of present output?

(b) To increase its output?

2. How many workers can be obtained from occupied countries, or how many can still be gained in the Reich by suitable means (increased output)? For one thing, it is this matter of making up for losses by death, infirmity, the constant fluctuation of workers, and so forth, and for another it is a matter of procuring additional workers.

The Plenipotentiary for the Employment of Labour, Sauckel, declared that, in order to maintain the present pool of workers, he would have to add at least 2.5 but probably 3 million new workers in 1944.

Otherwise production would fall off. Reichsminister Speer declared that he needed an additional 1.3 million labourers. However, this would depend on whether it would be possible to increase production of iron ore. Should this not be possible, he would need no additional workers. Procurement of additional workers from occupied territory would, however, be subject to the condition that these workers would not be withdrawn from armament and auxiliary industries already working there, for this would mean a decrease of production of these industries which he could not tolerate. Those, for instance, who were already working in France in industries mentioned above must be protected against being sent to work in Germany by the Plenipotentiary for the Employment of Labour. The Fuehrer agreed with the opinions of Reichsminister Speer and emphasised that the measures taken by the Plenipotentiary for the Employment of Labour should under no circumstances lead to the withdrawal of workers from armament and auxiliary industries working in occupied territories, because such a shift of workers would only cause disturbances of production in occupied countries.

The Fuehrer further called attention to the fact that at least 250,000 labourers would be required for preparations against air attacks in the field of civilian air raid protection. For Vienna alone 2,000- 2,500 were required immediately. The Plenipotentiary for the Employment of Labour must add at least 4 million workers to the manpower pool, considering that he required 21 million workers for maintenance of the present level, that Reich Minister Speer needed 1.3 million additional workers, and that the above-mentioned preparations for security measures against air attacks called for 0.25 million labourers."

Referring again to Page 2, the first full paragraph of the English text of this document, and Page 5, Paragraph 1 of the German text:

"The Reichsfuehrer S.S. explained that the enforcement agents put at his disposal were extremely few, but that he would try to help the Sauckel project to succeed by increasing them and working them harder. The Reichsfuehrer S.S. made immediately available 2,000 to 2,500 men from concentration camps for air raid preparations in Vienna."

Passing the next paragraph of this document and continuing with the paragraph entitled "Results of the Conference", and quoting it directly after the small figure II:

"The Plenipotentiary for Employment of Labour shall procure at least 4,000,000 new workers from occupied territories."

Moreover, as Document 3012-PS, which has already been offered as Exhibit USA 190, revealed, the defendant Sauckel in requesting the assistance of the Army for the recruitment of 1,000,000 men and women from the occupied Eastern territories informed the defendant Keitel that prompt action was required and that, as in all other occupied countries, pressure had to be used if other measures were not successful. Again, as revealed by Document 018-PS, which has been offered and from which excerpts have been read, the defendant Sauckel was informed by the defendant Rosenberg, that the enslavement of foreign labour was achieved by force and brutality.

Notwithstanding his knowledge of conditions, the defendant Sauckel continued to request greater supplies of manpower from the areas in which the most ruthless methods had been applied. Indeed, when German Field Commanders on the Eastern Front attempted to resist or restrain the defendant Sauckel's demands, because forced recruitment was swelling the ranks of the partisans and making the Army's task more difficult, Sauckel sent a telegram to Hitler, in which he implored him, Hitler, to intervene.

I make reference to Document 407-II-PS, which is Exhibit USA 226. This document is a telegram from the defendant Sauckel to Hitler, dated 10th March, 1943, It is a rather long message, but I wish to call particularly to the attention of the Tribunal the last paragraph on Page 1 of the English text. It is Page 2, Paragraph 5 of the German text. Quoting the last paragraph of the English text:-

"Therefore, my Fuehrer I ask you to abolish all orders which oppose the compulsion of foreign workers for labour, and to report to me kindly whether the concept of the mission presented here is still right."

Turning to Paragraph 5 on the first page of this English text, we find these words, quoting them directly:

"If the compulsion for labour and the forced recruiting of workers in the East is not possible any more, then the German war industries and agriculture cannot fulfil their tasks to the full extent."

The next paragraph:-

"I myself have the opinion that our Army leaders should not give credence under any circumstances to the atrocity and propaganda campaign of the partisans. The Generals themselves are greatly interested that the support for the troops is made possible in time. I should like to point out that hundreds of thousands of excellent workers going into the field as soldiers now cannot possibly be substituted by German women not used to work, even if they are trying to do their best. Therefore, I have to use the people of the Eastern territories."

THE PRESIDENT: I think you should read the next paragraph.

MR. DODD:

"I myself report to you that the workers belonging to all foreign nations are treated humanely and correctly and cleanly, are fed and housed well and are even clothed. On the basis of my own services with foreign nations I go as far as to state that never before in the world were foreign workers treated as correctly as is now happening, in the hardest of all wars, by the German people."

In addition to being responsible for the recruitment of foreign civilian labour by force defendant Sauckel was responsible for the conditions under which foreign workers were deported to Germany and for the treatment to which they were subjected within Germany.

We have already referred to the conditions under which these imported persons were transported to Germany and we have read from Document 2241-PS-3 to show that Sauckel knew of these conditions. Yesterday we referred at length to the brutal, degrading, and inhuman conditions under which these labourers worked and lived within Germany. We invite the attention again of the Tribunal to Document 3044-PS, already offered as Exhibit USA 206. It is Regulation No. 4 of 7th May, 1942, issued by Sauckel, as the Plenipotentiary General for the Mobilisation of Labour, concerning recruitment, care, lodging, feeding and treatment of foreign workers of both sexes. By this decree defendant Sauckel expressly directed that the assembly and operation of rail transports and the supplying of food therefor was the responsibility of his agents until the transports arrived in Germany. By the same regulation defendant Sauckel directed that within Germany the care of foreign industrial workers was to be carried out by the German Labour Front, and that the care of foreign agricultural workers was to be carried out by the Reich Food Administration. By the terms of the regulation, Sauckel reserved for himself ultimate responsibility for all aspects of care, treatment, lodging and feeding of foreign workers while in transit to and within Germany.

I refer particularly to the English text of this Document 3044-PS, Exhibit USA 206, and the part of it that I make reference to is at the bottom of Page 1 in the English text, and it appears at Page 518 of the volume in the German text. Quoting directly from the English text:-

"The care of foreign labour will be carried out.

(a) Up to the Reich border by my commissioners or-in the occupied areas-by competent military or civil labour mobilisation agencies. Care of the labour will be carried out in co- operation with the respective competent foreign organisation.

(b) Within the area of the Reich

(1) By the German Labour Front in the cases of non-agricultural workers.

(2) By the Reich Food Administration in the case of agricultural workers.

The German Labour Front and the German Food Administration are bound by my directives in the carrying out of their tasks of caring for the workers.

The agencies of the labour mobilisation administration are to give far-reaching support to the German Labour Front and the German Food Administration in the fulfilment of their assigned tasks.

My competence for the execution of the care for foreign labour is not prejudiced by the assignment of these tasks to the German Labour Front and the Reich Food Administration."

THE PRESIDENT: Mr. Dodd, do not you think that that is the sort of passage which might be summarised and not read, because all that it is really stating is that Sauckel, his department and commissioners were responsible, and that is what he is saying.

MR. DODD: Yes, indeed, your Honour, we spelled it out, thinking that perhaps under the rule of getting it into the record it must be read fully. I quite agree.

THE PRESIDENT: A summary will be quite sufficient, I think.

MR. DODD: In the same document, I should like to make reference to the data on Page 3, Paragraph 3 of the English text, which indicates, under the title of "Composition and Operation of the Transports", that this function is the obligation of the representatives of the defendant Sauckel; and in Paragraph "c", on Page 5 of the English text, under the title of "Supply for the Transport", after setting out some responsibility for the office of the German Workers Front, the defendant Sauckel states that for the rest his offices effect the supply for the transport.

The defendant Sauckel had an agreement with the head of the German Labour Front, Dr. Robert Ley, and in this agreement, the defendant Sauckel emphasised his ultimate responsibility by creating a Central Inspectorate, charged with examining the working and living conditions of foreign workers. We refer to Document 1913-PS, Exhibit USA 227. This agreement between the defendant Sauckel and the then Chief of the German Labour Front is published in the 1943 edition of the Reichsarbeitsblatt, Part 1, at Page 588. It is a rather lengthy agreement, and I shall not read it all or any great part of it, except such part as will indicate the basic agreements between the defendant Sauckel and Ley, with respect to the foreign workers and their living conditions and working conditions.

On the first page of the English text:-

> "The Reichsleiter of the German Labour Front, Dr. Ley, in collaboration with the Plenipotentiary General for the Arbeitseinsatz, Gauleiter Sauckel, will establish a 'Zentral Inspektion' for the continuous supervision of all measures concerning the care of the foreign workers mentioned under 1. This will have the designation: 'Central Inspection for Care of Foreign Workers.'"

Paragraph 4, marked with the Roman numeral IV, in the same text, states:-

> "The offices of the administration of the Arbeitseinsatz will be constantly informed by the 'Central Inspection for the Care of Foreign Workers' of its observations, in particular, immediately in each case in which action of State organisations seems to be necessary."

I should also like to call the attention of the Tribunal to this paragraph, which is quoted on the same page. It is the fourth paragraph down, after the small number 2, and it begins with the words:-

> "The authority of the Plenipotentiary General for the Arbeitseinsatz to empower the members of his staff and the presidents of the State employment offices to get direct information on the conditions regarding the employment of foreigners in the factories and camps, will remain untouched."

We have already offered to the Court, proof that the defendant Sauckel was responsible for compelling citizens of the occupied countries, against their will, to manufacture arms and munitions and to construct military fortifications for use in war operations against their own country and its allies. He was, moreover, responsible for compelling prisoners of war to produce arms and munitions for use against their own countries and their actively resisting allies.

The decree appointing Sauckel indicated that he was appointed Plenipotentiary General for Manpower for the express purpose, among others, of integrating prisoners of war into the German war industry; and in a series of reports to Hitler, Sauckel described how successful he had been in carrying out that programme. One such report states that in a single year, the defendant Sauckel had incorporated 1,622,829 prisoners of war into the German economy.

I refer to Document 407-V-PS, which is Exhibit USA 228. It is a letter from the defendant Sauckel to Hitler, on 14th April, 1943. Although the figures in the document have been contained in another one, this is the first introduction of this particular one. Quoting from Paragraphs 1 and 2 of the English text, it begins:-

> "My Fuehrer,

After having been active as Plenipotentiary for Arbeitseinsatz for one year, I have the honour to report to you that 3,638,056 new foreign workers have been added to the German war economy between 1st April of the last year and 31st March of this year."

THE PRESIDENT: Are you reading Paragraph I?

MR. DODD: Yes, your Honour.

THE PRESIDENT: It says 5,000,000, not three.

MR. DODD: I think it is 3,000,000, if your Honour pleases.

THE PRESIDENT: It should be three?

MR. DODD: I think so. The original looks to us like three.

Passing on a little bit, with particular reference to the prisoners of war, we find this statement:-

"Besides the foreign civilian workers another 1,622,829 prisoners of war are employed in the German economy."

A later report states that 846,511 additional foreign labourers and prisoners of war were incorporated into the German war industry, and quoting from Document 407-IX-PS, Exhibit USA 229, which is also a letter from the defendant Sauckel to Hitler, I read in part from Page I, Paragraphs 1 and 2:-

"My Fuehrer,

I beg to be permitted to report to you on the situation of the Arbeitseinsatz for the first five months of 1943. For the first time the following number of new foreign labourers and prisoners of war were employed in the German war industry: Total, 846,511."

This use of prisoners of war in the manufacture of armaments allocated by the defendant Sauckel was confirmed by the defendant Speer, who stated that 40 per cent. of all prisoners of war were employed in the production of weapons and munitions and in subsidiary industries. I wish to refer briefly to Paragraphs 6, 7 and 8, on Page 15 of the English text of an interrogation of the defendant Speer on 18th October, 1945, which was offered and referred to yesterday Exhibit USA 220.

Quoting from Paragraphs 6, 7 and 8, on Page 15, Paragraph 1, on Page 2 of the German text. There are three questions which will establish the background for this answer:-

"Q. Let me understand, when you wanted labour from prisoners of war did you requisition prisoners of war separately, or did you ask for a total number of workers?

A. Only Schmelter can answer that directly. As far as the commitment of prisoners of war for labour goes, it was effected through employment offices of the Stalags. I tried several times to increase the total number of prisoners of war that were occupied in the production at the expense of the other demand factors.

Q. Will you explain that a little more?

A. In the last phase of production, that is, in the year 1944, when everything collapsed, I had 40 per cent. of all prisoners of war employed in the production. I wanted to have this percentage increased.

Q. And when you say 'employed in the production', you mean in these subsidiary industries that you have discussed, and also in the production of weapons and munitions, is that right?

A. Yes. That was the total extent of my task."

THE TRIBUNAL (Mr. Biddle): What do you mean by "subsidiary industries", Mr. Dodd? Is that war industries?

MR. DODD: Yes, sir; war industries, as we understand it. It was referred to many times by these defendants as the component parts of the plans.

I also would like to call the attention of the Tribunal again to the "Minutes of the 36th Meeting of the Central Planning Board", Document R-124, from which we read a number of excerpts yesterday, and remind the Tribunal that in the report of the minutes of that meeting the defendant Speer stated that:-

> "90,000 Russian prisoners of war employed in the whole of the armament industry are for the greatest part skilled men."

We should like, at this point, to turn to the special responsibility of the defendant Speer, and to discuss the evidence of the various crimes committed by, the defendant Speer in planning and participating in the vast programme of forcible deportation of the citizens of occupied countries. He was the Reich Minister of Armaments and Munitions and Chief of the Organisation Todt, both of which positions he acquired on 15th February, 1942, and by virtue of his later acquisition of control over the armament offices of the Army, Navy and Air Force and the production offices of the Ministry of Economics, the defendant Speer was responsible for the entire war production of the Reich, as well as for the construction of fortifications and installations for the Wehrmacht. Proof of the positions held by him is supplied in his own statement, as contained in Document 2980-PS, which has already been offered to the Tribunal and which is Exhibit USA 18.

The industries under the defendant Speer's control were really the most important users of manpower in Germany; and thus, according to the defendant Sauckel, Speer's labour requirements received unconditional priority over all other demands for labour. We refer to the transcript of the interrogation of the defendant Sauckel on 22nd September, 1945, It is Exhibit USA 230. It is next to the last document in the document book. I wish to refer to Page 1 of that document, Paragraph 4. It is a brief reference, the last answer on the page. The question was asked of the defendant Sauckel:-

> "Q. Except for Speer, they would give the requirements in general for the broad field, but in Speer's work he would get them allocated to industry, and so on; is that right?
>
> A. The others only got whatever was left. Because Speer told me once in the presence of the Fuehrer that I was there to work for Speer and that mainly I was his man."

The defendant Speer has admitted under oath that he participated in the discussions, during which the decision to use foreign forced labour was made. He has also said that he concurred in the decision and that it was the basis for the programme of bringing foreign workers into Germany by compulsion. I make reference to the interrogation of this defendant of 18th October, 1945. It is Exhibit USA 220. We have already read from it; and I particularly refer to the bottom of Page 12 and the top of Page 13 of the English text:-

> "Q. But is it clear to you, Herr Speer, that in 1942 when the decisions were being made concerning the use of forced foreign labour you participated in the discussions yourself?
>
> A. Yes.
>
> Q. So that I take it that the execution of the programme of bringing

foreign workers into Germany by compulsion under Sauckel was based on earlier decisions that had been made with your agreement?

A. Yes, but I must point out that only a very small part of the manpower that Sauckel brought into Germany was made available to me; a far larger part of it was allocated to other departments that demanded it."

This admission is confirmed by the minutes of Speer's conference with Hitler on 10th, 11th and 12th August, 1942, in Document R-124, which has been offered here and from which excerpts have been read. Page 34 of that document, Paragraph 1 of the English text, has already been quoted, and those excerpts were read before the Tribunal yesterday. The Tribunal will recall that the defendant Speer related the outcome of his negotiations concerning the forcible recruitment of 1,000,000 Russian labourers for the German armaments industry, and this use of force was again discussed by Hitler and Speer on 4th January, 1943, as shown by the excerpts read from the Document 556-PS-13, where it was decided that stronger measures were to be used to accelerate the conscription of French civilian workers.

We say the defendant Speer demanded foreign workers for the industries under his control and used those workers with the knowledge that they had been deported by force and were being compelled to work. Speer has stated under oath in his interrogation of 18th October, 1945, Page 5, Paragraph 9 of the English text, quoting it directly:-

"I do not wish to give the impression that I want to deny the fact that I demanded manpower and foreign manpower from Sauckel very energetically."

He has admitted that he knew he was obtaining foreign labour, a large part of which was forced labour; and referring again to that same interrogation of 18th October, 1945, and to Pages 8 and 9 of the English text and Page 10 of the German text:-

"Q. So that during the period when you were asking for labour, it seems clear, does it not, that you knew you were obtaining foreign labour as well as domestic labour in response to your requests, and that a large part of the foreign labour was forced labour.

A. Yes.

Q. So that, simply by way of illustration, suppose that on 1st January, 1944, you require 50,000 workers for a given purpose, would you put in a requisition for 50,000 workers, knowing that in that 50,000 there would be forced foreign workers?

A. Yes."

The defendant Speer has also stated under oath that he knew at least as early as September, 1942, that workers from the Ukraine were being forcibly deported for labour into Germany. Likewise he knew that the great majority of the workers of the Western occupied countries were slave labourers, forced against their will to come to Germany; and again referring to his interrogation of this 18th day of October, 1945, and beginning with the fourth paragraph from the bottom of Page 5 of the English text, Paragraph 10 on Page 6 of the German text, we find this series of questions and answers:

"Q. When did you first find out then that some of the manpower from the Ukraine was not coming voluntarily?

A. It is rather difficult to answer this here, that is, to name a certain

360

date to you. However, it is certain that I knew that at some particular point of time that the manpower from the Ukraine did not come voluntarily.

Q. And does that apply also to the manpower from other occupied countries; that is, did there come a time when you knew that they were not coming voluntarily?

A. Yes.

Q. When in general, would you say that time was, without naming a particular month of the year?

A. As far as the Ukraine situation goes, I believe that they did not come voluntarily any more after a few months, because immense mistakes were made in their treatment by us. I should say off-hand that this time was either in July, August or September, 1942."

Turning to Paragraph 11 on Page 6 of the English text of this same interrogation and Page 7 and Paragraph 8 of the German text, we find this series of questions and answers - and I am quoting:-

"Q. But many workers did come from the West, did they not, to Germany?

A. Yes.

Q. That means, then, that the great majority of the workers that came from the Western countries, the Western occupied countries, came against their will to Germany?

A. Yes."

These admissions are borne out, of course, by other evidence, for, as Document R-124 shows, and as we have shown by the readings from it, in all countries conscription for work in Germany could be carried out only with the active assistance of the police, and the prevailing methods of recruitment had provoked such violence that many German recruiting agents had been killed.

And again, at a meeting with Hitler to discuss the manpower requirements for 1944, which is reported in Document 1292- PS, Speer was informed by the defendant Sauckel that the requirements - including Speer's requirement for 1,300,000 additional labourers - could be met only if German enforcement agents were furnished to carry out the enslavement programme in the occupied countries.

Now we say that, notwithstanding his knowledge that these workers were conscripted and deported to Germany against their will, Speer nevertheless continued to formulate requirements for the foreign workers and requested their allocation to those industries which were subject to his control. This is borne out by the minutes of the Central Planning Board, as contained in Document R-124, and particularly Page 13, Paragraph 4 of the English text; and that is Page 6 and Paragraph 4 of the German text.

Speer speaking:-

"Now, to the labour problem in Germany. I believe it is still possible to transfer some workers from the Western territories. The Fuehrer stated only recently that he wished to dissolve these foreign volunteers as he had the impression that the army groups were carting around with them a lot of ballast. Therefore, if we cannot settle this matter ourselves, we shall have to call a meeting with the Fuehrer to clear up the coal situation. Keitel and Keitzler will be invited to attend in order to determine the number of Russians from the rear army territories that can be sent to us. However, I see another possibility: We might organise another drive to screen out workers for the mines from the Russian Prisoners of War in the Reich. But this possibility is none too promising."

At another meeting of the Central Planning Board the defendant Speer rejected a suggestion that labour for industries under his control be furnished from German sources instead of from foreign sources. And again, in this Document R-124, on Page 16, Paragraphs 3, 4 and 5 of the English text, and Page 12, Paragraphs 6 and 7 of the German text - I quote Speer:-

"We do it this way: Kehrl collects the demands for labour necessary to complete the coal-and-iron plan and communicates the numbers to Sauckel. Probably there will be a conference at the Reich Marshal's next week, and an answer from Sauckel should have arrived by then. The question of recruitment for the armaments industry will be solved together with Weger."

Then Kehrl speaking:-

"I wish to urge that the allotments to the mines should not be made dependent on the recruitment of men abroad. We were completely frustrated these last three months because this principle had been applied. We ended December with a deficit of 25,000 and we never get replacements.

The number must be made up by men from Germany.

Speer: No, nothing doing."

We say also that the defendant Speer is guilty of advocating terror and brutality as a means of maximising production by slave labourers. And again I refer to this Document R-124. At Page 42 there is a discussion concerning the supply and exploitation of labour. That excerpt has been read to the Tribunal before, and I simply refer to it in passing. It is the excerpt wherein Speer said it would be a good thing; the effect of it was that nothing could be said against the S.S. and the police taking a hand and making these men work and produce more.

We say he is also guilty of compelling allied nationals and prisoners of war to engage in the production of armaments and munitions and in direct military operations against their own country.

We say that, as Chief of the "Organisation Todt," he is accountable for its policies, which were in direct conflict with the laws of war, for the "Organisation Todt," in violation of the laws of war, impressed allied nationals into its service.

Document L-191, Exhibit USA 231, is an International Labour Office study of the exploitation of foreign labour by Germany. We have only one copy of this document, being this International Labour Office study, printed at Montreal, Canada, in 1945. We ask that the Tribunal take judicial notice of it as an official publication of the International Labour Office.

I might say to the Tribunal, with some apology, that this arrived at a time when we were not able even to have the excerpt mimeographed and printed, to place in your document book, so this is the one document which is missing from the document book which is in your hands. However, I should like to quote from Page 73, Paragraph 2, of this study by the International Labour Office. It is not long; it is very brief. I am quoting directly. It says:-

"The methods used for the recruitment of foreign workers who were destined for employment in the Organisation did not greatly differ from the methods used for the recruitment of foreigners for deportation to Germany."

The Organisation, by the way, is the "Organisation Todt."

"The main difference was that, since the principal activities of the Organisation lay outside the frontiers of Germany, foreigners were not transported to Germany but had either to work in their own country or in some other occupied territory.

In the recruitment drives for foreign workers for the Organisation methods of compulsion as well as methods of persuasion were used, the latter usually with very little result."

Moreover, conscripted allied nationals were compelled by this same Organisation to actually engage in operations of war against their country.

Document 407-PS, VIII, discloses that the foreign workers who were impressed into the "Organisation Todt," through the efforts of the defendant Sauckel, did participate in the building of the Atlantic Wall fortifications.

As Chief of German War Production this defendant Speer sponsored and approved the use of these prisoners of war in the production of armaments and munitions. This has been made plain by the evidence already discussed.

To sum it up briefly, we say that it shows first that, after Speer assumed the responsibility for the armament production, his concern, in his discussions with his co- conspirators, was to secure a larger allocation of prisoners of war for his armament factories. That has been shown by the quotations from the excerpts of Document R-124, the minutes of the meeting of the Central Planning Board; and in this same meeting the Tribunal will recall that Speer complained because only 30 per cent. of the Russian prisoners of war were engaged in the armaments industry.

We have referred to a speech of Speer, Document 1435-PS - we quoted from it - in which he said that 10,000 prisoners of war were put at the disposal of the armaments industry upon his orders.

And, finally, Speer advocated the returning of escaped prisoners of war to factories as convicts. That is shown again by Document R-124, Page 13, Paragraph 5 of the English text, where Speer says that he has come to an arrangement -

THE PRESIDENT: Mr. Dodd, do not you think that we really have got this sufficiently now?

MR. DODD: Yes, sir.

THE PRESIDENT: We have Speer's own admission and any number of documents which prove the way in which these prisoners of war and other labourers were brought into Germany.

MR. DODD: Well I just wanted to refer briefly to that passage in that Document R-124 as showing that this defendant advocated having escaped prisoners of war returned to the munitions factories. I do not want to enlarge on this responsibility of the defendant Speer. I was anxious - or perhaps I should say we are all over-anxious - to have the documents in the record and before the Tribunal.

THE PRESIDENT: Which is the passage you want to refer to on Page 13?

MR. DODD: I just referred in passing to the statement which begins with the words "We have come to an arrangement with the Reichsfuehrer S.S." And in the next to the last sentence says: "The men should be put into the factories

363

as convicts."

Finally, with reference to this defendant, I should like to say to the Tribunal that he visited the concentration camp at Mauthausen and he also visited factories such as those conducted by the Krupp industries, where concentration camp labour was exploited under degrading conditions. Despite this first-hand knowledge of these conditions in Mauthausen and places where these forced labourers were at work in factories, he continued to direct the use of this type of labour in factories under his own jurisdiction.

THE PRESIDENT: How do you intend to prove it as to these concentration camps?

MR. DODD: I was going to refer the Tribunal to Page 9 of the interrogation of 18th October, 1945, and I refer to Page 11, Paragraph 5 of the German text and Page 9, beginning with Paragraph 9, of the English text:-

"Q. But, in general, the use of concentration camp labour was known to you and approved by you as a source of labour?

A. Yes.

Q. And you knew also, I take it, that among the inmates of the concentration camps there were both Germans and foreigners?

A. I did not think about it at that time.

Q. As a matter of fact, you visited the Austrian concentration camp personally, did you not?

A. I did not - well, I was in Mauthausen once, but at that time I was not told just to what categories the inmates of the concentration camps belonged.

Q. But in general everybody knew, did they not, that foreigners who were taken away by the Gestapo or arrested by the Gestapo, as well as Germans, found their way into the concentration camps?

A. Of course, yes. I did not mean to imply anything like that."

And on Page 15 of this same interrogation, beginning with the 13th paragraph of the English text, and Page 20 in the German text, we find these questions:

"Q. Did you ever discuss, by the way, the requirements of Krupp for foreign labour?

A. It is certain that it was reported to me what shortage Krupp had in foreign workers.

Q. Did you ever discuss it with any of the members of the Krupp firm?

A. I cannot say that exactly, but during the time of my activities I visited the Krupp factory more than once and it is certain that this was discussed, that is, the lack of manpower."

Before closing, I should like to take two minutes of the time of the Tribunal to refer to what we consider to be some of the applicable laws of the case for the assistance of the Tribunal in considering these documents which we have offered.

We refer, of course, first of all, to Sections 6 (b) and 6 (c) of the Charter of this Tribunal. We also say that the acts of the conspirators constituted a flagrant violation of Articles 46 and 52 of the Regulations annexed to the Hague Convention No. IV of 1907.

Article 46 seeks to safeguard the family honour, the rights and the lives of persons in areas under belligerent occupation.

Article 52 provides in part that: "Requisitions in kind and services shall not be demanded from municipalities or inhabitants except for the needs of the army of occupation. They shall be in proportion to the resources of the country".

We say that these conspirators violated this Article because the labour which they conscripted was not used to satisfy the needs of the army of occupation, but, on the contrary, was forcibly removed from the occupied areas and exploited in the interest of the German war effort.

Finally, we say that these conspirators, and particularly the defendants Sauckel and Speer, by virtue of their planning, of their execution, and of their approval of this programme which we have been describing yesterday and today, the enslavement and the misuse of the forced labour of prisoners of war - that for this they bear a special responsibility for their Crimes Against Humanity and their War Crimes.

THE PRESIDENT: Are you finishing, Mr. Dodd?

MR. DODD: Yes, I have finished.

THE PRESIDENT: I should like to ask you why you have not read Document 3057-PS, which is Sauckel's statement.

MR. DODD: Yes. We had intended to offer that document. Counsel for the defendant Sauckel informed me a day or two ago that his client maintained that he had been coerced into making the statement. Because we had not ample time to ascertain the facts of the matter, we preferred to withhold it, rather than to offer it to the Tribunal under any question of doubt.

THE PRESIDENT: He objects to it, and therefore you have not put it in?

MR. DODD: No, we did not offer it while there was any question about it.

THE PRESIDENT: Very well.

MR. DODD: Might I suggest to the Tribunal that a recess be taken at this time? I am sorry to have to say that I am due to be before the Tribunal for some little time - that is, I am sorry for the Tribunal - with the matters on the concentration camps.

THE PRESIDENT: You mean a recess now?

MR. DODD: If your Honour pleases.

THE PRESIDENT: Certainly, yes; ten minutes.

[A recess was taken.]

MR. DODD: May it please the Tribunal, we propose to offer additional evidence at this time concerning the use of Nazi concentration camps against the people of Germany and allied nationals. We propose to examine the purposes and the role of the concentration camp in the larger Nazi scheme of things. We propose to show that the concentration camp was one of the fundamental institutions of the Nazi regime, that it was a pillar of the system of terror by which the Nazis consolidated their power over Germany and imposed their ideology upon the German people, that it was really a primary weapon in the battle against the Jews, against the Christian Church, against Labour, against those who wanted peace, against opposition or non-conformity of any kind. We say it involved the systematic use of terror to achieve the cohesion within Germany which was necessary for the execution of the conspirators' plans for aggression.

We propose to show that a concentration camp was one of the principal instruments used by the conspirators for the commission on an enormous scale of Crimes Against Humanity and War Crimes; that it was the final link in a chain of terror and repression which involved the S.S. and the Gestapo, and which resulted in the apprehension of victims and their confinement, without trial, often without charges, generally with no indication of the length of their detention.

My colleagues will present full evidence concerning the criminal role of the S.S. and Gestapo in this phase of Nazi terrorism, the concentration camp, but at this point, I wish simply to point out that the S.S., through its espionage system, tracked down the victims, that the criminal police and the Gestapo seized them and brought them to the camps, and that the concentration camps were administered by the S.S.

This Tribunal, we feel, is already aware of the sickening evidence of the brutality of the concentration camp from the showing of the moving picture. More than that, individual prosecutions are going on, going forward before other courts, which will record these outrages in detail. Therefore, we do not propose to present a catalogue of individual brutalities, but, rather, to submit evidence showing the fundamental purposes for which the camps were used, the techniques of terror which were employed, the large number of victims and the death and the anguish which they caused.

The evidence relating to concentration camps has been assembled in a document book bearing the letter "S". I might say that the documents in this book have been arranged in the order of presentation, rather than, as we have been doing, numerically. In this book we have put them in as they occur in the presentation. One document in this book, 2309- PS, is cited several times, so we have marked it with a tab with a view to facilitating reference back to it. It will be referred to more than once.

The Nazis realised early that, without the most drastic repression of actual and potential opposition, they could not consolidate their power over the German people. We have seen that, immediately after Hitler became Chancellor, the conspirators promptly destroyed civil liberty by issuing the Presidential Emergency Decree of 28th February, 1933. It is Document 1390-PS, and it sets forth that decree, which has already been introduced in evidence before the Tribunal and is included in Exhibit USA B. It was this decree which was the basis for the so-called "Schutshaft ", that is, protective custody - the terrible power to imprison people without judicial proceedings. This is made clear by Document 2499-PS, which is a typical order for protective custody. We offer it for that purpose, as a typical order for protective custody which has come into the possession of the prosecution. It is Exhibit USA 232. I should like to quote from the body of that order:-

"Order of Protective Custody.

Based on Article 1 of the Decree of the Reich President for the Protection of People and State of 28th February, 1933 (Reichsgesetzblatt, Page 83), you are taken into protective custody in the interest of public security and order.

Reason: Suspicion of activities inimical toward the State."

Defendant Goering in a book entitled Aufbau einer Nation, published in 1934, sought to give the impression, it appears, that the camps were originally directed at those whom the Nazis considered Communists and Social Democrats. We refer to Document 2324-PS, Exhibit USA 233. This document is an excerpt from Page 89 of the German book. We refer to the third and fourth paragraphs of the document, which I read as follows:

"We had to deal ruthlessly with these enemies of the State. It must not be forgotten that at the moment of our seizure of power over 6,000,000 people officially voted for Communism and about 8,000,000 for Marxism in the Reichstag elections in March.

Thus the Concentration Camps were created, to which we had to send first, thousands of functionaries of the Communist and Social Democratic parties."

In practical operations, the power to order confinement in these camps was almost without limit. The defendant Frick, in an order which he issued on 25th January, 1938, as Minister of the Interior, made this quite clear. An extract from this order is set forth in Document 1723-PS, to which we make reference. It is Exhibit USA 206. I wish to read Article 1, beginning at the bottom of Page 5 of the English translation of this order:-

"Protective custody can be decreed as a coercive measure of the Secret State Police against persons who endanger the security of the people and the State through their attitude, in order to counter all aspirations of enemies of the people and State."

I wish also to read into the record the first two paragraphs of that order, which are found at the top of Page 1 of the English translation:-

"In a summary of all the previously issued decrees on the co-operation between the Party and the Gestapo I refer to the following and ordain:-

1. To the Gestapo has been entrusted the mission by the Fuehrer to watch over and to eliminate all enemies of the Party and the National Socialist State, as well as all disintegrating forces of all kinds directed against both. The successful solution of this mission forms one of the most essential prerequisites for the unhampered and frictionless work of the Party. The Gestapo, in their extremely difficult task, are to be granted support and assistance in every possible way by the N.S.D.A.P."

The conspirators then were directing their apparatus of terror against the "enemies of the State", against "disintegrating forces", against those people who endangered the State "with their attitude". Whom did they consider as belonging to those broad categories? Well, first, there were the men in Germany who wanted peace. We refer to Document L-83, Exhibit USA 231.

THE PRESIDENT: What was the date of that document that you have been referring to, 1723-PS?

MR. DODD: 25th January, 1938. This document consists of an affidavit of Gerhart H. Segar, and I wish to read only from Page 1, Paragraph 2 of that affidavit:

"2. During the period after World War One, up to my commitment to the Leipzig Gaol and Oranienburg Concentration Camp in the spring of 1933, following the Nazi accession to power in January of that year, my business and political affiliations exposed me to the full impact of the Nazi theories and practice of violent regimentation and terroristic tactics. My conflict with the Nazis by virtue of my identification with the peace movement and as a duly elected member of the Reichstag representing a political faith (Social Democratic Party) hostile to

367

National Socialism, clearly demonstrated that, even in the period prior to 1933, the Nazis considered crimes and terrorism a necessary and desirable weapon in overcoming democratic opposition."

Passing to Page 5 of the same document, and the paragraph marked (e):-

"That the Nazis had already conceived the device of the Concentration Camp as a means of suppressing and regimenting opposition elements, was forcefully brought to my attention during the course of a conversation which I had with Dr. Wilhelm Frick in December, 1932, Frick at that time was Chairman of the Foreign Affairs Committee of the Reichstag, of which I was a member. When I gave an emphatic answer to Frick concerning the particular matter discussed, he replied, 'Do not worry, when we are in power we shall put all of you into Concentration Camps.' When the Nazis came into power, Frick was appointed Reichsminister of the Interior and promptly carried out his threat in collaboration with Goering, as Chief of the Prussian State Police, and Himmler."

This paragraph shows that, even before the Nazis had seized power in Germany, they had conceived the plan to repress any potential opposition by terror, and Frick's statement to Segar is completely consistent with an earlier statement which he made on the 18th October, 1929. We refer to Document 2513-PS, Exhibit USA 235, which has also been received in evidence and has been included in Exhibit USA B. We refer to the first page of the English translation, Page 48 of the German text. On Page 1 the quotation begins:-

"This fateful struggle will first be taken up with the ballot, but this cannot continue indefinitely, for history has taught us that in a battle blood must be shed and iron broken. The ballot is the beginning of the fateful struggle. We are determined to promulgate by force that which we preach. Just as Mussolini exterminated the Marxists in Italy, so must we also succeed in accomplishing the same through dictatorship and terror."

THE PRESIDENT: This is the defendant, is it?

MR. DODD: Yes, the defendant Frick.

There are many additional cases of the use of the concentration camp against the men who wanted peace. There was, for example, a group called the Bibelforschers, that is, Bible Research Workers, most of whom were known as Jehovah's Witnesses. They were pacifists, and so the conspirators provided not only for their prosecution in the regular courts but also for their confinement in the concentration camps after they had served the judicial sentences, and we refer to Document D-84, Exhibit USA 236.

This document is dated 5th August, 1937, and it is an order by the Secret State Police at Berlin, and I refer particularly to the first and last paragraphs of this order, as follows:-

"The Reichsminister of Justice had informed me that he does not share the opinion voiced by subordinate departments on various occasions, according to which the arrest of the Bibelforschers, after they have served a sentence, is supposed to jeopardise the authority of the Law Courts. He is fully aware of the necessity for measures by the State Police after the sentence has been served. He asks, however, not to bring the Bibelforschers into protective custody under circumstances detrimental to the respect of the Law Courts."

And then, the paragraph (2):-

"If information regarding the impending release of a Bibelforscher from arrest is received from the authorities carrying out the sentence, my decision regarding the ordering of measures by the State Police will be asked for in accordance with my circular decree dated 22nd April, 1937, so that transfer to a Concentration Camp can take place immediately after the sentence has been served. Should a transfer into concentration camp immediately after the serving of the sentence not be possible, Bibelforschers will be detained in police prisons."

The Labour Unions, of which I think it is safe to say the majority are traditionally opposed to wars of aggression, also felt the full force of Nazi terror. A member of the American staff, Major Wallis, has already submitted evidence before this Tribunal concerning the conspirators' campaign against the trade unions. But the concentration camp was an important weapon in this campaign, and the Tribunal will recall that in Document 2324-PS, to which I made reference this morning, the defendant Goering made it plain that members of the Social Democratic Party were to be confined in concentration camps. Now labour leaders were very largely members of that Party, and they soon learned the horrors of protective custody. We refer to Document 2330-PS, Exhibit USA 237, which has already been received as part of Exhibit USA G, which consists of an order that one Joseph Simon should be placed in protective custody. We refer to the middle of the first page of the English translation of that order, beginning with the material under the word "Reasons".

THE PRESIDENT: I think you should read the sentence before that the two lines before it. The words are: "The arrestee has no right to appeal against the decree of protective custody."

MR. DODD: "The arrestee has no right to appeal against the decree of protective custody." Then comes a title "Reasons":-

"Simon was for many years a member of the Socialist Party and temporarily a member of the Union Socialists Populaire. From 1907 to 1918 he was Lantag deputy of the Socialist Party; from 1908 to 1930 Social Democratic City Counsellor (Stadtrat) in Nuremberg. In view of the decisive role which Simon played in international socialism, and in regard to his connection with international Marxist leaders and central agencies, which he continued after the national recovery, he was placed under protective custody on the 3rd May, 1933, and was kept, until 25th January, 1934, in the Dachau Concentration Camp. Simon was strongly suspected, even after this date, of playing an active part in the illegal continuation of the Socialist Party. He took part in meetings which aimed at the illegal continuation of the Socialist Party and propagation of illegal Marxist printed matter in Germany. Through this radical attitude, which is hostile to the State, Simon directly endangered public security and order."

We do not wish to burden these proceedings with a multiplication of such instances, but I refer the Tribunal to documents which have already been offered in connection with the presentation of the evidence concerning the destruction of the trade unions. In particular, we wish to refer to Document 2334-PS and Document 2928-PS, Exhibits USA 238 and 239, both of which are included within Exhibit USA G.

Thousands of Jews, as the world so well knows, were, of course, confined in these concentration camps. The evidence on this point will be developed in a later presentation by another member of the prosecuting staff of the United States. But among the wealth of evidence available on this point showing the confinement of Germans only because they were Jews, we wish to offer a Document 3051-PS, Exhibit USA 240. This is a copy of a teletype from S.S. Gruppenfuehrer Heydrich, and it is dated 16th November, 1938. It was sent to all Headquarters of the State Police and all Districts and Sub-districts of the S.D. We refer to Paragraph 5 of this teletype. Paragraph 5 is found on Page 3 of the English translation. It begins at the bottom of Page 2 and runs over to Page 3. Quoting from Paragraph 5:

"As soon as the course of events of this night allows the use of the officials employed for this purpose, as many Jews, especially rich ones, as can be accommodated in the existing prisons are to be arrested in all districts. For the time being only healthy men, not too old, are to be arrested. Upon their arrest, the appropriate concentration camps should be contacted immediately, in order to confine them in these camps as soon as possible.

Special care should be taken that the Jews arrested in accordance with these instructions are not mistreated."

Himmler in 1943 indicated that use of the concentration camp against the Jews had been motivated not simply by Nazi racialism. He indicated that this policy had been motivated by a fear that the Jews might have been an obstacle to aggression. There is no necessity to consider whether this fear was justified. The important consideration is that the fear existed, and with reference to it we refer to Document 1919-PS, Exhibit USA 170. The document is a speech delivered by Himmler at the meeting of the S.S. Major Generals at Posen on 4th October, 1943, in the course of which he sought to justify the Nazi anti-Jewish policy. We refer to a portion of this document of this speech which is found on Page 4, Paragraph 3, of the English translation, starting with the words "I mean the clearing out of the Jews".

"I mean the clearing out of the Jews, the extermination of the Jewish race. It is one of those things it is easy to talk about. 'The Jewish race is being exterminated', says one party member, 'that is quite clear, it is in our programme, elimination of the Jews, and we are doing it, exterminating them'. And then there come 80,000,000 worthy Germans, and each one has his 'decent Jew'. Of course, the others are vermin, but this one is 'an A-1 Jew'. Not one of all those who talk this way has witnessed it, not one of them has been through it. Most of you must know what it means when 100 corpses are lying side by side, or 500 or 1,000. To have stuck it out and at the same time - apart from exceptions caused by human weakness - to have remained decent fellows, that is what has made us hard. This is a page of glory in our history which has never been written and is never to be written, for we know how difficult we should have made it for ourselves, if - with bombing raids, the burden and privations of war - we still had Jews today in every town as secret saboteurs, agitators and trouble-mongers."

It is clear, we say, from the foregoing that prior to the launching of the Nazi aggression, the concentration camp had been one of the principal weapons by which the conspirators achieved the social cohesion which was needed for the execution of their plans for aggression. After they launched this aggression and their armies swept over Europe, they brought the concentration camp to occupied countries, and they also brought the citizens of the occupied countries to Germany and subjected them to the whole apparatus of Nazi brutality.

Document R-91 is Exhibit USA 241. This document consists of a communication dated 16th December, 1942, sent by Muller to Himmler, for the Chief of the Security Police and S.D., and deals with the seizure of Polish Jews for deportation to concentration camps in Germany. I am beginning with the first paragraph. It says, quoting directly:-

"In connection with the increase of the transfer of labour to the concentration camps, ordered to be completed by 30th January, 1943, the following procedure may be applied in the Jewish section:

1. Total number: 45,000 Jews.

2. Start of transportation: 11th January, 1943. End of transportation: 31st January, 1943. The Reich railroads are unable to provide special trains for the evacuation during the period from 15th December, 1942, to 10th January, 1943, because of the increased traffic of Armed Forces leave trains.

3. Composition: The 45,000 Jews are to consist Of 30,000 Jews from the district of Byalystock. 20,000 Jews from the Ghetto Theresienstadt, 5,000 of whom are Jews fit for work who heretofore had been used for smaller jobs required for the ghetto, and 5,000 Jews who are generally incapable of working, also Jews over 60 years old."

And passing the next sentence:-

"As heretofore only such Jews would be taken for the evacuation who have no particular connections and who are not in possession of any high, decorations. 3,000 Jews from the occupied Dutch territories, 2,000 Jews from Berlin - 45,000. The figure Of 45,000 includes the invalid (old Jews and children). By use of a practical standard the screening of the arriving Jews in Auschwitz should yield at least 10,000 to 15,000 people fit for work."

The Jews of Hungary suffered the same tragic fate. Between 19th March, 1944, and the 1st August, 1944, more than 400,000 Hungarian Jews were rounded up. Many of these were put in wagons and sent to extermination camps, and we refer to Document 2605-PS, Exhibit USA 242. This document is an affidavit made in London by Dr. Rudolph Kastner, a former official of the Hungarian Zionist Organisation. We refer to Page 3 of the document, the third full paragraph:-

"In March, 1944," - quoting - "together with the German Military Occupation arrived in Budapest a 'Special Section Commando' of the German Secret Police, with the sole object of liquidating the Hungarian Jews. It was headed by Adolf Aichmann, S.S. Obersturmbannfuehrer, Chief of Section IV. B of the Reich Security Head Office. His immediate collaborators were: S.S. Obersturmbannfuehrer Hermann Krumcy, Hauptsturmfuehrer Wisliczeny, Hunsche, Novak, Dr. Seidl, and later Danegger, Wrtok. They arrested and later deported to Mauthausen all the leaders of

371

Jewish political and business life, and journalists, together with the Hungarian democratic and anti-Fascist politicians. Taking advantage of the 'interregnum' following upon the German occupation and lasting four days, they placed their Quislings in the Ministry of the Interior."

On Page 7 of that same document, the eighth paragraph, beginning with the words "Commanders of the death camps", and quoting:-

"Commanders of the death camps gassed only on direct or indirect instructions of Aichmann [sic]. The particular officer of IV. B who directed the deportations from some particular country had the authority to indicate whether the train should go to a death camp or not, and what should happen to the passengers. The instructions were usually carried by the S.S. - N.C.O. escorting the train. The letter 'A' or "M" - capital letters "A" or "M" - "on the escorting instruction documents indicated Auschwitz or Majdanck; it means that the passengers were to be gassed."

And passing over the next sentence, we come to these words:-

"Regarding Hungarian Jews the following general ruling was laid down in Auschwitz: children up to the age of 12 or 14, older people over 50, as well as the sick, or people with criminal records, who were transported in specially marked wagons, were taken immediately on their arrival to the gas chambers.

The others passed before an S.S. doctor who, on sight, indicated who was fit for work and who was not. Those unfit were sent to the gas chambers, while the others were distributed in various labour camps."

In the so-called "Eastern territories" these victims were apprehended for extermination -

THE PRESIDENT: Mr. Dodd, do not you want Page 5 for the numbers which you have stated-up to 27th June, 1944? You have not yet given us any authority for the numbers that you have stated.

MR. DODD: Oh, yes. On Page 5 of that same Document, 2605-PS, quoting: "Up to 27th June, 1944, 475,000 Jews were deported."

In the so-called "Eastern territories" these victims were apprehended for extermination in concentration camps without any charges having been made against them. In the Eastern occupied territories charges seemed to have been made against some of the victims. Some of the charges which the Nazi conspirators considered sufficient basis for confinement in the concentration camps are shown by reference to Document L-215, which becomes Exhibit USA 243. This document is the summary of the file, the dossier, of 25 persons arrested in Luxembourg for commitment to various concentration camps and sets forth the charges made against each person. Beginning with the paragraph after the name "Henricy", at the bottom of the first page, and quoting:-

"The name: Henricy. Charge: For associating with members of illegal resistance movements and making money for them, violating legal foreign exchange rates, for harming the interests of the Reich and being expected in the future to disobey official administrative regulations and act as an enemy of the Reich. Place of confinement: Natzweiler."

Next comes the name of "Krier" and the charge:-

"For being responsible for advanced sabotage of labour and causing fear because of his political and criminal past. Freedom would only further his anti-social urge. Place of confinement: Buchenwald."

Passing to the middle of Page 2, after the name "Monti":-

"Charge: For being strongly suspected of aiding desertion. Place of confinement: Sachsenhausen."

Next, after the name "Junker":-

"Charge: Because as a relative of a deserter he is expected to endanger the interests of the German Reich if allowed to go free. Place of confinement: Sachsenhausen."

"Jaeger" is the next name and the charge against Jaeger, quoting:-

"Because as a relative of a deserter he is expected to take advantage of every occasion to harm the German Reich. Place of confinement: Sachsenhausen."

And down to the name "Ludwig" and the charge against Ludwig:-

"For being strongly suspected of aiding desertion. Place of confinement: Dachau."

Not only civilians of the occupied countries but also prisoners of war were subjected to the horrors and the brutality of the concentration camps; and we refer to Document 1165-PS, Exhibit USA 244. This document is a memorandum to all officers of the State Police signed by Muller, the Chief of the Gestapo, dated 9th November, 1941. The memorandum has the revealing title of, and I quote, "Transportation of Russian Prisoners of War, Destined for Execution, into the Concentration Camps."

I wish to quote also from the body of this memorandum which is found on Page 2 of the English translation and I quote directly:-

"The commandants of the concentration camps are complaining that 5 to 10 per cent. of the Soviet Russians destined for execution are arriving in the camps dead or half dead. Therefore the impression has arisen that the Stalags are getting rid of such prisoners in this way.

It was particularly noted that, when marching, for example, from the railroad station to the camp, a rather large number of prisoners of war collapsed on the way from exhaustion, either dead or half dead, and had to be picked up by a truck following the convoy.

It cannot be prevented that the German people take notice of these occurrences.

Even if the transportation to the camps is generally taken care of by the Wehrmacht, the population will attribute this situation to the S.S.

In order to prevent, if possible, similar occurrences in the future, I therefore order that, effective from today on, Soviet Russians, declared definitely suspect and obviously marked for death (for example with typhus) and therefore not able to withstand the exertions of even a short march on foot, shall in the future, as a matter of basic principle, be excluded from the transport into the concentration camps for execution."

More evidence of the confinement of Russian prisoners of war in concentration camps is found in an official report of the investigation of the Flossenburg concentration camp by the Headquarters of the United States Third Army, the Judge Advocate Section, and particularly the War Crimes Branch, under the date of 21st June, 1945. It is our Document 2309- PS, and is

Exhibit USA 245. At the bottom of Page 2 of the English text the last two sentences of that last paragraph say, and I quote:-

"In 1941 an additional stockade was added at the Flossenburg Camp to hold 2,000 Russian prisoners. Of these 2,000 prisoners only 102 survived."

Soviet prisoners of war found their allies in the concentration camps too and at Page 4 of this same Document 2309-PS it will show, particularly Paragraph 5, on Page 4, and I quote it:-

"The victims of Flossenburg included among them Russian civilians and prisoners of war, German nationals, Italians, Belgians, Poles, Czechs, Hungarians, British and American prisoners of war. No practical means was available to complete a list of victims of this camp; however, since the foundation of the Camp in 1938 until the day of liberation it is estimated that more than 29,000 inmates died."

Escaped prisoners of war were sent to concentration camps by the conspirators, and these camps were specially set up as extermination centres ; and we refer to Document 1650-PS, being Exhibit USA 246. This document is a communication from the Secret State Police of Cologne and it is dated the 4th March, 1944. At the very top of the English text it says "To be transmitted in secret - to be handled as a secret Government matter." In the third paragraph, quoting:-

"Concerns: Measures to be taken against captured escaped prisoners of war who are officers or non-working non- commissioned officers, except British and American prisoners of war. The Supreme Command of the Army has ordered as follows:

1. Every captured escaped prisoner of war who is an officer or a non-working non-commissioned officer, except British and American prisoners of war, is to be turned over to the Chief of the Security Police and of the Security Service under the classification 'Step III', regardless of whether the escape occurred during a transport, whether it was a mass escape or an individual one.

2. Since the transfer of the prisoners of war to the Security Police and Security Service must not become officially known to the outside under any circumstances, other prisoners of war must by no means be informed of the capture. The captured prisoners are to be reported to the Army Information Bureau as 'escaped and not captured'. Their mail is to be handled accordingly. Inquiries of representatives of the Protective Power of the International Red Cross and of other aid societies will be given the same answer."

The same communication carried a copy of an order of S.S. General Muller, acting for the Chief of the Security Police and S.D., directing the Gestapo to transport escaped prisoners directly to Mauthausen; and I quote the first two paragraphs of Muller's order, which begins on the bottom of Page 1 and runs over to Page 2 of the English text. Quoting:-

"The State Police Directorates will accept the captured escaped officer prisoners of war from the prisoner of war camp commandants and will transport them to the concentration camp Mauthausen following the procedure previously used, unless the circumstances render a special transport imperative. The prisoners of war are to be put in irons on the transport - not on the station if it is subject to view by the public. The camp commandant at Mauthausen is to be notified that the transfer occurs within the scope of the action 'Kugel'. The State Police Directorates will submit semi-yearly reports on these transfers giving merely the figures, the first report being due on 5th July, 1944."

Passing the next three sentences, we come to this line:-

"For the sake of secrecy the Supreme Command of the Armed Forces has been requested to inform the prisoner of war camps to turn the captured prisoners over to the local State Police Office and not to send them directly to Mauthausen."

It is no coincidence that the literal translation for the German word 'Kugel' is the English word 'bullet', since Mauthausen, where the escaped prisoners were sent, was an extermination centre.

Nazi conquest was marked by the establishment of concentration camps over all Europe. In this connection we refer to Document R-129. It is a report on the location of concentration camps, signed by Pohl, who was an S.S. General in charge of concentration camp labour policies. Document R- 129 is Exhibit USA 217.

I wish to refer particularly to Section 1, Paragraphs 1 and 2 of this document, which are found on Page 1 of the English translation. It is addressed to the Reichsfuehrer S.S. and bears the stamp "Secret":-

"Reichsfuehrer: Today I report about the present situation of the concentration camps and about measures I have taken in order to carry out your order of the 3rd March, 1942:

1. At the outbreak of war there existed the following concentration camps:

(a) Dachau-1939, 4,000 prisoners; today, 8,000.

(b) Sachsenhausen-1939, 6,500 prisoners; today, 10,000.

(c) Buchenwald-1939, 5,300 prisoners; today, 9,000.

(d) Mauthausen-1939, 1,500 prisoners; today, 5,500.

(e) Flossenburg-1939, 1,600 prisoners; today, 4,700.

(f) Ravensbruek-1939, 2,500 prisoners; today, 7,500."

And then it goes on to say in Paragraph 2, quoting:

"In the years 1940 to 1942 nine further camps were erected:

(a) Auschwitz.

(b) Neuengamme.

(c) Guson.

(d) Natzweiter.

(e) Gross-Rosen.

(f) Lublin.

(g) Niederhagen.

(h) Stutthof.

(i) Arbeitsdorf."

In addition to the camps in the occupied territory mentioned in this Document R-129, from which I have just read these names and figures, there were many, many others. I refer to the official report by the United States Third Army Headquarters, to which we have already made reference,

Document 2309-PS, on Page 2 in the English text, Section IV, Paragraph 4, quoting:_

"Concentration Camp Flossenburg was founded in 1938 as a camp for political prisoners. Construction was commenced on the camp in 1938 and it was not until April, 1940, that the first transport of prisoners was received. From this time on prisoners began to flow steadily into the camp. (Exhibit B-1.) Flossenburg was the mother camp and under its direct control and jurisdiction were 47 satellite camps or outer-commandos for male prisoners and 27 camps for female workers. To these outer- commandos were supplied the necessary prisoners for the various work projects undertaken.

Of all these outer-commandos Hersbruck and Leitmeritz (in Czechoslovakia), Oberstaubling, Mulsen and Sall, located on the Danube, were considered to be the worst."

I do not wish to take the time of the Tribunal to discuss each of the Nazi concentration camps which dotted the map of Europe. We feel that the widespread use of these camps is commonly known and notorious. We do, however, wish to invite the Tribunal's attention to a chart which we have had prepared. The solid black line marks the boundary of Germany after the "Anschluss", and we invite the Tribunal's attention to the fact that the majority of the camps shown on the chart are located within the territorial limits of Germany itself. They are the red spots, of course, on the map. In the centre of Germany there is the Buchenwald camp located near the city of Weimar, and at the extreme bottom of the chart there is Dachau, several miles outside Munich. At the top of the chart are Neuengamme and Bergen-Belsen, located near Hamburg. To the left is the Niederhagen camp in the Ruhr Valley. In the upper right there are a number of camps near Berlin, one named Sachsenhausen (formerly Oranienburg, which was one of the first camps established after the Nazis came into power). Near to that is the camp of Ravensbruck, which was used exclusively for women. Some of the most notorious camps were indeed located outside Germany. Mauthausen was in Austria. In Poland was the infamous Auschwitz; and to the left of the chart is a camp called Hertogenbosch which was located in Holland, as the chart shows; and below it is Natzweiler, located in France.

The camps were established in networks, and it may be observed that surrounding each of the major camps-the larger red dots - is a group of satellite camps, and the names of the principal camps, the most notorious camps, at least, are above the map and below it on the chart; and those names, for most people, symbolise the Nazi system of concentration camps as they have become known to the world since May or a little later in 1945.

I should like to direct your attention briefly to the treatment which was meted out in these camps. The motion picture to which I have made reference a short time ago and which was shown to the members of this High Tribunal, has disclosed the terrible and savage treatment which was inflicted upon these Allied nationals, prisoners of war and other victims of Nazi terror. Because the moving picture has so well shown the situation, as of the time of its taking at least, I shall confine myself to a very brief discussion of the subject.

The conditions which existed inside these camps were, of course, we say, directly related to the objectives which these Nazi conspirators sought to achieve outside the camps through their employment of terror.

It is truly remarkable, it seems to us, how easily the words "concentration camps" rolled off the lips of these men. How simple all problems became when they could turn to the terror institution of these camps. I refer to Document R-124, which is already before the Tribunal as Exhibit USA 179. It is again that document covering the minutes of the Central Planning Committee on which the defendant Speer sat, and where the high strategy of the high Nazi armament production was formulated. I do not intend to read from the document again, because I read from it this morning, to illustrate another point, but the Tribunal will recall that it was at this meeting that the defendant Speer and others were discussing the so-called slackers, and the conversation had to do with having drastic steps taken against these workers, who were not putting out sufficient work to please their masters. Speer suggested that "there is nothing to be said against the S.S. and Police taking steps and putting those known as slackers into concentration camps," and he used the words "concentration camps ". And he said "Let it happen several times and the news will soon get around."

Words spoken in this fashion, we say, sealed the fate of many victims. As for getting the news around, as suggested by the defendant Speer, this was not left to chance, as we shall presently show.

The deterrent effect of the concentration camps upon the public was a carefully planned thing. To heighten the atmosphere of terror, these camps were shrouded in secrecy. What went on in the barbed wire enclosures was a matter of fearful conjecture in Germany and countries under Nazi control; and this was the policy from the very beginning, when the Nazis first came into power and set up this system of concentration camps. We refer now to Document 778-PS, Exhibit USA 247. This document is an order issued on the 1st October, 1933, by the camp commander of Dachau. The document prescribed a programme of floggings, solitary confinement and executions for the inmates for infractions of the rules.

Among the rules were those prescribing a rigid censorship concerning conditions within the camp ; and I refer to the first page of the English text, paragraph numbered Article 11, and quoting:-

"By virtue of the law on revolutionaries, the following offenders, considered as agitators, will be hanged: anyone who, for the purpose of agitating, does the following in the camp, at work, in the quarters, in the kitchens and workshops, toilets and places of rest: talks politics, holds inciting speeches and meetings, forms cliques, loiters around with others; who, for the purpose of supplying the propaganda of the opposition with atrocity stories, collects true or false information about the concentration camp and its institution, receives such information, buries it, talks about it to others, smuggles it out of the camp into the hands of foreign visitors or others by means of clandestine or other methods, passes it on in writing or orally to released prisoners or prisoners who are placed above them, conceals it in clothing or other articles, throws stones and other objects over the camp wall containing such information, or produces secret documents; who, for the purpose of agitating, climbs on barracks roofs and trees, seeks contact with the outside by giving light or other signals, or induces others to escape or commit a crime, gives them advice to that effect or supports such undertakings in any way whatsoever."

The censorship in the camps themselves was complemented by an officially inspired rumour campaign outside the camps. Concentration camps were spoken of in whispers, and the whispers were spread by agents of the Secret Police. When the defendant Speer said that if the threat of the concentration camp were used, the news would get around soon enough, he knew whereof he spoke.

We refer to Document 153I-PS. With reference to this document, I wish to submit a word of explanation. The original German text, the original German document, the captured document was here in the document room and was translated into English as our translation shows. Yesterday we were advised that it had either been lost or misplaced, the original German text, and unfortunately no photostatic copy was available here in Nuremberg. A certified copy is, however, being sent to the office here from Frankfurt and it is on its way today, and I ask the Tribunal's permission to offer the English translation of the German original, which is certified to be accurate by the translator, into evidence, subject to a motion to strike it from the record if the certified copy of the original German document does not arrive.

I now refer to the Document 1431-PS. It is Exhibit USA 248. This document is marked "Top Secret" and it is addressed to all State Police District Offices and to the Gestapo Office and for the information of the Inspectors of the Security Police and the S.D. It is an order relating to concentration camps, issued by the head of the Gestapo, and I read from the English text, beginning with the second paragraph, and quoting directly:-

"In order to achieve a further deterrent effect, the following must, in the future, be observed in each individual case.

3. The length of the period of custody must in no case be made known, even if the Reichsfuehrer S.S. and Chief of the German Police or the Chief of the Security Police and the S.D. has already fixed it.

The term of commitment to a concentration camp is to be openly announced as 'until further notice'.

In most serious cases there is no objection to the increasing of the deterrent effect by the spreading of cleverly carried out rumour propaganda, more or less to the effect that, according to hearsay, in view of the seriousness of his case, the arrested man will not be released for two or three years.

4. In certain cases the Reichsfuehrer S.S. and Chief of the German Police will order flogging in addition to detention in a concentration camp. Orders of this kind will, in the future, also be transmitted to the State Police District Office concerned. In this case, too, there is no objection to spreading the rumour of this increased punishment as laid down in Section 3, Paragraph 3, in so far as this appears suitable, to add to the deterrent effect.

5. Naturally, particularly suitable and reliable people are to be chosen for the spreading of such news."

THE PRESIDENT: Mr. Dodd, the Tribunal think that they will take judicial notice of that United States Document, 2309- PS, and, for the convenience of the defence counsel, the Tribunal having sat until one, will not sit again until two- fifteen.

MR. DODD: Very well, your Honour.

MR. DODD: May it please the Tribunal, the deterrent effect of the concentration camps was based on the promise of brutal treatment. Once in the custody of the S.S. guards, the victim was beaten, tortured, starved, and often murdered through the so-called "extermination through work" programme which I described the other day, or through the mass execution gas chambers and furnaces of the camps, which were shown several days ago on the moving picture screen in this court room.

The reports of official government investigations furnish additional evidence of the conditions within the concentration camps.

Document 2309-PS, which has already been referred to and of which the Tribunal has taken judicial notice, I now refer to again, particularly to the second page of the English text, beginning with the second sentence of the second paragraph:-

"The work at these camps mainly consisted of underground labour, the purpose being the construction of large underground factories, storage rooms, etc. This labour was performed completely underground and as a result of the brutal treatment, working and living conditions, a daily average of 100 prisoners died. To the one camp Oberstaubling 7,000 prisoners were transported in February, 1945, and on the 15th April, 1945, only 405 of these men were living. During the 12 months preceding the liberation, Flossenburg and the branch camps under its control accounted for the death of 14,739 male inmates and 1,300 women. These figures represent the number of deaths as obtained from the available records in the camp. However, they are in no way complete, as many secret mass executions and deaths took place. In 1941 an additional stockade was added to the Flossenburg Camp to hold 2,000 Russian prisoners. From these 2,000 prisoners only 102 survive.

Flossenburg Concentration Camp can best be described as a factory dealing in death. Although this camp had in view the primary object of putting to work the mass slave labour, another of its primary objectives was the elimination of human lives by the methods employed in handling the prisoners.

Hunger and starvation rations, sadism, herding, inadequate clothing, medical neglect, disease, beatings, hangings, freezing, forced hand hanging, forced suicides, shooting, all played a major role in obtaining their objective. Prisoners were murdered at random, spite killings against Jews were common. Injections of poison and shooting in the neck were everyday occurrences. Epidemics of typhus and spotted fever were permitted to run rampant as a means of eliminating prisoners. Life in this camp counted for nothing. Killing became a common thing, so common that a quick death was welcomed by the unfortunate ones."

Passing to the next to the last sentence of this same paragraph, quoting directly -

THE PRESIDENT: What are those exhibits that are referred to?

MR. DODD: They are in evidence with the affidavit. They are attached to it.

THE PRESIDENT: They are not, I suppose, mimeographed in our copy?

MR. DODD: No, we have not had an opportunity to mimeograph each one of them.

THE PRESIDENT: Are they documents or photographs or what?

MR. DODD: They are principally documents. There are some few plans and photographs, and so on.

THE PRESIDENT: Are they affidavits or what?

MR. DODD: Some of them are in the form of affidavits taken at the time of the liberation of the camp from prisoners who were there, and others are pictures of writings that were found there and of the plans and so on - that sort of thing.

THE PRESIDENT: Yes. Well the Tribunal will take judicial notice of those exhibits as well.

MR. DODD: Very well, your Honour.

Reading from the last sentence of this same paragraph on the same page and quoting:-

> "On Christmas, 1944, a number of prisoners were hanged at one time. The other prisoners were forced to view this hanging. By the side of the gallows was a decorated Christmas tree, and, as expressed by one prisoner, 'It was a terrible sight, that combination of prisoners hanging in the air and the glistening Christmas tree'."

In March or April, 13 American or British parachutists were hanged. They had been delivered to this camp some time before and had been captured while trying to blow up bridges.

We will not burden the Tribunal with a recital of all of these reports. We wish, however, to make reference to the Concentration Camp Mauthausen, one of the most notorious extermination centres, and I refer particularly to Document 2176-PS, which I have already placed in evidence as Exhibit USA 249. This is also an official report of the office of the Judge Advocate General of the United States Third Army, dated 17th June, 1945. I wish to refer to the conclusions on Page 3 of the English text, at paragraph numbered Roman V, beginning with the second sentence as follows:-

> "V. Conclusions:
>
> There is no doubt that Mauthausen was the basis for long- term planning. It was constructed as a gigantic stone fortress on top of a mountain flanked by small barracks. Mauthausen, in addition to its permanency of construction, had facilities for a large garrison of officers and men, and had large dining rooms and toilet facilities for the staff. It was conducted with the sole purpose in mind of exterminating any so-called prisoner who entered within its walls. The so-called branches of Mauthausen were under direct command of the S.S. officials located there. All records, orders, and administrative facilities were handled for these branches through Mauthausen. The other camps, including Gusen and Ebensee, its two most notorious and largest branches, were not exclusively used for extermination but prisoners were used as tools in construction and production until they were beaten or starved into uselessness, whereupon they were customarily sent to Mauthausen for final disposal."

Both in the showing of the moving picture and from these careful reports, which were made by the Third Army of the United States on their arrival at those centres, we say it is clear that the conditions in those concentration camps over Germany, and in a few instances outside the actual borders of the Old Reich, followed the same general pattern. The widespread incidents of these conditions make it clear that they were not the result of sporadic excesses on the part of individual jailers, but were the result of policies deliberately imposed from above. The crimes committed in these camps were on so vast a scale that individual atrocities pale into insignificance.

We have had turned over to us two exhibits which we are prepared to show to this Tribunal only because they illustrate the depths to which the administration of these camps had sunk, at least shortly before the time that they were liberated by the Allied Army. The Tribunal will recall that in the exhibit of the moving picture, with respect to one of the camps, there was a showing of sections of human skin taken from human bodies in the Buchenwald Concentration Camp and preserved as ornaments. They were selected, these particular hapless victims, because of the tattooing which appeared on the skin. This exhibit, which we have here, is USA 252. Attached to the exhibit is an extract of an official U.S. Army report describing the circumstances under which this exhibit was obtained, and that extract is set forth in Document 3420-PS, which I refer to in part. It is entitled:-

"Mobile Field Interrogation Unit No. 2.

P.W. Intelligence Bulletin.

13. Concentration Camp, Buchenwald.

Preamble. The author of this account is P.W. Andreas Pfaffenberger, 1 Coy, 9 Landesschuetzen Bn., 43 years old and of limited education. He is a butcher by trade. The substantial agreement of the details of his story with those found in P.W.I.S. (H) /LF/736 establishes the validity of his testimony. This P.W. has not been questioned on statements which, in the light of what is known, are apparently erroneous in certain details, nor has any effort been made to alter the subjective character of the P.W.'s account, which he wrote without being told anything of the intelligence already known. The results of interrogation on personalities at Buchenwald have already been published (P.W.I.B. No. 2/12, Item 31).

In 1939 all prisoners with tattooing on them were ordered to report to the dispensary."

THE PRESIDENT: Is this what Pfaffenberger said?

MR. DODD: Yes, sir.

"No one knew what the purpose was, but after the tattooed prisoners had been examined the ones with the best and most artistic specimens were kept in the dispensary and then killed by injections administered by Karl Beigs, a criminal prisoner. The corpses were then turned over to the pathological department where the desired pieces of tattooed skin were detached from the bodies and treated. The finished products were turned over to S.S. Standartenfuehrer Koch's wife, who had them fashioned into lamp shades and other ornamental household articles. I myself saw such tattooed skins with various designs and legends on them, such as 'Haensel and Gretel', which one prisoner had on his knee, and ships from prisoners' chests. This work was done by a prisoner named Wernerbach."

I also refer to Document 3421-PS, which bears Exhibit USA 253.

"I, George C. Demas, Lieutenant, U.S.N.R., associated with the United States Chief of Counsel for the Prosecution of Axis Criminality, hereby certify that the attached exhibit, consisting of parchment, was delivered by the War Crimes Section, Judge Advocate General, U.S. Army, to me in my above capacity, in the usual course of business, as an exhibit found in Buchenwald Camp and captured by military forces under the command of the Supreme Commander, Allied Expeditionary Forces."

And the last paragraph of Document 3423-PS, Exhibit USA 252, is a conclusion reached in a United States Army report, and I quote it:-

"Based on the findings in Paragraph 2, all three specimens are tattooed human skin."

This document is also attached to this exhibit on the board. We do not wish to dwell on this pathological phase of the Nazi culture, but we do feel compelled to offer one additional exhibit, which we offer as Exhibit USA 254 This exhibit, which is on the table, is a human head with the skull bone removed, shrunken, stuffed, and preserved. The Nazis had one of their many victims decapitated, after having had him hanged, apparently for fraternising with a German woman, and fashioned this terrible ornament from his head.

The last paragraph of the official United States Army report from which I have just read deals with the manner in which this exhibit was acquired. It reads as follows:-

"There I also saw the shrunken heads of two young Poles who had been hanged for having relations with German girls. The heads were the size of a fist, and the hair and the marks of the rope were still there."

Another certificate by Lieutenant Demas is set forth in Document 3422-PS, Exhibit USA 254, and is similar to the one which I have read a few minutes ago with relationship to the human skin, excepting that it applies to this second exhibit. We have no accurate estimate of how many persons died in these concentration camps and perhaps none will ever be made, though as the evidence already introduced before this Tribunal indicates, the Nazi conspirators were generally meticulous record keepers. But the records which they kept about concentration camps appear to have been quite incomplete. Perhaps the character of the records resulted from the indifference which the Nazis felt for the lives of their victims. But occasionally we find a death book or a set of index cards. For the most part, nevertheless, the victims apparently faded into an unrecorded death. Reference to a set of death books suggests at once the scale of the concentration camp operations, and we refer now and offer Document 493-PS as Exhibit USA 251. This exhibit is a set of seven books, the death ledger of the Mauthausen concentration camp. Each book has on its cover the word "Totenbuch" or Death Book-Mauthausen.

In these books were recorded the names of some of the inmates who died or were murdered in this camp, and the books cover the period from January, 1939 to April, 1945. They give the name, the place of birth, the assigned cause of death, and time of death of each individual recorded. In addition each corpse is assigned a serial number, and adding up the total serial numbers for the five-year period one arrives at the figure of 35,318.

An examination of the books is very revealing in so far as the camp's routine of death is concerned, and I invite the attention of the Tribunal to Volume 5 from Pages 568 to 582, a photostatic copy of which has been passed to the

Tribunal. These pages cover death entries made for the 19th March, 1945, between 1.15 in the morning and 2 o'clock in the afternoon. In this space of 12 3/4 hours, on these records, 203 persons are reported as having died. They were assigned serial numbers running from 8390 to 8592. The names of the dead are listed. And interestingly enough the victims are all recorded as having died of the same ailment - heart trouble. They died at brief intervals. They died in alphabetical order. The first who died was a man named Ackermann, who died at 1.15 a.m., and the last was a man named Zynger, who died at 2 o'clock in the afternoon.

At 2.20 of that same afternoon, according to these records, on 19th March, 1945, the fatal roll call began again and continued until 4.30. In a space of two hours, 75 more persons died, and once again they died all from heart failure and in alphabetical order. We find the entries recorded in the same volume, from Pages 582 to 586.

There was another death book found at Camp Mauthausen. It is our Document 495-PS and is Exhibit USA 250. This is a single volume, and again has on its cover the words "Death Book - Prisoners of War." And I invite the attention of the Tribunal in particular to Pages 234 to 246. Here the entries record the names of 208 prisoners of war, apparently Russians, who at 15 minutes past midnight on the 10th May, 1942, were executed at the same time. The book notes that the execution was directed by the chief of the S.D. and Sipo, at that time Heydrich.

There was called to my attention as late as this morning a publication of a New York newspaper published in the United States, part of which is made up of three or more pages consisting of advertisements from the families, the relatives, of people who once resided in Germany or in Europe, asking for some advice about them. Most of the advertisements refer to one of these concentration camps or another. The paper is called Der Aufbau. It is a German language newspaper in New York City, published on 23rd day - this particular issue on 23rd November, 1945 - I do not propose to burden the record of this Tribunal with the list of the names of all of these unfortunate individuals, but we refer to it as a publication in the City of New York, a German language newspaper of recent date, which illustrates the horrible extent of this terrible tragedy, which has affected so many people as a result of this concentration camp institution. We feel that no argument, no particular argument, is necessary to support our statements that the Nazi conspirators used these concentration camps and the related instruments of terror in them, to commit Crimes against Humanity and to commit War Crimes.

More about concentration camps will of necessity be involved in the presentation concerning the persecution of the Jews, but this concludes our presentation with respect to the concentration camp as a specific entity of proof.

THE PRESIDENT: Mr. Dodd, speaking for myself, I should like to know what these headings mean.

MR. DODD: Yes, I have them here.

THE PRESIDENT: Document 495-PS.

MR. DODD: Yes, Document 495-PS. Column 1 is the serial number assigned to the prisoners in the order of their deaths.

THE PRESIDENT: Yes.

MR. DODD: Column 2, prisoners of war serial number. Column 3 is the last name, Column 4 is the first name.

THE PRESIDENT: Yes.

MR. DODD: Column 5 is the date of birth. Column 6, the place of birth. Column 7, cause of death. In these cases their cause of death is stated as follows.

"Execution pursuant to order of the Chief of the Sipo and S.D. dated 30th April, 1942," and the ditto marks beneath indicate that the same cause of death was assigned to the names which come beneath it. In the eighth column is the date of death and the hour of death. The first one being 9-5- 42 at 23.35 hours. In the ninth column there is a space which says it is reserved for comments.

THE PRESIDENT: There are numbers there too - M1681 is the first one.

MR. DODD: Well, the German word, I am told, means that it confirms the death with that number. Apparently the number of the -

THE PRESIDENT: I think you said the number of the corpse.

MR. DODD: The number of the corpse, I think that is what it is as distinguished from the number of the prisoner. Each corpse was given a number as well, after the individual died.

COLONEL STOREY: If the Tribunal please, the next phase of War Crimes and Crimes against Humanity, the Persecution of the Jews, will be presented by Major Walsh.

THE PRESIDENT: Major Walsh.

MAJOR WALSH: If the Tribunal please, on behalf of the United States Counsel, I now present to this august Tribunal the evidence to establish certain phases of the Indictment alleged in Count I under War Crimes and Crimes against Humanity, and by agreement between the prosecutors, the allegations in Count IV, Paragraph 10 (b), Crimes against Humanity. The topical title of this presentation is: "The Persecution of the Jews."

At this time I offer in evidence a document book of translations, lettered "T". The documents contained in the book are arranged according to the D, L, PS, and R series; and under the series the translations are listed numerically. This title, "The Persecution of the Jews," is singularly inappropriate when weighed in the light of the evidence to follow. Academically, I am told, to persecute is to afflict, harass, and annoy. The term used does not convey, and indeed I cannot conjure a term that does convey the ultimate aim, the avowed purpose to obliterate the Jewish race.

This presentation is not intended to be a complete recital of all the crimes committed against the Jews. The extent and the scope of the crimes was so great that it permeated the entire German nation, its people, and its organisations.

I am informed that others to follow me will offer additional evidence under other phases of the prosecution's case. Evidence relating to the Party organisations and State organisations, whose criminality the prosecution will seek to establish, will disclose and emphasise the part that these organisations played in the pattern and plan for annihilation.

The French and the Soviet Prosecutors, too, have a volume of evidence all related to this subject, which will be submitted in the course of the trial.

Before I begin a recital of the overt acts leading to the elimination of the Jews, I am prepared to show that these acts and policies within Germany from the year 1933 to the end of the war, related to the planning, preparation, initiation, and waging of aggressive wars, thus falling within the definition of

"Crimes against Humanity" as defined in Article 6 (c) of the Charter.

It had long been a German theory that the first world war ended in Germany's defeat because of a collapse in the zone of the interior. In planning for future wars it was determined that the home front must be secure, to prevent a repetition of this 1918 debacle. Unification of the German people was essential to successful planning and waging of war, and the Nazi political premise must be established - "One race, one State, one Fuehrer."

Free trade unions must be abolished, political parties (other than the National Socialist Party) must be outlawed, civil liberties must be suspended, and opposition of every kind must be swept away. Loyalty to God, church, and scientific truth was declared to be incompatible with the Nazi regime.

The anti-Jewish policy was part of this plan for unification because it was the conviction of the Nazis that the Jews would not contribute to Germany's military programme, but on the contrary would hamper it. The Jew must therefore be eliminated.

This view is clearly borne out by a statement contained in Document 1919-PS, Exhibit USA 170. This document is a transcript of a Himmler speech at a meeting of the S.S. Major Generals on 4th October, 1943, and from Page 4, Paragraph 3, of the translation before the court, I read a very short passage:

"We know how difficult we should have made it for ourselves if with the bombing raids, the burdens and privations of war, we still had Jews today in every town as secret saboteurs, agitators, and trouble mongers; we would now probably have reached the 1916-1917 stage when the Jews were still in the German national body."

The treatment of the Jews within Germany was therefore as much of a plan for aggressive war as was the building of armaments and the conscription of manpower. It falls within the jurisdiction of this Tribunal, as an integral part of the planning and preparation to wage a war of aggression.

It is obvious that the persecution and murder of Jews throughout the conquered territories of Europe following 1939 are War Crimes as defined by Article 6 (b) of the Charter. It further violates Article 46 of the Regulations of the Hague Convention of 1907, to which Germany was a signatory.. I quote Article 46 and ask the Court to take judicial notice thereof.

"Family honour and rights, the lives of persons, and private property, as well as religious convictions and practice, must be respected."

I know of no crime in the history of mankind more horrible in its details than the treatment of the Jews. It is intended to establish that the Nazi Party precepts, later incorporated within the policies of the German State, often expressed by the defendants at bar, were to annihilate the Jewish people. I shall seek to avoid the temptation to editorialise or to draw inferences from the documents, however great the provocation; rather I shall let the documentary evidence speak for itself - its stark realism will be unvarnished. Blood lust may have played some part in these savage crimes, but the underlying purpose and objective to annihilate the Jewish race was one of the fundamental principles of the Nazi plan to prepare for and to wage aggressive war. I shall from this point limit my proof to the overt acts committed, but I venture to request the Court's indulgence, if it is necessary in weaving the pattern of evidence, to make reference to certain documents and evidence previously submitted.

Now this ultimate objective, that is, the elimination and extermination of the Jews, could not be accomplished without preliminary steps and measures. The

German State must first be seized by the Nazi Party, the force of world opinion must be faced, and even the regimented German people must be indoctrinated with hatred against the Jews.

The first clear-cut evidence of the Party policies concerning, the Jews was expressed in the Party programme in February, 1920. I offer in evidence Document 1708-PS, Programme of the National Socialist Party, Exhibit USA 255. With the Court's permission, I would like to quote the relevant part of that programme.

Paragraph (4):-

"Only a member of the race can be a citizen. A member of the race can only be one who is of German blood without consideration of confession."

THE TRIBUNAL (Mr. Biddle): May I interrupt a minute. It is a little hard to know where these exhibits are or what volume you are now quoting from.

MAJOR WALSH: This, Sir, is Document 1708-PS.

THE TRIBUNAL (Mr. Biddle): Volume 2?

MAJOR WALSH: Volume 2.

THE TRIBUNAL (Mr. Biddle): And what page of the document?

MAJOR WALSH: That is Paragraph 4 and Paragraph 6, Sir, on the first page.

Paragraph (4)

"Only a member of the race can be a citizen. A member of the race can only be one who is of German blood, without consideration of confession. Consequently, no Jew can be a member of the race."

And again, in Paragraph (6):-

"The right to determine matters concerning administration and law belongs only to the citizen; therefore, we demand that every public office of any sort whatsoever, whether in the Reich, the county or municipality, be filled only by citizens."

I now offer Document 2662-PS, Mein Kampf, Exhibit USA 256. On Pages 724-725, Hitler, in this book, speaking of the Jew, said that if the National Socialist movement was to fulfil its task - and I quote:

"It must open the eyes of the people with regard to foreign nations and must remind them again and again of the true enemy of our present-day world. In the place of hate against Aryans - from whom we may be separated by almost everything, to whom, however, we are tied by common blood or the great tie of a common culture - it must dedicate to the general anger the evil enemy of mankind as the true cause of all suffering. It must see to it, however, that at least in our country he is recognised as the most mortal enemy and that the struggle against him may show, like a flaming beacon of a better era, to other nations too, the road to salvation for a struggling Aryan mankind."

A flood of abusive literature of all types and for all age groups was published and circulated throughout Germany. Illustrative of this type of publication is the book entitled Der Giftpilz.

I offer in evidence Document 1778-PS, Exhibit USA 257.

This book brands the Jew as a persecutor of the labour class, as a race defiler, a devil in human form, a poisonous mushroom, and a murderer. This particular book instructed school children to recognise the Jew by caricature of his physical features, shown on Pages 6 and 7, taught them that the, Jew abuses little boys and girls, on Page 30, and that the Jewish Bible permits all crimes, Pages 13-17. The defendant Streicher's periodical Der Sturmer No. 14, April, 1937, in particular, went to such extremes as to publish the statement that Jews at the ritual celebration of their Passover slaughtered Christians.

I offer Document 2699-PS, Exhibit USA 258. On Page 2, Column 1, Paragraphs 6 to 9, I quote:-

"Also numerous confessions made by the Jews show that the execution of ritual murders is a law to the Talmud Jew. The former Chief Rabbi, and later monk, Teofite, declared that the ritual murders take place especially on the Jewish Purim in memory of the Persian murders and Passover in memory of the murder of Christ. The instructions are as follows:

The blood of the victims is to be tapped by force. On Passover it is to be used in wine and matzos. Thus a small part of the blood is to be poured into the dough of the matzos and into the wine. The mixing is done by the Jewish head of the family. The procedure is as follows:

The family head empties a few drops of the fresh and powdered blood into the glass, wets the fingers of the left hand and with it sprays and blesses everything on the table. The head of the family then says, 'Thus we ask God to send the ten plagues to all enemies of the Jewish faith'. Then they eat, and at the end the head of the family exclaims, 'May all Gentiles perish, as the child whose blood is contained in the bread and wine'.

The fresh, or dried and powdered blood of the slaughtered is further used by young married Jewish couples, by pregnant Jewesses, for circumcision and so on. Ritual murder is recognised by all Talmud Jews. The Jew believes he absolves himself thus of his sins."

It is difficult for our minds to grasp that falsehoods such as these could fall on fertile soil, that a literate nation could read, digest, or believe these doctrines. We must realise, however, that with a rigidly controlled Press which precluded an expose of such lying propaganda, some of the ignorant and gullible would be led to believe.

I now offer in evidence Document 2697-PS, a copy of Der Sturmer, Exhibit USA 259.

This publication, Der Sturmer, was published by the defendant Streicher's publishing firm. In this publication, Streicher, speaking of the Jewish faith, said:-

"The Holy Scripture is a horrible criminal romance abounding with murder, incest, fraud and indecency."

And again he said:-

"The Talmud is the great Jewish book of crimes that the Jew practises in his daily life."

This is contained in Document 2698-PS, Der Sturmer, which I now offer in evidence, Exhibit USA 260.

This propaganda campaign of hate was too widespread and notorious to require further elaboration. Within the documents offered in evidence in this and in other phases of the case will be found similar and even more scurrilous statements, many by the defendants themselves, and others by their accomplices.

When the Nazi Party gained control of the German State, a new and terrible weapon against the Jews was placed within their grasp, the power to apply the force of the State against them. This was done by the issuance of decrees

Jewish immigrants were denaturalised 1933 Reichsgesetzblatt, Part I, Page 480, signed by defendants Frick and Neurath.

Native Jews were precluded from citizenship: 1935 Reichsgesetzblatt, Part 1, Page 1146, signed by defendant Frick.

Jews were forbidden to live in marriage or to have extra marital relations with persons of German blood: 1935 Reichsgesetzblatt, Part 1, Page 1146, signed by Frick and Hess.

Jews were denied the right to vote: 1936 Reichsgesetzblatt, Part 1, Page 133, signed by defendant Frick.

Jews were denied the right to hold public office or civil service positions: Reichsgesetzblatt 1933, Part 1, Page 277, signed by defendant Frick.

It was determined to relegate the Jews to an inferior status by denying them common privileges and freedoms. Thus, they were denied access to certain city areas, sidewalks, transportation, places of amusement, restaurants: 1938 Reichsgesetzblatt, Part 1, Page 1676.

Progressively more and still more stringent measures were applied, even to the denial of private pursuits. They were excluded from the practice of dentistry: 1939 Reichsgesetzblatt, Part 1, Page 47, signed by defendant Hess.

The practice of law was denied: 1938 Reichsgesetzblatt, Part 1, Page 1403, signed by defendants Frick and Hess.

The practice of medicine was denied: 1938 Reichsgesetzblatt, Part 1, Page 969, signed by defendants Frick and Hess.

They were denied employment by Press and Radio: 1933 Reichsgesetzblatt, Part 1, Page 661.

From stock exchanges and stock brokerage: 1934 Reichsgesetzblatt, Part 1, Page 169 ; and even from farming: 1933 Reichsgesetzblatt, Part 1, Page 685

In 1938 they were excluded from business in general and from the economic life of Germany: 1938 Reichsgesetzblatt, Part 1, Page 1580, signed by the defendant Goering.

The Jews were forced to pay discriminatory taxes and huge atonement fines. Their homes, bank accounts, real estate and intangibles were expropriated.

To digress for a moment from a recital of decrees and to refer specifically to the atonement fines, I wish to offer Document 1816-PS, Exhibit USA 261. This exhibit is a stenographic report of a conference under the chairmanship of the defendant Goering, attended by the defendant Funk, among others, held at 11 o'clock on 12th November, 1938, at the Reich Ministry for Air.

From Pages 8 and 9 of Section 7, I quote the defendant Goering:

"One more question, gentlemen, what would you think the situation would be if I announced today that Jewry-"

THE TRIBUNAL (Mr. Biddle): What page are you on?

MAJOR WALSH: From the English, sir, the middle of Page 22.

"One more question, gentlemen, what you would think the situation would be if I announced today that Jewry would have to contribute this one billion as a punishment."

And then the last paragraph on Page 22 of the Translation before the Court - I quote:-

"I shall choose the wording this way, that German Jewry shall, as punishment for their abominable crimes, etc., etc., have to make a contribution of one billion. That will work, the pigs will not commit another murder. I would like to say again that I would not like to be a Jew in Germany."

It was whimsical remarks such as these that originated decrees, for following this meeting, a decree was issued placing upon the German Jews the burden of a billion Reichsmark fine.

1938 Reichsgesetzblatt, Part I, Page 1579, dated 12th November, 1938, signed by the defendant Goering.

Similar decrees are contained in 1939 Reichsgesetzblatt, Part 1, Page 282, signed by defendant Goering, and 1941 Reichsgesetzblatt, Part 1, Page 72Z, signed by defendants Frick and Bormann.

Finally, in the year 1943, the Jews were placed beyond the protection of any judicial process by a decree signed by the defendants Bormann and Frick and others, and the police became the sole arbiters of punishment and death: 1943 Reichsgesetzblatt, Part 1, Page 372, signed by Frick and Bormann.

I ask the Court to take judicial notice of the Reichsgesetzblatt decrees cited.

Side by side with the passage of these decrees and their execution went still another weapon, wielded by the Party and Party-controlled State. These were the openly sponsored and official anti-Jewish boycotts against Jews. I now offer Document 2409-PS, the published diary of Joseph Goebbels, Exhibit USA 262, and I invite the Court's attention to Page 290, where, under date Of 29th March, 1933, he wrote - the Court will find the quotation on the top of Page 1 of the translation Of 2409-PS.

"The boycott appeal is approved by the entire cabinet."

And again, on 31st March, 1933, he wrote on Page 1, first sentence of Paragraph 2:-

"We are having a last discussion among a very small circle, to decide that the boycott is to start tomorrow with all severity."

The defendant Streicher and the defendant Frank, together with Himmler, Ley and others, were members of a central committee who conducted the 1933 boycott against the Jews. Their names are listed in Document 2156-PS, National Socialist Party correspondence, 29th March, 1933, Exhibit USA 263.

As early as 1933, violence against the Jews was undertaken. Raids were conducted by uniformed Nazis on services within synagogues. Attending members of the synagogues were assaulted and religious insignia and emblems were desecrated. A report of such an occurrence was contained in the official dispatch from the American Consul General in Leipzig, dated 5th April, 1933.

I offer in evidence Document 2709-PS.

THE PRESIDENT: What do you refer to 2156 for?

MAJOR WALSH: Only, sir, to show the names of the defendants Streicher and Frank as members of the boycott committee.

THE PRESIDENT: I see.

MAJOR WALSH: Document 2709 will be Exhibit USA 265. From Paragraph 1 of Page 1, I quote:-

"In Dresden, several weeks ago, uniformed Nazis raided the Jewish prayer house, interrupted the evening religious service, arrested 25 worshippers, and tore the holy insignia or emblems from their head-covering worn while praying."

At a meeting here in Nuremberg, before the representatives of the German Press, the defendant Streicher and Mayor Liebel of Nuremberg revealed in advance to the gathered members of the Press that the Nuremberg synagogue was to be destroyed.

I offer in evidence Document 1724-PS, Exhibit USA 266, which is the minutes of this meeting, dated 4th August, 1938. From Page 1, Paragraph 4 of the original, I quote the translation before the Court:

"The breaking-up of the synagogue (information must still be secret).

On 10th August, 1938, at 10 a.m., the break-up of the synagogue will commence. Gauleiter Julius Streicher will personally set into motion the crane with which the Jewish symbols, Star of David, etc., will be torn down. This should be arranged in a big way. Closer details are still unknown."

The defendant Streicher himself supervised the demolition.

In support of this, I offer Document 2711-PS, a newspaper account of 11th August, 1938, Exhibit USA 267, Paragraph 1 of the translation before the Court:

"In Nuremberg the synagogue is being demolished; Julius Streicher himself inaugurates the work by a speech lasting more than an hour and a-half. By his order then - as a prelude, so to speak, of the demolition - the tremendous Star of David comes off the cupola."

These accounts of violence were not localised anti-Semitic demonstrations but were directed and ordered from a centralised headquarters in Berlin. This is established by a series of teletype messages sent by the Berlin Secret State Police Headquarters to chiefs of police throughout Germany on 10th November, 1938, which contained instructions pertaining to the prearranged demonstration.

I now refer to Document 3051-PS, previously offered in evidence as Exhibit USA 240. I shall quote the relevant part of one of these confidential orders signed by Heydrich, the translation before the Court, the last half on Page 2.

"Because of the attempt on the life of the Secretary of the Legation, von Rath, in Paris tonight, 9th-10th November, 1938, demonstrations against Jews are to be expected throughout the Reich. The following instructions are given on how to treat these events:

1. The Chiefs of the State Police, or their deputies, must get in telephonic contact with the political leaders who have jurisdiction over their districts and must arrange a joint meeting with the appropriate inspector or commander of the Order Police to discuss the organisation of the demonstrations. At these discussions the political leaders must be informed that the German Police have received from the Reichsfuehrer S.S. and Chief of the German Police the following instructions, in accordance with which the political leaders should adjust their own measures.

(a) Only such measures should be taken as do not involve danger to German life or property. (For instance, synagogues are to be burned down only when there is no danger of fire to the surroundings.)

(b) Business and private apartments of Jews may be destroyed but not looted. The police are instructed to supervise the execution of this order and to arrest looters."

Up to this point we have found a gradual and a mounting emphasis in the campaign against the Jews, one of the basic tenets of the Nazi Party and of the State. The flame of prejudice has now been lighted and fanned. The German people have been to a large degree indoctrinated, and the seeds of hatred have been sown. The German State is now armed and is prepared for conquest and the force of world opinion can now safely be ignored. Already they have forced out of Germany 200,000 of its original 500,000 Jews. The Nazi-controlled German State is therefore emboldened and Hitler, in anticipation of the aggressive wars already planned, casts about for a "whipping boy" upon whose shoulders can be placed the blame for the world catastrophe yet to come. The speech before the Reichstag on 30th January, 1939, is set forth in Document 2663-PS, which I now offer in evidence as Exhibit USA 268. I quote -

THE PRESIDENT: What is the number please?

MAJOR WALSH: 2663-PS-a very short extract, Sir. "If the international Jewish financiers within and without Europe succeed in plunging the nations once more into a world war, the result will not be the Bolshevisation of the world and the victory of Jewry, but the obliteration of the Jewish race in Europe."

THE PRESIDENT: We will adjourn for 10 minutes.

[A recess was taken.]

THE PRESIDENT: Major Walsh, it would, I think, assist the Tribunal if you were careful to state the PS number, which we have, rather more clearly and slowly. You see, we have not got the United States exhibit number and I do not know whether it would be better to state the United States exhibit number first and then give us the PS number; I am not sure it would. Anyhow, if you would go a little more slowly and make certain we get the PS number, it would be helpful.

MAJOR WALSH: Yes, your Honour.

The Chief Editor of the official organ of the S.S., the Schwarze Korps, expressed similar sentiments on 8th August, 1940.

I offer in evidence Document 2668-PS; this is Exhibit USA 269, Page 2 of the original and the full excerpt before the Court in translation, as follows:

"Just as the Jewish question will be solved for Germany only when the last Jew has been deported, so the rest of Europe should also realise that the German peace which awaits it, must be a peace without Jews."

These were not the only officials of the Party and of the State to voice the same views. The defendant Rosenberg wrote for the publication World Struggle. I offer in evidence Document 2665-PS, Exhibit USA 270. This publication, Nos. 1 and 2, April and September, 1941, Page 71 of the original, reads: "The Jewish question will be solved only when the last Jew has left the European continent."

The Court will recall Justice Jackson's reference to the apologetic note contained in the diary of Hans Frank when he wrote, and I quote from Document 2233-C-PS, Exhibit USA 271, bottom of Page 1 of the translation:

"Of course, I could not eliminate all lice and Jews in only one year's time. But in the course of time and, above all, if you will help me, this end will be attained."

THE PRESIDENT: I forgot to say, Major Walsh, it would help us too, when you do not begin at the beginning of a paragraph, if you would indicate where abouts it is.

MAJOR WALSH: Yes, sir, I will do that.

While this presentation is not necessarily intended to be a chronological narrative of events in the treatment of the Jewish people, it would appear at this point that we should pause to examine the record to date. We find that the Nazi Party and the Nazi-dominated State have, by writings and by utterances, by decrees and by official acts, clearly expressed their intent the Jew must be eliminated.

How do they now progress to the accomplishment of this purpose? The first requirement was a complete registration of all Jews and, inasmuch as the policy relating to the Jews followed on the heels of German aggression, such registration was required not only within the Reich but successively within the conquered territories. For example, within Germany registration was required by decree (Reichsgesetzblatt Part 1, 1938, Page 922, 23rd July, signed by the defendant Frick); within Austria (Reichsgesetzblatt, Volume I, 1940, Page 694, 29th April); within Poland (Kurjer Krakowski, 5th October, 1939); in France (Journal Officiel No. 9, Page 92, 30th September, 1940); in Holland (Verordnungsblatt, No. 16, 20th January, 1941, signed by the defendant Seyss-Inquart).

The second step was to segregate and concentrate the Jews within restricted areas, called ghettos. This policy was carefully worked out, and perhaps the confidential statement taken from the files of the defendant Rosenberg will best serve as an illustration.

I offer in evidence a copy of memorandum from defendant Rosenberg's file, entitled "Directions for Handling of the Jewish Question", Document 212-PS, Exhibit USA 272. I quote from the top of Page 2 of the translation before the Court:-

> "The first main goal of the German measures must be strict segregation of Jewry from the rest of the population. In the execution of this, first of all is the seizing of the Jewish population by the introduction of a registration order and similar appropriate measures -"

And then, in the second sentence, in the second paragraph on Page 2, I continue:-

> " - all rights of freedom for Jews are to be withdrawn. They are to be placed in ghettos and at the same time are to be separated according to sexes. The existence of many more or less closed Jewish settlements in White Ruthenia and in the Ukraine makes this mission easier. Moreover, places are to be chosen which make possible the full use of the Jewish manpower in case labour needs exist. These ghettos can be placed under the supervision of a Jewish self-government with Jewish officials. The guarding of the boundaries between the ghettos and the outer world is, however, the duty of the Police.
>
> Also, in the cases in which a ghetto cannot yet be established, care is to be taken through strict prohibitions and similar suitable measures that a further intermingling of blood of the Jews and the rest of the populace does not continue."

In May, 1941, Rosenberg, as the Reich Minister for the Eastern Regions, issued directions confining the Jews to ghettos in the Ukraine.

I offer in evidence Document 1028-PS, Exhibit USA 273, and from the first sentence of the translation before the Court, I read:-

"After the customary removal of Jews from all public offices, the Jewish question will have to have a decisive solution through the institution of ghettos."

The policies expressed in the quoted Rosenberg memoranda were not isolated instances nor the acts of one individual. It was the expressed State policy. Defendant von Schirach played his part in the programme of forming ghettos. I offer in evidence Document 3048-PS, Exhibit USA 274. Before the Court is a full translation of that which I wish to quote. The defendant von Schirach spoke before the European Youth Congress held in Vienna on 14th September, 1942, and from Page 2, Column 2, of the Vienna edition of the Volkischer Beobachter of 15th September, I quote:

"Every Jew who exerts influence in Europe is a danger to European culture. If anyone reproaches me with having driven from this city, which was once the European metropolis of Jewry, tens of thousands upon tens of thousands of Jews into the ghetto of the East, I feel myself compelled to reply: I see in this an action contributing to European culture."

One of the largest ghettos was within the City of Warsaw. The original report made by S.S. Major General Stroop concerning this ghetto is entitled "The Warsaw Ghetto is no More". I now offer this in evidence, if the Court please, and request leave to refer to it later on in this presentation, as Exhibit USA 275, top of Page 3, of the translation, Document 1061-PS:

"The ghetto thus established in Warsaw was inhabited by about 400,000 Jews.

It contained 27,000 apartments with an average of two and a-half rooms each.

It was separated from the rest of the city by partitions and other walls and by walling-up of thoroughfares, windows, doors, open spaces, etc."

Some idea of the conditions within this ghetto can be gathered from the fact that an average of six persons lived in every room. Himmler received a report from the S.S. Brigadefuehrer Group A, dated 15th October, 1941, which further illustrates the establishment and operation of the ghettos. I offer Document L-180 in evidence as Exhibit USA 276. The translation, if the Tribunal please, is from the second paragraph from the bottom of Page 9:-

"Apart from organising and carrying out measures of execution, the creation of ghettos was immediately begun in the larger towns during the first days of operations. This was especially urgent in Kowno because there were 30,000 Jews in a total population of 152,400."

And from the last paragraph on Page 9 continuing to Page 10 I quote:-

"In Riga the so-called 'Moscow Suburb' was designated as a ghetto. This is the worst dwelling district of Riga, already mostly inhabited by Jews. The transfer of the Jews into the ghetto district proved rather difficult because the Latvian dwellings in that district had to be evacuated and residential space in Riga is very crowded. 24,000 of the 28,000 Jews living in Riga have been transferred into the ghetto so far. In creating the ghetto the Security Police restricted themselves to mere policing duties, while the establishment and administration of the ghetto as well as the regulation of the food supply for the inmates were left to Civil Administration; the Labour Offices were left in charge of Jewish Labour.

In the other towns with a larger Jewish population, ghettos shall be established likewise."

Jews were also forced into ghettos in the Polish Province of Galicia. No words in my vocabulary could describe quite so adequately the conditions as those found in the report from Katzmann, Lt. General of Police, to Kruger, General of the Police East, dated 3rd June, 1943, entitled "Solution of Jewish Question in Galicia". I offer Document L-18 in evidence as Exhibit USA 277. From the translation, if the Court please, we will begin with the last three sentences on Page ii, that is, the last three sentences prior to the word "nothing" which is there on that page: "Nothing but catastrophical conditions were found in the ghettos of Rawa- Ruska and Rohatyn."

THE PRESIDENT: Where is this?

MAJOR WALSH: Sir, it is on Page 11, it would be about eight lines above the ending or bottom of the page; the story beginning with the words "Nothing but catastrophical conditions".

THE PRESIDENT: Yes.

MAJOR WALSH:

"The Jews of Rawa-Ruska, fearing the evacuation) had concealed in underground holes those suffering from spotted fever. When evacuation was to start the police found that 3,000 Jews suffering from that disease lay about in this ghetto. In order to destroy this centre of pestilence at once, every police officer inoculated against spotted fever was called into action. Thus we succeeded in destroying this plague-boil, losing thereby only one officer. Almost the same conditions were found in Rohatyn."

On Page 19 of this same Document L-18, the last paragraph, I wish to quote further.

THE PRESIDENT: Yes.

MAJOR WALSH:

"Since we received more and more alarming reports on the Jews becoming armed in an ever increasing manner, we started during the last fortnight in June, 1943, an action throughout the whole of the District of Galicia, with the intention of using the strongest measures to destroy the Jewish gangsterdom. Special measures were found necessary during the action to dissolve the ghetto in Lwow where the dug-out mentioned above has been established. Here we had to act brutally from the beginning in order to avoid losses on our side; we had to blow up or to burn down several houses. On this occasion the surprising fact arose that we were able to catch about 20,000 Jews instead of the 12,000 who had registered. We had to pull at least 3,000 Jewish corpses out of every kind of hiding place; they had committed suicide by taking poison."

On Page 20 of this document, the third paragraph I read

"Despite the extraordinary burden heaped upon every single S.S. Police officer during these actions, the mood and spirit of the men were extraordinarily good and praiseworthy from the first to the last day."

These acts and actions of removal and slaughter were not entirely without profit. The author of this report on the ninth page of this translated copy stated, and I quote the last paragraph:-

"Together with the evacuation action we executed the confiscation of

Jewish property. Very high amounts were confiscated and paid over to the Special Staff 'Reinhard'. Apart from furniture and many textile goods, the following amounts were confiscated and turned over to Special Staff 'Reinhard'."

I would like to read a few of the many and assorted items listed under this confiscation:-

20.952 kilograms of golden wedding rings.

7 stamp collections, complete.

1 suitcase with pocket knives.

1 basket of fountain pens and propelling pencils.

3 bags filled with rings - not genuine.

35 wagons of furs.

I will not burden the Court with the detailed lists of objects of value and of the money confiscated, but the foregoing is cited to illustrate the thoroughness of the looting of a defenceless people, even to the 11.73 kilograms of gold teeth and inlays.

By the end of 1942, Jews in the Government General of Poland had been crowded into 55 localities, whereas before the German invasion there had been approximately 1,000 Jewish settlements within this same area. This is reported in the 1942 Official Gazette for the Government General, No. 94, Page 665, 1st November, 1942.

The Jews having been registered and confined within the ghettos now furnished a reservoir for slave labour. It is believed pertinent at this time to point out the difference between the slave labour and labour duty. The latter group were entitled to reasonable compensation, stated work hours, medical care and attention, and other social security measures, while the former were granted none of these advantages, being in fact on a level below a slave.

Defendant Rosenberg, as Reich Minister for the Eastern Occupied Territories, set up within his Organisation a department which, among other things, was to seek a solution for the Jewish problem by means of forced labour. His plans are contained in another Document, 1024-PS, which I now offer in evidence, Exhibit USA 278.

I quote the first part of Paragraph 3 Of Page 1 of the document entitled "General Organisations and Tasks of our Office for the General Handling of Problems in the Eastern territory". This is dated 29th April, 1941. This brief excerpt reads as follows:-

"A general treatment is required for the Jewish problem for which a temporary solution will have to be determined (forced labour for the Jews, creation of ghettos, etc.)."

Thereafter he issued instructions that Jewish forced labour should be effected and utilised for every manual labour, and I refer to Document 212-PS, - already in evidence, as Exhibit USA 272 - from Page 3 of that document, Paragraphs 5 and 7. I quote Paragraph 5:-

"The standing rule for the Jewish labour employment is the complete and unyielding use of Jewish manpower regardless of age in the reconstruction of the Eastern Occupied Territories."

And from Paragraph 7 of the same page I read:-

"Violations of German measures, especially of the forced labour regulations, are to be punished by death in the case of the Jews."

From the ghettos Jewish labour was selected and sent to a concentration area. Here the usable Jews were screened from those considered worthless. For example, a contingent Of 45,000 Jews would be expected to yield 10,000 to 15,000 usable labourers. My authority for this statement is contained in a R.S.H.A. telegram to Himmler, marked "urgent" and "secret", dated 16th December, 1942.

I offer this Document, 1472-PS, in evidence, Exhibit USA 279, and from the translation before the Court I read the last four lines:

"In the total of 45,000 are included physically handicapped and others (old Jews and children). In making a distribution for this purpose, at least 10,000 to 15,000 labourers will be available when the Jews arriving at Auschwitz are assigned."

From Document L-18, a report from the Lieutenant General of the Police, Katzmann, to General of the Police East, Kruger, already in evidence as Exhibit USA 277, we find the clearly outlined nature of the forced labour situation for the Jews. On Page 2 of the translation, starting with Paragraph 6, I read:-

"The best remedy consisted in the formation by the S.S. and Police Leader of Forced Labour Camps. The best opportunity for labour was offered by the necessity to complete the 'Dg. 4' road which was extremely important and necessary for the whole of the southern part of the front, and which was in a catastrophically bad condition. On 15th October, 1941, the establishment of camps along the road was commenced, and despite considerable difficulties there existed, after a few weeks only, seven camps containing 4,000 Jews."

From Page 2, Paragraph 7, I read:-

"Soon more camps followed these first ones, so that after a very short time the completion of 15 camps of this kind could be reported to the Superior Leader of S.S. and Police. In the course of time about 20,000 Jewish labourers passed through these camps. Despite the hardly imaginable difficulties occurring at this work I can report today that about 16o kilometres of the road are completed."

And from Page 2, Paragraph 8, I read:-

"At the same time all other Jews fit for work were registered and distributed for useful work by the labour agencies."

And on Page 5, last part of Paragraph 1 -

THE PRESIDENT: Do you not want the remainder of that paragraph on Page 2?

MAJOR WALSH: It is such a lengthy document I hesitated to burden the record with so much of it, and had extracted certain portions therefrom, but I shall be very glad to read it into the record.

THE PRESIDENT: Then, for instance, the Municipal Administration at Lwow had no success in their attempts to house the Jews within a closed district which would be inhabited only by Jews. This question, too, was solved quickly by the S.S. and the Police Leader through his subordinate officials.

MAJOR WALSH: With the Court's permission, I add that to the record.

Reading the last paragraph of Page 2:

"When the Jews were marked by the Star of David, as well as when they were registered by the labour agencies, the first symptoms

396

appeared in their attempts to dodge the order of the authorities. The measures which were introduced thereupon led to thousands of arrests. It became more and more apparent that the Civil Administration was not in a position to solve the Jewish problem in an approximately satisfactory manner. For instance, the Municipal Administration at Lwow had no success in their attempts to house the Jews within a closed district which would be inhabited only by Jews. This question, too, was solved quickly by the S.S. and Police Leaders through their subordinate officials. This measure became the more urgent as in the winter, 1941, big centres of spotted fever were noted in many parts of the town."

And on Page 5 of this Document L-18, last half of Paragraph 1, I read:-

"During the removal of the Jews into a certain quarter of the town several sluices were erected at which all the work-shy and asocial Jewish rabble were caught during the screening and treated in a special way.

Owing to the peculiar fact that almost 90 per cent. of artisans working in Galicia were Jews, the task to be solved could be fulfilled only step by step, since an immediate evacuation would not have served the interest of War Economy."

And again, on Page 5, Paragraph 2, the latter part, beginning with "cases were discovered":-

"Cases were discovered where Jews, in order to acquire any certificate of labour, not only renounced all wages, but even paid money themselves. Moreover, the organising of Jews for the benefit of their employers grew to such catastrophical extent, that it was deemed necessary to interfere in the most energetic manner for the benefit of the German name.

Since the Administration showed itself too weak to master this chaos, the S.S. and Police Leader simply took over the entire disposition of labour for Jews. The Jewish labour agencies, which were manned by hundreds of Jews, were dissolved. All certificates of labour given by firms or administrative offices were declared invalid, and the cards given to the Jews by the labour agencies were revalidated by the police offices by stamping them.

In the course of this action, again, thousands of Jews were caught in possession of forged certificates or certificates of labour surreptitiously obtained by all kinds of pretexts. These Jews also were exposed to special treatment."

If the Court please, at this time I would like to arrange for the showing of a very short motion picture, perhaps one of the most unusual exhibits that will be presented during the trial. With the Court's permission I would like to call upon Commander Donovan to assist.

THE PRESIDENT: Need we adjourn for it or not?

MAJOR WALSH: No, sir. The picture itself is very, very short, sir.

THE PRESIDENT: Very well.

COMMANDER DONOVAN: May it please the Tribunal, the United States now offers in evidence Document 3052-PS, Exhibit USA 280, entitled "Original German eight millimetre Film of Atrocities against Jews".

This is a strip of motion pictures taken, we believe, by a member of the S.S., and captured by the United States military forces in an S.S. barracks near Augsburg, Germany, as described in the affidavits now before the Tribunal.

We have not been able to establish beyond doubt in which area these films were made, but we believe that to be immaterial.

The film offers undeniable evidence, made by Germans themselves, of almost incredible brutality to Jewish people in the custody of the Nazis, including German military units.

It is believed by the prosecution that the scene is the extermination of a ghetto by Gestapo agents, assisted by military units. And, as the other evidence to be presented by the prosecution will indicate, the scene presented to the Tribunal is probably one which occurred a thousand times all over Europe under the Nazi rule of terror.

This film was made on an eight millimetre home camera. We have not wished even to reprint it, and so shall present the original, untouched film captured by our troops. The pictures obviously were taken by an amateur photographer. Because of this, because of the fact that part of it is burned because of the fact that it runs for only one and a- half minutes, and because of the confusion on every hand shown on this film, we do not believe that the Tribunal can properly view the evidence if it is shown only once. We therefore ask the Tribunal's permission to project the film twice as we did before the defence counsel.

This is a silent film. The film has been made available to all defence counsels, and they have a copy of the supporting affidavits, duly translated.

[The film was shown.]

May it please the Tribunal, while the film is being rewound I wish to say that, attached to the affidavits offered in evidence, is a description of every picture shown in this film. And, with the Tribunal's permission, I wish to read a few selections from that at this time, before again projecting the film, in order to direct the Tribunal's attention to certain of the scenes.

Scene 2: A naked girl running across the courtyard.

Scene 3: An older woman being pushed past the camera, and a man in S.S. uniform standing at the right of the scene.

Scene 5: A man with a skull-cap and a woman are manhandled.

Scene 14: A half-naked woman runs out of the crowd.

Scene 15: Another half-naked woman runs through the house.

Scene 16: Two men drag an old man out.

Scene 18: A man in German military uniform, with his back to the camera, watches.

Scene 24: A general shot of the street, showing fallen bodies and naked women running.

Scene 32: A shot of the street, showing five fallen bodies.

Scene 37: A man with a bleeding head is hit again.

Scene 39: A soldier in German military uniform, with a rifle, stands by as a crowd concentrates on a man coming out of the house.

Scene 44: A soldier with a rifle, in German military uniform, walks past a woman clinging to a torn blouse.

Scene 45: A woman is dragged by her hair across the street.

[The film was shown again.]

We submit to the Tribunal for its permanent records this strip of eight millimetre film.

MAJOR WALSH: It is difficult from this point to follow the thread of chronological order or a topical outline. So numerous are the documents and so appalling the contents that in this brief recital the prosecution will make no effort to itemise the criminal acts. Selected documents, however, will unfold the crimes in full detail.

Before launching a discussion of the means utilised to accomplish the ultimate aim, that is the extermination of the Jewish people, I now turn to that fertile source of evidence, the diary of Hans Frank, then Governor General of Occupied Poland. In a cabinet session on Tuesday, 16th December, 1941, in the Government Building at Cracow, the defendant Frank made a closing address to the session. I offer now in evidence that part of Document 2233D-PS, Exhibit USA 281, identified CV 1941, October to December, and from Page 76, Line 10 to Page 77, Line 33 of the original and of the entire translation before the Court, I quote:

> "As far as the Jews are concerned, I want to tell you quite frankly that they must be done away with in one way or another. The Fuehrer said once: 'Should united Jewry again succeed in provoking a world-war, not only will the blood of the nations which have been forced into the war by them, be shed, but the Jew will have found his end in Europe.' I know that many of the measures carried out against the Jews in the Reich at present are being criticised. It is being done intentionally, as is obvious from the reports on the morale, to talk about cruelty, harshness, etc. Before I continue, I want to beg you to agree with me on the following formula: We will on principle have pity on the German people only and nobody else in the whole world. The others, too, had no pity on us. As an old National Socialist I must say this: This war would be only a partial success if the whole of Jewry should survive it, while we had shed our best blood in order to save Europe. My attitude towards the Jews will, therefore, be based only on the expectation that they must disappear. They must be done away with. I have entered into negotiations to have them deported to the East. A great discussion concerning that question will take place in Berlin in January, a discussion to which I am going to delegate the State Secretary, Dr. Buehler. It is to take place in the Reich Security Main Office with S.S. Lt. General Heydrich. A great Jewish migration will begin, in any case.
>
> But what should be done with the Jews? Do you think they will be settled down in the 'Ostland' in villages? This is what we were told in Berlin: Why all this bother? We can do nothing with them either in the 'Ostland' or in the 'Reichskommissariat'. So liquidate them yourselves.
>
> Gentlemen, I must ask you to rid yourselves of all feeling of pity. We must annihilate the Jews, wherever we find them and wherever it is possible, in order to maintain the structure of the Reich as a whole. This will, naturally, be achieved by other methods than those pointed out by Bureau Chief Dr. Hummel. Nor can the Judges of the Special Courts be made responsible for it because of the limitations of the framework of the legal procedure. Such outdated views cannot be applied to such gigantic and unique events. We must find in any case a

way which leads to the goal, and my thoughts are working in that direction.

The Jews represent for us also extraordinarily malignant gluttons. We have now approximately 2,500,000 of them in the Government General, perhaps with the Jewish mixtures and everything that goes with it, 3,500,000 Jews. We cannot shoot or poison those 3,500,000 Jews, but we shall nevertheless be able to take measures which will lead, somehow, to their annihilation, and this will be done in connection with the gigantic measures to be determined in discussions from the Reich. The Government General must become free of Jews, the same as the Reich. Where and how this is to be achieved is a matter for the offices which we must appoint and create here. Their activities will be brought to your attention in due course."

This, if the Tribunal please, is not the planning and scheming of an individual, but is the expression of that official of the German State, the appointed Governor General of Occupied Poland. The methods used to accomplish the annihilation of the Jewish people were varied and, although not subtle, were highly successful.

I have from time to time made reference to certain utterances and actions of the defendant Rosenberg as one of the leaders and policy makers of the Nazi Party and German State. It is perhaps reasonable to assume that the defendant Rosenberg will claim for many of his actions that he pursued them pursuant to superior orders. I have before me, however, a captured document, 001-PS, marked "secret," dated 18th December, 1941, entitled "Documentary Memorandum for the Fuehrer - Concerning: Jewish Possessions in France ", Exhibit USA 282. I dare say that no document before this Tribunal will more clearly show the defendant Rosenberg's personal attitude, his temperament and convictions toward the Jews, than this memorandum, wherein he, in his own initiative, urges plundering and death. I offer in evidence Document 001-PS. The body of the memorandum reads as follows:-

"In compliance with the order of the Fuehrer for protection of Jewish cultural possessions, a great number of Jewish dwellings remained unguarded. Consequently, many furnishings have disappeared because a guard could, naturally, not be posted. In the whole East the administration has found terrible conditions of living quarters, and the chances of procurement are so limited that it is not possible to procure any more. Therefore, I beg the Fuehrer to permit the seizure of all the home furnishings of Jews in Paris, who have fled or will leave shortly, and those of Jews living in all parts of the occupied West, to relieve the shortage of furnishings in the administration in the East.

2. A great number of leading Jews were, after a short examination in Paris, again released. The attempts on the lives of members of the Armed Forces have not stopped; on the contrary they continue. This reveals an unmistakable plan to disrupt the German-French co-operation, to force Germany to retaliate and, with this, evoke a new defence on the part of the French against Germany. I suggest to the Fuehrer that, instead of executing 100 Frenchmen, we substitute 100 Jewish bankers, lawyers, etc. It is the Jews in London and New York who incite the French Communists to commit acts of violence, and it seems only fair that the members of their race should pay for this. It is

not the little Jews but the leading Jews in France who should be held responsible. That would tend to awaken the anti-Jewish sentiment.

Signed A. Rosenberg."

[Dr. Thoma approached the lectern.]

THE PRESIDENT: May I ask you to speak slowly so that your application will come to me through the earphones correctly.

DR. THOMA (Counsel for defendant Rosenberg): I request to take this opportunity, at a moment when the prosecutor has presented extensive documentary evidence against my client, Rosenberg, to voice an objection to Document 212-PS, Exhibit USA 272. The prosecutor claims that this document was an instruction by the Minister for the East. It begins with the words -

THE PRESIDENT: None of that has come through on the earphones. I do not understand you. You had better begin again.

DR. THOMA: The prosecutor presented a short while ago Document 212-PS, Exhibit USA 272, claiming its contents to be instructions given by the Minister for the East about the treatment of Jews. In this document he is supposed to have given instructions that violations of German regulations, especially violations of the compulsory labour laws, could only be punished by death in the case of Jews. This document did not originate with the defendant Rosenberg; also I do not consider it relevant -

THE PRESIDENT: More slowly, please.

DR. THOMA: This document did not originate with the defendant Rosenberg, It bears neither date nor address nor his signature. I, therefore, object to the assumption that this document originated with the defendant Rosenberg.

THE PRESIDENT: Wait a minute. I do not think that counsel for the prosecution said that the Document 212-PS, emanated from Rosenberg. I did not so understand him.

DR. THOMA: I understood him to say that it was an instruction given by the Minister for the East. If I am not mistaken, he also said it was dated April, 1941. At that time there was no Ministry for the East. Rosenberg was only named Minister for the East in July, 1941.

THE PRESIDENT: I will ask the counsel for the prosecution.

MAJOR WALSH: It is my understanding, sir, that that Document 212-PS, was taken from the captured files of Rosenberg.

DR. THOMA: That is true, it was found among the papers of the defendant Rosenberg; the defendant Rosenberg claims, however, that he has never seen this document, that he knows nothing about it and that it has never passed through his hands.

THE PRESIDENT: Rosenberg, when he is called as a witness, or when you appear to speak for him, will be able to say that he has never seen the document before. All that counsel for the prosecution has said - and it appears to be true - is that the document was found in Rosenberg's file. You can say or prove by Rosenberg's evidence when you call Rosenberg - if you do call him - that he never saw the document. Do you understand?

DR. THOMA: Yes.

THE PRESIDENT: It is 5 o'clock now, so we will adjourn.

[The Tribunal adjourned to 1000 hours on 14th December, 1945.]

Twentieth Day:
Friday, 14th December, 1945

DR. KAUFFMANN (Counsel for the defendant Kaltenbrunner): I permit myself to present two points to the Court with regard to yesterday's and future presentation of evidence, particularly with respect to the section on "Crimes against Humanity".

First, I should like to have stricken from the record yesterday's affidavit of the witness Pfaffenberger. Eventually one will have to cross-examine the witness in person. His testimony is fragmentary in most important points. It cannot be seen whether in many cases it is a matter of his personal observations or of assertions from hearsay. From this it is all too easy to draw false conclusions. The witness did not say that the Camp Commander Koch, along with his inhuman wife, was condemned to death by an S.S. court precisely because of these occurrences among other things. It is possible to ascertain the entire truth by questioning the witness in a later part of the trial. Until then every one, judges, defence counsel and prosecution, is impressed by this terrible testimony.

The content of this testimony is so terrible and so degrading for the human spirit that one would like to turn one's eyes and ears away from it. In the meantime such statements make their way through the Press of the whole world. Civilisation is justifiably indignant. The consequences of such premature statements are not to be calculated. The Prosecuting Attorney well recognises the significance of this testimony and exposed the sorry documents yesterday in court.

If it is only after weeks or months that such perverted testimony can be set aright, the previous effects of it can never be eliminated entirely. Truth suffers and justice is endangered. According to the 19th Article in the Charter, such a condition should not have been brought about.

Secondly, I should, therefore, like to suggest at this point in the procedure, that we do not read the testimony of witnesses who live in Germany and whose appearance here is, therefore, possible; because at this point of the procedure accusations are involved, the subject of which is even more terrible than the accusations referring to aims of aggression, since it is a question here of the tortured life and of the death of human beings.

At the beginning of this trial the Court refused to hear the testimony of the witness Schuschnigg, and it is my opinion that what was valid then should be all the more valid at this point in the trial.

I should like to emphasise by suggestion particularly as regards the defendant Kaltenbrunner himself, since it was not until the spring of 1943 that he became Chief of the Reich Main Security Office and since then, according to the testimony of the defence, many, if not all, of his signatures were forged, and the entire executive function of the administration of camps and happenings connected with them lay exclusively in Himmler's hands. That I hope to be able to prove at a later date. I have mentioned that in order to justify my next suggestion.

THE PRESIDENT: The Tribunal would like to hear counsel for the Chief

Prosecutor of the United States.

MR. JUSTICE JACKSON: May it please the Tribunal, Mr. Dodd, who had charge of the matter which is under discussion, left for the United States yesterday, and I shall have to substitute for him as best I may.

This Tribunal sits under a Charter which recognises the impossibility of covering a decade of time, a continent of space, a million acts, by ordinary rules of proof, and at the same time finishing this case within the lives of living men. We do not want to have a trial here, that, like the trial of Warren Hastings, lasted seven years. Therefore, the Charter set up only two standards by which, I submit, any evidence may be rejected. The first is that the evidence must be relevant to the issue. The second is that it must have some probative value. That was made mandatory upon this Tribunal in Article 19, because of the difficulty of ever trying this case if we used the technical rules of Common Law.

One of the reasons this was constituted as a military tribunal, instead of an ordinary Court of Law, was to avoid the precedent-creating effect of what is done here on our own law and the precedent control which would exist if this were an ordinary judicial body.

Article 19 provides that the Tribunal should not be bound by technical rules of evidence. It shall adopt and apply, to the greatest possible extent, expeditious and non-technical procedure, and shall admit any evidence which it deems to have probative value. That was made mandatory, that it shall admit any evidence which it deems to have probative value. The purpose of that provision, your Honours, I may say, was this: that the whole controversy in this case - and we have no doubt that there is room for controversy - should be centred upon the value of evidence and not on its admissibility.

We have no jury. There is no occasion for applying jury rules. Therefore, when a piece of evidence is offered, there are two questions which arise: The first is, does it have probative value? If it has no probative value, then it should not encumber the records, of course. The second is, does it have relevancy? If it has not, of course it should not come in.

The evidence in question has relevance. No one questions that, no one can say that an affidavit, duly sworn, does not have some probative value. What probative value it has, the weight of it, should be determined on the submission of the case. That is to say, if a witness has made a statement in an affidavit, and it is denied by Kaltenbrunner, and you believe that the denial has weight and credibility, then, of course, the affidavit should not be considered in the final consideration of the case. But we are dealing here with events that took place over great periods of time and great distances. We are dealing with witnesses widely scattered and a situation where communications are almost at a standstill.

If this affidavit stands at the end of this case undenied, unchallenged, it is not, then, beyond belief that you would give it value and weight. An affidavit might bear internal evidence that it lacked credibility, such as evidence where the witness was talking of something of which he had no personal knowledge. I do not say that every affidavit that comes along has probative value just because it is sworn to. But it seems to me that, if we are to make progress with this case, this simple system envisioned by this Charter, which was the subject of long consideration, must be followed; that if when a piece of evidence is presented, even though it does not comply with technical rules governing

403

judicial procedure, it is something which has probative value in the ordinary daily concerns of life, it should be admitted. If it stands undenied at the close of the case, as many of these things will, then, of course, there is no issue about it, and it saves the calling of witnesses, which, as we have already seen, will take an indefinite period of time. I may say that the testimony of the witness Lahousen, which took nearly two days, could have been put in, in this Court, in 15 minutes in affidavit form, and all that was essential to it could have been placed before us; and if it were to be denied you could then have determined its weight.

We want to adhere to this Charter. I submit, it is no reason for deviating from the Charter that an affidavit recites horrors. I should have thought that the world could not be more shocked by recitals of horrors in affidavits than it has been in the documents that have proceeded from sources of the enemy itself. There is no reason in that for departing from the plain principles of the Charter.

I think the question of orderly procedure and the question of time are both involved in this. I think that the Tribunal should receive affidavits, and we have prepared them - we hope carefully, we hope fairly - to prevent a great many things that would take days and days of proof. I may say that this ruling is more important in subsequent stages of this case than it is on this particular affidavit.

There is another reason, perhaps. We have some situations in which a member of an accused organisation, who is directly hostile to our position because the accusation would reach him within the accused class, has made an affidavit or affidavits, which constitute admissions against interest; but on some other issue he makes statements which we believe are untrue and incredible, and we do not wish to vouch for his general credibility by calling him as a witness, but we wish to avail ourselves of his admission. We have to make our proof largely from enemy sources. All this proof, and every witness, eight months ago were in the hands of the enemy. We have to make our proof from them. God alone knows how much proof there is in this world that we have not been able to reach. We submit that the orderly procedure here is to abide by this Charter and admit these affidavits. If they stand unquestioned at the end of the case, there is no issue about them. If they are questioned, then their weight is a matter which you would determine on final submission.

THE PRESIDENT: Mr. Justice Jackson, I have three questions I should like to ask you. The first is: where is Pfaffenberger?

MR. JUSTICE JACKSON: That I cannot answer at the moment, but I will get an answer as quickly as I can. It is unknown to me at the moment. If we are able to ascertain, I will inform you at the conclusion of the noon recess.

THE PRESIDENT: The second point to which I wish to draw your attention is Article 16 (e) of the Charter, which contemplates cross-examination of witnesses by the defendants. The only reason why it is thought that witnesses who are available should not give evidence by affidavit is because it denies to the defence the opportunity of cross- examining them.

MR. JUSTICE JACKSON: I think that this provision means just exactly what it says. If we call a witness, they have the right of cross-examination. If he is not called, they have the right to call him, if he is available, as their witness, but not, of course, the right of cross-examination. The provision itself, if your Honour notices, reads that they have the right to cross-examine any witness

404

called by the prosecution, but that does not abrogate or affect Article 19 - that we may obtain and produce any probative evidence in such manner as will expedite the trial.

THE PRESIDENT: Then the next point to which I wish to draw your attention to is Article 17 (a). As I understood it, you were arguing that it was mandatory upon the Tribunal to consider any evidence which was relevant. Therefore, I draw your attention to Article 117 (a) which, gives the Tribunal power to summon witnesses to the trial.

MR. JUSTICE JACKSON: That is right. I think there is no conflict in that whatever. The powers of the Tribunal to summon witnesses, and to put questions to them, was introduced into this Charter through the continental systems of jurisprudence. Usually there are not Tribunal witnesses in the States. Witnesses are called only by one of the parties, but it was suggested by the continental scholars that in this kind of case, since we were utilising a mixture of the two procedures, the Tribunal itself should have the right to do several things. One is to summon witnesses, to require their attendance, and to put questions to them. I submit that this witness, whose affidavit has been received, can be called, if we can find him, by the Tribunal and questioned.

The next provision - and it bears on the spirit of this-of Article 17 is that the Tribunal has the right to interrogate any defendant. Of course, under our system of jurisprudence the Tribunal would have no such right, because the defendant has the unqualified right to refrain from being a witness; but, in deference again to the continental system, the Tribunal was given the right to interrogate any defendant; and his immunities, which he would have under the Constitution of the United States, if he were being tried under our system, were taken away.

I submit that the perfect consistency in those provisions empowers the Tribunal on its own motion (Article 17) to summon witnesses, to supplement anything that is offered, to put any questions to witnesses, and to any defendant.

If any witness is called, the right of cross-examination cannot be denied, but that does not abrogate Article 19, which was intended to enable us to put our case before the Tribunal, so that the issue would then be drawn by the defendants and the weight of what we offer determined on final submission.

THE PRESIDENT: Lastly, there is Article 17 (e), which I suppose, in your submission, would entitle the Tribunal, if they thought right, after receiving the affidavit, to take the evidence of Pfaffenberger on commission.

MR. JUSTICE JACKSON: Yes, I think it would, your Honour. I may say, in reference to that section, and it may perhaps be surprising to those accustomed to our system of jurisprudence - that it was one of the most controversial issues we had in the framing of this Charter. We had in mind the authorisation of what we call "Masters" to go into various localities, perhaps, and take testimony, not knowing what might be necessary. Our practice, however, of appointing "Masters in Equity" to take testimony and make recommendations was not acceptable to the continental system, and we finally compromised on this provision which authorises the taking of testimony by commissions.

THE PRESIDENT: Thank you.

GENERAL RUDENKO: Your Honours, I have come forward after my colleague, Mr. Jackson, in order to make my own statement, inasmuch as the petition of the defence is fundamentally incorrect from my point of view and cannot be complied with.

We are submitting our objections for your examination. I fully share the viewpoint exposed here by the Chief Prosecutor of the U.S.A., Mr. Jackson. I should like, your Honours, to point out the following circumstances. The defence counsel, in his petition, raises the question whether the prosecution should refer to or publish documents in connection with affidavits from persons residing in Germany. A statement of this nature is completely out of order since, as is known, the defendants committed the greater part of their atrocities in every country in Europe, and it will be readily understood that the witnesses of these atrocities live in different parts of these countries, and it is essential that the prosecution have recourse to the testimony of such persons, whether the testimonies be written or oral. Your Honours, we have entered a stage in the Trial when we shall have to set forth the atrocities connected with so-called War Crimes and Crimes Against Humanity, atrocities committed by the defendants over extensive areas. We shall show you, your Honours, in evidence, documents originating from the defendants themselves or from persons who had suffered at the hands of the war criminals. And it would be impossible to summon to the Trial all these witnesses in order that they might give their evidence orally. It is essential to have affidavits and written testimonies from the witnesses.

As his Honour the President remarked, Article 17 determines the power of summoning witnesses to the Trial. That is correct; Article 17 determines this, but it is impossible to summon to the Trial all such witnesses who could give affidavits on the crimes committed by the defendants. Therefore, your Honours, I should like to refer to Article 19 of the Charter, reading as follows:

"The Tribunal shall not be bound by technical rules of evidence. It shall adopt and apply to the greatest possible extent expeditious - and I emphasise, your Honours, expeditious - and non-technical procedure and shall admit any evidence which it deems to have probative value."

I would also ask your Honours to proceed upon this regulation which definitely admits, as evidence, written affidavits of witnesses. This, I wish to say, is my statement, which supplements the statement made by Mr. Jackson.

MR. ROBERTS: May it please the Tribunal, as far as the British Delegation is concerned, they desire to support what the American Chief Prosecutor has said, and we do not feel we can usefully add anything.

THE PRESIDENT (To M. Faure of the French Delegation): Do you wish to add anything?

M. FAURE: Mr. President, I wish simply to inform the Court that the French Prosecution is entirely in accord with the remarks which were made by the American and the Soviet prosecutors.

I think, as the representative of the American prosecution said, that it is not possible to settle the questions of evidence in this trial solely by the practice of oral testimony in the courtroom, for under these conditions it might be opportune to call to the witness stand - a step which is obviously impossible - all the inhabitants of the territories who have been involved, and which have been occupied. The defence will have every opportunity to discuss later on the documents which have been presented by the prosecution and, notably, the written testimony.

THE PRESIDENT: I do not think that counsel for Kaltenbrunner was suggesting that every witness must be called, but that witnesses who were in Germany and available should be called and that their evidence should not be given by affidavit.

M. FAURE: The defence has a right to call them as witnesses if it desires to hear them.

DR. KAUFFMANN (Counsel for defendant Kaltenbrunner): Excuse me if I add just a few words to this important question. Those who have just spoken have said that one of the main principles of this trial is the circumstance that the trial should proceed speedily. That is also expressed in Article 19 of the Charter. No one can more hope that this principle be carried through than we defence counsel ourselves; but it is nevertheless my opinion that one principle, which is the highest that mankind knows, must not suffer in the interests of speed, and that principle is the principle of truth; and, if it were clearly a possibility that an over-hasty trial might give offence to truth, then the formal methods of procedure must step into the background. There are in mankind principles that are unspoken and that do not have to be spoken.

This spirit of truth hovers also over Article 19, and is its irrevocable content. The objections I raised to the testimony of the witness in question seem to me so justified, that the important principle of speed should be confronted with the principle of truth and should withdraw in its favour. It is a question of humanity. Humanity is in question here, and we want to find the truth for our children. If such testimony remains uncontradicted for months, then a part of mankind might despair of humanity and also the German people in particular, would suffer.

DR. BERGOLD (Counsel for defendant Bormann): If it please the Court, I am Dr. Bergold, defence counsel for Bormann.

In this debate I should like to bring up one other point. It appears important to me because it has apparently been the source of this debate. According to our system of jurisprudence the prosecution has the duty of producing not only the incriminating evidence but also that which serves to help the defendants. I can well understand that the defence counsel for Kaltenbrunner protests because the prosecution failed to mention an important point, namely, that the German authorities indicted this inhuman S.S. leader and his wife and condemned them to death. It is highly probable that the prosecution knew of this fact, and that the horrible exhibits of erring human nature, as presented to us, were found in the files of the German Courts.

I believe this entire debate would not have arisen if the prosecution had made the statement that the German authorities themselves passed judgment against so inhuman a character, and condemned him to death.

We find ourselves here in difficulties because, in contrast to our procedure, the prosecution for the most part simply presents incriminating evidence and on the basis of a single document or a single witness - but, of its own accord, does not produce the exculpating evidence which may present itself in the introduction of evidence. If that procedure had been followed in this present case, and if the prosecution had stated that this man had been condemned to death, then, first of all, the impression about Kaltenbrunner would have carried less weight, and public opinion, on the whole, would have been left with a different impression. Then my colleague Kauffmann would presumably have limited himself in this case to proving in the further course of this trial that Kaltenbrunner had nothing to do with this matter; but the inhuman character of the procedure and the terrible impression which it made on us would have been avoided.

THE PRESIDENT: Will you explain the part of the German law to which you were referring, where you say it is the duty of the prosecution, not only to produce evidence for the prosecution, but also to produce evidence for the defence.

DR. BERGOLD: That is a general principle of jurisprudence. In Paragraph 161 of the Reich Penel Code that has been established. That is one of the basic principles of law that we have in Germany in order to -

THE PRESIDENT: Give me that reference again.

DR. BERGOLD: Paragraph 161. This principle, according to German law, is to make it possible that against an accused person who frequently, when he -

THE PRESIDENT: 161 of what ?

DR. BERGOLD: Reichsstrafprozessordnung (Reich Penal Code). The same thing is true of Austria. There is a similar paragraph in the Austrian Penal Code. This principle is supposed to permit that a defendant should have the whole truth said about him, since frequently he himself is not in a position to produce all the evidence in his favour. Therefore, German law has commissioned the prosecution to present exculpating evidence also, along with its incriminating evidence.

DR. KUBUSCHOK (Counsel for defendant von Papen): The question of Pfaffenberger does not concern the defendant von Papen specifically, because that part of the Indictment does not apply to his case. I am simply discussing this question in respect to the principle. I believe that the practical effect of the opinions expressed by the prosecution and the defence counsel cannot be of very great importance. Mr. Justice Jackson agrees with us that every witness whose affidavit can be presented can be called as a witness by the defence if he is available. In every case in which the defence holds that an affidavit, evidence of secondary value, is insufficient, and that only first-hand evidence, such as oral testimony given by the witness, should be taken, there would always be a duplication of the evidence- taking; namely, the reading of the affidavit, and the hearing and cross-examination of the witness. This undoubtedly would lead to a prolongation of the trial. In each such case, the Court would, right from the outset, object to the reading of the affidavit, in order to prevent this delay. Consequently it is probably futile for the prosecution to present affidavits where it can be expected that the witness will later be heard again.

I believe that the prosecution does not need in any way to be worried about this. It is a matter of course that we, the defence, want nothing but that which we assume to be true in the case of the prosecution also; namely, that conduct of the trial which is as speedy as possible, but which is also as safe as possible in regard to the establishment of the truth. And, finally, if in a trial evidence is introduced by means of an affidavit, which can be a monstrous source of untruths, if such evidence is introduced first, it is natural that this evidence will have to be clarified in a more complicated and time-consuming fashion at a later date, when the witness is examined.

THE PRESIDENT: The Tribunal will consider the objection that has been raised when the Court adjourns.

MR. JUSTICE JACKSON: May I have one word?

THE PRESIDENT: Mr. Justice Jackson, it is unusual to hear counsel who opposes an objection, a second time.

MR. JUSTICE JACKSON: I merely want to give you the answer to the question which you asked me as to the whereabouts of Pfaffenberger. My information is that these affidavits were taken by the American Army at the time it liberated the people in these concentration camps, when the films were taken and the whole evidence that was available was gathered. This witness was present at the concentration camp, and at that time his statements were taken. We do not know his present whereabouts, and I see no reasonable likelihood that we will be able to locate him within any short time. We will make an effort.

MR. ROBERTS: May it please the Tribunal, might I endeavour to assist? I think I have now found the German order to which the defence counsel referred, Paragraph 161. It is, of course, an order in German. Perhaps I might hand it up, and the Court translators will no doubt deal with the paragraph.

MR. JUSTICE JACKSON: I think one bit of additional information must be furnished, in view of the statements made here that we have information that we are withholding. Kaltenbrunner has been interrogated. At no time has he made such a claim, so I am advised by our interrogators; and under the Charter our duty is to present the case for the prosecution. I do not, not in any purpose, serve two masters.

THE PRESIDENT: Now, I call upon Major Walsh. Major Walsh, did you give a lettering to the document books with which you are dealing?

MAJOR WALSH: Yes. If your Honour please, it is the letter "T".

May it please the Tribunal, during the last session the prosecution presented briefly the preliminary steps leading to the ultimate objective of the Nazi Party and the Nazi controlled State, that is, the extermination of the Jews. Propaganda, decrees, the infamous Nuremberg Laws, boycotts, registration and the creation of ghettos were the initial measures in the programme. I shall, with the Court's permission, continue with a discussion of the methods utilised for the annihilation of the Jewish people.

I would like first to discuss starvation. Policies were designed and adopted to deprive the Jews of the most elemental necessities of life. Again the defendant Hans Frank, then Governor General of Poland, wrote in his diary that hunger rations were introduced in the Warsaw Ghetto and, referring to the new food regulations in August, 1942, he callously, and perhaps casually, noted that by these food regulations he virtually condemned more than 1,000,000 Jews to death. I offer in evidence that part of Document 2233 E- PS, Diary of Hans Frank, Conference Volume, 24th August, 1942, Exhibit USA 283.

And I quote:-

> "That we sentence 1,200,000 Jews to die of hunger should be noted only marginally. It is a matter of course that, should the Jews not starve to death, it would, we hope, result in a speeding-up of the anti-Jewish measures."

Frank's diary was not the only guide to the deliberate policy of starvation of the Jews. They were prohibited from pursuing agricultural activities in order to cut them off from access to the source of food. I offer Document 1136-PS in evidence, Exhibit USA 284. I refer the Court to Page 4 of the translation, marked with the Roman numeral V, Paragraphs (a) and (b). The document is entitled "Provisional Directives on the Treatment of Jews", and it was issued by the Reichskommissar for the Ostland, I read:-

"Jews must be cleaned out from the countryside. The Jews are to be removed from all trades, especially from trade with agricultural products and other foodstuffs".

Jews were excluded from the purchase of basic food, such as wheat products, meat, eggs and milk.

I offer in evidence Document 1347-PS, Exhibit USA 285, and I quote from Paragraph 2, on the first page of the translation before the Court. This is an original decree dated 18th September, 1942, from the Ministry of Agriculture. I quote:-

"Jews will no longer receive the following foods, beginning with the 42nd distribution period (19th October, 1942): meat, meat products, eggs, wheat products (cake, white bread, wheat rolls, wheat flour, etc.), whole milk, fresh skimmed milk, as well as such food distributed not on food ration cards issued uniformly throughout the Reich, but on local supply certificates or by special announcement of the Nutrition Office on extra coupons of the food cards.

Jewish children and young people over ten years of age will receive the bread ration of the normal consumer".

The sick, the old, and the pregnant mothers were excluded from the special food concessions allotted to non-Jews. Seizure by the State Police of food shipments to Jews from abroad was authorised, and the Jewish ration cards were distinctly marked with the word "Jew", in colour, across the face of the cards, so that the storekeepers could readily identify and discriminate against Jewish purchasers.

The Czechoslovakian Government published in 1943 an official document entitled "Czechoslovakia Fights Back". I offer this book in evidence, Document 1689-PS, Exhibit USA 286. To summarise the contents of Page 110, it states that the Jewish food purchases were confined to certain areas and to certain days and hours. As might be expected, the period permitted for the purchases was during the time when food stocks were likely to be exhausted.

By Special Order No. 44 for the Eastern Occupied Territories, dated 4th November, 1941, the Jews were limited to rations as low as only one-half of the lowest basic category of other people, and the Ministry of Agriculture was empowered to exclude Jews entirely or partially from obtaining food, thus exposing the Jewish community to death by starvation.

I now offer in evidence Document L-165.

THE PRESIDENT: Did you read anything from 1689-PS?

MAJOR WALSH: Just to summarise, sir, the contents of Page 110.

THE PRESIDENT: I see. Now you are offering L -

MAJOR WALSH: L-165, your Honour, Exhibit USA 287.

I refer the Court to the last half of the first paragraph of the translation. This is a Press bulletin issued by the Polish Ministry of Information, dated 15th November, 1942. The Polish Ministry concludes that, upon the basis of the nature of the separate rationing and the amount of food available to Jews in the Warsaw and Cracow ghettos, the system was designed to bring about starvation, and from the quotation I read:-

"In regard to food supplies they are brought under a completely separate system, which is obviously aimed at depriving them of the most elemental necessities of life".

I would now like to discuss annihilation within the ghettos. Justice Jackson in his opening address to the Tribunal made reference to Document 1061-PS, "The Warsaw Ghetto is No More", marked Exhibit USA 275.

This finest example of ornate German craftsmanship, leather bound, profusely illustrated, typed on heavy bond paper, is the almost unbelievable recital of a proud accomplishment by Major General of the Police Strupp, who signed the report with a bold hand. General Strupp in this report first pays tribute to the bravery and heroism of the German forces who participated in the ruthless and merciless action against a helpless, defenceless group of Jews, numbering, to be exact, 56,065, including, of course, the infants and the women. In this document he proceeds to relate the day-by-day account of the ultimate accomplishment of his mission - to destroy and to obliterate the Warsaw Ghetto.

According to this report, the ghetto, which was established in Warsaw in November, 1940, was inhabited by about 400,000 Jews, and prior to the action for the destruction of this ghetto, some 316,000 had already been deported. The Court will note that this report is approximately 75 pages in length, and the prosecution believes that the contents are of such striking evidentiary value that no part should be omitted from the permanent records of the Tribunal, and that the Tribunal should consider the entire report in judging the guilt of these defendants.

The defendants were furnished with several photostatic copies of the document at least 20 days ago, and have had ample time, I am sure, to scrutinise it in detail. If the Court, in the exercise of its judgment, determines that the report may be accepted in toto, the prosecution believes that the reading of a portion of the summary, together with brief excerpts from the daily teletype reports, will suffice for the oral record. I would like the Court to examine it, and I present it to the Court, together with the duplicate original thereof, and ask that the Court rule that the entire document may be accepted.

THE PRESIDENT: Major Walsh, the Court will take that course, provided that the prosecution supplies, as soon as possible, both to the Soviet and to the French members of the Tribunal, copies in Russian and French of the whole document.

MAJOR WALSH: Yes, sir; may I consult with -

THE PRESIDENT: I do not say present immediately, but present as soon as possible.

MAJOR WALSH: Yes.

THE PRESIDENT: You are going to read the passages that you think necessary?

MAJOR WALSH: Yes. From Page 6 of the translation before the Court of Document 1061-PS I would like to read the boastful but none the less vivid account of some of this ruthless action within the Warsaw Ghetto. I quote, second paragraph, Page 6:

"The resistance put up by the Jews and bandits could be broken only by relentlessly using all our forces and energy by day and night. On 23rd April, 1943, the Reich Fuehrer S.S. issued through the Higher S.S. and Police Fuehrer East at Cracow his order to complete the combing out of the Warsaw Ghetto with the greatest severity and relentless tenacity. I therefore decided to destroy the entire Jewish residential area by setting every block on fire, including the blocks of residential buildings near the armament works. One concern after

411

another was systematically evacuated and subsequently destroyed by fire. The Jews then emerged from their hiding places and dug-outs in almost every case. Not infrequently the Jews stayed in the burning buildings until, because of the heat and the fear of being burned alive, they preferred to jump down from the upper stories after having thrown mattresses and other upholstered articles into the street from the burning buildings. With their bones broken they still tried to crawl across the street into blocks of buildings which had not yet been set on fire, or were only partially in flames. Often the Jews changed their hiding places during the night by moving into the ruins of burnt-out buildings, taking refuge there until they were found by our patrols. Their stay in the sewers also ceased to be pleasant after the first week. Frequently from the street we could hear loud voices coming through the sewer shafts. Then the men of the Waffen S. S., the Police, or the Wehrmacht Engineers courageously climbed down the shafts to bring out the Jews and not infrequently they then stumbled over Jews already dead, or were shot at. It was always necessary to use smoke candles to drive out the Jews. Thus one day we opened 183 sewer entrance holes and at a fixed time lowered smoke candles into them, with the result that the bandits fled from what they believed to be gas into the centre of the former ghetto, where they could then be pulled out of the sewer holes there. A great number of Jews who could not be counted were exterminated by blowing up sewers and dug-outs.

The longer the resistance lasted, the tougher the men of the Waffen S.S., Police, and Wehrmacht became. They fulfilled their duty indefatigably in faithful comradeship and stood together as models and examples of soldiers. Their duty hours often lasted from early morning until late at night. At night search patrols, with rags wound around their feet, remained at the heels of the Jews and gave them no respite. Not infrequently they caught and killed Jews who used the night hours for supplementing their stores from abandoned dug-outs and for contacting neighbouring groups or exchanging news with them.

Considering that the greater part of the men of the Waffen S.S. had only been trained for three to four weeks before being assigned to this action, high credit should be given to the pluck, courage and devotion to duty which they showed. It must be stated that the Wehrmacht Engineers, too, executed the blowing up of dug- outs, sewers and concrete buildings with indefatigability and great devotion to duty. Officers and men of the Police, a large part of whom had already been at the front, again excelled by their dashing spirit.

Only through the continuous and untiring work of all involved did we succeed in catching a total of 56,065 Jews whose extermination can be proved. To this should be added the number of Jews who lost their lives in explosions or fires, but whose number could not be ascertained."

THE PRESIDENT: Major Walsh, in the section that you are just upon now, ought you not to read the opening paragraphs of this document, which set out the amount of the losses of the German troops?

MAJOR WALSH: I will do so, Sir. On Page 1 of the translation, I quote.

The title: "The Warsaw Ghetto is No More".

"For the Fuehrer and their country the following fell in the battle for the destruction of Jews and bandits in the former ghetto of Warsaw."

Fifteen names are thereafter listed.

"Furthermore, the Polish Police Sergeant Julian Zielinski, born 13th November, 1891 8th Commissariat, fell on 19th April, 1943, while fulfilling his duty. They gave their utmost, their life. We shall never forget them. The following were wounded."

Then follow the names of 60 Waffen S.S. personnel; 11 watchmen from training camps, probably Lithuanians; 12 Security Police Officers in S.S. units; 5 men of the Polish Police; and 2 regular army personnel, engineers.

Permit me to read some brief excerpts of the daily teletype reports. Page 13 of the translation, from the teletype message of 22nd April, 1943, I read:-

"The result of our setting the block on fire was that during the night those Jews whom we had not been able to find despite all our search operations, left their hide- outs under the roofs, in the cellars, and elsewhere and appeared on the outside of the buildings, trying to escape the flames. Masses of them - entire families - were already aflame and jumped from the windows or tried to let themselves down by means of sheets tied together or the like. Steps had been taken so that these Jews as well as the remaining ones were liquidated at once."

And from Page 28 of the translation, the last part of the first paragraph, I read:-

"When the blocks of buildings mentioned above were destroyed, 120 Jews were caught and numerous Jews were killed when they jumped from the attics to the inner courtyards, trying to escape the flames. Many more Jews perished in the flames or were killed when the dug-outs and sewer entrances were blown up."

And on Page 30, second half of the second paragraph, I read:-

"Not until the blocks of buildings were well aflame and were about to collapse did a further considerable number of Jews emerge, forced to do so by the flames and the smoke. Time and again the Jews tried to escape even through burning buildings. Innumerable Jews whom we saw on the roofs during the conflagration perished in the flames. Others emerged from the upper stories in the last possible moment and were only able to escape death from the flames by jumping down. Today we caught a total of 2,283 Jews of whom 204 were shot; and innumerable Jews were killed in dug-outs and in the flames."

And from Page 34, the second paragraph, I read, beginning the second line:-

"The Jews testify that they emerge at night to get fresh air, since it is unbearable to stay permanently within the dug-outs owing to the long duration of the operation. On the average the raiding parties shoot 30 to 50 Jews each night. From these statements it was to be inferred that a considerable number of Jews are still underground in the ghetto. Today we blew up a concrete building which we had not been able to destroy by fire. In this operation we learned that the blowing up of a building is a very lengthy process and takes an enormous amount of explosives. The best and only method for destroying the Jews therefore still remains the setting of fires".

And from Page 35, the last part of the second paragraph, I read

"Some depositions speak of 3,000 to 4,000 Jews still remaining in underground holes, sewers and dug-outs. The undersigned is resolved not to end the large-scale operation until the last Jew has been exterminated."

And from the teletype message of 15th May, 1943 on Page 44, we gather that the operation is in its last stage. I read the end of the first paragraph on Page 44:-

"A special unit once more searched the last block of buildings which was still intact in the ghetto, and subsequently destroyed it. In the evening the chapel, mortuary, and all other buildings in the Jewish cemetery were blown up or destroyed by fire."

On 24th May, 1943, the final figures have been compiled by Major General Strupp. He reports on Page 45, last paragraph:-

"Of the total of 56,065 caught, about 7,000 were killed in the former ghetto during large-scale operation. 6,929 Jews were killed by transporting them to T. II" - which we believe to be Trablinka [sic], Camp No. 2, which will later be referred to - "the sum total of Jews killed is therefore 13,929. Beyond the number Of 56,065 an estimated number of 5,000 to 6,000 Jews were killed by being blown up or by perishing in the flames."

The Court has noted within the report 1061-PS a number of photographs, and with the Court's permission I should like to show a few of these photographs, still pictures, on the screen, unless the Court believes that reference to the original text will be sufficient for the Court's purpose.

THE PRESIDENT: No, if you want to put them on the screen you may do so. Perhaps it would be convenient to adjourn now and you can put them on the screen afterwards.

[A recess was taken.]

[Still pictures were projected on the screen in the courtroom.]

MAJOR WALSH: This first picture is shown on Page 27 of the photographs in Document 1061-PS. It is entitled "The Destruction of a Block of Buildings". The Court will recall those portions of the teletype messages that referred to the setting of fires for the purpose of driving out the Jews. This picture, taken from the record, portrays such a scene.

This picture is from Page 21 of the photographs contained in the exhibit, and the caption is "Smoking out of the Jews and Bandits". Excerpts from the teletype messages read in the record relate to the use of smoke as a means of forcing Jews out of the hiding places.

This picture is from Page 36 of the photographs in the exhibit and it is called "Fighting a Nest of Resistance". It is obviously a picture of an explosive blast being used to destroy one of the buildings, and the Court may recall the message of 7th May, 1943, that related to the blowing up of buildings as a lengthy process requiring an enormous amount of explosive. The same message reported that the best method for destroying the Jews was the setting of fires.

This picture is taken from Page 36 of the photographs. The Court's attention is invited to the figure of a man in mid- air who appears in the picture about half-way between the centre and the upper right-hand corner. He has jumped from one of the upper floors of the burning building. A close examination of this picture by the Court, in the original photograph, will disclose other figures in the upper floor windows, who apparently are about to follow him. The teletype message of 22nd April reported that entire families jumped from burning buildings and were liquidated at once.

This picture is from Page 39 of the photographs. It is entitled "The Leader of the Large-Scale Action". The Nazi- appointed commander of this action was S.S. Major General Strupp, who probably is the central figure. I cannot refrain from commenting at this point on the smiling faces of the group shown there, in the midst of the violence and destruction.

THE PRESIDENT: Are you passing from that document now?

MAJOR WALSH: Yes, sir.

THE PRESIDENT: Will you tell the Tribunal where the document was found?

MAJOR WALSH: Where the document itself was found?

THE PRESIDENT: Found, yes.

MAJOR WALSH: It is a captured document, sir. I have not the history, but I shall be very pleased to submit the background and history to the Court at the beginning of the afternoon session, sir.

THE PRESIDENT: The Tribunal, I think, would like to know where it was found and to whom it was submitted.

MAJOR WALSH: I have it. I believe that is contained in the document. The teletype messages, sir, that are contained in this exhibit, were all addressed to the Higher S.S. and Police Fuehrer, S.S. Obergruppenfeuhrer and General of the Police Kruger or his deputy.

It was not always necessary, or perhaps desirable, to first place the Jews within the ghettos to effect the elimination. In the Baltic States a more direct course of action was followed. I refer to Document L-180, now in evidence, which is Exhibit USA 276. This is a report by S.S. Brigade Fuehrer Stahlecker to Himmler, dated 15th October, 1941, entitled "Action Group A", found in Himmler's private files. He reported that 135,567 persons, nearly all Jews, were murdered in accordance with basic orders directing the complete annihilation of the Jews. This voluminous document provides me with the following statement by the same S.S. Brigade Fuehrer, and from the translation at the bottom of Page 6, the second sentence of the last paragraph, I read:-

> "To our surprise it was not easy, at first, to set in motion an extensive pogrom against the Jews. Klimatis, the leader of the partisan unit, mentioned above, who was used for this purpose primarily, succeeded in starting a pogrom on the basis of advice given to him by a small advanced detachment acting in Kowne, and in such a way that no German order or German instigation was noticed from the outside. During the first pogrom in the night from 25th to 26th June the Lithuanian partisans did away with more than 1,500 Jews, setting fire to several synagogues or destroying them by other means and burning down a Jewish dwelling district consisting of about 60 houses. During the following nights about 2,300 Jews were made harmless in a similar way..."

From the last part of Paragraph 3, Page 7, I read:-

> "It was possible, though, through similar influences on the Latvian auxiliary, to set in motion a pogrom against the Jews also in Riga. During this pogrom all synagogues were destroyed and about 400 Jews

were killed."

Nazi ingenuity reached a new high mark with the construction and operation of the gas van as a means of mass annihilation of the Jews. A description of these vehicles of horror and death, and the operation of them is fully set forth in captured top secret document dated 16th May, 1942, addressed to S.S. Obersturmbannfuehrer Rauff, 8 Prince Albrecht- strasse, Berlin, from Dr. Becker, S.S. Untersturmfuehrer. I offer this Document 501-PS as Exhibit USA 288. I quote:-

> "The overhauling of vans by groups D and C is finished. While the vans in the first series can also be put into action if the weather is not too bad, the vans of the second series (Saurer) stop completely in rainy weather. If it has rained for instance for only one half hour, the van cannot be used, because it simply skids away. It can only be used in absolutely dry weather. It is now merely a question of whether the van can be used only when it stands at the place of execution. First, the van has to be brought to that place, which is possible only in good weather. The place of execution is usually 10 to 15 Km. away from the highway and is difficult of access because of its location; in damp or wet weather it is not accessible at all. If the persons to be executed are driven or led to that place, then they realise immediately what is going on and get restless, which is to be avoided as far as possible. There is only one way left; to load them at the collecting point and to drive them to the spot.
>
> I ordered the vans of group D to be camouflaged as house- trailers by putting one set of window shutters on each side of the small van and two on each side of the larger vans, such as one often sees on farmhouses in the country. The vans became so well known that not only the authorities but also the civilian population called the van 'death van' as soon as one of the vehicles appeared. It is my opinion the van cannot be kept secret for any length of time, not even camouflaged."

And then I read the fourth paragraph on this page:-

> "Because of the rough terrain and the indescribable road and highway conditions, the caulkings and rivets loosen in the course of time. I was asked if in such cases the vans should not be brought to Berlin for repairs. Transportation to Berlin would be much too expensive and would demand too much fuel. In order to save these expenses I ordered them to have smaller leaks soldered and, if that should no longer be possible, to notify Berlin immediately by radio, that Pol Nr . is out of order. Besides that I ordered that during application of gas all the men were to be kept as far away from the vans as possible, so that they should not suffer damage to their health by the gas which eventually would escape. I should like to take this opportunity to bring the following to your attention: after the application of gas several commands have bad the unloading done by their own men. I brought to the attention of the commander of these S.K. concerned the immense psychological injuries, and damage to their health which that work can have for those men, even if not immediately, at least later on. The men complained to me about headaches which appeared after each unloading. Nevertheless they do not want to change the orders,

because they are afraid prisoners called for that work could use an opportune moment to flee. To protect the men from those risks, I request orders be issued accordingly.

The application of gas is not usually undertaken correctly. In order to come to an end as fast as possible, the driver presses the accelerator to the fullest extent. By doing that the persons to be executed suffer death from suffocation, and not death by dozing off as was planned. My directions now have proved that by correct adjustment of the levers death comes faster and the prisoners fall asleep peacefully. Distorted faces and excretions, such as could be seen before, are no longer noticed.

Today I shall continue my journey to group B, where I can be reached with further news.

Signed Doctor Becker, S.S. Untersturmfuehrer."

On Page 3 in Document 501-PS we find a letter signed by Hauptsturmfuehrer Truehe on the subject of S-vans, addressed to the Reich Security Main Office, Room 2-D-3-A, Berlin, marked "Top Secret". This letter establishes that the vans were used for the annihilation of the Jews. I read this "Top Secret" message, subject: "S-vans".

"A transport of Jews, which has to be treated in a special way, arrives weekly at the office of the commandant of the Security Police and the Security Service of White Ruthenia.

The three S-vans which are there are not sufficient for that purpose. I request assignment of another S-van (5 tons). At the same time I request the shipment of 20 gas hoses for the three S-vans on hand (two Diamond, one Saurer), since the ones we have are leaky already.

Signed: the Commandant of the Security Police and the Security Service, Ostland."

It would appear from the documentary evidence that a certain amount of discord existed between the officials of the German Government as to the proper means and methods used in connection with the programme of extermination. A secret report dated 18th June, 1943, addressed to defendant Rosenberg, complained that 5,000 Jews killed by the police and S.S. might have been used for forced labour, and chided them for failing to bury the bodies of those liquidated. I offer in evidence this file, Document R-135, Exhibit USA 289

THE PRESIDENT: Is it in these volumes, Major Walsh?

MAJOR WALSH: I think, sir, that will be found in the assembly of the document book in our case that has been placed in front of R-124.

I quote from the letter referred to addressed to the Reich Minister for the Occupied Eastern Territories, the first paragraph of the translation.

"The fact that Jews receive special treatment requires no further discussion. However, it appears hardly believable that this was done in the way described in the report of the General Commissioner of 1st June, 1943. Imagine only that these occurrences might become known to the other side and be exploited by them. Most likely such propaganda would have no effect, only because people who hear and read about it simply would not be ready to believe it."

The last part of Paragraph 3 on this page reads:

"To lock men, women and children into barns and to set fire to them does not appear to be a suitable method for combating bands, even if it is desired to exterminate the population. This method is not worthy of the German cause and hurts our reputation severely."

Gunther, the prison warden at Minsk, in a letter dated 31st May, 1943, addressed to the General Commissioner for White Ruthenia, subject: "Action Against Jews", was critical by implication. With the Court's permission I would like to read this entire letter, part of Document R-135, Page 5, subject: "Action Against Jews".

"On 13th April, 1943, the former German dentist Ernst Israel Tichauer and his wife, Elisa Sara Tichauer, nee Rosenthal, were committed to the court prison by the Security Service. Since that time all German and Russian Jews who were turned over to us had their golden bridgework, crowns, and fillings pulled or broken out. This happens always one to two hours before the respective action. Since 13th April, 1943, 516 German and Russian Jews have been finished off. On the basis of a definite investigation gold was taken in only two actions - on 14th April, 1943, from 172, and on 27th April, 1943, from 164 Jews. About 50 per cent. of the Jews had gold teeth, bridgework, or fillings. Hauptscharfuehrer Rube of the Security Service was always personally present, and he took the gold along, too.

Before 13th April, 1943, this was not done. Signed Gunther, Prison Warden."

This letter was forwarded to the defendant Rosenberg as Reich Minister for the Occupied Eastern Territories on 1st June, 1943. I will read the covering letter, part of Document R-135, Page 4, to the Reich Minister of the Occupied Eastern Territories, Berlin, through the Reich Commissioner for the Eastland, Riga.

Subject: "Actions Against Jews in the Prison of Minsk."

"The enclosed official report from the warden of the prison in Minsk is submitted to the Reich Minister and the Reich Commissar for Information. Signed, The General Commissar in Minsk."

THE PRESIDENT: Does "respective action", as indicated in the letter dated 31st May, 1943, mean execution?

MAJOR WALSH: Yes, sir; we interpret it as such. The Court will recall that the ridding of the Jews via gas vans ties in very closely with the second letter of the transport of Jews arriving for that purpose.

THE PRESIDENT: Was this document found in Rosenberg's file?

MAJOR WALSH: I am so informed, sir. A further complaint is contained in a secret letter addressed to the General of the Infantry Thomas, Chief of the Industrial Armament Department, dated 2nd December, 1941. It might be noted with interest that the apprehensive writer of this letter stated that he did not forward the communication through official channels. I offer in evidence captured Document 3257-PS, and I quote from the first paragraph, - this is Exhibit USA 290.

"For the personal information of the Chief of the Industrial Armament Department I am forwarding a complete account of the present situation in the Reichskommissariat Ukraine in which the difficulties and tensions encountered so far, and the problems which give rise to serious anxiety, are stated with unmistakable clarity.

I have intentionally refrained from submitting such a report through official channels or from making it known to other departments interested in it because I do not expect any results that way, but on the contrary, I am apprehensive that the difficulties and tensions and also the divergent opinions might only be increased because of the peculiarity of the situation."

"Jewish problem" (Paragraph 7, Page 1):-

"Regulation of the Jewish question in the Ukraine was a difficult problem because the Jews constituted a large part of the urban population. We therefore have to deal - just as in the Government General - with a mass problem of policy concerning the population. Many cities had a percentage of Jews exceeding 50 per cent. Only the rich Jews had fled from the German troops. The majority of Jews remained under German administration. The latter found the problem more complicated through the fact that these Jews represented almost the entire trade and even a part of the manpower in small and medium industries, besides businesses, which had in part become superfluous as a direct or indirect result of the war. The elimination therefore necessarily had far-reaching economic consequences and even direct consequences for the armament industry (production for supplying the troops)."

Paragraph 1 on Page 2:

"The attitude of the Jewish population was anxiously obliging from the beginning. They tried to avoid everything that might displease the German administration. That they hated the German administration and army inwardly, goes without saying and cannot be surprising. However, there is no proof that Jewry as a whole or even to a greater part was implicated in acts of sabotage. Naturally there were some terrorists or saboteurs among them, just as among the Ukrainians. But it cannot be said that the Jews, as such, represented a danger to the German Armed Forces. The output produced by Jews who, of course, were prompted by nothing but the feeling of fear, was satisfactory to the troops and the German administration.

The Jewish population remained temporarily unmolested shortly after the fighting. Only weeks, sometimes months later, specially detached formations of the police executed a planned shooting of Jews. This action as a rule proceeded from East to West. It was done entirely in public with the use of the Ukrainian militia, and, unfortunately, in many instances also with members of the Armed Forces taking part voluntarily. The way these actions, which included old men, women, and children of all ages, were carried out was horrible. The great masses executed made this action more gigantic than any similar measure taken so far in the Soviet Union. So far about 150,000 to 200,000 Jews may have been executed in the part of the Ukraine belonging to the Reichskommissariat; no consideration was given to the interests of economy.

Summarising, it can be said that the kind of solution of the Jewish problem applied to the Ukraine, which obviously was based on ideological theories as a matter of principle, had the following results:

(a) Elimination of a part of partly superfluous caters in the cities.

(b) Elimination of a part of the population which undoubtedly hated us.

(c) Elimination of badly needed tradesmen who were in many instances indispensable even in the interests of the Armed Forces.

(d) Consequences as to foreign policy propaganda which are obvious.

(e) Bad effect on the troops which in any case get indirect contact with the execution.

(f) Brutalising effect on the formations which carry out the execution regular police."

Lest the Court be persuaded to the belief that these conditions related existed only in the East, I invite attention to the official Netherlands Government report by the Commissioner for Repatriation as indicative of the treatment of the Jews in the West.

This document is a recital of the German measures taken in the Netherlands against the Dutch Jews. The decrees, the anti-Semitic demonstrations, the burning of synagogues, the purging of Jews from the economic life of their country, the food restrictions against them, forced labour, concentration camp confinement, deportation, and death - all follow the same pattern that was effected throughout Nazi-occupied Europe.

I now refer to Document 1726-PS, Exhibit USA 195, already in evidence. It is not intended to read this document in evidence, but it is deemed important to invite the Court's attention to that portion of the report relating to the deportation of Dutch Jews, shown on Page 5 of the translation. There the Court will note that full Jews being liable to deportation number 140,000, The Court will also note that the total number of deportees was 117,000, representing more than 83 per cent. of all the Jews in the Netherlands. Of these 115,000 were deported to Poland for slave labour, according to the Netherlands report, and after departure all trace of them was lost. Regardless of victory or defeat to Germany, the Jew was doomed. It was the expressed intent of the Nazi State that, whatever the German fate might be, the Jew would not survive.

I offer in evidence Document L-53, stamped "Top Secret", Exhibit USA 291. This message is from the Commandant of the Sipo and S.D. for the Radom District, addressed to S.S. Hauptsturmfuehrer Thiel on the subject: "Clearance of Prisons". I read the body of this message.

"I again stress the fact that the number of inmates of the Sipo and S.D. prisons must be kept as low as possible. In the present situation particularly those suspects handed over by the Civil Police, need only be subjected to a short, formal interrogation, provided there are no serious grounds for suspicion. They are then to be sent by the quickest route to a concentration camp, should no court martial proceeding be necessary or should there be no question of discharge. Please keep the number of discharges very low. Should the situation at the front necessitate it, early preparations are to be made for the total clearance of prisons. Should the situation develop suddenly in such a way that it is impossible to evacuate the prisoners, the prison inmates are to be liquidated and their bodies disposed of as far as possible (burning, blowing up the building, etc.). If necessary, Jews still employed in the armament industry or on other work are to be dealt with in the same way.

The liberation of prisoners or Jews by the enemy, be it the W.B. or the Red Army, must be avoided under all circumstances, nor may they fall into their hands alive."

THE PRESIDENT: What is the W.B.?

MAJOR WALSH: I have inquired about the W.B., your Honour, from several sources and have not found an understanding or a statement of it. Perhaps before the afternoon session I may be able to enlighten the Court. I have not yet been able to find out.

THE PRESIDENT: Where was the document found?

MAJOR WALSH: It is a captured document, sir.

THE PRESIDENT: Does it relate to prisoners of war, did you say?

MAJOR WALSH: No, sir; though it includes, of course, prisoners of war as well as all Jews. The history of the document, sir, I will try to gather for the Court's information.

THE PRESIDENT: Yes. Did you tell us what the Sipo were ?

MAJOR WALSH: Yes, sir; I furnished the Court with that information, they are the Security Police, sir. This presentation, if the Court please, would be incomplete without including a reference to the concentration camps in so far as they relate to the hundreds of thousands - millions - of Jews who died by mass shooting, gas, poison, starvation, and other means. The subject of concentration camps and all its horrors was shown to this Tribunal not only in the motion picture film but by the most able presentation of Mr. Dodd yesterday, and it is not intended, at this time, to refer to the camps except in so far as they relate to the part they played in the annihilation of the Jewish people. For example, in the Camp Auschwitz, during July, 1944, Jews were killed at the rate of 12,000 daily. This information is contained in Document L-161, Exhibit USA 292. The Document L-161 is an official Polish report on Auschwitz Concentration Camp. It is dated 31st May, 1945. I have taken a short excerpt from this report on the original marked -

THE PRESIDENT: I think you made a mistake, did you not? It is not a Polish report; it is a British report.

MAJOR WALSH: I understand, sir, it was compiled originally by the Polish Government and perhaps distributed from London.

THE PRESIDENT: I see. Very well.

MAJOR WALSH: I quote:-

"During July, 1944, they were being liquidated at the rate of 12,000 Hungarian Jews daily, and, as the crematorium could not deal with such numbers, many bodies were thrown into large pits and covered with quicklime."

I offer in evidence Document 3311-PS, Exhibit USA 293. This is an official Polish Government Commission report on the investigation of German crimes in Poland. The document described the concentration camp at Treblinka, and from Page 1, Paragraphs 3 and 4, I read as follows:-

"In March, 1942, the Germans began to erect another camp, Treblinka B, in the neighbourhood of Treblinka A, intended to become a place of torment for Jews.

The erection of this camp was closely connected with the German plans aimed at the complete destruction of the Jewish population in Poland which necessitated the creation of machinery by means of which the Polish Jews could be killed in large numbers. Late in April, 1942, the erection of the first chambers, in which these general massacres were to be performed by means of steam, was finished. Somewhat later, the erection of the real death building, which contained ten death chambers, was finished. It was opened for wholesale murders in early autumn 1942."

And on Page 3 of this report, beginning with the second paragraph, the Polish Commission describes graphically the procedure for the extermination within the camp:-

"The average number of Jews dealt with at the Camp in the summer of 1942 was about two railway transports daily, but there were days of much higher efficiency. From autumn, 1942, this number fell off.

After unloading in the siding, all victims were assembled in one place, where men were separated from women and children. In the first days of the existence of the camp the victims were made to believe that after a short stay in the camp, necessary for bathing and disinfection, they would be sent farther East, for work. Explanations of this sort were given by S.S. men who assisted at the unloading of the transports, and further explanations could be read in notices stuck up on the walls of the barracks. But later, when more transports had to be dealt with, the Germans dropped all pretences and only tried to accelerate the procedure.

All victims had to strip off their clothes and shoes, which were collected afterwards, whereupon all of them, women and children first, were driven into the death chambers. Those too slow or too weak to move quickly were driven in by rifle butts, by whipping and kicking, often by Sauer himself. Many slipped and fell; the next victims pressed forward and stumbled over them. Small children were simply thrown inside. After being filled up to capacity, the chambers were hermetically closed and steam was let in. In a few minutes all was over. The Jewish menial workers had to remove the bodies from the platform and to bury them in mass graves. By and by, as new transports arrived, the cemetery grew, extending in the Eastern direction.

From reports received it may be assumed that several hundred thousand Jews were exterminated in Treblinka."

I now offer in evidence the document identified by L-22, Exhibit USA 294. This is an official United States Government report issued by the Executive Office of the President of the United States, War Refugee Board, on the German camps at Auschwitz and Birkenau, dated 1944. On Page 33 of this report is set forth the number of Jews gassed in Birkenau in the two-year period between April, 1942 and April, 1944. I have been assured that the figure printed in this report is not a typographical error. The number shown is 1,765,000.

I would now like to turn to the German book-keeping and statistics for enlightenment on the extermination of Jews in Poland. Referring again to the diary of Hans Frank, already in evidence, Document 2233-PS, Exhibit USA 231, I read briefly from the beginning of the fourth paragraph on Page 1:-

"For us the Jews also represent extraordinarily malignant gluttons. We have now approximately 2,500,000 of them in the Government General -"

THE PRESIDENT: Major Walsh, you have read this already yourself.

MAJOR WALSH: Yes, Sir, that is true. I just want to make reference to it again, Sir, for comparison with other figures.

THE PRESIDENT: Very well.

MAJOR WALSH: " ... perhaps with the Jewish mixtures, and everything that goes with it, 3,500,000 Jews."

Now this figure, if the Court please, was as of 16th December, 1941 I now wish to turn to 25th January, 1944, three years and one month later, and make reference to another excerpt from Frank's diary, Document 2233-PS, loose- leaf volume, Exhibit USA 295. This volume covers the period from 1st January, 1944 to 28th February, 1944, and Page 5 of the original reads:-

"At the present time we still have in the Government General perhaps 100,000 Jews."

In this period of three years, according to the records of the then Governor General of Occupied Poland, between 2,400,000 and 3,400,000 Jews had been eliminated.

The prosecution could offer this Tribunal a wealth of evidence on the total number of Jews who died by Nazi hands, but it is believed that cumulative evidence would not vary the guilt of these defendants.

I do wish, however, to offer one document, a statement, to establish the deaths of 4,000,000 Jews in camps and the deaths Of 2,000,000 Jews at the hands of the State Police in the East, making a total of 6,000,000, Document 2738-PS, Exhibit USA 296. This is a statement - Adolph Eichmann, Chief of the Jewish Section of the Gestapo, is the source of the figures quoted - made by Dr. Wilhelm Hottl, Deputy Group Leader of the Foreign Section of the Security Section, Amt. VI of the R.S.H.A. Dr. Wilhelm Hottl, in affidavit form, made the following statement, and I quote from Page 2:-

"Approximately 4,000,000 Jews had been killed in the various concentration camps, while an additional 2,000,000 met death in other ways, the major part of whom were shot by operational squads of the Security Police during the campaign against Russia."

May I, in conclusion, emphasise that the captured documents in evidence are, almost without exception, from the official sources of the Nazi Party.

THE PRESIDENT: You only read that one statement, but where does the person who made the affidavits get his information from?

MAJOR WALSH: I shall be pleased to read that in there, sir. I made the statement that Eichmann was the source of the information given to Dr. Wilhelm Hottl, one of his assistants, and on Page 1 it says:-

"According to my knowledge Eichmann was at that time the leader of the Jewish Section of the Gestapo, and in addition he had been ordered by Himmler to get hold of the Jews in all the European countries and to transport them to Germany. Eichmann was then very much impressed with the fact that Roumania had withdrawn from the war in those days. Moreover, he had come to me to get information about the military situation which I received daily from the Hungarian Ministry of War and from the Commander of the Waffen S.S. in

Hungary. He expressed his conviction that Germany had lost the war and that he personally had no further chance. He knew that he would be considered one of the main war criminals by the United Nations, since he had millions of Jewish lives on his conscience. I asked him how many that was, to which he answered that, although the number was a great Reich secret, he would tell me since I, as an historian, would be interested, and that he would probably not return anyhow from his command in Roumania. He had, shortly before that, made a report to Himmler, as the latter wanted to know the exact number of Jews who had been killed."

It was on that basis of this information, sir, that I read the following quotation -

THE PRESIDENT: The Tribunal will adjourn now.

[A recess was taken until 1400 hours.]

THE PRESIDENT: The motion that was made this morning on behalf of the defendant Kaltenbrunner is denied, and the affidavit is admitted and will not be stricken from the record. But the Tribunal wished me to say that it is open to the defendants' counsel, in accordance with the Charter and the Rules, to make a motion, in writing, if they wish to do so, for the attendance of Pfaffenberger for cross- examination and to state in that motion the reasons therefor.

DR. KURT KAUFFMANN (Counsel for defendant Kaltenbrunner): I am here in a similar position. The case in question is that of Pfaffenberger, and I beg that the evidence given by Dr. Hottl, which was incorporated into the record this morning, be stricken from the record for two reasons. As far as I know Dr. Hottl is here in Nuremberg.

THE PRESIDENT: One minute. Do you understand that the Tribunal has just denied the motion that you made this morning?

DR. KAUFFMANN: Yes, I understood that correctly.

THE PRESIDENT: What is your motion now?

DR. KAUFFMANN: I should like to ask that the evidence given by Dr. Hottl be stricken from the record for a reason - and several other reasons depend on it - which is different from the one I gave this morning in the Pfaffenberger case.

As can be seen from the affidavit, Dr. Hottl was interrogated on 26th November; that is but three weeks ago. Moreover, I heard that Dr. Hottl is kept under arrest here in Nuremberg. No delay would result if we ask that this witness be brought before the Court.

This man held a significant position in the S.S. and, therefore, I suggested some time ago, in writing, that he be called as a witness. I am convinced that there is a large amount of important evidence which he can reveal to the Court. Dr. Hottl's disposition is infinitely important. The death of millions of people is involved. His evidence is based in the greater part on conclusions drawn by him, and he knew the facts described only from hearsay. I am of the opinion that the case will look entirely different and request that the Tribunal will not direct me later on, after weeks or months, to bring this witness into Court.

MAJOR WALSH: If the Court please: Dr. Hottl's affidavit, Document 2738-PS, was read in part into the record this morning for the sole purpose of showing the approximate number of Jews, according to his estimates that had met death at the hands of the German State. No other portion of his testimony was referred to and the evidence offered was for the sole purpose of establishing his estimate of the number. His position in the Party and in the State, as well as the position of Adolf Eichmann, the source of his information, was also stated for the record.

I believe that Dr. Hottl, if he is desired for any other purpose by the defence, may be called by the defence, but the prosecution had no other purpose in utilising his evidence.

THE PRESIDENT: Do you wish to add anything more?

MAJOR WALSH: That is all I have, sir.

THE PRESIDENT: The Tribunal makes the same ruling in this case as in the case of Pfaffenberger, namely, that the affidavit is admitted in evidence but that it is open to defendants' counsel to make a motion, in writing, for the attendance of the witness for cross-examination and to state in that motion the reasons for it.

MAJOR WALSH: During the morning session the Court requested certain information concerning documents that had been offered and accepted in evidence. I refer to Document 1061- PS, the report "The Warsaw Ghetto Is No More". This report, I am told, was prepared for presentation at a meeting of the S.S. Police Leaders to be held on 18th May, 1943. This is indicated on Page 45 of the translation before the Court.

This document was captured by the Seventh United States Army and delivered by them to the G-2 of the United States Forces in the European theatre. In turn they were delivered to Colonel Storey of the United States Prosecutors' Staff some months ago.

THE PRESIDENT: Major Walsh, I think the Tribunal also wished to know whether you could tell us to whom the report had been made?

MAJOR WALSH: The report, sir, according to the teletypes, the daily teletypes, sir, were addressed to the higher S.S. and Police Fuehrer, S.S. Obergruppenfuehrer and General of the Police Kruger, or his deputy.

THE PRESIDENT: Thank you.

MAJOR WALSH: The Court further inquired about Document L-53 and I have obtained some information concerning this document. This document was captured by T-Force of the Counter Intelligence Corps Detachment No. 220, found among the German records at Weimar, Germany, some time prior to 10th May, 1945.

The Court further inquired concerning this document the meaning of the letters "W.B." I regret that I have been unable to obtain definite information as to the meaning of "W.B." but it has been suggested to me that it might mean West-Bund or Western Ally because it is used in connection with the capture or the destruction of all prisoners, before capture by either the W.B. or the Red Armies, and I presume that it may mean West-Bund.

The slaughter of the Jews in Europe cannot be expressed in figures alone, for the impact of this slaughter is even more tragic to the future of the Jewish people and mankind. Ancient Jewish communities with their own rich, spiritual, cultural and economic life, bound up for centuries with the life of the nations in which they flourished, have been completely obliterated. The contribution of the Jewish people to civilisation, the arts, the sciences, industry and culture, need not, I am sure, be elaborated before this Tribunal. Their destruction, carried out continuously, deliberately, intentionally and methodically by the Nazis, represents a loss to civilisation of special qualities and abilities that cannot possibly be restored.

I have not attempted to recount the multitudinous and diabolical crimes committed against the Jewish people by the State which these defendants ruled, because, with sober regard for contemporary and historical truth, a detailed description of some of these crimes would transcend the utmost resources of the human faculty of expression. The mind already recoils and shrinks from the acceptance of the incredible facts already related. Rather is it my purpose to elucidate the pattern, the successful and successive stages, the sequence and concurrence of the crimes committed, the predetermined means to a preordained end.

Yet, these cold, stark, brutal facts and figures, drawn largely from the defendants' own sources, and submitted in evidence before this Tribunal defy rebuttal.

From conception to execution, from Party Programme Of 1920 to the gloating declarations of Himmler and defendant Frank in 1943 and 1944, the annihilation of the Jewish people in Europe was man-made - made by the very men sitting in the defendants' box, brought to judgment before this Tribunal.

Before closing, may I acknowledge with appreciation the untiring services of that group of the Staff of the United States Prosecution, through whose painstaking search, analysis and study, this presentation of evidence was made possible, Captain Seymour Krieger, Lt. Brady Bryson, Lt. Frederick Felton, Sgt. Isaac Stone and Mr. Hans Nathan.

COLONEL STOREY: If the Tribunal please, the next presentation, concerning Germanisation and spoliation in occupied countries, will be presented by Captain Sam Harris.

CAPTAIN SAM HARRIS: May the Tribunal please. Documents relating to the Nazi programme of Germanisation and Spoliation have been assembled in a document book bearing the letter "U". These document books are now being distributed for the use of the members of the Tribunal. I ask your Honours to note that the tabs on the side of the document book are numbered 1 to 30. The index sheet at the front of the book keys these numbers to the EC and PS numbers.

For your Honours' convenience we have also numbered the pages of each exhibit in pencil at the upper right-hand corner.

The documents which we shall introduce were collected by Lt. Kenyon, who sits at my right, and by Doctors Derenberg and Jacoby. Without their untiring efforts, this presentation would not have been possible.

Evidence has already been introduced by Mr. Alderman to prove that the defendants conspired to wage aggressive war. It has also been proved that the desire for "Lebensraum" was one of the chief forces motivating the conspirators to plan, launch and wage their wars of aggression. We propose, at this time, to present evidence disclosing what the conspirators intended to do with conquered territories, called by them "Lebensraum", after they had succeeded in overpowering the victims of their aggressions.

We have broadly divided this subject into two categories; Germanisation and spoliation. When we speak of plans to Germanise, we mean plans to assimilate conquered territories politically, culturally, socially and economically into the German Reich. Germanisation, we shall demonstrate, meant the obliteration of the former national character of the conquered territories and the extermination of all elements which could not be reconciled with the Nazi ideology. By spoliation, we mean the plunder of public and private property and, in general, the exploitation of the people and natural resources of occupied countries.

We propose, with the permission of your Honours, to introduce at this time, in all, 30 documents. These documents lay bare some of the secret plans of the conspirators, to Germanise, to plunder, to despoil, and, to destroy. They do not, of course, tell the whole story of all the conspirators' plans in this field. In some instances proof of the plan is derived from the acts committed by the conspirators. But these few documents are particularly illuminating with respect to their plans for Poland, Czechoslovakia and Russia, and they indicate the outlines of carefully conceived plans for the rest of Europe. Others who follow will fill in this outline by showing a series of outrages committed on so vast a scale that no doubts will exist that they were committed according to plan.

Poland was, in a sense, the testing ground for the conspirators' theories upon "Lebensraum", and I turn to that country first.

The four Western provinces of Poland were purportedly incorporated into Germany by an order of 8th October, 1939. This order, which was signed by Hitler, Lammers and defendants Goering, Frick and Hess, is set forth in Reichsgesetzblatt, 1939, Part 1, Page 2042, and we ask the Tribunal to take judicial notice thereof. These areas of Poland are frequently referred to in correspondence between the conspirators as "incorporated Eastern territories". The remainder of Poland which was seized by the Nazi invaders was established as the Government General of Poland by an order of Hitler, dated 12th October, 1939. By that same order defendant Hans Frank was named Governor General of the newly created Government General, and defendant Seyss- Inquart was named Deputy Governor General. This order is set forth in Reichsgesetzblatt, 1939, Part 1, Page 2077, and we ask the Tribunal also to take judicial notice of it.

The plans with respect to Poland were rather complicated and I believe that the significance of specific items of proof may be more readily apparent if, in advance of the introduction of documents, I am permitted briefly to indicate the broad pattern of those plans.

We submit that the documents we are about to introduce on Poland show the following:-

First, the conspirators specifically planned to exploit the people and material resources of the Government General of Poland in order to strengthen the Nazi war machine, to impoverish the Government General, and to reduce it to a vassal State. At a later stage plans were formulated for creating islands of German settlements in the more fertile regions of the Government General, in order to engulf the native Polish population and accelerate the process of Germanisation.

Secondly, the incorporated area of Poland, which was deemed to be a part of the German Reich, was to be ruthlessly Germanised. To that end, the conspirators planned:

(a) To permit the retention of the productive facilities in the incorporated area, all, of which, of course, would be dedicated to the Nazi war machine.

(b) They planned to deport to the Government General many

hundreds of thousands of Jews, members of the Polish intelligentsia, and other non-compliant elements. We shall show that the Jews who, were deported to the Government General were doomed to speedy annihilation. Moreover, since the conspirators felt that members of the Polish intelligentsia could not be Germanised and might serve as a centre of resistance against their New Order, they too were to be eliminated.

(c) They planned to deport all able-bodied Polish workers to Germany for work in the Nazi war machine. This served the two-fold purpose of helping to satisfy the labour requirements of the Nazi war machine and of preventing the propagation of a new generation of Poles. Mr. Dodd has already produced abundant proof on this topic, and I shall do no more than refer to it.

(d) They planned to mould all persons in the incorporated area who were deemed to possess German blood into German subjects, who would religiously adhere to the principles of National Socialism. To that end, the conspirators set up an elaborate racial register. Those who resisted or refused to co-operate in this programme were sent to concentration camps.

(e) They planned to bring thousands of German subjects into the incorporated area for purposes of settlement. Finally, they planned to confiscate the property - particularly the farms - of the Poles, the Jews and all dissident elements. The confiscation of the property of Jews was part of the conspirators' larger programme of extermination of the Jews. Confiscation likewise served three additional purposes: (1) it provided land for the new German settlers and enabled the conspirators to reward their adherents; (2) dispossessed Polish property owners would be shipped to Germany for work in the production of implements of war; and (3) by the separation of Polish farmers from their wives furthered the plan to prevent the growth of a new generation of Poles.

We turn now to the specific items of proof.

I first offer in evidence Document EC 344-16, which is Exhibit USA 297. This document is a report of an interview with defendant Frank on 3rd October, 1939, and was found among the files of the O.K.W., which were assembled in bulk at the Fechenheim Document Centre. This particular document was included in a large report prepared in the O.K.W. by one Captain Varain at the direction of General Thomas, then Chief of the Military Economic Staff of the O.K.W. I quote from the first 19 lines of Page 3 of the English text. The German text appears on Page 29, Lines 25-36 and Page 30, Lines 1-6. The report states, and I quote:-

"In the first interview which the chief of the Central Division and the liaison officer between the Armament Department Upper East and the Chief Administrative Officer (subsequently called Governor General) had with Minister Frank on 3rd October, 1939, in Posen, Frank explained the directive and the economic and political responsibilities which had been conferred upon him by the Fuehrer and according to which he intended to administer Poland. According to these directives, Poland can only be administered by utilising the country through means of ruthless exploitation; deportation of all supplies, raw materials, machines, factory installations, etc., which are important for the German war economy; availability of all workers for work within Germany; reduction of the entire Polish economy to the absolute minimum necessary for the bare existence of the population; and the closing of all educational institutions, especially technical schools and colleges in order to prevent the growth of the new Polish intelligentsia. Poland, defendant Frank stated (and this is an exact quotation), 'Poland shall be treated as a colony; the Poles shall be the slaves of the Greater German World Empire.'"

I should like also to quote from the last six lines of the English text. In the German text it is Lines 18 to 23 of Page 30.

Defendant Frank further stated:

"By destroying Polish industry, its subsequent reconstruction after the war would become more difficult, if not impossible, so that Poland would be reduced to its proper position as an agrarian country which would have to depend upon Germany for the importation of industrial products."

As further proof of the defendants' plan to plunder and despoil the Government General of Poland, I next offer in evidence Document EC-410, which is Exhibit USA 298. In addition to the proof of the defendants' plans to plunder and despoil the Government General, this document demonstrates the difference in treatment which the conspirators planned for the incorporated area of Poland and the Government General. It is a copy of a directive issued and signed by defendant Goering on 19th October, 1939, and was likewise found among the captured O.K.W. files. I quote from Lines 1 to 19 on Page 1 of the English text, Page 1514, Paragraph 4, Line 11. In the German text it is all of Page 1 and the first line of Page 2. Defendant Goering's directive states, and I quote:-

"In the meeting of 13th October, I have given detailed instructions for the economical administration of the occupied territories. I will repeat them here in short:

1. The task for the economic treatment of the various administrative regions is different, depending on whether a country which will be incorporated politically into the German Reich is involved, or whether we are to deal with the Government General, which, in all probability, will not be made a part of Germany.

In the first-mentioned territories the reconstruction and expansion of the economy, the safeguarding of all their production facilities and supplies must be aimed at, as well as a complete incorporation into the Greater German economic system at the earliest possible time. On the other hand, there must be removed from the territories of the Government General all raw materials, scrap materials, machines, etc., which are of use for the German war economy. Enterprises which are not absolutely necessary for the mere maintenance of the naked existence of the population must be transferred to Germany, unless such transfer would require an unreasonably long period of time, and would make it more practical to exploit these enterprises by giving them German orders to be executed at their present location."

Once the Government General had been stripped of its industrial potential, the defendants planned to leave the country desolate. Not even the war damage was to be repaired. This is the clear import of the documents previously introduced, and is likewise made clear by Document EC-411, which is Exhibit USA 299. I offer this document in evidence. This is a copy of an order dated 20th November, 1939, by defendant Hess, in his capacity as Deputy Fuehrer. This document was also found in the captured O.K.W. files. I quote the English and German texts in their entirety. Defendant Hess stated, and I quote:-

"I hear from Party members who came from the Government General that various agencies, as, for instance, the Military Economic Staff, the Reich Ministry for Labour, etc., intend to reconstruct certain industrial enterprises in Warsaw. However, in accordance with a decision by Minister Dr. Frank, as approved by the Fuehrer, Warsaw shall not be rebuilt nor is it the intention of the Fuehrer to rebuild or reconstruct any industry in the Government General."

Turning from the defendants' programme of economic spoliation in the Government General to their programme of deportation and resettlement, I next offer in evidence Document 661-PS, which is Exhibit USA 300. This is a secret report prepared by the Academy of German Law in January, 1940, upon plans for the mass migration of Poles and Jews from incorporated areas of Poland to the Government General, and for the forcible deportation of able-bodied Poles to Germany. This document was obtained from the Ministerial Collecting Centre at Kassel, Germany. The date does not appear in the English translation, but it is clearly set forth on the cover page of the original document as January, 1940. Before quoting from this document, I ask first, that the Tribunal take judicial notice of the decree of 11th July, 1934, embodied in the Reichsgesetzblatt, Part 1, Page 605, which provided that the Academy of German Law would be a public corporation of the Reich under the supervision of the Reich Ministers of Justice and the Interior, and that their task would be:-

"To promote the reconstruction of German legal life and to realise, in constant close collaboration with the competent legislative organisations, the National Socialist programme in the entire sphere of law."

Secondly, before quoting from the afore-mentioned report of the Academy of Law, I should like to offer in evidence Document 2749-PS, which is Exhibit USA 301. This is the title page of the publication of the Academy of German Law for 1940. It is offered for the purpose of showing that defendant Frank was the president of the Academy of German Law during the period that the above-mentioned secret report of the Academy was made. The document specifically states, and I quote:-

"Reich Minister Dr. Hans Frank, President of the Academy for German Law: 7th year 1940."

Now, if I may ask your Honours to turn to Document 661-PS, I should first like to quote Lines 6 to 24 of Page 1 of the English text. In the German text, these extracts appear at Page 6, Lines 6 to 10; and Line 22, Page 6 to Line 4, Page 7. I quote:-

"For the carrying out of costly and long term measures for the increase of agricultural production the Government General can, at most, absorb 1 to 1.5 million resettlers, as it is already over-populated. By further absorption of 1.6 million resettlers the 1925 Reich census figure of 133 inhabitants per square kilometre would be reached, which, because of already existing rural over-population and lack of industry, would practically result in a double over-population.

This figure of 1.6 million will barely suffice to transfer from the Reich: The Jews from the liberated East (over 600,000), groups of the remaining Jews, preferably the younger age groups from Germany proper, Austria, Sudetengau and the Protectorate (altogether over 1 million)."

Continuing the quotation, the report goes on with respect to transfers from the Reich:

"The Polish intelligentsia, who have been politically active in the past, and potential political leaders; the leading economic personalities, comprising owners of large estates, industrialists and business men, etc.; the peasant population, so far as it has to be removed in order to carry out, by strips of German settlements, the encirclement of Polish territories in the East."

Next I quote the last paragraph on Page 1 of the English text. The German text is at Page 8, Lines 3-10:-

"In order to relieve the living space of the Poles in the Government General as well as in the liberated East, one should temporarily remove cheap labour by the hundreds of thousands, employ them for a few years in the Old Reich, and thereby hamper their native biological propagation. (Their assimilation into the Old Reich must be prevented.)"

Finally, I quote from the last paragraph of Page 2 of the English text. In the German text it is the last five lines of Page 40:-

"Strictest care is to be taken that secret circulars, memoranda and official correspondence which contain instructions detrimental to the Poles are kept steadily under lock and key so that they will not some day fill the White Books printed in Paris or the U.S.A."

Your Honours will recall, from your own experiences, the vicious propaganda campaigns conducted by Nazi Germany to discredit the Polish books when they made their appearance in countries friendly to Poland. The last paragraph from this document which I have just read gives the lie to that whole Nazi propaganda campaign.

The plans for the deportation of thousands of innocent people, which are set forth in the document from which I have just quoted, were not mere theories spun by lawyers. They represented, as the next three documents to be offered in evidence will show, a programme which was, in fact, ruthlessly executed.

I next offer in evidence Document 2233-PS-G, the Frank Diaries, 1939, from 25th October to 15th December, which is Exhibit USA 302. This document was obtained from the 7th Army Documentation Centre at Heidelberg. I quote from the last paragraph of Page 1, carrying over to the first two lines of Page 2 of the English text. In the German text, the statements appear at Page 19, Lines 19 to 28. Defendant Frank stated, and I quote:-

"The Reichsfuehrer S.S." - meaning Himmler - "wishes that all Jews be evacuated from the newly gained Reich territories. Up to February approximately 1,000,000 people are to be brought in this way into the

Government General. The families of good racial extraction present in the occupied Polish territory (approximately 4,000,000 people) should be transferred into the Reich and individually housed, thereby being uprooted as a people."

I next offer in evidence Document EC-305, which is Exhibit USA 303. This exhibit is the top secret minutes of a meeting held on 12th February, 1940, under the chairmanship of the defendant Goering on "Questions Concerning the East." The document was found in the captured O.K.W. files. Himmler and defendant Frank, likewise, were present at this meeting.

I first quote Lines 15 to 17 of Page 1 of the English text. These extracts are found in the front page, Lines 1 to 8 of the German text. The minutes state, and I quote:-

"By way of introduction the General Field Marshal" - meaning defendant Goering - " explained that the strengthening of the war potential of the Reich must be the chief aim of all measures to be taken in the East."

I next quote the first two lines of the last paragraph on Page 1 of the English text. The German text appears at Page 2, Lines 2 to 4.

"Agriculture:
The task is to obtain the greatest possible agricultural production from the new Eastern Gaus without regard to questions of ownership."

I then quote from the first sentence of the second paragraph of Page 2 of the English text. This is at Page 3, Lines 22- 24 of the German text.

"Special questions concerning the Government General:
The Government General will have to receive the Jews who are ordered to emigrate from Germany and the New Eastern Gaus."

Finally, I quote paragraph numbered 2 under Roman numeral II of Page 2 of the English text. These statements appear in the German text at Page 4, Lines 3-19.

"The following reported on the situation in the Eastern territories: 2. Reichsstatthalter Gauleiter Forster, who said, 'The population of the Danzig/West Prussia Gau (newly acquired territories) is 1.5 million, of whom 240,000 are Germans, 850,000 well-established Poles and 300,000 immigrant Poles, Jews and asocials (1,800 Jews). 87,000 persons have been evacuated, 40,000 of these from Gotenhafen. From there also the numerous shirkers, who are now looked after by welfare, will have to be deported to the Government General. Therefore an evacuation of 20,000 additional persons can be counted on for the current year.'"

Comparable reports were made by other Gauleiters at the meeting. These figures, it may be noted, were only as of February, 1940. The forcible deportations which are reported in the exhibits from which I have just read, did not involve merely ordering the unfortunate victims to leave their homes and take up new residences elsewhere. These deportations were accomplished according to plan, in an utterly brutal and inhuman manner. Document 1918-PS, which is Exhibit USA 304, affords striking proof of this fact, and I offer it in evidence. This is a speech delivered by Himmler to officers of the S.S. on a day commemorating the presentation of the Nazi flag. It is contained in a compilation of speeches delivered by Himmler, which was captured by the U.S. Counter Intelligence Corps. The exact date of the speech does not appear in the exhibit, but its contents plainly show that it was delivered some time after Poland had been overrun. I quote from the second to the eighth lines of Page 1 of the English text. In the German text, this quotation appears on Page 52, Lines 2 to 10. In this speech Himmler said, and I quote:-

"Very frequently a member of the Waffen S.S. thinks about the deportation of the people living here. These thoughts came to me today when watching the very difficult work out there performed by the Security Police, supported by your men, who help them a great deal. Exactly the same thing happened in Poland in weather 40 degrees below zero, where we had to haul away thousands, tens of thousands, hundreds of thousands; where we had to have the toughness - you should hear this but also forget it again - to shoot thousands of leading Poles."

I repeat the latter part of the statement:

"Where we had to have the toughness - you should hear this but also forget it again - to shoot thousands of leading Poles."

Those Poles from the incorporated area who managed to survive the journey to the Government General could look forward, at best, to extreme hardship, and exposure to every form of degradation and brutality. Your Honours will recall defendant Frank's statement contained in Document EC-344-16, now Exhibit USA 297, which was introduced a short while ago, that the Polish economy would be reduced to the absolute minimum necessary for the bare existence of the population.

Your Honours will also recall defendant Goering's directive in Document EC-410, now Exhibit USA 298, also introduced a few moments ago, that all industrial enterprises in the Government General not absolutely necessary for the maintenance of the naked existence of the Polish population must be removed to Germany. A bare and naked existence, by the precepts of the conspirators, meant virtual starvation.

For the Jews who were forcibly deported to the Government General there was, of course, absolutely no hope. They were, in effect, deported to their graves. The defendant Frank, by his own admissions, had dedicated himself to their complete annihilation. I refer your Honours to the Frank Diaries, Conference Volume, 1941, October to December, which is Document 2233-PS-D, and which was introduced by Major Walsh as Exhibit USA 281. The particular statement to which I want to call your attention particularly is on Page 4, Document 2233-PS. I believe it appears at Page 77, Lines 9 and 10 of the German text. I quote the following from defendant Frank's statement:-

"We must annihilate the Jews, wherever we find them, and wherever it is possible."

I turn next to that aspect of the conspirators' programme which involved the forcible Germanisation of persons in the incorporated area who were deemed to possess German blood. I refer now again to the incorporated area, to those persons who were deemed to possess German blood. Such persons, the evidence will show, were given the choice of the concentration camp or submission to Germanisation. Himmler was the chief executioner of this programme, and initially I should like to introduce a few documents which disclose the powers bestowed upon him, and his conception of his task.

First, I offer in evidence Document 686-PS. This is Exhibit USA 305. This is a copy of a secret decree signed by Hitler and defendants Goering and Keitel, dated 7th October, 1939, entrusting Himmler with the task of executing the conspirators' Germanisation programme. This particular document came from the Ministerial Collection Centre of Kassel, Germany. I quote from Page 1, Lines 9 to 21 of the English text. In the German text this extract appears at Page 1, Lines 13 to 25. Page 1, Lines 13 to 25. I quote:-

"The Reichsfuehrer S.S." - that was Himmler - "has the obligation in accordance with my directives:

1. To bring back for final return into the Reich all German nationals and racial Germans in the foreign countries.

2. To eliminate the harmful influence of such alien groups of the population as represent a danger to the Reich and the German folk community.

3. To form new German settlements by resettling and, in particular, by settling returning German citizens and racial Germans from abroad.

The Reichsfuehrer S.S. is authorised to take all necessary general and administrative measures for the execution of this obligation."

Himmler's conception of his task under this decree is plainly stated in the foreword which he wrote for the Deutsche Arbeit issue of June/July, 1942. The foreword is contained in Document 2915-PS, now Exhibit USA 306. I quote from the first four lines of the English text. The German text appears at Page 157:-

"It is not our task," Himmler wrote, "to Germanise the East in the old sense, that is, to teach the people there the German language and German law, but to see to it that only people of purely German, Germanic blood live in the East.

Signed, Himmler."

I next offer in evidence Document 2916-PS, which is Exhibit USA 307. This document contains various materials taken out of Der Menscheneinatz 1940, a confidential publication issued by Himmler's Office for the Consolidation of German Nationhood. I quote initially from Lines 7 to 11 of Page 1. In the German text these extracts appear at Page 51, first four lines under the letter "D". I quote:-

"The removal of foreign races from the incorporated Eastern territories is one of the most essential goals to be reached in the German East. This is the chief national political task, which has to be executed in the incorporated Eastern territories by the 'Reichsfuehrer' S.S., Reich Commissioner, for the strengthening of the national character of the German people."

I next quote from Lines 33 to 39 of Page 1 of the English text. In the German text, these extracts appear on Page 52, Lines 14 to 20. I quote:-

" ... there are the following two primary reasons which make the regaining of lost German blood an urgent necessity:

1. Prevention of a further increase of the Polish intelligentsia through families of German descent, even if they are Polonised.

2. Increase of the population by racial elements desirable for the German nation, and the acquisition of ethno-biologically un-objectionable forces for the German reconstruction of agriculture and industry."

Further light is thrown upon the goals which the conspirators had set for their Germanisation programme in conquered Eastern areas by a speech delivered by Himmler on 14th October, 1943. This speech was published by the National Socialist Leadership Staff of the O.K.W. The document came to us through the Document Section, 3rd U.S. Infantry Division. Excerpts from this speech are set forth in L-70, which is Exhibit USA 308. I quote all of the English text, and in the German text these excerpts appear at Page 23, Lines 6 to 11, 12 to 15, 20 to 23, and Page 30, Lines 7 to 16. Himmler said, and I quote:-

"I consider that in dealing with members of a foreign country, especially of some Slav nationality, we must not start from German points of view, we must not endow these people with decent German thoughts and logical conclusions of which they are not capable, but we must take them as they really are .

Obviously in such a mixture of peoples there will always be some racially good types. Therefore I think that it is our duty to take their children with us, to remove them from their environment, if necessary, by abducting them. Either we win over any good blood that we can use for ourselves and give it a place in our people, or we destroy that blood."

Continuing the German text on Page 30, Lines 7 to 16 Himmler stated. I quote:-

"For us the end of this war will mean an open road to the East, the creation of the Germanic Reich in this way or that . . . the bringing home of 30,000,000 human beings of our blood, so that during our lifetime we shall be a people of 120,000,000 Germanic souls. That means that we shall be the sole decisive power in Europe. That means that we shall then be able to tackle the peace, during which we shall be willing for the first 2o years to rebuild and spread out our villages and towns, and that we shall push the borders of our German race 500 kilometres further to the East."

In furtherance of the unlawful plans disclosed by the last four exhibits, which have been offered in evidence, the conspirators contrived a Racial Register in the incorporated area of Poland. The Racial Register was, in effect, an elaborate classification of persons deemed to be of German blood, and contained provisions setting forth some of the rights, privileges and duties of the persons in each classification. Persons were classified into four groups:-

1. Germans who had actively promoted the Nazi cause.

2. Germans who had been more or less passive in the Nazi struggle, but had retained their German nationality.

3. Persons of German extraction who, although previously connected with the Polish nation, were willing to submit to Germanisation.

4. Persons of German descent, who had been "politically absorbed by the Polish nation", and who would be resistant to Germanisation.

The Racial Register was inaugurated under a decree of 12th September, 1940, issued by Himmler as Reich Commissioner for the Consolidation of German Nationhood, and it is contained in Document 2916-PS, previously introduced in evidence. It is Exhibit USA 307, that is Document 2916-PS. I quote from Page 4 of the English text, Lines 14 to 16. In the German text, these extracts appear at Page 92, Lines 29 to the end of the page, and Lines i

"The list of ethnic Germans will be divided into four parts (limited to inter-office use).

1. Ethnic Germans who fought actively in the ethnic struggle. Besides membership in a German Organisation, every other activity favouring the German against a foreign nationality will be considered an active manifestation.

2. Ethnic Germans who did not actively intervene in favour of the German nationality but had proof of their German nationality.

3. Persons of German descent who became connected with the Polish nation in the course of the years but have, on account of their attitude, the prerequisites to become full-fledged members of the German national community. To this group belong also persons of non- German descent who live in mixed marriage with an ethnic German in which the German spouse has the prevailing influence. Persons of Masurian, Slonzak, or Upper Silesian descent, who are to be recognised as ethnic Germans usually belong to this group 3.

4. Persons of German descent, politically absorbed by the Polish nation (renegades).

Persons not included on the list of ethnic Germans are Poles or foreign nationals.

Their treatment is regulated by B II.

Members of groups 3 and 4 have to be educated as full Germans, that is, have to be re-Germanised in the course of time through an intensive educational training in old Germany.

The establishment of members of group 4 has to be based on the doctrine that German blood must not be utilised in the interest of a foreign nation. Against those who refuse re-Germanisation, Security Police measures are to be taken."

The basic idea of creating a Racial Register for persons of German extraction was later incorporated in a decree Of 3rd March, 1941, signed by Himmler and the defendants Frick and Hess. This decree is dated 4th March, 1941, and is set forth in the Reichsgesetzblatt, 1941, Part 1, Page 118. We ask the Tribunal to take judicial notice thereof.

The entire apparatus of the S.S. was thrown behind the vigorous execution of these decrees. Proof of this fact is contained in Document R-112, which is Exhibit USA 309, and I now offer it in evidence. This exhibit contains directives issued by Himmler as the Reich Commissioner for the Consolidation of German Nationhood. I quote first from the last two paragraphs of the English text of the directives, 16th February, 1942, which is on Page 3 of this exhibit. In the German text this provision appears on Page 1 of the first decree, dated 16th February, 1942, Paragraphs 1 and 2. The directive provided, and I now quote:-

"I. Where racial Germans have not applied for entry in the German Ethnical List you will instruct the subordinate agencies to turn over their names to the State Police (Superior) Office. Subsequently, you will report to me.

II. The Local State Police (Superior) Office will charge the persons whose names are turned over to them to prove within eight days that they have applied for entry in the German Ethnical List. If such proof is not submitted, the person in question is to be taken into protective custody for transfer to a concentration camp."

The measures taken against persons in the fourth category - "Polonised Germans" as the conspirators called them - were particularly harsh. These persons were resistant to Germanisation, and ruthless measures calculated to break their resistance were prescribed. Where the individual's past history indicated that he could not be effectively Germanised, he was thrown into a concentration camp.

Some of these measures are set forth in Sub-paragraph A of Paragraph II on Page 5 of Document R-112, and I quote in full from the English text of that particular paragraph. This passage is set forth in the German text at Pages 2 and 3 of the second decree dated 16th February, 1942, under II. This is what the directive provides:-

"II. The re-Germanisation of the Polonised Germans presupposes their complete separation from Polish surroundings. For that reason the persons entered in Division 4 of the German Ethnical List are to be dealt with in the following manner:

1. They are to be resettled in Old Reich territory. 1. The Superior S.S. and Police Leaders are charged with evacuating and resettling them according to instructions which will follow later.

2. Asocial persons and others who are of inferior hereditary quality will not be included in the resettlement. Their names will be turned over at once by the Higher S.S. and Police Fuehrer (Inspectors of Security Police and Security Service) to the competent State Police (Superior) Office. The latter will arrange for their transfer to a concentration camp.

3. Persons with a particularly bad political record will not be included in resettlement action. Their names will also be given by the Higher S.S. and Police Fuehrer (Inspectors of Security Police and Security Service) to the competent State Police (Superior) Office for transfer to a concentration camp.

The wives and children of such persons are to be resettled in old Reich territory and to be included in the Germanisation measures. Where the wife also has a particularly bad political record and cannot be included in the resettlement action, her name, too, is to be turned over to the competent State Police (Superior) Office with a view to imprisoning her in a concentration camp. In such cases the children are to be separated from their parents and dealt with according to III, Paragraph 2 of this decree.

Persons are to be considered as having a particularly bad political record who have offended the German nation to a very great degree - e.g., who participated in persecutions of Germans or boycotts of Germans, etc."

Coincident with the programme of Germanising persons of German extraction in the incorporated areas, the conspirators, as previously indicated, undertook to settle large numbers of Germans of proved Nazi convictions in that area. This aspect of their programme is clearly shown by an article by S.S. Obergruppenfuehrer and General of the Police Wilhelm Koppe, who was one of Himmler's trusted agents.

Excerpts from this article are contained in Document 2915- PS, which was earlier introduced as Exhibit USA 306. I quote from the second paragraph of the English text of this exhibit. The German text appears at the third line from the bottom of Page 170 and continues to the first full paragraph of Page 171. I now quote Koppe's statement:-

"The victory of German weapons in the East must, therefore, be followed by the victory of the German race over the Polish race, if the regained Eastern sphere - according to the Fuehrer's will - shall henceforth remain for all time an essential constituent part of the Greater German Reich. It is therefore of decisive importance to infiltrate German farmers, labourers, civil servants, merchants, and artisans into the regained German region so that a living and deep-rooted bastion of German people can be formed as a protective wall against foreign penetration, and possibly as a starting point for the racial infusion of the territories farther East."

THE PRESIDENT: We will adjourn now for 10 minutes.

CAPTAIN HARRIS: Yes, sir.

[A recess was taken.]

CAPTAIN HARRIS: Up to this point we have been speaking of the Germanisation measures in the incorporated areas. I should like now briefly to turn to the Germanisation programme in the Government General.

In the Government General there were relatively few persons at the outset who qualified as Germans according to the conspirators' standards. Hence little would be served by the introduction of a Racial Register categorising persons of German extraction on the model of the one instituted in the incorporated area, and, to our knowledge, no such Racial Register was prescribed in the Government General. Rather, the plan seems to have been (a) to make the Government General a colony of Germany, which - as your Honours will recall from Document EC-344-16 which has been introduced as Exhibit USA 297 - was the objective expressed by the defendant Frank, and (b) to create so-called "German Island Settlements" in the productive farming areas. These Island Settlements were to be created by an influx of German persons who faithfully adhered to the principles of National Socialism.

In this connection I offer in evidence Document 910-PS. This is Exhibit USA 310. These are secret notes bearing the date line: Department of the Interior, Cracow, 3oth March, 1942, and they concern Himmler's statements upon the "planned Germanisation" of the Government General. This document was obtained from the Third Army Intelligence Centre at Freising, Germany, and I now quote from Page 2 of the English text, from Line 3 to the end of the report. This appears in the German text at Page 2, Line 21, continuing to the end of the report. The document states, and I quote:-

"The Reichsfuehrer S.S. (Himmler) developed additional trains of ideas to the effect that in the first Five Year Plan for resettlement after the war the new German Eastern territories should first be filled; afterwards it is intended to provide the Crimea and the Baltic countries with a German upper-class at least. Into the Government General perhaps further German Island Settlements should be newly transplanted from European nations, an exact decision in this respect, however, has not been issued. In any case, it is wished that at first a heavy colonisation along the San and the Bug be achieved so that these parts of Poland are encircled with alien population. Hitherto, it has been always proved that this kind of resettlement leads most quickly to the desired nationalisation."

In this same connection, I offer in evidence Document 2233- PS-H. This is defendant Frank's Diary, 1941, Volume II, Page 317. This is Exhibit USA 311. I quote from the last sentence at the bottom of our Page 3 of the English text of this exhibit. In the German text this passage appears on Page 317, Lines 25 to 28; the English text is at the bottom of Page 3, the last sentence. Defendant Frank stated in this diary, and I quote:-

"Thanks to the heroic courage of our soldiers, this territory has become German, and the time will come when the valley of the Vistula, from its source to its mouth at the sea, will be as German as the valley of the Rhine."

I now turn to another phase of the programme that I mentioned earlier, that is, the conspirators' plan to confiscate the property of Poles, Jews and dissident elements. As I previously mentioned, the evidence will show that these plans were designed to accomplish a number of objectives. In so far as the Jews were concerned, they were part and parcel of the conspirators' over-all programme of extermination. Confiscation was also a means of providing property for German settlers and of rewarding those who had rendered faithful service to the Nazi State. This phase of their programme likewise made available dispossessed Polish farmers for slave labour in Germany, and operated to further the conspirators' objective of preventing the growth of another generation of Poles.

Proof of the fact that the conspirators confiscated the property of Poles in furtherance of their Germanisation and slave labour programme is contained in Document 1352-PS, previously introduced by Mr. Dodd as Exhibit USA 176. This exhibit contains a number of reports by one Kusche, who appears to have been one of Himmler's chief deputies in Poland. Mr. Dodd quoted from one of Kusche's confidential reports, dated 22nd May, 1940, at our Page 4, Paragraph 5 of the English text. In the German text it is at Page 9, Lines 16 to 18. In this statement Kusche pointed out that it was possible, without difficulty, to confiscate small farms and that - and I now quote - "The former owners of Polish farms together with their families will be transferred to the Old Reich by the employment agencies, for employment as farm workers."

I now desire to quote from another report by Kusche contained in the same exhibit and bearing the same date - 22nd May, 1940. I think the upper right-hand corner numbers might simplify it. The report from which I now quote is marked secret and is entitled "Details of the Confiscation in the Bielitz Region." Initially, I should like to quote from the last paragraph at the bottom of Page ii of this exhibit. This document, you will recall, is 1352-PS, Exhibit USA 176, last paragraph at the bottom of Page 1. The German text is at Page 11, Paragraphs 1 and 2. Kusche stated, and I quote:-

"Some days ago the commandant of the concentration camp being built at Auschwitz called on Staff Leader Muller and requested support for the carrying out of his assignments. He said that it was absolutely necessary to confiscate the agricultural enterprises within a certain area around the concentration camp, since not only the fields but also the farmhouses of these border directly on the camp. A local inspection held on the 21St of this month revealed the following: there is no room for doubt that agricultural enterprises bordering on the concentration camp must be confiscated at once. In addition, the camp commandant requests that further plots of farmland be placed at his disposal, so that he can keep the prisoners busy. This too can be done without further delay since enough land can be made available for the purpose. The owners of the plots are all Poles."

I next quote from Page 2, Lines 22 to 31, of the English text of this same exhibit. The German text is at Page 12, Paragraph 2, continuing through to Line 22 from the top of the page. I quote:-

"I had the following discussion with the head of the labour office in Bielitz:

The lack of agricultural labourers still exists in the Old Reich. The transfer of the previous owners of the confiscated enterprises, together with their entire families, to the Reich, is possible without any further consideration. It is only necessary for the labour office to receive the lists of the persons in time in order to enable it to take the necessary steps (collection of transportation, distribution over the various regions in need of such labour)."

Finally, I quote from Page 3 of this same exhibit, Lines 6 to 13 of the English text. The German text appears at Page 13, the last three lines, continuing through to Page 14, Line 9:-

"The confiscation of these Polish enterprises in Alzen will also be carried out within the next few days. The commandant of the concentration camp will furnish S.S. men and a truck for the execution of the action. Should it not yet be possible to take the Poles from Alzen to Auschwitz" - and Auschwitz, your Honours will recall, is where the concentration camp was - "they should be transferred to the empty castle at Zator. The liberated Polish property is to be given to the needy racial German farmers for their use."

In order to regularise the programme of confiscation, defendant Goering issued a decree on 17th September, 1940. This decree appears in the Reichsgesetzblatt, 1940, Part 1, Page 1270, and I ask the Tribunal to take judicial notice of it. Under Section 2 of this decree, sequestration of movable and immovable property, stores, and other intangible property interests of Jews and "persons who have fled or are not merely temporarily absent" was made mandatory. In addition, sequestration was authorised under Section 2, Subsection 2, if the property were required "for the public welfare, particularly in the interests of Reich defence or the strengthening of Germanism." By Section 9 of this decree, issued by defendant Goering, confiscation of sequestrated property was authorised "if the public welfare, particularly the defence of the Reich, or the strengthening of Germanism, so requires." However, Section 1, Subsection 2, of the decree provided that property of German nationals was not subject to sequestration and confiscation; and Section 13 provided that sequestration would be suspended if the owner of the property asserted that he was a German. The decree, on its face, indicates very clearly a purpose to strip Poles, Jews, and dissident elements of their property. It was, moreover, avowedly designed to promote Germanism.

We ask the Court to take judicial notice of it. It is in the Reichsgesetzblatt.

Apparently, some question arose at one point as to whether the decree required that a determination be made, in each case involving the property of a Pole, that the property was required "for the public welfare, particularly in the interests of Reich defence or the strengthening of Germanism." The answer supplied by the conspirators was firm and clear. In any case in which the property of a Pole is involved, the "strengthening of Germanism" required its seizure. In this connection I offer in evidence Document R- 92, which is Exhibit USA 312. This document, which is dated 15th April, 1941, bears the letterhead of the Reich Leader S.S., Commissioner for the Consolidation of German Nationhood, and is entitled "Instruction for internal use on the application of the law concerning property of the Poles Of 17th September, 1940." This document was captured by the U.S. Counter-Intelligence Corps. I quote from Page 2, Lines 11 to 14 of the English text. In the German text this statement appears at Page 3, Paragraph 2, Sub-paragraph. I quote: -

"The conditions permitting seizure according to Section 2, Subsection 2, are always present if the property belongs to a Pole, for the Polish real estate will be needed without exception for the consolidation of the German nationhood."

In the Government General defendant Frank promulgated a decree on 24th January, 1940, authorising sequestration "in connection with the performance of tasks serving the public interest" and liquidation of "anti-social or financially unremunerative concerns." The decree is embodied in the Verordunngsblatt of the Government General, No. 6, 27th January, 1940, Page 23, and we ask the Tribunal to take judicial notice of it. The undefined criteria in this decree obviously empowered Nazi officials in the Government General to engage in wholesale seizure of property.

The magnitude of the conspirators' confiscation programme in Poland was staggering. I ask your Honours to turn to the chart on the sixth page of Document R-92, which was introduced into evidence a moment ago as Exhibit USA 312.

This chart shows that as of 31st May, 1943, the staggering total of 693,252 estates, comprising 6,097,525 hectares, had been seized, and 9,508 estates, comprising 270,446 hectares, had been confiscated by the Estate Offices Danzig, West Prussia, Poznan, Zichenau, and Silesia. This, it will be noted, represented the seizure and confiscation by only four offices.

That, your Honours, concludes our discussion on Poland, and I now turn to Czechoslovakia. At this point of the proceedings we shall introduce only one document upon Czechoslovakia. This one document, however, contains a startling revelation of the conspirators' plans to Germanise Bohemia and Moravia. It relates how three plans, each characterised by its severity, were discussed, and finally how the Fuehrer decided on plan (c), which involved the assimilation of about one-half of the Czech population by the Germans, and the extermination of the other half. Moreover, the plan envisaged a large influx into Czechoslovakia of Germans whose loyalty to the Fuehrer was unquestioned. I offer this document in evidence. It is Document 862-PS, and it is Exhibit USA 313. This is a top secret report dated 15th October, 1940, which was written by General Friderici, Deputy General of the Wehrmacht in Bohemia and Moravia. On the face of the document, it appears that only four copies were made. The document we offer in evidence is the original document, which was found among the captured files of the O.K.W. This document bears the hand-written letters "K" and "J" on the first page on the left-hand side, and I am advised that the handwriting is unquestionably that of defendants Keitel and Jodl. I quote the document in its entirety:-

"On 9th October of this year, the office of the Reich Protector held an official conference in which State Secretary S.S. Lt. General K. H. Frank spoke about the following" - S.S. Gruppenfuehrer K. H. Frank, it may be noted, was Secretary of State under defendant von Neurath, who at the date of this report was the Protector of Bohemia and Moravia.

Continuing this quotation-

THE PRESIDENT: Who did you say Frank was?

CAPTAIN HARRIS: Frank was an S.S. Gruppenfuehrer, and Secretary of State under defendant von Neurath. He is not the defendant Hans Frank. At the date of this particular report von Neurath, under whom K. H. Frank served was the Protector of Bohemia and Moravia. Continuing the quotation:-

"Since creation of the Protectorate of Bohemia and Moravia, Party agencies, industrial circles, as well as agencies of the central authorities of Berlin, have considered a solution for the Czech problem.

After ample deliberation, the Reich Protector expressed his views about the various plans in a memorandum. In this, three ways of solution were indicated:

(a) German infiltration of Moravia and confinement of the Czech nationals to a residual Bohemia. This solution is considered unsatisfactory, because the Czech problem, even if in diminished form, will continue to exist.

(b) Many arguments can be brought up against the most radical solution, namely, the deportation of all Czechs. Therefore, in the memorandum it is concluded that it cannot be carried out within a reasonable period of time.

(c) Assimilation of the Czechs, i.e., absorption of about half of the Czech nationals by the Germans, in so far as this is of racial or other value. This can also be effected in other ways, e.g., by increased employment of Czechs in the Reich territory (with the exception of the Sudeten-German border districts), in other-words, by dispersing the concentrations of Czech nationals.

The other half of the Czech nationals must be deprived of their power, eliminated and shipped out of the country by all sorts of methods. This applies particularly to the racially Mongoloid part and to the major part of the intellectual class. The latter can scarcely be converted ideologically and would become a burden by constantly making claims for the leadership over the other Czech classes, and thus interfering with a rapid assimilation.

Elements which counteract the planned Germanisation ought to be handled roughly and eliminated.

The above development naturally presupposes an increased influx of Germans from the Reich territory into the Protectorate.

After a discussion, the Fuehrer has chosen solution (c) (Assimilation) as a directive for the solution of the Czech problem and decided that, while keeping up the autonomy of the Protectorate on the surface, the Germanisation will have to be carried out in a centralised way, by the office of the Reich Protector, for years to come.

From the above no particular conclusions are drawn by the Armed Forces. This is the line which has always been taken here. In this connection I refer to my memorandum submitted to the Chief of the High Command of the Armed Forces, dated 12th July, 1939, file No. 6/39, top secret, entitled: The Czech Problem (Attached as annex).

The Representative of the Armed Forces with the Reich Protector in Bohemia and Moravia.

Signed, Friderici, General of Infantry."

With the permission of your Honours, I should like to comment further upon some parts of this memorandum. First, I invite your attention to solution (a). This solution would have called for German infiltration into Moravia and the forcible removal of the Czechs from that area to Bohemia. As your Honours know, Moravia lies between Bohemia and Slovakia. Thus solution (a) would have involved the erection of a German State between Bohemia and Slovakia, and would have prevented effective intercommunications between the Czechs and the Slovaks. In this manner, the historic desire for unity of these two groups of peace-loving people and the continued existence of their Czechoslovakian State would have been frustrated. Solution (a), it may be noted, was rejected because the surviving Czechs, even though compressed into a "residual Bohemia" would have remained to plague the conspirators.

Solution (b), which involved the forcible deportation of all Czechs, was rejected, not because its terms were deemed too drastic but rather because a more speedy resolution of the problem was desired.

Solution (c), as shown in the exhibit, was regarded as the most desirable, and was adopted. This solution first provided for the assimilation of about one half of the Czechs. This meant two things: (a) enforced Germanisation for those who were deemed racially qualified and (b) deportation to slave labour in Germany for others. "Increased employment of Czechs in the Reich territory," as stated in the exhibit meant, in reality, slave labour in Germany.

Solution (c) further provided for the elimination and deportation "by all sorts of methods" of the other half of the Czech population, particularly the intellectuals and those who did not meet the racial standards of the conspirators. Intellectuals everywhere were an anathema to the Nazi conspirators, and the Czech intellectuals were no exception. Indeed, the Czech intellectuals, as the conspirators well knew, had a conspicuous record of gallantry, self-sacrifice, and resistance to the Nazi ideology. They were, therefore, to be exterminated. As will be shown in other connections, that section of the top secret report which stated "elements which counteract the planned Germanisation are to be handled roughly and eliminated " meant that intellectuals and other dissident elements were either to be thrown into concentration camps or immediately exterminated.

In short, the provisions of solution (c) were simply a practical application of the conspirators' philosophy as expressed in Himmler's speech, part of which we have quoted in L-70, already presented in evidence as Exhibit USA 308. Himmler said that "Either we win over any good blood that we can use for ourselves or we destroy this blood."

I now turn briefly to the conspirators' programme of spoliation and Germanisation in the Western occupied countries. Evidence which will be presented at a later stage of this proceeding will show how the conspirators sought to Germanise the Western occupied countries; how they stripped the conquered countries in the West of food and raw materials, leaving to them scarcely enough to maintain a bare existence; how they compelled local industry and agriculture to satisfy the inordinate wants of the German civilian population and the Wehrmacht; and finally, how the spoliation in the Western occupied countries was aided and abetted by excessive occupation charges, compulsory and fraudulent clearing arrangements, and confiscation of their gold and foreign exchange. The evidence concerning these matters, which will be presented in great detail by the prosecutor for the Republic of France, is so overwhelming that the inference is inescapable that the conspirators' acts were committed according to plan.

However, it will not be until after the Christmas recess that the evidence concerning the execution of the conspirators' plans in the West will be presented to this Tribunal. Accordingly, by way of illustration, and for the purpose of showing in this presentation that the conspirators' plans embraced the occupied Western countries as well as the East, we now offer in evidence a single exhibit on this aspect of the case, Document R-114, which is Exhibit USA 314. This document was obtained from the U.S. Counter-Intelligence Branch. This exhibit consists of a memorandum dated 7th August, 1942, and a memorandum dated 29th August, 1942, from Himmler's personal files. The former memorandum deals with a conference of S.S. officers, and bears the title "General Directions for the Treatment of Deported Alsatians". The latter memorandum is marked secret and is entitled "Shifting of Alsatians into Germany Proper". The memoranda comprising this exhibit show that plans were made and partially executed to remove from Alsace all elements which were hostile to the conspirators, and to Germanise the province. I quote from Page 1, Lines 21 to 31 of the English text entitled "General Directions for the Treatment of Deported Alsatians". These extracts contained in the German text at Page 1, the last eight lines, and Page 2, Lines 1 to 5. I now quote:-

"The first expulsion action was carried out in Alsace in the period from July to December, 1940; in the course of it 105,000 persons were either expelled or prevented from returning. They were in the main Jews, gypsies and other foreign racial elements, criminals, asocial and incurably insane persons, and in addition Frenchmen and Francophiles. The patois-speaking population was combed out by this series of deportations in the same way as the other Alsatians.

Referring to the permission the Fuehrer had given him to cleanse Alsace of all foreign, sick or unreliable elements, Gauleiter Wagner has recently pointed out the political necessity of new deportations (zweite Aussiedlungsaktion) which are to be prepared as soon as possible."

I should like your Honours to permit me to defer the remainder of this presentation until Monday. Mr. Justice Jackson would like to make a few remarks to the Tribunal.

MR. JUSTICE JACKSON: May it please the Tribunal, I wish to bring to the attention of the Tribunal and of the defence counsel some matters concerning the case as it will take its course next week, in the belief that it will result in expediting our procedure if over the week-end our programme can be considered.

Captain Harris's presentation will take a little longer on Monday, and when it has concluded, the presentation by the United States will have reached that part of the indictment which seeks declaratory judgment of this Tribunal that six of the organisations named therein are criminal organisations. They effect such a finding only that they they constitute a basis for prosecution against individual members in other courts than this, proceedings in which every defence will be open to an accused individual, except that he may not deny the findings made by this Tribunal as to the character of the organisation of which he was a member.

The United States desires to offer this evidence under conditions which will save the time of the Tribunal and advance the prosecution as rapidly as possible so that United States personnel can be released.

We also desire defendants' counsel to have before them as much as possible of our evidence against organisations before the Christmas recess, so that they may use that recess time to examine it and to prepare their defences, and that we may be spared any further applications for delay for that purpose.

The substance of our proposal is that all of the ultimate questions on this branch of the case be reserved for consideration after the evidence is before the Tribunal. The real question we submit is not whether to admit the evidence. The real question is its value and its legal consequences under the provisions of this Charter. All of the evidence which we will tender will be tendered in the belief that it cannot be denied to have some probative value, and that it is relevant to the charges made in the Indictment. And those are the grounds upon which the Charter authorises a rejection of evidence.

At the time we seek no advantage from this suggestion except the advantage of timesaving to the Tribunal and to ourselves to get as much of the case as possible in the hands of the defendants before the Christmas recess, and to urge the ultimate issues only when they can be intelligibly argued and understood on the basis of a real record, instead of on assumptions and hypothetical statements of fact.

In offering this evidence as to the organisations, therefore, we propose to stipulate as follows:-

Every objection of any character to any item of the evidence offered by the United States as against these organisations, may be deemed to be reserved and fully available to defence counsel at any time before the close of the United States case, with the same effect as if the objection had been made When the evidence was offered. All evidence on this subject shall remain subject to a continuing power of the Tribunal, on motion of any counsel or on its own motion, to strike, unprejudiced by the absence of objection. Every question as to the effect of the evidence shall be considered open and unprejudiced by the fact that it has been received without objection.

Now we recognise the adherent controversial character of the issues which may be raised concerning this branch of the case. What this evidence proves, what organisations it is sufficient to condemn, and bow the Charter applies to it are questions capable of debate, and which we are quite ready to argue when it can be done in orderly and intelligible fashion. We had expected to do it in a final summary, but we will do it at any time suggested by the Tribunal, after there is a record on which to found the argument, and we are willing to do it either before or after the defendants take up the case. But we do suggest that if it is done step by step as the evidence is produced, and on questions of admissibility, it will be disorderly and time consuming. Piecemeal argument will consume time by requiring counsel on both sides either to recite evidence that is already in the case or to speculate as to evidence that is not yet in, to resort to hypothetical cases, and to do it over and over again to each separate objection. It will also be disorderly because of our plan of presentation.

Questions which relate to these organisations go to the very basis of the proposal made by President Roosevelt to the Yalta Conference, agreement upon which was the basis for this proceeding. The United States would not have participated in this kind of determination of question of guilt, but for this or some equivalent plan of reaching thousands of others, who, if less conspicuous, are just as guilty of these crimes as the men in the dock. Because of participation in the framing of the Charter, and knowledge of the problem it was designed to solve, I shall expect to reach the legal issues involved in these questions.

The evidence, however, will be presented by the lawyers who have specialised in the search for the arrangement of evidence on a particular and limited charge or indictment. Piecemeal argument, therefore, would not be orderly but would be repetitious, incomplete, poorly organised, and of little help to the Tribunal. The issues deserve careful, prepared presentation of the contentions on both sides.

We will ask, then, for these conditions, which we think protect everybody's rights and enable the defence, as well as ourselves, to make a better presentation of their questions - because they will have time to prepare them-to lay before the Tribunal, as rapidly as possible next week and as uninterruptedly as possible, the evidence which bears upon the accusations against the organisations.

THE PRESIDENT: Mr. Justice Jackson, have you yet communicated that to the defendants' counsel in writing, or not?

MR. JUSTICE JACKSON: I have not communicated it, unless it has been sent to the Information Centre since noon.

THE PRESIDENT: I think, perhaps, it might be convenient that you should state what you have stated to us, as to objections to the evidence, in writing, so that they may thoroughly understand it.

MR. JUSTICE JACKSON: I have prepared to do that and to supply sufficient copies for members of the Tribunal and for all defence counsel.

THE PRESIDENT: Yes.

DR. GEORG BOEHM: I represent the members of the S.A. who have reported themselves to the Tribunal for examination. I understood the statements made by Mr. Justice Jackson only partially. As counsel I have no one who can supply me with information and I cannot under any circumstances agree to reply, in the course of this trial, to speeches that I do not understand or which are presented to me in such a way that I am not in a position to get information.

I should like to ask first that care be taken that I receive a German translation of the statements which the prosecution has made in regard to the future course of the trial, so that I can reply to these statements. I do not represent only one person in this trial but millions of people, people who will make all sorts of accusations, in part perhaps even justified accusations against me, once this trial has ended. The responsibility, which I, as well as those colleagues of mine who represent organisations have, is terribly great. I should therefore like to request, as a matter of principle, that everything which is presented in this trial be submitted to me in the German language, because I am not in a position to have translated into German from day to day whole volumes of documents which could easily be given to me in the original German. This circumstance makes it dreadfully hard for me, as well as for a number of my colleagues, to follow the trial at all.

In the previous sessions I found little that I could consider incriminatory evidence against the organisations. Since however, according to today's statements, the evidence against the organisations is to be presented in the future, I should like to ask urgently, if we are to remain as counsel for these organisations, that the trial be ordered in such a way that, in regard to technical matters too, we shall be in a position to carry on the defence in a responsible manner.

THE PRESIDENT: As you know or have been told, only those parts of those documents which are read before the Tribunal are treated as being in evidence and, therefore, you hear through your earphones everything that is in evidence read to you in German. You know, also, that there are two copies of the documents in your Information Centre which are in German. So much for that. That has been the procedure up to now.

In order to meet the legitimate wishes of German counsel, the proposal which Mr. Justice Jackson has just made is perfectly simple, as I understand it, and it is this:

That the question of the criminality of these organisations should not be argued before the evidence is put in; that the United States counsel should put in their evidence first, and that they hope to put the majority of that evidence in before the Christmas recess, but that the German counsel, defendants' counsel, shall be at liberty at any time, up to the time the United States case is finished, to make objection to any part of the evidence on these criminal organisations. Is that not clear?

DR. GEORG BOEHM: Yes, that is fairly simple.

THE PRESIDENT: Have you any objection to that procedure?

DR. GEORG BOEHM: I am rather of the opinion that it is highly inadequate. I have had no opportunity yet to get into my hands either of those two copies, which are supposed to lie downstairs in Room 54. It may be that two copies are not sufficient for the purposes of 25 lawyers, especially since these copies in German are placed in Room 54 at 10.30 in the morning, while the session has already started at 10.00 in the morning. It would also not suffice, if these two copies for 25 people were to be placed there the day before, because it is not possible in this short period of time for all 25 of us to make satisfactory use of these two copies. I should therefore like to request just how the prosecution will do that, or just how it can do it I cannot say that arrangements be made so that we are in position to know at the proper time and, I emphasise this once more, in the German language, everything that the prosecution desires to use, in order that we can act, so that our work will be of use to the Court.

THE PRESIDENT: What you have just stated is a general objection to the procedure which has been adopted up to now and has nothing to do with the procedure which has been suggested by Mr. Justice Jackson with reference to these criminal organisations. His suggestion was that argument on the law of the criminal issue or the criminal nature of these organisations should be postponed until the evidence was put in, and that the right of counsel for the defence should be to make objection at any stage or, rather, to defer their, objections until the evidence had been put in, and it was hoped that the evidence would be completed or nearly completed by the Christmas recess. What you say about the general procedure may be considered by the Tribunal.

So far as the particular question is concerned, namely, the question of the procedure suggested by Mr. Justice Jackson, have you any objection to that?

DR. GEORG BOEHM: I will object only if through this proceeding - and for this purpose I reserve for myself all liberties and all rights in the interest of my large clientele - I am in any way handicapped or hindered in representing the interests of so many people before the Tribunal.

THE PRESIDENT: We are aware of that fact, but that does not seem to be material to the question whether the legal argument should be deferred until after the evidence is presented. The fact that you have millions of people to represent has nothing to do with the question whether the legal argument shall take place before or in the middle of or at the end of the presentation of the evidence. What I am asking you is: "Have you any objection to the legal argument taking place at the end of the presentation of the evidence?"

DR. GEORG BOEHM: I have no objection to these suggestions in so far as my defence is not hindered in any way thereby.

THE PRESIDENT: The Tribunal will now adjourn.

[The Tribunal adjourned until 1000 hours on 17th December, 1945.]

About Coda Books

Most Coda books are edited and endorsed by Emmy Award winning film maker and military historian Bob Carruthers, producer of Discovery Channel's Line of Fire and Weapons of War and BBC's Both Sides of the Line. Long experience and strong editorial control gives the military history enthusiast the ability to buy with confidence.

The series advisor is David McWhinnie, producer of the acclaimed Battlefield series for Discovery Channel. David and Bob have co-produced books and films with a wide variety of the UK's leading historians including Professor John Erickson and Dr David Chandler.

Where possible the books draw on rare primary sources to give the military enthusiast new insights into a fascinating subject.

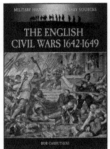
The English Civil Wars

The Zulu Wars

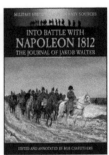
Into Battle with Napoleon 1812

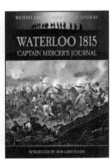
Waterloo 1815

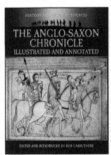
The Anglo-Saxon Chronicle

The Battle of the Bulge

The Normandy Campaign 1944

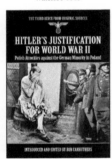
Hitler's Justification for WWII

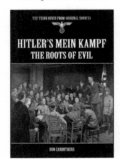
Hitler's Mein Kampf -
The Roots of Evil

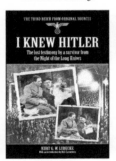
I Knew Hitler

Mein Kampf - The 1939
Illustrated Edition

The Nuremberg Trials Volume 1

450

For more information, visit codahistory.com

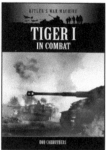
Tiger I in Combat

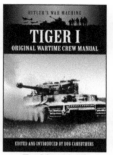
Tiger I Crew Manual

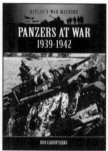
Panzers at War 1939-1942

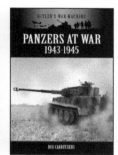
Panzers at War 1943-1945

Wolf Pack - the U boats

Poland 1939

Luftwaffe Combat Reports

Eastern Front Night Combat

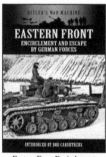
Eastern Front Encirclement

Panzer Combat Reports

The Panther V in Combat

The Red Army in Combat

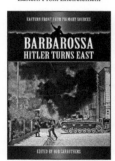
Barbarossa - Hitler Turns East

The Russian Front

The Wehrmacht in Russia

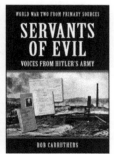
Servants of Evil